"Raising our Daughters *is loaded with hands-on practical advice and action steps that will help any parent or caregiver raise a healthier, happier daughter. Nice work!"*

Christiane Northrup, MD, author of *The Secret Pleasures of Menopause, The Wisdom of Menopause, Women's Bodies, Women's Wisdom,* and *Mother-Daughter Wisdom*

"Raising Our Daughters *is one of the most practical books I've ever seen about the challenging and exciting journey of raising healthy girls. Filled with many different voices of experts and parents, the book gives parents and stepparents concrete ways to take positive action collectively and within their own families. Plus,* Raising Our Daughters *is an outstanding, research-based resource for professionals and programs working with families."*

Joe Kelly, author of *Dads & Daughters®: How to Inspire, Understand and Support Your Daughter* and editor of Daughters.com.

"*What an incredible wealth of information, resources, guidance, and processes which* Raising Our Daughters *offers to parents and caregivers in every community. This material is so rich and comprehensive, yet it is presented in a step-by-step format so that the parent groups can gradually gain knowledge, exchange experiences and wisdom, reflect on their own practices as well as hopes and dreams, and develop skills and mindful strategies to influence their daughters' lives so positively. One of the very best aspects of this guide is the core approach in which you recommend it be delivered: parents making connections together to jointly increase their confidence, find support, gain understanding, and strengthen their own safety network.*

The relationship between a girl and her parents is always, in the end, the central bond of influence. Raising Our Daughters *acknowledges, celebrates, and empowers adults to empower their daughters with wide-reaching tools through the power of group connections. Get together with a group of parents and start this journey now! You will be so glad you did."*

Beth Hossfeld, MFT, co-founder of the *Girls Circle Association* and *Boys Council*

"*It's hard for busy parents of girls to get together and share their concerns and ideas.* Raising Our Daughters *gives them an easy-to-use framework for getting together, learning and supplying each other with much-needed support. The book overflows with great information that will help all of us raise confident, creative and caring daughters."*

Nancy Gruver, Founder of *New Moon Girls* magazine at newmoon.com and author of *How to Say It to Girls®: Communicating with Your Growing Daughter.*

"*What a powerful, positive resource!* Raising Our Daughters *truly guides parents through the terrain of adolescence, offering diverse voices, detailed information and clear directions for creating small supportive communities in which teens and families can stay connected and thrive."*

SuEllen Hamkins, MD, co-author of *The Mother-Daughter Project: How Mothers and Daughters Can Band Together, Beat the Odds and Thrive Through Adolescence.*

Raising Our Daughters Parenting Guide
...a new, unique way to support you,
as a parent or caring adult, to:

- Create a thriving family now and prepare for the teen and tween years.
- Learn from the perspective of many different voices from over 100 authors.
- Get a broad exposure to many parenting books, DVDs and other resources.
- Gain clarity on parenting by reading, discussing and exploring what works.
- Discover which of these parenting resources are the "best fit" for you.
- Learn the power of focusing early on preventive, proactive parenting.
- Connect to your own "inner wisdom."
- Be empowered to be the best mom, best dad, or best caring adult with your unique approach.
- Understand the incredible power you have as an adult who reaches out to connect with kids.
- Learn many ways to weave a network of support for your daughter and other children you care about.
- Be empowered to contribute to a community that takes action to show they care about children.

Form a discussion group with these *Parenting Guides,* and you will:

- Have a format to share honestly, create connections with other concerned parents, and find allies on your parenting path.
- Discover you are not alone, as you learn about other family's struggles and issues.
- Gain wisdom from other parents.
- Support each other and be encouraged to focus on long-term parenting.
- Create the life, the family, and the community you want to see in the world.
- Enjoy your family and have fun.

The magic that can happen when using Raising Our Daughters Parenting Guide *with a group is that you create a support network of people who not only care about you, but also care about your children. In essence, you can create a group of "aunties" and "uncles" who look out for all the children in your everyday life.*

—Kathy Masarie, MD

RAISING
OUR DAUGHTERS

The Ultimate Parenting Guide
For Healthy Girls and Thriving Families

Kathy Masarie, MD
with
Jody Bellant Scheer, MD
Kathy Keller Jones, MA

Family
Empowerment
Network

Jody Bellant Scheer, MD, Kathy Masarie, MD, and Kathy Keller Jones, MA (pictured left to right), created *Raising our Sons, Raising our Daughters* and *Kids Social Lives* with a diverse, insightful group of volunteers and co-authors.

We would like to thank the many writers, contributors, family photographers, organizations, and our own families for their contribution and support on this ten-year project.

Binoy Bahuleyan	Claire Ersan	Kaitlin Masarie	Leann Scotch
Michelle Bailey	Adrienne Greene	Ruthie Matinko-Wald	Peter Serrell
Harmony Barrett	Chris Harrington	Ann Matschiner	Lisa Sloan
Ann Baumgartner	Sally Hersh	Glenda Montgomery	Madelyn Stasko
Chithra Binoy	Nancy Huppertz	Christine Nelson	Elizabeth Stevens
Cindy Broder	Annette Kleinfelter	Nelle Nix	Cynthia Thomas
Francis Bubalo	Dana Lodhie	Michelle Roehm	Susan Thomson
Kathy Bunn	Lindsey Lodhie	Alice Rose	Debra Tomsen
Ann Cleveland	Trudy Ludwig	Carol Sherman Rogers	June Tremain
Karen Costello	Chip Masarie	Karen St. Clair	Tim Turner
Mary d'Autremont	Jon Masarie	Eileen Schmidt	

Graphic design   Anita Jones at www.anotherjones.com
Cover design   Machele Brass at www.brassdesign.net
Proof Editors   Bridget Weber, Leslie O'Neill and Glenda Montgomery
Marketing Consultant Michael Kosmala, The Canoe Group at www.thecanoegroup.com
Published by   Kathy Masarie at www.family-empower.com

We thank the 2001 7th and 8th grade art students of the West Linn-Wilsonville School Districts who contributed their drawings from Charcoal Challenge Art Class, taught by Sally Nelson: Brittany Baartlein, Drew Bardana, Caelen Bensen, Sarah Bernert, Matt Boggess, Katie Bonham, Kamon Bryck, Tom Flannery, Stephani Graap, Liana Hochhalter, Shelby Lindstedt, Andrea Millen, McKenna Miller, Carley Nelson, Lindsay Nelson, Lee Ogle, Eric Ramfjord, Thomas Ramfjord, Amanda Russel, Kara Tucker, and Danny Walinsky.

Finally, we would like to acknowledge Northwest Earth Institute, founded by Dick and Jeanne Roy, whose own courses were the model for this discussion guide.

Family Empowerment Network

Please contact us at:
Family Empowerment Network™
6663 SW Beaverton Hillsdale Highway PMB 158, Portland, OR 97225
coach@kathymasarie.com   www.family-empower.com

Preface

You are on a parenting journey, one that can bring more joy, more worry and occasionally more despair than you probably ever imagined. How can you both enjoy yourself and be your best, while maximizing precious moments with your children and nurturing them to discover their best selves and unique talents? As parents, we feel stretched in many directions with higher expectations than previous generations. We are constantly bombarded by cultural messages to buy more and be more while receiving little support in exchange.

Mary Pipher, author of *Reviving Ophelia,* says, "Raising your family in isolation is like buying a first class ticket on the Titanic." In today's culture, it is easy to feel alone. In her pediatric practice, Dr. Kathy Masarie saw parents of teens struggling in isolation with big problems: pregnancy, depression, risky drinking and drug use. With her own teens, she experienced how hard and sometimes embarrassing it was to share her struggles with others. Dr. Masarie wanted to encourage the networking she saw among parents of young kids and to provide a continuum of support as families evolved. In 1996, she founded the non-profit, *Full Esteem Ahead,* to "support parents to support kids and one another" and created these parenting guides in the process.

Since then, *Raising Our Daughters* and *Raising Our Sons* have provided parents, schools and caring adults with powerful vehicles for learning, self-discovery, networking, and the importance of connecting with all kids. These guides respond to parents' crucial needs: to talk to each other honestly and authentically, to support each other's families, and to collaborate in building family-friendly communities. Initially created by a team of volunteers who gathered the best information from over 200 new and timeless resources, Kathy and her co-writers, Jody Bellant Scheer, a pediatrician, and Kathy Keller Jones, a school counselor, have updated and expanded *Raising Our Sons* and *Raising Our Daughters.*

Busy parents and other caring adults often look for quick, easy answers from the "experts." At *Family Empowerment Network*, we believe that you have the best answers. You know yourself and your children better than anyone. When you take the time to read and discuss common concerns with other parents, your mind opens to new ideas. You recognize which of many effective solutions are a "good fit" and then you become the expert in your own life. You have the power to come together as parents, school communities, and neighborhoods to create alliances and communities that nurture thriving, healthy children. **And most importantly, you connect with young people so they know they matter.**

Thank you for your participation from all of us at Family Empowerment Network.

Kathy Masarie, MD	Kathy Keller Jones, MA	Jody Bellant Scheer, MD
Pediatrician	School Counselor	Pediatrician
Parent/Life Coach	Parent Coach	Compassionate Communication

Contents

Introduction

Discover the overall purpose of these Parenting Guides, an overview of topics and articles covered in each session, and how to run your own group. Also see a list of all the authors and organizations who contributed to this project, along with a permissions list for reprint information.

In spite of the challenges they face today, parents have the power to make a positive difference in their daughter's lives and the lives of other children. Learn how the 40 Developmental Assets can guide you.

Become familiar with the powerful media influence in your daughter's world, as well as the ways commercialism creates her culture. In becoming more media literate, parents can reduce the harm of the media and guide their families in making wise decisions about what to watch, play and purchase.

Explore parenting strategies that help avoid sabotages and encourage open and compassionate communication. Learn about the importance of fathers, family rituals, meetings and meals together.

Focus on your daughter's transition into womanhood, including understanding puberty, cultural pressures, and how to share this with her. Learn about the female brain and girls' friendships.

Support your daughter as she develops her own identity and pursues her dreams. Surround her with positive messages about her strength and her ability to resist gender stereotypes. Encourage financial independence.

Recognize the value of partnership between families and schools in preparing children for the future. Raise your awareness about gender equity. Learn how to reduce relational aggression among our daughters.

Explore your priorities in life and become more aware of the choices you are making regarding work, busyness, and stress. Realign your time with your true priorities and have more quality time with loved ones.

Understand that a goal of adolescence is to form one's own identity and that this often involves experimentation and risk taking. Know that as a parent you are the first line of defense between you daughter and common health and safety risks. Establish support structures which help keep her safe.

Develop "safe havens" where your daughter can be herself and develop relationships with other caring adults. Design a rite of passage. Understand the importance of fitness to mental and emotional well-being.

Solidify your vision and plan to create a nurturing, supportive, and connected family and community using the 40 Developmental Assets. Include volunteering. Keep connected to other families.

The permission's list acknowledges the wonderful authors and organizations who contributed to this project, along with sharing contact and reprint information.

Contents: Articles

GUIDELINES FOR DISCUSSION GROUPS

These guidelines will help you create a supportive parent discussion group and effectively share this *Parenting Guide*. Parent groups most often meet once or twice a month to discuss a chapter of the *Parenting Guide*. Group leadership rotates—then each participant is empowered to have an equal voice and the group's shared wisdom can be maximized.

HOW TO START YOUR OWN PARENTING DISCUSSION GROUP
- Talk to your friends, parents of your child's friends, scout or soccer team parents ... Find a co-leader.
- Share the *Parenting Guide* with your school counselor and ask if s/he would like to get involved.
- Talk to the principal about putting an ad in your school newsletter to announce an "info meeting."
- Host a parenting seminar with a local speaker. Send around a sign-up sheet to tap interest in a class.

OPENER GUIDELINES
- The role of **opener** rotates each session among participants.
- The purpose of the opening is to transition from the outside distractions of daily life to the discussion group.
- Start on time. Late members can join in as they arrive. Groups committed to starting on time may add fifteen minutes to the beginning of the meeting for greetings and snacks.
- The opening is an opportunity for the opener to express appreciation of parenting or their child(ren). This may be done by relating a personal experience, sharing a family ritual, reading a poem or a passage from a favorite book, doing a short activity with the group, singing a song or doing a dance or a meditation.

FACILITATOR GUIDELINES
- The role of **facilitator** rotates each session among participants. Facilitators generally take time to read all of the materials of the chapter. They are not expected to be experts on the topic.
- Start on time with the opening. End on time with the action steps. Groups generally meet for one-and-a-half hours.
- The session starts off with the **Circle Question**. Each participant takes a turn so everyone's voice is heard over about 20 minutes. The group then chooses the most relevant **Discussion Questions** and the facilitator guides the discussion for about 30 minutes, leaving time for solutions and action steps.
- The facilitator's principal role is to keep the focus on the topic and to foster a comfortable environment for everyone to share ideas fairly and respectfully. The articles and the discussion questions are only a guide to the topic. Add in your own, and if the group discussion is branching off in a relevant, fruitful direction, follow it. Conversation that drifts off topic too far can be gently brought in with a comment such as, "I noticed we are talking about ... rather than ..."
- When a participant or two dominates discussion, thank them for their opinions. Then ask someone else for their opinion. If it continues, share your experience with that person privately later.
- Listen carefully and talk less to help guide the discussion effectively. Keep in mind:
  › Consensus is not the goal of the group. Disagreements should be expected and welcomed.
  › Interrupt any discussions where respect is being jeopardized or one person is monopolizing.
  › Agree ahead of time how you are going to handle one or two people dominating discussions.
  › Consider having a visible clock, using a sand timer or a talking stick to foster fair sharing.
  › Keep the discussions moving along, so there is time to discuss the **Putting It Together** action steps and solution ideas.
- This course is for personal exploration and to discover how the participants can make a difference in their own lives in connection with their families, communities, and schools. Write down your personal ideas you want to implement in **Putting it Together—Your Version**.

CLASS SCHEDULE AND SIGN-UP

All participants fill out this sheet at the first session. Two volunteers are needed for each session: someone to provide an Opening and someone to serve as Facilitator. Snacks are provided by the hosting member.

	SESSIONS	DATE	OPENER	FACILITATOR	LOCATION
1	What is Happening to Her?				
2	What Influences Her?				
3	Parenting Her				
4	Celebrating Womanhood				
5	Empowering Her				
6	Teaching Her				
7	Making Time for Her				
8	Keeping Her Safe				
9	Supporting Her				
10	Creating Community				
	Gathering to Celebrate				

TIPS FOR A MEANINGFUL, CONNECTED, SUPPORTIVE DISCUSSION GROUP
- Bring an open mind and acceptance to each meeting. Share honestly.
- Attend every meeting, and show up on time for the opening.
- Prepare for each session by doing as much reading as you can. At least, try to read the overview.
- List one or more goals for what you want to create in your life during this discussion group time.
- Take your turn with the co-leader roles: **opener and facilitator.**
- Ideally everyone monitors his/her own talking and makes sure it is a "fair amount of time." This is critical. Putting structures in place to support equal sharing can be helpful.
- Allow time for discussion of solutions and action steps in each session.
- Take ownership of solutions. Focus your energy on what you can change personally or contribute as a group. Avoid "should" as in: "my child, partner, the media, school, counselor … should …"
- **Set ground rules for the group** at the first meeting and share how you are best supported by others:
  › Observe confidentiality of personal stories.
  › Seek clarity, not consensus. Maintain respect for everyone's opinions.
  › Avoid finger pointing, blaming others or ganging up on someone with a differing opinion.
- Handle conflict directly and early, such as one or two people dominating the discussions
  › Avoid third party talk.
  › If you have a problem with a fellow participant, talk with them directly and when the problem is small and easier to resolve. Everyone matters and the group success depends on honest interactions.
  › If the problem continues, or a group problem arises bring it up at the next meeting to discuss together.
- Participants with serious problems with their adolescent or with themselves will find more effective support from outside, for example, from professional counseling.

What's Happening to My Daughter?

Lee Ogle, Asst. Teacher and Artist

What's Happening to My Daughter?

> "What we are teaches the child far more than what we say, so we must be what we want our children to become." —Joseph Chilton Pearce
>
> "A hundred years from now, it will not matter what my bank account was, the sort of house I lived in, or the make of car I drove. But the world may be different, because I was important in the life of a child." —Anon
>
> "There is a story about a town where people were falling off its cliffs. The city elders met to debate whether to build a fence at the top of the cliff or put an ambulance down in the valley. This story summarizes the essential differences between treatment and prevention." —Mary Pipher
>
> "Nothing in life is to be feared, it is only to be understood. When you dare to face the things that scare you, you open the door to freedom." —Anon

GOALS

- To understand the power parents have to make a positive difference in their children's lives and in the lives of other people's children

- To understand the 40 Developmental Assets that help every child navigate childhood and adolescence in a positive and healthy manner

- To empower parents to make more connections with the children in their lives

- To acknowledge the difficult challenges that girls and parents are facing today

- To get acquainted with the other parents in your parenting group

OVERVIEW

You are on an exciting, wonderful journey called parenting. We are honored you chose this parenting guide to support you. We believe that through the voices of more than 100 authors you will find your own voice, your inner wisdom. No one knows your deepest values as well as you do. No one cares for and is as invested in the well-being of your daughter as you are. By reading these different perspectives and having discussions with other dedicated parents, you can discover a renewed confidence in yourself and your ability to support your child as they discover who they are.

One of the best activities to start you on this journey is to take a moment and think about what inspired you to make the commitment to read this parenting guide. What would you most like to gain from this activity? What is it that you most want for your daughter? Taking the time to make a list of the positive visions and wishes that you have for your daughter will support you in your parenting journey. It is a lot easier to be an empowered and effective parent when you are in touch with these long-term goals. Focusing on what you don't want to happen and what you fear is a common parenting pitfall, especially as children approach their teens. Unfortunately, this encourages a high state of parental anxiety and hopelessness, with feelings of impotence towards protecting your daughter from the dangers of adolescence. Actually, there are many things you can do to help your daughter grow up safely and successfully. That is what *Raising Our Daughters* is all about: working with other involved parents to create a positive vision for your daughters' futures and looking at preventive strategies that will strengthen our girls and ensure their success in the long run. Holly Nishimura shares her parenting goals in the first article of this chapter, **"What I Want for My Daughter and All Young Women"** (p. 1:11).

Family Empowerment Network™ (FEN) offers this parenting guide to acquaint parents with a variety of preventive parenting strategies that instituted **now**, will help your children navigate adolescence with safer and better decision-making skills. Furthermore, we would like to introduce you to a variety of issues that affect the mental, social and emotional health of girls as they grow up in contemporary American society. We would like to empower parents to support each other and to network within their community to create a nurturing and healthy environment for all youth. Lastly, we would like to support parents in their parenting struggles. Although parents may at times feel inadequate or overwhelmed, FEN believes that parents are the very best resource for helping their kids survive the transition from childhood to adulthood, and for creating an environment that will support their children's emerging competence, caring, and responsibility. Parents, however, may need some help along the way, as this is a difficult if not impossible task to do all alone. Children are social creatures and require relationships with adults and children outside of their own homes to ensure their full and healthy development. The African wisdom that "it takes a village to raise a child" is truly applicable in our modern lives as well. It is also true that adults **can** create healthy contemporary "villages" that will support and nurture our children, if they so choose. Family Empowerment Network is making the assumption that you are one of the parents who chooses to make a difference.

Our introductory chapter addresses the power parents have to make a positive difference in the lives of their own children and in the lives of other youth. Family Empowerment Network is excited to introduce you to a grassroots movement called "asset building" that is based on the Search Institute's twenty-five years of research on resiliency and protective factors for children. The Search Institute, a nonprofit organization based in Minneapolis, Minnesota, began their project by asking, "Why do some kids from an incredibly impoverished neighborhood do well, while others who have plenty of advantages do poorly? What internal resources and external supports are necessary for a child from any background to become successful, resilient and healthy?"

By researching scientific literature, conferring with child health and educational professionals, and by talking extensively with children and families themselves, the Search Institute found that there are 40 building blocks or assets that all kids need in their lives to succeed. These Developmental Assets represent 40 essential socialization experiences that have been shown in extensive testing to support health-promoting behaviors and to decrease risky behaviors in all youth, consistent across gender, racial, economic and cultural lines. These assets entail actions which adults can readily promote and over which a family and community of people can exert considerable influence.

The list of **"40 Developmental Assets"** is the second handout in your parenting guide (p. 1:12). Please copy this list and POST IT ON YOUR REFRIGERATOR! These assets are grouped into 20 external assets (including the categories of support, empowerment, boundaries and expectations, and constructive use of time) and 20 internal assets (with the categories of commitment to learning, positive values, social competencies, and positive self-identity). Assets have been shown to be cumulative; the more kids possess, the better off they are. As the number of assets in a child's life increases, so does that child's well-being, as assets help inoculate youth against high-risk behaviors. Having 30 of 40 assets is protective against high-risk behaviors. Sadly enough, even though most people will recognize the importance of these 40 Developmental Assets, the vast majority of our nation's youth possess less than one half of them

in their lives. Only 8% have 30 or more assets. What may sound like good common sense is not yet common practice for most of our youth.

Using the assets as a guide, parents can find ways to strengthen their own child's potential to do well in life, as well as to positively impact the lives of other children. Time and again during the Search Institute's research, it was impressive to see the positive power of growing up in a neighborhood where multiple adults took an interest in the well-being of children, and where these adults also helped set boundaries and monitor out-of-bounds behaviors. Taking an active interest in the children and adolescents in your own community can be a huge step towards improving the lives and Developmental Assets of all of your community's children. It is interesting to note that only nine of the 40 Developmental Assets are built within the family. This helps explain why parents so desperately need the help and support of others—adults, schools, neighborhoods and communities—to ensure the success and healthy development of their daughters.

Asset building within your community can be as simple as showing up at your daughter's school and greeting all the children there by name, volunteering as a sports coach, arranging constructive after-school activities for kids on your block or in your community, or encouraging your local newspaper to run more articles with positive stories about local youth and families. The assets framework can be a great tool for increasing the impact and interactions of adults in the lives of a community's children, which exactly complements the goals and work of Family Empowerment Network. Of course, we hold high hopes that you will make good use of this helpful tool. Our hope is to see parents, families, organizations and neighborhoods pitching in to reclaim their own personal capabilities and responsibilities for raising a community of healthy and resilient youth.

What we find most attractive about asset building is that it is a positive, proactive approach that builds on what's right in a community, and creates changes that become a part of the ongoing infrastructure of schools, homes and neighborhoods. This approach empowers parents and communities by looking at

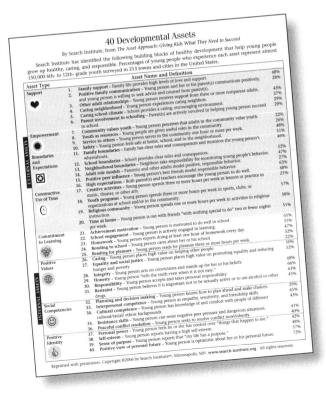

youth as resources, by involving everyone (including kids) in creating a healthy, cooperative and hopeful community, and by paying attention to all children, not just the troublemakers. Family Empowerment Network bases much of its philosophy on these assets. We are not alone. Over a thousand communities have adopted these assets around the nation, including the entire State of Colorado. You will be introduced to the key aspects of asset building in this chapter. In subsequent chapters, the assets relevant to that chapter will be listed and related asset-building articles will be included.

There are five articles from the Search Institute on Developmental Assets that are included in your syllabus. These are: **"Fast Facts about Developmental Assets," "The Power of Assets: Protecting Youth from High-Risk Behaviors and Promoting Positive Attitudes and Behaviors," "How You Can Build Assets,"** and **"The Asset-Building Difference"** (pp. 1:13 - 1:16). Two articles, **"Adults Who Cared in My Life"** and **"Tips for Adults to Connect with Children"** (p.1:17 and 1:19), discuss the essential need for meaningful relationships between adults and teenagers and include suggestions on how to create them. The next article, **"Are Americans Afraid of Teens?"** (p. 1:20) discusses the fears adults have of teens, which are largely due to the influences of negative media messages, derogatory stereotypes, unrecognized racism and lack of opportunities to interact with teenagers. The article includes tips for connecting with teens, including increasing opportunities for positive interactions and taking the time to listen to teens' stories and concerns.

In fact, children born in the last two decades of the 20th century (1981-1999), "The Millennials," also known as "Generation Y," may be the key to a more peaceful future, according to Life Coach Sally Gardiner who wrote **"The Millennials—Our Future Hope"** (p.1:23). Millennials, the most technologically advanced generation ever, are global citizens who are tolerant and value diversity. They love working collaboratively since they have been involved in family decision-making throughout their lives by child-focused parents. As parents, we may need to help Millennials find a balance between the attitude that they can have, be, or do anything they want, and the reality that success takes hard work and determination.

So, just how are our girls faring in today's society? The answer is certainly mixed. Girls now benefit from tremendous opportunities for self-expression, independence and career advancement that no previous generation of women has ever been able to experience. The past 30 years have seen steady gains by girls in academics, such that there are now more females than males taking high level math and science courses, leading extracurricular clubs and activities, earning high school diplomas, enrolling in college, and graduating from colleges and universities. Girls are also more active in sports than ever before. However, there are also many indicators that our girls are engaging in risky behaviors that can severely alter the course and success of their lives. Our adolescent girls are increasingly faced with the risks of sexual activity, sexually transmitted diseases, depression, eating disorders, drug abuse, date rape, verbal and relational aggression, pregnancy and violent crime during their childhoods, when we all agree they are not best prepared to deal with them. These high-risk behaviors are not simply the result of poor parenting. They are a consequence of the fact that our girls are more stressed and less protected than they were 30, or even 10, years ago. Girls are growing up in a society that is toxic—more dangerous, sexualized and media saturated than in any previous era. At the same time, our communities and families are more stressed and fragmented as well. There is less time available to nurture teens or provide a counterpoint to the youth culture created by commercial media.

Dr. Mary Pipher, a psychologist who works primarily with adolescent girls, wrote *Reviving Ophelia: Saving the Selves of Adolescent Girls* in 1994. She sounded an alarm about the self-esteem of our adolescent girls and fundamentally changed the way our nation looks at the resiliency and problems of adolescent girls. Dr. Pipher contends that adolescence has always been hard, but it is harder now because of cultural changes that have diminished the protected place in space and time that we once called childhood. She notes that our once vital and curious preadolescent girls become less resilient, assertive and active, and are inclined to take fewer healthy risks once they hit puberty. Girls' psychological wellbeing and academic performance can also falter as girls try to fit their whole selves into a small, feminine role of looking good to please others. High-risk behaviors seem to multiply as girls deny their "true selves" in order to comply with cultural prescriptions for becoming "properly female."

It helps parents to understand that their daughters still need their love and presence, even if the girls are stressed by adolescence and the commercialized, sexist culture. As Mary Pipher says in *Reviving Ophelia*:

> *Wholeness is shattered by the chaos of adolescence. Girls become fragmented, their selves split into mysterious contradictions. They are sensitive and tenderhearted, mean and competitive, superficial and idealistic. They are confident in the morning and overwhelmed with anxiety by nightfall. They rush through their days with wild energy and then collapse into lethargy. They try on new roles every week—this week the good student, next week the delinquent and the next, the artist. And they expect their families to keep up with these changes.*

We can help our adolescent girls by being there with them and allowing them to be their REAL selves, while not insisting they always please others. If we listen deeply to them and teach them to respect and care for themselves, they will find their authentic selves. Dr. Pipher challenges parents and all adults to become active agents in making our communities more child-friendly and, especially, less toxic for our girls.

Parents who want to help their daughters navigate this modern mine-field of adolescence with strength and resiliency can be helped by looking at current research in the field. The National Council for Research on Women has compiled its findings in **"The Girls Report: What We Know & Need to Know About Growing Up Female"** (p. 1:24), a brief summary of which is included in your syllabus. This report reminds us that helping girls begins with creating a supportive and nurturing environment with rich relationships that can build on girls' strengths, so that they can grow and explore meaningful options for their futures. Lyn Mikel Brown, EdD, founder of Hardy Girls, Healthy Women at www.hghw.org, echoes these same recommendations. Dr. Brown notes that the problems that young girls face cannot be looked at solely at the personal level. Girls are influenced by the cultural and political landscape of their lives and need to have nurturing, supportive "hardiness zones" in which to develop and mature.

> *The stress and distress that so many girls experience can be understood as a loss of control in many arenas of their lives, a struggle to create an identity and belief system to which they can wholeheartedly commit, and a sense of isolation within the challenges that face them. Girls need experiences in which they exert control over more than their body's sexuality or appearance, where they can connect to their own worth, a positive belief system, and others who will commit to them, and where they can experience support and encouragement to learn and persist in the face of struggles.*

The chapter **"Hardy Girls"** (p. 1:27), from Tim Flinder's online book, *Parent Promise: Helping School Girls Hold on to Their Dreams*, is included in your syllabus as an overview of how parents can encourage hardiness in their girls. Mr. Flinders emphasizes that girls who show resilience and success tend to have three traits that set them apart: they tend to be connected to at least one caring, competent adult and to their home, community and culture; they are both caring and achievement oriented; and they have a balance of traditionally feminine and masculine attributes. Parents who help their daughters develop hardiness increase the chances that their daughters will survive adolescent storms intact.

Family Empowerment Network agrees that girls are in need of our support. What this curriculum won't do is to compare who has it worse—girls or boys. All of our children face risk factors in being raised in our complex, modern society and they all need our support. Rather than pitting the needs of girls against those of boys, it is better to commit ourselves to raising boys and girls who respect themselves and each other, and who are willing to work together to make the world a more humane place for all. Supporting girls *more* does not mean we have to support boys *less,* or vice versa.

Also included at the end of this chapter is a **"Girl in a Box"** exercise and **"An Asset Checklist"** (p. 1:31 and 1:32) to fill out at your first ROD meeting. These two activities can help you better understand your daughter's world. It would be interesting to also have your daughter fill out these forms from her own perspective. An active discussion about how your answers differ would be a great starting point toward understanding your daughter's own unique point of view.

To sum up, all of our kids need the active support of the adults in their communities. This support will come from people like you, the involved parents who care a lot and who are not willing to be discouraged. We are the ones who can turn this culture around by taking action to support all kids—not just our own. This includes the kids in our neighborhoods, schools, and places of worship. By working together to create resources and support systems that truly encourage all children to develop into competent and caring adults, and by focusing on strengths, we parents can truly create a more hopeful world for ourselves and for our children—if we will only choose to take the time.

ACTIVITIES TO DO BEFORE YOU MEET WITH YOUR GROUP

Imagine you were raising your daughter in a perfect environment. What would this vision look like? What support would be there for her from her family, community, government, and school? Write these down and refer back to them as you read this book.

Take the "Asset Checklist" for every child in your family and for the adults in the family when they were children. What are your family's strengths? Name the area you would most like to improve.

CIRCLE QUESTION

Take some time to do the "Girl in a Box" activity together as a group.
Then, have each of you share something that you learned from doing this activity.
Compare life for your daughter to your own experience growing up.

POSSIBLE DISCUSSION QUESTIONS

1. What does your vision for your daughter look like? What kinds of support would you like there to be for her?
2. Draw a family tree. Who were the powerful influences in the family both male and female? Keep this in your book.
3. What are the differences in expectations between girls (women) and boys (men) in your family? In your family of origin?
4. Review the protective power of assets against drugs, alcohol, sexual activity and violence. Why do you think that having more than 30 assets has such power?
5. Fill out the asset checklist on page 1:34 for your daughter and discuss how you can build and maintain assets.
6. How many adults (other than parents) does your child have involved in her life? How could you get more adults involved in her life? How many children's lives, other than your own, do you influence?
7. What top 3 activities does your daughter do with her time? What would you like to see less of? More of?
8. Describe 3 top issues your daughter struggles with now or you worry she will soon struggle with.
9. Describe the qualities of two women you admire—one who you know personally and one who is famous (alive or dead).
10. List the traits you would like to see in an ideal role model in your daughter's life.
11. How aware are you of the culture your child lives in? What are some ways to learn more?
12. Have you had an experience of being "pleasantly surprised" by connecting with teens, finding they weren't as frightening as you thought?

PUTTING IT INTO PRACTICE

-   Get all adults who live in the household involved in this curriculum, either by attending the class together or reading this book alongside you and discussing it. For single parent households, get your support adults involved too.
-   Evaluate how you are spending time. Are you really doing what you care most about?
-   Get into the world of your daughter: watch the TV she watches, get to know her friends she hangs out with, be available to talk when she needs it.
-   Examine carefully how your expectations of girls and boys differ.
-   Ask your daughter who her role models are.
-   Ask your daughter who she would feel comfortable talking with if she were having problems.
-   Ask your daughter what she is most worried about now and in her future.
-   Use the asset checklist to assess your family's strengths. What areas could be actively worked on?
-   Post the assets on your refrigerator and look at them a few times every week.
-   Form support groups for your daughter and for yourself.

PUTTING IT TOGETHER—YOUR VERSION

Write down three or four ideas you have been inspired to implement in your own life after reading and discussing this chapter.

1. _____

2. _____

3. _____

4. _____

TOP RESOURCES FOR RAISING OUR DAUGHTERS

1. *Reviving Ophelia, Saving the Selves of Our Adolescent Girls* by Mary Pipher
2. *Mother Daughter Wisdom: Creating a Legacy of Physical and Emotional Health* by Christiane Northrup
3. *Things Will Be Diferent for My Daughter* by Mindy Bingham and Sandy Stryker
4. *Growing a Girl: Seven Strategies for Raising a Strong, Spirited Daughter* by Barbara MacKoff
5. *The Mother-Daughter Project: How Mothers and Daughters Can Band Together, Beat the Odds, and Thrive Through Adolescence* by SuEllen Hamkins, MD and Renee Schultz, MA
6. *How To Say It® to Girls: Communicating with Your Growing Daughter* by Nancy Gruver

TOP RESOURCES FOR RAISING OUR CHILDREN

1. *Parenting From the Inside Out: How a Deeper Self-Understanding Can Help You Raise Children Who Thrive* by Daniel Siegel, MD and Mary Hartzell, MEd
2. *How to Talk So Your Kids Will Listen, and How to Listen So Your Kids Will Talk* by Adele Faber and Elaine Mazlish
3. *Positive Discipline: A Classic Guide for Parents and Teachers to Help Children Develop Self-discipline, Responsibility, Cooperation, and Problem-solving* by Jane Nelsen, EdD, MFT and *Positive Discipline for Teenagers: Empowering Your Teen and Yourself Through Kind and Firm Parenting* by Jane Nelsen, EdD, MFT and Lynn Lott, MA, MFT
4. *Uncommon Sense for Parents of Teenagers* by Michael Riera, PhD
5. *The Parent as Coach Approach: The Seven Ways to Coach Your Teen in the Game of Life* by Diana Sterling
6. *The Good Father: On Men, Masculinity, and Life in the Family* by Mark O'Connell
7. *Parenting From Your Heart: Sharing the Gifts of Compassion, Connection, and Choice* by Inbal Kashtan
8. *Respectful Parents, Respectful Kids: Seven Keys to Turn Family Conflict into Cooperation* by Sura Hart and Victoria Kindle Hodson
9. *Putting Family First: Strategies for Reclaiming Family Life in a Hurry-Up World* by William Doherty, PhD and Barbara Carlson
10. *Best Friends, Worst Enemies: Understanding the Social Lives of Children* by Michael Thompson, PhD

TOP RESOURCES FOR TEENS

1. *Six Most Important Decisions You'll Ever Make* by Sean Covey
2. *Seven Habits of Highly Effective Teens* by Sean Covey
3. *Perfectionism: What is Bad about Being Too Good* by Mariam Adderholdt and Jan Goldberg

Full Esteem Ahead's Wings Newsletter
What I Want for My Daughter and All Young Women

By Holly Nishimura

I WANT A COMMUNITY and environment that teaches and supports development of the whole person. If sports are to be our model, I want it to be based on good sportsmanship, not superstardom and win-loss records. If soft drinks are the model, then base it on nutritional content and contributions to one's health, not the image and sizzle of a model or the promise of cool you can attain simply by taking a sip. I want her to know it is not the size of her bra or the status of her friends or the clothing she wears that has true meaning: what she owns and wears is only a detail in her life. The content of her character, her actions and contributions, the truth as she knows it, and her beliefs and values are what define her. I want her to be strong, independent and self-sufficient so she can make clear and positive decisions for herself throughout her life. I want her to be strong, independent and self-sufficient so she can love herself, and if she so chooses, she can wisely select a partner who will provide her with love and support.

I want her to understand her sense of responsibility and her place in a community. I want her to know we all bear responsibility for our society and environment and we can contribute in one thousand ways.

I want her to experience true joy because life can be a great deal of fun. I want her to know that even on a bad hair day she can meet a new friend, that with a run in her stockings, she can have a rich and rewarding experience, that when she steps outside herself and her immediate surroundings and parameters, she can experience the entire world. And if she can manage her feelings and life, she can have whatever she wants. I believe in the potential of her individual spirit, and want her to have that belief as well.

And finally, I always want her to know unconditional love —from her parents and family, from at least one friend, from a partner if that is her choosing, and how to give love and how to share it. I believe these will give her the emotional strength to survive anything and choose to thrive in everything.

Holly Nishimura worked for the Ophelia Project in Erie, PA in 2001 when she wrote this article.

Reprinted with permission from Full Esteem Ahead, *Wings,* Winter, 1998.

40 Developmental Assets

By Search Institute, from *The Asset Approach: Giving Kids What They Need to Succeed*

Search Institute has identified the following building blocks of healthy development that help young people grow up healthy, caring, and responsible. Percentages of young people who experience each asset represent almost 150,000 6th- to 12th- grade youth surveyed in 213 towns and cities in the United States.

Asset Type		Asset Name and Definition	
Support	1.	**Family support** – Family life provides high levels of love and support.	68%
	2.	**Positive family communication** – Young person and her or his parent(s) communicate positively, and young person is willing to seek advice and counsel from parent(s).	28%
	3.	**Other adult relationships** – Young person receives support from three or more nonparent adults.	43%
	4.	**Caring neighborhood** – Young person experiences caring neighbors.	37%
	5.	**Caring school climate** – School provides a caring, encouraging environment.	29%
	6.	**Parent involvement in schooling** – Parent(s) are actively involved in helping young person succeed in school.	29%
Empowerment	7.	**Community values youth** – Young person perceives that adults in the community value youth.	22%
	8.	**Youth as resources** – Young people are given useful roles in the community.	26%
	9.	**Service to others** – Young person serves in the community one hour or more per week.	48%
	10.	**Safety** – Young person feels safe at home, school, and in the neighborhood.	51%
Boundaries and Expectations	11.	**Family boundaries** – Family has clear rules and consequences and monitors the young person's whereabouts.	46%
	12.	**School boundaries** – School provides clear rules and consequences.	52%
	13.	**Neighborhood boundaries** – Neighbors take responsibility for monitoring young people's behavior.	47%
	14.	**Adult role models** – Parent(s) and other adults model positive, responsible behavior.	27%
	15.	**Positive peer influence** – Young person's best friends model responsible behavior.	63%
	16.	**High expectations** – Both parent(s) and teachers encourage the young person to do well.	48%
Constructive Use of Time	17.	**Creative activities** – Young person spends three or more hours per week in lessons or practice in music, theater, or other arts.	21%
	18.	**Youth programs** – Young person spends three or more hours per week in sports, clubs, or organizations at school and/or in the community.	57%
	19.	**Religious community** – Young person spends one or more hours per week in activities in religious instruction.	58%
	20.	**Time at home** – Young person is out with friends "with nothing special to do" two or fewer nights per week.	51%
Commitment to Learning	21.	**Achievement motivation** – Young person is motivated to do well in school.	65%
	22.	**School engagement** – Young person is actively engaged in learning.	55%
	23.	**Homework** – Young person reports doing at least one hour of homework every day.	47%
	24.	**Bonding to school** – Young person cares about her or his school.	52%
	25.	**Reading for pleasure** – Young person reads for pleasure three or more hours per week.	22%
Positive Values	26.	**Caring** – Young person places high value on helping other people.	50%
	27.	**Equality and social justice** – Young person places high value on promoting equality and reducing hunger and poverty.	52%
	28.	**Integrity** – Young person acts on convictions and stands up for her or his beliefs.	68%
	29.	**Honesty** – Young person "tells the truth even when it is not easy."	66%
	30.	**Responsibility** – Young person accepts and takes personal responsibility.	63%
	31.	**Restraint** – Young person believes it is important not to be sexually active or to use alcohol or other drugs.	45%
Social Competencies	32.	**Planning and decision making** – Young person knows how to plan ahead and make choices.	29%
	33.	**Interpersonal competence** – Young person has empathy, sensitivity, and friendship skills.	45%
	34.	**Cultural competence** – Young person has knowledge of and comfort with people of different cultural/racial/ ethnic backgrounds.	43%
	35.	**Resistance skills** – Young person can resist negative peer pressure and dangerous situations.	41%
	36.	**Peaceful conflict resolution** – Young person seeks to resolve conflict nonviolently.	40%
Positive Identity	37.	**Personal power** – Young person feels he or she has control over "things that happen to me."	42%
	38.	**Self-esteem** – Young person reports having a high self-esteem.	48%
	39.	**Sense of purpose** – Young person reports that "my life has a purpose."	57%
	40.	**Positive view of personal future** – Young person is optimistic about her or his personal future.	72%

EXTERNAL ASSETS

INTERNAL ASSETS

Fast Facts
About Developmental Assets for Youth
By Search Institute, from *Pass It On! Ready-to-Use Handouts for Asset Builders*

IMMUNIZATIONS KEEP young children healthy and protect them from disease. Similarly, Developmental Assets help kids make healthy choices and inoculate them against a wide range of risk-taking behaviors, including substance abuse, violence, and school failure. The more assets young people have, the more likely they are to be healthy.

Other Facts About Developmental Assets:

- **Young people with more assets are less likely to engage in risk-taking behaviors.** Young people with 10 or fewer assets say they are involved in an average of about 4.5 high-risk behaviors. Young people with 31 assets or more report an average of less than one high-risk behavior.

- **As young people's assets increase, their positive behaviors also increase.** While young people with 10 or fewer assets report an average of

fewer than 3 positive behaviors, those with 31 assets or more average 6 positive behaviors. This includes school success, informal helping, valuing diversity, and exhibiting leadership.

- **The average young person surveyed has 18.0 of the 40 assets.** But levels of assets decrease for older youth. While the average sixth grader surveyed has 21.5 assets, the average 12th grader surveyed has 17.2 assets.

- **The most common asset is #40: positive view of personal future.** Seventy percent of young people surveyed report having this asset.

- **The least common asset is #17: creative activities.** Only 19 percent of young people report having this asset.

- **Girls typically have more Developmental Assets than boys.** However, boys are more likely to have #10: safety; #18: youth programs; #38: self-esteem; and #39: sense of purpose.

- **Assets that decrease in frequency between 6th and 12th grades are** #31: restraint (71 percent of 6th graders vs. 21 percent of 12th graders); #12: school boundaries (70 percent vs. 34 percent); and #15: positive peer influence (82 percent vs. 49 percent).

- **Assets that increase in frequency between 6th and 12th grades are** #10: safety (45 percent vs. 68 percent); #37: personal power (40 percent vs. 55 percent); and #28: integrity (63 percent vs. 75 percent).

The Developmental Assets are 40 opportunities, skills, relationships, values, and self-perceptions that all young people need to succeed.

The Power of Assets

By Search Institute, from *The Asset Approach: Giving Kids What They Need to Succeed*

On one level, the 40 Developmental Assets represent common wisdom about the kinds of positive experiences and characteristics that young people need and deserve. But their value extends further. Surveys of almost 150,000 students in grades 6–12 (ages appoximately 11–18 years) reveal that assets are powerful influences on adolescent behavior. Regardless of gender, ethnic heritage, economic situation, or geographic location, these assets both promote positive behaviors and attitudes and help protect young people from many different problem behaviors.

0–10 assets   **11–20** assets   **21–30** assets   **31–40** assets

Promoting Positive Attitudes and Behaviors

Our research shows that the more assets students report having, the more likely they are to also report the following patterns of thriving behavior.

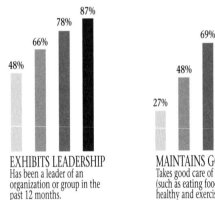
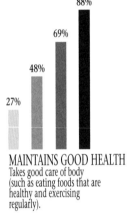
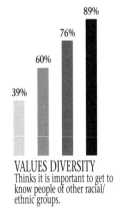
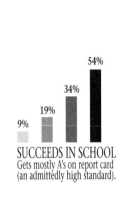

EXHIBITS LEADERSHIP
Has been a leader of an organization or group in the past 12 months.

MAINTAINS GOOD HEALTH
Takes good care of body (such as eating foods that are healthy and exercising regularly).

VALUES DIVERSITY
Thinks it is important to get to know people of other racial/ethnic groups.

SUCCEEDS IN SCHOOL
Gets mostly A's on report card (an admittedly high standard).

Protecting Youth from High-Risk Behaviors

Assets not only promote positive behaviors, they also protect young people: The more assets a young person reports having, the less likely he or she is to make harmful or unhealthy choices. (Note that these definitions are set rather high, suggesting ongoing problems, not experimentation.)

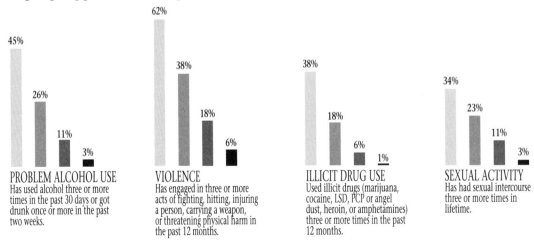

PROBLEM ALCOHOL USE
Has used alcohol three or more times in the past 30 days or got drunk once or more in the past two weeks.

VIOLENCE
Has engaged in three or more acts of fighting, hitting, injuring a person, carrying a weapon, or threatening physical harm in the past 12 months.

ILLICIT DRUG USE
Used illicit drugs (marijuana, cocaine, LSD, PCP or angel dust, heroin, or amphetamines) three or more times in the past 12 months.

SEXUAL ACTIVITY
Has had sexual intercourse three or more times in lifetime.

How You Can Build Assets

By Search Institute, from *The Asset Approach: Giving Kids What They Need to Succeed*

...On Your Own

Everyone—parents and guardians, grandparents, teachers, coaches, friends, youth workers, employers, youths, and others—can build assets. It doesn't necessarily take a lot of money. But it can make a tremendous difference in raising confident, caring young people. What it takes is building relationships, spending time together, and being intentional about nurturing positive values and commitments. Some things you can do:

- Get to know the names of kids who live around you. Find out what interests them,
- Get to know what young people around you are really like, not just how they are portrayed in the media,
- Eat at least one meal together every day as a family. Take time to talk about what's going on in each other's lives,
- Volunteer as a tutor, mentor, or youth leader in a youth-serving program.

...In Your Organization

If you're involved in an organization such as a school, youth organization, family service agency, health-care provider, or business—either as an employee or volunteer—you can encourage asset-building action within that organization. Some possibilities:

- Educate your constituency, employees, or customers about their potential as asset builders,
- Develop policies that allow parents to be involved in their children's lives and that encourage all employees to get involved with kids in the community,
- Contribute time, talent, or resources to support community asset-building efforts,
- Develop or strengthen programs and activities that build assets, such as mentoring, service-learning activities, peer helping, and recreation.

...In Your Community

Hundreds of communities across the Unites States are discovering the power and potential of uniting efforts for asset building. They involve people from all parts of the community in shaping and coordinating strategies that will help all young people be more likely to succeed. You can use your influence in the community to:

- Talk about asset building with formal and informal leaders and other influential people you know. Get their support for asset building,
- Conduct a survey to measure the asset levels of young people in your community. (Call Search Institute for information.),
- Develop opportunities for youth to contribute to the community through sharing their perspectives and taking action and leadership,
- Celebrate and honor the commitments of people who dedicate their lives and time to children and youth.

Six Keys to Asset Building

It doesn't cost a lot of money or require special training to build Developmental Assets. Here are six key ways to guide asset-building action.

1. Everyone can build assets. Building assets requires consistent messages across a community. All adults, youth, and children play a role.

2. All young people need assets. While it is crucial to pay special attention to those youth who have the least (economically or emotionally), nearly all young people need more assets than they have.

3. Relationships are key. Strong relationships between adults and young people, young people and their peers, and teenagers and children are central to asset building.

4. Asset building is an ongoing process. Building assets starts when a child is born and continues through high school and beyond.

5. Consistent messages are important. Young people need to receive consistent messages about what's important and what's expected from their families, school, communities, the media, and other sources.

Intentional redundancy is important. Assets must be continually reinforced across the years and in all areas of a young person's life.

The Asset-Building Difference

By Search Institute, from *Pass It On! Ready-to-Use Handouts for Asset Builders*

For healthy community development to occur for all children and youth, we need to rebuild communities where young people and organizations feel connected, engaged, responsible, and committed to young people. In order to do this, some essential shifts in thinking need to happen.

Moving From...

- Talking about problems
- Focusing on troubled and troubling youth
- Focusing primarily on ages 0 to 5
- Age segregation
- Viewing young people as problems
- Reacting to problems
- Blaming others
- Treating youth as objects of programs
- Relying on professionals
- Competing priorities
- Conflicting signals about values and priorities
- Managing crises
- Despair

To...

- Talking about positives and possibilities
- Focusing on all children and adolescents
- Focusing on all young people, ages 0 to 18
- Intergenerational community
- Seeing youth as resources
- Being proactive about building strengths
- Claiming personal responsibility
- Respecting youth as actors in their own development
- Involving everyone in the lives of young people
- Cooperative efforts
- Consistent messages about what is important
- Building a shared vision
- Hope

The Developmental Assets are 40 opportunities, skills, relationships, values, and self-perceptions that all young people need to succeed.

Adults Who Cared in My Life

By Julie Salmon

THERE'S A GIRL in my neighborhood who, like so many 16-year-olds, is going through a rough time right now. I don't know why. But I do know she used to be a sunny, confident little kid and she has turned into a sullen, unhappy teenager. She doesn't speak to her parents, skips school and, in general, tries to harm herself in any way she can. I saw her walking by one day after my family and others had finished playing a pick-up soccer game. I called out to her and said she ought to play with us sometime. She looked interested, and I thought of calling her the next week to remind her, but chickened out. What would she think, a 42-year-old neighbor lady, calling to ask her to play? How uncool. So I didn't do it, and she didn't show up.

Last week we went to interview Chris Tebbin of "Take the Time," an asset-building program in Portland, Oregon. She talked about the benefits of getting involved in kids' lives, both for them and for us. She especially noted the impact just one adult can have on one child's life. She said almost every adult who has overcome a troubled adolescence can point to a person whose influence or concern somehow turned them around. I told her about the girl in my neighborhood. "Is it as easy as that?" I asked. "Is it just picking up the phone and inviting this neighborhood kid to play soccer? Even if it feels a bit weird?" "Absolutely!"

That set me to thinking about the adults in my own childhood. I was lucky: I had two parents who cared. I was also the youngest of four children and had seen my parents go through a lot with my older siblings. I wanted to protect my parents, not confront them. So anytime I broke the rules (which I did often), I kept it very quiet. I lived by the "'what they don't know won't hurt them" philosophy. Basically I had a secret life my parents knew nothing about.

Fortunately there were other adults in my life I was unable to fool—for example, Coach Keay, the assistant

principal at my middle school. I logged many hours between grades six and eight in his office. I didn't mind getting kicked out of class for some misdemeanor because it meant I could spend time with him. I knew he thought well of me, had high expectations for me, and while I didn't always agree with his interpretations of my capabilities, I appreciated his high regard. He helped me think well of myself.

There were others as well—a host of them, it seems to me now. Some helped in big ways, some in small. Mr. Benton, the retired man across the street who always had a toy in his pocket for me. Mr. Morley, the crossing guard. I used to go to school early just to hang out and chat with him. Mrs. Adelman, my fourth grade teacher who gave up her lunch hours to give me individual instruction in math. The school nurse who called my mom when I was in 9th grade and told her to pick me up and take me out for a treat. She thought I needed a break because I seemed stressed out. I was actually faking a headache. But maybe that nurse was right. Maybe I WAS stressed out and DID need a break. Maybe she was a perceptive adult who reached out to me when I needed help. For that, I was grateful.

Paul Armstrong, my college English teacher who volunteered to work with me on my thesis on Jane Austen. He brought out the best in me, made me work harder and think more analytically than I had ever done. All these people contributed to a sense that I was worth something—their time, their interest, their concern. Where would I be now, if they hadn't "taken the time"?

I was a kid who could have gotten into big trouble. Lots of my friends did. A few of them did not live to tell the tale. I came of age in the '70s in an affluent community where drinking, drugs, and promiscuity ran rampant. But something always kept me from going too far. Some instinct of self-preservation, even self-worth, kept me safe. Undoubtedly, my parents' love kept me on track. But parents can't watch you every second. Mine certainly didn't.

There were always other adults along the way, encouraging me just by taking an interest. Without them I might not have been able to maintain that fragile sense of self that made it seem worthwhile to "be careful." So now I have this new theory. Maybe if we all make an extra effort to interact with the youth we see daily, we—like Jimmy Stewart in "It's a Wonderful Life"—will unknowingly have some profound effect on them. Each one of us just might take it upon ourselves to reach out to, say, one kid a week. Or one kid a month.

Not necessarily in a big way.

Sure, it's great if you can volunteer in the schools or start a youth group at your church or go to work for an organization that supports children. But it's also great if you can remember the name of the teenager down the street and say hello to her (or him). It's great if you can take five minutes to chat with the kid waiting for the bus at your corner. And it's great if you can invite the sullen teenager down the street to play soccer. Like I plan to do!

Julie Salmon is a freelance writer/editor and mother of three.

Reprinted with permission from Full Esteem Ahead, *Wings*, Spring 2000

Tips for Adults to Connect with Children: What Can We Do???
by Kathy Masarie, MD

Mary Pipher, author of *Reviving Ophelia: Saving the Selves of our Adolescent Girls* and *The Shelter of Each Other, Rebuilding our Families,* gets to the heart of what parents can do to help their children. Here are some of her ideas from a talk given in Portland, Oregon.

- **Take It Easy on Ourselves.** The role of parenting today is more complicated than ever. Instead of having community support to gently introduce our children to our culture, we have little support and want to hide them from our culture. Troubled kids often have pretty balanced families, but we all need to slow down.

- **Form Support Groups.** Everyone's as dysfunctional as you are. Sharing problems and solutions helps.

- **Learn About The World Your Children Are Living In.** Check out the malls, movies, and video arcades. Know their friends. The author's family had a rule that any kid could come over to the house for the evening, but their kids were not allowed to go out with anyone the parents didn't know.

- **Share Your Values With Your Kids.** One of the best times to talk to your kids is over dinner. Only 7% of families in America eat their meals together. Go over what happened in the world, as well as what happened in their and your day.

- **Teach Kids Resistance Training.** Saying "No" to a good friend or a popular kid can be very difficult for our peer-pressure-driven teens. The D.A.R.E. (Drug Awareness Resistance Effort) and the Drug Free Years (for parents) courses help with this.

- **Choose Your Media As Carefully As Your Friends.** They are living in your home and influencing your kids as powerfully as any live friends. Fund PBS. Control bad TV with letters of protest.

- **Satisfy Their Needs For:**
  o **Meaningful Work** - There is no more important work for a child than school. Put in effort to help.
  o **Challenging Talents And Interest** - Sports, music, collections, languages, Scouts....
  o **Learning Skills To Cope With Stress** - Exercise is a healthy outlet for stress for everyone.
  o **Sense Of Purpose** - This comes from a combination of all the things we have talked about.

- **Provide The Opportunity For Volunteer Work.** The author's daughter wanted to help the homeless and volunteered at a shelter. It got her away from her peers and got her around people whose smoking and drinking didn't look so glamorous. Homeless people have plenty of time and could talk with her as long as she wanted—not an option with most adults who are "too busy." She also learned she could help and that her actions could make a difference!

- **Have Them Read Books About Competent Girls And Women.** Have your daughters, read the magazine "New Moon, A Magazine For Girls And Their Dreams," P.O. Box 3587, Duluth, MN 55803 or *Great Books for Girls* by Kathleen Odean summarizing 600 books to inspire girls.

- **Form Alliances / Support Groups For Kids.** Ideally groups start as young as 8 (12 at the latest) and last until 18, with 2 adult facilitators of different ages, who shouldn't be one of the kids' parents. It may take a year of activities and outings before the kids will start talking about issues you feel are important. Perhaps a girl's club could agree to not talk about weight or appearances for one month. It could be called the "Fearless Club." Have a physician come to the school to talk about eating disorders and discuss it afterwards.

- **Get To Know Other People's Children.** Bring back that community spirit and be an available caring adult. Sometimes kids can't talk to their own parents and you, as their "mentor," may literally save them. The children of America are all "our children."

- **Celebrate Adolescence With Coming Of Age Ceremonies.** One family had all the women involved in the girl's life, draw or sew quilt pieces that represented their relationship with her. Then, they all got together and promised one thing they would each do to help her become an adult.

- **Encourage Situations Where Your Child Can Have Friends Of All Ages.** Being influenced by only single age peers can be very dangerous. Scouts or church groups are excellent opportunities for 17-year-olds to talk to struggling 13-year-olds. Single gender experiences are very important.

- **Encourage Your Child To Keep A Journal.** Teens could write down things they like about themselves and are proud of. It is very therapeutic to write down your thoughts when you are angry. It helps take it out of your head where it spins around in a vicious circle and place it on the paper in an organized way. A child may prefer taping his or her thoughts, rather than writing them.

Are Americans Afraid

Assets Magazine, Summer 1998

'Teens these days'

Like millions of American adults, they perceive that teens today are unruly, rude, lacking in basic civility, and oftentimes, downright dangerous. Are they right?

If one relies on mass media for an image of teenhood today, the answer would be certain. Consider the grizzly scenes of the school killings in Jonesboro, Ark., at the hands of youth ages 11 and 13; the shootings in Springfield, Ore., the work of a troubled teen; or the gritty photos of streetwise teens, pierced, tattooed, and gun-toting, as portrayed in *George* magazine in its feature, "Why Kids Are Ruining America."

But what do the statistics say? The Federal Bureau of Investigation (FBI) reported in 1995 that only 6.2% of all people arrested in the nation were under the age of 15. Only one-half of 1% of teens are arrested for a violent crime in any given year, says the FBI.

Still, this is not to say that teens never commit crimes. And it's not to say that violence by teens should be glossed over or dismissed. The point is that the vast majority of teens are not hoodlums or dangerous and don't aspire to be. So why is fear that should be reserved for genuinely dangerous teens often overlaid on virtually all teens?

In a middle-income neighborhood in a Midwest community known for its nice homes, clean environment, safe streets, and good schools, a shy 15-year-old girl rose nervously from her chair during a heated neighborhood hearing on how to spend a government grant.

Face flushed, voice shaking, she made her case: "Please, won't you think about us teens? We don't have anywhere to go, especially in the winter. We really need something to do in our neighborhood. We could really use a community center."

Her poignant plea notwithstanding, the neighborhood council decided to use the money to refurbish a school playground. The rationale? One argument raised was that building facilities that encouraged teens to "hang out" could create an intimidating environment for toddlers and preschoolers.

No one raised the obvious question: Just what would these younger kids do and where would they go 10 years from now when they come of age in a community that clearly values childhood innocence over adolescent awakenings?

And how is it that these well-educated, typically well-meaning adults could leapfrog logic, ignoring the fact that these teens were the same ones they depend on to babysit their toddlers, mow their lawns, and shovel their sidewalks?

In a word, fear.

Out of the **mouth of teens...**

The Mall of America in Bloomington, Minn., is a favorite gathering place for hundreds of teens and a destination for thousands of shoppers worldwide. *Assets* Editor Kathleen Kimball-Baker spent a recent afternoon at the mall interviewing teens. Here's what she heard:

Hector,* 17, is a tall lanky Latino youth who dressed in baggy black pants, a black shirt, a backwards baseball cap. He was walking the mall.

KKB: *Do you think Americans are afraid of teens?*

H: Yeah. They're scared when someone like me walks by–scared something will happen to them. But I give no one reason to be afraid.

KKB: *How do you know they're afraid of you?*

H: (Grins) When I pass by they lock their doors or walk on the other side of the street

KKB: *Why do you think they're afraid?*

H: The movies they see about wild teenagers. My town has a lot of old people in it. They shouldn't be scared. They should understand us, get to know us, pay attention to us to see how we are.

# of Teens?

Appearances can be deceiving

The problem is perceptual, often confounded by racism, classism, and stereotypes. Can the average adult, for example, tell the difference between a kid in sagging, baggy pants who's only trying to "fit in" from one who's armed for a fight? Not always. Maybe never.

And then there are the facial expressions. Can adults tell if the teen with the angry look is ready to lash out violently, or is she simply trying to process a perceived slight by her best friend? And what about those loud teens sitting on the sidewalk in front of the dollar cinema: Are they about to accost and embarrass the moviegoers in line—or are they just trying to figure out if they have enough change to buy a ticket?

Without knowing, many adults may simply be taking caution too far. If so, the result is ever-growing alienation and misunderstanding. And worse, such perceptions may be chipping away at a fundamental faith that teens will grow into adults who may actually make the world a better place some day.

A Princeton survey sponsored by Newsweek and NBC News in April found that three-quarters of American adults held the belief that teens with poor education, dim job prospects, and worrisome values pose a greater danger to this country than any foreign threat.

A recent poll of Colorado adults, conducted by Search Institute, together with Norwest Public Policy Research Program at the University of Colorado – Denver, found that two-thirds of the 934 adults polled think youth don't respect adults and that teens get into more trouble today than youth did years ago.

The 'enemy' within: youth or fear?

According to Kids These Days: What Americans Really Think About the Next Generation, a report published by Public Agenda, a nonprofit research organization based in New York: "Americans are convinced that today's adolescents face a crisis – not in their economic or physical well-being but in their values and morals. Most Americans look at today's teenagers with misgiving and trepidation, viewing them as undisciplined, disrespectful, and unfriendly." Public Agenda based its findings on telephone surveys of 2,000 adults and 600 young teens, focus groups, and follow-up interviews.

But, at the same time that Americans are extremely critical of teens, they also refuse to give up on them.

Shireen,* 17, is a young woman of Middle-Eastern descent. She was wearing jeans, a t-shirt, and a black head covering. She was sitting on a bench, talking with her friend, Ali.

KKB: *Do you think Americans are afraid of teens?*

S: Actually, I don't think people are really afraid of teens. I just think they think there's no use trying to do anything about them, that they're just going through a phase.

Mara,* 16, a white youth, hangs out regularly at the mall. Heavily made up and chain-smoking, she sat with a group of friends just outside the mall.

KKB: *Do you think Americans are afraid of teens?*

M: I used to dress better than I dress now…but I don't see why people should be afraid of me.

KKB: *How long have you been smoking?*

M: (Counts on her fingers.) Four years.

KKB: *Don't you think that the fact that you smoke and are so young may intimidate some adults?*

M: That shouldn't intimidate you.

KKB: *What do you want adults to know about you?*

M: We're not bad kids. They shouldn't judge us by our appearance. Our

group here is the nicest little group of people you could ever meet, aren't we? (Chuckles among group follow.) I want them to make an effort to get to know us.

KKB: *Some adults think teens today don't have good values. Do you have values?*

M: What are values?

KKB: *Well, things like honesty, respect, responsibility.*

(No response)

KKB: *Good-heartedness…*

M: Yeah, I've got a good heart! (Laughter follows.) I'm honest to an extent, but you can't trust that many people.

KKB: *What about drugs? Do you think drugs can make kids violent?*

M: Drugs don't make you violent if you're not violent to begin with. I'll tell you a violent drug, though: alcohol.

*Names have been changed.

According to the report, adults "care deeply" about young people and "are stubbornly optimistic about the chances of reclaiming the lives of even the most troubled teens." Respondents were unified in their belief that solutions center on building character. Parents, they said, need to spend more time with their kids, schools need to do a better job of teaching kids "discipline, honesty, and respectfulness towards themselves and others," teens need to be involved in more constructive activities, and such boundaries as curfews and sanctions for wrongdoings must be firm.

Helping Adults Overcome Their Fear of Teens

How do we address the fears and negative attitudes people have about teens? The perceptions are complex and deeply embedded in our society and culture. However, here are ways asset-building communities can begin helping people shift from fearing to valuing youth:

- **Name the issue**—Negative stereotypes of teenagers are so much a part of the culture that many people don't even notice them...until you point them out. Naming the assumptions begins to disarm them.
- **Listen to young people**—Having young people tell their own stories and experiences personalizes the issue and brings it close to home. Just asking teenagers in your community how adults treat them in stores, on street corners, in parks, and other public places can start powerful conversations.
- **Provide opportunities for interaction**—One of the best ways to overcome stereotypes is to provide safe, comfortable places for interaction across generations.
- **Highlight the positives**—Go out of your way to recognize, affirm, and tell about ways young people (particularly those who defy the stereotypes) contribute to the community.
- **Challenge negative stereotypes**—When you see or hear blanket negative statements about teenagers in public settings, the media, or your own social network, find ways to challenge them—or at least offer balance. (This response may be as simple as offering an alternative perspective in a conversation.)
- **Put crises into perspective**—Too often, major crises involving youth (such as the recent school shootings) only confirm people's negative stereotypes of all youth. It's important to remember that the perpetrators of these tragedies are seriously disturbed teenagers–just as adult murderers are seriously disturbed adults. We must find ways as a society to prevent these kinds of tragedies–not use them to reinforce our stereotypes.
- **Recognize the influence of racism**—Complicating adult fears of youth is racism. Many men of color, for example, can easily recount episodes of being regarded with suspicion and fear by white persons. Being intentional about addressing this issue adds a particular focus to the strategies suggested above.

Moving through fear and discomfort

If Americans agree on solutions when it comes to teens, can they actually enact them? If so, first they must come to terms with their fear, and next with their discomfort.

One of the sponsors of the Public Agenda report is the Advertising Council, based in New York, which plans to launch a decade-long effort to mobilize citizens to volunteer in their own communities on behalf of children and teens. Ruth Wooden, executive director of the Ad Council, believes important messages emerged from the study that can guide how her organization approaches its efforts.

Of great importance, says Wooden, is "humanizing the struggle of parents to raise their children" and emphasizing their need for help from the community. Surveys and interviews showed that many people know they need to pitch in, but they fear embarrassing those who they are trying to help. To change perceptions, says Wooden, a television spot could, for example, show a struggling single mom working several jobs and expressing appreciation for help from neighbors or community organizations.

One-on-one works, too

While the Ad Council works on a national scale, a good deal can happen locally. In Hardwick, Vt., for example, students stunned a group of adults in one day-long workshop by repeating back the frighteningly negative messages they have gotten from adults. The alternative list of how young people wished to be perceived led to a community education project called "Flip the Page."

On an individual level, many adults have to overcome a very basic fear–that of the unknown. But adults who've pushed past their discomfort with teens are often startled at how rewarding interactions with them can actually be, even very simple ones like greeting a teen neighbor by name or smiling at a young person cruising the shopping mall.

A security guard named Carol, who works at one of Minnesota's favorite teen hang-outs, the Mall of America, offered the following observation: "Most of the kids, even the regulars, the ones who dress up like vampires, are good kids. Yeah, they may walk around with what looks like an attitude. But adults are always downing them. It's not an attitude–it's a shield. I'd be doing that too if I was treated that way."

Kathleen Kimball-Baker is Editorial Director and Eugene C. Roelkepartain is Director of the Publishing & Communications Division at Search Institute in Minneapolis, Minnesota

The Millennials—Our Future Hope?
By Sally Gardiner

WILL THIS GENERATION (born 1981-1999) be the greatest generation? Some think so. Others are worried they will never be able to lead the world of tomorrow or even care to. Why such opposite views? Those who have studied the generations have high expectations. Those who only pay attention to the media hype and tragic events involving teens believe the worst. What's real?

The Millennials have some of the best characteristics of all who have come before. They show up as loyal, much like their traditionalist grandparents, optimistic like their boomer parents tempered with caution from their Gen X older siblings. In a word, they are realists.

They are the most technically advanced generation of all time, born with cell phones stitched into their onesies. They are true "Global Citizens" as the world has always been available to them with the click of a mouse or a remote. They assimilate information at a rapid pace from multiple sources at the same time and make decisions quickly. Thus they may appear cocky or less than thorough. Growing up with constant and immediate information, is it any wonder that they can move quickly when problem solving?

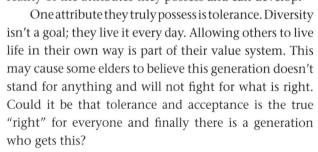

Their parents have involved them in family decision making. Being part of the solution is what they understand. They book vacations online for the family and do comparison shopping over the Internet. They expect to "play" as soon as they hit the job market and are not interested in and don't understand why "paying dues" is relevant with today's rate of change. They are communicative and tough to bully and can fend for themselves, yet they love being part of a team and collaboration is their middle name.

This generation has been raised by child-focused parents, overprotective and involved. The overprotection comes from fear of child abduction, molestation, AIDS and terrorism. This generation lives with fear for their personal safety COUNTERED with the support of involved parents. This balance was lacking for Gen Xers (whose parents both worked or who came from single parent families due to a 50% divorce rate), so the Millennials are emerging as cautious but confident team players.

This confidence is showing up in other ways as well. This generation has been raised to believe that they are "special." They have been told by their parents and teachers that they can have, be and do anything they choose. Many expect to be "famous & rich." Take for example the hit TV reality show "American Idol." In the early auditions, young people with virtually NO SINGING talent whatsoever, audition to be the next Idol! Do they do it for their "15 minutes of fame" (often the "really bad" auditions are shown on TV) or do they do it because of this belief that they can be, do and have whatever they want? As adults, have we inadvertently taught them that "believing" is all that is required for success? Have we stopped stressing hard work, determination, ability and talent? Is this specialness evolving into "entitlement"? As parents we need to help Millennials find the balance between being special (because they certainly are) and the reality of the attributes they possess and can develop.

One attribute they truly possess is tolerance. Diversity isn't a goal; they live it every day. Allowing others to live life in their own way is part of their value system. This may cause some elders to believe this generation doesn't stand for anything and will not fight for what is right. Could it be that tolerance and acceptance is the true "right" for everyone and finally there is a generation who gets this?

The Millennials may be the key to a more peaceful future. Their confidence, team mentality, technological expertise and tolerance of others ensure their influence will be nothing short of remarkable!

Written for Family Empowerment Network by Sally Gardiner, Certified Professional Coach, Reality Therapy Certified © 2008. For reprint requests, contact www.family-empower.com.

The Girls Report
What We Know & Need To Know About Growing Up Female
An overview of the 121-page report written by the National Council for Research on Women

The National Council for Research on Women (NCRW) is proud to issue The Girls Report: What We Know and Need to Know About Growing Up Female, *its second report on adolescent girls in this decade. Much has changed in what we know about adolescent girls, how they are viewed, and how they view themselves since 1991, when the first report,* Risk, Resiliency, and Resistance: Current Research on Adolescent Girls, *was released. Today, researchers and activists increasingly perceive girls as smart, bold, and determined, and call on them to help shape programs and research that address their special concerns and needs. Although the findings in this report are anchored in the proliferating research on, and programs for, girls in the United States, the expanding attention to this age group-- and the perception of girls as partners with important perspectives to share--has become a global phenomenon, as demonstrated by the active participation of girls at the United Nations Fourth World Conference on Women, held in Beijing in 1995.*

The Girls Report provides an important baseline of knowledge on adolescence as we approach the new millennium. Lynn Phillips, its author, has done an admirable job of synthesizing the present state of research on this pivotal phase in girls' lives. In contrast to most research reports, which tend to focus on single issues, The Girls Report *employs a holistic perspective, exploring adolescent girls' health, sexuality, education, experiences with violence, and economic realities and viewing them across the divides of race, ethnicity, class, and sexual orientation. In so doing, it also assesses how what we know can guide future research and programs. While the report identifies programs and achievements that engender a sense of vitality and empowerment, it also delineates the underbelly of girls' experiences, the many areas in which they remain victimized, harassed, and diminished, and the very real risks that still constrain their healthy development. Throughout, the voices of girls themselves provide a counterpoint to the analyses of researchers. These statements, drawn from interviews and focus groups, express girls' struggles and aspirations, and their views of how their situations could be improved.*

"Considering the rich input to this project from so many sources, we are convinced that The Girls Report *will inform, enlighten, and inspire all those interested in making the world a better place for girls and women."*

—Linda Basch, Executive Director, National Council for Research on Women

Executive Summary Of *The Girls Report:*

ADOLESCENCE CAN BE both a rich and challenging time for girls as they confront new ideas, explore life's possibilities, and navigate through the stormy seas of physical, social, behavioral, and emotional changes. How are girls meeting these challenges? The research and policy studies reviewed and analyzed for this report provide a mixed picture of progress and continuing struggles. Several large-scale national studies suggest that girls are as likely as boys of the same age to smoke cigarettes, that they have inadequate access to sports programs that offer physical, social, and psychological benefits, that they are twice as likely as boys to be depressed, and that they often are the victims of violence.

On the other hand, new evidence identifies other, more encouraging trends. In school, girls continue to do well in reading and language, and their math achievement now almost matches that of boys. The teen birth rate has declined steadily since 1992, after rising by 25 percent between 1986 and 1991, and although access to contraception and abortion services has been restricted in many states, more teens appear to be using contraception than ever before.

These are some of the key findings of this report, which is a sequel to *Risks, Resiliency, and Resistance: Current Research on Adolescent Girls,* produced by the National Council for Research on Women for the Ms. Foundation in 1991.

The current report strives to present a balanced picture of the status of adolescent girls today. Its goal is to provide useful information about what we do and don't know about adolescent girls that can guide future research, policy decisions, and programs designed to improve the climate and life possibilities for all girls, regardless of where they live, their racial or ethnic background, or their social or economic status.

The report contains three additional sections that will be helpful to people who want to advocate for girls. "What Do Adolescent Girls Need for Healthy Development?" outlines specific actions that individuals and groups, including parents, teachers, and funders, can take to support girls. The "Resource Guide" includes descriptions of diverse programs created by NCRW member centers and related organizations aimed at improving the situation of girls, as well as publications that illuminate adolescent girls' development. "Looking Ahead: Developing a New Research Agenda" points to areas that need future research. These range from further investigation of girls' needs to the impact of programs and policies addressing those needs.

Introduction

What exactly do adolescent girls need for healthy development? What do we know about these needs? What can families, schools, other public agencies, and private organizations and communities do to ensure that girls thrive as they make the transition from adolescence to adulthood? These are the basic questions addressed throughout this report. Its structure and findings should be interpreted with the following context in mind:

- Adolescent boys face many of the same issues and challenges that confront girls. The report focuses on girls because they and their issues traditionally are underrepresented in research and policy debates, but it also recognizes that measures to improve the climate for girls almost inevitably benefit boys as well,
- Girls face gender-related issues throughout their development, but many of these issues come into especially sharp relief during adolescence,
- Research on girls often has focused on risks and negative trends, rather than exploring positive aspects of their lives,
- Research often does not take into account the social and cultural context--for example, the availability of health care in inner-city neighborhoods--that influence girls' life experiences,
- The voices of girls are rarely heard in research reports or in discussions of policies that affect their lives.

Framing Gender, Identity, and Adolescence

Adolescence traditionally has been characterized as a period of "storm and stress." However, recent research suggests that many of the difficulties associated with adolescence are due more to social factors such as poverty, family stresses, and societal ambivalence toward youth than to some inevitable, internal process or characteristics of adolescents themselves.

Discussions of girls' identity development are based too often on narrowly defined notions of self-esteem, tending frequently to emphasize overall gender differences

without probing the interconnections among race, culture, social class, and sexuality. The structure of future research and of programs and policies devised to improve girls' lives must strive to understand and account for these complexities.

Perspectives On Girls' Lives and Health: Adolescence is a potentially healthy time for girls, but the leading causes of premature death among women—including lung cancer, other cancers, heart disease, and AIDS—are associated with behaviors that often begin during adolescence. Evidence that sparks concern includes the rise in the percentage of girls who smoke (from 13 percent of eighth graders in 1991 to 21 percent five years later); a report that 30 percent of adolescent girls have thought about suicide, compared with 18 percent of boys; and the fact that 90 percent of cases of eating disorders are found among girls and young women. Society must search for ways to encourage young women to take a holistic approach to their health, educate them to take responsibility for their behavior, and provide universal access to reliable information and health services.

Sexuality: National data exists on the age of first intercourse, but little or no data has been gathered on the prevalence of other types of girls' sexual experiences. The rate of births to teens is declining and teens' use of contraception is increasing, but many adolescents are still not using contraception or are having abortions. More quantitative information about sexual behaviors among adolescents, and more qualitative research on the nature of their experiences is needed, as are affordable and confidential access to both sexuality education and health services.

Violence and Victimization: Girls are a proportionally higher percentage of victims of violence—including rape—than boys. Their perception that rape is committed by strangers may inhibit girls from reporting rape or other violence perpetrated by family members or acquaintances. Other causes for concern include the rate of arrest for violent crimes, which is rising more quickly for girls than for boys, and the inadequate preparation of the justice system to address the special needs of girls, especially those who are pregnant or who have children. Schools as well as parents need to play a role in educating children about violence, and schools must have strictly enforced policies against sexual harassment on the premises.

Schooling: As in other aspects of girls' lives in recent years, the record of change in schooling is mixed. Girls' performance has improved in math (on standardized tests) but not in science. Girls say that they like these subjects less than do boys and that they have less confidence in their abilities in these areas. In general, girls are less likely to drop out of school than are boys. However, female dropouts are much more likely than their male counterparts of the same race or ethnic group to live in poverty. Researchers need to explore further the positive and negative effects of single-sex schools, classes, and programs. Educators should create learning environments that practice gender equity and are peopled by strong female role models and mentors from diverse cultural backgrounds. Schools should offer sexuality education as well as opportunities for critical discussion of issues including racism, class distinctions, and sexism.

Economic Realities: Women and children account for more than three-quarters of households with incomes below the poverty level. Contrary to stereotypes, only 11 percent of mothers on welfare are teenagers. Children from racial minority groups are much more likely to live in poverty than are white children. Recent changes in the welfare system discourage some girls from continuing their education and becoming economically self-sufficient. Unmarried teen mothers should not have to live in a home situation that is dangerous to receive a benefit; they need access to day care, transportation, and other supports that will enable them to work and pursue their education.

Conclusions and Recommendations

This review of an extensive body of recent work on key issues in the lives of adolescent girls leads to five overarching conclusions. These perspectives should underlie efforts by adults, communities, and all others working to meet the needs of adolescent girls and enrich their opportunities.

- Girls are multi-dimensional individuals with diverse perspectives, needs, and developmental contexts. Researchers, policymakers, and people who work directly with girls must be sensitive to the

interactions of gender with other aspects of their identities--including race, ethnicity, social class, sexuality, disability, and the communities where they live--that influence girls' actions, attitudes, and, ultimately, their futures.

- Girls can benefit from programs and strategies that build on their strengths and encourage them to explore meaningful possibilities for their futures. In many fields, including education, health care, athletics, and juvenile justice, adults have worked successfully over the last decade to create school- and community-based programs that provide support to many girls and that could be replicated.

- Research must continue to play a role in deepening our understanding of girls' needs and how to respond to them. Researchers, advocates, public officials, and funders should collaborate to articulate, fund, and promote a research agenda.

- Girls require and deserve the awareness, attention, and commitment of a wide range of individuals and institutions to promote their healthy development. Parents should continue to play the primary role in supporting girls' development. However, educators, a range of professionals, public officials, and other members of the community should strengthen their efforts to create a safe and supportive climate that nurtures girls and encourages them to pursue their goals.

- Adults should listen to what girls have to say about their own lives. Adults who want to help girls must collaborate not only with one another, but also with girls themselves. Adults should listen to girls' concerns and perspectives and include girls as partners in designing and implementing programs and research that address their needs.

The National Council for Research on Women, founded in 1981, is a working alliance of 95 women's research and policy centers, more than 3,000 affiliates and a network of over 200 international centers. NCRW's mission is to enhance the connections among research, policy analysis, advocacy, and innovative programming on behalf of women and girls. The full 121-page copy of The Girls Report can be purchased from the NCRW website at: www.ncrw.org/research/girlsrpt.htm

Hardy Girls

By Tom Flinders, from Chapter Three of the online book
Power and Promise: Helping School Girls Hold Onto Their Dreams

THE LOSSES THAT many girls experience as they enter adolescence are neither necessary nor inevitable. They come largely from the dislocation of self that most girls experience as they try to find their way through the "force fields" of biases and stereotypes that still pervade our culture. There's probably no way to completely buffer young girls from these forces. But parents can support and empower their daughters in ways that help them get through their adolescence with their self-confidence intact. I've kept in touch with a number of my former girl students as they went through high school and on to college, and their resilience and confidence have caused me to take a closer look at the self-esteem data of the past decade to see how it accounts for their success. What I found has been especially encouraging, as it confirms these girls' more hopeful experience and forms a basis of hope for others.

Though all girls have to pass through the adolescent gauntlet of pressures, stereotypes, and biases, self-esteem studies show a fair number of them making it through with their confidence intact. When you look more closely at the self-esteem data of the past decade—what the media missed and what you probably haven't read

or heard about—you find that some girls get through adolescence with high levels of self-esteem. In fact, a fair proportion of them manage it: twenty-nine percent of the high-school girls in the AAUW study, for instance, reported high levels of self-esteem, as did twenty percent of the young women in the UC Berkeley study.

As you break down self-esteem data, you can find a core set of qualities that these more resilient girls seem to share. In fact, they form a pattern of qualities and experiences that parents can use as guidelines for their own daughters. Looking more closely at the literature on self-esteem, we can find three traits that appear to be common to these more resilient survivors: these are connection, competence, and complimentarity or gender balance.

1. Connection: Connectedness to a caring, competent adult is a strong predictor of high self-esteem.

A close correlation has been found between a girl's level of self-confidence and the amount of support she receives from the adults in her life. Girls who indicate that their parents care about their opinion and that teachers listened to what they say, report that they feel much more comfortable in expressing themselves.

Psychologist Dr. Susan Harter of the University of Denver reviewed the literature on adolescent self-esteem and found two primary components that seem consistently predictive. The first is what she calls the "looking-glass" concept, based on how a person feels she is being perceived by other people. Here a young person incorporates the attitudes of significant other people towards herself, and unconsciously imitates them: If Ms. X likes me, then I must be OK. The AAUW survey found that it was girls' parents and teachers, and not their peers, who had the greatest impact on their self-esteem.[1] The poll found that teachers act as especially important role models for young women. (Nearly three out of four elementary-school girls and over half of the high-school girls indicated they wanted to become teachers.)

Dr. Michael Resnick is Director of Research at the University of Minnesota's Adolescent Health Program and his studies have found that the single most important predictor of an adolescent positively weathering attacks on self-esteem is "connectedness to at least one competent adult."[2] Resnick identified the second most important predictor of resiliency among teens as "academic connectedness"—when teens identify school as an arena where they felt competent, naming one or two special teachers. A third component of connection Resnick calls "spiritual connectedness." This does not necessarily imply church-going, but "spirituality in terms of some kind of belief in a higher being or higher order." So, despite predictable generational conflicts, parents continue to play a central role in helping their daughters hold on to their self-esteem. Carol Gilligan's five-year Laurel School study reinforced this conclusion: "This came to be the message of the study," Gilligan's co-investigator Lyn Mikel Brown reported,

> ..that one woman can make a huge difference in a young girl's life. Girls around eleven start to look to women almost as touchstones to reality, so it's very meaningful when women really align with girls and start to listen carefully and say, 'Yes, this does seem unfair. I understand what you're seeing. I don't know what to do about it, but let's think about it together.'"[3]

2. Competence: A sense of personal competence correlates highly with high levels of self-esteem.

In her survey of the literature on self-esteem, Harter identified a cluster of attributes that are grounded in competence: how well a girl performs in areas of life *that are important to her.* For girls this is especially true of their school performance, which the AAUW study found was the most important contributor to their self-esteem.

A sense of competence in math and science is especially important, as it correlates strongly with high self-esteem. In fact, the AAUW survey found its highest correlations here. "Students who like math and science possess significantly greater self-esteem; students with higher self-esteem like math and science more."[4]

Competency in athletics also correlates with high self-

esteem. Girls who play sports have higher self-esteem, and are more likely to stay in school, assume leadership roles, do well academically and perform better in science. (This appears to be especially true for Latina girls.)[5] 80 percent of the women among the top echelons of Fortune 1000 companies have been involved in team sports at the high-school or college level.[6] Adolescent girls who play high-school sports are three times more likely to graduate from high-school, eighty percent less likely to have an unwanted pregnancy and ninety-two percent less likely to use drugs.[7]

It turns out that the self-esteem research supports what we all know anyway about ourselves, that, when we are good at something, we feel good about ourselves. This is not rocket science, and it opens a number of avenues for parents and teachers working with young girls. From my experience with hundreds of young people over the past twenty-five years, at both ends of the academic spectrum, I've developed three maxims that parents and educators can use as touchstones to children's competence and, therefore, their self-confidence.

Three Keys to Competence

1. Everyone is good at something. Given the opportunity to experiment, combined with instruction, every child can become competent in something.

2. It doesn't matter what that something is. Working with clay, playing the piano, shooting baskets, chess, computer facility, singing, dancing, athletics—as long as a child finds it enjoyable and significant to her, she can reach a satisfying level of competence. We all have at least one gift.

3. Parents can play a central role in helping their daughters find out what they're good at. It takes time, persistence, and perhaps a fair amount of trailing a youngster from tennis camp to gymnastics until she finds her métier. Help her become competent at something.

3. Gender Balance: Girls who exhibit both feminine and masculine attributes have higher levels of self-esteem.

Men and women have traditionally occupied such different spaces, women confined to the home, men going out to their work, that personality traits have become gendered.

Because certain traits are considered "masculine" or "feminine" qualities—the strong, independent male, the convivial, loving woman—we overlook the fact that these are, first of all, *human* qualities which have nothing to do with one's sex.

Not surprisingly, given the pronounced tilt towards success and achievement in our culture, positive masculine qualities cluster around our notions of achievement, success and power: *assertive, physical, independent, confident, ambitious, competitive, independent, self-reliant, risk-taking.* Positive feminine qualities cluster around service, emotional sensitivity, and appearance: *nurturing, emotional, cheerful, loyal, sensitive, soft-spoken, understanding, sweet, cute, enticing.* (Whatever may be said about these, they are not the qualities you'd be looking for on the resume of a corporate CEO.) That feminine qualities are so strongly linked in our minds to service and appearance, while decidedly *disassociated* from achievement, speaks volumes for our culture's disregard (despite lip service to the contrary) for traditional "women's work"—homemaking, child rearing, and caretaking.

Like it or not, we've all been conditioned to view ourselves as mature and emotionally developed only when we have fully achieved those qualities associated with our gender. We have our modern mythic heroes and heroines to remind us at every turn: John Wayne still stands for many as the epitome of the properly

acculturated male—independent, self-reliant, take-charge, the tough guy with a big heart. Jackie Kennedy was a powerful icon for the smiling, compliant, savvy woman, ready to stand by her man, raise their children, and look good while doing it. When she married the Godfather-like Aristotle Onassis, Jackie Kennedy sent

alarms through the culture for stepping so precipitously out of her perceived gender mold.

The need for such gender specialization is largely a myth. In fact, psychological studies find that it is not uncommon for a woman or a man to combine personality traits that were considered mutually exclusive to one or the other sex. More significant, they found that people who combined masculine and feminine traits were psychologically better adjusted than their more stereotypical counterparts.[8] Other studies found that women who expressed a combination of feminine and masculine qualities tended to have higher self-esteem than women who exhibited a more traditional version of femininity. Women who were stereotypically feminine tended to suffer greater anxiety, and lower self-esteem than their more gender-balanced counterparts.[9]

Something of the same is being found with the more resilient and confident teen-aged girl. Harter found in her review of the self-esteem literature that the girl who describes herself as both caring and competitive, for instance, both nurturing and assertive, seemed most likely to remain self-confident throughout adolescence.[10] On the other hand, girls who most strongly endorsed an exclusive feminine gender orientation reported greater loss of voice.

The idea of linking a balance of gender qualities with emotional health and self-confidence mirrors my own experience in working with high-achieving girls these past twenty years. The girls I have found to be the most promising have generally combined their feminine sensibilities with a sturdy self-reliance, a robust sense of their selves and their capacities, and a ready access to risk-taking and problem solving. (It's also my observation that many of my most promising boys possessed ample measures of sensitivity and connectedness: of the three male stars most prominent in my memory, one teaches handicapped kids to swim, another spent much of his sixth-grade year studying and drawing birds, and the third was deeply connected to and seemed more or less the caretaker of a younger sister who later came into the program.)

Beyond Gender

In raising and schooling girls, we need to break personality traits free of their traditional gender moorings, and view them as qualities and skills appropriate to us all. Freeing the most common personality traits from their sex stereotypes, we can classify them loosely into two broad categories. First, the *qualities of achievement,* which include independence, self-reliance, risk-taking, problem-solving, and many of those we've traditionally associated with socially successful males. Second are the *qualities of connection,* the traditional feminine qualities I mentioned above. Both connection and achievement are central to the human experience, both can serve women and men at home, in the workplace, alone and with others.

Parents, then, should try to help their daughters develop a *range* of skills and qualities that embrace both connection and achievement. Girls with such a range will have at their disposal a broad set of qualities and skills that can help them master any given set of circumstances, wherever they choose to employ them. This maximizes their potential for surviving the perils of adolescence and for leading satisfactory adult lives.

Buffering Your Daughters

Though you cannot shelter your daughter from the culture in which she is growing up, you can play a major role in equipping her to withstand its worst effects. From what we've seen so far, there are several basic keys to her self-esteem that you should understand. Girls need to be aware of essential information about themselves as females, and about their experience growing up female in a culture that has traditionally disadvantaged them. Your daughter needs to know:

- **The power of the feminine.** For too long, Western culture has devalued the feminine, especially women's ways and women's work. Girls need know that women have played a vital historical role in developing culture, and in what scholar Peggy MacIntosh calls the "mending and minding of the social fabric,"
- **That institutional bias still persists.** Despite the passage of the Civil Rights Act and Title IX decades ago, deep and pervasive forms of gender bias still infect our institutions, schools and the workplace,
- **That they will need to balance the competing claims of home and work.** Ninety percent of the female high school graduates will work outside the home for at least twenty-five years. The increasing presence of women in the workplace has not

diminished the demands and expectations made upon them at home,
- **That they can find the autonomy they need without separating from their mothers.** Adolescent girls need to be aware of their competing need for autonomy and for connection, and that they can achieve autonomy without emotionally separating from their mothers.

Finding Balance

While we empower girls to develop the skills of achievement, we have to make certain that we do not devalue the traditional feminine skills of connection. Our work is double-edged. In our eagerness to equip girls for an increasingly competitive workplace, we so do not want to strip them of their capacity for connection and nurturance, traits which the workplace will require if it is to serve all human needs. Girls should understand early that they can lay claim to traditional masculine qualities with as much entitlement as boys. They can be fully feminine and as capable of self-reliance and decision-making as they are of nurturing and caring. All girls should carry within them an image of rich possibilities for themselves—that they can be as loving or as assertive as they need to be, wherever they find themselves.

Endnotes

1. Greenberg-Lake,1991, 10.
2. Michael Resnick, in Sundra Flansburg, 1991, 4.
3. Lyn Mikel Brown, San Francisco Examiner, March 23, 1994, B3.
4. Greenberg-Lake, "Shortchanging Girls, Shortchanging America: Executive Summary," AAUW, 1994, 12.
5. Messner, Michael, in "Fear No Man, Trust No Woman," NCSEE News, Fall, 1995, 5.
6. Senator Olympia Snowe, quoted in AAUW Outlook, Spring 1996, 21.
7. "For Title IX: Court ruling protects equality for menand women athletes," Santa Rosa Press Democrat, April 22, 1997,B4.
8. Mindy Bingham and Sandy Stryker, *Things Will be Different for My Daughter: A Practical guide to building Her Self-Esteem and Self-Reliance,* Penguin Books, New York , NY , 1995, 43-47.
9. Ibid, 44-45.
10. Susan Harter, "Girls Face Risks Entering Adolescence," on "All Things Considered," National Public Radio, February 16, 1995, audiotape available through NPR, 635 Massachusetts, NW, Wash 20001.

Reprinted with permission from website www.tworocks.org

"Girl in the Box" Activity

Adapted from *Queen Bees and Wannabes* by Rosalind Wiseman
and *Boys Will Be Men: Raising our Sons for Courage, Caring and Community* by Paul Kivel

This exercise can be used with adults and girls from 4th grade and up. It helps participants see the cultural pressures on our girls and women to be stereotypically feminine, which can limit their full and active participation in the world.

THE ACTIVITY:

- Have the group brainstorm and list all of the messages from our culture and the media about how a young woman should look or act. Draw a box around these words.
- On the right side of the box, have the group list how others (especially other girls) act to reinforce behaving "like a woman," and try to keep a girl "in the box." These actions can include physical and verbal aggression (bullying), shaming, shunning, gossip, exclusion, name-calling, etc.
- On the left side of the box, have the group list all of the thoughts a girl might create within her own head to reinforce her own attempts to stay in the box. If you are having trouble thinking of examples, fill in the following blanks: "If I don't act or look like ..., I won't ... (get a guy, have friends, be popular, etc.)," or "I can't ... (be smart, take risks, sweat, be a normal weight, act loud and crazy, etc.) because people will put me down," or "In order to fit in, I'll have to ... (fill in the blank), even if I don't feel like it."

THE LESSON:

From a very early age, girls are taught to want to please. As girls enter adolescence, the culture and the media place increased pressure on them to hide their true selves and become someone else. This unhealthy process drives girls' and women's feelings underground, and when they do surface, they can be expressed in indirect and often very hurtful ways.

The "Girl Box" represents everything that a "real woman" is supposed to be, as portrayed by our confused culture. Girls who are different (i.e., too forward, too opinionated, gay, overweight, with acne, wear unstylish clothes, etc.) or who don't care what other people think and do their own thing in spite of disapproving public opinion, are at risk for being targeted. Girls also face a difficult societal double standard: while boys are expected to be sexually active "studs," girls can be targeted whether or not they act sexual. Girls can be labeled "sluts" for sexual exploration (although some girls may get away with it if they are popular and do it with the "right guy"), or be put down as prudes if they won't act sexual. Women in the box are valued for the guy that they catch. This drives a competition among women and girls.

When a girl tries to step outside of the box, she is pushed back inside by verbal and relational aggression from her peers, her culture and herself. Her peers are the most powerful "patrollers"—on the lookout for anyone who is different. The result is that girls (and women) hide their true selves, putting up a false front that they are uncomfortable with because it is dishonest. Thus, girls experience a loss of connection to themselves and others, and suppress their own feelings, joy and passion. This kind of disconnection often results in hurtful aggression against self and others.

This exercise is designed to help girls and women to defy the "box" and the media lie that looks are the most important value of a woman. The old dogma that a woman is only as valuable as the man she can snatch does not help girls to grow up independent and empowered. Every young woman and girl needs to feel accepted and loved for who they are inside, not for their outside packaging. In order to encourage this, it is important to look at the forces, both external and internal, that keep girls from venturing out of their box and into the world of more authentic self-expression and self-exploration. When you are done constructing the box, talk about how you would like the world to be for girls.

Example: "Girl in the Box"

How A Girl Keeps Herself in the Box:		Verbal and Relational Aggression and Shaming from others:
"I have to hide what I think." →	Pretty, very thin / Popular for wrong reasons / Sexy, maybe sexual / Cool clothes / Wears make-up / Hangs out with "right" crowd / Has a boyfriend / Has money / Hides personality and intelligence / Defers to men & authority figures / Popular / Nice on the outside / Sadness is OK, anger isn't / Insecure / Afraid to make waves	← Exclusion, silent treatment, gossip, rumor, shunning, shaming, etc.
"I have to have sex to keep my boyfriend." "I need to buy more clothes to be okay."		← Name Calling: Fat, Dike, Prude, Bossy, Bitch

An Asset Checklist

By Search Institute, from The Asset Approach: Giving Kids What They Need to Succeed

Many people find it helpful to use a simple checklist to reflect on the assets young people experience. This checklist simplifies the asset list to help prompt conversation in families, organization, and communities. ***Note:*** *This checklist is not intended nor appropriate as a scientific or accurate measurement of Developmental Assets.*

❏ 1. I receive high levels of love and support from family members.

❏ 2. I can go to my parent(s) for advice and support and have frequent, in-depth conversations with them.

❏ 3. I know some nonparent adults I can go to for advice and support.

❏ 4. My neighbors encourage and support me.

❏ 5. My school provides a caring, encouraging environment.

❏ 6. My parent(s) or guardian(s) help me succeed in school.

❏ 7. I feel valued by adults in my community.

❏ 8. I am given useful roles in my community.

❏ 9. I serve in the community one hour or more each week.

❏ 10. I feel safe at home, at school, and in the neighborhood.

❏ 11. My family sets standards for appropriate conduct and monitors my whereabouts.

❏ 12. My school has clear rules and consequences for behavior.

❏ 13. Neighbors take responsibility for monitoring my behavior.

❏ 14. Parent(s) and other adults model positive, responsible behavior.

❏ 16. My parent(s)/guardian(s) and teachers encourage me to do well.

❏ 17. I spend three hours or more each week in lessons or practice in music, theater, or other arts.

❏ 18. I spend three hours or more each week in school or community sports, clubs, or organizations.

❏ 19. I spend one hour or more each week in religious services or participating in spiritual activities.

❏ 20. I go out with friends "with nothing special to do" two or fewer nights each week.

❏ 21. I want to do well in school.

❏ 22. I am actively engaged in learning.

❏ 23. I do an hour or more of homework each day.

❏ 24. I care about my school.

❏ 25. I read for pleasure three or more hours each week.

❏ 26. I believe it is really important to help other people.

❏ 27. I want to promote equality and reduce world poverty and hunger.

❏ 28. I can stand up for what I believe.

❏ 29. I tell the truth even when it's not easy.

❏ 30. I can accept and take personal responsibility.

❏ 31. I believe it is important not to be sexually active or to use alcohol or other drugs.

❏ 32. I am good at planning ahead and making decisions.

❏ 33. I am good at making and keeping friends.

❏ 34. I know and am comfortable with people of different cultural/racial/ethnic backgrounds.

❏ 35. I can resist negative peer pressure and dangerous situations.

❏ 36. I try to resolve conflict nonviolently.

❏ 37. I believe that I have control over many things that happen to me.

❏ 38. I feel good about myself.

❏ 39. I believe my life has a purpose.

❏ 40. I am optimistic about my future.

What Influences Her? 2

1
2
3
4
5
6
7
8
9
10

Kara Tucker, 8th Grade, Rosemont Ridge Middle School

What Influences Her?

"Average six-year-old children have spent more time watching TV than they will spend talking to their fathers in their lifetimes."
Television, Violence, and Children —U of O Thesis Paper, by Carla Kalin (1997)

"Advertising has a thousand principles, one purpose, and no morals." —Humorist Finley Peter Dunne, 1909

"Kids are the epicenter, the top agents in decisions about what the family buys."
—Juliet Schor, author of *Born to Buy*

"Marketing to teens is like untapped Africa—a market segment worth $150 billion." —*Merchants of Cool* video

"Three minutes spent looking at models in a fashion magazine caused 70% of women to feel depressed, guilty and shameful." —1995 psychological study

"The best screening device is between the ears of your child."
—Nancy Willard, author of *Cyber-Safe Kids*

GOALS

- To become familiar with the research about the media culture our girls are growing up in today and how powerfully the media influences them

- To explore the power of advertising not only on our daughters directly, but also the ways in which commercialism creates their culture

- To become more media literate so that we can reduce the harm of the media and guide our families in making wise decisions about what to watch, play and purchase

OVERVIEW

Media as Teacher

Where do children learn their values and develop a vision of their future? That can depend upon where you live, according to Dr. Bill Daggett of the International Leadership Institute. Children in Europe learn from family, religion and national leaders. Media is a distant fourth. Children in Japan learn from leaders and family (a close tie) with religion a distant third and media fourth. However, children in America learn from TV first, then leaders (these being leaders in entertainment and sports, such as Bart Simpson, sports and reality stars). Family is a distant third and religion is fourth. What values are American children learning? What is the "vision of the future" that our children hold?

Viewed from this standpoint, parents can see how important it is to become empowered to lessen the grip that the media has over their own kids' lives and to teach their children critical media-viewing skills. Becoming an educated, conscientious, media-literate parent goes a long way towards putting your own family values first in your child's life. The purpose of this media chapter is to give parents a better understanding of the ways in which the media bombards children with messages, and to learn how to mitigate the negative effects that the media has on our children's lives. Our hope is that parents will become more conscious "consumers" of the media, will buffer their children from the negative effects of media violence and consumerism, and will start taking an active role in holding corporations accountable for their children's programming and entertainment.

The Research

Look around you. "Some Media Facts to Get Us Started" (p. 2:15) explores how children in the United States are surrounded by influences from the media, from intense advertising, exposure to violence, and loss of time that could have been spent on reading, homework, using their imagination, getting outside, exercising or interacting with friends and family. And our children start young with their screen time, with babies less than 18 months old spending, on average, two hours per day in front of the TV, in spite of the strong recommendation of the

Academy of Pediatrics that children under two should not watch television at all.

A 2005 Kaiser Family Foundation study called "Generation M: Media in the Lives of 8-18 Year Olds" looked at screen time. The average American child spends almost 4 hours a day watching TV/movies, 1 hour on the computer outside of school work (Internet and instant messaging) and just under 50 minutes a day playing videogames. Over the last five years the total amount of media content children consume has increased one hour per day, but because kids multitask their media, the total number of hours has stayed the same. "Summary of Generation M" (p. 2:17) shares more details on this study. Today's teens experience the world as a multi-media network of instant connections.

Consumerism and Cool Hunting

The media certainly has also latched on to our teenagers as consumers. "Our Children and Consumerism" (p. 2:18) discusses the moral cost of advertisers preying on the vulnerabilities of our children and using them to the marketer's advantage. Juliet Schor's book *Born to Buy*, as summarized in "The Silver Bullet" (p. 2:19), shares how deeply consumerism affects our families. Two-year-olds know brand names. Consider the impact of the "Nag Factor" in your life? Do you work longer hours for the stuff your children say they need?

The video *Merchants of Cool* (PBS Frontline) talks about the teen market in 2002 which was 32 million strong—the largest generation ever, even bigger than the baby boomers. Teens spent $100 billion a year on themselves and they influenced their parents to spend another $50 billion yearly. Retailers have taken note. Everywhere our teens look, they are bombarded with marketing messages—over 3000 per day!

Teens do not respond to traditional marketing, but they do respond to "cool." Major media outlets (like Rupert Murdock's NewsCorp, Disney, Viacom, AOL/Time Warner and Universal/Vivendi) are always looking for "cool." They employ "cool hunters," or culture spies, to study our teenagers. Cool hunters look for the 20% of kids who are trend-setters or early adopters. They pick up their ideas and styles and then sell them back to the masses. Ironically, as soon as something is successfully marketed to teens as "cool," it is no longer "cool." "Cool" has a very short shelf life thus the frenzy to keep it all going.

If your daughter is older than 12, consider watching the "Merchants of Cool" together. Discuss how corporations use the media to sell to kids for their own profit and with no thought about how it affects the kids to whom they sell. When watching this show with your daughter, it helps to remember that it is more important to share and respect each other's opinions and interpretations than to agree on everything.

Media and Health

"Impact of Media on our Children's Health" (p. 2:20) presents some of the positive and negative impacts the media can have on our kids. The first section of "When Children Walked the Earth: Is the Active Child Becoming Extinct" is a sad commentary on the state of affairs of our children's physical health. There is a clear link between screen time, overeating and lack of activity. This contributes to the epidemic of obesity and diabetes. Some believe that the lack of time spent playing and interacting with other kids and adults has even led to decreased social skills and problem-solving ability. In addition, other problems for avid media consumers can include depression, low self-esteem, and addiction to cigarettes, alcohol and drugs. Alcohol is heavily marketed to our children. Beer ads in sports games equate drinking beer with popularity, being "cool" and attracting boys. Magazines with high youth readership, advertise beer and hard liquor so heavily that youth actually see MORE alcohol advertising than adults, according to The Center on Alcohol, Marketing and Youth.

Of course, media can also be used for good purposes. For example, the "Elmo/Broccoli Study" found that broccoli with an Elmo sticker was preferred over a chocolate bar with an unknown character. Other studies show that just a "little bit" of media literacy education can reduce teen smoking choices.

"Fear Sells: Is No News Good News?" (p. 2:21) reminds us that children don't see the media with the same screening lens that we do. The evening news can promote the "mean world syndrome" in our children, as well as in ourselves. The more bad news we watch, the more we think the world is a bad place. Children need to develop a joyful, hopeful sense of place, before they face the distorted perspective of bad news. Our own fears can interfere with thinking clearly about how to parent wisely. Today, many parents imagine that their kids are safer watching screens full of strangers than playing in their own neighborhood.

Lookism

Lookism is "discrimination against or prejudice towards others based on their appearance." Most of us are susceptible to media messages of how to look, which exaggerates and distorts how we think we "should" look. There are 3 billion women in the world trying to look like eight supermodels. One 1995 study of women showed that after 3 minutes of viewing a fashion magazine, 70% of women felt depressed, guilty and shamed. Comparing themselves to airbrushed, unreal images, these women felt inadequate, that they did not measure up to that beauty standard. Our girls are affected, too. What marketers have discovered is that the quality to add in is "cool." The sad thing about "cool" is that it really hits our teenagers' insecurity hot button. "Cool" implies that without a certain product or a certain look, you will never be popular, independent, masculine/feminine, successful or good looking enough. Our teens are encouraged to become obsessed with their appearance.

For boys, there are also various popular looks or images. In an effort to be "buff" enough, some boys become obsessed with working out and taking steroids to improve their appearance and performance. Another image marketed to our sons is called, in the media industry, the "mook." A mook is crude, loud, obnoxious and in your face. He thinks that sexual harassment is entertaining. He does not care what other people think. (Think of Howard Stern or the stars of *Jackass*.) One female look being marketed is called, in the corporate media world, a "midriff." (Think Britney Spears.) A midriff is a premature adult, consumed by appearance, seeing herself primarily as a sexual object and proud of it. Sexuality is equated with power and liberation. And, she had better be skinny! Teen girls particularly fall victim to "lookism" which can drive them to eating disorders and death. Eating disorders are covered in depth in our "Safety" Chapter and in the article **"Sick and Ailing"** (p. 2:22) in this chapter. A mook and a midriff may not be true to life, but these are the images being marketed to our children, along with the unprecedented sexual sophistication of many shows on MTV, sitcoms and in the movies. And, sadly enough, because the major media outlets go out of their way to "understand" teens and their culture and deliver what teens "want," our teens tend to view their parents and teachers as nerds and geeks who simply don't understand them. Corporate sponsors can become the superheroes who do understand.

Sexuality

As our daughters transition from childhood to adolescence, messages in the media pressure girls to "lead" with their newly developing sexuality (see "Girl in the Box," Chapter 1). Girls may feel pressured to look sexy. They may also feel that they need to act sexual. However, if they agree to this they may be called "sluts" and if they stand up for themselves and say "No" they may also be put down for being prudes. In this way, girls may feel "darned if they do, darned if they don't." When alcohol enters a girl's world she can be at even greater risk, both for unplanned and sometimes unwanted sexual advances, as well as for alcohol abuse. Our commercial culture actually uses the concept that beer will encourage popularity and sexual behavior in order to sell more beer. Teen girls can support each other in being themselves in spite of the media messages and stick together to make sure they are all safe in teen social situations. As with all negative media messages, communicative parents and a warm stable home provide a critical counterpoint to the stresses of the teen world. Girls need to be encouraged to lead with their personalities, intelligence, and talents rather than their sexuality.

Media and Violence

Ninety percent of the violence in our culture is perpetrated by men and the ten percent of violence caused by women is usually self-defense. Surprisingly 70% of the time, the recipients of violence are also men. So men cause and receive the lion's share of violence. That is not to diminish the impact on women. **"Media and Violence"**

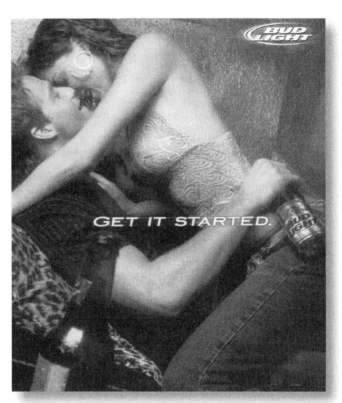

GET IT STARTED.

(p. 2:23) is an excellent summary of the negative effects of violence in our media and our media-linked toys. The wrestling action toy, Al Snow, marketed to children as young as four years of age, is holding the severed head of a woman. Why are manufacturers making media-linked toys for such young children and trying to lure children into media rated for older children? It is very hard to argue that there is positive value for children in these toys. Obviously, these toys are made to make money. The media targets even our youngest children as consumers. The reality is that the current childhood media culture described above is a relatively recent development. It only became possible in 1984 when children's television was deregulated in the US. Prior to 1984, FCC regulations limited the number of advertising minutes per hour allowed on children's television. The FCC also had a rule which stated that marketing toys with a TV show constituted a program-linked commercial, and therefore violated the limit on the number of advertising minutes per hour. Deregulation has led to dramatic changes in children's media, children's toys and children's play.

Media violence encourages children to act more aggressively and it desensitizes them to violence, thus interfering with their capacity for empathy. For example, there is a serious impact on our psyches when any of us see media where sexuality and violence are combined. For males, this can lead to a feeling of sexual entitlement, increasing the frequency of acquaintance rape or assault. On a lighter note, in **"Reviewing my Movie Choices"** (p. 2:24) one mom changed her mind, once she realized the potential harm of violent movies, and talked about it with her daughter. This led both of them to choose healthier venues.

Music

Music can be another media quagmire for parents. For many girls music will be the medium they use to express their emerging sense of self. Music can really help kids to connect to their feelings and emotions, which may otherwise be hard to name or express. But it is easy to worry about our kids when they only want to listen to depressing or angry music. Is this a cry for help? Not necessarily.

The article **"Music in the Millennium"** (p. 2:25) discusses tips on how to evaluate the influence of music in your own daughter's life. Remember that our kids may just be trying to exert their independence by being a little rebellious, or fit in with the crowd, or may just like the way something sounds without even paying attention to the lyrics. Think back to the way your own parents reacted to your music choices. If the lyrics to a song really offend you, then it is time to start a dialogue with your daughter. Talk about what she believes, what she likes and who she is. This conversation could be a window to your daughter's life and emotions. If you come down on her hard and try to forbid her listening to a particular song or group, you may miss the opportunity to learn more about her. What William Pollack, author of *Real Boys*, says about boys, also applies to girls:

> *Music provides an important way for a boy to connect with and release his emotions, evolve an aesthetic sense, and act as a creative person. It's also a way for him to practice his developing critical intelligence, if adults will pay respectful attention to his choices and tastes. If a parent can possibly stand not to set limits on a boy's musical choices, it's an especially good place to back off and let him be himself.*

Music videos, however, as opposed to listening to music, introduce a whole new, often troubling dimension to today's popular music and require limits and supervision for our younger teens. Some families avoid MTV altogether by not paying for extended cable since they do not want their children to conclude that the most important aspect of a woman is her sexuality.

The Internet

Several years ago, if our daughters spent a lot of time on their computers we probably wouldn't have been alarmed. After all, computers are educational. But with the advent of the Internet and all that it exposes our girls to, parents are now worried about their daughters' computer use. For example, how can we monitor what our daughters find on the Internet? How can we protect our girls from harm resulting from her Internet use? How can we prevent Internet use and instant messaging from dominating our daughter's time, even if they are an important part of her social life? Is text messaging interfering with learning at school? To learn more on this important topic see the PBS Frontline *Growing up Online* (2008) and the related discussion at www.pbs.org/frontline.

In working hand-in-hand with our daughters, parents can come up with guidelines that make sense for their own situation. We must be sure that our younger daughters know that they can't believe everything they read. Parents need to also be aware that even child-centered chat rooms, like a children's author's site, can expose children to relationships and conversations that are confusing and can draw them out of their own reality. Just as we warned our daughters about personal safety in the neighborhood, they likewise must be warned that there are people who prey on innocent children on the Internet. We need to be assured that at each stage of use our children know the ground rules of being safe on the Internet, e.g., never give any personal information to anyone they do not know in person. Our daughters also need to know not to post anything on the Internet in writing or photos that they would not want a future college or employer to see. Older teens may also have to search to make sure no one else has posted information which includes their name. Tips on Internet and chat room use by your daughter are included in the article, **"Internet Literacy"** (p. 2:27).

Basic Internet Use Guidelines

- Set limits on the amount of time a child spends online each day or week.
- Do not let the Internet take the place of homework, dinner time, playing outside or with friends or pursuing other interests.
- Never use bad language or send mean messages online.

Basic Internet Safety Rules (Net Smart Rules)

- Do not give out any personal information or fill out details to "win" a prize.
- Never share passwords—even with friends.
- Never arrange a face-to-face meeting with someone online, unless your parent approves the meeting and is with you to meet him or her.
- Make sure you are aware that people online are not always who they say they are and that online information is not private.
- Be careful of any advice given to you on a website, especially if you are advised to not "tell anyone" or keep it a secret.

The Internet is unfortunately an excellent medium for social aggression among our teens. Therefore your daughter needs to be aware of her responsibility to use kindness, restraint, respect and the Golden Rule in her written communications as well as in her face-to-face communications. She may also need a plan and a listening ear if she discovers that her peers are using the Internet in mean ways, i.e., cyberbullying. The article "CyberbullyingNOT: Stopping Online Social Aggression" (p. 2:28) explains the definition of cyber-bullying, the harm it causes, how your child can avoid being a target or aggressor, and what to do when it happens. Girls need to know that it is important to report cyberbullying just like one would any other type of bullying.

Social networking sites frequently play a powerful role, for better or for worse, in the social lives of teens. Parents have a responsibility to become familiar with the power of these sites while modeling appropriate computer-use behavior themselves, so that they can design boundaries for their teens. Adults use the term "social networking sites" but teens refer to these sites by their names such as MySpace, Facebook, Stickam (web-cam), or Youtube (video sharing). Candice M. Kelsey is the author of a great resource for parents called *Generation MySpace – Helping Your Teen Survive Online Adolescence: How Social Networking is Changing Everything About Friendship, Gossip, Sex, Drugs, and Our Kids' Values*. She reminds us that social networking sites teach our teens that they deserve to be entertained at all times, that voyeurism, exhibitionism, and even narcissism are normal and expected, and that success means having the "right" image. As a high school teacher, Kelsey has seen how easily kids get addicted to these sites and exposed to the prevalent messages about sexuality, drug use, and consumerism. The book describes how to set age-appropriate limits such as turning off (collecting, securing) electronics at 9 PM, keeping computers out of bedrooms, setting profiles to "Private" (while knowing they may not be), supervising profile settings, setting time limits, and creating an Internet contract.

Media Literacy

Who wants an hour of meaningful conversations with your family members each day or a kid who rarely pressures you to buy brand names and popular toys? Need inspiration to unplug? Read "TV-Free Families" (p. 2:29). Maybe you are not ready to totally get rid of the TV, but reducing exposure can reduce the harm. "12 Tips to Tame the Tube: Ideas to Give You Control over Television" (p. 2:32) has excellent tips to get you started. Taking the TV out of the children's bedroom alone, reduces their TV viewing, on average, by 1½ hours per day, reduces video game playing by 30 minutes per day and increases reading time. Tivo (www.Tivo.com), which pretapes shows, is an excellent way to fast forward through commercials and manage TV time wisely. Parents need to think carefully about the location of computers as well. No one wants their child online or text messaging at 2 AM.

In our homes we can set up screen standards which reflect our family values. However, what are we to do when our children are watching DVDs, playing games or watching TV in their friend's homes? By adolescence, we trust our children to handle themselves away from home and to feel relaxed about discussing any confusion they may have about what they see. Before then, it pays to be in close communication with other parents and set limits as needed. We can also let our children know that they always have the option of taking a book along and not watching the movie being shown even if it does have appropriate ratings.

Your family may also benefit from one of the excellent blocking devices for both TV and computers that can be found on www.familysafemedia.com, such as BOB:

BOB helps parents monitor and manage the time their children spend using in-home media. BOB is an easy-to-use, small device that sits next to a TV, video-game system or computer. The power cord from one of these devices plugs into the back of BOB and is locked in place. Then, BOB plugs into an electrical outlet. After set up—a process that takes about three minutes—the machine monitors the amount of time a child spends using that media device. Parents decide an acceptable amount of viewing time for each child per day or per week. Specific time periods can be blocked entirely for studying, chores, family time, or sleeping. Each child in the house (up to 6 users) has a four-digit PIN that they enter before they can turn on the attached device. BOB tracks the time used. A "master pin" allows a parent to turn on the connected device at any time.

Media literacy is a key skill that will help parents and families analyze, understand and mitigate the effects of the media on their lives. Media literacy is about understanding the workings of the media and having the ability to analyze, investigate, evaluate, and create one's own media interpretation. Being media literate requires critical thinking. Some people may think they are immune to advertising or the mass media, but in reality, no one is unaffected. Other than our own immediate experience, our perception of the rest of the world is filtered for us directly via the media. An excellent review of media literacy is included in the article **"Media Literacy in Action"** (p. 2:33). Parents who educate themselves and their children in the skills of media literacy can greatly diminish the negative effects the media has on their lives.

Media Activism and Advocacy

It is the hope of Family Empowerment Network that parents will use the information in this chapter to consider the role that media plays in their own families and take positive action to mitigate any untoward effects they might see on their children. **"Examples of Media Activism Successes"** (p. 2:35) share a few of the inspiring stories of success that we have heard. Some of you may want to take a more active role in holding the creators of media programming and entertainment accountable for their products.

THE 40 DEVELOPMENTAL ASSETS Essential to Every Young Person's Success

Those families practicing media literacy and decreasing screen time will suffer less from the effects of media and will have more time to foster healthy behaviors. If you know you've made bad media choices in the past, don't worry; it is never too late to change. Screens steal time from our families that could be spent conversing, playing, reading, drawing, or helping out with a chore. At Family Empowerment Network, we would say time spent in front of a screen is time a child is not building assets. Asset building for this chapter focuses on replacing screen time with activities that build assets instead.

- Asset #2 **Positive Family Communication:** Young person and his/her parent(s) communicate positively, and young person is willing to seek advice and counsel from parent(s).
- Asset #9 **Service to Others:** Young people volunteer one hour or more per week to help others.
- Asset #17 **Creative Activities:** Young people are involved in music, theater or other arts three hours per week.
- Asset #18 **Youth Programs:** Young people are involved in sports, clubs or organizations at least three hours per week.
- Asset #25 **Reading for Pleasure:** Young people enjoy reading on their own for at least three hours per week.
- Asset #33 **Interpersonal Competence:** Young person has empathy, sensitivity, and friendship skills.

CIRCLE QUESTION

What are the primary ways in which you and your daughter are affected by the media and what are you doing to counter the negative effects?

POSSIBLE DISCUSSION QUESTIONS

1. What screen time monitoring systems work and don't work for you?
2. Would your family consider giving up TV for a short or long period of time? What are the pros and cons?
3. How does the "mean world syndrome" influence the extent to which your kids have freedom in their neighborhood and their community?
4. How involved do you get in your daughter's screen time at friend's homes?
5. How did your parents feel about the music you listened to? How do you feel about your kid's music?
6. Is your daughter more Internet and computer savvy than you are? What are the challenges you've experienced in monitoring her computer time?
7. Do you see the cultural diversity you'd like to see in mass media?
8. How do you feel about the concept of "cool hunting" by corporate interests?
9. Large corporations market to kids because they know kids have buying power. Can parents increase, moderate or limit their kids' buying power? And, would it have any effect on how corporations market to kids?
10. What can we do to influence the media to stop producing violent movies, TV shows, and video games?

PUTTING IT INTO PRACTICE

- Avoid television for children less than two years of age per advice of American Academy of Pediatrics.
- Provide young children with toys that encourage creative play.
- Keep all TVs, video game consoles, computers, and cell phones (after 9pm) used by kids in the shared spaces of your home (at least until later in adolescence when your emerging independent young person benefits from having privacy and experiencing choice).
- Let your daughter be part of the decision making on any screen time rules in your home.
- Plan ahead. Teach children to watch TV with a purpose. No channel surfing!
- Agree on a set number of hours of screen time and turn them off when the limit is reached.
- Use blocking devices, such as BOB at http://hopscotchtechnology.com/products.html to help you enforce your rules.
- Don't have extended cable at your house.
- Preview TV shows, video games, music CDs, movies for violence and harmful content.
- Read reviews at www.gradingthemovies.com and www.teachwithmovies.org.
- Limit your own TV viewing—model the behavior you'd like from her.
- Tape the kids' favorite TV shows and watch them later without the commercials.
- Use TIVO at www.TiVo.com to help plan viewing and fast forward through commercials.
- Try her video and computer games with her. It will show her you are trying to relate to her on her level and you will see first hand what she is playing.
- Watch TV/movies with your kids and ask questions about the program and commercials.

- Encourage your schools to offer classes on media literacy and do a yearly school-wide TV Turnoff Week.
- Let your voice be heard! Speak out when you see programming or ads that offend you.
- Watch PBS Frontline's "Merchants of Cool" and "Growing up Online" with your adolescent daughter (or on your own).
- Encourage the PTA to buy videos for your school library from the Media Education Foundation (see below), who make documentary films to inspire critical reflection on the social, political and cultural impact of American mass media. Host a parent educational evening using them.
- Stay informed and connected to media activism. Pick a favorite media website or subscribe to it. We recommend: National Institute on Media and the Family, Campaign for a Commercial Free Childhood.

PUTTING IT TOGETHER—YOUR VERSION

Write down three or four ideas you have been inspired to implement in your own life after reading and discussing this chapter.

1. _____

2. _____

3. _____

4. _____

FURTHER READING

Websites

National Institute on Media and the Family: www.mediafamily.org; www.mediafamily.org/research
   FREE parent guides on online social networking at www.mediafamily.org/network_pdf/Social_Networking_2008.pdf

Center for Media Literacy: excellent all around source at www.medialit.org/focus/par_home.html

Campaign for a Commercial Free Childhood: fantastic advocacy for children at www.commercialfreechildhood.org

Media Literacy: resources for advancing media education at www.medialiteracy.com

Media Matters by American Academy of Pediatrics: www.aap.org/advocacy/mediamatters.htm

Media Education Foundation: fantastic source of educational videos (see below) at www.mediaed.org

Center for Safe and Responsible Internet Use: wonderful current information by Nancy Willard at www.csriu.org

American Library Association: promotes healthy reading habits at www.ala.org

Dads and Daughters: excellent support, advocates for a healthy culture for girls at www.dadsanddaughters.org

Girls, Women, and Media Project: www.mediaandwomen.org/resources.html

About-Face: combats negative and distorted images of women in media at www.about-face.org/

Geena Davis Institute on Gender in Media: www.thegeenadavisinstitute.org, www.seejane.org

Media Awareness Network: www.media-awareness.ca/english/index.cfm. Resources and support for everyone interested in media and information literacy for young people

Media Literacy Clearinghouse: a website designed for K-12 educators at www.frankwbaker.com

ESRB Entertainment Software Rating Board: www.esrb.org

PBS Teacher Source: multimedia resources and professional development for America's pre-K through 12 educators at www.pbs.org/teachers/, search for Media Literacy

New Mexico Media Literacy Program: great resources on media literacy programs at www.nmmlp.org

Media Watch: challenging racism, sexism and violence in the media through education and action at www.mediawatch.com

Center for Screen Time Awareness: sponsors Turn Off TV Week at www.tvturnoff.org, www.screentime.org

Media Think: media literacy courses and resources at www.mediathink.org

Parent Books: Media and Children: up-to-date list of books at www.parentbooks.ca/Media_&_Children.html

Books

The Other Parent: the Inside Story of the Media's Effect on our Children by James Steyer

Remote Control Childhood? Combating the Hazards of Media Culture by Diane E Levin

The Children are Watching: How the Media Teach About Diversity by Carlos E. Cortes
Looks at how TV and other media influence how children think about race, ethnicity and gender.

Television and Movies

The Big Turnoff: Confessions of a TV-Addicted Mom Trying to Raise a TV-Free Kid by Ellen Curry Wilson, a fun book which is thought provoking

Mommy I'm Scared: How TV and Movies Frighten Children and What We Can Do to Protect Them by Joanne Cantor
This book for parents discusses how TV viewing may be influencing children's sense of fear.

Talking Pictures: A Parent's Guide to Using Movies to Discuss Ethics, Values, and Everyday Problems with Children by Ronald J. Madison. This book offers parents suggestions for using films to talk about ideas and issues.

TV-Proof Your Kids, A Parent's Guide to Safe and Healthy Viewing by Lauryn Axelrod

The Smart Parent's Guide to KID'S TV by Milton Chen

Computers and the Internet

E-Parenting: Keeping up with Your Tech-Savvy Kids by Sharon Miller. Learn how to make the most of what the Internet, your computer and other technologies have to offer your family.

Imagination and Play in the Electronic Age by Dorothy and Jerome Singer. With guidance from parents and teachers, empathy, creativity and imagination can expand and intensify in the electronic age.

Cyber-Safe Kids, Cyber Savvy Teens by Nancy Willard, supporting kids to use the Internet safely at www.cyber-safe-kids.com

Cyberbullying and Cyberthreats: Responding to the Challenge of Online Social Aggression, Threats, and Distress by Nancy Willard at www.csriu.org

Youth Risk Online: A Guide for Adults Who Work with Children and Teens by Nancy Willard

Consumerism

Born to Buy: The Commercialized Child and the New Consumer Culture by Juliet Schor

Consuming Kids: Protecting our Children from the Onslaught of Marketing and Advertising by Susan Linn

Packaging Girlhood: Rescuing our Daughters from Marketers' Schemes by Sharon Lamb and Lyn Mikel Brown
"Girl power" has been co-opted by the media to mean the power to shop and attract boys; helps guide parents through attempts to claim them by marketers at www.packaginggirlhood.com

Violence

Stop Teaching Our Kids to Kill by Lt. Col. Dave Grossman and Gloria DeGaetano

Kid Stuff: Marketing Sex and Violence to America's Children by Diane Ravitch and Joseph Viteritti

See No Evil: A Guide to Protecting our Children from Media Violence by M. Levine, PhD

Articles

Cyberbullying: 8-page summary of information under Resources at www.empower-family.com

Generation M: Media in the Lives of 8-18 Year Olds: 2005 Survey by Kaiser Family Foundation at www.kff.org/entmedia/entmedia030905pkg.cfm

Magazines & Journals

Adbusters Magazine: an ad-free critique of consumer culture and the machine that drives it at www.adbusters.org

Good Reads for Girls

***New Moon Magazine for Girls and Their Dreams:* girl-edited, strong on the total girl (ages 8-14) at www.newmoon.org (our personal favorite)

Teen Voices: written by teen women for teen women, challenging media images and serving as a vehicle of change, improving young women's social and economic status at www.teenvoices.com

American Girls: celebrates girlhood and the total self (ages 8-12) at www.americangirl.com

Products to Support Healthy Viewing

BOB at www.hopscotchtechnology.com/products.html, can set limit to #/hours of TV viewing

Media Literacy Toolbox-$79; Teaches basic media literacy concepts like "language of persuasion" and how to deconstruct a media message. Examine media messages about body image, alcohol, tobacco, race, class, aging, and other topics, and explore new marketing techniques, like stealth marketing and viral marketing. New Mexico Media Literacy Project at www.nmmlp.org

TIVO at www.tivo.com, tapes TV programs so you can watch them later and fast forward commercials

Videos from PBS (1-877-PBS-SHOP for $19.99 apiece, fantastic educational investment)

Growing up Online: PBS Frontline examines the ways online activities have taken over teen life and the struggles of parents to handle various situations at www.pbs.org/wgbh/pages/frontline/kidsonline

Merchants of Cool: PBS Frontline examines the energy spent to market cool to our teens who have $150 billion in expendable income at www.pbs.org/wgbh/pages/frontline/shows/cool/view.

Videos from Media Education Foundation: Challenging Media at www.mediaed.org

**Reviving Ophelia: Saving the Selves of Adolescent Girls* with Mary Pipher

Slim Hopes: Advertising and our Obsession with Thinness with Jean Kilbourne

Killing Us Softly 3: Advertising's Image of Women with Jean Kilbourne

**Spin the Bottle: Sex, Lies and Alcohol* with Jean Kilbourne and Jackson Katz, focuses on the normalization of alcohol abuse despite the fact that use leads to deaths, sexual assaults, violence among our youth

Deadly Persuasion: The Advertising of Alcohol and Tobacco with Jean Kilbourne

*Tough Guise: Violence, Media and the Crisis in Masculinity with Jackson Katz

Game Over: Gender, Race and Violence in Video Games

*Dream Worlds 2: Desire, Sex and Power in the Music Industry

Teen Sexuality in an Age of Confusion

Girls Moving Beyond Myth, sexual dilemmas and difficult life choices young girls face today

Date Rape Backlash: Media and the Denial of Rape

Beyond Good and Evil: Children, Media and Violent Time

Advertising and the End of the World

Captive Audience: Advertising Invades the Classroom, exposé of schools becoming advertising vehicles

Money for Nothing: The Political Economy of Pop Music

No Logo: Brand Globalization Resistance, Naomi Klein addresses the dynamics of corporate globalization

Mickey Mouse Monopoly: Disney, Childhood and Corporate Power, Disney gender, race, commercialization

Behind the Scenes: Hollywood Goes Hypercommercial, product placement, toy and fast food promotion

Off the Straight and Narrow: Lesbians, Gays, Bisexuals and Television

Playing Unfair: The Media Image of the Female Athlete, journalism is lagging far behind Title IX

The Military in the Movies

Getting the Message Across: A Video About Making Videos

Some Media Facts to Get Us Started

By Carol Ann McKay and Dr. Riva Sharples

As DIFFERENT AS WE ALL ARE from each other, most parents seem to have similar hopes and dreams for their children. We want children to be strong and healthy, successful in school, to have good interpersonal skills, and be proud of who they are. While there are wonderful television programs available for children, too much television and specifically too much of the "wrong" television can infringe on each of these goals. Television isn't the only culprit, as parents must also consider the lyrics of music, the images in video games, and the subject matter of e-mail chat rooms.

What Is All of This Costing Us?

- An hour spent being passively entertained is time that could be spent reading, doing homework, interacting with friends and family members, or getting fresh air and exercise.

- Many advertisements for children's shows are for foods with high sugar and fat content, encouraging poor dietary habits.

Consider These Statistics:

- By the time the average American child turns 5, he or she has spent the equivalent of 8 months, 24 hours a day, in front of the television. By age 18, he or she will have watched an average of 18,000 hours of television and videos. Meanwhile, that child will have averaged a whopping 15 minutes each day of real interaction with his or her parents while spending approximately 3.9 hours each day in front of the television.

- More children can identify and name the main characters in a popular video game than they can their real life neighbors. As people move farther away from their extended families, the imaginary relationships with characters on television become more important than real relationships with people.

A majority of US children know more about the history of fictional television families than they do about their own.

Are We Selling Out Our Children?

Children's television exists to sell products. Children are exposed to a barrage of advertisements telling them they need to buy certain toys, eat a specific brand of cereal or buy the right brand name of clothes so that they can look a certain way. Advertisers work by making us dissatisfied with the lives we have. They know that this effect is enhanced with children who often can't distinguish between a television program and its advertisements. It is sobering to consider that every five hours of television watched contains one full hour of advertisements.

Loss of Creativity and Imagination

One of the biggest problems with children and television, movies, and video games is the loss of creativity and imagination that occurs. Studies show that young children (particularly those under the age of 5) exposed to TV, movies, and video games never fully develop the ability to imagine, dream and entertain themselves. Television, movies and video games provide visuals and a story line for a child so there is nothing left for the child to do but sit and stare, and perhaps (with a video game) follow a mostly pre-ordained path. In a study of six-year-olds in California, those children who watched a lot of television, movies, and video games often recreated scenes from movies or video games while the children with limited television and game time (or no TV or game time at all) created plots and ideas from their own surroundings and experiences that were unique and individual.

How Far Will It Go?

Television shows keep "upping the ante" as violence, conflict and shock value can grab the audience's attention. Even "wholesome" shows like "Malcolm in the Middle" (praised because it is "realistic") contains more drama, violence, and conflict in one episode than most families see in 6 months. Television, movies and video games are visual mediums, fulfilling our growing need to be constantly entertained and meeting the stations' demands for higher ratings. It's understandable why most television shows are "must see" shows with amazing twists every week.

Effect on Education

Consider that not only does all this exposure take up precious time that can be spent reading or doing homework, it creates difficulties for educators. Our children, with their fleeting attention spans, expect to be entertained. Educators are not entertainers and must try to impart knowledge to children who are used to slick presentations, flashing images and surround sound. Is it realistic to expect these same children to focus on a calculus problem or ponder the meaning of Tennyson's "Crossing the Bar"?

Desensitization to Violence

Studies have shown that not only does violence on television lead to more aggressive behavior in children, it may make them more fearful as they come to believe that violence is as common in the real world as it is on television. Children blur the lines between reality and fantasy all the time. Television, in particular, makes this confusion worse for children because the news is real, and some shows are real, but others are not.

Where Can We Start?

There are some wonderful programs out there but parents must guide their children toward them. PBS channels have no advertisements and programmers take into consideration the wishes of the viewing public who contribute to the station. There are programs that teach about science and offer positive role models for conflict resolution and moral dilemmas. Most parents know instinctively what is a positive message for children and what is a negative message. Parents

can steer children toward programming and images to enable them to grow into strong healthy adults. All messages are "educational" to children. Parents must decide what sort of an education they want their children to have.

Carol Ann McKay has worked as a nurse and an attorney and cuurently teaches law in upstate New York. Dr. Riva Sharples is an Associate Professor of Contemporary Media and Journalism Department at University of South Dakota. She has studied the effect of television on children extensively.

Summary of Generation M: Media in the Lives of 8- to 18-Year-Olds

THE KAISER FAMILY FOUNDATION released its first major study of children's media use in 1999. In 2005 they published their follow-up survey documenting the dramatic changes taking place in family media use in our country. The report is based on a large national sample (2,032 anonymous questionnaires) of 8- to 18-years-olds and their families. The study also included nearly 700 young people who completed a detailed 7-day diary of their media use. Over the last 5 years there has been almost no change in the amount of time young people spend watching or listening to some kind of media (6+ hours per day). This includes watching TV (3 hours per day or almost 4 hours including DVDs/videos), 1 hour per day on the computer outside of school work, up to 50 minutes per day on video games and 1.75 hours per day listening to music. However, the presence of media has substantially expanded. A higher percentage of families have cable or satellite TV and premium TV channels, 3 or more VCR or DVD players, and multiple video game consoles. And more of these media have migrated to kids' bedrooms. Children have increased the amount of time they spend consuming more than one type of media at a time, i.e., multitasking - instant messaging while doing homework and watching TV, so they are actually exposed to 8 hours of media total. Home Internet access rocketed from 47% to 74%. In a typical day 62% of 8- to 18-year-olds used a computer. Important findings for parents trying to parent wisely in today's times are listed below:

- In a typical day, 81% of children watch TV, 47% go online, 46% read a book, 41% play console and 35% play hand-held video games, and 34% read a newspaper,
- For many young people, TV is a constant companion. Two-thirds live in homes where the TV is usually on during meals, and half live in homes where the TV is on most of the time whether anyone is watching it or not,
- Children's bedrooms: 68% have TV in their bedrooms, 54% have a VCR/DVD and a video game console (49%) and nearly one-third have a computer in their bedroom. The percentages for boys are even larger than for girls,
- Children with TVs in their rooms spend almost 1.5 hours more per day watching TV than those without a set in their room and read less than other kids,
- Children from homes where the TV is on most of the time watch an hour more of TV per day and read less than children from homes where the TV is on less often,
- Young people who live in homes where the TV is usually on during meals or is simply left on most of the time are less likely to talk their problems out with parents,
- Children who are heavy TV users spend less time engaged in homework,
- Boys spend more than twice as much time playing video games as girls do. Sixty-five percent of 7th to 12th graders have played the violent video game Grand Theft Auto,
- African-American youth spend far more time watching TV, going to movies, and playing video games than do white youth,
- Over half of 8- to 18-year-olds say their families have no rules about TV. Of the 46% who have rules, only 20% say that their rules are enforced most of the time. Even among the youngest children, 55% say they have no TV rules in their home. Parents are more likely to restrict the amount of time on the computer (23%) than video games (17% have rules),
- Those children who are the least content or get the poorest grades spend more time with video games and less time reading than their peers.

For the full Generation M report, researched by the Kaiser Family Foundation, check out: www.kff.org/entmedia/ entmedia030905pkg.cfm.

Our Children and Consumerism

By Carol Ann McKay and Dr. Riva Sharples

THE REACH OF THE MEDIA, including television, magazines, video games, music and the Internet, is profound. Imagine our children living in a culture that inundates them with negative messages. We as parents and teachers may think our positive messages supersede the culture, but they often don't. They are often diluted by powerful external messages from the media. On a macro level all of us need to work to change the culture, but on a micro level—right now, in our homes—we have to change the environment. The culture is sending our children messages through our televisions, radios, CD's, video games and newspapers. We have to look at the media presences in our homes and take action to protect our children.

The Media Is Selling a Lie: How Bad Is It?

The primary concern of advertisers is not the wellbeing of our children. To the market, children are simply consumers in training. Our children are rushed along through those golden, once-in-a-lifetime years of childhood in the push to turn them into mini- adults. The buying habits of the young are the "cash crop" for advertisers as they hope to develop brand loyalty early. The messages of greed and consumerism are everywhere, preying on the vulnerabilities of children and using them to the marketer's advantage.

Advertising, in general, is geared to make us dissatisfied with the life that we have, convincing us that buying is good and will make us happy. Children and teens are the most naïve consumers and are very sensitive to these tactics—being led to believe that they are not cool enough unless they have the right product, look or attitude.

The Moral Cost Is High

The research has not supported the assumption that an environment teeming in consumerism is a happy one—especially for children. It's not an environment rooted in principle, faith or community. The moral cost is high as it promotes the sort of world where you don't think anything matters unless it serves your material gain. Why

be honest? Why have integrity? Why care about other people? No matter how many times we tell our children that happiness and self-esteem comes from within, the culture is saying that happiness is found in having things. We try to raise our children to be altruistic, kind and generous while the culture says "get all you can for yourself" and "the one with the most toys wins."

The frenzy of buying exaggerates the economic inequalities in our society and has families staggering under loads of debt. A broader environmental consequence of our uncontrolled buying is even more sobering. As we throw away still usable items to get the latest gadgets and material trappings, we are placing enormous strain on the world's resources.

Imagine Fish Swimming in a Fish Bowl

When we bring them home they are bright-eyed and energetic. They swim around like happy little fishes do. After a while we notice their fins starting to flop, their eyes clouding up, their swimming slowing down. They are ill. We try to make them well by adding some additional ingredients to their water. We add medicine to the water, but the medicine dilutes. But we don't check the quality of the water. It's impure. Fish absorb everything in their water, it is their very existence and if the water is impure and we don't change the water, the fish will continue being ill.

Now imagine our children living in a culture that inundates them with negative messages. Like a fish does water, they depend on the culture for survival. We may think our positive messages supersede the culture, but they often don't. They are often diluted by powerful external messages from the media.

Think of your children as the fish swimming in the fish bowl with tainted water. Children absorb everything in their environment. The culture is sending your children impure messages and they're gobbling up these messages. This is the water your children "swim in." We need to change the water.

Reprinted with permission from Carol Ann McKay and Dr. Riva Sharples. From The Ophelia Project® Newsletter, August, 2003

The Silver Bullet

Summary of Juliet Schor's talk, author of *Born to Buy*

New York Times best-selling author Juliet Schor strikes at the core of one of most insidious, powerful influences in our children's lives: advertising. Ads aimed at kids are virtually everywhere— in classrooms and textbooks, on the Internet, even at slumber parties and the playground. Product placement and other innovations have introduced more subtle advertising to movies and television. Companies are enlisting children as guerrilla marketers, targeting their friends and families. Even trusted social institutions such as the Girl Scouts are teaming up with marketers. Drawing on her own survey research and unprecedented access to the advertising industry, Juliet Schor, author of *The Overworked American* and *The Overspent American*, examines how a marketing effort of vast size, scope, and effectiveness has created "commercialized children."

Consider the impact of the "Nag Factor" in your life. When parents were asked, "Are you working longer hours for stuff your children say they need?" 30% said YES. Kids, 0-12 years, spend $30 billion of their own money and influence $670 billion spent on them by parents. Kids influence not only toy and clothes purchases, but also groceries, junk food, cars, hotels, and tourist destinations. Kids are now the "epicenter," the top agents in decisions about what the family buys.

What Schor's Research Shows Is That:

- As marketing has gotten more sophisticated, it has infiltrated every aspect of their lives. For example, the combination of "money-starved schools" and the appeal of a "captive audience" has led to the adoption of Channel 1 in 40% of our middle and high schools. This gives youth a daily mandatory infusion of ads, which include a strong push of junk food,
- Curriculums are being developed by corporations with propaganda (i.e. the logging and energy industry says clear-cutting is good and the ozone layer isn't a problem) to counter environmental information in the schools,
- In 1970's kids saw 20,000 TV commercials per day; they now see 40,000 per day,

- Kids watch TV an average of 5.5 hours/day,
- 20% of preschoolers have TVs in their rooms,
- 2-year-olds are asking for brand names,
- 3-year-olds identify their personalities with brand (I'm cool if I use...),
- For many years, the favorite commercial for 8-year-old boys has been Budweiser ads.

Why is advertising so successful? Over the last 10-15 years, advertisers have committed lots of money to researching kids to find strategies that work. There are 1000s of studies to show how to do it best (Nickelodeon alone has 100s of studies). Word of mouth remains the most powerful way to market kid-to-kid. An example is the *Girls Intelligence Agency,* which helps girls organize slumber parties to help with marketing research. Girls get money and/or prizes to sell out their friends.

What is the impact on advertising on kids? Studies have shown that the effects include depression, anxiety, low self-esteem, and obesity. The more kids watch TV, the more they:

- are depressed, anxious, and have headaches, low self-esteem and stomach aches,
- think their parents aren't cool,
- fight with parents,
- feel like their parents don't understand them,
- are vulnerable to peer pressure.

A silver bullet to reduce these problems is to **TURN OFF THE TV** or, at least, reduce it significantly. Blocking devices, such as BOB, can be incredibly helpful tools to help keep the TV limited. Adults must break through the "cycle of denial" that there is a problem. Media literacy is good too, but not enough. Kids will still buy products, even after being educated about how they are influenced.

Check out Parents' Bill of Rights, a legislative agenda created by Commercial Alert (www.commercialalert.org) to "keep corporations from meddling in the relationship between parents and children."

Impact of Media on Our Children's Health:
How Much Proof Do We Need?

This is the first generation that may actually live shorter lives than their parents—they are unhealthier, more overweight, and more sedentary with all the attendant complications these conditions create

When Children Walked the Earth: Is the Active Child Becoming Extinct?©

By Carol Ann McKay and Dr. Riva Sharples

Childhood obesity has hit epidemic proportions in this country with greater than 30% of children categorized as overweight. Besides low self-esteem issues, these children also face a higher incidence of asthma and hormone disturbances. A disturbing trend, noticed by pediatricians, is the emergence of diseases in children that were previously reserved for adults. These include type II diabetes, high blood pressure, and joint damage.

The sedentary lifestyle many children now have is one of the greatest contributors to this problem. Physical education programs have been decreased in many schools and much more of a child's leisure time is likely to be spent watching television, playing video games and working or playing on the computer. The American Academy of Pediatrics has suggested that obesity is greater among children and adolescents who frequently watch television not only because less energy is expended while viewing but also because of the concurrent consumption of high calorie snacks.

It is no surprise that we see such a dramatic increase in the media's influence on our children—junk values and consumerism are absorbed during those long hours in front of the tube or computer. And not only is the moral cost high, the future health of American children is at stake.[1] **Editors Note:** According to an International Journal of Pediatric Obesity report, researchers predict that <u>nearly</u> <u>half</u> of the children in North and South America will be overweight by 2010. Europe will go from 25% to 38% and even China will start seeing a problem.

Consumerism Leads to Poor Health

Juliet Schor, author of *Born to Buy*, found youth consumerism correlates strongly with alcohol, drug and cigarette consumption, emotional and mental health problems, poor nutrition and obesity. She studied 300 5th/6th graders and found that those who were more materialistic and consumer-oriented develop higher levels of depression, low self-esteem, headaches and poor relationships with parents. Being depressed did not lead to more consumerism but consumerism did lead to depression.

Marketing: Junk Food vs. "Elmo/Broccoli" Study

Addictions often begin during youth and some researchers suspect changes in brain chemistry occur that make early dependence difficult to break. Fast food marketers are taking advantage of the fact that in many households parents don't have a lot of time. They think that junk food saves time and money.

Food companies spend $11 billion per year marketing to kids. They often use popular characters to influence food choices, and kids go for it. What is very inspiring is that this can positively influence food choices, too. The Sesame Workshop's recent "Elmo/Broccoli" Study, supported by the Dr. Robert C. Atkins Foundation, concluded that children would choose broccoli over chocolate when the vegetable was labeled with an Elmo sticker, and an unknown character was placed on a chocolate bar. Yea!

More recently, another study conducted by the Institute of Medicine reinforced this concept and went on to recommend that licensed TV characters should only promote healthy foods. Now if we can just get lawmakers to value the health of our children over the corporations that produce junk food.

—Health and Wellness Directory, Lake Tahoe

Proof: Media Literacy Can Improve Teens' Health

One study found that if teens increase their "Smoking Media Literacy Scale" by only <u>one</u> point using basic media literacy education addressing (1) authors and audiences, (2) messages and meanings, and (3) reality and representation, they significantly reduced current smoking and susceptibility to future smoking. It is amazing that even a "little bit" of information can go a long way for schools daunted by adding yet another comprehensive program.[2]

Another study, has shown that even one media literacy training session can increase early adolescents' skepticism toward advertising, and that taking a more emotional rather than only fact-based approach may be most effective with middle-schoolers.[3]

[1] Reprinted with permission from Carol Ann McKay / Dr. Riva Sharples.
[2] Primack et al., "Association of cigarette smoking and media literacy about smoking among adolescents," *J Adolesc Health*. 2006; 4(39):465–472.
[3] Austin et al. "Benefits and costs of Channel One in a middle school setting and the role of media-literacy training," *Pediatrics*. 2006; 117: 423–433

Fear Sells
Is No News Good News?
By Carol Ann McKay

What Kids See...	The Message They Get...
• Horrible plane and car crashes	• It is not safe to travel
• Child abductions, Amber Alerts	• Children aren't safe, not even in their own homes
• Replays of events such as the World Trade Center bombings	• Terrorist attacks happen frequently
• SARS, West Nile Virus, Mad Cow Disease coverage	• Children will get these diseases; it is not safe to go outside
• Certain foods may cause cancer	• Not even our food is safe to eat
• Celebrity scandals	• Divorce, drug addiction, sex scandals, and adultery are common, even "cool."
• Bloody, dead bodies as a result of war	• Violence and death are the inevitable result of conflict

THE STYLE OF NEWS REPORTING has raised attention grabbing to an art form. The problem is that it is the extraordinary that gets our attention and that is what is reported. War, the attacks on the World Trade Center, and the frightening string of child abductions in the summer of 2002 all have horrific images that grab our attention and keep us glued to the set. Even our weather has become attention grabbing with our storm Doppler and the flashes of warnings that run across our set in bright colors. Tornadoes and hurricanes provide lots of footage from the tedious preparations to their tragic aftermath.

The problem children have when they are confronted with these messages is that they don't have the life experience to put them into perspective. There is even a name for it—"mean world syndrome." They don't understand that the news stories are about things that DON'T happen every day. They are unable to understand that these images are happening, often, half a world away and not on the next street over. Even though the news is real it doesn't mean it is going to happen to them.

Tips for Newsworthy Parents

- Watch or read the news with your child so that you can fill in the facts and answer the questions on issues they don't understand. Remember that TV news is usually not appropriate for younger children.
- Share your feelings about the news, expressing your own morals or values concerning the subject matter
- Select "kid-friendly" news sources for your child where children are more likely to understand and less likely to be frightened.
- Explain that even though the news is real, you are hearing only a portion of the facts.
- Try getting your own news from sources such as public television or radio. These sources answer to the public, not to advertisers interested only in ratings.

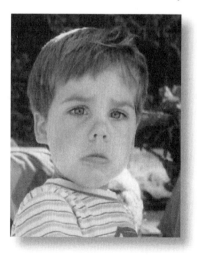

Carol Anne McKay has worked as a nurse and an attorney and is currently teaching law in upstate New York.

Reprinted with permission from Carol Ann McKay. From The Ophelia Project® Newsletter, August, 2003

Sick and Ailing: Teen Girls' Magazine Health Coverage

By Lynette Lamb

Let's hope your girl isn't relying on teen magazines for all her health and wellness information. If she is, she's sunk.

THE BIG SEPTEMBER 2000 issue of *Seventeen*, which weighed in at more than 300 pages, contained a grand total of 6 pages of health information, 3 of which were focused on how to improve a tennis serve. Another 2 pages were devoted to a first-person account of a teen girl's addiction to crystal meth, and the final page was a reasonably good nutrition piece on how to eat right before a big test or sports match.

Addiction got even more pages in *Seventeen's* August 2000 issue, which held a lengthy feature on the hazards of binge drinking and the high incidence of it among college women. Although plenty of high school and even junior high school girls drink too, the magazine didn't acknowledge this fact. Nevertheless, the college feature, which said that 23 percent of young women frequently indulge in binge drinking, probably served as a cautionary tale to younger girls.

Most "fitness" articles found in teen magazines appeal largely to a girl's concern about her weight and body shape rather than to her concern about her overall health. For example, *Jump* (August 2000) ran a piece about a girl who had lost 40 pounds, but her most pressing concern was not her cardiac health and overall fitness (despite having a strong family history of heart disease), but her appearance. That same issue also contained an exercise feature called "Backyard Buff-up," whose subhead said it all: "Get back to school buff." Although purportedly about exercise, the buff-up regime's true purpose was made obvious by the inclusion of beauty instructions for hair conditioning, fitness gear, and hair straighteners.

Teen (August 2000) had some genuine medical news for teen girls—including short pieces about ovarian cysts and sports injuries—but devoted just 1 of its 144 pages to health information. Despite its sleazy reputation, *Cosmo Girl* (August 2000) did much better than most on health care. This issue contained 9 pages of health/fitness information, including a page of questions directed toward a doctor, a page of health shorts, a page about yoga and pilates, and a really terrific 6-page feature called "Getting Strong on the Inside" in which six superstar women athletes discussed what sports have taught them about discipline, communication, teamwork, etc.

In the midst of lots of boy-crazy stuff, *Seventeen's* Summer 2000 "love issue" did redeem itself somewhat by including a straightforward 5-page guide to sexually transmitted diseases, and another 3-page guide to birth control. Given how many teenage girls are sexually active, it would be great if these articles could be regular features.

One more note about *Seventeen's* fall issue. Since guns are the cause of so many deaths of young people these days, it's only fair to report that the September issue of *Seventeen* contained a thorough look at guns and teens, as seen through the eyes of four teenagers (two girls, two boys) who had various opinions and experiences with firearms.

And finally, the great weight debate that just won't die. *Glamour* magazine ran an editorial in its October 2000 issue called "Diet is not a four-letter word," in which it argued that excessive weight is a big killer in America. "Skeleton chic is unhealthy, but the supersize alternative is even worse," *Glamour* wrote.

While it's true that gross obesity can be problematic for health, keep in mind that *Glamour's* audience is mostly made up of middle-class females between the ages of 13 and 30. This is hardly a group that fails to worry sufficiently about staying thin. Indeed, it could be argued that telling a group already at high risk for eating disorders that "Americans need to stop celebrating fat and start dropping pounds," is downright irresponsible.

Most teen magazines, in other words, are designed to sell makeup and clothes, and the best way to do that is to make their readers feel inadequate about their looks. This atmosphere is antithetical to providing good and thorough health information. Please don't let these publications be your daughter's major source for that kind of news.

> Indeed, it could be argued that telling a group already at high risk for eating disorders that "Americans need to stop celebrating fat and start dropping pounds," is downright irresponsible.

Media and Violence

By Jody Bellant Scheer, MD

WHAT ARE CHILDREN WATCHING? Even animated films with a 'G' rating contain "a significant amount of violence" that may not be acceptable for young viewers.[1] And prime-time TV, as well as network news programming, brings a violent world right into our living rooms. According to The National Center for Violence Prevention, by the age of 18 the average teenager has seen 16,000 murders and 200,000 acts of violence on television.

Since 1950 there have been more than 3,500 research studies about the negative effects of media violence on the general population, and on children in particular.[2] Unfortunately, many of these studies are in professional journals and are not readily available to the general public. In addition, the media have tried to denigrate these studies, just as the tobacco industry executives have tried to deny a link between smoking and cancer.

Young children can also be introduced to violence and sex through toys. Traditionally, one might not consider a toy part of "the media" but we now have media-linked toys. We've all seen them—characters from recent TV shows, movies, video games (many with PG-13 and Teen ratings)—all marketed to children as young as 4 years old. Products run the gamut from fast food toys,

clothes, lunchboxes, bed sheets, soda and candy. Consider the World Wide Wrestling Federation action figure toy "Sable," recommended for children aged 4 and up. Based on the real-life female wrestler of the same name, Sable comes complete with an angry face, a whip and chair, minimal black leather clothing and spiked red high heels. Her breasts are enormous and her leather bra is unzipped in front. The pictures on the box show other WWF wrestlers—all males. One, Al Snow, is holding the severed head of a woman. A toy like this, especially because it is connected to "real"

people children see on the weekly TV show, these characters cannot help but contribute to increasing confusion for children about gender roles, sexuality, violence and relationships between males and females.

Why are manufacturers making media-linked toys for such young children and trying to lure children into media rated for older children? Obviously, these toys are made to make money even from our youngest children. The reality is that the current childhood media culture described above is a relatively recent development. Prior to 1984, FCC regulations limited the number of advertising minutes per hour allowed on children's television. The FCC also had a rule which stated that marketing toys with a TV show constituted a program-linked commercial. Deregulation has led to dramatic changes in children's media, children's toys and children's play.

Video games add a new and horrifying dimension because our kids can now participate personally in media violence. Video game technology has changed so rapidly that it is hard for many parents to understand how the new games differ from those of just a few years ago.

How much is media/screen violence contributing to the violence in our society? The answer is clear. Voluminous research shows that media/screen violence affects our children and contributes to violence in our society. The effects can be summarized as follows:
- Media violence encourages children to act more aggressively,
- Media violence encourages attitudes that are distorted, fearful and pessimistic,
- Media violence desensitizes children to real-life violence,
- Desensitized children are more likely to be aggressive than children who are not desensitized,
- Desensitization interferes with a child's capacity for empathy critical for healthy relationships.

[1]*Violence in G-Rated Animated Films*, JAMA, May 2000
[2]*Stop Teaching Our Kids to Kill* by Grossman, pg 24

Reviewing My Movie Choices

By Holly H. Nishimura

I AM A CHILD OF THE 50's, flower child of the 70's and parent of the 90's—maybe you can identify. Every 20 years I boldly move into a new mode and only realize it when a landmark movie tells me so. **Forrest Gump** gave me a sweeping summary of my life and **The Big Chill** reminded me of earlier idealism. **Then and Now** brought back girlhood where friendships were everything and so very fragile all at once. As a child, I spent Saturday afternoons at the local theater where 35 cents bought a double feature with great cartoons in the beginning. We lined up with our tickets and nickel candy bars that were as big as the 50 cent ones of today.

I introduced a love of movies to my daughter and we've been watching since she was 2 when I'd lug a booster seat to the theater [yes, Virginia, there were movies before Tinsel Town]. But when I consider what she's been exposed to, I'm not proud. We are now well versed on the plastic explosive C4, could easily spot a bomb wired to the ignition of the car, know to swim under and away from a burning oil slick, and could land a 747 with only minor coaching from the tower. We could find the safety on most handguns, change Uzi clips as quickly as we change earrings, and know never to enter a darkened room because that's ALWAYS where the bad guy is waiting [duh!]. Together we have witnessed buildings blown up, countless train wrecks and derailments, murders, rapes, stabbings, robberies, torture, alien beings bursting out of unsuspecting co-stars' chests, flesh-eating monsters, mutant human-like life forms who swim in sewers, and so much more. We've witnessed kidnappings, hostage meltdowns, enough births to populate New Hampshire, drownings, every form of drug paraphernalia being used, more surgical procedures than any 6 months in a trauma unit, drunken spectacles and heroic acts of courage and death. We know for a fact—because these were BASED on fact—that parents can and will sell, kill, torture, rape and desert their children, adults will do the same to their parents, and kids will do the same to their friends and parents. But we don't live in Sarajevo or Nairobi where acts of terror and war are routine, and humanity is lost among political issues, hateful factions and everyday survival. No, we buy tickets to see this for fun!! We call this "Entertainment" and sit in quiet anticipation with our popcorn while the multiple speaker system brings us every blood-curdling scream and the special effects-laden images flash the brightest of reds and pyrotechnics. This is what I passed on to my child. Sound familiar?

> **After seeing all those cut-kill-destroy-explode movies with my daughter, how can I suddenly decide they are not okay?**

I'm not here to pass judgment or justify my earlier choices. Those choices seemed sound at the time [what WAS I thinking??] and passed for mother-daughter activities. After seeing all those cut-kill-destroy-explode movies with my daughter, how can I suddenly decide they're not okay? [I'd bought the tickets after all!!] Like this: I changed my mind. Those violent, sexual, exploitive movies had changed my mind over time and I chose to change it back. It's mine again! As a swan song we rented **Aliens: The Resurrection** for our last gross-me-out-athon that I first refused to watch. But the ritual had meaning so I sat and squirmed and looked away and wondered how they made that slimy thing look so disgustingly real. Then it was over and we were done. We'll still see an occasional action movie but will be much more selective about the amount of violence, sex, pain and harm I'll pay to witness.

Not everyone can or will make a change after so long —it's a big move. But if you're wondering whether you can change your vote, take back your acceptance and again define what you consider acceptable, the answer is only two words: YOU CAN. You'll save the time previously spent 'explaining' that the vile language, sexual activity, violent outbursts and acts of torture in the movie are not real AND not allowed in your house. You can spend that time watching movies about all the other topics that don't involve horrific and negative themes. Or not. You could spend that time NOT doing movies and witnessing someone else's vision of a story and plot, of character development and human emotion. Maybe you will read about or live or share your vision of those same things with your child, and listen to hers. The initial silence could be filled with ideas and ideals and experiences you'd otherwise have missed while watching a movie.

Holly Nishimura was a board member and active volunteer with the Ophelia Project, of Erie, PA, dedicated to saving the selves of girls by protecting and reconnecting families.

Music in the Millennium: An Interview with Peter Christenson

By Julie Salmon

PICTURE THIS SCENE: Your fifteen-year-old daughter, formerly of the khaki pants and t-shirt set, starts showing up in combat boots and black lucre. Earrings, which once graced her lobes, now start appearing in even stranger places—her nose, her navel, the center of her tongue. And her music—forget about it! The slightly tinny strains of Spice Girls and Britney Spears have given way to another sound altogether, one in which young girls like your daughter are not held in high esteem. Do you panic? Ship her off to boot camp? Is this daughter of yours irretrievably lost?

Not necessarily, according to Peter G. Christenson, professor of Communications at Lewis and Clark College. Christenson, co-author of *It's Not Only Rock & Roll, Popular Music in the Lives of Adolescents* (Hampton Press, 1997) believes you need to examine all areas of the child's life in order to determine if that child is heading for trouble. "I would tell parents, with music or video games, that the way to find out if there's a problem is not so much to pay attention to that behavior but to pay attention to the rest of the kid's life," says Christenson. "If the kid doesn't have friends or doesn't interact when interaction is what to do, that's when you should worry."

Christenson does not deny the power of music to influence kids, however. In fact, he believes it is the single most important medium in an adolescent's life. He cites a study in which researchers asked adolescents to choose what mass media they would take with them if stranded on a desert island. Most of the teens picked music over television, newspapers, magazines and books. "It's not that they watch less television and listen to more music," he explains, "it's just that the most important moments of their lives, the times they're with friends, having a great time, or the times they're depressed or they're searching for something of meaning in the media, it's music they turn to. Television is kind of vegetation time."

Since music clearly has the power to influence our kids, should parents monitor the lyrics, even censor some songs? "There's a lot of argument about whether kids pay attention to lyrics. Sometimes they do, and sometimes they don't," says Christenson. Kids process lyrics in different ways. When listening to songs on the radio, kids may be completely unaware of the significance of the words. Other times they may write the lyrics down and pour over them, just as their parents did before them.

Communication, rather than censorship, is the key to influencing your child's attitude towards any medium. "I think people should talk to their children about the values that are imbedded in the music," says Christenson. Tell kids what you like and don't like in music, television and on the Internet. Help them understand your values and discuss their own. Then set guidelines. "You can say, 'I know enough about that music to know that some of the things in it are personally offensive to me,' and, frankly, the kid probably knows that too," says Christenson.

It is much easier for parents to evaluate the television shows or movies their children will watch than to review their music, their video games, or their Internet activity. Christenson makes a distinction between "visible" and "invisible" media as a way of understanding the difficulty a parent faces in monitoring the media. "Television and movies are very visible," he explains, but when it comes to music and video games, and certainly the Internet, parents are less likely to encounter them. These activities are easier to ignore because they usually happen in the bedroom. They're alien and a little bit frightening. As a result, many parents may want to simply forbid some of the "invisible" activities outright, particularly in regard to Internet use. But Christenson points out that these new technologies can have a positive effect on our kids as well as a negative one. Any kid entering the 21st century will certainly have to know his or her way around a computer. "Forbidding [computer use] entirely is a projection of our values onto a technology which may be rather neutral," says Christenson. Better to promote the wise use of technology than to ban it.

When your children are young, you should make a concerted effort to monitor their use of any media. As Christenson points out, it's easy to guide kids up to the ages of five and six towards, for example, TV shows on PBS or educational software. "When it's appropriate to control the child, then steer them to good stuff and away from bad stuff. Steer them away from the media to the extent you can without alienating them totally and steer them towards the good stuff by example, if possible." In other words, don't let them catch you sitting around watching *Terminator II* or listening to Snoop Doggy Dog. Let them find you reading a good book instead. Better yet, read a good book with them and talk about it. As your child matures, continue setting an example and keep the lines of communication open. "By the time your kid's a teenager," says Christenson, "you have to accord them a certain amount of freedom to make their own cultural choices and the best you can hope for is that those [choices] will reflect the good values of your family."

Parental Advisory

The parental warning "explicit lyrics" labels put on CD's are at the discretion of the music industry; there are no formal rules or regulation. The recognizable black and white "Parental Advisory Explicit Lyrics" label is the most commonly used. Another common one is "Parental Advisory-Explicit Content."

Can the music rating system help parents monitor what comes into their homes? Yes and no. These labels are used by three groups—music stores, parents, and the kids themselves. Music stores occasionally use them to restrict sales to those less than 18 years of age. "These

ratings are good as long as it's parents who use them," Christenson says.

On the other hand, if they are not used by the parents, the kids may actually gravitate towards the higher ratings simply as a way of testing their limits or showing their sophistication—the 'forbidden fruit' theory. This may be why the record companies are "cooperating" so well with the voluntary system. One study in Portland showed that out of a random sampling of 1000 records the following had the parent warning label: Rap 59%, Heavy metal 13%, Alternative 8%, Pop 1%, and Misc 8%.

If parents use them, ratings can give a logical standard to apply to this vast array of material. Still a parent's best defense is familiarizing yourself with the music and the lyrics and setting your own standards.

Julia Salmon is a freelance writer/editor and mother of three children.

Reprinted with permission from Full Esteem Ahead, *Wings* Newsletter, Fall 1999

Internet Literacy: Safe Surfing in the Online World

THE INTERNET IS NOW A major part of the media mix that surrounds us, and an important component of media literacy—especially for young people. The under-18 demographic comprises over 20% of the US online population, and nearly one-half of all kids and teens are online. The average teenager spends about 9 ½ hours a week online (and another 18 hours a week watching TV), with an even 50/50 split of male and female online teens, doing different activities. Their online time is typically spent on email, instant messaging, doing homework, and playing games.

With so many young people spending so much time online, this market has become a focus for advertisers. According to eMarketer, a leading advertising publication, "marketers all across the Web are working overtime to win over kids and teens." In addition, the Internet presents new risks around privacy, safety and the manipulation of facts.

Fortunately, there is also a growing base of online resources to help with the challenges of building "Internet literacy." Individuals should determine their own comfort level with limit-setting, filtering software, online safety rules and other available techniques, but it is essential to make the Internet a significant part of any media literacy effort. The annotated list (at right) provides selected sites that offer research, suggestions, tools, and further links.

5 Things You Can Do Today

1. Start a conversation about Internet usage—make sure you know what sites your kids are using, with whom they are using chat rooms, and the importance of protecting their personal information.
2. Share some Internet time with your kids. By using the Internet together you can learn a lot about their familiarity and level of online sophistication, and also help to set age-appropriate limits.
3. Help them understand authenticity issues by using the Internet to verify information as fact or fiction.
4. Become familiar with your computer's "history" and "cookies" folder, and explore software that can limit or monitor online usage.
5. Become aware of online commercial messages in all their guises, and help your kids to identify which parts of a website are sponsored for advertisements.

RESOURCES FOR PARENTS:
www.getnetwise.org/
A public service website providing extensive resources about online child safety, privacy, security, and email issues. Includes lists of relevant computer software.

www.media-awareness.ca/english/special_initiatives/web_awareness/
A comprehensive educational resource from Web Awareness Canada. This site is designed to offer parents and teachers with "practical information and hands-on activities to help give kids the cyber smarts they need to make wise, safe, and responsible online decisions."

www.familyInternet.about.com/
Extensive list of articles about making your Internet experience more "family friendly." Be sure to see the list of "Articles and Resources" that deal specifically with kids and online safety.

www.nsbf.org/safe-smart/
Research and guidelines for children's use of the Internet (based on a national survey of parents and children by the National School Boards Foundation).

RESOURCES FOR KIDS
www.pbskids.org/license/
An interactive test that challenges kids to understand Internet protocol and safety practices for online surfing.

www.safekids.com and www.safeteens.com/
Good general resource sites – created by syndicated technology columnist, Larry Magid (author of "Child Safety on the Information Highway" and "Teen Safety on the Information Highway" from The National Center for Missing and Exploited Children.)

CyberbullyNOT: Stopping Online Social Aggression

Cyberbullies use the Internet or cell phones to send hurtful messages or post information to damage the reputation and friendships of others.

Types of Cyberbullying
- Flaming. Angry, rude arguments.
- Harassment. Repeatedly sending offensive messages.
- Denigration. "Dissing" someone online by spreading rumors or posting false information.
- Outing and trickery. Disseminating intimate private information or tricking someone into disclosing private information, which is then disseminated.
- Impersonation. Pretending to be someone else and posting material to damage that person's reputation.
- Exclusion. Intentionally excluding someone from an online group.
- Cyberstalking. Creating fear by sending offensive messages and engaging in threatening activity.

How, Who, and Why
- Cyberbullying occurs via personal Web sites, blogs, e-mail, discussion groups, message boards, chat, instant messaging, or voice, text, or image cell phones.
- A cyberbully may be a person whom the target knows or an online stranger. A cyberbully may be anonymous and enlist the aid of others, including online "friends."
- Cyberbullying may be a continuation of, or in retaliation for, in-school bullying. It may be related to fights about relationships or be based on hate or bias. Some teens think cyberbullying is a fun game.
- Teens might think...
  o They are invisible, so they think they can't be punished.
  o No real harm has been caused online
  o They should have a free speech right to post whatever they want, regardless of the harm

The Harm
Cyberbullying can cause great emotional harm. The communications can be vicious and occur 24/7. Damaging material can be widely disseminated and impossible to fully remove. Teens are reluctant to tell adults for fear they will be restricted from online activities or the cyberbully will retaliate. Cyberbullying can lead to youth suicide and violence.

Responsible Management of Internet Use
- Keep the computer in a public place and supervise.
- Find out what public online sites and communities your child uses and review what your child is posting. Emphasize that these are public places!

Prevent Your Child from Being a Cyberbully
- Make it clear that all Internet use must be in accord with family values of kindness and respect for others.
- Recognize that you can be held financially liable for harm your child causes to another through cyberbullying.
- If your child is being bullied at school, work with the school to stop the bullying and make sure your child knows not to retaliate online.
- If you know your child has cyberbullied others, be very proactive in preventing any continuation.

Prevent Your Child from Becoming a Target
- Make sure your child knows not to post information that could be used maliciously.
- Visit your child's online communities and discuss the values demonstrated by those who participate.
- Bully-proof your child by reinforcing your child's individual strengths and fostering healthy friendships.

Warning Signs
- Sadness or anger during or after Internet use
- Withdrawal from friends and activities, school avoidance, decline of grades, and depression
- Indications that your child is being bullied at school

Action Steps and Options
- Make sure your child knows not to retaliate, to save the evidence, and to ask for help if he/she is having difficulties.
- Identify the cyberbully or bully group. Ask your Internet service provider for help.
  There are different ways that your child or you can respond to cyberbullying:
  o Calmly and strongly tell the cyberbully to stop and to remove any harmful material.
  o Ignore the cyberbully by leaving the online environment, blocking communications, or both.
  o File a complaint with the Internet or cell phone company.
  o Send the cyberbully's parents a letter that includes the evidence of cyberbullying. Demand that the actions stop and harmful material be removed
  o Seek assistance from the school.
  o Contact an attorney to send a letter or file a lawsuit against the cyberbully's parents.
  o Contact the police if the cyberbullying involves threats of violence, coercion, intimidation based on hate or bias, or any form of sexual exploitation.

TV-Free Families: Why—and How—They Unplug

By Nelle Nix

"We were afraid that it could foster a short attention span. It was so fast-paced, so loud, so frenetic that we became concerned that it was a negative influence. And with that, we just quit watching TV." —Steve Cook

TELEVISION NEVER HELD MUCH CHARM for Jody Bellant Scheer. So when the part-time pediatrician had children of her own, it seemed quite natural to declare her family's home a TV-free-zone.

"We made the choice that it wasn't worth the negatives," she says of the decision she and her husband, Stephen Scheer, made. "It wasn't a forbidden fruit. They had access to television—at friends' houses and at their grandparents'—and it wasn't like they never watched it. But it wasn't something they were focused on."

Instead, Gabe and Maya Scheer, about two years apart in age, developed a talent for entertaining themselves. When they were little, their mom says, she did spend perhaps more time than some parents do reading books to them and playing with them outside. But Gabe and Maya could also spend hours amusing themselves with imaginative play, and when they were older, they spent lots of time playing outdoors with the many kids who lived in the neighborhood.

Occasionally a friend would come over for a play date and immediately ask where the television was. "We say, 'We don't have one,'" Scheer recalls. "It would take them about 40 minutes then to figure out how to play, but they would figure it out. Some kids really had forgotten how to play. That's one of the things that motivated me to stick with the no-TV resolve," says Scheer.

That resolve made the Scheer family a rarity. Just two percent of America's families forgo having a television in the house, according to a Nielsen Media Research study published in 2000. That same study found that the average American child, ages 2 to 19, spends 19 hours and 40 minutes each week watching TV.

The idea of families going without television intrigued Eastern Washington University professor Barbara Brock. Four years ago, she placed ads searching for some of these families in Parents magazine, the Chinaberry Book catalog and the TV-Free America newsletter. The response overwhelmed her. She signed up 385 families from 43 states for the 22-page, 100-question survey. In the end, 280 families responded.

Some of Brock's findings, which she titled "TV Free Families: Are They Lola Granolas, Normal Joes or High and Holy Snots?" include the following:

- **TV-free families have an hour of meaningful conversation each day with their children (compared to the national average of 38 minutes per week),**
- **While they come from all walks of life, income brackets, levels of education, races, etc., most are in their 30's, married with two children, have college degrees, earn $60,000 to $80,000 per year, and have religious affiliations,**
- **41 percent send their kids to public schools, with private and home school equally dividing the rest,**
- **92 percent of parents say their children "never or rarely" complain about the lack of TV or pressure them to buy brand names and popular toys,**
- **51 percent of the children receive mostly or all A's in school,**
- **81 percent of the families responded that they were "very satisfied with life."**

Brock says that with a growing body of research indicating a relationship between sedentary watching of media and obesity, lack of physical activity and aggression, more and more families are choosing to shelve their TVs.

"They were NOT Lola Granolas or High and Holy Snots!" says the recreation management professor, whose tentatively titled book *"No TV? No Big Deal! (How Hundreds of Americans are Living Outside of the Box),"* will be published in the spring of 2005 by the Eastern Washington University Press. "They were Normal Joes who found a ton of benefits attached to the TV-free lifestyle."

"I truly feel the trend is upon us and that more families are choosing to go TV-free," Brock says. "Lots of studies (over 4,000) have already been done of the negative effects [of television viewing]. My research was the first to point out that hundreds of families have made the choice and are not only surviving, but thriving!"

At the home of Steve Cook and Marianne Parshley, the television exists but it's mostly a silent guest instead of a constant companion.

"With [oldest daughter] Mimi, we were careful from the start," says Cook, an attorney. "When she was like 3, we did let her watch 'Sesame Street.' Initially we thought it was a great show. But one of the things we began to notice is that she would just sit there and stare."

"The second thing we noticed is that 'Sesame Street' is boom, boom, boom—sort of like music videos. We were afraid that it could foster a short attention span. It was so fast-paced, so loud, so frenetic that we became concerned that it was a negative influence. And with that, we just quit watching TV."

Now, with Mimi at 16, Gwen, 13, and Kathleen, 8, the family is far too busy pursuing their various interests including drama, soccer, basketball, and reading—not

Teaching Your Child to Be Media Literate

The average American child sees some 20,000 TV commercials each year, according to the American Academy of Pediatrics.

But even if you decide to turn off your own TV – for good – the influence of the media is inescapable, according to Peter Christenson, professor of communication at Lewis and Clark College.

"The impact spreads way beyond the actual viewing," Christenson says. "The extent to which kids are bombarded with commercial messages is amazing. They're on every surface."

That's why, Christenson says, it's critical for parents not to ignore the television entirely, but to talk about it. In fact, Vanessa Hughes of the Northwest Media Literacy Center says that while participating in events such as TV-Turn-off Week, April 19-25, is important as a way of heightening awareness of the media's influence, she does not like to see people tune out entirely.

"Opting out is not really the solution," says Hughes, an artist, filmmaker, and educator. "To be truly media literate," Hughes says, "we need to turn the tables on the passive relationship most of us have and start being much more intentional." The goal, according to experts, is for both parents and kids to be able to critically analyze the media that they're consuming.

So how can parents help their children become more media literate? Here are some tips:

Talk about what you see in the media, whether it's television, magazines, billboards or Internet sites. Media literacy experts call this "deconstructing"— essentially taking apart the media in question and analyzing it. By doing so, you can help your kids to fully understand media's role and impact. Hughes suggests some questions you might ask your children (depending on their age):

- Who created this message? Or if it's a commercial, what product are they selling and what audience are they selling to?
- What techniques did they use to get their message across—humor, sex, science ...? (Be sure to point out that the famous people kids may see in commercials—like basketball and rock stars—are paid big bucks to endorse products.)
- How might different people understand this information differently?
- What are the lifestyles, values and points of view represented in this message?
- What's left out of this message?
- How does it make you feel?

Be intentional about what you watch. With all its promotional spots for future programming and sometimes seamless transitions from one show to the next, it's easy to get pulled along and find yourself spending far more time in front of the television than you'd intended. Hughes suggests looking at the TV schedule with children, deciding which programs are important, and then sticking to that plan.

Interact with the media. Complain when it's bad, but be willing to offer praise when it's good, too, Hughes says. "I believe there are a lot of talented people in the industry, and if consumers demand high-quality media, they'll start producing it," she says.   —Nelle Nix to mention homework—to worry about what they're missing on television.

Everyone in the family reads voraciously, and the family typically starts its day with the newspaper at the breakfast table. In recognition of the kids' need to participate at least to a degree in pop culture, the family does rent occasional movies and enjoys debating their merits.

But for the most part, the kids don't seem to feel like they're missing out by not being up-to-date on the latest round of "Survivor" or the final episode of "Friends." "I expected more of a battle," Cook says, "but it really is not an issue."

Like the Cooks, the Scheer family also has a TV now, though it spends weeks at a time tucked away in a cabinet. "We got it when the kids were in high school," Scheer says. "They didn't ask for it, but we wanted them and their friends to come around more. And we noticed that TV was a help ... it was an icebreaker."

Now, with Maya at 21 years old and Gabe at 19, the television is pulled out only occasionally. Certainly, Gabe says, when he was younger, there were times he felt ever-so-slightly isolated as his friends talked about their favorite shows.

"It was just stupid stuff, like 'Did you see the new episode of 'The Simpsons,'" he says. "I kind of felt left out then. But in retrospect, it was so much better, not having a TV. Instead of coming home from school, sitting and watching TV, we'd come home and go out and build forts in the woods or go fishing. It was definitely way better."

And, in perhaps the ultimate testament to the advantages of a TV-free lifestyle, Gabe adds, "I think I would even go so far as to raise my kids with less TV than I got if possible."

Nelle Nix is a Portland freelance writer and mother of two.

Ideas for unplugging

How can you move toward less—instead of more—TV viewing in your house? Parents Jody Bellant Scheer and Steve Cook offer the following advice:

- **Be vigilant about your own television viewing because kids do tend to imitate what their parents do,**
- **Avoid making TV the focus of any room. "Have it be something that may be watched, but don't make it have to be watched," Cook says. One**

solution is to make TV viewing inconvenient by, for example, relegating your television to a basement room or closing it off in a cabinet, as the Scheers have done,
- **Set viewing limits and stick with them. This means turning off the television after a favorite program rather than sitting through the next not-so-great program just because the TV is still on,**
- **Avoid making TV a "forbidden fruit," Scheer says. Instead, when kids watch a program, talk about what you've seen,**
- **Intervene early. It's much easier to control what a toddler watches than what a 12-year-old watches, Cook says, and a child's viewing pattern as a toddler is predictive of what the pattern will be when they're older.**

Resources

Turnoff Week encourages children and adults to decrease screen time in order to promote healthier lives and communities. See "Take Action Programs" and "Turnoff Week" at http://www.screentime.org. Barbara Brock shares more in *Living Outside the Box: TV-Free Families Share Their Secrets.*

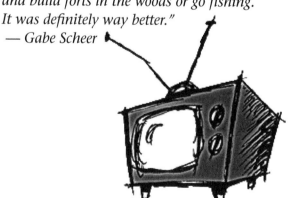

"It was so much better, not having a TV. Instead of coming home from school, sitting and watching TV, we'd come home and go out and build forts in the woods or go fishing. It was definitely way better."
— *Gabe Scheer*

12 Tips to Tame the Tube: Ideas to Give You Control Over Television
National Institute on Media and the Family

Avoid Using TV/Computer as a Babysitter: Think of how careful you are about choosing a baby-sitter and day care. Try to be just as careful about what your children watch on TV every day.

Know What Your Kids Are Watching: It is important to be aware of program content as well as the content of the daily news. The younger the child, the more impressionable he or she is, and the less experienced in evaluating content against the values of family and community. Additionally, emotional images may intrude upon and interrupt sleep.

Keep TV's and Computers Out of Kids' Bedrooms: It is difficult to monitor what your children are watching when they are watching TV in their own room. Having a TV in a child's room discourages participation in family activities and encourages them to watch TV when they could be studying, reading, or sleeping.

Set Some Guidelines About When and What Children Watch: This can be done in conversation with your children, but the final call belongs to the adults. The clearer the rules (i.e., no TV before school, or until homework is completed, etc.), the better. Setting new limits may be upsetting to your children at first, but consistency is very important.

Practice "Appointment" TV. Decide in Advance What's Good and Watch it as a Family: Go through the TV guide in the paper on Sunday and make family decisions on shows to watch for the week. Discuss reasons for the decisions with your children. If in doubt, get more information. In choosing TV shows or videos, make use of independent evaluations, like **KidScore®**, TV and movie guides, articles in magazines, etc. Discuss issues and ideas with other adults, friends, and parents of your children's playmates.

Talk to Your Child About What He or She is Watching: Discuss what you are watching and ask specific questions. Ask what they see, as it may be very different from what you see. Ask them to tell you what things mean to them. Ask them why they watch specific shows, what characters they like and don't like. Discuss the commercials and their perception of toys, cereals, etc. and the people who sell them.

Turn TV Off During Meals: Catch up with one another. Focus on each other. Share stories and activities from each family member's day.

Use the VCR to Your Advantage: Tape a good show and schedule a special family viewing—complete with popcorn. If a show is on at an inconvenient time such as meal time, homework time, or family time, tape it to watch later.

Put the Family on a TV Diet: Schedule some fun alternative activities. When you do watch television, watch it with your children.

Create a TV Coupon System: Kids get coupons and turn them in when they watch a program. Unused coupons can be "cashed in" for a special family activity.

Don't Make TV the Focal Point of the Room: Make your children the focus of your attention, not the TV. Research shows that people watch less TV if it is not in the most prominent location in the room.

Patronize Good Programs & Games and Demand More of Them: Express your opinions to TV and radio stations, network executives, and advertisers. Tell them not only what you do not like, but also what you like. Addresses for networks and local stations are in your TV guide. Also, remember that your money has its own voice.

Check out National Institute on Media and the Family: Building Healthy Families through the Wise Use of the Media at www.mediafamily.org. They have many reports on the latest in recommendations for games, TV, and movies that are healthy and are unhealthy, research on impact of the media on children's health, learning, social skills and tips on how to reduce the harm of media in your child's life.

Media Literacy in Action

Since the year 2000, the organization Media Think has given many presentations to groups throughout the area. As a result of hearing and answering concerns about the media, Media Think has compiled a list of actions to improve media and our relationship to them.

Here are some major points we make to groups and individuals.

1. Start With Yourself

Ask yourself how much you spend on media...in both time and money. If you are like the others, you will be surprised on both counts.

We are both active and passive media consumers. When active, we sometimes binge without paying attention to the consequences. We fill each waking moment with media, whether it be the radio in the background or the television during dinner. Many of us screen out the sounds of the natural environment with portable audio players.

When we are passive consumers, we don't realize how much media we are exposed to. While reading the newspaper, we are exposed to dozens of ads; while driving down a major street, we scan hundreds of signs; and while strolling a supermarket aisle, we face thousands of alluring labels.

Whether active or passive consumers, we need to be media aware.

Accounting for the money we spend on media is another form of awareness. Add up the monthly costs of your magazine or newspaper subscriptions, of the Internet service, the cable bill, movie tickets, the telephone and the cost of newsstand purchases or CDs. Your monthly media bill can easily run to $200 a month.

Realize that the choices you make become part of the economics of the multi-billion dollar media business. One of the five main principles of media literacy is that all media messages have an economic underpinning—starting with your dollars.

Finally, think about how your media consumption habits set examples for other family members—particularly children. The media habits of friends can also influence you and vice versa. Whether you go on a walk together or watch a sitcom is determined by your habits.

2. Communicate

When you watch TV (or read a book or magazine for that matter), talk about it. Experience media together. One of the enjoyments about going to a movie with a friend is sharing perceptions about it afterwards. What is the first thing we do when we walk out of a theater? We ask the other person what he or she thought.

Another of the principles of media literacy is that no two people "read" a media message in the same way.

Without such sharing, media can be isolating. We become lone, unprotected "targets" of messages. But if we engage in the media together and discuss its content, it can bring us together. Ask this: If a program isn't worth talking about, is it worth watching?

3. Change Behavior

To discover more about your relationship with media, try going without it for a set period.

Every third week in April, thousands of families across the country participate in "TV Turn-off Week." The experience of removing television from our daily lives often reminds us of constructive activities we have lost and how little time many of us have been spending together. Without television on, we actually talk at the dinner table. Without television, we become acquainted with the fun of games and the joy of reading to each

other. And without TV, we also learn what programs we truly miss and which ones we literally can do without.

Of course, many people go on "media fasts" on their own and under their own terms. Computer games, the daily newspaper, magazines—all can be subjected to "fasts."

4. Know The Effects Of Media

Very often changing our relationship with media will tell us what its effects have been on us. In spite of that, we often are unaware of how media affects us and others around us. We need to stay informed of what researchers are learning. For example, recently links between attention deficit disorder and television viewing have been found. Low self-esteem among adolescent girls, obesity, low grades and heightened fear has also been linked to certain habits of media consumption. There are hundreds of studies about such media effects.

Numerous media literacy websites will keep you informed of the latest findings. You can find a list of resource links at Media Thinks' web site: www.mediathink.org. Remember that media literacy is an on-going process, not a goal, so return to these sites routinely.

Excellent books have also been written alerting the public to harmful effects of the misuse of media. "Screen Smarts" by Gloria DeGaetano and Kathleen Bander and "The Other Parent" by James Steyer are just two among many.

5. Work To Change The Media

We often complain about the media, but how often do we complain to those who are responsible for media decisions? We become part of the problem if we don't. Phone a television station to complain about gratuitous violence or demeaning stereotypes. Write sponsors of programs that you disagree with. Letters to the editor are among the most read parts of newspapers—use the newspaper as a forum for your criticism.

Just as important as complaining is complimenting when you see something you like. Media can seem impersonal and distant, but it is run by real people who want to know what others think of their work. Tell them.

> **MEDIA ACTIVISM**
> **A RECAP IN BRIEF**
> 1. **Start with yourself**
> 2. **Communicate**
> 3. **Change behavior**
> 4. **Know the effects of media**
> 5. **Work to change the media**
> 6. **Don't media bash**

6. Don't Media Bash

Likewise, remember the problem isn't the media themselves; it is how media are used. Nicolas Johnson, one of the most critical commissioners ever to serve on Federal Communications Commission, once said, "All television is educational television. The only question is: what is it teaching?"

By educating ourselves, by being selective, by speaking out, we can shape media to be a positive force in society and in our lives. Media Think was founded on the premise that a public that is knowledgeable about the media and acts on that knowledge will ultimately change the media for the better.

Reprinted with permission from Media Think. Media Think (formerly the Northwest Media Literacy Center) is a group of volunteers committed to strengthening critical thinking skills for understanding media, and empowering people to shape media that better serve the needs of individuals and communities. www. MediaThink.org

Examples of Media Activism Successes

Never Underestimate the Power of Angry, Intelligent Girls: A boycott of Abercrombie & Fitch by a group of 23 Pennsylvania girls gained national attention and ended when the retailer agreed to stop selling two controversial T-shirts: "Who Needs Brains When You Have These?" and "All Men Like Tig Old Bitties." (Other A&F shirts say. "Muck Fe" and "You Blow I'll Pop"). The girls dubbed their action a "girlcott." This inspired Women and Girl Foundation to submit their own T-shirt ideas to A&F. (Story from *Chicago Tribune's* "Red Eye," 11/7/05.)

Stand for Children Supports Families by Helping to Get Rid of Junk Food in Oregon Schools: Junk food got into our schools under the guise of "helping" by bringing in money, but research shows that schools can actually make more money selling healthy food than junk food. Although revenues drop at first, they increase as more parents give their kids money to eat in the cafeteria and more teachers and staff buy meals at the school. Furthermore, the schools tend to discover they have fewer behavior problems when kids are not hopped up on sugar and empty calories. When you add in the savings in future health care costs as kids develop healthy eating habits, getting rid of junk food makes financial sense. California became the first state to ban soft drinks in 2003 and then junk food in 2005. Stand for Children (www.stand.org). addressed this problem in Oregon in 2007 by helping craft and win passage of statewide legislation requiring the replacement of high-sugar, high-fat junk food and soda with healthier snacks in school vending machines, student stores, and à la carte bars.

Bringing Media Literacy to Hollywood: Where better to introduce media literacy than in a community situated near Hollywood, "the entertainment capital of the world." Father Bill Kerze at Our Lady of Malibu Parish and School in Malibu, California says, "The world we live in is clearly permeated with media. We teach our kids how to read and write, yet we're not really cognizant of the language of media and its powerful effect. My goal is to help people become better aware so they can make more informed choices." Components included: grade-specific lesson plans in consumerism and violence prevention, a 7th-grade video project, newspaper article production and an animation workshop for 5th- to 8th-grade students. The Center for Media Literacy (www.medialit.org) helped develop the curriculum.

Although media literacy education has been practiced in Canada, Great Britain, and Australia for three decades or more, it is just now gaining a foothold in the US. The movement has spawned two national organizations that advance media education training, networking, and information exchange through professional conferences and media list-serves: Alliance for a Media Literate America (AMLA) and Action Coalition for Media Education (ACME).

Celebrating "Beauty on the Inside": To counter *People Magazine's* yearly report of the 25 most beautiful women, *New Moon Magazine for Girls and Their Dreams* publishes "25 Beautiful Girls" every June which celebrates inner beauty—the beauty of conviction, caring, and action. All *New Moon* content is geared for girls age 8-15. It is for girls, written by girls, and is about girls and their interests. They remain free of advertising and external media influences in order to avoid "perfect girl" stereotyping, and to remain accountable only to girls and their needs.

Girls Get the Message from Girls Inc.:

Girls Incorporated (www.girlsinc.org) has a unique program to help girls develop the skills to wade through the media messages that bombard them. Girls Get the Message® is a national program that encourages girls and other media consumers to evaluate the messages in media such as television shows, films, CDs, newspapers, websites, music videos, magazines and video games. The program helps girls recognize stereotypes in media and differentiate between those stereotypes and their own lives. Girls learn to "read" media messages with a critical eye as they consider issues of ownership, media business and the roles of women and minorities "behind the scenes" in media careers. In Girls Get the Message, girls learn how to directly communicate with media industry professionals to make their voices heard. Girls Inc. continues this dialogue by hosting events that bring girls and media industry leaders together. At these events girls express their views on how to create more positive and realistic portrayals of girls and women in media.

McDonalds Gets Out of Report Cards:

McDonald's has ended its controversial report card advertising in Seminole County, Florida. Children in kindergarten through fifth grade had been receiving their report cards in envelopes adorned with Ronald McDonald promising a free Happy Meal to students with good grades, behavior, or attendance. The Campaign for a Commercial-Free Childhood (CCFC) at www. commercialfreechildhood.org, was alerted to the advertising by Seminole County parent Susan Pagan and launched a campaign which resulted in nearly 2,000 letters to McDonalds and plenty of bad publicity for the fast food giant. The following is CCFC's statement on McDonald's decision to end the program. *In the absence*

of needed government regulation to protect school children from predatory companies like McDonalds, the burden is on parents to be vigilant about exploitative marketing aimed at children. One parent can make a difference. There is no doubt that the Seminole County ads would have continued—and violated McDonald's pledge to stop advertising in elementary schools—had one parent not called attention to the problem. And when that parent was joined by other parents and CCFC members, one of our nation's largest corporations was forced to back down. What we accomplished in Seminole County should put all marketers on notice: advertising has no place in our nation's schools. Working together, we can reclaim childhood from corporate marketers.

You can keep updated and get involved by simply signing up for the CCFC newsletter.

Media Literacy Resources to Combat Sexualization of our Girls:

Girls get one message repeatedly: What matters is how "hot" they look. It plays on TV and across the Internet. You hear it in song lyrics and music videos. You see it in movies, electronic games, and clothing stores. It's a powerful message which harms girls. Sexualization occurs when:

- a person's value comes only from his or her sexual appeal or behavior, to the exclusion of other characteristics;
- a person is held to a standard that equates physical attractiveness (narrowly defined) with being sexy;
- a person is sexually objectified—that is, made into a thing for others' sexual use, rather than seen as a person with the capacity for independent action and decision making; and/or
- sexuality is inappropriately imposed upon a person

All four conditions need not be present; any one is an indication of sexualization. As parents, you are powerful, too. You can teach girls to value themselves for who they are, rather than how they look. You can teach boys to value girls as friends, sisters, and girlfriends, rather than as sexual objects. You can advocate for change with manufacturers and media producers. Check out: www.apa.org/pi/wpo/sexualizationres.html.

Parenting Her 3

Liana Hochhalter, 8th Grade, Rosemont Ridge Middle School

Parenting Her

> *"Effectiveness as a parent is much more from what you hear than from what you say."*
> —Mira Kirshenbaum, author of *Parent Teen Breakthrough*
>
> *"Parents have become so convinced that educators know what is best for children that they forgot that they themselves are really experts."*
> —Marian Wright Edelman, Children's Defense Fund
>
> *"Motherhood: 24/7 on the frontlines of humanity. Are you man enough to try it?"*
> —Maria Shriver
>
> *"The most important thing she had learned over the years was that there was no way to be a perfect mother and a million ways to be a good one."*
> —Jill Churchill

GOALS

- To explore and implement positive parenting strategies for today's world and avoid common sabotages

- To provide support for each other in our struggles, recognizing that there are often no easy answers and many possible solutions

- To develop strategies for encouraging open and compassionate communication, including family rituals, family meetings and meals together

- To explore the impact your own childhood has on the way you parent your children

- To recognize and embrace the important role of a father, as well as a mother, in raising a daughter

OVERVIEW

Modern parenting is a complicated business. When we "signed-up" for parenting and were holding that darling little baby—we thought THAT was complicated. Little did we know what was to come. The poem, **"Letting Go,"** reminds us that in the process of supporting our children as they grow, we develop right along beside them, and expand our capacity and flexibility in ways we could never have imagined before we had children. Through all of the difficulties of maintaining family relationships, there is one thing that is clear: when times get tough, it is our families that we turn to and our families that help pull us through. The article **"Family Comes First"** (p. 3:14), reminds us of this fact. Our busy lives often distract us as parents from what is most important in our lives: the lifelong relationships we are building with our children.

Connected Parenting

There is simply no easy rulebook for parenting. Parenting strategies and advice abound and there are thousands of books written on the subject. You will find that no one technique works for any single child in all situations. As our kids grow and develop, the strategies we use with them must also change, so as they grow, we grow. However, we would like to acquaint you with one overall parenting approach, which we call **"Connected Parenting"** (p. 3:16). Connected parenting helps children of all ages develop into happy, self-reliant and capable individuals, and respects the dignity and wholeness of both parents *and* child. Jane Nelsen, author of *Positive Discipline,* is one of a number of experts who encourage connected parenting, which:

1. Helps children feel a sense of connection (belonging and significance),
2. Is mutually respectful and encouraging (kind and firm at the same time),
3. Is effective long-term (gets inside the kid's head about what she is thinking, feeling, learning and deciding about her world),
4. Teaches important social and life skills (respect, concern for others, problem solving, and cooperation, as well as the skills to contribute to the home, school, and community).

In **"Comparison of Common Parenting Styles"** (p. 3:17) you can get a feel for three parenting styles:
1. Permissive child-centered
2. Connected, authoritative, Adlerian
3. Strict, authoritarian, parent-centered.

A common scenario is "yo-yo" parenting when we go from overly permissive (because it's easier, fun and child-centered) to overly strict (because the kids "crossed the line" and we are exhausted and angry). This is why it can benefit everyone to strive for the middle-ground where everyone's needs for respect are met. Jane Nelsen's positive discipline is an excellent model. Positive discipline, as described in **"Positive Discipline Guidelines"** (p. 3:18), is based on understanding the underlying positive intentions that hide behind a child's mis-behaviors. Parents can then create a response which supports the self-esteem, growth and self-discipline of the child that is also respectful, loving and non-punitive. Parents and kids both feel better with this approach.

Connected parenting acknowledges that children make decisions about their lives every day. Parenting is focused on helping children to develop good decision-making skills by letting them practice making choices and learning from the natural and logical consequences of those choices. Children who are allowed to learn from their mistakes when they are young are less likely to act out in dangerous ways as teenagers. They understand that there are personal consequences for the choices that they make that are a direct result of their actions. Connected parenting encourages parents to see mistakes as wonderful opportunities to learn. Setting clear and appropriate boundaries that are wide enough to allow children plenty of room to make lots of choices and mistakes is the hallmark of positive, compassionate parenting.

An important element to parenting is a deep regard for preserving the humanity and dignity of the child and the parents. Learning to discipline with compassion, kindness and firmness, instead of guilt, shame, or coercion, is a skill any parent can learn. Few of us, however, were raised with this model ourselves. The articles **"Connected Parenting"** (p. 3:16), and **"Taking Charge: Basic Concepts of JoAnne Nordling's Caring**

Discipline" (p. 3:19), will help you to gain your child's cooperation and enhance their mastery of important life skills. The other payoff to parenting with humanity and respect is that a parent usually feels better about him or herself.

Spanking is a common parenting tool used in our culture that carries a number of negative long-term side effects, as outlined in **"Spanking: A Slap at Thoughtful Parenting,"** (p. 3:20) originally written by developmental-behavioral pediatrician, Dr. Barbara Howard. Spanking can lead to a belief that those who are the strongest have "power over" those who are weaker. Learning to use positive parenting techniques rather than spanking respects the dignity and humanity of the child and teaches children that there are ways other than hitting to resolve disputes.

"Monster Mother from the Black Lagoon" (p. 3:21) and the **"The Mistaken Goal Chart"** (p. 3:23) remind us how easily our own feelings can get the best of us when we are parenting, and how to use our emotional reactions to inform our parenting. Lionel Fisher's article, **"Parent's Job: Step Aside, Let Kids Become Heroes,"** (p. 3:24) encourages us to guide children in finding their own path based on their own inner compass.

Parenting Teens

Parenting teenagers can be a challenge for any parent, and due to the developmental changes in adolescence, your effectiveness as a parent will greatly increase if you change too. The article, **"Overview of One of Our Favorites:** *Positive Discipline for Teenagers"* (p. 3:25) highlights key points from the excellent book, *Positive Discipline for Teenagers: Resolving Conflict with Your Teenage Son or Daughter,* by Jane Nelsen and Lynn Lott. This book is especially useful for helping parents to understand that teenagers, more than ever, need opportunities in their lives for decision-making. By age 18, teenagers are expected to be fully functioning within adult society. Learning to respectfully guide and trust our teenagers through adolescence, while allowing teens to learn from their own experiences and mistakes, is truly one of the most difficult tasks that any parent faces. This book is a blessing for anyone wanting to learn how to parent their

teenagers effectively, in a way that preserves everyone's dignity, respect, sanity and safety.

Effective communication and connection with your child continues to be the most powerful protection against future risky behaviors. A US study, titled "Protecting Adolescents from Harm"[1] surveyed 12,000 youth and showed that the single most protective factor against risky behaviors was good connection with parents. A great way to seek more connection and fulfillment as a parent is to simply become curious about who our daughters are and what they think.

Listening to our daughters' stories, as well as to their nonverbal behaviors, can be immensely helpful for understanding our girls better. It also sends them a loud and clear message that they are valued, loved and cared about. Listening is a skill that can be learned, and parents who make a point to listen more and lecture less will be rewarded with more intimacy and connection with their child. We can use our curiosity and observation to hone our listening skills. **"Curiosity Kills the Cat but Connects the Family"** (p. 3:26), speaks to the power of curiosity—just wondering what is going on inside the head of your child. It can help to let go of your agenda and focus on what is important to your child; what are the needs behind her actions? Your child will then be in a more receptive state to listen to your needs.

Compassionate Communication

"Peaceful Parenting," by Sura Hart and Victoria Kindle Hodson, introduces a powerful communication approach called nonviolent or compassionate communication. It is based on the idea that every action we do is motivated by attempts to meet needs or values, and that trusting relationships are built through attentiveness to those needs. When a child says "no" to your request (or demand), ask yourself to what underlying need she may be saying "yes"? The **"Feelings and Needs Inventories"** (p. 3:29) can support you in exploring the values that are behind the behavior. When both sides get clarity on their underlying needs, new solutions arise that meet everyone's desires.

Family Rituals

"**Family Rituals: The Ties that Bind**" (p. 3:30) is written by William Doherty, author of *Putting Family First.* We live in a culture that tears the family in many different directions: work, school, sports, and lessons. Rituals can create a "gravitational field" that connects the family. When adults are asked what they remember about their childhood, they remember three things, all of which are rituals: meals, vacations and holidays (many add getting tucked into bed). You could start with meals; set out candles, and turn off the phone, the TV and the scolding. This keeps dinner time "safe." If each family member tells about the best and worst thing that happened that day you will learn a lot about each other. "**At the Heart of Parenting: Eating Together**" (p. 3:32) describes why family meals are incredibly powerful protective factors. Research shows that family meals are correlated with school success and reduction of risky behavior. Meals together is one of the most important ways to strengthen your family. One-on-one dates and vacations are powerful rituals, too. Dad might go on a regular ice cream run once a week with one kid, and play golf every other week with the other. Mom might go camping with one of the kids.

Family Meetings

Regular family meetings are a fabulous "ritual" that sets up open communication between family members. Little things that are bothering a family member get addressed in these regular meetings and prevent a big "blow-out" later. Meetings that are friendly and comfortable, including some favorite treats, put everyone at ease. All family members add to the agenda, participate in problem solving and voice their opinions so that they feel empowered. This simple tool is reviewed in the article "**Tips on Running a Successful Family Meeting**" (p. 3:34). A family meeting can be used to lessen family conflict over chores. At a family meeting, in response to nagging and pleading to get the kids to routinely finish their chores on time, the family establishes a set of agreements and consequences around chores. Because the kids are involved in setting up the agreements as well as the consequences for chores not done, they become more invested in carrying through on their agreements.

The entire family benefits as chores get done without conflict, and the kids learn accountability and feel good about their contribution to the family's welfare.

Fathers and Daughters

Fathers are becoming more involved in their daughters' lives than ever before and we hope this trend just keeps growing, until all children see both their parents as equally involved caregivers. The role of a father is critical for both daughters and sons. The power of a dad to make his daughter feel self-assured, capable and confident is tremendous. He, particularly, can help her appreciate that her body is powerful and functional and not just an ornament for others to admire. The many ways that a Dad can help his daughter gain important life skills is reviewed in the article "**The Important Role of Fathers in Raising Daughters**" (p. 3:36).

In summary, parenting is not a perfect science, but more of an art. With the myriad of influences that our daughters are exposed to on a daily basis through peers, media, institutions, and the ever-increasing pace of life in our society, we parents can provide a "haven" where our children and teens can feel at rest, safe, accepted and understood. Our daughters deserve our love and support, so they can experiment and experience who they are without fear of harsh judgment. In this way, they can truly discover and grow into the persons they are meant to be.

Parenting for mothers and fathers of daughters is not easy. It requires endless patience, tenacity, energy, and attentiveness combined with unconditional love. It requires believing in, protecting, and celebrating your daughter's inner sense of worth. Although the responsibility of raising a daughter can be daunting, the journey can be filled with joy and love. Our goals as parents were aptly summed up by Hodding Carter, Jr., when he said,

> *"There are only two lasting bequests we can hope to give to our children … one of these is roots, the other, wings."*

[1] "Protecting Adolescents from Harm," *Journal of the American Medical Association*, 9/10/97, Vol. 278, pp. 823-32.

THE 40 DEVELOPMENTAL ASSETS Essential to Every Young Person's Success

The 40 Developmental Assets are research-proven building blocks that support the healthy development of our youth and help them to grow up to be caring and responsible. The following assets relate directly to a child's experiences with her parents and within the home:

- **Asset #1** **Family Support:** Family life provides high levels of love and support.
- **Asset #2** **Positive Family Communication:** Young person and her parents communicate positively and young person is willing to seek advice and counsel from parents.
- **Asset #6** **Parent Involvement in Schooling:** Parents are involved in helping young people succeed in school.
- **Asset #11** **Family Boundaries:** Family has clear rules and consequences and monitors the young person's whereabouts.
- **Asset #14** **Adult Role Models:** Parents and other adults model positive, responsible behaviors.
- **Asset #16** **High Expectations:** Both parents and teachers encourage the young person to do well.

CIRCLE QUESTION

What were the advantages and disadvantages of the parenting style your parents used raising you? Specifically, what contributed to your well-being and health that you would like to include in your parenting? Name one thing you are doing differently.

POSSIBLE DISCUSSION QUESTIONS

1. What do you love about your daughter? What is special and unique about her?
2. What positive qualities does she bring out in you? How does she challenge you to grow?
3. Share a successful parenting story. How did some of the most rewarding moments with your daughter come about? What is your biggest parenting struggle right now?
4. What other adults are involved in your child's life and how did these relationships evolve? How do you seek out support for your parenting from other adults? Who are they? How do they help?
5. What are effective alternatives to nagging?
6. Have you found rewards to be useful in parenting? In what situations? Do you think they might be potentially damaging?
7. How do you and your child "match" in terms of temperament?

Connection/Listening

8. What is your parenting style along the spectrum of strict versus permissive?
9. How do you as a parent balance/assert your own needs with those of your children?
10. How do you express anger constructively in your family? What constitutes "confrontation" at your house?
11. Describe an instance where you allowed your daughter to experience some difficult consequences of a mistake, without rescuing or buffering her. What did you both learn?
12. How difficult would it be for you to start allowing your daughter to make more choices and mistakes in her life? In what areas of her life would it be easiest for you to start this new tactic?
13. What is the difference between punishment and positive discipline?
14. How do you react when your daughter makes a mistake, acts out in front of others, or expresses her outrageous individuality? How might she interpret your response and how might she feel?
15. Go over the needs list and decide what your biggest unmet needs are, as a parent. Imagine your life if these needs were met and describe it to each other.

Rituals

16. What are the rituals in your home that increase connection and communication?
17. What do you like/dislike about family meals in your home?
18. Describe the one-on-one activities you do with each of your kids.

Teens

20. How is your teen different from you when you were a teen?
21. How do parents balance setting limits with allowing independence?
19. Did you learn some of your most important life lessons from your own experiences or other's advice?
20. What preconceived ideas do you have of the type of person your child will become as a grown-up? Has that idea changed over time? How realistic is it?
21. What type of relationship do you imagine having with your child when she is an adult?
22. What boundaries are most important for your daughter to have?

Fathers/Mothers

23. Whether you are a mom or a dad taking this course, how can you share what you are learning with your spouse?

24. How involved are male relatives—father, grandfather, uncles—and close family friends in your daughter's life? If your daughter would benefit from more time with them, how can you foster that?

PUTTING IT INTO PRACTICE

- Shift parenting style to a more positive approach that supports relationships, teaches responsibility, sets reasonable boundaries and respects the dignity of the child and integrity of the parent.
- Encourage independence and interdependence.
- Respect your adolescent's privacy.
- Accept your teen's grumblings as normal and natural—don't take it personally.
- Develop family rituals aimed at strengthening your family structure and relationships.
- Consider establishing a family mission statement and having regular family meetings.
- As your daughter grows, include her more and more in making decisions that affect her.
- Maintain your balance and assert your own needs, especially for stress reduction and self-care.
- Seek out a support system for you and a mentoring system for her.
- Spend more one-on-one time with your daughter.
- When in conflict with your daughter, re-examine the content when calm, connect with your underlying need or value behind what you want, and consider your daughter's point of view.

PUTTING IT TOGETHER—YOUR VERSION

Write down three or four ideas you have been inspired to implement in your own life after reading and discussing this chapter.

1. _____

2. _____

3. _____

4. _____

FAVORITE PARENTING RESOURCES

Connection and Empathy (Nonviolent Communication)

Nonviolent Communication (NVC), by Marshall Rosenberg, introduces the basic concepts of the compassionate communication approach to interacting with others, leading to a deep connection both to ourselves as well as the other person. It is based on the premise that we are motivated by attempts to meet needs, and trusting relationships are built through attentiveness to those needs. Sura Hart and Victoria Kindle, authors of *Respectful Parents, Respectful Kids: 7 Keys to Turn Family Conflict Into Cooperation*, get to the heart of family conflict with powerful insights. In her book *Parenting from Your Heart: Sharing the Gifts of Compassion, Connection, and Choice*, Inbal Kashtan applies these NVC principles to parenting. Instead of focusing on authority and discipline, attachment parenting and NVC provide theoretical and practical grounds for nurturing compassionate, powerful, and creative children who will have resources to contribute to a peaceful society.

How to Say It® to Girls: *Communicating with Your Growing Daughter* by Nancy Gruver, founder of *NewMoon: the Magazine for Girls and Their Dreams*, is an expert guide to girl talk. Talking with your daughter can be difficult, but knowing the right words can help. *How to Say It® to Girls* provides a wellspring of practical advice on how to broach uncomfortable subjects, or simply open the lines of communication, with girls of all ages. This book offers concrete words, phrases, and sample dialogues to help parents figure out what to say and how best to say it. Whether you're dealing with toddlers or teens, you'll find useful information to help you discuss relevant topics—from bedtime to body image from creativity to cliques.

Understanding Temperament

Raising Your Spirited Child by Mary Sheedy Kurchinka is an important resource for understanding the effects of temperament. As you know, there is no one simple answer for what to do in any given situation. Each of our own children may need different approaches. Parents have different personalities, and so do kids. Sometimes the problem is simply that the two sets of personalities are just not matching up well. There are nine temperament traits we are born with that remain fairly consistent our entire lives. They are: activity level, intensity, persistence, distractibility, regularity, approach-withdrawal, adaptability, mood and sensory threshold. The better we understand temperament, the more we can match our parenting to these differences and help children value and understand themselves.

Teens

Parenting a teenage girl is an especially difficult task for most parents, who may be frightened not only by the growing autonomy of their daughter, but also by the myriad of toxic influences in our modern culture. Parents are also influenced by their own experiences as teenagers, when they likely rebelled against their own parents and culture. The following parenting resources can help parents to support their teens with love, connection, and respect during the turbulent teen years. The bonus is that you can be closely connected with your daughter and actually enjoy yourself, too.

Positive Discipline for Teenagers by Jane Nelsen and Lynn Lott provides one of the best all-round approaches to parenting teens. When our children are struggling and we jump in and "solve" it for them, it turns the situation into "our problem." When we can let go enough to hold our tongue and help them think through their own solutions, children learn about responsibility and how to cope with their own problems.

Parent as Coach by Diana Sterling is an easy-to-read book that is just packed with powerful, new ideas encouraging parents to switch from administrating to coaching their teen. It is based on a poem, titled "Message to Parents," written by teens who had received coaching. By focusing on respect, listening, understanding, appreciation, and support, our teen will have the resources to become responsible and independent.

> *If you Respect me,*
> *I will hear you.*
> *If you Listen to me,*
> *I will feel understood.*
> *If you Understand me,*
> *I will feel appreciated.*
> *If you Appreciate me,*

I will know your support.
If you Support me as I try new things,
I will become responsible.
When I am Responsible,
I will grow to be independent.
In my Independence,
I will respect you and love you all of my life.

Mira Kirshenbaum and Charles Foster, PhD, authors of *Parent/Teen Breakthrough: The Relationship Approach,* help parents to switch from control to connection. Children are already making hundreds of decisions in their daily lives independent of parental control. Parents who connect with their budding teen rather than attempting to control her, will have a far greater chance of supporting her through the "rocky roads" of adolescence towards adulthood.

The Romance of Risk: Why Teenagers Do The Things They Do, by Dr. Lynn Ponton, helps parents to recognize that risk-taking in teenagers is a normal and developmentally-appropriate behavior. Helping your teenage daughter to find positive challenges and risks and steer clear of dangerous behaviors is a special parenting skill that will help your teenager immensely. Current thinking is beginning to acknowledge that adolescence is a time of risk-taking that is not solely harmful. On the contrary, risk-taking is a normal, healthy behavior for adolescents. It is during adolescence that young people experiment with many aspects of life, taking on new challenges, testing out how things fit together, and using this process to define and shape both their identities and their knowledge of the world.

Rituals

Bill Doherty, author of *The Intentional Family* and *Putting Family First,* believes in increasing family connection through the use of rituals. He has an entire chapter on how to create a rich bonding and social time around family mealtimes. In the face of the complex obstacles and distractions of our busy society, families breaking bread together can enrich themselves body and soul.

Seven Habits of Highly Effective Families by Stephen Covey and *Seven Habits for Highly Effective Teens* by his son, Sean Covey, outline a list of habits that can be practiced by any family to strengthen their relationships: Be Proactive, Begin with the End in Mind, Put First Things First, Think "Win-Win," Seek First To Understand … Then to Be Understood, Synergize and Sharpen the Saw. Sean also wrote a wonderful book for teens, called *The Six Most Important Decisions You'll Ever Make,* asking teens what they are going to decide about: school, friends, parents, dating and sex, addictions and self-worth

FURTHER READING

General

How to Talk So Kids Will Listen and Listen So Kids Will Talk by Adele Faber and Elaine Mazlish, a mainstay for all those raising school-aged children
Liberated Parents, Liberated Children: Your Guide to a Happier Family by Adele Faber and Elaine Mazlish, ways to use language to build self-worth, and encourage responsibility in children of all ages
Growing Up Again: Parenting Ourselves, Parenting our Children by Jean Illsley Clarke and Connie Dawson

Taking Charge: Caring Discipline That Works, at Home and at School, 4th edition by JoAnne Nordling, MS, MEd

Positive Discipline by Jane Nelsen, EdD, MFT an approach that leaves your child feeling respected and valued

Parenting with Love and Logic: Teaching Kids Responsibility by Foster Cline MD and Jim Fay

Parenting Teens with Love and Logic: Preparing Adolescents for a Responsible Adulthood by Foster Cline MD and Jim Fay

Whole Parenting Guide: Strategies, Resources and Inspiring Stories for Holistic Parenting and Family Living by Alan Reder, Phil Catalfo, and Stephanie Renfrow Hamilton

Compassionate Communication

Raising Children Compassionately: Parenting the Nonviolent Communication Way by Marshall Rosenberg

Empathy Magic website of Holley Humphrey: videos and books to use with kids at www.empathymagic.com

Fathers

Fatherneed: Why Father Care is as Essential as Mother Care for Your Child by Kyle D. Pruett MD

Dads & Daughters: How To Inspire, Understand and Support Your Daughter When She is Growing Up So Fast by Joe Kelly

The Dads & Daughters Togetherness Guide: 54 Fun Activities to Help Build a Great Relationship by Joe Kelly

Mothers

Surviving Ophelia: Mothers Share Their Wisdom in Navigating the Tumultuous Teenage Years by Cheryl Dellasega

Keep Talking: Mother Daughter Guide to Teen Years by Lynda Madison

Whatever, Mom: Hip Mama's Guide to Raising a Teenage by Ariel Gore with Maia Swift

---

HOW IS THE DISCUSSION GROUP WORKING FOR YOU?
If you are part of a parenting group, this is a great time to talk with each other about how things are going. What's working, not working? Is everyone getting a fair chance to talk? Are you getting a fair chance to talk? Do you feel safe in the group so that there is comfort in sharing deeply and honestly? Brainstorm solution ideas. Make a commitment to each other to share when your needs, such as fairness, honesty, consideration, acceptance, support, appreciation, or openness are not being met.

Letting Go

To "let go" does not mean to stop caring;

it means I can't do it for someone else.

To "let go" is not to cut myself off;

it's the realization I can't control another.

To "let go" is not to enable,

but to allow learning from natural consequences.

To "let go" is to admit powerlessness,

which means that the outcome is not always in our hands.

To "let go" is not to try to change or blame another;

it's to make the most of myself.

To "let go" is not to "care for,"

but to "care about."

To "let go" is not to "fix,"

but to support.

To "let go" is not to judge,

but to allow another to be a human being.

To "let go" is not to be in the middle arranging outcomes, but to

allow others to affect their destinies.

To "let go" is not to be protective;

it's to permit another to face reality.

To "let go" is not to deny, but to accept.

To "let go" is not to nag, scold, or argue,

but instead to search out my own shortcomings and correct them.

To "let go" is not to adjust everything to my desires,

but to take each day as it comes.

To "let go" is not to criticize and regulate anybody,

but to try to become what I can be.

To "let go" is not to regret the past,

but to grow and live for the future.

To "let go" is to fear less . . . and love more.

—Unknown

Family Comes First

By William J. Doherty, author of *Putting Family First*

ON SEPTEMBER 11, 2001 our nation's boundaries were violently breached and our sense of invulnerability shattered. After the initial shock, the reaction most people had was to contact loved ones. When hijacked airline passengers found telephones, they called their spouses or parents to say, "I love you" and "goodbye." When office workers in the World Trade Center felt the shock of the airplane collisions and saw the smoke, they called a family member to offer reassurance that they would get out safely. When the rest of us heard the news of the attacks, we called our spouses, children, parents, or siblings. Parents everywhere gathered their children around them.

We know that not all families are connected enough to be helpful in such a crisis. A mental health worker in New York recounted that the most distressed survivors he encountered during the aftermath of the attacks were people who were cut off from family members and uncertain if they could contact them.

The message could not be clearer: family relationships are the irreplaceable core of a full human life. However, a rich family life alone is not enough because we also need strong neighborhoods, schools, communities, governments, nations, and a cooperative international community. But none of these, alone or together, can substitute for family life.

The frantic pace of contemporary American family life is eroding family closeness and depriving our children of their childhood. Today's families are sorely lacking time for spontaneous fun and enjoyment, for talking over the day's events and experiences, for unhurried meals, for quiet bedtime talks, for working together on projects, for teaching and learning life skills such as cooking and gardening, for visiting extended family and friends, for attending religious services together, for participating together in community projects, and for exploring the beauty of nature. Not enough time, that is, to be a family with a rich internal and external life.

There are many contributors to the "time famine" experienced by many families, including parents' work commitments, employers' expectations for increased work hours, and larger economic forces. Some of these forces can be controlled by individual families, and others cannot. One thing that parents can control is the problem of over-scheduling children in a competitive culture; maybe your child doesn't have to take up a

second musical instrument or join a traveling sports team. You might not have control over whether you can be home for dinner reliably at six o'clock, but your family can decide to snack early and then eat later in the evening when you can all be together. When you are scheduling your summer, you might not be able to claim the exact weeks for vacation that you would prefer, but you can hold sacred the vacation time you do have— and not surrender it to the vagaries of children's baseball schedules or French lessons.

You may feel regret or guilt at times as you read along. You may have surrendered your family dinners to over-scheduling and television watching. You may not have created bedtime rituals for your children because you don't need the hassle of getting them to bed. A certain amount of regret and guilt comes with the territory of being a caring parent, because it is a big job and we all make mistakes. But two ideas can help to offset the guilt and turn it into constructive action. First, the problems we are talking about are rooted in the broader culture we have created together; they are not primarily the fault of individual parents. Second, the solutions, both personal and communal, are within our grasp if we reach for them. We are not talking about solving an intractable social problem such as world poverty or ethnic hatred. We can do something right now, in our own lives and with our neighbors, about the problem of overscheduled kids and under-connected families. We can take back our kids and renew our family time.

Along with our fellow citizens, we will be processing for many years the meaning of the events of September 11, 2001. But our first conclusion is this: that everything has changed and nothing has changed. We have awakened as from a slumber to the sobering new world of the twenty-first century, where the risks and the rules are different. But we have also realized anew something we have known all along, something we lose sight of in our high speed, consumerist culture: that close families, immersed in vibrant democratic communities, have always been the source of our strength as a people.

Written for Family Empowerment Network by William J. Doherty, PhD, co-author of Putting Family First, *(Henry Holt, August, 2002) about reclaiming family time in a frantic world, and has a nonprofit for families at www.puttingfamilyfirst.org. For reprint requests, contact www.family-empower.com.*

Positive Discipline Guidelines

From the book *Positive Discipline* by Jane Nelsen, EdD, MFT

1. **Misbehaving children are "discouraged children"** who have mistaken ideas on how to achieve their primary goal—to belong. Their mistaken ideas lead them to misbehavior. We cannot be effective unless we address the mistaken beliefs rather than just the misbehavior.

2. **Use encouragement to help children feel "belonging"** so the motivation for misbehaving will be eliminated. Celebrate each step in the direction of improvement rather than focusing on mistakes.

3. A great way to help children feel encouraged is to **spend special time** "being with them." Many teachers have noticed a dramatic change in a "problem child" after spending five minutes simply sharing what they both like to do for fun.

4. When tucking children into bed, ask them to **share with you** their "saddest time" during the day and their "happiest time" during the day. Then **you share with them.** You will be surprised what you learn.

5. Have **family meetings** or **class meetings** to solve problems with cooperation and mutual respect. This is the key to creating a loving, respectful atmosphere while helping children develop self-discipline, responsibility, cooperation, and problem-solving skills.

6. Give children **meaningful jobs.** In the name of expediency, many parents and teachers do things that children could do for themselves and one another. **Children feel belonging when they know they can make a real contribution.**

7. **Decide together** what jobs need to be done. Put them all in a jar and let each child draw out a few each week; that way no one is stuck with the same jobs all the time. Teachers can invite children to help make class rules and list them on a chart titled, "We Decided." Children have ownership, motivation, and enthusiasm when they are included in the decisions.

8. **Take time for training.** Make sure children understand what "clean the kitchen" means to you. To them it may mean simply putting the dishes in the sink. Parents and teachers may ask, "What is your understanding of what is expected?"

9. **Teach and model mutual respect.** One way is to **be kind and firm at the same time**—kind to show respect for the child, and firm to show respect for yourself and the "needs of the situation." This is difficult during conflict, so use the next guideline whenever you can.

10. Proper **timing** will improve your effectiveness tenfold. It does not "work" to deal with a problem at the time of conflict—emotions get in the way. Teach children about cooling-off periods. You (or the children) can go to a separate room and do something to make you feel better—and then work on the problem with mutual respect.

11. **Get rid of the crazy idea that in order to make children do better, first you have to make them feel worse.** Do you feel like doing better when you feel humiliated? This suggests a whole new look at "time out."

12. **Use Positive Time Out.** Let your children help you design a pleasant area (cushions, books, music, and stuffed animals) that will help them feel better. Remember that children do better when they feel better. Then you can ask your children, when they are upset, "Do you think it would help you to take some positive time out?"

13. Punishment may "work" if all you are interested in is stopping misbehavior for "the moment." Sometimes we must **beware of what works** when the long-range results are negative—resentment, rebellion, revenge, or retreat.

14. Teach children that **mistakes are wonderful opportunities to learn!** A great way to teach children that mistakes are wonderful opportunities to learn is to model this yourself by using the Three R's of Recovery after you have made a mistake:
    (1) **Recognize your mistake.**
    (2) **Reconcile: Be willing to say "I'm sorry, I didn't like the way I handled that."**
    (3) **Resolve: Focus on solutions rather than blame.** (#3 is only effective if you do #1 & #2 first.)

15. Focus on **solutions** instead of **consequences.** Many parents and teachers try to disguise punishment by calling it a logical consequence. Get children involved in finding solutions that are (1) **Related** (2) **Respectful** (3) **Reasonable and** (4) **Helpful.**

16. **Make sure the message of love and respect gets through.** Start with "I care about you. I am concerned about this situation. Will you work with me on a solution?"

17. **Have fun!** Bring joy into homes and classrooms.

Connected Parenting

By Jody Bellant Scheer, MD and Glenda Montgomery

PSYCHOLOGISTS TEND TO divide parenting styles into three broad categories with varying levels of power and control. Although there are many different names for these three categories, they are generally referred to as:

- **Permissive:** low parent effectiveness, no limits, freedom without order
- **Connected or authoritative:** parenting based on relationships without need for punishment or humiliation, choices allowed within limits that respect all, freedom with order
- **Authoritarian or strict:** parent attempts to control child, few choices allowed, narrow limits, order without freedom.

Many parenting books offer strategies to produce happy, self-reliant and respectful children, and advocate a "connected" or authoritative approach to child-raising. This kind of approach is neither permissive nor punitive and places a high value on fostering relationship connections while working toward long-term goals. Providing opportunities for children to develop a sense of belonging and a sense of themselves as competent and worthwhile human beings are key components. Underlying this approach is a high regard for the humanity of children, for treating all family members with equal dignity and respect, and for the parents' message of love and support to shine through as the primary message even when the child has made a mistake.

Connected parenting approaches are designed to address the underlying motivations of a child's misbehavior instead of just reacting to their naughty deed. This is counterintuitive at times. A parent using a traditional approach may look at a child's annoying misbehavior and may either punish the child or say, "Oh, ignore him. He just wants attention." Whereas, a parent practicing a connecting approach may say, "Oh, it seems he really needs attention. I'll ignore this behavior and will ask for his help and get him involved in something useful so I can give him attention in a positive way."

This kind of parenting requires a long-term approach to parenting, and thoughtful reactions to misbehavior. Many parents lack experience with such approaches, having been raised for the most part in either permissive or over-controlling households themselves. It may take a bit of stretching and personal growth to understand how a connected parenting approach works, and to trust that learning these skills will improve all of your interpersonal relationships. But it makes sense that if we want our children to be in control of their emotions, to be patient and understanding, to be open to changing their behavior, and to take an active and respectful role in resolving conflicts, we should expect only the very same behaviors of ourselves.

Sometimes, all that is needed for motivation is to step back and imagine how your child sees you when you are angry and upset. Somewhere in our culture, we have developed the crazy notion that kids will want to do better only if we first yell, lecture, or punish them. This does not meet the child's needs for empathy or compassion, and only fuels the fires of feeling worse! Certainly adults are not motivated by such techniques, and neither are our kids. In our guilt, we sometimes do "yo-yo parenting," going from overly permissive (because it is easier, fun and is child-centered) to overly strict (because the kids "crossed the line" and we are exhausted and angry).

Children, like adults, learn best when their needs for respect and understanding are met. Finding ways to support and guide our children, while building their sense of worthiness and competence, their self-esteem and self-discipline, their ability to make choices, and their capacity to learn from their experience is at the heart of connected parenting.

The following two pages contain an overview of strategies involved in all three of the primary styles of parenting. It is never too late to change your parenting approach and to transform your family relationships. Choosing to parent with a connected approach is a sure way to enrich your family's competence, warmth, and long-term success.

Comparison of Common Parenting Styles:

(Note these styles are often practiced unconsciously, a legacy of our own upbringing)

	Permissive	Connected, Authoritative	Authoritarian, Strict
Beliefs about misbehavior	A child misbehaves because the parent is not doing enough for the child. A child will be motivated to do better when parents coddle, cajole and plead with them.	A child's behavior is driven by his attempts to meet his needs, especially the need to belong and to be loved. Misbehavior is often a sign of a child's discouragement, thinking he is insignificant or doesn't belong. A child will do better when his underlying needs for love and understanding are met, so this becomes one of the primary intervention goals of connected discipline.	A child misbehaves because he is bad and needs to be "fixed." A child will be motivated to do better when he is humiliated, threatened, intimidated, lectured at, or made to feel guilty. If a kid doesn't improve, the punishment is made more severe, as this will surely teach him or her a lesson.
Power	Freedom without order. Ruled by the child, assumes parent has little or no control or influence over child's behaviors.	Freedom with limits. Shared power, assumes parents can guide and support a child's behavior without having to punish or control, trusts that child can learn from his own mistakes and can be an independent and competent thinker/doer.	Order without freedom. Ruled by the parent, who assumes the child cannot behave in an appropriate manner without oversight by a parent or other authority figure.
Control	Lack of parental control or limits, lots of rescuing and buffering children from consequences of their behaviors (overprotection), often overly solicitous.	Parent acknowledges that child operates with free will. Parent holds high degree of control & integrity over what *parent* will do, guides and supports children instead of trying to control, allows choices within broad but clear limits.	Parent is over-controlling, doesn't allow child to make choices, maintains tight control and narrow limits.
Responsibility	Few and inconsistent rules. Parents expect child to become responsible naturally without much parental effort due to the gratitude the kid will feel for the constant parental sacrifices made on their behalf. Bribery is also often used as a motivator for responsible behavior.	Fewer rules as kids age. Kids are taught responsibility through parents modeling the behaviors they wish to see in their children and by parents keeping their own agreements with their kids. Parents also take time to train, to gain co-operation, to make and follow through on mutual agreements, and to empathically hold their kids accountable for all the consequences (good and bad) of the choices and behaviors they choose.	Lots of rules. Parents assume kids are irresponsible and need to be shown who is the boss. Use of demands, lectures, intimidation, threats, humiliation, ultimatums and guilt to teach kids responsibility.
Approach to Adolescence	Supports individuation (creating unique self & interests) somewhat, but parents often are enmeshed with child, hindering differentiation (ability to separate from family & establish one's own values).	Allows child to test and learn life skills so that by age 18, child is making most of his/her own life decisions. Supports individuation and differentiation as normal and expected developmental goals during adolescence.	Protects adolescents by placing more rules on them than on younger children. Low tolerance for exploration, rebellion or differing values. Hinders normal adolescent processes of individuation and differentiation.
Warmth	Usually high degree of warmth, relationship may be close but tends to be enmeshed and/or disrespectful.	High degree of warmth & empathy, value is placed on creating respectful, long-term relationships where needs of parents and kids are equally valued.	Usually low warmth and empathy, long-term relationship is often strained.

continued

	Permissive	Connected, Authoritative	Authoritarian, Strict
Short-term Parenting Goal	Give child whatever s/he wants to avoid disappointment or conflict, be "friends" with the child, rescue and buffer child from the negative consequences of his/her mistakes. Avoid hard decisions because it takes too much time and energy to create & enforce clear boundaries. Often unclear on what to do- waits and hopes problem will either get better or go away on its own	Parent models dignity and respect of child and parent by being in control of his/her own behaviors & by using good conflict resolution skills. Gains cooperation, uses discipline techniques that support a child's self esteem and competence, & allows a child to make choices within safe limits. Supports the child while s/he learns from the natural and logical consequences of his/her successes and failures.	Stop any misbehavior immediately. Punish and humiliate the child for mistakes. Force the child to do what the parent wants or what the parent thinks is in the best interest of the child.
Long-term Parenting Goal (often unconscious)	Dependence on parents.	Independence, success, self-discipline. Child is able to make decisions that actually meet his/her own needs, which at the same time take into consideration the needs of others.	Dependence on outside authorities: child often substitutes other voices for parents' (peers, romantic partners, bosses, pop culture idols, etc) as s/he grows up.
Likely Long-term Outcome for Child	A child who may appear to be selfish, demanding, irresponsible, and not responsive to social cues. Often exhibits high self-regard, low self-esteem, and high sense of entitlement (expects others or parents to take care of him/her).	A child with high self-esteem, in control of his/her own behaviors and emotions, able to operate with personal power to create positive results in their lives, able to make decisions and learn from the consequences of those decisions.	Children tend to appear either rebellious or submissive, have low self-esteem and high self-doubt, and have few opportunities to learn life skills. Often unable to handle the responsibility of learning by trial and error, tend to blame the world for their problems, & tend to seek sources outside themselves for validation and direction. Tendency towards unhappiness and addictions.
Likely Feelings Kids Hold Towards Parents	Love, often lacking empathy or understanding of parents/others	Love, connection, respect	Feelings of rebellion, anger, hatred, intimidation, resentment, sneakiness, withdrawal

A List of Books about Parenting with Empathy and Connection:

Positive Disicpline by Jane Nelsen, EdD, MFT

Positive Discipline for Teenagers: Resolving Conflict with Your Teenage Son or Daughter by Jane Nelsen, EdD, MFT and Lynn Lott, MA, MFT

Parenting with Love and Logic: Teaching Kids Responsibility by Foster Cline, MD and Jim Fay

Parenting Teens With Love and Logic: Preparing Adolescents for Responsible Adulthood by Foster Cline, MD and Jim Fay

Seven Habits of Highly Effective Families by Stephen Covey

The Seven Year Stretch: How Families Work Together to Grow Through Adolescence by Laura S. Kastner, PhD and Jennifer Wyatt, PhD

Parent as Coach: Helping Your Teen Build a Life of Confidence, Courage, and Compassion by Diana Sterling

Parenting from your Heart: Sharing the Gifts of Compassion, Connection and Choice by Inbal Kashtan

Respectful Parents, Respectful Kids: 7 Keys to Turn Family Conflict into Cooperation by Sura Hart & Victoria Kindle Hudson

Nonviolent Communication by Marshall Rosenberg, PhD

Raising Children Compassionately: Parenting the Nonviolent Communication Way by Marshall Rosenberg PhD

Raising Self-Reliant Children in a Self-Indulgent World: Seven Building Blocks for Developing Capable Young People by H. Stephen Glenn and Jane Nelsen

How to Talk so Kids Will Listen and Listen so Kids Will Talk by Adele Faber and Elaine Mazlish

Liberated Parents, Liberated Children, Your Guide to a Happier Family by Adele Faber and Elaine Mazlish

Raising Your Spirited Child. A Guide for Parents Whose Child is More Intense, Sensitive, Perceptive, Persistent, and Energetic by Mary Sheedy Kurcinka

Temperament Tools: Working with your Child's Inborn Traits by Helen Nelville and Diane Clark Johnson

Parent/Teen Breakthrough: The Relationship Approach by Mira Kirshenbaum and Charles Foster

Taking Charge: Basic Concepts of JoAnne Nordling's *Caring Discipline*

Child's Staircase of Needs: This is based on Maslow's Heirachy of Needs. Lower needs need to be satisfied before higher needs can be met. We all regress during stressful times.

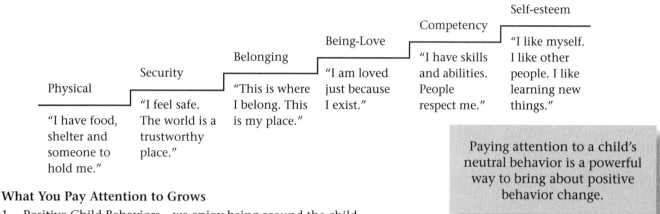

Physical
"I have food, shelter and someone to hold me."

Security
"I feel safe. The world is a trustworthy place."

Belonging
"This is where I belong. This is my place."

Being-Love
"I am loved just because I exist."

Competency
"I have skills and abilities. People respect me."

Self-esteem
"I like myself. I like other people. I like learning new things."

> Paying attention to a child's neutral behavior is a powerful way to bring about positive behavior change.

What You Pay Attention to Grows

1. Positive Child Behaviors—we enjoy being around the child
2. Neutral Behaviors—child entertaining him/herself—no problem for parent
3. Negative Behaviors—child is angering or irritating us—parent's problem

Paying attention to a child's neutral behavior is a powerful way to bring about positive behavior change. Message to the child: "You are loved just because you exist." Paying undue attention to negative behaviors may cause them to misbehave to connect with you.

How Parents and Teachers Sabotage Their Discipline: There are five ways that even the best-intentioned parents get in the way of their own goals when they are teaching and disciplining.

1. **Procrastination**
   Act when you first see the misbehavior, and avoid the anger that arises when we repeat ourselves. Try not to give children the emotional energy they crave when they are misbehaving; you are encouraging the negative behavior.

2. **Talking and Talking about the Misbehavior**
   Rudolf Dreikurs said, "Act, don't talk." If possible carry out your discipline action calmly and do not mention it again. When negative emotions are present in the adult and/or the child, lecturing or verbally trying to teach in any way can cause the child to turn off their listening or even rebel in order to maintain their self integrity. Power struggles ensue. Teach and talk in neutral or positive situations.

3. **Forgetting to Pay Attention to the Child's Positive and Neutral Behaviors**
   Each child needs at least four positive attentions for every negative one for the child to feel and act well. Nonverbal attention is even more powerful than verbal.

4. **Negative Scripting**
   Children believe what they hear us say about them. Avoid negative scripts "He is just so unorganized!" and use positive scripting "Josh was so supportive of Jen!"

5. **Lack of Self-Care and Self-Love**
   Parents who take care of themselves and their unmet needs are much more able to be the kind of parent they want to be, even when the child is misbehaving.

Spanking: A Slap at Thoughtful Parenting

Summarized from an article by behavioral pediatrician Dr. Barbara Howard

SPANKING IS A FORM OF discipline that is both common in America and associated with unintended negative side effects. One quarter of American parents spank infants only 1 to 6 months old and three-quarters of parents hit their one-year-olds, even though these infants are not old enough to understand the lesson the parent is trying to teach. Spanking gets worse as toddlers get older: by age 3, 90% of children are being spanked. Hitting doesn't stop as children grow older, even when parents think it should: 60% of children ages 10-12, 40% of those aged 14 years, and 25% of those aged 17 years are still being hit by their parents. These, in spite of the fact that one half of the time, parents concede that hitting was a knee-jerk reaction that was inappropriate in light of the offense for which it was given.

Spanking is associated with a number of negative side effects. Children who are spanked are four times as likely to be aggressive, are less attentive to social cues, and are more likely to have delinquent behaviors outside the home than their peers who are not spanked. Children who are spanked are also at higher risk to become adults who approve of spanking and who hit their own spouse and children. Additionally, painful punishments have been shown to make non-painful punishments less effective. Kids who are spanked by their parents think time-out at school is a joke they are therefore more difficult for teachers to manage and are at increased risk for behavior problems in school or day care. Lastly, in order to be effective, a painful stimulus must be increased over time to maintain its effectiveness. Since toddlers and preschoolers misbehave on average every 6-8 minutes, it's not surprising that there is going to be a lot of hitting, and it's likely to get more intense once spanking is embedded in a parent's disciplinary repertoire.

Research confirms that spanking is no more effective than non-painful forms of discipline, which are more effective and less harmful to the child in both the long- and short-term. Why then, do so many parents spank? Parents learn to hit because they were hit. Also, hitting is a short-term parenting strategy that looks like it works in the moment. A child who gets a swat is no longer

participating in an undesired behavior because they are crying instead. The chance of the child going back to that behavior, however, is likely regardless of the consequence that is given, because that is how children learn: by repetition.

Parents may never have thought about the negative side effects of spanking. What can help many parents that were hit themselves as children is to look at the quality of their current relationships with their own parents. Close, warm, long-term relationships usually spring from parenting styles that include more positive strategies than negative. If spanking is one element of an otherwise overwhelmingly positive parenting strategy, that strategy may well work just as successfully without it. Parents would also do well to note if their own children are exhibiting negative side effects from spanking. Have their children started to hit them back? Are their children's relationships with other children going well?

What if a parent wants to change from spanking to alternative, non-painful forms of discipline? This can be a difficult, but successful task if parents are committed to long-term positive change. Non-punitive discipline alternatives, such as age-appropriate time-outs, natural and logical consequences and cooperative agreements, can take some time to establish. Parents need to think in terms of the long-term outcome: trying a new form of discipline may take 3-6 weeks of consistent use before changes in behavior are accomplished. It is helpful (but not necessary) for a parent to have the mutual support of their spouse during this transitional stage. In addition, ongoing professional or peer support can be beneficial. Parenting groups, pediatricians and school psychologists are good resources for parents to use if they need help. The benefits of establishing a positive disciplinary approach that uses respect and dignity, instead of pain and fear, to motivate desired behaviors include laying the foundation for your child to create warm, long-lasting, and secure connections with yourself and others.

> Kids who are spanked exhibit increased aggressive and delinquent behaviors and are at higher risk for behavior problems in school and daycare.
>
> Research confirms that non-painful forms of discipline are just as effective as spanking, and do not carry these negative side effects.

Complete original article first published in *Pediatric News,* July 2001.

Monster Mother from the Black Lagoon

How to Use Those Less-than-Lovely Emotions in a Positive Way:
The Positive Discipline Mistaken Goal Chart

By Glenda Montgomery

THIS WASN'T WHAT I SIGNED UP FOR. When my husband and I decided to have children, I signed up for the kind of experience where, in my benevolent wisdom, I would offer sage advice to my adoring children who would, of course, take that advice as it was sound and based on education and experience. They would love me because I was a good and kind mother and they would, of course, become good and kind children. THAT's what I signed up for. Sure, I had some inkling that it was going to be "difficult" at times, though I wasn't quite sure exactly what that meant. And because I was going to be a "good" mother, it surely wouldn't be too very difficult. Nothing prepared me for how much time I would feel like "The Mother from the Black Lagoon," a shrieking witch of a monster mother. The chaos of negative emotions surprised and appalled me. At times, when I passed a mirror, I was shocked to find that I did not, in fact, have warts and boils, black lips and red eyes.

Parenting is a tough job. Tougher than any of us could have imagined. We didn't have to get a license to become a parent and no children that I know came with operating instructions. We tend to muddle through, using parenting strategies that come naturally to us, which, logically, are the strategies that our parents used on us. When things are going well, we feel blessed to have such wonderful kids and we believe that we are doing a fine job of parenting. But, when things get difficult and the strategies our parents used aren't working, parenting can become a very emotional job. Our feelings can get the best of us: frustration, anger, worry, embarrassment, helplessness hopelessness, fear. We can feel challenged, threatened disappointed, disgusted, despairing and hurt. My kids haven't even hit the teen years and I think at some point or another I've felt every one of these emotions in the twelve years I've had children. Mostly, I am confused about why my child is "misbehaving" and am desperate to try to find a solution.

Though I was brought up in a home where misbehavior was punished, through my learning and work as a teacher, I was able to see that we don't have to make children feel worse in order for them to do better. Think about it: if you've messed up at work, do you feel inclined to do better if you've been shamed and punished? Or, are you more inclined to do better if someone supports you through figuring out what went wrong and why, and then being available to consult with you through the process of fixing the mistake. I know that in this way, children are no different. Children do best when they are *encouraged*...not punished, not pampered. As a parent, I was solution focused but didn't know where to turn to figure out WHY my children were doing what they were doing, nor what I should try in order to help them solve the problems and get the behavior to stop!

The most important piece of information I've received about parenting came from Positive Discipline parenting classes, based on Jane Nelsen's book, *Positive Discipline*. Now, when I am feeling completely perplexed and am in some negative emotional chaos over the behavior of one of my children, I have a place to begin. It is called the Positive Discipline Mistaken Goal Chart.

Positive discipline is based on the work of famous psychiatrists from the past century, Alfred Adler and Rudolf Driekurs, who proposed the idea that human beings are goal driven. As human beings, our top two goals are **to feel significant (that we matter)** and **to feel a sense of belonging.** We act in order to achieve our goals. In other words, much of our behavior is driven, often subconsciously of course, by the need to feel both important, and an integral part of something cohesive and larger than ourselves. Sometimes our kids have mistaken ideas about *how* to feel significant and *how* to get that sense of belonging, which leads them to do things that look like misbehavior to us. Our children's perplexing misbehavior truly does make sense when looked at with this understanding.

Rudolf Driekurs saw *4 mistaken understandings* that children sometimes have about significance and be-longing. Children may feel that:

1. They belong/are significant only if they are getting special service and special attention from others,
2. They belong or are important only if they are the boss and are running the show,
3. They are NOT feeling important or connected and as a result they feel angry and hurt and so they are going to make everyone else feel as badly as they do,
4. They don't belong and are not significant, see no way to belong or become significant, and so they have given up and will avoid all challenges so they don't have to face their inadequacy.

Rudolf Driekurs called these mistaken under-standings, the mistaken goals of: *Undue Attention, Power, Revenge, and Assumed Inadequacy.*

It's logical to assume that your daughter is not going to understand WHY things are going so poorly for her during a time that she is discouraged. She'll just know she's going through a hard time and nothing feels right. She's trying to achieve that feeling of importance and belonging and is going at it in a way that is less than satisfying for both of you. It can be a time of confusion for her. The relief is, in order to successfully use the Mistaken Goal Chart you don't have to know exactly what your daughter is feeling, you only need to know how YOU'RE feeling! You are able to use those less-than-desirable emotions to get you on the right track. Using the Mistaken Goal Chart enables you to find out what mistaken belief is behind your daughter's misbehavior. Try to see the message underlying this belief emblazoned across your daughter somehow, on a T-shirt or on the front of a hat. Keep this image alive as you begin to work with your girl, because understanding her discouraged, mistaken thinking will help you to have more empathy and patience as you support her moving through this phase.

The first strategy to use is always to set up some one-on-one time with your daughter. One half-hour a week of one-on-one time with her will make an incredible difference in turning your daughter's behavior around because it fulfills both her primary goals: to feel a sense of importance and a sense of belonging. This time should be scheduled every week for when both of you are free. After consulting your daughter, mark your "dates" on the calendar for both of you to see. The time together needs to be a priority, but doesn't need to be elaborately spent. It can be simple: a run together, baking, a walk, sitting down to tea together, a card game, scrap-booking, shopping, kicking the soccer ball, etc. It can be used differently every week but can be just as powerful if it is always spent in the same way. Carving out of your busy schedule this time just for your daughter gives her the message that she is significant enough to spend regular uninterrupted time with, and that you and she belong together.

Next, use your negative emotion cues to find your entry into the Mistaken Goal Chart. Take time to understand your daughter's mistaken belief and its underlying message. Try the strategies listed there. Don't expect sudden miraculous change. Expect some time when things remain challenging, and perhaps even worse than they were as she tries to elicit the same responses from you but fails to get them. Then, be encouraged by gradual, steady, positive change as your daughter becomes less discouraged, more encouraged and more aware of other ways that she can achieve a sense of belonging and importance that don't support her mistaken belief.

In the past, I used to feel overwrought and ashamed by the strength and frequency of the negative emotions I felt when confronted with my child's misbehavior. Now I understand that there is no cause for shame. Now I tune into these emotions and use them proactively. I am able to sit down with the Mistaken Goal Chart, find myself there and know that I will be able to see where my daughter is, too. My emotions steer me toward solutions that I would not have seen otherwise, giving me specific strategies to use and allowing me to better understand the world that my daughter is experiencing. The ironic thing is, now that I understand the importance of "monster mother" feelings, they don't seem nearly as intense or as overwhelming! I now spend a lot less time in the Black Lagoon.

Reprinted with permission of Glenda Montgomery, parent coach and Certified Positive Discipline Instructor in Portland, OR and mother of a daughter and a son, at www.positiveparenting.pdx. com.

Mistaken Goal Chart

The parent FEELS:	The child's mistaken goal is:	The parent reacts by:	The child's response is:	The BELIEF behind the child's behavior is:	What the child's message is, and what you can do to encourage your child to find a sense of significance and belonging:
EXASPERATED ANNOYED IRRITATED WORRIED GUILTY	UNDUE ATTENTION To be the center of attention and keep others busy giving special service	Reminding Coaxing Nagging Scolding Doing things for the child that the child can do by him/herself.	Stops temporarily but later resumes same or other disturbing behavior.	I count only when I'm being noticed or getting special service. I'm only important when I'm keeping you busy with me or doing things for me.	<u>NOTICE ME! INVOLVE ME!</u> Together, set up regular, scheduled one-on-one special time. Refrain from doing for your child. Involve your child in setting up routines. Create charts together and help her learn to use them. Retrain for tasks she can do herself and tell her you trust her ability to do them. Train child for new chore or family responsibility she thinks will be appealing. Notice her accomplishments and any tasks of self-reliance. Encourage them. Remind once then act kindly and firmly. No nagging. Together make up non-verbal reminders. Ask child to help problem solve. Find some tasks to do together. Say, "I love you and _____" Example: I love you and will spend time with you in half an hour. Right now I am busy."
ANGRY PROVOKED CHALLENGED THREATENED DEFEATED	POWER To be boss	Arguing Fighting Thinking, "You can't get away with it" or "I'll make you!" Wanting to be right and have the last word. Giving in	Intensifies behavior. Defiant compliance. Feels s/he's won if the parent is upset. Passive power	I count only when I'm boss or in control or proving that no one can boss me. "You can't make me!"	<u>LET ME HELP! GIVE ME CHOICES!</u> Choose to withdraw from power struggles. Acknowledge that you can't make her, and ask for her help. Try to offer limited choices or alternatives whenever possible. Redirect to positive power by asking for help in problem solving and planning. Let routines be boss. Decide what YOU will do. Act, rather than talking or yelling. Practice kind, firm follow-through. Find leadership opportunities for your child.
HURT DISAPPOINTED DIS-BELIEVING DISGUSTED	REVENGE To get even	Retaliating Getting even Thinking, "How could you do this to me?" Taking behavior personally	Retaliates Hurts others Damages property Gets even Escalates behavior	I don't think I belong. I'm not feeling important. I'll hurt others, as I feel hurt. I can't be liked or loved.	<u>I'M HURTING! VALIDATE MY FEELINGS!</u> Don't take the behavior personally. Don't retaliate. Spend time dealing with her feelings. Listen well. Use reflective listening so that you're sure to understand. Share your feelings. Apologize for your part. Show you care. Agree to start anew. Avoid punishment. Instead, allow her to find ways to make reparations. Make an effort to find, encourage and support her strengths. Focus on positive.
DESPAIR HOPELESS HELPLESS INADEQUATE	ASSUMED INADEQUACY To give up and be left alone	Giving up Showing utter discouragement Over-helping Doing for	Retreats further Remains passive. No improvement No response	I don't believe I can belong. I am helpless and unable. It's no use trying because I won't do it right.	<u>HAVE FAITH IN ME! DON'T GIVE UP ON ME!</u> Break things into tiny steps. Celebrate tiny accomplishments. Take time for training and retraining. Show faith. Refrain from doing things for your child that she can do. Encourage any positive attempt, no matter how small. Share personal stories of struggle. Spend regular one-on-one time to enjoy your child. Build on her interests. Focus on strength areas. Encourage, encourage, encourage. Stop all criticism. Don't give up!

Adapted by Glenda Montgomery from *Positive Discipline for Working Parents* by Jane Nelsen and Lisa Larson.

RAISING OUR DAUGHTERS

Parents' Job: Step Aside, Let Kids Become Heroes

By Lionel Fisher

"I've been poor and I've been rich," Sophie Tucker once said. "Rich is better."

My sentiments exactly, only in regard to parenting: I've been a father and I've been a grandfather. Grandfather is better.

I base my opinion, mind you, not on the relative importance of the two roles, but on their degree of difficulty. And their vastly different potential for pleasure.

> My problem, I've come to realize, is that I took fatherhood too seriously.
>
> I thought it was my job to make my children the best they could be. I know now this was their responsibility.
>
> Mine was to love them, shield them from harm, keep them from want. And try not to get in their way while they became the heroes they were meant to be.

Something each of us has to do for ourselves.

If someone else could do it for us, particularly our parents, what an amazing, if boring, world this would be.

There's something else I've come to realize.

As a grandparent, I'm much better equipped to be a parent than I ever was as a parent.

Back then, I viewed the job as an adult.

Today, I see it from a much different perspective: the viewpoint of a child.

Shakespeare understood. "An old man," he said, "is twice a child."

And Edith Wharton put it this way: "The life of a man is a circle from childhood to childhood."

I know this for a fact. Certainly, I've been told it enough times.

And what better mentor for a child to have than another child, one past meridian on the journey of life, greatly experienced in the ways of the world, yet still childlike in all things vital to happiness?

There's something else I've come to realize, sadly of late, that raising children imposes a stern obligation on parents to examine their own habits, scrutinize their own attitudes, question their own behavior, each day of their lives, for one critical reason.

Their children will surely absorb them.

Try or not—like it or not—we make chips off the old block. We can't help it. We do it by being ourselves, sometimes with enormous consequences.

Our "shadow side," psychologist Carl Jung called all the negative elements we see in ourselves but steadfastly deny. They are the demons we stuff in the closets of our psyche and rationalize away, thinking we've safely hidden them—while we pass them along to our children.

And what happens later? Heartache.

It's a universal truth, says US Catholic magazine writer Dolores Curran that parents have difficulty relating with the children most like themselves because they see in their offspring the things they dislike and repress in themselves.

From my perch as a grandparent, I now know: If I could be a parent once more, I would not try to make my children the best they can be.

It's what kept me from enjoying them.

I would relish and love them, marvel daily at their wonder and uniqueness, knowing the rest would take care of itself. That they would see to it themselves.

So easily said as a grandparent. So hard to do as a parent.

The young adult I was didn't understand this simple, marvelous truth.

The child I'm becoming again does.

Lionel Fisher is the author of several personal growth self-help books, including Celebrating Time Alone: Stories of Splendid Solitude *(Beyond Word Publishing, 2001).*

Overview of One of Our Favorites: *Positive Discipline for Teenagers*
Authored by Jane Nelsen, EdD, MFT and Lynn Lott, MA, MFT

Brief Summary: *Positive Discipline for Teenagers* describes the normal developmental process of individuation during adolescence and how this affects parenting. Supporting a teen to explore their world, as well as to grow up into a self-reliant, resourceful and successful adult can be difficult, but will be infinitely more pleasant using positive parenting techniques. Nelsen and Lott support a positive parenting approach which educates, challenges and supports teenagers in an atmosphere of mutual respect, affirming the self-worth of both youth and parents. This is accomplished by using long-term parenting approaches as alternatives to punishments and control, the latter of which encourage long-term resistance, resentment and revenge. These rob teenagers of the opportunity to learn from their own experiences as they focus on their anger at adults. Parents are encouraged to support, empower and guide their teens to make as many decisions about their own lives as is reasonable. In this way, teens learn self-discipline and maturity by experiencing the consequences, both good and bad, of their own behaviors. A special section is included for differentiating normal from dysfunctional teen behavior and a study guide is included for further exploration and practice of positive discipline skills.

Issues Explored in Book:

The Individuation Process: Teenagers undergo individuation as a normal developmental process whereby they become their own unique selves. Knowing that adolescent experimentation is a normal and essential developmental task of adolescence can set many parents at ease. Teens learn best by making mistakes, by being held accountable for their own choices, and suffering (without parental rescuing or buffering) the consequences of all those choices. This section helps parents to understand their teen's world, to develop empathy and compassion for their teen's struggles, and to differentiate between long- and short-term parenting goals.

Nonpunitive Parenting: Alternatives to control and punishment are essential for developing mutual respect with teens. Alternatives include cooperative problem solving, setting and keeping agreements, family meetings, open communication and relationship building. Positive discipline does not advocate for the short-term parenting goal of controlling a teen's behavior (which is impossible), but rather for a long-term goal of supporting teens to learn from their own choices, while holding them accountable for their agreements. This can be a scary new approach for many parents. This book also helps parents to explore their own rational and irrational fears and unresolved issues around adolescence that could be hindering their ability to foster the optimum development of their teen.

Normal and Dysfunctional Teen Behavior: This section deals with a myriad of risk-taking behaviors in teens and helps parents differentiate between exploratory and dysfunctional patterns of behavior. Tips on discussing and resolving these issues with your teen are included.

Key Points: Parenting teens requires a different approach from younger children, due to a teen's need for individuating and for gaining essential life skills such that she can be fully responsible for all of her life decisions by the time she reaches age 18. This requires parents to stretch and grow during their child's adolescence, as they must learn to trust their teenagers to make choices, to learn from their own experiences, and to be able to handle more and more freedom and autonomy as they grow older. "Positive discipline" involves offering adolescents guidance and support without trying to control or punish, setting clear parental boundaries that establish what *parents* (not kids) will do and institutes mutual dignity and respect as key ingredients of the parent-teen relationship. This model of parenting requires parents to place a high priority on the long-term goal of supporting adolescents in their developmental tasks of learning self-discipline and self-control. By putting teenagers in charge of their own growth, responsibilities and lives, parents are removed from power struggles and from the impossible task of controlling their teenagers' behaviors. When faced with primary responsibility for their own lives, teens tend to move from reacting and rebelling to authority towards making positive and more self-affirming decisions. Supporting and guiding adolescents, without rescuing or abandoning them, is a process that can be learned by any parent. This process respects that teens are operating with free will and are able to make their own decisions, but it also holds them fully accountable for all the consequences of their behaviors. This book helps parents to learn and implement such long-term parenting strategies, which result in enhancing a family's self-esteem, self-reliance, competency, and ability to communicate respectfully.

Curiosity Kills the Cat but Connects the Kid

By Kathy Masarie, MD

OK, I AM THE FIRST TO ADMIT IT. I read over and over again the importance of listening to my children, especially my teens, and I said, "Of course, I listen to my kid. I am a good parent. All good parents listen."

But was I really listening? When my son was 16, he taught me to listen better than anyone else. That year, many of our interactions were filled with struggling, yelling and arguing. It led to nowhere for either of us. I realized it had to be me that changed. When I stopped trying to control his behavior and focused my energy on understanding where he was coming from—that is when I actually started listening. We both calmed down. And, he started talking.

I was busily cooking dinner one night, trying to get it done "on time" when Jon started talking. As he talked, I realized how important and serious this was. I turned off the stove to give him my full attention. We talked for a solid half hour. Dinner was a little late, but I gained a new perspective on an issue he was struggling with that I didn't have before.

So what were the ingredients for this success?

First Step: Be Present

Would I have gotten the same information if I thought dinner had to be served at 6:00 instead of letting it go until 6:30? In *Putting Family First,* William Doherty talks about three kinds of parent/kid time: "being around" time, logistics time, and connecting time.

- "Being around" time is the building block of family time. As a preschooler my son would hang out wherever I went. As a teen, he still wants me to "be around" at four times during the day—morning, after school, at dinner and going to bed. We may or may not talk to each other, but I am there if needed.
- "Logistics-getting-things-done" time is what makes the "family business" run, where we talk about everyday routine and where most of us spend most of our talking time.
- "Connecting" talk is the most important! It's when you find out what really is going on with your child— what happened, how they're feeling, what they are worried about. It is the first to go when we are busy. It often happens when we are just "hanging out" with no agenda.

Stop Talking

With Jon, when I listened, he talked. Think about when you are with someone who talks too much and your energy drains just blocking their words from coming at you. **If you want your teen to talk, stop talking.** Imagine there are only a limited number of words that can be said between you and your child. If you say more, they say less, and now you know less. "**Effectiveness as a parent comes much more from what you hear than from what you say,**" says Mira Kirshenbaum in *Parent/Teen Breakthrough: The Relationship Approach.*

Be Curious and Actively Listen

I asked questions so I could really understand what he meant. This is not plying him for information with 20 questions. These are questions that keep teens talking and help them get clarity about their priorities and values. It also keeps me from jumping to conclusions, helps me see his point of view and have empathy for him. Questions like: How do you feel about that? Tell me more. What do you think about what happened? Just how important is this to you? Why is this so important to you? How do you think things will turn out if they go on as they are? What do you want to have happen? What are you going to do now? How can I be helpful? Is there anything else bothering you? Is there anything else I should know about this? What else could you tell me to help me better understand? What else?

> **Effectiveness as a parent comes much more from what you hear than from what you say.**

Be Honest

When I shared some of the things I did as a teen and why I did them, Jon was able to be more honest. This "honest talk" helped him be more open about his mistakes so we could deal with them together. It also helped to be honest and accountable for my mistakes, like when I lost my temper and yelled, I said, "Here is what I wish I would have done."

Keep It Simple: Brainstorm and Compromise

Jon had lots of ideas for solutions on his own. I didn't offer my ideas without asking permission. When I did, it was short, not a lecture. I didn't repeat myself later. After we brainstormed some solutions, we compromised and picked ones that worked for both of us. You know what? A lot of his ideas sounded like solutions I might have offered. What goes around comes around—and, in this case, I liked it.

Peaceful Parenting: How to Turn Parent-Child Conflict into Cooperation

By Sura Hart and Victoria Kindle Hodson

IT'S NINE O'CLOCK ON a school night and 12-year-old Jesse is absorbed in his favorite video game until his mother comes into his bedroom and announces that it's bedtime.

Jesse: No, I don't want to go to bed!

Mom: But it's already past your bedtime, and you know you have to get your rest.

Jesse: But I'm not tired!

Mom: Well, you will be in the morning if you don't go to sleep soon.

Jesse: Shut up. Anyway, you can't make me go to sleep.

The conversation might go on this way until Mom, exhausted and angry, shouts something like, "I quit! Suit yourself!" Sound familiar? It does to us. In our experiences leading parenting workshops in Nonviolent Communication—a way of communicating that facilitates honest, respectful, and compassionate connection between people—we've seen countless parents frustrated by the combative exchanges they have with their children. Their conflicts are especially intense around daily activities such as going to sleep, waking up, and completing homework. Indeed many parents today find themselves engaged in what seems like a constant power struggle with their kids. As they engage in arguments like the one between Jesse and his mother, both sides stake out their territory and resist giving in to the other. Parents come away feeling worn out and irritated; children feel threatened and even more determined to resist their parents' demand.

Based on our years of observation, we believe the way through these conflicts lies in shifting the way parents use their power, from using power *over* kids to using power *with* them. In the example above, the mother's attempt to control her son, though well-intended, triggers resistance as will any attempt by one person to control another, no matter the age or relationship. As Christopher Boehm demonstrates in his essay in *Greater Good*, humans have been genetically predisposed to resent and resist being dominated for at least seven million years. While we may temporarily submit, we often do so with anger or resentment that will surface later. And when parents try to manage and control their

children, everyone pays a high price especially in the loss of trust, goodwill, and willing cooperation among family members. This does not mean that parents should give up their power and permit their children to do whatever they want, whenever they please. Instead, what matters is *how* parents use their power. Parents who use their considerable power *over* children—by making demands and enforcing them with threats of punishment and promises of reward—often find themselves locked into bitter struggles. Fiercely protecting their autonomy, wary children test us to find out where they can get some power of their own. And, very early on, they take charge of two crucial realms of their lives: where and when they sleep;

and what, where, and when they eat. Try as they might, parents can't make children eat, nor can they make them sleep. Their needs for power and autonomy are so strong that kids will sometimes deny themselves their basic needs for food and rest in order to assert control over their lives.

Even when children don't immediately or obviously resist parental demands, parents may still be creating an unhealthy environment for their family when they attempt to exert power over their kids. Marshall Rosenberg, the founder of Nonviolent Communication, makes this point when he asks parents two questions: *What do you want your children to do?* and *What do you want their reason to be for doing it?*

Many parents ask themselves only the first question and find they can, at times, get what they want by using threats, punishments, and rewards. However, when parents ask themselves the second question, *What do you want your child's reason to be?*, they realize why they feel so dissatisfied with their family's interactions. Their children are doing what they are told because they are afraid not to, not because they understand either what is important to their parents (and why), or what is important for themselves.

The parents we've met in our workshops say they want their children to develop strong inner characters and the skills to make the best choices for themselves, yet none of this can be developed when children act out of fear of blame or punishment. What's more, when parents use power-over tactics, anger and resentment often build up, even in children who seem to submit easily to parental control. Such anger and resentment may be expressed through self-destructive choices later in life, including extreme rebellion against authority or by relying excessively on the judgments of others.

Sometimes parents see only one alternative to the power-over strategy: to deny their own needs for rest, order, safety, and connection and give in to what their kids want.

What we advocate instead are ways parents can use power *with* their children. This third way is facilitated by the practice of Nonviolent Communication, which is based on equal concern and care for the needs of all. Parents, in daily interactions with their children, can model and teach their children how to take one's own needs and the needs of others into consideration. Let's revisit the scene between Jesse and his mother—but this time, with Mom taking a power-with approach.

Mom: It's time to get ready for bed.

Jesse: No, I don't want to go to bed

Mom: You're having a lot of fun playing now, huh?

Jesse: Yeah, and I'm not even tired.

Mom: So you just want to keep playing until you're tired?

Jesse: Yeah.

Mom: It must be frustrating to be asked to stop doing something that's so much fun when you don't feel tired.

Jesse: I never have time for what I want to do. I just have to come home and do homework.

Mom: Hmm. It sounds like this time between homework and bedtime is really important to you, and you wish it were longer?

Jesse: Yeah, Mom, I do.

Mom: Thanks for helping me understand that. You know, I'd like you to have as much time as you want for the things that interest you. At the same time, I've also noticed that when you stay up after nine on school nights, you're tired the next morning. Do you hear?

Jesse: Yeah, you want me to get a good night's sleep.

Mom: Yes. Thanks for hearing that.

Jesse: I just need five more minutes to finish this game. Okay?

Mom: Okay. I'll get out your pajamas.

In this dialogue, Mom first chose to connect with her son's feelings and his needs for play and choice. When Jesse felt heard and realized that his needs mattered to his mom, he opened up to hearing her needs while also standing up for his own. Then he was willing to cooperate.

It's true that learning and implementing these communication skills, and reaching this kind of mutual understanding, can take time and effort. It is also true that children who are already accustomed to a power-over model often need time to develop trust that parents mean it when they say their child's needs matter. But these are skills we've seen many parents use and parents tell us they see more trust and cooperation within their family afterwards, which they say justifies all the early energy they invest.

Each time parents come to a workshop in Nonviolent Communication, we all ask ourselves, *What do we want for ourselves and for our children?* The answers we hear are always the same: kindness, respect, communication, cooperation, and responsibility. From the time they're young, we can prepare our children for a lifetime of power struggles, arguments, fights, and wars. Or we can help them learn skills to create a world that embraces cooperation and understanding as the only true ways to lasting peace and satisfying, sustainable relationships. When parents use their power *with* their children, they are subtly teaching them skills and strategies for practicing compassion and cooperation in all areas of their lives.

Reprinted with permission of Sura Hart and Victoria Kindle Hodson MA. Sura and Victoria are co-authors of three books: *The Compassionate Classroom: Relationship Based Teaching & Learning; Respectful Parents, Respectful Kids: 7 Keys to Turn Family Conflict into Cooperation;* and *The No-Fault Classroom: Tools to Resolve Conflict & Foster Relationship Intelligence (2008).* They also offer consultation workshops, see website at www.k-communication.com. Originally published in *Greater Good Magazine,* Vol. 4, Issue 3, Winter 07-08.

Feelings and Needs Inventories

Needs Inventory:

"A need is life seeking expression within us." Marshall Rosenberg, PhD

Autonomy
- To choose one's dreams, goals, & values
- To choose one's plan for fulfilling one's dreams, goals, & values
- Freedom
- Choice
- Independence
- Space
- Spontaneity

Connection
- Acceptance
- Affection
- Appreciation
- Belonging
- Closeness
- Community
- Consideration
- Emotional Safety
- Inclusion
- Inspiration
- Interdependence
- Intimacy
- Love
- Reassurance
- Respect
- Self-love
- Support
- Sympathy
- Trust
- Understanding
- Warmth

Meaning
- Awareness
- Celebration of life
- Challenge
- Clarity
- Competence
- Consciousness
- Contribution
- Creativity
- Discovery
- Efficacy
- Effectiveness
- Growth
- Learning
- Making a contribution
- Making a difference
- Mourning
- Participation
- Purpose
- Self-expression
- Stimulation
- Understanding

Physical Nurturance
- Air
- Food
- Exercise
- Movement
- Physical Safety
- Rest/sleep
- Sexual expression
- Shelter
- Touch
- Water

Celebration
- Gratitude
- To celebrate the creation of life and dreams fulfilled.
- To celebrate losses: loved one, dreams, etc. (mourning)

Integrity/Honesty
- Authenticity
- Creativity
- Honesty
- Presence
- Self-worth

Play and Recreation
- Exercise
- Fun
- Humor
- Joy
- Laughter

Spiritual Communion
- Beauty
- Communion
- Ease
- Empathy
- Equality
- Harmony
- Inspiration
- Order
- Peace
- Unconditional Love

Adapted by Kathy Masarie and Jody Bellant Scheer from <u>Nonviolent Communication</u> by Marshall Rosenberg, PhD, the Center for Nonviolent Communication www.cnvc.org.

Feelings Inventory:
How We Are Likely to Feel When Our Needs ARE Being Met:

Adventurous	Compassionate	Enthusiastic	Invigorated	Reassured
Affectionate	Composed	Fascinated	Involved	Rejuvenated
Alive	Confident	Free	Intrigued	Relaxed
Amazed	Contented	Friendly	Joyous	Satisfied
Animated	Curious	Fulfilled	Lively	Secure
Appreciated	Dazzled	Glad	Loving	Serene
Aroused	Delighted	Glowing	Moved	Stimulated
Astonished	Eager	Grateful	Optimistic	Tender
Blissful	Ecstatic	Gratified	Overjoyed	Tickled
Calm	Elated	Happy	Peaceful	Thankful
Carefree	Empowered	Helpful	Pleased	Upbeat
Cheerful	Encouraged	Hopeful	Proud	Wonderful
Comfortable	Energetic	Inspired	Radiant	etc...

Feelings Inventory:
How We Are Likely to Feel When Our Needs AREN'T Being Met:

Afraid	Depressed	Flustered	Lethargic	Repulsed
Aggravated	Despairing	Forlorn	Listless	Resentful
Agitated	Detached	Fragile	Livid	Sad
Alarmed	Devastated	Frazzled	Lonely	Scared
Alienated	Disappointed	Frightened	Mad	Self-conscious
Aloof	Disconnected	Frustrated	Mean	Shocked
Ambivalent	Discouraged	Furious	Miserable	Sorrowful
Anguished	Disengaged	Gloomy	Morose	Startled
Angry	Disgusted	Guilty	Mortified	Surprised
Annoyed	Dismayed	Harried	Mystified	Suspicious
Anxious	Distaste	Heartbroken	Nervous	Tepid
Apathetic	Distracted	Heavy	Nostalgic	Terrified
Ashamed	Distressed	Helpless	Numb	Torn
Baffled	Disturbed	Hopeless	Outraged	Troubled
Bewildered	Downhearted	Horrible	Overwhelmed	Uncomfortable
Bitter	Dull	Hostile	Pained	Uneasy
Bored	Edgy	Hurt	Panicky	Unhappy
Brokenhearted	Embarrassed	Impatient	Passive	Unsteady
Burned out	Embittered	Indifferent	Perplexed	Upset
Concerned	Envious	Insecure	Pessimistic	Vulnerable
Confused	Exasperated	Irate	Puzzled	Wary
Dazed	Fatigued	Irritated	Rattled	Weary
Dejected	Fearful	Jealous	Reluctant	Worried
Depleted	Fidgety	Lazy	Remorseful	etc...

Family Rituals: The Ties that Bind

By William J. Doherty, author of *Putting Family First*

IF YOU RECALL YOUR FAVORITE memories of childhood, they are likely to center around family rituals such as bedtime, an annual vacation, or patriotic and religious holidays. Your worst memories might also be connected with these family rituals. Interestingly, many family researchers and family therapists have learned only recently how important family rituals are to the glue that holds families together.

What are family rituals? They are repeated and coordinated activities that have significance for the family. To be a ritual, the activity has to have meaning or significance; otherwise it is a routine, not a ritual. To be a ritual, the activity must be repeated; an occasional, unplanned trip to a cabin would not make for a family ritual, whereas an annual trip that family members look forward to would. Also, a ritual activity must be coordinated; a meal that each person fixes and eats separately would not qualify as a family ritual, whereas one that everyone deliberately eats together would be a family ritual if done regularly and with meaning for the family.

Family rituals give us *predictability*—the sense of regularity and order that families require, especially those with children. Knowing that a father will talk to his child and read a story every night makes bedtime something to savor.

Family rituals give us *connection.* The bedtime ritual may be the main one-to-one time between a father and his child. Trips to see grandparents provide the glue in the grandparent-grandchild relationship. A family meal is a place for the telling of family stories.

Family rituals give us *identity*—a sense of who belongs to the family and what is special about the family. You may know whom your core family members are by who is invited to the Thanksgiving meal. Including non-relatives in core family rituals also makes them "family." Families who do interesting vacations together acquire the self-image of a fun-loving family. They will say, "We are campers" or "We are hikers."

Family rituals give us a *way to enact values.* They help us demonstrate what we believe and hold dear. Religious rituals are a good example, as is a family's collective volunteering for community work, or expecting the children to join in regular family visits to a grandparent in a nursing home.

Family rituals by definition involve more than one family member. Not all family rituals necessarily involve the whole family. Some rituals involve just two members, say, a married couple's dinner out or a parent reading to a child. Some involve sub-groups, as when my father took my sister and me to Philadelphia Phillies baseball games. Some involve the larger extended family, such as family reunions and holiday rituals. Some involve close family friends, and some involve a larger community like a church/synagogue or a volunteer group.

I like to classify family rituals by the function they play for families, or what needs they serve. Thus, there are rituals for connection or bonding, rituals for showing love to individual family members, and rituals that bind the family to the larger community.

There is no universal yardstick for measuring family rituals for all of our diverse, contemporary families. Remarried families will have different needs than first-married families, as will single-parent families than two-parent families. Different ethnic traditions will expect different degrees of flexibility or structure in family rituals. Some families have young children, some have adolescents, and some have no children. Some families are experiencing peaceful periods in their life, and thus feel free to be creative with their rituals, while others are undergoing tremendous stress and need to just hang on to what they have. There is no formula for all this diversity, but at the core of each kind of family are its rituals of connection, love and community.

How can we become more intentional about our family rituals in the face of the time shortage most of us experience? What if you are already an overwhelmed single parent, or a married person who barely has time to talk to your spouse? Will thinking about enhancing your family rituals just make you feel even more guilty than you already are? I offer two general strategies:

1. Make better use of the time you already spend on family activities. You have to feed your children, so start with improving the quality of those feeding rituals. You have to put your kids to bed; work on making it more pleasurable. You probably have birthday parties, holiday celebrations, and countless other family activities. You can work on enhancing their quality while not extending their number or their time burden.

2. Experiment with carving time out of another activity that occupies more than its fair share of your attention. Here is the place for taming

technology. We live in an era of the "Wired American Family." The average American spends over four hours per day watching television, half of our non-sleep, non-work time. Perhaps carve ritual time from there!

Once you capture time for family rituals, how can you put new rituals into place, or turn routines into rituals? Here are some practical ways:

1. Make something happen one time without major comment, and then ask other family members how they liked it and whether they would like to do it again. You might say, "Why don't we try something different this time?" If family members go along with it, they may have a new experience they want to continue. I did this once with my wife and children when I proposed that during the Christmas meal we each express some appreciation to the other family members, as a kind of verbal Christmas gift. I brought it up a few days before Christmas so that everyone could think about what they might want to say. No one objected. During the meal, we had a lovely exchange of appreciations, a real moment of family intimacy. Now it's a Christmas ritual.

2. Elevate a routine into a ritual by giving it meaning. After moving to Minnesota in 1986, my family started going to Davanni's restaurant for pizza with no thought of starting a family ritual. After several months of going every Friday night, we began to realize that we had the makings of a ritual, and decided together to commit to it as a going-out ritual of connection. Even when my kids were in their 20's, they still signaled that they wanted family time by calling home to suggest we do pizza at Davanni's.

3. Negotiate a new ritual or change an existing one. Bring up your idea at a calm moment and without criticism. Just say that you are feeling the need for a change. Say what is missing for you, or what you would add. Make a suggestion to try something different. See if other family members are willing to give this a try for a period of time to see how it works. And do your best to make it special. It may take a while for family members to get used to a new ritual, but give it time. And be willing to make adjustments and compromises that seem to be reasonable and do not defeat the purpose of ritual.

Once you have good family rituals in place, keeping them alive takes work and vigilance. Here is a summary of the major principles I have developed for managing family rituals over time:

- **Adult Agreement:** If you and your spouse or co-parent do not agree on the ritual, it will not work well. Take the time to negotiate the needs, values, and goals of your family rituals with your adult partner.

- **Eventual Buy-In from the Children:** Older children especially may resist changes at first, particularly if the changes diminish their freedom and spontaneity. A ritual that works well will eventually win the allegiance of the children. If they continue to complain and resist over time, consider overhauling, substituting, or dropping the ritual.

- **Maximum Participation:** The more that family members are involved in planning and carrying out the ritual, the more meaningful it is likely to be.

- **Clear Expectations:** Rituals of all kinds require enough coordination that people know what to do and when to do it.

- **Minimal Conflict:** Although conflict can always pop up in families, the most successful rituals occur without regular tension and conflict.

- **Protection from Erosion:** Entropy threatens all family rituals. Good rituals must be fought for and management means protecting the ritual from the inevitable threats to its consistency and integrity.

- **Openness to Change:** Rituals have their seasons for planting, cultivating, pruning, and harvesting. Intentional families are forever changing while holding on to their important traditions.

Most families have some rituals they enjoy, some they don't enjoy but feel stuck with, and some they could benefit from creating or refurbishing. I encourage you to develop an agenda of current rituals you might want to remodel and new ones you might want to try. The payoffs for your family can be enormous.

Written for Family Empowerment Network by William J. Doherty, PhD, professor of family social science at the University of Minnesota and a practicing marriage and family therapist. He is author of The Intentional Family: Simple Rituals to Strengthen Family Ties *(1999); and* Take Back Your Kids: Confident Parenting in Turbulent Times *(2000) and co-author with Barbara Carlson of* Putting Family First *(2002). He helped found a grassroots parents' initiative: www. puttingfamilyfirst.org. He is father to a son and a daughter. For reprint requests, contact www.family-empower.com.*

At the Heart of Parenting: Eating Together

By Kathy Keller Jones, MA

IN TODAY'S BUSY WORLD, what was once considered an inevitable part of family life—eating together—is becoming an "endangered species." In the busyness of our modern consumer-driven world, we either defend our family time or we lose it. When we eat together regularly, as in all family rituals, the family's culture is created and maintained, and family life is enhanced by the sense of order, the emotional bonding, the sense of being part of a larger whole, and the modeling of family values and communication. When we spend time together, the family provides a critical counterpoint to the negative aspects of the consumer culture which teaches a maladaptive attitude of personal entitlement: "I will fuss as much as necessary to have my own way and have it now." Contrast this with the sense of teamwork and belonging that can come when family members work together to plan, prepare and enjoy good food. Eating together is one of the critical ways we can support our children of all ages as they grow and find their way in the world.

Becoming organized enough to share regular meals can be a challenge, and it is also a step which can help us become more proactive in many areas of our lives. As our ability to plan ahead and organize the week improves, the entire family benefits since their needs for order and security are met. As our children enter elementary school, they too need to learn to look ahead and plan the week, and family meetings can become a vehicle for this, as long as they are kept short and end with fun. I was inspired by one large blended family who organized eating together in the following way: the father cooked breakfast every morning and oversaw the bagged lunch preparation. Each week an older and younger team (parent and child or older child and younger child) signed up to be in charge of each dinner, which included planning the menu, listing and shopping for the items needed, cooking and cleaning up. Most families have

fewer family members than my friends had, but it is a reminder that meals provide wonderful opportunities for learning about teamwork. Meals are family affairs and even the youngest children can help out in some way. Some families, for example, call the kids 10 minutes before the meal is ready and have the kids prepare the table. Others ask everyone to stay in the kitchen until cleanup is 100% done and then they all sit down and do quiet work/homework together. Dinner and work time are times when TV screens and phones are off. For adolescents, the computer can be at hand, and in sight, for writing and research.

Why is eating together so important? Family dinners are incredibly powerful protective factors for our children and adolescents. Research by the National Center on Addiction and Substance Abuse (CASA) at Columbia University (2007)[1] has clearly shown that children who eat 5 or more weekly dinners with their family are significantly more successful than kids who eat 1 or 2 meals weekly:

- They are less likely to smoke, drink or use illegal drugs. The fewer family dinners a teen has in a

typical week the more likely they are to use.
- They have higher grades.
- They are at lower risk for depression and thoughts of suicide.
- They are more emotionally content and have fewer behavior problems.
- They have healthier eating habits and fewer eating disorders
- They are less likely to have sex at younger ages.

These findings held regardless of gender, socio-economic status, and whether there were one or two parents in the household[3]. A University of Michigan longitudinal study of how children use their time (1999) [2], found that mealtime at home was the strongest predictor of achievement and behavior. Mealtime was more powerful than time in school, studying, church activities, playing sports or art activities! Family meals directly compete with the problematic tendency for teens to bond exclusively with peers and leave adults out, thus putting themselves at risk.

The key ingredients of family meals involve gathering together without distractions and having face-to-face interactions. Of course, families with very young children may only be approximating this ideal while they teach the basic skills of sitting and staying at the table for 15 to 20 minutes. Over time, however, family meals are an opportunity to share the "best and worst" thing that happened that day and to learn to listen to others. Some families have the delightful habit of sharing one thing about the day for which they are grateful. Telling and creating family stories can take place during meals and greatly enrich our children's language and concept development while creating community. Without saying a word, parents are modeling a healthy relationship to food. As a counselor, I have found that children are less likely to exhibit behaviors related to food disorders when they eat daily family meals. Although the companionship at family dinners is more important then the quality of the food, families with frequent meals together expose children to more natural and homemade foods and therefore the entire family is less likely to become overweight. When we snack or eat meals individually, we are more likely to eat lower quality, more highly processes and thus less nutritious foods[4]. In the CASA study[1], 84% of teens surveyed said they would rather eat dinner with their family. Let's make eating together a top priority; it is at the heart of good parenting!

[1] CASA., *"The Importance of Family Dinners IV,"* 2007. www.casacolumbia.org.
[2] Sandra L. Hofferth, *"Changes in American Children's Time, 1981–1997,"* U. of Michigan's Institute for Social Research, Center Survey, January, 1999.
[3] Council of Economic Advisors to the President. *"Teens and Their Parents in the 21st Century: An Examination of Trends in Teen Behavior and the Role of Parental Involvement."* May, 2000.
[4] Make Healthy Eating Fun for Kids. www.nationalfamilymonth.net/JoinTheFight/MakeHealthyEatingFun.pdf

Tips on Running a Successful Family Meeting

By JoAnne Nordling, MS, MEd

The purpose of this article is to give you some basic guidelines on how to run successful family meetings, meetings that will give you and your children the opportunity to 1) learn the art of problem solving, negotiation and compromise, 2) share responsibility for family operating rules, and 3) strengthen emotional bonds among members of the family.

Schedule a regular meeting time, rather than holding family meetings only when a crisis arises. Weekly meetings held on a regular basis help ensure a calm and supportive atmosphere. Before holding your very first family meeting, ask each member of the family when would be the best time to meet. Thereafter, before the closing of each meeting, ask the family, "Shall we meet at the same time next week?" Give everyone a chance to check their schedules. Then write the date on a calendar, which you display in a prominent place, such as the refrigerator door.

No voting is allowed at family meetings. While voting is a great system for a nation, voting in the intimate family setting can tear the group apart. Whenever there is a vote, someone wins and someone loses. People who lose are likely to feel misunderstood and put down. The losing minority will also often resist the will of the majority, and sabotage in subtle and not so subtle ways.

The process of searching for a solution is more important than actually finding a solution. Not voting means that the meeting might end with everyone still not agreed on a solution. Believe it or not, this is perfectly okay. The most important outcome of the meeting is that every individual in the family has had a chance to speak and to be heard. People of all ages who have their needs met for being treated as competent and respected human beings are much more likely, in the long run, to be cooperative and trusting members of the group.

Do not let yourself be baited into a power struggle by getting involved in an argument with any other member of the family. This is probably the hardest idea to put into practice, but is a rock-bottom necessity for conducting a successful family meeting. Remember that when children are nervous about being blamed for the problem, it is common for them at first to attempt to sabotage the process. And when a child makes some apparently outrageous and self-indulgent remark in an attempt to deflect blame, the indignant adult can hardly resist trying to "talk some sense" and saying "listen to reason."

Here's an example of how two parents sabotaged their first attempt at a family meeting. Every night when the mother, Naomi, got home from work, she walked into a messy house where her four children had left behind a trail of books, clothes, and half-eaten food. At the family meeting, she presented the problem to her kids, being careful not to place blame, and used good describing language to state the problem, "When I come home from work, I see coats and books and food in the living room and dining room. I get so tired when I come home to a messy house. I need some help in figuring out a plan for keeping things picked up." Her thirteen-year-old daughter said, "Why can't the baby sitter pick things up?" The ten-year-old son added, "Why should I have to work on this? I never leave my stuff around."

Imagine Naomi's feelings. She immediately launched into a lecture to her daughter on the need for everyone to be responsible for his or her own things. Next, her husband told their son (in a sarcastic tone of voice) that even if the son was Mr. Perfect, which he clearly was not, he had an obligation to participate in the meeting to help his mother find a solution. All doors to communication promptly slammed shut. Here's how the parents might have sidestepped their children's attempt to sabotage the meeting:

Daughter's attempt to sabotage:

1. Describe what your daughter just said by repeating her exact words: "You think the baby-sitter should pick things up." Try to look thoughtful and keep calm. Turn to the rest of the group and ask, "Anybody else have any ideas?" Or,

2. Use an inner-reality listening response. If you can't think of anything to say, just say, "Hmm…" Then turn to the group and ask, "Anybody else have any ideas?" Try to keep your tone of voice accepting and unemotional.

Son's attempt to sabotage:

1. Describe what he just said, "You never leave your stuff around so you don't think you should have to work on the problem." Keep your voice even and calm (no sarcastic overtones please!). Turn to the rest of the group and ask, "Anyone have any ideas?" Or,

2. Use an inner-reality listening response: "Hmm…" If you think of it, you can add, "You don't think it's fair." Then ask, "Anybody else have any ideas?" Your new response to these kinds of self-indulgent statements opens up lines of communication and reduces power struggles.

Establish a relaxed and upbeat atmosphere for the meeting. It's okay to sprawl on the floor.

Use an opening ritual. Rituals should be done on a regular basis so they help set the mood for the meeting to follow. Rituals can be as simple as tinkling a bell, turning off the fluorescent lights, passing out the popcorn, lighting a candle, or building a fire in the fireplace.

Ruth, who grew up in a Jewish family, looked forward to the meetings her parents held when she was a child. These meetings always opened with a short reading. Then each person was asked to tell something interesting that had happened to them during the week. Ruth remembers how important she felt when her opinion was asked for and listened to.

Involve everyone in setting the agenda. Use a blank sheet of paper and fasten it to the refrigerator door. Tell everybody this is the place to write down items anyone, whether parent or child, wants to discuss at the next family meeting (or use a shoebox with a slot on top.) If children are only writing down problem topics, be sure to add at least one fun topic like, "Should we do something fun together as a family next week?" or "Something that happened recently that made you feel happy or proud."

Keep focused on the general problem. Emphasizing specific names makes it easy to turn the meeting into a blaming session, where the "good guys" blame the "bad guys" and the "bad guys" blame everybody else. Try to keep the group focused on the general problem of teasing, for example, instead of on the specific complaints.

Watch out for hidden agendas. If mother comes to the meeting convinced she has already found the correct solution for convincing her children to pick up their clutter, it will be almost impossible for her to listen to their ideas. Since children are smart, they will soon realize mother is not able to listen to their ideas.

Use brainstorming to think about possible solutions. Even though it is okay if a solution is not found, it is important to sincerely explore all possibilities for a solution. Have the recorder for the week write down all ideas so they can be referred to throughout the process. 1) Clarify the problem so that everyone agrees as to the exact nature of the problem. 2) Brain-storm possible solutions; accept and write down even the zany ones. 3) Attempt to choose a solution from your list. Remember, every single person in the family must agree on any proposed solution. If no unanimous solution is found, just say, "Well, at least we tried and we did a lot of good thinking about it. Maybe someone will come up with a good idea this coming week. In the meantime, we'll just have to keep on doing it the way we always have."

Rotate leadership of the group when you think your children are ready. Adults have to continue to exercise informal leadership in all areas that are beyond the capabilities of a child, but you will be amazed at the extent to which your children will learn effective leadership and human relationship skills by observing your behavior as you participate in the family meeting.

For more information on how to conduct family meetings and brainstorming sessions, read the entire chapter on family meetings in Taking Charge: Caring Discipline That Works, at Home and at School, *4th ed. by JoAnne Nordling. A videotape featuring the author and two examples of family meetings is also available from Parent Support Center (503) 796-9665. CDs and audiotapes are available from North American Parenting Institute at (616) 738-0848 or www.parenting-institute.com.*

Reprinted with permission from JoAnne Nordling, the author of *Taking Charge: Caring Discipline That Works, at Home and at School* and director of Parent Support Center at www.parentsupport.org.

The Important Role of Fathers in Raising Daughters
By Jody Bellant Scheer, MD

The Role of a Father in the Tween Years: Ages 8 to 12

Girls ages 8 to 12 are full of enthusiasm, confidence, energy and emotion. Dads rank very high on the popularity list of tween girls, who crave their dad's undivided attention to their feelings, uniqueness and inner beauty[1]. Listening to your daughter, finding out what she thinks, believes, feels, dreams and does, shows a girl that you value her for her true self, and helps to counteract society's strong claim that a woman is valued only for her physical attributes. By building this strong relationship, a father can help increase his daughters' self-reliance, inner strength and problem-solving skills. Fathers who involve themselves fully with their daughters at this age will have a profound, positive effect on the ease with which their daughters' make the transition into adolescence.

Preteen girls have a rich feeling life, and wish deeply to be able to share their hearts and souls with their fathers. "They especially want their feelings to be heard, understood and respected. Daughters feel diminished when fathers are critical, overly-rational, withholding or impatient around the expression of emotion."[1] This offers a new challenge to many fathers, who often don't know how to support a girl who is buffeted by powerful emotions. When faced with raw emotion, some fathers withdraw from their daughters.[2] Many men in our culture were taught in their own childhoods to hide their emotions, thinking they were a sign of weakness.[3] This creates a challenge for fathers to adapt in order to maintain strong connections with their daughters. Learning to express emotions in healthy ways—crying over losses, expressing frustration at behaviors instead of at persons, or celebrating joyful events, for example—will help fathers model emotional maturity, as well as connect with their daughters.[3] Fathers are also challenged to develop good listening skills, which means giving their daughters their full attention, asking open-ended questions, remaining calm, and fighting the urge to lecture.[4]

Anger is an emotion that is used and expressed differently by men and women. If men do express emotion, it tends to be anger: verbal outbursts, criticism, withdrawal, or even violence.[3] Expressions of anger can be used to get things off one's chest, to bully, to get one's way, or to make an impact. Women tend both to fear anger, and to be socialized not to express it. A far more acceptable emotion in women is sadness, such that many women will actually cry when angry.[1] Women therefore learn to disassociate from angry feelings, which de-prives them of a powerful internal guidance system.[1] Anger denotes a violation, an injustice, or an act out of integrity with one's values. It is important for both men and women to be able to notice their anger, as well as to be careful and intentional about the behaviors they resort to when angry. Dads who are overly angry and controlling, and who are then mortified when their daughters express these same emotions, may forbid such outbursts from their daughters. These girls are at risk of growing into women who think that they cannot directly express anger with those who have provoked it, and as a result may feel powerless, vulnerable and weak.[1] Fathers can have a tremendous positive impact on their daughters' emotional health by first accepting and encouraging their daughters to feel and express anger, and secondly, by modeling for their daughters constructive ways to act on those angry feelings.

Girls in the tween years want to be included in their Dad's world, to feel loved and accepted by their Dad. Even though her interests and activities may be different, there are lots of opportunities for Dads to include their daughters on trips to the store, to ballgames, to special lunches, to work or to help on special projects around the house. A girl who is asked may not accept each invitation, but she will know that her Dad values her company and help. Encouraging physical activity and rough-and-tumble play is an arena where many fathers feel at home with their daughters. Team sports are known to teach kids valuable life lessons…responsibility, assertiveness, competence, strength, good sportsmanship, conflict resolution and how to be a team player. [1] Girls now have more athletic opportunities than ever before, and fathers can play an important supportive role by coaching, encouraging and advocating for their daughters.

Many girls from ages 8 to 12 know how to work their Dads. By batting their eyelashes and being "cute," girls can often manipulate their fathers into solving their problems or giving them money, protection or favors. Dads who encourage such behaviors from their daughters are teaching them to be compliant, charming, and manipulative. [5] This does not help these young women succeed in relationships or in the modern world.

More difficult is to encourage girls to problem solve on their own, to make their own decisions and to learn from their own mistakes. Mistakes are wonderful opportunities to learn, but many parents interpret them as signs of failure and berate their children when they happen. "Where did we ever get the crazy idea that in order to make kids do better, first we have to make them feel worse? People cannot feel bad and learn at the same time. We only learn when we feel good." [6] When fathers can see mistakes as learning opportunities, our kids may shift: approach things differently the next time and have more faith in themselves. [6] This can lead to our long-term parenting goals of self-reliance, assertiveness and competence.

One area where a father can help a daughter gain mastery of essential skills is money. Money is a sign of power in our culture, and it is essential that your daughter learn to manage it. [1] It is great for your daughter to gain experience while the stakes are still low. Budgets are a good way to learn about money management, and can include more complex items as the child grows older. 8-year-olds can handle a simple weekly allowance that includes lunch money, for example. Allowances are very effective for teaching the child about spending money when the child is allowed to have some choice. Be clear about what the weekly allotment is to be used for. Some families choose a 3-allotment system: 10% charity of kid's choice, 45% spend anytime and 45% save for a big ticket item. Stick to your guns and allow your child to learn from mistakes when she overspends her money and has to go hungry for a few days at lunch. An empty stomach for a few days will teach her far more than any lecture about saving money! This is because kids (and adults too) learn best to save **only after** we've learned how to be broke. [7] As your daughter gets older, you can negotiate more items such as clothes, outings, bus fares, and so on. Consider opening a checking or savings account for her to teach her about keeping financial records, saving for short- and long-term purchases, stretching her money, and making reasonable choices. When it's her own money she's spending, you'll be surprised how often she may decide to buy a regular sweatshirt, instead of paying an extra $25 to get a specialized one. A side benefit is that you will be removed from shopping disputes, as it will now be solely your daughter's choice how she spends her own money for clothes.

You may want to encourage your daughter to work for pay to increase her budget. In general, it is best not to pay children for doing household chores, which are done as part of a family obligation. [7] You can pay her for special projects or enlist neighbors who might hire your daughter to help them. In this way, our daughters learn to pay their own way while gaining feelings of competence, self-reliance and self-worth from creating financial abundance.

A Father's Role During Adolescence

No period of life is marked by more self-doubt and self-consciousness than adolescence. [4] Girls are undergoing hormonal and bodily changes and are confused about how and where they fit in. Our culture tends to teach a girl that appearance is her most important asset, and that her ideas and opinions are less interesting than her dress size. Adolescent girls often measure their self-worth based on their complexion, their physical attributes and/or the ebb and flow of their friendships. [1] Emotions which were active in the preteen years are now felt and expressed at even more explosive levels. Girls at this age also tend to be less confident, active and assertive than in their preteen years. This is due to the fact that women are socialized as they grow up to please others, and they tend to think that they must hide or change themselves in order to maintain relationships or to be loved. [1] The result is that by age 15, twice as many girls show depressive symptoms as boys do, and many girls start experimenting with dangerous behaviors that may seriously affect their future. [9]

Fathers are especially important during these teen years. Research confirms, however, that many fathers retreat emotionally and physically when their daughters enter puberty, talking to them less and criticizing them more. [2] "The worst mistake for a father to make at this time in his daughter's life is to withdraw himself from her, because he does not know how to deal with his own response to her developing sexuality." [1] A daughter's transition from girl to woman provides a father with yet another opportunity to grow in order to stay connected with his daughter. Developing a respectful way to give affection and love to your developing daughter will help ensure that she will not go looking for the same in the arms of just any young hormonal admirer. This may require that a Dad look at his own feelings and thoughts about sexuality, and that he broaden his understanding of male sexuality. A man's sexuality is more than his ability to engage in the act of intercourse, it is about his total 'being' and his way of relating to the world. [1] Sexual energy is a normal part of life, and includes caring behaviors, affection, vitality and creativity.

A father is constantly modeling sexual expression to his daughter, whether he realizes it or not. How does he treat women? Does he comment on their beauty or on their ideas and actions? Does he demonstrate in his actions that women are valued for their character, integrity and femininity? Does he respect and act lovingly towards his daughter's mother, whether or not he is currently married to her? [1,3,4,10]

Actions speak much louder than words. Daughters tend to look for men who resemble their fathers. Would you be proud to see yourself reflected in your daughter's boyfriends? A daughter's adolescence can be a challenging time because many of a father's own values and beliefs can be severely tested. However, this can also be a time of great growth and personal enrichment, as a father learns to give healthy doses of attention, affirmation and physical affection to his adolescent daughter, while respecting that she is a

woman with her own need to explore her own sexual identity issues. Fathers are a vital force in showing daughters that there are good men in the world, who are consistent, trustworthy, loving and sensitive to her needs. [1,3] Fathers who want more input on how to father adolescent daughters may find enormous help from other fathers via parenting support groups. There is a host of information on father-daughter relationships in our libraries and on the Internet.

One of the greatest gifts a father can give an adolescent daughter is to encourage her to make her own decisions and to support (but not rescue) her as she learns from her own mistakes. Fathers tend to want to protect their daughters from any hurtful experience, but doing so rescues their daughters and prevents girls from learning from their own failed experiences. By the time a girl graduates from high school, she will need to be able to function as an adult in society. She therefore needs to learn all of the skills of independent living and decision-making during her years in high school. A father can best encourage this process by setting firm boundaries, and allowing his daughter to make more and more of her own life decisions as she gets older, until she is making nearly all of her own life decisions

by her senior year in high school. Most importantly, he will need to model the behaviors he wishes to see in his daughter. If men want to produce self-disciplined, confident daughters who make wise choices, take responsibility for their own actions, and proactively work to fix their problems, then they must demonstrate those same behaviors. [3] Daughters learn more from watching our lives than from listening to what we say. Each day, in hundreds of ways, we communicate to our daughters, "Follow me!" [3]

There may be times when your adolescent daughter openly rebels against your desires, your established routine, and even your values. Too many fathers respond to this behavior by desperately trying to exert strict control over their daughters and, in the process, drive them away.[4] "Our kids are their own people. We can teach them to make wise choices, but we can never control them. Instead, we need to focus on those things which are under our control and make appropriate adjustments."[4] We may control the purse strings, or the use of the family car, but behaviors are really up to our kids to choose. By practicing self-control ourselves when our daughters rebel, we can demonstrate that our kids' behaviors affect them way more than they affect us. "With self-control, we can let some responsibility slide onto our teens' shoulders. We can communicate trust in them, be patient and let them sharpen their decision-making skills."[4] By removing ourselves from the argument, we give our kids the opportunity to make decisions based on their own good sense. When allowed, kids will often make better decisions for themselves than we would make for them.

When my own daughter was 16, she was constantly coming home with her boyfriend ½ hour after my established weekend curfew of midnight. Finally, on the fifth weekend, when she asked what time she needed to be home, I asked her to let me know when she would be home instead. Then, I said I expected her to keep her agreement with me. After a few minutes of consultation, she informed me that she would be home at 10:30 pm, a full 2 hours earlier than she had arrived home the past 4 weekends! However, since I had not given her a time to rebel against, she made a decision based on her own needs. And, I was able to give her the opportunity to feel good about keeping her own agreement, which she did.

One of the most difficult of teenage developmental tasks is to move from simply "reacting" to authority (parents, schools, teachers, society) to behaving in a way that supports what they truly want in their own life. Sometimes, this shift involves learning lessons the most difficult way: by trial, error, and making mistakes. A father's most effective role at this developmental stage is to support and guide his daughter in making her own

behavior choices, to listen respectfully to her point of view, to set limits on what **HE** will do, and to respect that his daughter may chose differently than he would. After all, how many of us learned life's most important

lessons by listening to the advice of others? We had to rise and fall under the power of our own choices, and so do our children. It is essential to remember that our teenage daughters are **NOT** their untoward behaviors. Beneath any rebellious teenage girl is a young woman who desperately wants the love and acceptance of her father. It is a great act of unconditional love to support a daughter while she makes a choice we are at odds with. The long-term outcome of intimacy and mutual respect, however, is your reward.

Teaching daughters fiscal responsibility continues into the adolescent years. When daughters are not given their own money to manage, they often fall into the trap of "dipping into Dad's pocket." Daughters ply their Dads for money because they want to know that he still cares, and Dads give in because they feel guilty for distancing themselves from their teenage daughters.[1] This results in a vicious cycle of daughters begging for money, having tantrums and brooding if they don't get their way, and fathers feeling guilty and abused whether or not they give in to their daughter's antics. All this can be avoided by continuing to use a budget with a teenage daughter, and by sticking to your agreements around it. High school girls can manage a monthly or even yearly budget for clothes, transportation, toiletries, entertainment, etc. This works best if the responsibility for creating the budget is up to the daughter, who then must negotiate the final details with Dad. This ultimately gets a father out of the loop when a fiscal crisis hits his teen. Instead of doling out money, he can spend some quality time with his daughter helping her to problem-solve and find ways to supplement her income, if needed, with paid work. This teaches a daughter fiscal responsibility, a huge asset in today's consumer society, where impulse buying on credit feeds the burgeoning number of financially ruined borrowers.

A father can exert a tremendously important role in supporting his teenage daughter by guiding her toward a successful and independent future.[4] Practically speaking, this means that fathers actively encourage their daughters to stay invested in school, to explore math and science interests as well as creative and social ones, and to identify and express their own unique personalities, talents and gifts. This will be easier if a father stays involved in his daughter's high school and keeps in touch with her studies to see where she excels.[4] Expand your own interests and your daughter's by taking her on confidence-building adventures that involve a bit of healthy risk-taking, such as river rafting, rock climbing or kayaking. This will create a lifelong memory of special time together as well. Explore areas of interest with your daughter, and encourage her to try new physical or intellectual challenges. Notice her strengths and celebrate her accomplishments.

Fathering an adolescent daughter can be frustrating for both teens and fathers. A changing adolescent daughter and a changing father will either have a changing relationship over time, or else a very strained one. Sometimes, it seems easier to just give up, and many fathers do pull away at this stage. But hanging in there has many advantages. An actively involved father is associated with daughters who are less likely to engage in risky sexual activity, substance abuse, violence or suicidal behavior.[9] Daughters with engaged and active fathers are more likely follow their Dad's example when dating, driving, making moral choices, forming lasting relationships, and making choices about what to pursue in their futures.[3] Girls with effective fathers run a far smaller risk of getting into trouble for uncontrolled anger or aggression.[11] Fathers who hang in there benefit too. Those who report that they have learned to communicate effectively with their adolescent daughters also report the highest levels of parenting satisfaction.[4] Our daughter's transition from childhood to adulthood is full of drama and trauma. A father's influence may be diminished during this time, but it is still very powerful. Even when she won't admit it, your teenage daughter needs your love and acceptance now more than ever.

References:

1. *Raising a Daughter*, by Jeanne Elium and Don Elium, Ten Speed Press. 1994.
2. "Keeping Dad in the Loop: Father-Daughter Relationship is Crucial for Adolescent Girls," by Amy Lynch, June 1998. www.vanderbiltedu/WomensCenter/June98main.html
3. "Lasting Impressions: A Father's Model," by Ken Canfield. 2001, National Center for Fathering. www.fathers.com
4. "Fathering Your Teen: Thriving in Times of Change," Ken Canfield. 2001, National Center for Fathering. www.fathers.com
5. "Raising Girls," by Helena Sharpstone. The Parent Company. www.familiesonline.co.uk
6. *Positive Discipline for Teenagers: Resolving Conflict with your Teenage Son or Daughter*, by Jane Nelsen and Lynn Lott. Prima Publishing, 1994.
7. *Parenting with Love and Logic: Teaching Children Responsibility*, by Foster Cline, MD and Jim Fay. Pinon Press, 1990.
8. *Great Transitions: Preparing Adolescents for a New Century*. A report of The Carnegie Corporation of New York, 4/26/02.
9. "Protect Your Child with Limbic Bonding," by Dr. Daniel Amen, from *Change Your Brain, Change Your Life*. Times Books, January, 2000.
10. "Teenagers Need Fathers Who Love Their Moms," by Walt Mueller, www.fathers.com
11. "A Brief Quiz for Fathers," *Common Sense No Frills Plain English Guide to being a Successful Dad*. Center for Successful Fathering, Inc., 1997
12. "Ten Tips for Dads of Daughters," by Dads and Daughters, Inc. www.dadsanddaughters.org
13. "Ten Tips for Live-Away Dads," by Dads and Daughters, Inc. www.dadsanddaughters.org
14. "How Well Am I Doing As My Daughter's Father?" by Dads and Daughters, Inc. www.dadsanddaughters.org

Celebrating Womanhood

Carley Nelson, 6th Grade, Rosemont Ridge Middle School

Celebrating Womanhood

"Well behaved women rarely make history." —Laurel Thatcher Ulrich, historian

"Now that I'm growing, my body and feelings are changing. Sometimes I try to hide, but then I think about it and say, 'Hey! How come I have to hide it if it is the real truth.'" —Laura, 11, Los Angeles, California

"When women come together in one place to share their experiences, their dreams and wisdom, a very special resonance—a powerful energy—is created." —Marion Woodman, psychologist

"How might it have been different for you, if, on your first menstrual day, your mother had given you a bouquet of flowers and taken you to lunch, and then the two of you had gone to meet your father at the jeweler, where your ears were pierced, and your father bought you your first pair of earrings, and then your went with a few of your friends and your mother's friends to get your first lip coloring; and then you went, for the very first time, to the Women's Lodge, to learn the wisdom of women? How might your life be different?"
—Judith Duerk, author of *Circle of Stones*

"Can you imagine what would happen if girls took all the energy they spent worrying about their image and put it into painting, writing, theorizing, science, or sports?" —Joan Jacobs Brumberg, writer

GOALS

- To understand the pubertal development of girls and to share this with your daughter

- To understand some of the cultural myths, rituals and taboos about femininity that your daughter will be experiencing as she makes her transition to womanhood

- To help create a positive experience for your daughter as she enters womanhood

- To encourage your daughter to create healthy friendships and to express a full range of emotions

OVERVIEW

Watching our girls awaken into young women can be both wonderful and terrifying for parents. On the one hand, it is exciting to share with our daughters their sense of wonder, excitement and empowerment as they experience their emerging womanhood. We are often touched by the sweetness of our daughter's first crush or by her curiosity about the dynamics of romantic relationships. On the other hand, it can scare the daylights out of parents to watch their daughter exert her sexuality, while knowing her vulnerability and her naiveté in the outside world, where there are forces highly divergent from our own love and concern. We worry that our girls will fall prey to predators, sexual harassment or relationships that will turn too intimate or violent. We worry that our girls will become obsessed by boys, to the detriment of their studies. We worry that our daughter's sexual development, whether early or late, will make life difficult for her at school.

Dads can be intimidated by their daughter's developing sexuality and be confused about how to remain emotionally and physically connected to her. Mothers can find that they are revisiting their own bittersweet adolescent pasts when they find themselves battling their daughters' hormonal storms. Daughters often end up feeling confused and rejected by both of their parents at a time when they need them the most. That is why we are focusing an entire chapter on emerging womanhood, when girls start to embody the lessons their families and cultures teach them about being a woman.

Girls at this time are entering a difficult period of their lives, when their pubertal development is on display for everyone to see. They are both embarrassed by their bodily changes and enamored of the power their developing bodies exert over men. Parents can help create a more healthy transition into womanhood for their daughters by becoming more aware of their own conscious and unconscious feminine programming, and by counteracting negative messages that our daughters receive about their femininity and sexuality. Understanding this volatile time in your daughter's life

can be a great help toward making her transition into adulthood a successful one.

The fact is that many of our daughters will have difficulties and are at increased psychological risk during the transition into adolescence and womanhood. A girl undergoing puberty in our media-driven culture may imagine that her value in our culture is overwhelmingly as a sexual object, something to be desired and owned by others. This may cause her to "dumb down," to silence her own feelings and thoughts, to become less capable, and to lose connections in her relationships and with herself. She may also feel ashamed of her monthly cycles, her emerging sexual desire, and even of her own inner wisdom. A young girl on the path to womanhood may learn to lose herself in an effort to become the perfect female. Parents can be powerful insulators against these cultural patterns of feminine training, but only if they take the time to educate themselves and take action in their own homes to encourage more open and nourishing forms of feminine role-taking.

This chapter will acquaint parents with accurate information about puberty, sexuality, and psychological development. We will also look at the underlying myths, rules and taboos that surround girls growing up in our culture. We hope that by celebrating our daughter's emerging womanhood, we can help her to develop a healthier sense of self, a stronger voice, rightful personal power and meaningful relationships with herself and others. Each girl deserves to look forward to a positive experience of her future as a woman. Having men in her life who support her mind as well as her body, and having women in her life who exemplify empowered womanhood is a great help to any girl.

Puberty

To start with, it is important for girls to understand the process of puberty, sexual development and menstruation. Our first articles in this chapter, **"Pubertal Development in Girls"** (p. 4:13) and **"Surviving Puberty: A Handout for your Daughter"** (p. 4:16) discuss the physical and emotional changes that occur in girls during puberty. Discussing these facts with your daughter in a matter-of-fact way will help allay the fears that a girl can have if she has not been educated about the changes taking place in her body. This discussion may take some work for mothers (or female relatives stepping in for motherless daughters) who are themselves ashamed of this natural bodily process. One comfortable way to have this discussion with your daughter is to read aloud one of the excellent books written on this topic (see "Further Reading") when your daughter is 9- to 11-years-old. You can just skip over the chapters on advanced topics.

It is helpful to remember that menstruation is a monthly ritual experienced by half of the population of the earth. Something so commonplace and so important to the propagation of the species should not be considered shameful! Many indigenous cultures around the world consider the monthly cycle of women to be one of the most sacred of human traits, because it is associated with the creation and nurturing of life itself. It is helpful to learn about some of these more positive, alternative ways of looking at menstrual flow to see how our own cultural programming might shame women about their bodies, their monthly cycles and their sexual desire. Tami Lynn Kent, a physical therapist, has written a book entitled *Wild Feminine: Female Power, Spirit & Joy in the Root of the Female Body* which can help women reclaim their strength and better appreciate their bodies. How would our daughter's experience of menstruation change if she better understood the energetic patterns and preciousness of the pelvis? The article **"Moontime Celebrations"** (p. 4:17) talks about preparing our daughters more thoughtfully for menstruation, sexuality and child-bearing. Honoring a girl's first menstruation with a small ritual can help her to feel blessed to have a body that works so well, and one that is full of such wonderful, creative energy and potential.

Sexuality

Sexuality is another awkward yet important topic for parents to address. Study after study shows that women are portrayed in a sexual manner (postures that imply sexual readiness) or objectified (showing only body parts) more often than men. We all contribute when we emphasize a narrow unrealistic standard of beauty, focus on appearance, or allow our girls to be exposed to a high volume of media. When our girls are sexualized it can be an enormous impediment to empowerment, impacting

them cognitively, physically and emotionally. According to a 2006 American Psychological Association study[1], sexualization occurs when:

1. A person's value comes only from his or her sexual appeal or behavior,
2. A person is held to a standard that equates physical attractiveness with being sexy,
3. A person is sexually objectified—that is, made into a thing for others' sexual use—rather than seen as a person with the capacity for independent action,
4. Sexuality is inappropriately imposed on a child.

Girls in our culture are taught that any expression of sexual desire is equated to an invitation for male sexual aggression; therefore, they may suppress their desire into a passive stance of "being desired," or risk being called "sluts." This unhealthy cultural myth is a serious problem for girls; they often find themselves in sexual situations without adequate preparation and expose themselves to unwanted pregnancies and sexually transmitted diseases. Helping your daughter develop a healthy appreciation for and acceptance of her sexual desire can help her to protect herself, as noted in the article **"Girls and Desire"** (p. 4:19). Sexuality can be an enormous source of pleasure in her life. To have talked about this with her parents increases the chances that she will learn to experiment with her sexuality in ways that are both safe and healthy. Again, this will be unusually difficult for most contemporary parents, who themselves feel constrained by their own negative sexual upbringing and programming. That is why our girls' transformation at puberty can be a wonderful, and possibly challenging, opportunity to stretch our own boundaries and to revisit our own adolescence.

We cannot expect our children to avoid the sexual experimentation and mistakes that we ourselves made in adolescence. However, we can make it a bit easier on our daughters through education and thoughtful discussions about expressing our sexuality in responsible and safe ways. The article **"How I Dealt with my Teenagers' Sexuality"** (p. 4:21) outlines one family's approach to educating their children on sexual matters.

Girls and Alternative Sexual Orientations

Another sexual issue that may come up is that your daughter may worry that she is a lesbian. It helps to keep in mind that our cultural fears about homosexuality can sometimes cause innocent developmentally appropriate attachments between girls to be misinterpreted. Close friendships between girls are normal and also a psychological preparation for love relationships later in adolescence. Although about 5% of girls will eventually settle on an alternative sexual orientation, up to 40% of our daughters will experience sexual feelings toward another girl at least once during their adolescence. In fact, our culture is much more accepting of same-sex sexual experimentation for girls than in previous generations. Only a fraction of girls who question their sexuality, therefore, will end up being lesbians. It can take a girl many years—often into her 20's—to establish fully what her sexual orientation is.

If your daughter feels that she is different, and is able to discuss this with you, you will be in the best position to be able to support her. This kind of revelation carries with it many diverse feelings for most parents and children, and it is important for your daughter to realize that even though you may be disappointed or upset, you will still love, cherish and accept her regardless of what her sexual orientation ends up to be. Counseling can also be immensely helpful for adolescent lesbian girls, as they do suffer from higher rates of depression, substance abuse and promiscuity than do heterosexual girls. The article **"If She Thinks She's Lesbian"** (p. 4:22) gives more details on this difficult aspect of parenting.

Cultural Pressures

It is important to look closely at cultural myths and standards of femininity to understand the pressures our girls face as they enter adolescence. Mary Pipher, author of *Reviving Ophelia: Saving the Selves of Adolescent Girls,* has found that girls today are having a harder time than ever in adolescence. Pipher felt this was not explained by dysfunctional or inadequate parenting, but by our culture, which is violent, sexist, media-saturated, and "girl-poisoning." Girls now are bombarded by negative cultural messages about women and female sexuality in multitudes of violent and debasing images, stories

and programming broadcast daily into our lives by our modern, consumer society.

Pipher notes that many girls are not developmentally or psychologically equipped to meet the challenges that confront them during adolescence, and this results in a dramatic drop in self-esteem, confidence and academic performance. They also suffer from a lack of social and community support systems that used to shelter and support girls in the past as they faced adolescence. Pipher's findings were echoed in a landmark 1990 study from the American Association of University Women, "How Schools Short-change Girls," which found that girls' self-esteem and academic achievement both plummet as they reach adolescence. By sixth grade, both boys and girls equate masculinity with opportunity and assertiveness, and femininity with reserve and restraint.

Myra and David Sadker, authors of *Failing at Fairness,* have also documented this slide of self-esteem by girls entering adolescence. They note that girls must deal with two difficult transitions at once: the bodily changes from childhood through puberty along with the equally difficult transition from elementary to middle school. Their studies showed that girls, during this period, stop feeling capable of "doing things," of being athletic, of being attractive, or even of being able to speak their ideas or express their opinions openly. Some girls learn that being smart isn't OK, so they self-censure themselves and turn their energies towards looking good. Most telling is these authors' study of the reactions of over 1100 students who were asked what they would think if they woke up the next day as a member of the opposite sex. The girls' answers ran the gamut from preferring to stay girls to enthusiastically embracing their new roles as boys. Forty-two percent of the girls noted that there were advantages to being a boy, such as more freedom, the ability to make more money, more career choices and higher social status. Boys, however, overwhelmingly thought that being female would be appalling, disgusting and humiliating. Ninety-five percent of them saw no advantages to being female, and many of them invented fantasy escapes from their female bodies, the most common of which was some form of violent suicide. They most lamented the loss of their athletic prowess, as they perceived girls to have fragile, limited and incompetent bodies. If our girls at adolescence look to boys for their self-esteem, for some kind of approval and affirmation, it is no small wonder that their self-confidence and self-esteem plummet. What they see reflected in their male counterparts is a distorted view of femininity that emphasizes a loss of power, a lack of substance and value, and an appalling lack of respect for the important role women play in our lives and culture.

Research by Lyn Mikel Brown and Carol Gilligan in their book *Meeting at the Crossroads: Women's Psychology and Girls' Development,* also finds that adolescence is a time of increased psychological risk for girls, when they lose their vitality, their resilience and their sense of self. Girls learn to give up their voices and abandon their own feelings and emotions in order to fit into the role of being a "good girl." Girls learn to silence their anger, their strong emotions, and their opinions, feeling that they can no longer be honest in their relationships for fear of losing them. This causes girls to disconnect from their friends, their families and themselves, leaving them psychologically vulnerable. These behaviors were found to be learned first and foremost from the adult women in their lives; as such, this represents a form of negative cultural feminine programming. The article **"What's Happening from a Developmental Perspective"** (p. 4:23) discusses this trend and what we can do about it.

Why is it Important to Know about Brains?

At the core, girls and women's lives are about social connections. In her book on *The Female Brain,* Dr. Louann Brizendine writes that

> *The female brain has tremendous unique aptitudes —outstanding verbal ability, the ability to connect deeply in friendships, a nearly psychic capacity to read faces and tone of voice for emotions and states of mind, and the ability to defuse conflict. All of this is hardwired into the brains of women.*

Brain studies have revealed ways in which the female brain is wired for connections. This provides us with new insights into why women are the way they are and how their neurological strengths benefit our culture. Brain imaging studies have shown that the corpus callosum, the band that connects the right and left sides of the brain, is much thicker and has more neural connections in females, which may account for their ability to multitask and integrate right and left hemispheres easily.[2] Studies have shown the brain circuitry for language and hearing has 11% more neurons in female brains.[3] The hub for emotion and memory formation and the area for observing emotions in others are all larger in the female brain.[4] How this manifests is that the average woman is more adept at interpreting, expressing and remembering emotional events. Neural imaging will continue to explore the genetic wiring innate in men and women.

As we discover these new pathways and discover the "nature" behind our behavior, we also recognize that nurture has a tremendous influence no matter what the wiring is. There is even evidence that "nurture" can influence "nature." Parts of our brain will not develop if they are not used. For example, one visual part of the brain will not work if a lazy eye is not treated. The part of the brain where deep connection and attachments are made will not completely develop if a baby does not experience loving interaction by age 2. If we want our daughter to be everything that she can be, we need to expose her to experiences that foster growth in all areas of her life: mental, emotional, social, and physical.

Girls Friendships

Brain research helps us understand why girls' friendships are such a critical part of their development. **"The Nature of Girls' Friendships"** (p. 4:24) contrasts girls' friendships with boys' friendships. Girls are also particularly sensitive to rejection and conflict in friendships. One of the ways parents support their daughters is to help them strengthen their positive relationships, while also developing the ability to set appropriate limits with problematic relationships.

As parents, we need to acknowledge that our kids have the prerogative to choose their friends. Then we can focus our efforts on healthy friendship skills. Here are a few tips from the **"Supporting Healthy Friendships"** (p. 4:25) article:

1. Get to know your child's friends, especially those you are unsure about.
2. Make it comfortable for kids to be at your home.
3. There is not a "right" number of friends. One or two friends can be enough.

4. Encourage kids to be friendly and fair to everyone. As your child gets older, help her distinguish under what circumstances she can trust each of her friends.

5. When your daughter fights with a friend, listen carefully and empower her to solve her own problems. Focus on support rather than rescue.

"Relationships with Family, Friends, Self, and Others" (p. 4:26) is a teen's guide to starting and strengthening relationships. It is so easy for "mother/father bear" to jump in to protect and rescue, when what our kids need most is guidance to develop conflict resolution skills. In **"When Our Kids Fight with Friends"** (p. 4:29), Positive Discipline coach Glenda Montgomery shares how parents can strengthen their daughter's social skills by listening, coaching and encouraging her. Our girls also benefit from "home alone" time to regroup, process, and get grounded. **"Fun Things to Do When You're Alone"** (p. 4:30) lists several ways to strengthen one's relationship with one's self.

The following are additional ways that parents can help their daughters strengthen this important relational side of her. First of all, it is important to model respect in all of your own relationships with women and to point out the many strengths of women. What are the hidden messages your daughter is receiving at home? How do you treat women? Do you comment on their beauty or on their ideas and actions? Do you demonstrate in your actions that women are valued for their character, integrity and femininity? Do you respect and act lovingly towards your daughter's other parent, whether or not you are currently married? How do the divisions of labor in your household divide along gender lines? Do you remain respectfully affectionate with your daughter, even once she's fully developed? Parents are constantly broadcasting to their daughters their views and expectations of gender in all that they do. It is therefore a good thing to look consciously at what you are teaching her about femininity, both consciously and unconsciously, to make sure that it is consistent with the values you want to pass on to her.

Secondly, a daughter needs deep, honest relationships with adults who are accepting and encourage a girl's full range of emotions and ideas, in order to explore who she is and what she believes in. These relationships help her to learn that open and respectful conflict does not destroy, but can actually deepen relationships. Furthermore, our girls need to be exposed to empowered, assertive and happy women in order to envision such future roles for themselves. Hopefully, by establishing close, honest relationships with adults, a girl can learn to create similar relationships with her peers. *The Mother-Daughter Project: How Mothers and Daughters Can Band Together, Beat the Odds, and Thrive Through Adolescence* by SuEllen Hamkins, MD and Renee Schultz, MA is full of practical information on how to form a group for you and your daughter (see more about this in Session 9 - Supporting Her).

Emotional IQ and Compassionate Communication

Finally, it is important to help your daughter explore and express her full range of emotions and develop her "emotional intelligence." The expression of emotions tends to be very gender specific in our culture. While men are socialized to withhold and deny most emotions other than anger, women are expected to be "overly" emotional, with the exception of expressing anger. Women are socialized to fear anger, and are ostracized when they express it. A far more acceptable emotion in women is sadness, such that many women will actually cry when angry. Girls and women, therefore, learn to disassociate from angry feelings, which deprives them of a powerful internal guidance system. Anger denotes a violation, an injustice, or an act out of integrity with one's values. It is important for girls to be able to notice their anger, as well as to be able to choose respectful ways to express it. Girls think they cannot directly express angry feelings with those who have provoked it because it is '"unladylike" and likely to destroy relationships. As a result, they can feel powerless, vulnerable and weak. Parents can have a tremendously positive impact on their daughter's emotional health by first accepting and encouraging their daughters to feel and express anger, and secondly, by modeling for their daughters constructive ways to act on those angry feelings. The article **"Coping with Anger and Impulsivity"** (p. 4:31) reviews this topic.

Learning to understand, acknowledge and act responsibly on one's emotions is an empowering act. In fact, there are researchers who conclude that our "emotional intelligence" may be even more important than our IQ for getting along in our world. Because our brains developed emotional abilities before cognitive abilities, emotions often take precedence over our thought processes. A high "emotional intelligence" depends on three factors: self-awareness (an ability to step back from emotions and analyze them), self-discipline (an ability to withstand emotional storms), and empathy (an ability to understand how another person feels). Daniel Goleman's book, *Emotional Intelligence*, is a great resource for anyone wanting to support kids in developing their full emotional potentials.

Another approach to communication is **compassionate communication** which takes feelings as a signal that an underlying need or value is not being met. Exploring these unmet needs is an amazing way to empower yourself and your child with self-awarenesss and self-empathy, as well as empathy for and connection with others. It is based on the book *Nonviolent Communication* (NVC) by Marshall Rosenberg (www.cnvc.org). By getting connected to the values/needs that are behind our reaction, we can then look underneath the "behavior storm" or "brick wall" and see what is going on in the other person. The article **"Empathetic Connections"** (p. 4:35) by Inbal Kashtan, author of *Parenting from Your Heart: Sharing the Gifts of Compassion, Connection and Choice* gives some examples and depth to the power of connecting with needs.

"Empowering Girls with Empathy" (p. 4:41) discusses a similar but different approach to empathy from ideas shared in *Building Moral Intelligence* by Michele Borba and *Taking Charge* by JoAnne Nordling.

Summing up, your daughter's emergence into womanhood will be a time of great excitement, change and turmoil. Parents who choose to rise to the challenge can learn a great deal about themselves as well as their daughters during this time. Helping our daughters to develop a positive view of their femininity will help them to find a rightful sense of personal power. Our girls deserve our love, support and help as they work to explore who they are within the cultural dictates of femininity. Let us encourage them to grow into an empowered vision of womanhood: one that supports and celebrates each of them as lovable, capable and magnificent.

---

[1] Report of the American Psychological Association Task Force of the Sexualization of Girls: Executive Summary, 2007, www.apa.org/pi/wpo/sexualization.html
[2] Dubb, A. et. al., "Characterization of sexual dimorphism in the human corpus callosum." *NeuroImage* Vol 20, Issue 1, September 2003, pp. 512-519
[3] Witelson, S.F. (1995) "Women have greater density of neurons in posterior temporal cortex." J Neurosci 15 (5, Pt.1): 3418-28
[4] Baron-Cohen, s., and Ellis, B.J. (2005). "The empathizing system: A revision of the 1994 model of the mindreading system." In *Origins of the Social Mind: Evolutionary Psychology and Child Development*, 468-92. New York: Guilford Press.

THE 40 DEVELOPMENTAL ASSETS Essential to Every Young Person's Success

The 40 Developmental Assets are research-proven building blocks that support the healthy development of our youth and help them to grow up to be caring and responsible. The following assets relate to a child's experience with her femininity and her emergence into puberty and womanhood:

- Asset #1 **Family Support:** Family life provides high levels of love and support.
- Asset #10 **Safety:** Young person feels safe at home, school and in the neighborhood.
- Asset #14 **Adult Role Models:** Parent(s) and other adults model positive, responsible behavior.
- Asset #26 **Caring:** Young person places a high value on helping other people.
- Asset #28 **Integrity:** Young person acts on convictions and stands up for her beliefs.
- Asset #29 **Honesty:** Young person tells the truth even when it is not easy.
- Asset #33 **Interpersonal Competence:** Young person has empathy, sensitivity and friendship skills.
- Asset #35 **Resistance Skills:** Young person can resist negative peer pressure and dangerous situations.
- Asset #37 **Personal Power:** Young person feels she has control over "things that happen to me."

CIRCLE QUESTION

What are some of your spoken and unspoken family rules and
feelings about what women can or can't do?

POSSIBLE DISCUSSION QUESTIONS

1. What are some things that you do for your daughter that she could learn to do by herself? How could you empower her to learn some life skills that are culturally seen as predominantly men's work?

2. What kind of relationship do you have with your daughter's other parent? What does your relationship teach your daughter about men's and women's roles in a family/in the world?

3. Do you maintain an affectionate relationship with your daughter? Was this (or will it be) difficult, once she entered puberty? How might you increase the use of respectful touch in your own household?

4. How do you feel about female sexuality and menstruation? How did you (or will you) educate your daughter about menstruation? ? How does your daughter feel about the physical changes of puberty?

5. Do you think that a ritual at first menstruation is of any value for your family? What kinds of things might you do for such a ritual?

6. How do you feel about your daughter becoming a sexual being? What might you say to her about your own values about sex and sexuality? What might you do if her values in this arena are different from yours?

7. Can you imagine being able to talk to her about safe ways to express her sexuality outside of oral sex or intercourse? Can you imagine being able to talk to her about safe sex, contraception and sexual desire?

8. How will you handle your daughter's relationships with boys if you are afraid they are or might turn sexual?

9. Does your daughter have access to medical care and to reproductive health care? If not, how might you ensure that your daughter get such care if the need arises?

10. What are your views about homosexuality? Could you accept your daughter if she felt she was a lesbian?

11. Does your daughter have relationships with adults other than her parents? With female role models or mentors? If not, how might you find a mentor for her?

12. How does your family handle anger? Does your daughter express her anger openly, or does she tend to express her anger as sadness? How might you help your daughter to express her anger respectfully?

13. How does your daughter do emotionally? How do you think your daughter is faring with regards to her "emotional intelligence"?

14. Do you think that your daughter has strong personal power? How could you enhance it?

PUTTING IT INTO PRACTICE

- Become aware of the messages you are sending your daughter about what women can and cannot do.
- Discuss media images of women you see with your daughter and what messages they may portray.
- Help your daughter to do for herself. Teach her life skills in all areas of life, including those tasks that generally are considered men's work.
- Encourage your daughter to have adult mentors and support in her life.
- Give your daughter accurate information about puberty, menstruation, sexuality and safe sex.
- Consider some kind of ritual to honor your daughter's passage into womanhood near the onset of menses. At the least, a mother can discuss with her daughter why she is glad she is a woman.

- Respectfully discuss your own values about sexuality with your daughter.
- Accept that even if your daughter has sexual values different from your own, she will be more likely to listen to, consider and honor your values if you respect her as an independent decision-maker.
- Let your daughter know what you are willing to do to help her with issues of sexuality and reproductive health. Your daughter will then know how to factor this into her own decisions about her sexuality.
- Think about how you could support your daughter if she thinks she is a lesbian.
- Encourage your daughter to develop healthy relationships, and talk to her about the basics of making and keeping friends. Discuss your own values about healthy relationships, and use media images of relationships to spark discussions on this topic.
- Encourage the respectful expression of anger in your daughter, and be a good role model for her in this regard.
- Encourage your daughter to develop an understanding of her emotional life, and to learn good coping skills in dealing with her feelings. Again, be a good role model for her in this regard.

PUTTING IT TOGETHER—YOUR VERSION

Write down three or four ideas you have been inspired to implement in your own life after reading and discussing this chapter.

1. _____

2. _____

3. _____

4. _____

FURTHER READING

Womanhood

Reviving Ophelia: Saving the Selves of Adolescent Girls by Mary Pipher

Meeting at the Crossroads: Women's Psychology and Girls' Development by Lyn Mikel Brown and Carol Gilligan, top-notch researchers talk about what girls in America give up on the way to womanhood, i.e. self-esteem

Daughters of the Moon, Sisters of the Sun: Young Women and Mentors on the Transition to Womanhood by K. Wind Hughes and Linda Wolf

Our Bodies Ourselves For The New Century by The Boston Women's Health Book Collective

Always My Child: A Parent's Guide to Understanding Your Gay, Lesbian, Bisexual, Transgendered, or Questioning Son or Daughter by Kevin Jennings and contributors Pat Shapiro and Patricia Gottlieb Shapiro

Venus in Blue Jeans: Why Mothers and Daughters Need to Talk about Sex by N. Bartle and S. Lieberman, interviews of 24 mother-daughter pairs, addresses common barriers to communication on subject of sex

Defending Ourselves by Rosalind Wiseman, a complete course in self-defense for women

Moontime Celebrations: A Guide to Discovering, Honoring the Inner Gifts of Menses by Janet Rudolph

Wild Feminine: Finding Power, Spirit & Joy in the Root of the Female Body by Tami Lynn Kent

Friendship and Peer Aggression

Best Friends Worst Enemies by Michael Thompson

Mom, They're Teasing Me: Helping Your Child Solve Social Problems by Michael Thompson

Queen Bees and Wannabes by Rosalind Wiseman
Queen Bee Moms and Kingpin Dads by Rosalind Wiseman
Girls Wars: 12 Strategies That Will End Female Bullying by Cheryl Dellasega
Odd Girl Out: The Hidden Culture of Aggression in Girls by Rachel Simmons

Reading Recommended from the Article "Girls and Desire"

A Woman's Book Of Life. The Biology, Psychology, and Spirituality of the Feminine Life Cycle by Joan Borysenko
The Body Project. An Intimate History of American Girls by Joan Jacobs Brumberg
The Red Tent by Anita Diamant
The Vagina Monologues by Eve Ensler
Cherry: A Memoir by Mary Karr
School Girls: Young Women, Self-Esteem, and the Confidence Gap by Peggy Orenstein
By the Light of My Father's Smile by Alice Walker
Promiscuities: The Secret Struggle for Womanhood by Naomi Wolf

BOOKS FOR OUR DAUGHTERS

Womanhood

Ready, Set, Grow! A What's Happening to My Body Book for Younger Girls by Lynda Madaras
The What's Happening to my Body Book for Girls: a growing up guide for parents and daughters by Lynda Madaras
My Body, My Self for Girls: A 'What's Happening to My Body?' Quizbook and Journal by Lynda & Area Madaras
My Feelings, My Self: A Growing-Up Journal for Girls by Lynda Madaras, et al
The Care and Keeping of You – The Body Book for Girls by American Girl, for tweens

Friendship and Connection

Nobody Likes Me, Everybody Hates Me: The Top 25 Friendship Problems and How to Solve Them by Michelle Borba
Respect: A Girl's Guide to Getting Respect and Dealing when Your Line is Crossed by Courtney Macavinta
My Secret Bully, Trouble Talk, Sorry, Just Kidding by Trudy Ludwig, 4 picture books

Pubertal Development in Girls

By Kathy Masarie, MD

THERE ARE FOUR MAIN events that occur during puberty:

- Sexual organs mature and additional sexual characteristics develop
- A wide range of emotional changes also take place
- A significant growth spurt and weight gain occur
- Reproduction becomes possible

The process of sexual maturation in females usually starts about 2 years before the first menstrual period. The first sign of puberty can be seen as early as age 8 or 9 and still be perfectly normal. **Signs of pubertal development before eight require an evaluation by your physician.** The beginning of puberty can vary from 9 to 16, but the sequence is usually the same. Breast development usually begins at age 11. Shortly thereafter, pubic hair appears. Hair under the arms begins to increase at age 12. Between 12 and 13, a growth spurt results in a noticeable gain in height. Girls often grow and change so fast that they feel clumsy, and may even have uncomfortable growing pains, usually in their arms and legs. When she gets her first period, a girl has reached about 95% of her adult height. She might still grow another few inches. Menstrual periods begin around 12 ½. During this time fat is distributed over the body and particularly in the hips and buttocks. The hips widen and development of the uterus, vagina and external genital organs occurs.

Many girls have a white, sticky discharge from their vaginas. This is a perfectly normal sign that puberty has begun. Sometimes, this discharge gets on a girl's underwear. She shouldn't worry about it unless her vulva becomes itchy or irritated, which may reflect an infection. Soaking is a sitz bath of water daily for a few days can help distinguish infection from simple irritation.

There is debate that "girls are maturing earlier." The controversial study, done in a pediatric office in 1997, showed that many girls developed breast tissue earlier than the accepted norm of 8. However, the same study showed that menses onset remained the same steady 12.8 that it had been for the last forty years. Many physicians debate the validity of this study, wondering if breasts were really developing early or just had excess fat in them (obesity has increased tremendously in the last few decades). So the standards remain the same for now—if you see breast development before age 8, see your health care provider.

Sequence of events at puberty	Average Age	Range
Height spurt	10.5	9.5-14.5
Enlargement of areola and budding of breast	11	8-13.5
Pubic hair	11	8-14
Development of breast, pigmentation of areola, axillary hair and uterine enlargement	13	10-16
Menarche	12.8	10-16.5
Ovulation	14	11-18

Breast Development

Breasts begin to develop 1 to 2 years before the first period, but this may not occur for as long as 2 years after menstruation. Often one breast develops faster than the other and it may take until age 18 for them to even out. In about 75% of girls, the areola (the dark area around the nipple) is elevated and in the remainder it is not. Both patterns are normal, as are inverted nipples.

Breast size no longer seems to be the ultimate sign of sex appeal, but it still causes concern. A flat-chested girl may take until 2 years after her menstruation begins to develop and it may take until age 19 or 20 to be fully developed. It is possible one 13-year-old will have very little breast development while some of her friends have completed their development. Excessively large breasts will require physical support from a good bra and these girls may need emotional support from their parents. Surgical reduction can be considered for such girls, but because this surgery usually undermines breastfeeding success, many women will want to postpone this surgery until after their childbearing years.

Menstrual Cycle

Although a girl usually gets her period between ages 10-12, it may vary from 9 to 16. Many families celebrate menarche as the time when a girl becomes a woman. Sometimes parties, gifts and congratulations celebrate a young woman's first period. Other families are more private about menarche. But whether or not menarche is celebrated in your family, it is an important moment in a girl's life.

Periods usually last from 3 to 7 days. A normal menstrual cycle can be as short as 21 days or more than 35 days. Changes from month to month are also normal. Periods may be irregular, especially during the first year. Too much exercise can use up body fat to the point that periods stop. Stress from illness, worry about school or worry about being pregnant can delay a period.

If a tampon is used for menstrual flow, it must be changed every 3-5 hours. Sometimes women who use "high absorbency" tampons all day and night during their periods become ill. This happens when bacteria that sometimes grow in the vagina grow too much. This rare illness is called toxic shock syndrome. If your daughter develops vomiting and has a high fever, diarrhea and a sunburn-type rash while using a tampon, seek medical care immediately.

The hymen is very important to some people. They believe that a girl whose hymen is stretched open has let a boy put his penis in her vagina. But that isn't always true. Some girls are born without a hymen. Others stretch open their hymens by exercising a lot or riding a bike. Tampons may stretch the hymen a little bit. But they don't usually stretch it open all the way. It may be important to use a pad if it is important not to stretch the hymen.

Some girls have cramps with their periods. They usually get less and less crampy with time. Exercise and rest can help prevent cramps. Eating well can help protect against cramps: drink plenty of water and avoid salty foods; eat green, leafy vegetables or take 500 mg of magnesium each day; and eat whole-grain cereals or take vitamin B complex—especially B6—each day. A heating pad on her back or abdomen or pain relievers like ibuprofen can help.

Some girls and women may have physical or emotional discomfort up to 2 weeks before menstruating. This is called premenstrual syndrome (PMS). It happens in fewer than half of all women between the ages of 14 and 50.

Sometimes a girl will have some spotting of blood for a day or two after ovulation (mid-cycle). She may also feel some pain in her lower abdomen. This is normal, but it is not her period.

Here are some tips for girls to know about menstruation:

- Menstruation is not a "curse" or a "punishment."
- Menstruation has nothing to do with "bad blood."
- Losing normal menstrual blood doesn't make you weak.
- Menstruation doesn't need to put you in a bad mood.
- Menstruation doesn't mean being "sick" or "unclean."
- Women can enjoy sex while they have their periods.
- It is possible to become pregnant before your first period.
- It is possible to become pregnant when you are bleeding. It could be spotting after ovulation instead of your period.
- You don't need to stay in bed on the first day of your period.
- Cold drinks, showers, or baths do not cause menstrual cramps.
- Having your period is a sign that your body is healthy and working the way it should.

Masturbation

Children touch their sex organs for pleasure from the time they are babies. The clitoris is designed to give women and girls great pleasure when touched. (The penis, especially the tip of the penis, gives men and boys great pleasure when touched.) Touching our sex organs for pleasure, is a normal, healthy part of life. However, some people choose not to masturbate. And some people are ashamed to admit that they do. Masturbation is not harmful in any way. It is a healthier outlet for sexual arousal than having sexual intercourse or oral sex before a girl is ready.

Relationships

The emotional changes of puberty appear to parallel physical changes. In their early teen years, girls compare their secondary sexual changes, like breast growth and pubic hair, with those of other girls. These body changes become a major preoccupation.

Attaining independence from parents is a necessary and central task of adolescence. As girls decrease their dependence on their parents, they increase their dependence on others. For some, these "others" are exclusively their peers. What is best is if they have other adults to turn to for this new support they need: youth leaders, teachers, counselors, neighbors, etc. Initially girls hang out with other girls. Eventually they start dealing with the struggle of relating with boys. Dealing with feelings of sexual drive, attaining some social sophistication, and relating to members of one's own peer group about sexual matters all become areas of concern for the teenager. Some emotionally immature girls enter into intense relationships to feel good, to appear mature and even to "feel loved." The onset of mature heterosexual relationships usually does not come about until the end of adolescence or even later. For this to happen, a girl needs to become somewhat autonomous and develop caring feelings for another.

Parents must support their daughter's progress towards independence. However, if a child feels she is being pushed too fast by what she sees in the media and by what her peers say they are doing, she might feel anxiety, loneliness and abandonment. A girl may protect herself against these feelings by not actually achieving the necessary skills of independence. If she acts impulsively and pushes boundaries too far, it may force intensive parental involvement and a crackdown on rules to reel her back in. Another way a girl might manifest problems with separation is in the way she handles going off to college or breaking up with a boyfriend. She might panic or get depressed. Feelings of abandonment can feel urgent and acute and may be dealt with in a self-destructive fashion.

Summary of Emotional Changes in Girls During Puberty

- Experience moodiness: changes in their estrogen levels can cause mood swings (for males, changes in their testosterone levels can cause mood swings)
- Are concerned about how their bodies look, how other people look and how they compare to self, and what other people think in general
- Feel awkward or embarrassed, especially in times of change
- Feel sexual attraction and arousal very easily
- Experience sexual curiosity and are attracted to other people (for example, crushes and idol worship)
- Usually become more emotional and react to situations more intensely than before
- Typically try to gain more independence from parents.

Surviving Puberty: A Handout for Your Daughter

Puberty can be challenging if you are not prepared for what is happening to your body and either don't have someone you can reliably turn to for advice or are uncomfortable talking about it. Here are some guidelines to help:

1. Look for the information to understand what is happening to your body.
   - Ask questions of people you trust
   - Check out the web:
       www.teenwire.org; www.iwannaknow.org/puberty/girls.html; www.frombirthtopuberty.com
   - Look up information in books such as
     a. *Ready, Set, Grow! A What's Happening to My Body Book for Younger Girls* by Lynda Madaras
     b. *The Care and Keeping of You—The Body Book for Girls* published by American Girl (for tweens)
     c. *The What's Happening to My Body Book for Girls* by Lynda Madaras
     d. *My Body, My Self for Girls: A 'What's Happening to My Body?'* Quizbook and Journal by Lynda Madaras.
   - Call your local Planned Parenthood health center at 1-800-230-PLAN. They can provide you with information, too.

2. Respect your body. What are you going to do about alcohol, drugs, cigarettes, and other addictive stuff?
   - Smoking, using drugs and drinking alcohol are actions that do not respect your body.
   - If you love junk food, eat it infrequently and in moderation. Two slices of pizza with a side salad is healthier than four pieces of pizza.
   - If you must lose weight, do it sensibly. Eat several reasonably-sized meals a day. Studies show that people who skip breakfast end up eating more overall than those who don't.
   - Exercise 3-4 times a week. Walking is great and easy.

3. Accept the changes you see in your body. Try not to compare yourself with others. Know that everyone goes through puberty at his or her own rate.

4. If you are feeling down or confused about something, talk to somebody. Don't suffer in silence.

5. Your parents can give you a lot of support and information if you give them a chance. They are more interested in your well-being than anyone.

6. **Wait to have sex until you are ready. Don't be pushed into it.**
   - Sometimes, it seems that having sexual intercourse is more important than anything else. It isn't.
   - Sometimes, it seems that having sexual intercourse will solve all our problems. It won't.
   - Sometimes, people have sexual intercourse before they're ready and when they don't really want to. It's not worth it.
   - We have to remind ourselves of the risks, no matter what people say, no matter how "turned on" we are. An accidental pregnancy can change everything. Getting a serious sexually transmitted infection can damage our health for the rest of our lives.
   - Before things get really sexy, or you feel pressured, take time to think about your dreams and plans for the future. Think about what they mean to you. Then ask yourself and your partner if you are ready. If not, then cool down.
   - Sex can be exciting, satisfying, caring and rewarding—especially when you plan ahead and wait until you're ready for it. If you know what you're doing, and if you stay in charge, you can feel empowered.

Moontime Celebrations

By Janet Rudolph

HOW IS IT THAT GIRLS get such a thorough yet unconscious message that their bodies are flawed? I still remember with horror the day my exquisite, rail-thin 11-year-old first announced that she needed to diet.

There are messages everywhere that our female bodies just aren't up to perfection. Girls constantly hear women complaining about the shape and size of our hips, bellies, thighs, and even feet. In magazines and on TV, our daughters are exposed to impossibly beautiful supermodels discussing beauty secrets for covering up their supposed flaws. (If they're so flawed, what chance is there for us?)

My generation accepted that our female bodies are inadequate; that only diet, grueling exercise, makeup, and popular clothing will make us beautiful. Yet, what I accepted for myself became intolerably painful when I saw my own daughter develop these same attitudes.

Like many women, I began to wonder if things have to be this way. Perhaps long ago, we women did feel blessed by our physical bodies. Perhaps once upon a time we did not have to mutilate our feet (read: struggle with our bodies) to fit into the slipper (read: to belong to a culture) that would then confer queenship and a life lived happily ever after.

I wanted different messages for my daughter. I wanted her to learn to question the world around her. I wanted her to feel a pride and joy in her body—not only as a sexual gift, but as the source of her communicating and communing with the outer world. I wanted to teach her to howl at the moon, fly in the wind, sing with birds, dance among trees, and not feel ashamed, corny, or ugly. To this purpose, I looked to build a bridge between these possibilities and my daughter's world, so filled with intense pressures to conform and to be popular.

My foundation to this bridge became the blueprint of a ritual-celebration to honor my daughter's menarche, or mooncycle, as we now call it in our household. While girls look forward to this initiation into womanhood, there so often appears to be an underlying sense of shame. And why not? Ambivalence about our bodies pervades

our culture—from the Bible's calling menstruation "unclean" to modern industry pushing "sanitary" products in advertisements featuring a standard of beauty few can attain. I want my daughters to see their moontimes as a beautiful blessing, not as society's curse. (Interestingly enough, the word "blessing" is from the Old English word *bloedsen*, meaning blood.)

As I made my ritual plans, there was an unexpected boon—my daughter's anticipation. She knew I was planning something unusual and couldn't wait to learn what. Changes she anticipated with apprehension became infused with a sense of mystery and specialness.

My basic plan was simple. As Snow White received gifts of special virtues at her birth, I wanted to present special traits to my daughter as she was born into womanhood. The use of symbols offered a unique opportunity to do this. Symbols lie at the heart of religious tradition because they speak to us on many levels. They speak to the rational mind through verbal discussion and then penetrate hearts and souls through the unconscious. I searched my own traditions and my own heart to think about what I hold to be important. When I searched for a way to reveal my findings, it all came together. I would give my daughter gifts representing my chosen symbols in the tangible form of jewelry and objects d'art. How better to capture an adolescent's imagination!

In preparation for the ritual, I went on nature hikes and shopping trips, letting the spirit guide me to find affordable items that touched my heart. I chose gifts that were outward expressions of the inner gifts I wished to present to her.

When her menarche arrived, I set a small table in my daughter's room with a red rose, three bowls, and a cauldron/basket filled with my treasures. The bowls contained water, soil, and air.

We began by debunking negative views of women's bodies, everything from the need for "sanitary" products, as if our bodies were unclean, to anorexic fashion models. We took these negative feelings and symbolically threw them out the window to indicate our rejection of their message. I then offered her the rose to honor the fact that she had blossomed into womanhood.

Next came my first three gifts: air, soil, and water. These, I explained, are parts of the Earth's body, always to be treated with reverence and respect. Without them, life on Earth, including our own lives, would not exist. In ancient civilizations, the Earth was considered the living body of the Goddess. With or without the image of the Goddess, however, the Earth is the sacred foundation of our lives. Therefore, the Earth and her gifts are to be honored.

We touched each bowl and expressed our thanks. I then presented her with the special gifts I had gathered:

1. **A palm-sized pewter dragon.** This, I told my daughter, will remind you of your inner power. The dragon was an emblem of the ancient Goddess when she showed her inner strength. In an age when women are at risk for abuse, no one will victimize this face of a woman. She has the ability to throw fire where it is appropriate, such as when she needs to protect herself or great wrong is being done. This gift of dragon energy, I told my daughter, I give to you.

2. **A figure sitting in meditation.** This aspect of ourselves looks inward and understands that outward achievement is not the totality of life. It understands that the moontime has strong creative potential when inner dreams and thoughts are especially potent. Listen well, for moontime dreams are a guide to inner wisdom and self-knowledge. This gift, I told my daughter, I give to you.

3. **A pendant of the moon.** Like the cycles of life, I told her, the moon has a time to be full and a time to be dark. You, too, will find times when you are in the full bloom of creativity and those when you feel lost in the darkness. Both aspects of life contain treasures. By facing the dark directly, it can be transformed into a fertile foundation for new ideas and directions. This deep knowledge of the existence of treasures in all stages of the life cycles is a gift, I told my daughter, I give to you.

4. **Native American turquoise bear earrings.** The mother bear is powerful and strong, yet nurturing and loving to her offspring. The bear represents the power to overcome obstacles while maintaining the capability of love. The bear also represents the power to heal. These are gifts, I told my daughter, I give to you.

5. **Conch shell.** All life began in water, creating a deep connection within us. Listening carefully, we can feel the ebbing and flowing in our veins. The water beckons to us as the wellsprings of our birth and the substance of cleansing. It teaches us to "go with the flow" in good times and bad. These gifts, I told my daughter, I give to you.

6. **Driftwood.** All trees are descended from the Tree of Life (also known as the Tree of Knowledge) which in ancient lore grew from the center, the navel, of the Earth. From the roots that extend deep into the ground to the leaves that reach toward the sky and the enduring trunk that links them, the world tree connects the depths of the soil, Earth, and sky. The vital connections between the elements were once considered sacred knowledge. Being able to hear and appreciate nature's rhythms is a gift, I told my daughter, I give to you.

I closed the ritual: Your body knows ancient wisdom. Your river of blood connects you to all women past and future, your ancestors and descendents. It connects you to the creative life energy of the universe. Listen to your body and your dreams especially during moontimes. Slow down to hear. Not because the blood limits you. It does not. With the open pathways, you can gain new knowledge and develop old wisdom. It is a powerful time.

Whether you choose to have children or not, this is your body's great gift. Wear it proudly with honor.

A year has passed since my daughter and I shared this ritual, and I have already seen its power. It allowed us a rare and special space to grow closer because we opened avenues of communication surrounding this very important shared aspect of our lives. Menstruation was once a communal activity for women, and it is becoming so once again in our home.

She is growing into a strong, self-assured person, unafraid to follow her own paths in life. I am still looking forward to the time when she will be able to dance in the wind and howl at the moon. The seeds I planted at this ritual promise to blossom for many years to come.

Menstruation celebration can be personalized and changed according to each mother's and daughter's personalities and needs. It is one part of an evolving process to teach our children to honor their own bodies, those of other people, and the body of the earth.

Janet Rudolph is a social worker who does moontime work-shops and wrote Moontime Celebrations: A Guide to Discovering, Honoring the Inner Gifts of Menses *($8.95, Jancin Production, PO Box 568, Woodmere, NY 11598)*

Girls and Desire:

Sexuality Is an Awkward Yet Important Topic for Parents to Address

By Christine Schoefer

DESIRE IS TRICKY. Like fire, it is a volatile source of energy. It warms the heart and body and accomplishes all kinds of transformations when it's used wisely. But out of control, it destroys. Sexual desire, of course, is the most tricky desire of all, especially when it comes to girls.

We want girls to aim high, to be inspired by vision and fueled by desire. But when it comes to their sexual longing, we may feel less certain because our culture has enmeshed us in a paralyzing web of ignorance, shame, and fear. Yet this is an important topic for us to address. Our well-considered affirmation of a girl's blossoming sexual desire helps her to be at home in her body, and this makes her strong. Squelching or penalizing this natural desire will undermine her self-confidence and could diminish her ability to come forward in other areas of her life.

Navigating the tricky terrain of a girl's sexual desire may well be one of the greatest parental challenges. Most of us lack confidence in this area because our own conceptions and experiences are fraught with emotional distress. To make matters even more difficult, we have to work against virtually all of the media-driven images that girls encounter.

Adolescence is a time of longing: wanting to be part of the world, to make a difference, to be noticed. Instead of presenting role models that would feed this yearning, popular culture reduces it to sexual desire. Not only does this simplify the complexity of adolescence, it puts girls at a great disadvantage.

As we well know, sexual desire has historically been a male prerogative. Boys want, girls are wanted; boys demand, girls can either "put out" or hold out. Everyone expects girls to be in charge, not only of restricting their own desire, but of curbing boys' desire. But paradoxically, popular culture begins to sexualize girls even before puberty, urging them to stir boys' fantasies by wearing revealing clothes and provocative makeup. At the same time, colloquial references to girls' desire are inevitably derogatory. To say that a girl "wants it" is to judge her a slut, designate her as prey, and to invite and excuse lewd, invasive male conduct.

> To say that a girl "wants it" is to judge her a slut, designate her as prey, and to invite and excuse lewd, invasive male conduct.

Since any expression of sexual desire is likely to be misinterpreted as invitation, girls learn to transform their wanting into a passive stance of being desired. They begin evaluating themselves through a boy's eyes. Chances are their slinky mini-dresses and bare midriffs are not to express their own sexual yearning but rather their longing to be desired. Girls' role as sexual censors allows boys to extend their wanting in every direction. Imagine how it could be different: girls explore and assert their desire, knowing that boys will apply the brakes. Think of the energy this would free up for girls.

For girls, biology gets muddled with emotions. We all remember the breathlessness, the tingling bodies, and racing hearts that accompany puberty. Whereas boys are encouraged to seek a physical outlet for this, girls are told it is love. So when they want to kiss a boy, they embellish this straightforward physical urge with the complicated feelings of romantic love. This illusion emotionally ties girls to boys, encouraging them to give up their power and independence (Does he like me? Will he call me?).

Sex education classes reinforce our culture's disregard for girls' desire. Last fall, the *New York Times* reported that teachers and parents favor more detailed sex education. But neither pleasure nor desire made the list of topics they deemed most important. Yet talking about desire, urges, feelings, and girl-identified sexual awakening is important for both girls and boys. It would support our protective efforts and lay the groundwork for cultural transformation.

Girls need their mothers' guidance—I speak of mothers because I feel that this is women's territory. I don't see how fathers can do much more than stand by, appreciate and support their daughters, and continue to be as affectionate as possible with them. First of all, we need to protect them from the pernicious messages of popular culture, which leaves no room for awakening desire and tentative sexuality.

We see how vulnerable girls are to these messages. We know that the teen years are prime time for high drama, poses, and roles that alternately hide and express the authentic self. When our pubescent daughters go from gyrating their hips to hugging their teddy bears, we understand that this is the child playing hide-and-seek with the emerging adult.

Because we see that it's a long way from the first sexual stirrings to actual sexual activity, we are eager to protect the full range of girls' expression. If we joined forces with popular culture in interpreting every thrust or strut as an over-sexualized signal, we would surely curtail our daughters' ability to track and understand urges and feelings.

We can support girls as they struggle to fit in, to encourage them to channel their longing in many different directions. But at the same time, we need to support their sexual awakening. Feeling desire is an essential component of self-knowledge and a prerequisite for establishing boundaries. If a girl doesn't know what her "yes" could mean, how could her "no" come from the heart? But if it's true that we empower a girl by supporting her sexuality, why is this so difficult for mothers?

I believe we remain uneasy with girls' sexual desire for three reasons: one, because we know the world really is full of male predators; two, because we were also shaped by our culture's messages; and three, because our daughter's sexual awakening signals her inevitable separation from us.

We worry about teenage pregnancy, sexually transmitted diseases, and sexual violence. We understand that as long as teen culture promotes male-identified sexuality and portrays girls as objects of male lust, girls' bodies remain vulnerable.

Because we ourselves have experienced male predators, we worry about the safety of our daughters—who are often oblivious to the signals they're sending out. We recognize the subtext of their glossy cadmium-shaded lips, bare midriffs, and provocative dance moves. We see men take note when our girls walk down the street.

Though we have good reason to be protective, we must remember that our safeguarding could easily entrench the role that our culture assigns to girls: putting on the brakes. Help your daughter become aware of her body, gestures, and clothes. Whatever you do, don't stigmatize her for her identity-search efforts and don't frighten her into submission by carelessly conjuring the specter of sexual violence. That hobbles her efforts at self-assertion.

Our worry about the possible negative ramifications of girls arousing male desire is legitimate. But since our pubescent daughters' emerging sexuality probably also brings up our own issues with sexuality, we should be sure we're not hiding our discomfort behind talk of predators and dangers.

Our girls' pubescent transformation is a wonderful —if painful—opportunity to revisit our own adolescence. Girls' sexual desire, which awakens them to the world, is a wake-up call for us as well. It presents us with an opportunity to investigate the splendid, muddled terrain of our own sexuality and desire. Watching them will remind us of the losses, constraints, and violations we have suffered or are still suffering.

What messages were we given about masturbation, kissing, petting? Chances are our sex education was a mixture of detached anatomical instruction, girl talk, and street smarts. We learned to dichotomize behavior in terms of virgins and whores, abstinence or intercourse, and found ourselves guided by convention and ruled by fear. Did anyone tell us we had the right to pleasure? Or instruct us that sensual and sexual pleasure is as personal as fingerprints?

Begin by investigating your own attitude toward desire—what part does it play in your life, how does it ignite your vitality and feed your self-expression? Help your daughter develop a language of desire by telling stories about yourself, friends, or even fictional women. Tell her about your regrets, triumphs, pleasures, and discomforts.

But as much as possible, link sexuality with women's pleasure. We know that sexual desire can be fanciful, quirky, and varied, and that the intercourse/homerun equation is a sad reduction of possibility. But how would a girl who watches Hollywood movies know that unless we tell her? If you find this subject uncomfortable, enlist the help of a friend or relative.

Our daughters' sexual awakening may bring up sadness and ambivalence because it announces the inevitable separation that lies just around the bend. But supporting her pleasure and sexuality in adolescence will actually strengthen the mother-daughter bond, whereas denying it will promote separation.

The film *Tumbleweeds* has a poignant scene in which the mother grabs an apple from a bowl and uses it to teach her daughter how to kiss a boy. With that simple act, the mother acknowledges her daughter's desire, offers guidance, and nourishes the mother-daughter bond. Isn't that what we're all striving for?

Christina Schoefer is a freelance writer for Salon, UtneReader, The Nation, Mothering and many other national publications. She lives in Berkeley with her family and daughters.

Reprinted with permission from *New Moon® Network: For Adults Who Care About Girls;* Jan/Feb 2001. Copyright New Moon® Publishing, Duluth, MN; www.newmoon.org

Body
Head
Heart } *all ready*

How I Dealt With My Teenager's Sexuality

By Jody Bellant Scheer, MD

PARENTING IS FULL OF surprises and awakenings. Just as kids grow and change, parents must grow and change to keep up. Providing our kids with the experiences and knowledge they need to succeed in contemporary culture is a challenge parents must constantly face. Teenage sexuality is probably one of the most emotional challenges a parent will face in trying to balance one's own values, wishes and desires with those of our kids and with the realities of the world. Our kids live in a sexualized culture, unprecedented in any previous era. The media and teenage peer culture encourage ever-younger kids to experiment with sexual intercourse without stable relationships, marriage, contraception, safe sex or even emotional attachments. Rates of pregnancy and sexually transmitted diseases, including AIDS, occur in our culture's teenagers at rates far above those of any other developed country in the world. Faced with my own three teenagers' developing sexuality, I turned to my medical training background and experience with positive parenting. Now that they are young adults, they admit they're thankful for how I approached this subject, even though it did make them uncomfortable many times.

My approach to sexuality differed little from any other aspect of my parenting, other than it made me a lot more uncomfortable! However, I was committed to talking about sexuality and all of its ramifications, so I made it a priority to start talking about sex with my kids from the time they were little. As they approached puberty, I often brought up such discussions as we watched movies or TV shows together, where sexual behaviors were shown or hinted at. I made sure to provide my kids with accurate information about their bodies, puberty and sexual function, and I shared my values and opinions with them. Since I deal with the ramifications of unprotected and unsafe sex daily in my job, I shared stories from my work as well.

Finally, though, each of my kids started a dating life and each one of them, at some point in high school, developed a steady relationship. How different it was for me when it came time to deal with a potential sexual relationship, rather than a hypothetical one, and I needed all the positive parenting skills I could muster. Though this approach was diametrically opposed to the way I was raised, I was convinced that making my children's sexuality their own business AND responsibility was the best way to ensure that they would make sensible and healthy decisions.

My strategy was simple. First, I shared my own values, which included the opinion that intercourse is an adult behavior that carries with it a host of benefits, risks and responsibilities. I acknowledged the pleasures of sexual relationships. I also outlined what I considered the minimum of sexual responsbility: some sort of committed relationship, sharing of important sexual history (such as sexually transmitted diseases), testing for HIV, use of contraceptives, making plans in the event of an unplanned pregnancy, and being responsible about getting and paying for adequate medical and reproductive healthcare. People who were not responsible, or who couldn't talk with their partners about these details, were not ready for sex.

Secondly, I reiterated that I respected that my kids would and could make their own decisions about sex. I conceded that, although I didn't think they were ready at the time, they might feel otherwise. I noted that while I respected their ability to choose to become sexually active, I did not exempt them from being responsible about their sexuality. I talked about the many ways to be sexual without incurring the risks of intercourse. I also reminded my kids that the results of their sexual activities affected their lives way more than mine. I asked them to think wisely before acting.

Lastly, I explained that while adults can make independent decisions, and their sexual activity was none of my business, it really was my business to know about any sexually active kids who lived under my roof and who depended on me for their economic, emotional and bodily welfare. Part of becoming an adult is being accountable for one's actions. I did ask my kids to confide in me if they were thinking a relationship might be turning sexual. (Contrary to our society's puritanical myths, I believe that most couples KNOW when they are in a relationship on the verge of sexual intercourse.) I wanted to know that they had carefully considered this step and had been responsible in planning for it.

This approach has worked very well. It even scared off a suitor or two, when I included them in our "family discussions." Responsibility and respect around sexual behaviors must be taught, and the lessons are best learned at home in communication with parents. The payoff of this approach for me is my three healthy young adult children, who, to the best of my knowledge, have been responsible, safe and respectful in their significant relationships.

If She Thinks She Is a Lesbian

By Lynn E. Ponton, MD

In the quiet of my office, Noelle whispered, "I'm not here for the reason my parents said. I'm seriously turned on by my best friend." Listening closely, I heard the story of a 15-year-old girl who was sexually attracted to her friend. Nothing physical had happened between them, but Noelle's fantasies frightened her. "Does this mean I'm going to be gay?" she asked. I told her the truth —that I don't know, that no one could know whether she would be a lesbian as an adult. It's a complicated question.

First Reactions

If your daughter suspects she is gay, she may tell a counselor first, as Noelle did, or a friend or her diary. But sooner or later, she will tell you. As her parent, your reaction may be disbelief or anger. You may realize that you had sensed this already, or you may be totally unprepared. In either case, you will likely be overwhelmed by feelings of grief and guilt. When a girl reveals that she is or might be lesbian, most parents react by wondering if they could have caused her sexual orientation or have done something to prevent it. The answer to both questions is no. We don't cause our daughters' sexual orientation, nor can we change it.

Approximately 40% of our daughters experience sexual feelings toward another girl at least once during their adolescent or teen years. But this doesn't mean they will be lesbians. Research indicates that a girl's sexual orientation is established during early childhood, and that genetics almost certainly plays a role. Lesbian girls usually have an awareness of being different early in childhood. They feel they don't fit in, but they don't know why. At about 14, they first identify this difference as being lesbian or bisexual. Even then, a girl's sexual orientation isn't necessarily set. For many women, orientation changes over the course of a lifetime, sometimes more than once. Noelle's feelings for her friend at 15 were no guarantee that she would still have sexual feelings for girls at 18 or 21.

If your daughter has told you she is lesbian, your feelings of loss are natural. She may not have the kind of adulthood you planned for her. Whatever your beliefs about homosexuality, this is not likely to be an easy time for you.

> **Nearly 40% of our daughters experience sexual feelings for another girl at least once during adolescence.**

Accepting and Learning

After Noelle talked with me, she found courage to talk with her parents. Her mother was deeply worried about the problems Noelle might face, but she let herself listen as her daughter talked. Noelle's father had more difficulty with her revelation. He believed homosexuality was immoral, and he disapproved of the life he foresaw for her. Later, when Noelle became more certain of her orientation, he joined a support group for the parents of gay children. He was never able to talk directly with her about her orientation. For him, learning more and withholding judgment were the best he could do. This showed Noelle that in his own way, he loved her. If a girl you love identifies herself as lesbian or bisexual, these ideas may help:

Treat her feelings seriously. Listen to her admission with respect. Don't dismiss her with "This is just a phase," which amounts to a rejection of who she knows herself to be at this point in her life.

Talk about your fears for her. Many people in our society fear and hate homosexuality. Bisexual and lesbian girls are often targets of verbal and physical abuse. Lesbian girls have higher rates of depression, anxiety, smoking, and alcohol and drug abuse than other girls. Let your daughter know you're aware of these risks, and emphasize how much you care about her safety.

Find support for both of you. Don't hesitate to talk with a support group or therapist. This can help you cope with your feelings. Above all, remember that your daughter needs your acceptance. You don't have to agree with everything she tells you, but she depends on you to acknowledge what is true for her.

Resources:
- *The Sex Lives of Teenagers: Revealing the Secret World of Adolescent Boys and Girls* by Lynn Ponton (Dutton, 2000). Insight into the complicated lives of our daughters and our sons.

What's Happening from a Developmental Perspective

By Kathy Keller Jones, MA

IN THEIR FIVE-YEAR study of 100 girls, Brown and Gilligan in *Meeting at the Crossroads: Women's Psychology and Girls' Development,* attempted to find an explanation for the loss of self-esteem that occur in girls' adolescence. This study documented that adolescence is a time of increased psychological risk for girls. Girls' resilience and vitality can suffer, and the occurrence of anxiety and depression increases.[1] Both the Brown and Gilligan study and Brizendine's book on *The Female Brain* emphasize the importance of responsive relationships in women's development. Yet in adolescence, girls often feel that they have to give up both their voices and their authentic relationships. This disconnection from self and others leaves them psychologically vulnerable.

Brown and Gilligan found that 9- to 11-year-old girls had voices that showed clear evidence of strength, courage, and a healthy ability to stand up for themselves. They speak freely of feeling angry, and open conflict in relationships, and tend to expect differences and disagreement to be a normal part of daily life. However, during adolescence, girls tend to silence themselves or are silenced in relationships, rather than risk open conflict that might lead to isolation or to violence. In this struggle, they begin to lose connection with themselves as they lose the battle to hold on to what they know to be true. This struggle affects their feelings about themselves, their relationships, their ability to take themselves seriously, and their ability to act in the world. Girls begin moving from real to idealized relationships.[2]

Real relationships are critical for girls' strength and development, as well as for bringing women's voices fully into the world. The women who participated in Brown and Gilligan's study began to see how their behavior was serving as a model for the girls. They saw that, like the girls, they had silenced themselves; they didn't publicly disagree with policy, with each other, with men, with the Administrator or even the lunch menu.

"It was first with a sense of shock and then a deep, knowing sadness that we listened to the voices of the girls tell us that it was the adult women in their lives that provided the models

for silencing themselves and behaving like 'good little girls.' We wept."[3]

What can we do with what we have learned? The first thing is to examine our own voices and relationships to see what we are modeling. Then we need to support and keep in relationship to our girls and their friends at all stages. Bingham and Stryker in *Things Will be Different for My Daughter: A Practical Guide to Building her Self-Esteem and Self–Reliance,* suggest that girls go through 5 stages of self-esteem:

1. Birth to 8: Developing the hardy personality,
2. 9 to 12: Forming an identity as an achiever,
3. 13 to 16: Skill building—friendships, liking herself, assertiveness,
4. 17 to 22: Developing strategies for emotional and financial self-sufficiency,
5. Adulthood: Finding satisfaction in work and love.[4]

While helping our daughters to build skills, we can allow disagreement and rambunctiousness, encourage our girls to question and argue and risk conflict, and honor their voices by listening with an open heart to all they are experiencing. Ideally they will learn that the reward of risking honesty and engaging conflict is real relationships.

---

[1] Brizendine, L,. *The Female Brain,* p. 53.
[2] Brown, L. and Gilligan, C., *Meeting at the Crossroads,* p. 39.
[3] Brown, L. and Gilligan, C., *Meeting at the Crossroads,* p. 221.
[4] Bingham, M. and Stryker, S., *Things will be Different for My Daughter,* p. 100.

The Nature of Girls' Friendships

"Female friendship is most of all about sharing who we are . . .
It doesn't matter to me what I do with my friend, as long as I am with her."

—Janet F. Quinn, Nurse, Professor, Researcher

- Girls are relationship-oriented, concerned more than boys with their standing among friends.
- Girls tend to socialize in pairs which exist within larger cliques.
- Girls have "face-to-face" relationships, where they center their play around talking and socializing within a small circle of friends.
- Friendships solidify via shared confidences and feelings.
- Girls need constant reassurance from one another that they look good and fit in.
- Girls are swayed by their friends more easily than boys are.[1]
- The top three popularity traits[2] in girls are: 1) looks; 2) clothes; and 3) charisma.

The Nature of Boys' Friendships

"Start with action and energy, throw in loyalty, laughter, and 'doing together.' Add covert verbal expressions
of caring, earnestness and hidden physical touching—and you get a good friend."

— Author William Pollack, PhD, *Real Boys*

- Boys play and socialize in packs or tribes.
- Boys typically have "side-by-side" relationships, using action-oriented behavior to express their connection to other boys.
- Boys engage in active competitive games, with set rules and procedures to enhance camaraderie.
- Boys use nonverbal bonding and affectionate insults.
- Pecking order is important.
- Humor is used to gain popularity.
- The top three popularity traits[2] in boys are: 1) sports; 2) stature; and 3) humor.

[1] Interview with Dianne Hales on peer pressure, *Daughters*, Vol. 6, No. 5, July 2001.
[2] Michael Thompson found one study that showed the top three traits of popular 4th grade boys and girls. Those traits are listed in the nature of boys' and girls' friendships above.

Supporting Healthy Friendships

Kathy Keller Jones, MA

As PARENTS, IT IS normal to be invested in our children's friendships. We all want our kids to be well-liked. Some of us even venture into wanting our kids to be popular. One thing that is very true for our children is that every one of them is unique. What attracts them to one kid and not another is sometimes a mystery.

Suggestions:
- **Your kids will choose their own friends.**
- **If you don't like a friend or friends they choose, find ways to spend time with those kid(s).** You may start to see what your child sees and actually like them. You may have a good influence on them and be a person they turn to. You can encourage them to play at your house.
- **If you are worried about the negative influence of a friend, do the same as above and really strive to keep communication open with your child.** Under some circumtances with younger children, you may restrict play to your house and school.
- **When your child has a fight with a friend, listen attentively and with caring and empower your child to solve his/her problem.** Focus on support rather than rescue. You are your child's consultant and they need to feel free to come to you when they are feeling overwhelmed by any size problem.
- **If your child and a friend get in trouble, make sure you are calm and have remembered that mistakes are great learning opportunities before you help with processing the situation.** Be empathetic about the fact that they have a problem and support them in making amends and experiencing logical consequences.
- **There is no right number of friends. Some kids will have one or two and others will have more than they can handle.**
- **When your child says, "no one will play with me," listen very carefully and allow space for the story to unravel. Often kids exaggerate from one kid who wouldn't play with them that one day to "I don't have any friends." Remind them that every day is a new day.**

Prevention Strategies
- Teach your child to be friendly and fair to everyone and to use the Golden Rule.
- If your child has trouble making friends, expose them to new and different environments. You may find a child who doesn't do well in a crowded school does extremely well in scouts or a youth group.
- Don't force your child to play with your friend's children. It helps if your families spend time together when your children are young so they grow up like cousins, or if you allow the children to bring along other friends who are inclusive.
- Clothing styles are very important to help a child feel comfortable and "fit in." Let them choose the style.
- Stock your place with good food and provide space and acceptance so your kid will hang out with his friends at your house. This is a great investment of energy in the long run.
- Watch your baggage. You may hang onto friends forever, but your child may move on to new ones frequently. Accept his/her style.
- If a parent has a chemical dependency problem, it can make it very difficult for your child to have friends over. The environment can be embarrassing and unpredictable. Get help.
- As they get older, kids need to learn how to be friendly with a peer who tends to get them in trouble. They need to know under what circumstances they can trust that friend and have a good, safe time.
- Clear behavioral expectations are important for all of our children, but especially our sons. Communicate how you expect them to behave at home and wherever they go.
- When your child needs help with social skills, role-playing, rehearsing and direct teaching can be very important, especially in today's times when they are exposed to so much negative modeling.

For more information see the texts listed below.

Resources:
The Friendship Factor by Kenneth Rubin
Best Friends, Worst Enemies by M. Thompson, et. al.
Positive Discipline from A to Z by Jane Nelsen

Relationships with Family, Friends, Self, and Others

By Barbara A. Lewis, author of *What Do You Stand For? A Kid's Guide to Building Character*

"Personal relations are the most important thing forever and ever." —E. M. Forster

You may have heard or read about the three-year-old boy who fell into a gorilla exhibit at the Brookfield Zoo in Illinois in 1996. Binti Jua, an eight-year-old female gorilla who was carrying her own baby, Koola, on her back, hurried over to the unconscious boy, who had climbed a railing and fallen 18 feet. Binti gently picked him up, cradled him in her arms, and held him. Then she carried him over to the door where the zookeepers could reach him, and carefully placed him on the floor. She continued to protect him from the advances of the other gorillas until help came.

Onlookers were astounded at the seemingly understanding and sensitive behavior of the mother gorilla toward the human boy. Some animal behavior specialists think that Binti might have acted differently if the boy had been running around in a threatening way, because gorillas, while not normally aggressive, will act to defend their territory and their babies. Nevertheless, Binti's behavior sparked a lot of discussion across the country.

It's difficult to know why Binti behaved the way she did, because she can't tell anyone how she felt at the time. Is it possible that Binti protected the boy because she had her own baby and had experienced the mothering instinct? What do you think?

You first learned about loving and caring in your relationship with your parents and family. When you are loved and nurtured, you can love and nurture in return. Babies who aren't loved and nurtured don't grow as well, and sometimes they die. If they live to be adults, they often have a difficult time developing relationships with other people.

You probably received tender loving care from your parents, and you're all set. But what if you didn't? What if your relationships with family members weren't as nurturing as you might have hoped or wanted them to be? Here's good news: You can *learn* to develop good relationships with your family, friends, yourself, and

other. Following are some tips and suggestions you can try:

12 Ways to Start and Strengthen Relationships[1]

1. **Be a person of good character.** When you're positive, honest, loyal, and respectful, other people are naturally drawn to you. They recognize you as someone worth getting to know.

2. **Be kind and caring.** Notice and reach out to other people, especially when they're hurting. *Example:* Your friend is caught cheating on a test and he's embarrassed and ashamed. You might write a note telling him something you admire about him. By doing this, you're not condoning the cheating. Instead, you're letting him know that you still see his good qualities.

"The greatest healing therapy is friendship and love."
—Hubert Humphrey

[1] Sometimes people who haven't been loved and cared for need professional help learning how to love and care for others. If you think you might need professional help, talk to an adult you trust—a teacher, school counselor, religious leader, family member, or a friend.

3. **True love is unconditional.** You love your friend even when she makes poor choices. You love your little brother in spite of the fact that he constantly raids your hidden cache of candy. IMPORTANT: Unconditional love doesn't mean that you sacrifice your beliefs or values for another person. You can stay true to yourself and be a true friend.

"If we would build on a sure foundation in friendship, we must love our friends for their sake rather than for our own." —Charlotte Brontë

4. **Be a good listener.** Show that you're interested in other people and their lives. Ask questions about their talents, passions, plans, goals, hopes, dreams, fears, and anxieties; find out what makes them happy or sad. Example: If your sister suddenly starts spending a lot of time alone in her room, try to find out why. She might not be willing to tell you when you first approach her. But if you're patient, persistent, and kind, you'll eventually gain her confidence and she may tell you what's bothering her.

"You can make more friends in two months by becoming interested in other people than you can in two years by trying to get other people interested in you." —Dale Carnegie

5. **Spend time together and share experiences.** As much as you might like and appreciate another person—a parent, sibling, close friend, or acquaintance—your relationship won't grow if you don't do things together and connect in other ways. You might plan special adventures to share—or you might spend quiet time together reading, doing homework, studying, or watching the clouds go by.

6. **Recognize when you have problems with others.** The first step in healing a wound is acknowledging that one exists. But don't just scratch it or put a band-aid on it and hope it will go away. Try to find the cause of the wound. Was it something you said or did? How can you make up for it? Was it something another person said or did? How can you find out what's bothering him or her, and what, if anything, can you do to make things better? What might you do to improve the relationship?

7. **Be willing to compromise.** When you compromise with another person, you *both* get something you want. You might not get *everything* you want, but you reach an agreement that seems fair to everyone involved. *Example:* You're 15, and your dad still wants you to be home each night by 8:30 p.m. You'd like to be able to stay out later. You and your dad sit down together to talk about your curfew. You each express your point of view, and you listen carefully to each other. You agree to a compromise: 8:30 p.m. on school nights (unless there's a school activity), later on Fridays and Saturdays. Neither you nor your dad gets *everything* you want, but you both get *something* you want.

8. **Talk about your feelings**, especially when problems arise. Be assertive. Address the problem without blaming the person. *Example:* A friend borrows $10 from you and doesn't pay it back. You might say "I'm wondering how soon you'll be able to pay back the $10 I loaned to you. I have to buy some books tomorrow and I really need the cash. Could you have the money for me by tomorrow morning?" Or you might say "You're such a loser! You never pay me what you owe me. Don't ever ask me for a loan again!" Which approach is most likely to get your $10 back?

9. **Don't play the blame game.** If you think your parents, siblings, friends, and others have wronged you in any way, try to forgive them. Let it go.

There's a story about an old man who gathered kindling for a living and sold it to others. He was an angry guy who held many grudges. Whenever someone did something mean to him, he wrote the person's name on a stick and put the stick in a sack on his back so he could eventually get even. At night, he'd pull out all the sticks and plan strategies for revenge. Often just thinking about what he might do to get back at someone made him feel better. One day, as he was climbing a hill to collect dead branches from a tree, he lost his balance from the burden of sticks on his back and fell backwards to the bottom of the hill.

Holding grudges can weigh you down. When you let things go, you're free to move on and improve your relationships.

10. **Try not to judge others**, not even when you're absolutely, positively sure that you're right and they're wrong. Nobody's perfect all of the time—not even you. It's your job to improve *yourself*, not everyone else you know.

> *"Every man should have a fair-sized cemetery in which to bury the faults of his friends."*
> —Henry Brooks Adams

11. **Expand your circle of friends** to include people who are different from you. Sometimes these friendships can bring the most rewards. You'll learn to see things from a new perspective. You'll become more tolerant and accepting. Your world will grow in many positive ways.

12. **Be friendly.** You might say "But I'm too shy!" Or "Being friendly is too risky. I don't want to get hurt." Many people are shy or go through periods in their lives when they're shy. Being shy is okay. And most people are afraid of getting hurt—so you're not alone. But if you want to be friendlier, here are some tips you can try:

Friendliness starts with a simple "Hello." Say "Hello" (or "Hi" or "How's it going?" or whatever feels comfortable to you) to people you see often, even if you don't know

them well. Practice by standing in front of the mirror and watching yourself. Practice on your family. Tell your mom or brother that this is your goal. Try doing it once a day, then three times, and so on. The more you do it, the easier it gets, like learning to ride a bike.

Reach out to others. Join groups, organizations, and clubs. Sit with someone you usually don't sit with at lunch. Get a pen pal. Call someone on the phone.

Include others. Look for people who are left out of activities and groups and invite them to join you. The more people you're nice to, the more friends you'll have. I know a young man who once ran for president of his high school. He didn't hang out with the popular group, but he always talked to everyone and looked for people who were alone so he could include them. Some students laughed when he ran for school president, but they didn't laugh when he won.

Eye contact. If you look at people when you say "Hi" or talk with them, they'll pay more attention to you. Practice on your family. Practice in the mirror. Try making eye contact with teachers, then with friends, and so on.

Names. Learn and remember them. To most people, the most beautiful sound in the world is the sound of their own name. When you first meet someone new, repeat his or her name. To help you remember it in the future, make up a mnemonic or "hook." *Example:* You're just met someone named Justin Harmon. You might think "*Justin* is *just* and he *harmonizes* well." It's corny, but it works.

Don't focus only on yourself. Think of the person you're with. If you hang a picture of yourself in your window, you can't see through it to the world (and the people) on the other side. Ask questions and listen to the answers.

Smile. Your smile might warm up a person who doesn't know you exist. If you combine your smile with eye contact, you might start a fire of friendship. If you're not used to smiling very much, you may need practice.

When Our Kids Fight with Friends
based on the approach of the *Positive Discipline* books by Jane Nelsen
By Glenda Montgomery

ONE OF THE MOST difficult times to be a parent is when we witness our child experiencing the intense emotional pain which is inherent, at times, in human relationships. We all remember that gut-wrenching feeling that accompanies the trauma of fighting with or being rejected by our friends. So, as concerned parents, we will often leap into what I call my "mother bear" mode: bristling, ready to pounce, eager to protect and to rescue. However, as difficult as it is for us, what is most helpful for our children in these times is to allow them to experience the trials, tribulations and challenges that come along with the joys of friendships. Rather than being a rescuing mother bear, we are more helpful and productive long term if we choose the roles of listening heart, coach and cheerleader.

As a listening heart, we listen with empathy, identifying with our child's emotions. We refrain from judging the behavior of our own child or of the other child involved. We refrain from treating our children like victims or they will begin to see themselves as victims. We don't explain other points of view at this point, we just LISTEN. This is extremely hard to do but unless we listen in this respectful way, we will risk losing our child's confidence.

As a coach, we can be available to encourage our children. We can help them to brainstorm some potential solutions or action plans. We can describe

some ways we might have approached a similar problem when we were little. We can stimulate creative thought and ways of looking at other points of view. But we cannot force our child to take our advice. We are *available as needed,* but the creation of plans or any action must come from our child, not from us.

As a cheerleader, we can let our children know that we have faith in their ability to confront difficult situations, deal with pain, and be strong enough to withstand rejection. We can celebrate with them when they have successes, and let them know that no matter what, we love them completely.

When we listen, encourage and offer faith in our children's abilities, rather than jumping in and making the problem go away, our children learn that:

- They can handle emotional pain and that it eventually does lessen and go away,
- They can deal with rejection and the whole world does not fall apart,
- They are capable human beings, able to solve friendship problems,
- They can fight with friends AND make up with friends,
- They can stand up for themselves.

This is the time for our children to learn about themselves and the world of human relationships. They need practice and support. Should your child be the victim of bullying, abuse, sexual abuse or racism, you **would** need to step in and take an active role in getting help, as this trouble is beyond a child's ability to manage. However, in cases of normal relationship turmoil, do choose to be a listening heart, a coach and a cheerleader. Keep that "mother bear" at bay and then stand back, allowing your children to build their friendship skills, their problem-solving skills and their faith in themselves.

Reprinted with permission of Glenda Montgomery, parent coach and Certified Positive Discipline Instructor in Portland, OR and mother of a teenage boy and girl. All rights reserved. www.positiveparenting.pdx

Fun Things To Do When You're Alone

By Barbara A. Lewis

"Friendship with oneself is all-important, because without it one cannot be friends with anyone else in the world."
—Eleanor Roosevelt

To *have* a good friend, you must *be* a good friend. And that means with yourself as well as others. Here are some ways to strengthen your relationship with Y-O-U:

• Find a quiet, private place where you can hang out with yourself and just think—an attic, basement, tree, under the porch, under your bed, or in your closet,

• Write in your journal about how you feel about things that happen to you each day or each week. Or write poems, stories, or letters to yourself,

• Dress up in a friend's or parent's clothes, or go to a department store or sports shop and try on clothes you don't normally wear,

• Do something physical. Jog, practice throwing, shoot baskets, kick balls, skate, walk, lift weights, swim, dance, or whatever gets your heart beating and your blood circulating,

• Draw or paint. Copy characters from comic books or the comics section in your local newspaper. Check out books on drawing from your library and practice. Instead of *writing* in your journal, try *drawing* in your journal,

• Surprise your parents and wash the dishes, clean out a closet, or bake a treat,

• Practice a skill you'd like to learn, such as singing, dancing, playing a musical instrument, doing card tricks, or blowing bubbles,

• Make something, such as jewelry, wood carvings, model cars or airplanes, or clothes,

• Read something. Read anything that interests you —books, comic books, encyclopedias, cookbooks, newspapers, magazines,

• Make a time capsule. Bury it in your backyard or hide it on a closet shelf. Plan to dig it up or take it out in five or ten years,

• Lie in your bed, under the clouds, or somewhere you're comfortable and just dream. Listen to soft, soothing music and let your mind wander.

Excerpted from *What Do You Stand For? A Kid's Guide to Building Character* by Barbara A. Lewis, copyright © 2005. Used with permission from Free Spirit Publishing Inc., Minneapolis, MN; 1-800-735-7323; www.freespirit.com. All rights reserved.

Coping with Anger and Impulsivity

By Kathy Masarie, MD

Anger: a feeling of great annoyance or antagonism as the result of some real or supposed grievance; rage; wrath.
—The Collins English Dictionary, 2000

"The world we presently live in has chosen to ignore the message that patience is a virtue. We want things instantly, and if we don't get our own way, we have a tendency to flare up with anger. All too often that anger results in our own personal destruction and humiliation or the destruction of others."
—John Crudele & Dr. Richard Erickson

Aggression: 1) violent action that is hostile and usually unprovoked, 2) deliberately unfriendly behavior, 3) act of initiating hostilities, 4) disposition to behave aggressively, 5) feeling of hostility that arouses thoughts of attack
—WordNet Dictionary

"ANGER IS A NORMAL and natural emotion that arises from our interpretation of the 'fight or flight' arousal we all experience at times," according to Michael Obsatz, author of *Raising Nonviolent Children in a Violent World.* "It is a warning signal that lets you know when something is going on around you that needs your attention." We feel angry when our boundaries are being violated or we feel some injustice. Violent individuals do not know how to vent their anger appropriately. They often interpret events in a negative or blaming way and become cynical and hostile. Their stress builds to a boiling point and a violent explosion occurs.

It is common to worry about anger in perpetrators of violence or aggression. But this emotion is also operating within the psyche of the victim. Anger may be even more pronounced in victims because they are the ones who have the least control, and anger commonly occurs when someone feels powerless in a situation. According to Jane Nelsen in *Positive Discipline: Solutions From A*

to Z, "When children are bossed or controlled and have no choices, they will probably feel angry." In a similar way, victims of aggression will also likely feel anger.

When this occurs, a child victim may turn this anger outward by acting aggressively toward self or others, thereby moving from target to perpetrator. Or the child may turn the anger inward, which can lead to depression, anxiety, eating disorders, social withdrawal or suicide. In a 2001 study reported in *Adolescence* magazine, results indicated that adolescents who internalized their anger were more likely to be depressed and to experience feelings of hopelessness. In addition, teens who internalized their anger made more serious suicide attempts than did those who externalized their anger. Internalized anger has also been shown to be a significant factor in the pathology of female anorexic patients. Teens who externalized anger, however, were shown to have a higher than average addiction to alcohol and drugs.

Does this mean it's better for your child to externalize her anger and act aggressively in order to avoid the serious implications of internalizing that anger? Obviously not, but what are the other choices? Here are some suggestions for helping your daughter identify and deal with normal angry feelings and for learning some

safe, non-violent responses to these passionate emotions and sometimes aggressive behaviors.

Model coolness

- Parents, your kids are watching! How do you act when you are in a crisis, after a hard day with your patience sagging, or when you think no one is watching?
- Do you follow the same rules you set for your kids? Do you talk only when calm and treat your daughter with respect and dignity, even when she is misbehaving?
- Have you made a strong commitment to teaching self-control and healthy anger management by example? When angry yourself, do you treat your spouse and loved ones in a way you'd like your daughter to treat you?

Acknowledge anger

- Let your daughter know that anger is a normal and important feeling and that its purpose is to act as a signal that her needs are not being met.
- Encourage your child to express her anger in words. Those who can't may need to draw it.
- Show her that you really have listened by repeating what she has said and expressing some understanding of her feelings.
- Discuss the reason for being angry. Help her to see that it's a normal reaction to having our boundaries, our needs or our sense of justice violated.

Watch for the warning signs

- Try to relieve stress before it becomes an angry outburst by recognizing your own early signs of distress that usually precede loss of control. That way you can do something to calm yourself down instead of blowing up.
- Become aware of the physiological signs of stress: flushed cheeks, rapid breathing, dry mouth, etc.
- Become aware of the physical signs of stress: clenched fists, loud voices, hunched shoulders, aggressive stance, etc.

Encourage healthy outlets

- Let her cool off. Encourage "time-outs" as a way to regain self-control, not to punish.
- Teach the use of self-talk, such as "I can calm down," "Slow down," "Keep control," "Be cool," "Be calm."
- Teach relaxation techniques, such as taking deep, slow breaths, contracting and relaxing muscles (such as the fists), or visualizing a calming experience or place.
- Exercise! Physical activity helps expend energy, as anger and aggression create lots of energy. Have kids beat pillows or a punching bag, let them scream out their frustration in a designated place, etc. Taking an active "time-out" (such as running around the perimeter of the house, for example) helps dissipate anger along with the desire to seek immediate retaliation.

Look for those things that tend to trigger anger

- Desensitize yourself to these triggers by convincing yourself that you won't be bothered by it. Choose not to become enraged.
- With children, it is very important to help them identify and validate their emotions as they are feeling them. If we can point out—you feel sad, you feel disappointed, etc. we help our daughters to identify all their emotions including anger. And, by recognizing anger, girls are more able to make conscious choices about how to respond to their anger, rather than just internalizing it or blowing up.

Long-term solutions to anger management

- Focus on finding creative solutions to deal with anger.
- Distract her by involving her in something that requires attention and energy.
- Share a lesson about how you managed your anger in a similar situation.
- Suggest she write a poem, story, letter or draw a picture that describes the anger. Consider tearing up the paper afterwards as a symbolic way to "throw your anger away."
- Establish a house rule to talk only when calm, or remind your daughter that your house is a no-hit, no-hurt home. While exact words might later be forgotten, yelling, hitting and out-of-control behaviors rarely are.

Teach and practice the 1+3+10 rule:

- This is one of the most effective formulas for self-control in both kids and adults, according to Dr. Michele Borba, author of *No More Misbehavin'—38 Difficult Behaviors and How to Stop Them.*
- Here's how it works: As soon as you feel you're losing control (when you feel your stress warning signs), do three things:
  1) Tell yourself inside your head to "Be Calm."
  2) Take three deep, slow breaths from your tummy (getting oxygen to the brain helps to calm you down).
  3) Count slowly to ten inside your head.
- Putting this together makes 1+3+10: an easy way to stop the tide from anger to outburst.

Work through the following questions/ideas together with your daughter to help her learn to vent her anger nonviolently

- What makes you really mad?
- When was the last time you were really mad? How did you handle it?
- Brainstorm five nonviolent ways of venting anger.
- What are some of the benefits of anger? How can anger teach you some things about yourself?
- List five ways of venting anger that are hurtful and destructive to yourself or others.
- Role-play a situation that might make your child angry—such as a friend being unfair in a game—and brainstorm some new ideas on handling the situation.
- Help her practice calming herself down and figuring out nonviolent ways to vent her feelings.

It is important that your child understand that angry feelings are normal, and that there are healthy ways to display and manage these feelings. By learning self-control, your daughter will feel more confident about responding to anger in an appropriate manner that lets her remain in control of herself, while retaining a sense of personal power and dignity.

Impulsivity

Dr. Michael Obsatz, who wrote *Raising Nonviolent Children in a Violent World,* believes that many children do not learn to control impulsive behaviors. They watch adults who act impulsively while driving, watching a sports game or shopping—to name a few. They watch movies and TV programs which not only show impulsive and selfish behavior, but show people being rewarded for these behaviors. "When we act impulsively, we act without thinking. We don't consider our options, the consequences of our behavior or how we affect others." While "impulsive behaviors can be positive, loving

and life-affirming, they can also be self-destructive and hurtful to others. We may move quickly into anger or quickly follow through on a thoughtless act without thinking about the harm it may cause another. Some ADD/ADHD kids especially have trouble with their friendships when impulsivity rules."

Impulse control requires a certain level of experience and maturity. A child needs to be able to consider the outcome of her behavior, as impulse control means not always getting your own way; and it requires finding safe, nonviolent alternatives for the expression of disappointment, frustration or rage. Children need support, guidance, and tools to learn how to stop, take a time-out and think before they act.

So, how can parents teach their children to control their impulses? Dr. Obsatz recommends the following:

- Parents can discuss with children "both positive and negative impulsive behaviors—such as driving without considering other drivers, fighting back when you feel wronged, buying on impulse and sending flowers to a friend." What makes some of these behaviors okay and others unacceptable? What are some other, more acceptable ways, to express our feelings at these times?

- Role-play with children about how to stop themselves when they are acting impulsively. Practice deep breathing or time-outs.

- During the time-out, they can use reason to consider other ways to handle a situation or communicate their feelings without hurting someone either physically or emotionally.

- Most importantly, adults must model the behavior they desire to see in their child. They must show children that they can control their own impulses. They may need to tell their child when they've done it—"See, I just stopped myself from shouting at that bad driver!"—then they tell her why they believe it was a wise decision and how glad they are that they took a time-out before reacting.

Controlling anger and impulses are key skills that parents can teach and encourage in their daughters. While many in our culture never become competent in these pro-social skills, those kids and adults who do

will experience unequaled success, connection and happiness in their lives. Imagine how much your own close relationships would be enriched if your family practiced consistently safe, respectful and conscious conflict resolution. The benefits of such personal accountability around anger and impulse control can be summed up in the following quote:

"Real freedom is the ability to pause between stimulus and response, and in that pause, to choose."
—Rollo May, author of *Love and Will*

Choose to teach your daughter to be accountable for her reactions to anger and impulses, and you will empower her to have deep and meaningful friendships and an actualized, authentic life.

Resources:
- *Adolescence*, 2001 Spring; 36 (141): pages 163-70.
- *Building Moral Intelligence: The Seven Essential Virtues that Teach Kids to Do the Right Thing,* by Michele Borba, Eddy. (Jossey Bass, 2001)
- *Cliques: Eight Steps to Help Your Child Survive the Social Jungle,* by Charlene C. Giannetti and Margaret Sagarese (Broadway, 2001)
- *Journal of Psychosomatic Research,* 2000 Oct; 49(4): pages 247-53.
- *Positive Discipline Solutions From A to Z* by Jane Nelsen, EdD, (Prima Lifestyles, 1999)
- *No More Misbehavin' - 38 Difficult Behaviors and How to Stop Them,* by Michele Borba, EdD (Jossey Bass, 2003)
- *Raising Nonviolent Children in a Violent World,* by Michael Obsatz, PhD (Augsburg Fortress Publishers, 1998)

Compassionate Connection

By Inbal Kashtan, author of *Parenting from Your Heart: Sharing the Gifts of Compassion, Connection, and Choice*

Attachment Parenting and Nonviolent Communication

How do we deal with a two-year-old when he grabs every toy his friend plays with? What do we say to a four-year-old who screams in rage when her baby brother cries? How do we talk with a ten-year-old about the chores he has left undone, again? What strategies will keep our teenager open with us—and safe?

NONVIOLENT COMMUNICATION (NVC), sometimes referred to as Compassionate Communication, offers a powerful approach for extending the values of attachment parenting beyond infancy. A process for connecting deeply with ourselves and others, and for creating social change, NVC has been used worldwide in intimate family settings as well as in organizations, schools, prisons, and war-torn countries.

NVC shares two key premises with attachment parenting: human actions are motivated by attempts to meet needs, and trusting relationships are built through attentiveness to those needs. Both premises contrast with prevailing child rearing practices and with the assumptions about human beings that underlie these practices. Instead of focusing on authority and discipline, attachment parenting and NVC provide theoretical and practical grounds for nurturing compassionate, powerful, and creative children who will have resources to contribute to a peaceful society.

Human Needs and Human Actions

Unlike conventional views of babies as manipulative and in danger of being spoiled, attachment parenting suggests that our babies' cries are always attempts to get their needs met. NVC, too, shifts attention away from judgments about our own and others' actions (as manipulative, wrong, bad, inappropriate—or even good), focusing instead on our own and others' feelings and needs. (See end of the article, "The Steps of NVC.") Consider the following common situation:

A child, Anna, leaves her clothes and toys strewn about the house. Dad may reprimand, remind, offer incentives, or punish. These tactics may or may not lead to the immediate outcome he intends. They will, however, likely result in unwanted long-term outcomes, such as hindering Anna's intrinsic desire to keep her home orderly and impairing the sense of connection and trust in the family.

Anna's mom may choose to say nothing out of confusion about what might work. Not getting her needs met, and lacking trust that her needs even matter to Anna, Mom might feel resentful and frustrated. The relationship is again impaired, and Anna loses the opportunity to practice finding solutions that will work for everybody—a powerful skill she needs in order to live in harmony with others.

NVC offers parents two key options that foster connection: empathy for others' feelings and needs and expression of one's own. In this situation, Dad can guess—and thus connect with— Anna's deeper feelings and needs. He can ask, "Are you excited because you want to play?" Or, "Are you annoyed because you want to choose what to do with your space?" Often, simply shifting to an empathic guess of the child's feelings and needs eases the parent's reaction. Dad no longer sees Anna as an obstacle to getting his needs met; rather, he is ready to connect with this other human being. For Anna, having the experience of being understood may nurture her willingness to listen to Dad's feelings and needs and to contribute to their fulfillment.

Mom may choose to express her own emotions. She may start with an observation: "I see clothes, books, markers, and toys on the living room floor." The observation, instead of an interpretation or judgment ("the house is a mess"), can make a tremendous difference in Anna's readiness to hear Mom's perspective. Then, when Mom follows with her feelings and needs instead of going immediately to a solution, she humanizes herself to Anna: "I feel frustrated because I enjoy order in the house." Mom clearly expresses that her feelings are caused by her own unmet needs, not by Anna's actions, thereby taking full responsibility for her feelings and for meeting her needs. She continues with a doable request: "Would you be willing to pick up your things and put them in their places?" Or if she wants to explore the broader pattern: "Would you be willing to talk with me about how we can meet your needs for play and choice and my need for order?"

Even if Anna were not willing to talk at that moment, her parents could continue to use empathy and expression until mutually satisfying strategies were found—in that moment or over time. In fact, one of the most profoundly connecting moments in relationships can occur when one person says "No" and the other empathizes with what that person is implicitly saying "Yes" to: "When you say you don't want to talk about this, is it because you want more confidence that I care about your needs?"

Every interaction we have with our children contains messages about who they are, who we are, and what life is like. The parent who takes a toy away from a toddler who just took it from another child while saying "No grabbing," teaches her child that grabbing is okay—for those with more power. Instead, in both words and actions, a parent could convey three key things: I want to understand the needs that led to your actions, I want to express to you the feelings and needs that led to mine, and I want to find strategies that will meet both of our needs.

By hearing the feelings and needs beneath our children's words and behaviors, we offer them precious gifts. We help them understand, express, and find ways to meet their needs; we model for them the capacity to empathize with others; we give them a vision of a world where everyone's needs matter; and we help them see that many of the desires that human beings cling to—having the room clean, right now!, watching television, making money—are really strategies for meeting deeper needs.

Allowing ourselves to be affected by our children's feelings and needs, we offer ourselves the blessing of finding strategies to meet our needs that are not at a cost to our children. Conversely, by sharing our inner world of feelings and needs with our children, we give them opportunities all too rare in our society: to know their parents well, to discover the effects of their actions

without being blamed for them, and to experience the power of contributing to meeting others' needs.

Power With versus Power Over

When we want our children to do something they don't want to do, it is almost impossible to resist the temptation to use the enormous physical and emotional power we have over them. Yet attempting to coerce a child to do something she doesn't want to do neither works effectively in the short term nor supports our long-term needs. (The only exception comes when there is threat to health or safety, in which case NVC suggests that we use non-punitive, protective force.)

Marshall Rosenberg, founder and education director of the Center for Nonviolent Communication, asks parents two questions to point out the severe limitations of using power-over tactics such as reward and punishment: "What do you want the child to do?" and "What do you want the child's reasons to be for doing so?" Do we really want our child to do something out of fear? Guilt? Shame? Obligation? Desire for reward? Most of us have experienced the deadening effect—and the ensuing anger and resentment—of doing things out of these motivations. Human beings do not respond with joy to force or demands. It follows that if people get their needs met at a cost to others, there is an attendant cost to themselves. Our needs are met most fully and consistently when we find strategies that also meet others' needs.

While helping us meet our needs without coercion, NVC also helps us resist giving in to our children's every wish by teaching us to express our feelings, needs, and requests clearly, and to expect our needs to be considered. When we consistently express our commitment to attending to everyone's needs—not just theirs, not just our own—we model a way of life to our children and create power with them: the power of choosing to contribute to making life more wonderful for everyone.

Neither coercive nor permissive, NVC focuses on human needs and helps us realize that we, our children, and all human beings share these needs. I draw profound hope from the knowledge that by living this way, I can foster harmony in my family—and contribute to peace in our troubled world.

Parenting for Peace

When my son was four years old he asked me to read a book about castles that he had picked up at the library.

He picked the book because he loves the Eyewitness Series and was methodically going through as many of those books as we could find, irrespective of their subject matter. I didn't like this one. It depicted not only castles but also knights, armor and weapons of all kinds used in battles in centuries past.

I am not ready for weapons. One of the things I enjoy about my son not going to preschool and not watching TV is that his exposure to violence has been extremely limited. He has never said the word "gun" or played pretend violent games—yet. He doesn't know about war and people purposely hurting one another—yet. But here was the castle book, and he wanted to read it.

I am not trying to shield my son from the reality of violence and suffering in the world—but I am in a (privileged) position to choose, often, how and when these realities enter our lives. I read him some of the book, with numerous editorials. But when he asked to read the book again a few days later, I found myself saying that I feel a lot of sadness about people being violent with one another because I believe human beings can find peaceful ways to solve their conflicts.

Questions, of course, ensued. In response to one of my son's questions, I shared with him that my sadness was related not only to the past, when there were knights and castles, but to the present as well: people in the area where I grew up, Israelis and Palestinians, are also fighting. "Why are they fighting?" my son asked. "Because they both want the same piece of land and they haven't figured out how to talk about it," I replied. "I'll teach them!" he volunteered. "What will you teach them?" I asked. "I'll teach them that they can each have some of the land, they can share," he replied easily. "The only problem," he continued, "is that I don't know how to find them."

I felt a mixture of joy and grief at his words. How wondrous to hear from my son—and from so many children—a desire to contribute to the world and a trust in the possibility of solving conflicts peacefully. Yet how apt his words were—"I don't know where to find them." How do we find the hearts of "enemies" so we can reach them with a message of peace? How do we find our own hearts and open them to those whose actions we object to profoundly?

This search for our own and others' hearts is at the core of my hope for peace and has been the greatest influence on my parenting, including the decision to practice attachment parenting when my son was a baby. It has also led me to teach a process called Nonviolent Communication (developed by Dr. Marshall Rosenberg and taught around the world). I lead workshops for parents, couples, teachers, social change activists, and others who want to connect more deeply with themselves and with others and who want to contribute more effectively to mutual understanding, safety and peace in families, schools, organizations, and in the wider world.

My experience convinces me that what happens in our families both mirrors and contributes to what happens in our societies. Just as "enemies" fail to see each other's humanity, so we, too, at times fail to relate with others, even loved ones, with compassion. Probably the primary challenge most parents tell me about is, though they yearn for peace and harmony in their families, they find themselves getting angry with their children more often and more quickly than they would like. Because the problem-solving model we follow so often relies on threat of consequences or promise of reward, it's almost guaranteed that anger will crop up regularly. For what children learn from this model is not cooperation, harmony and mutual respect; it's more often the hard lesson of domination: whoever has more power gets to have his or her way, and that those who have less power can only submit or rebel. And so we continue the cycle of domination that is leading human beings close to self-destruction.

What alternative do we have? As parents, we have a remarkable opportunity to empower our children with life skills for connecting with others, resolving conflicts, and contributing to peace. Key to learning these skills is our concept of what human beings are like. Nonviolent Communication teaches that all human beings have the same deep needs, and that people can connect with one another when they understand and empathize with each other's needs. Our conflicts arise not because we have different needs but because we have different strategies for how to meet our needs. It is on the strategy level that we argue, fight, or go to war, especially when we deem someone else's strategy a block to our own ability to meet our needs. Yet Nonviolent Communication suggests that behind every strategy, however ineffective, tragic, violent or abhorrent to us, is an attempt to meet a need. This notion turns on its head the dichotomy of "good guys" and "bad guys" and focuses our attention on the human being behind every action. When we understand the needs that motivate our own and others' behavior, we have no enemies. With our tremendous resources and creativity, we can and—I hope—we will find new strategies for meeting all our needs.

We can teach our children about making peace by understanding, reflecting, and nurturing their ability to meet their needs while we also understand, express and attend to our own. One of the needs human beings have is for autonomy, for the ability to make decisions about things that affect us. This leads us on a path of self-interest and a search for confidence and power. Yet if we nurture this need in our children to the exclusion of others, it can be difficult for us to get our own needs met. Thankfully, our need for autonomy is balanced by another shared human need, for contribution to others. This need leads us on a path of consideration, care and generosity to others. NVC enables us to look at both needs (and many others) and find a way to balance them with each other so that we recognize our need to give, to consider others and contribute to them, as an autonomous choice. When giving is done freely, out of mutual care and respect, it does not conflict with autonomy and choice, but rather complements them.

From this perspective, parents may find that we don't need punishments or rewards in parenting our children—we can instead invite our children to contribute to meeting our needs just as we invite ourselves to contribute to meeting theirs: with joy and willingness instead of guilt, shame, fear of punishment or desire for reward. This is not permissive parenting—it is parenting deeply committed to meeting the needs of both parents and children through a focus on connection and mutual respect.

Transforming parenting is hugely challenging in the context of the daily, overwhelming reality of parenting. Yet this transformation enables a profound depth of connection and trust among family members. Perhaps more poignantly for me, choosing to parent this way gives me hope for peace for our world—perhaps for our children's generation, perhaps for future generations, when human beings have learned to speak the language of compassion. As the world enters our home and my son's exposure to life's realities grows, I hope he will

sustain these lessons and carry them into his own life. I hope he will know that the path to peace is most effectively followed not by rewarding the "good" guys and punishing the "bad" ones, but by striving to find strategies that will meet people's needs—not just our own, but everyone's. I hope he will have the confidence and trust in his own peaceful resources and in human beings' capacity for peace. I hope he remembers that we can find other people's hearts by seeing their humanity.

Copyright © Inbal Kashtan. Excerpted from her book, *Parenting from Your Heart* and also published in *Paths of Learning (Spring 2003).*

Transforming Children's Anger

NVC invites us to explore a different paradigm when we face challenges with and between our children: connection and compassion for all, of mutual care and the possibility of contributing to everyone's needs. Perhaps most importantly for our troubled times, this paradigm supports children with models and skills for making peace in our world.

How does this paradigm shift work in real-life families who practice NVC? Here is a story from one mother of three boys, who participated in BayNVC's family camp in 2004:

My 13-year-old son, David, was really angry one day and about to hurt one of his twin younger brothers as they sat near each other on the couch. So, I did what I now do whenever physical violence is about to happen between them and got in the middle of the two. David was breathing heavily and had his fists clenched as he sat in a chair next to me. His brother was on the other side of me on the couch. I went with habit and started to tell David about anger management and how he needed to go for a walk or go to his room until he cooled off. He continued to breathe heavily and clench his fists.

Then his brother said something like, "David did you just want to be included?" I realized then that what David needed was empathy and started guessing, too. My first guess simply echoed what his brother already guessed: "Are you needing to be included?" I saw David's fist relax just slightly. I guessed again: "Are you needing to feel that you belong?" His fist relaxed even more and his breathing began to slow down some. Then I guessed that his need for belonging had been unmet for a really long time with his twin brothers.

David's fist relaxed more along with his body. Then I guessed that maybe if his need for belonging were met, his need for love would be met, and tears began to roll down his cheeks.

I will be forever grateful for the tools of NVC for allowing me to get to this place of awareness and healing with my son.

I celebrate this mother's honesty about her struggle to remember to turn to connection. Like most of us, she has habits that point in another direction. Yet she is willing to be awakened by her son's initiative and remembers to return to the focus on the heart. This reinforces my trust in the possibility of transformation for all of us. We can always be reminded and can always choose to return to connection. I also celebrate this mother's modeling for her sons. It's her dedication to trying, again and again, to focus on holding everyone's needs with compassion and care that made it possible for her son to do the same when she could not.

Copyright © Inbal Kashtan. From "Transforming Children's Anger: How Empathetic Connection Can Reduce Sibling Rivalry and Family Conflict" PuddleDancer Press Quick Connect, October 2006 at www.nonviolencecommunication.com

The Steps of NVC

Expressing Ourselves:
NVC includes stating our observations, feelings, needs, and requests.

Step 1—Observations: Descriptions of what is seen or heard without added interpretations. For example, instead of "She's having a temper tantrum," say "She is lying on the floor crying and kicking."

Step 2—Feelings: Our emotions rather than our story or thoughts about what others are doing. For example, instead of "I feel like you're irresponsible," which includes an interpretation of another's behavior, say "I feel worried." See **Feelings Inventory** (p. 3-29).

Step 3—Needs: Feelings are caused by needs, which are universal and ongoing and not dependent on the actions of particular individuals. State your need rather than the other person's actions as the cause; for example, "I feel annoyed because I need support" rather than "I feel annoyed because you didn't do the dishes." See **Needs Inventory** (p. 3-29).

Step 4—Requests: Doable, immediate, and stated in positive action language (what you want instead of what you don't want); for example, "Would you be willing to come back tonight at the time we've agreed?" rather than "Would you make sure not to be late again?" By definition, when we make requests we are open to hearing a "No," taking it as an opportunity for further dialogue.

Example of NVC Statement:
Original statement: "You're irresponsible! You made me so worried when you didn't get home on time! If you come home late again, you'll be grounded."

NVC statement: "When you came home at midnight after agreeing to come home at 10 p.m., I felt so worried because I need peace of mind about your safety. Would you be willing to spend time right now coming up with a plan that will give you the autonomy you want and also help me feel more peaceful?"

Empathizing with Others:
In NVC, we empathize with others by guessing their feelings and needs: "Are you feeling _____ because you need _____?" Instead of trying to "get it right," we aim to understand. In the example above, the teen's response may be, "No!" The parent can then switch from expression to listening with empathy: "Are you feeling annoyed because you need your ability to choose how to spend your time to be trusted?" From here, the dialogue can continue with empathy and expression until both people's needs for connection and understanding are met.

Copyright © Inbal Kashtan. Excerpted from her book, *Parenting from Your Heart* and also published in *Mothering,* Jan/Feb 2002.

© by Inbal Kashtan.

Inbal Kashtan, co-founder of BayNVC and the NVC Leadership Program, focuses on training for trainers and occasionally also workshops and retreats for parents, couples, and the general public. She is the founder of the Center for Nonviolent Communication's Peaceful Families, Peaceful World project, and the author of Parenting from Your Heart: Sharing the Gifts of Compassion, Connection, and Choice, *a booklet about parenting with NVC. She also has a CD,* Connected Parenting: Nonviolent Communication in a Family Life. *Both are available at www.baynvc.org. For more information about Nonviolent Communication see www.cnvc.org. For more information about Inbal's work, see www.baynvc.org.*

Reprinted with permission of Inbal Kashtan for: "Attachment Parenting and Nonviolent Communication", 'Parenting for Peace," "The Steps of NVC" and "Transforming Children's Anger."

Empowering Girls with Empathy

By Kathy Keller Jones, MA

EMPATHY IS THE ability to put yourself in another's shoes and to identify with the feelings or thoughts of another. This is an essential skill that helps kids to succeed in life, to have healthy friendships, and navigate safely through the ethical challenges and pressures that will inevitably face them. It is important to remember that while all children are born with an innate potential to grow up empathic and generous, these traits are not guaranteed. Researchers have found that kids who exhibit empathy and generosity have one strong commonality: how they were raised. They have parents with a strong commitment toward modeling caring behaviors in their home, and who support and encourage empathic and compassionate behaviors. Again, parents have tremendous power to empower their daughters with empathy.

How can parents encourage empathy in their girls? Here is a list of suggestions for parents who wish to raise empathic, compassionate and moral daughters:

- **Be a strong empathic example:** Your daughter learns first and foremost from you. Model behaviors you are proud of, and that reflect your own moral values and beliefs, caring and empathy. Commit to raising a compassionate daughter, and do whatever it takes to achieve this.

- **Engineer gratitude into daily acts of living:** Institute dinner or bedtime ritual to talk about what each member of your family is grateful for, so that kids can become more aware of the many small acts of help and goodwill that they benefit from each day. It is important for parents to participate in these rituals, as kids learn most from behaviors parents are modeling.

- **Switch roles:** When your daughter is in a conflict, or criticizing another person's behavior, try to get her to stop and think about what the other person is thinking or feeling. Can your daughter talk about the issue or her behavior as if she were that other person? Being able to walk in another's moccasins is key to building empathy and compassion.

- **Reinforce empathic behaviors:** One of the best ways to teach kids compassion is to reinforce acts of kindness when you see them happen. Regularly catch your daughter being kind, considerate or acting morally, and acknowledge her. Describe what you see your daughter doing or saying, what you suspect the other person felt as a result, and why you appreciate it.

- **Call attention to insensitive behaviors:** Without shaming, discuss unkindness or insensitivity that you observe. To diminish defensiveness and increase the chances that your daughter will really hear you, it is most effective to describe what you saw, how you think the other person involved might have felt, and then ask your daughter what she thinks about your observation. This calls attention to your own perception of events, and leaves your daughter's dignity intact. Be willing to acknowledge your own insensitivity, and take the time to discuss these with your daughter, including how you might make amends for your mistakes.

- **Make some family rules or a family caring covenant to encourage desirable behaviors:** As a family, write down how you will work together to build each other up, instead of putting each other down. Think about some consequences for put downs or negative comments: some families use a monetary fine or an extra chore list for this purpose.

- **Make family rules about how to deal with conflict in a caring and supportive way:** Conflict is a normal part of life, but how people deal with conflict is largely learned from those within the family. Children need to learn that, although anger and conflict are normal, they alone are responsible for responding to conflict in safe, appropriate and caring ways. The best way to teach this is to model it.

- **Help your daughter to become aware of her own emotions and of the feelings of others:** Help your daughter to identify her feelings by taking a guess at what her feelings are and sharing this with her. Help her learn to read non-verbal emotional cues from others by making games of guessing other people's feelings. Reading nonverbal cues is important for making friends and nourishing good relationships. Most important, make sure that your home is a safe place for your daughter to express a full range of emotions, without shame or ridicule.

References:

Building Moral Intelligence: The 7 Essential Virtues Teach Kids to Do the Right Thing by Michele Borba

Taking Charge: Caring Discipline That Works, at Home, and at School by JoAnne Nordling

Empowering Her 5

Kim Millen, Asst. Teacher/Art Teacher at a Private School

Empowering Her

> *"Remember, no one can make you feel inferior without your consent."* —Eleanor Roosevelt

> *"There's an insane amount of media and peer pressure on girls to be thin, to be beautiful, to be air-headed and only care about going shopping, to always be wearing the latest trends...most girls won't have the courage to go against the media and do what they love."* —12th Grade Girl, *Girls Inc.* website

> *"Let me find out who I am before you tell me. Be supportive of my decisions no matter what. Understand that we are a different generation with different issues."* —Teenage Girl, *AAUW's Voices of a Generation*

> *"To be nobody but yourself—in a world which is doing its best, night and day, to make you everybody else—means to fight the hardest battle which any human being can fight, and never stop fighting."* —EE Cummings

> *"I didn't belong as a kid and that always bothered me. If only I'd known that one day my differences would be an asset, then my early life would have been much easier."* —Bette Midler

> *"Positive self-esteem operates as, in effect, the immune system of spirit, providing resistance, strength, and a capacity for regeneration."* —Dr. Nathaniel Brandon, *New Woman*, Jan. 1993

GOALS

- To support your daughter as she develops her own identity, encouraging her to pursue her dreams, her passions and her interests

- To help your daughter to be herself and to resist gender stereotypes

- To surround your daughter with positive messages about her value, her strengths, her capacity to learn and succeed, and her ability to be successful at whatever she chooses to be and do

- To model in your own life the kind of personal empowerment that you want for your daughter

- To encourage the skills of financial independence in our girls

OVERVIEW

Empowering our girls is really what this *Raising Our Daughters Parenting Guide* is all about: finding ways to support our daughters to be strong, smart and bold in a culture that often puts limits on what girls can be and do. As we have seen in previous chapters, girls have a tendency to lose their voice, self-identity and feelings of connection and competence as they enter the adolescent years. Parents can feel confused and disconnected. Mary Pipher, author of *Reviving Ophelia*, describes this time in a girl's life well:

They (parents) know that something is happening to their daughters. Calm, considerate girls grow moody, demanding and distant. Girls who loved to talk are sullen and secretive. Girls who liked to hug now bristle when touched. Mothers complain that they can do nothing right in the eyes of their daughters. Involved fathers bemoan their sudden banishment from their daughters' lives. But few parents realize how universal their experiences are. Their daughters are entering a new land, a dangerous place that parents can scarcely comprehend. Just when they most need a home base, they cut themselves loose without radio communications. Parents often end up feeling like failures at this time. They feel shut out, impotent and misunderstood. They often attribute the difficulties of this time to their daughters and their own failings. They don't understand that these problems go with the developmental stage, the culture and the times ... wholeness is shattered by the chaos of adolescence. Girls become fragmented, their selves split into mysterious contradictions. They are sensitive and tenderhearted, mean and competitive, superficial and idealistic. They are confident in the morning and overwhelmed with anxiety by nightfall. They rush through their days with wild energy and then collapse into lethargy. They try on new roles every week—this week the good student, next week the delinquent and the next, the artist. And they expect their families to keep up with these changes.

Parents who are aware of these trends can do a lot to ensure that their daughters are strong and proud of whom they are, able to honor their inner voices and confident enough to make choices based on their own convictions. Girls who are helped by their parents to learn resiliency and hardiness will be more able to persevere through the difficulties of adolescence and to create fulfilling and joyful lives.

Girls Incorporated® Girls Bill of Rights℠

Girls Incorporated®, a nonprofit organization that inspires all girls to be strong, smart, and bold℠, provides an example for empowering girls. With local roots dating to 1864 and national status since 1945, Girls Inc. has responded to the changing needs of girls through research-based programs and public education efforts that empower girls to understand, value, and assert their rights. In 2008, Girls Inc. reached over 900,000 girls through Girls Inc. affiliates, the website at www.girlsinc.org, and educational publications. Their Girls Inc. Girls Bill of Rights℠ is a worthy list of goals to empower our daughters:

- *Girls have the right to be themselves and to resist gender stereotypes.*
- *Girls have the right to express themselves with originality and enthusiasm.*
- *Girls have the right to take risks, to strive freely, and to take pride in success.*
- *Girls have the right to accept and appreciate their bodies.*
- *Girls have the right to have confidence in themselves and to be safe in the world.*
- *Girls have the right to prepare for interesting work and economic independence.* © 2009 Girls Incorporated®

These rights will be addressed not only in this "Empowerment" chapter, but throughout this entire parenting guide. Girls who are listened to, allowed to experiment with various roles and activities and learn from their own mistakes are more able to trust themselves and feel empowered. Girls can be helped to find their voices by creating a nurturing support group of peers, attending a school environment that is safe, caring and sensitive to issues of gender equity, and having numerous adults in their lives who are interested in their ideas and concerns. Clubs, sports and other extracurricular activities help girls to explore and appreciate their bodies, as well as experience making a contribution to their community and to the welfare of others. In Session 9: "Supporting Her," we will cover support groups, sports, volunteerism, and coming of age rituals to honor her as she grows up.

Modeling Assertiveness and Strength

It is important for mothers to remember that they are especially vital role models for their girls, with up to 99% of young girls in a recent Girls Inc. survey replying that their mothers were their heroines and their guides to planning their own lives. Whether they realize it or not, mothers model for their daughters the struggles involved in balancing a woman's life and her dreams. The best way for mothers to encourage their daughters to be assertive, clear, and strong is to find it within themselves to be that way too! Being an impassioned, empowered role model for your daughter can be challenging, but it is also a way to keep learning and growing through parenting. The article, **"Passionate Parenting: Finding Your Exceptional Selves"** (p. 5:14), is written by a personal development specialist who encourages all parents to focus on and celebrate the exceptional qualities within themselves and their children as a way to enrich their family relationships. How we parent is one of the important ways that we model respect for feelings and needs. As our children become teens, we can model respect by shifting our parenting style into a "parent coach" style. Diana Sterling's article on her book **"Parent as Coach Approach"** (p. 5:16) introduces us to a model which encourages parents to coach their pre-teen and teen by focusing on respecting, listening, understanding, appreciating, and supporting her. She will then become more responsible and independent.

Women Supporting Women

Balancing the needs of self, work and family is a modern challenge that American women (and men) must face. All too often, parents feel guilty about how they structure their lives, no matter how much time they spend at home, in the office, or on themselves. While there are no right answers on how to juggle all these competing needs, it certainly doesn't help when people criticize themselves or others for the decisions that they have made in this regard. The article **"Women Supporting Women in their Work"** (p. 5:17) discusses women supporting each other in the choices they have made, whatever they look like. Naturally, dads

who choose to stay at home can benefit from collaborating with others, too. Sharing our experiences and accepting that our choices are just one of many, will help parents to feel better about themselves and to be resourceful about finding ways to meet everyone's needs. Families who feel empowered in their own choices, whatever they are, will in turn empower their daughters to live according to their values and dreams. Furthermore they can be teaching their daughters to be supportive of other women and girls.

There is no shame in accepting help from others to meet our family's needs; on the contrary, by reaching out for help within our community, we expose our children to other families and adults who will in turn enrich their lives. The fact remains that it does "take a village to raise a child." Our girls need close relationships with other adults, as there will be things they will not and cannot tell you, but will desperately need to tell someone. The advice a girl gets from a mature, caring mentor will differ markedly from that which she gets from her peers.

Hardiness

Books and publications that celebrate girls and women can empower girls by counteracting media influences that portray women as weak, in need of rescuing, and as sidekicks to the action. A great resource for parents is *Great Books for Girls,* by librarian Kathleen Odean, which compiles a list of over 600 annotated book titles for girls ages 2-14 where the heroines are bold, capable and confident. *Women Who Rocked the World* is an excellent book written for girls that contains stories of girls who became famous before age 19. Your daughters will also enjoy several magazines and publications that offer a forum for girls' voices, such as *New Moon Magazine for Girls and Their Dreams* and *Girls Know Best,* both written by girls themselves, and *Teen Voices Magazine,* which encourages teen girls around the world to use their skills to speak out on issues, create positive and powerful media, and lead change in their communities. There are also numerous books for parents that deal with the empowerment of girls. You will find a list of these excellent resources at the end of this Chapter 5 overview.

It is helpful to awaken girls to the biases they will face in our patriarchal society, where males dominate in our media, history classes, political leadership, video games and corporate world. It is hard for a girl to believe she "can be anything" if she can't see it! "Take Your Child To Work Day," Women's History Month activities, Girls Career Conferences, and job-shadowing opportunities are all helpful tools to show your daughter that many options exist for women, and to show her how far women have come in the past century. You can help protect your daughter from negative media portrayals of women, by having discussions about TV shows and movies you watch together. While many young girls who are outgoing and tomboyish in their pre-adolescent years become shy, deferential, quiet middle-schoolers, others do not. Teaching girls to stand up for what is right, to believe in themselves and to be resilient in the face of conflict can be extremely empowering. **"Learning to Stand Up for What's Right"** (p. 5:18) summarizes this aspect of empowerment. Self-defense classes can teach her to also use her voice, among other things, to protect herself. It is an excellent empowering mother-daughter activity.

Mindy Bingham and Sandy Stryker, in their book *Things Will Be Different for My Daughter,* devote a whole chapter to developing a girl's hardy personality. These authors identify 8 skills that empower girls to form a strong personal identity, become achievers and maintain their self-esteem. Mastering these skills takes time and support and is essential for preparing our daughters to approach life with enthusiasm and to weather its challenges:

* Recognize and tolerate anxiety and act anyway,
* Separate fantasy from reality and tackle reality,
* Set goals and establish priorities,
* Project into the future and understand how today's choices affect the future,
* Discriminate in relationships and make choices consistent with her goals and values,
* Set boundaries and limits,
* Ask assertively for what she wants,
* Trust herself and her own perceptions.

As parents we can have a great influence over our daughters' development of hardiness. We can begin when our daughters are toddlers to ensure that they have plenty of opportunities: to be physical and get dirty, experience freedom and take risks, make mistakes, solve problems, play sports, speak their mind, and use tools to build and fix things.

Bingham and Stryker remind us how "loving parents and other adults often begin early in a child's life to undermine anxiety tolerance in girls." (From "Developing a Hardy Personality" in *Things Will Be Different for My Daughter* by Mindy Bingham and Sandy Stryker, w/ Susan Neufeldt, copyright © 1995 by Mindy Bingham, Sandy Stryker and Alison Brown Cerier Book Development, Inc. Used by permission of Penguin, a division of Penguin Group Inc.)

Mindy recently had dinner with a dear friend and his eighteen-month old grandchildren, Scott and Sara, who are fraternal twins. After dinner her friend decided to give Sara a piggyback ride and hoisted her up on his shoulder. She'd never experienced this before and began to cry and show signs of stress. He put her down immediately, cuddled her, and sympathized with her. A few minutes later, though, he tried the same thing with Scott. Scott, too, was clearly uncomfortable and responded the same way as Sara, but instead of putting him down, his grandfather persisted, told Scott he would be fine, and encouraged him to be brave. In a few minutes Scott was having the time of his life. Sara didn't get another chance.

Girls benefit from being treated as sturdy and capable from an early age. In raising both our girls and boys, if we focus on our children's "happiness," we tend to rescue and "overdo." This can sabotage their hardiness and self-esteem and fuel an inappropriate sense of entitlement.

The article, **"Cultivating Hardiness Zones for Adolescent Girls"** (p. 5:19), also discusses how to create hardiness in our daughters, so that they will be equipped to negotiate a balance between pursuing their dreams and fulfilling their commitments to others. Girls need us to create safe relational hardiness zones, such as home, school, neighborhood, community organizations and clubs, where they feel known, can be themselves, and have a sense of personal control and commitment that prepares them to take on new challenges.

Self-Esteem

Another topic that invariably comes up when talking about girls' empowerment is self-esteem. Self-esteem is a term that has been used to describe many aspects of a person's self-concept and their positive or negative adjustments to their world. Self-esteem can be seen as a measure of how much a person really believes that they are whole, lovable, capable and magnificent at their core, in spite of what they do, achieve or how they look. How a girl defines herself highly influences her motivations, attitudes and behaviors. Girls with healthy self-esteem tend to handle conflicts and resist negative pressures better, enjoy life more, and are generally optimistic and realistic. Girls who have low opinions of themselves will find challenges to be a source of major anxiety and frustration. They tend to become plagued by self-critical thoughts, and are prone to depression, passivity and withdrawal. Parents can help their daughters develop a positive sense of self by supporting them to learn from their own experiences, encouraging them to keep trying and working towards success, and by loving them unconditionally.

Parents create the background against which children initially explore their self-worth and capabilities. The messages that we send them verbally, physically and emotionally can take a great toll on their self-esteem if we are overly critical. Researchers have studied the messages that 2-year-olds receive throughout the day, by placing recording devices on them that monitored all their verbal interactions. Eighty percent of the average daily verbal interactions with these toddlers consisted of negative and/or punitive messages! An interesting experiment for parents wanting to become aware of the flavor of their interactions with their kids is to carry around two punch counters, one in each of two pockets. On one counter, keep track of positive messages and interactions with your child. On the other counter, track your negative messages, interactions, judgments, and demands. Analyzing a few days of data will give you a good way to assess your own parenting style, and to really look at how you might better create a positive, caring, and unconditionally loving climate for your child to grow up in. Remember from Chapter 3 that we all need at least four positive attentions for every negative one to

feel and act well, and that paying attention to another's neutral (rather than positive or negative) behavior most clearly gives the message that they are loved just because they exist.

An April, 2004 episode of the Oprah Winfrey show featured Maria Shriver, who is an example of a highly empowered woman with healthy self-esteem. During the interview, Ms. Shriver gave an impassioned testimonial honoring equally the art of motherhood, and the way her parents helped her to succeed. Her parents, Sergeant Shriver and Eunice Kennedy Shriver, have created life-long careers in politics, social activism and philanthropy, having among their credits the creation of the Head Start, Peace Corps and Special Olympics programs. Furthermore, they are inspired parents. Ms. Shriver related that her parents told her over and again that people were truly blessed whenever she entered the room, as she would surely have something important to contribute. They also reminded her often that she was capable and strong. Maria's parents made it clear that they expected all three of their children to make a positive difference in the world, and would constantly query them as to what they were doing to make life better for others. They surrounded their children with positive messages about who they were, how much they were loved and what they could accomplish.

Can you imagine what the world would be like if all children were raised in such an atmosphere of acceptance, positive expectation, community spirit and support? Children will often not hear or experience such supportive messages from our larger culture, but parents have a high level of control over the messages they give to their children at home. Do we support the inherent goodness of our children, or do we berate them with our words and actions? Are we striking a good balance for their age between providing parental structure and following their lead? Do we allow them to experience the consequences of their own actions and to learn from them, or do we try to control them with our own well-intentioned ideas of how to behave? It is easy to imagine why it is so hard for the average person to believe she is whole and worthy just how she is, when her environment is constantly telling her otherwise. One wonders how children might grow up differently if they were instead surrounded by encouraging and accepting words and messages. Supporting your daughter's developing self-esteem can mean simply choosing your messages carefully when you speak with her. Her self-esteem will also be enhanced when you show her that she has worth in spite of her behaviors, encourage her to believe in herself, raise her to be capable and accountable for her own life choices, and model healthy self-esteem yourself. Self-esteem is not something that you can buy and not something that you can GIVE to your children. It is derived from a child's own exploration of self within her own world, and the degree to which she believes in her capacity to learn, grow and thrive in spite of adversity.

The articles on self-esteem that we have included in this study guide include "**Exploring Self-Esteem,**" and "**Developing Healthy Self-Esteem in Children**" (pp. 5:26-5:28). These articles will give parents an overview of steps they can take to empower their daughters and to support the development of healthy self-esteem within their families. Courage is an important part of self-esteem and Tom Flinders' article "**Taking Risks: Teaching Her to Be Daring**" (p. 5:29) is a thorough examination of how we can help girls overcome learned helplessness and anxiety and become daring young women. It is important to recognize that if you as the parent have low self-esteem, it is often passed on to your child by your self-deprecating comments and actions. Therefore, another way to build self-esteem in your child is to start with yourself. *Breaking the Chain of Low Self-Esteem* by Marilyn Sorenson is a helpful resource.

In supporting your child's developing self-esteem and hardiness, it is important to understand the evolution of their "moral intelligence," as Laurence Kohlberg, a developmental psychologist explains. Our younger children are in self-centered stages and gradually grow into a more rule-oriented morality. Some adults stay stuck in lower levels, other people attain advanced stages based on universal principles and personal integrity. It's exciting when we see teens and young adults moving into those levels. Michele Borba is an expert on building moral intelligence and "**Building Moral Intelligence: 10 Tips for Raising Moral Kids**" (p. 5:35) gives practical ideas

on how to build our children's moral IQ. "**Developing Capable People Guidelines**" (p. 5:36), based on the work of Jane Nelsen, author of *Positive Discipline,* and Stephen Glenn, author of *Raising Self-Reliant Children in a Self-Indulgent World,* lists seven characteristics of resilient people and some of the parenting skills that help develop these skills:

1. Strong perceptions of personal capabilities,
2. Strong perceptions of significance,
3. Strong perceptions of personal influence over life,
4. Strong intrapersonal skills (e.g. self-control),
5. Strong interpersonal skills,
6. Strong systemic skills,
7. Strong judgmental skills.

Financial Responsibility

Finally, encouraging girls to seek fulfilling life work and economic independence will empower them to face their futures with self-confidence and success. The American dream of being able to stay home to raise children, while your husband takes sole care of the family's financial needs is long gone. The average American woman works at least 26 years outside the home; more than half of mothers of 1-year-old babies are working; and many of the women who give birth will be single mothers by the time their children graduate from high school. Assisting girls in setting their sights on jobs that offer both personal satisfaction and living wages will help them to be resilient in spite of whatever they might face in their futures. A girl who receives the lessons of financial stability from her parents knows that she can provide for her own security and be independent in the world. This is one of the greatest gifts a parent can bestow upon their daughter.

The tools for financial security are best taught to children in the same way that any other skill is taught: by practical experience. Dr. Kenneth Doyle, a University of Minnesota psychologist who specializes in the psychology of money, advises that "the more important money is to you as a parent, the more important it is to give freer rein to your children." The purpose for an allowance is to share the economic resources of the family, and more importantly, to teach kids to spend and save money by the direct experience of doing so.

This means that parents will need to make agreements with their kids over what purchases they are to cover with their allowance, and then work hard to not rescue their kids when they overspend and run out of money for that lunch or pair of jeans that they really want. Kids will never learn to save until they first experience the sorrows of being broke. And, the repercussions of being broke at age 8 are much less serious than those that can occur at age 23! The following examples about two boys pertain to girls, too. One mom who took care of her busy son's financial needs until he was 18. When he went off to college, she felt this would be a good time to learn. He spent all of his first semester money in six weeks and did not become financially responsible until he was 28. Another mother was very frustrated with her middle school son's desire for the newest pair of sneakers every three months. She decided to give him a clothing allowance of $40/month, in addition to his regular allowance for incidentals. She agreed to buy one pair of sneakers and one coat per year, and turned over the rest to him. He became incredibly frugal when it was HIS money: buying fewer clothes, trading clothes with friends, shopping at thrift stores. He actually had leftover money to save. As he got older and saw the power of compound interest, he decided he wanted to set aside money for long-term investing. His parents encouraged it by matching his savings up to a certain amount. At 22, he has $9,000 in his retirement account.

Exploring the emotional side of money can be valuable for you as well as your child. "Adults use money to buy security, affection, power, and recognition" says Dr. Doyle. Children learn the value of money from their parents. When your child wants something, look at the emotion behind it. What does the item symbolize? With a younger child, it may be simply impulse buying that quickly dissipates. With older kids it may be to "fit in" with their peers, as in wanting expensive sneakers or designer jeans as a way into the popular group. Or it may be an unrealistic view of what is "normal" from the TV shows they watch.

Good money management and business skills are best taught to girls from an early age, as outlined in the article **"Nine Steps to Raising Money-Smart Kids"** (p.

5:37). There is an incredible wealth of information here, including:

- Get children interested in money early.
- Make saving a habit.
- Open a savings account in child's name.
- Encourage goal-setting.
- Give regular allowances (starting age 6).
- Help plan a budget.
- Show them the effects of inflation.
- Give them a head start.

There is more media pressure to buy things to be "cool" than ever before. There is a FDIC article titled: *Start Smart: Money Management for Teens—How to Save, Spend and Protect Your Cash … and Still Get to DO and Buy Cool Things,* which suggests five ways to cut spending:

- Practice self-control.
- Research before you buy to get the best value. Take a day or two before you buy something, so you are really clear that you want it.
- Keep track of your spending so you only spend what you have.
- Think "used" instead of "new." Consider borrowing.
- Take good care of what you buy. (Don't lose it.)

Whether parents are aware of it or not, modeling is very important. Parents will become their child's primary financial teacher, guide and resource through their own daily examples of money management and financial responsibility. In today's times the wise use of debit cards and credit cards is an essential skill. It is helpful to become more conscious of your own spoken and unspoken values around money, so that you can share them directly with your daughter. The article, **"Empowering Our Girls to Gain Financial Independence"** (p. 5:40) further explores this issue. Becoming conscious about the financial habits and experiences you are passing on to your children will empower your family in the ways you most value. Spending some time looking at the spoken and unspoken rules around money in your own upbringing and within your current household will help you to pass on to your daughter the financial habits and experiences that you most value.

Discussing money issues with other parent-daughter pairs can help clarify the struggles today and brainstorm solutions. There are programs and books that can help with that. Bankers are also often willing to talk to teens about money management. When our daughter is empowered with financial skills, she can then use money in a way that reveals what she values, what she believes in and what she hopes for.

To sum up, parents who invest in empowering their girls will raise young women who can leave home with the skills to be successfully independent and to offer their unique talents to the world. It is helpful to remember that this does not mean that our daughters won't make mistakes. The difference is that hardy, empowered young women will not fall apart when they have made a mistake. Instead they will have the attitude and skills to learn from their mistakes and fortitude to carry on. Our girls will face many challenges in their lives, and what we hope for is that we have created strong daughters who know how to seek out hardiness zones, and who will be able to meet challenges as great opportunities to learn. With a healthy sense of self, the knowledge of her dreams and passions, and a solid foundation in fiscal management, our daughters will be able to enter the world and truly be empowered to be and do whatever they desire.

THE 40 DEVELOPMENTAL ASSETS Essential to Every Young Person's Success

The 40 Developmental Assets are research-proven building blocks that support the healthy development of our youth and help them to grow up to be caring and responsible. The following assets relate to a child's experience of empowerment in her world:

- **Asset #2** **Positive Family Communication:** Young person and her parent(s) communicate positively and young person is willing to seek advice and counsel from parent(s).
- **Asset #21** **Achievement motivation:** Young person is motivated to do well in school
- **Asset #14** **Adult Role Models:** Parent(s) and other adults model positive, responsible behavior.
- **Asset #28** **Integrity:** Young person acts on convictions and stands up for her beliefs.
- **Asset #30** **Responsibility:** Young person accepts and takes personal responsibility.
- **Asset #32** **Planning and Decision making:** Young person knows how to plan ahead and make choices.
- **Asset #37** **Personal Power:** Young person feels she has control over "things that happen to me."
- **Asset #38** **Self-esteem:** Young person reports having a high self-esteem.
- **Asset #39** **Sense of Purpose:** Young person resorts that "my life has a purpose."
- **Asset #40** **Positive View of Personal Future:** Young person is optimistic about her personal future.

CIRCLE QUESTION

In what ways are you empowering your daughter? How is she empowering herself? What areas do you feel need to be strengthened and what steps can you take to support her? What are some things that you do for your daughter that she could learn to do by herself?

POSSIBLE DISCUSSION QUESTIONS

Hardiness

1. What is difficult about achievement for you as a woman? For you as a man?
2. If you could tell your daughter one thing to help her through life, what would it be?
3. What words of wisdom do you repeat over and over to your daughter?
4. How can you help your daughter to develop and trust her inner voice, intuition and thinking functions?
5. Think of an area of your life where you would have liked to have been more empowered before leaving home.
6. Who are the positive and negative male and female role models in your daughter's life? How have they influenced your daughter's character development? Have you discussed these people with your daughter?
7. What has your daughter taught you? How have you grown as a result of parenting?

Values Empowerment

8. Have you talked with your daughter about what good character is? What tools have you used to promote it?
9. What are your celebrations and your regrets in your relationship with your daughter?
10. How have you allowed your daughter to see your feelings? Which feelings have you shared?
11. Do you allow your daughter to respectfully disagree with you? How do you handle conflict?

Financial Empowerment

12. What kinds of unconscious values around money are you passing on to your daughter? What were the unspoken rules around money in your family of origin? Which of these have you forsaken and which do you still hold dear?
13. Share what has worked (or not) for you to help your child learn about money. How do you handle allowance? Do you tie chores with allowance or keep them separate? Have you worked together to make a monthly family budget? Have you worked as a family to save money for something (an animal, a trip, etc.)? How much about your finances do you feel comfortable sharing with your children and why?
14. What more can you do to you increase the level of awareness about money and promote economic empowerment in your family?

PUTTING IT INTO PRACTICE

- Give girls a voice!
- Live your own life with passion and according to your values, so you will be a good role model for your daughter, no matter how you balance your home, work and social life.
- Read books on girls' empowerment and work in your community to support the success of girls of all ages.

- Think carefully about the messages you give your daughter about her worth, her abilities and her capacity to succeed. Create a positive and nurturing environment for her to learn, make mistakes and grow up.
- Support your daughter to explore her interests and to find her passion!
- Connect your daughter with adult mentors. Help girls focus on friendships and resiliency.
- Expose your daughter to powerful role models and the exciting world that extends beyond her classrooms.
- Celebrate Women's History Month in your school. Set up a bulletin board or poster display. Encourage your school to buy books and videos about famous women or act out the roles of famous women. For more information, visit the National Women's History Project web site at http://www.nwhp.org or call (707) 838-6000. They have a fabulous catalogue.
- Take Your Child to Work on the fourth Thursday of April each year (or take someone else's daughter). Check out www.daughtersandsonstowork.org.
- Help your daughter develop financial skills and independence.
- Give her a budget and talk to her about money. Form an Investment Club that explores ways to invest money and invite knowledgeable professionals.
- Buy one of the books and pamphlets available on teaching financial independence to your daughter.
- Check out *"Teenagers and Money"* at www.drkutner.com/parenting/articles/money.html
- Check out *"Money Matters: An Economic Literacy Kit for Girls"* at www.girlsinc.org/resources/publications/index.html.

PUTTING IT TOGETHER—YOUR VERSION

Write down three or four ideas you have been inspired to implement in your own life after reading and discussing this chapter.

1. _____

2. _____

3. _____

4. _____

FURTHER READING

Websites

Hardy Girls Hardy Women: dedicated to the health and well being of girls and women so that all girls and women experience equality, independence and safety in their everyday lives at www.hardygirlshealthywomen.org or www.hghw.org

Uniquely ME! - Girl Scout Self-Esteem Program: empowers girls by helping them develop the skills necessary to face life's challenges at www.girlscouts.org/program/program_opportunities/leadership/uniquelyme.asp

Girls Incorporated: Inspiring Girls to Be Strong, Smart and Bold: great articles in resources at www.girlsinc.org Publications include: "Know Your Rights: An Action Kit for Girls," "Money Matters: An Economic Literacy Kit for Girls," "In Their Own Words: Young Women Write About Their Lives," and "Luann Becomes a Woman"

Institute for Girls Development: wonderful articles about girls' social/ emotional health at www.instituteforgirlsdevelopment.com/publications.html

New Moon Magazine for Girls and Their Dreams: honest talk for girls written by girls at www.newmoon.org

Teen Voices Magazine and Teen Voices Online!: for teens and young women at www.teenvoices.com

Books and Articles

Empowerment

Things Will Be Different For My Daughter by Mindy Bingham and Sandy Stryker

Celebrating Girls: Nurturing and Empowering our Daughters by Virginia Beane Rutter

Growing a Girl: Seven Strategies for Raising a Strong, Spirited Daughter by Barbara Mackoff

Letters to Our Daughters: Mother's Words of Wisdom by Kristin Van Raden and Molly Davies

A Toolbox for Our Daughters: Building Strength, Confidence and Integrity by Annette Geffert and Diane Hughes Brown

Meeting at the Crossroads by Lyn Mikel Brown and Carol Gilligan

Raising Strong Daughters by Jeanette Gadeberge

Strong, Smart and Bold: Empowering Girls for Life by Carla Fine

Defending Ourselves by Rosalind Wiseman Rosalind Wiseman – a complete course in self-defense for women

Self-Esteem

How to Develop Self-Esteem in Your Child: 6 Vital Ingredients by Bettie B. Youngs PhD

Self-Esteem, A Family Affair by Jean Illsley Clarke

The Handbook for Building Healthy Self Esteem in Children and Breaking the Chain of Low Self-Esteem by Marilyn Sorensen

Moral Intelligence

Building Moral Intelligence: The Seven Essential Virtues that Teach Kids to Do the Right Thing by Michelle Borba

Financial Empowerment

Free article: "Teenagers and Money" at www.drkutner.com/parenting/articles/money.html

Free Pamphlet: *Start Smart: Money Management for Teens How to Save, Spend and Protect Your Cash* by FDIC Consumer at www.fdic.gov/consumers/consumer/news/cnsum06/

More Frogs to Kiss: 99 Ways to Give Economic Power to Girls by Joline Godfrey

Smart Kid, Rich Kid and Rich Dad, Poor Dad by Robert T. Kyosaki

The Energy of Money: Spiritual Guide to Financial and Personal Fulfillment by Maria Nemeth PhD

The Kids Guide to Money: Earning It, Saving It, Spending It, Growing It, Sharing It by Steven Otfinoski

Your Money or Your Life – Transforming Your Relationship With Money by Joe Dominguez and Vicki Robin

An Asset Builder's Guide to Youth and Money by the Search Institute at www.search-institute.org

Money Matters. An Economic Literacy Kit for Girls at www.girlsinc.org/resources/publications/index.html

RESOURCES FOR GIRLS

The Six Most Important Decisions You'll Ever Make by Sean Covey

Stick Up For Yourself! Every Kid's Guide to Personal Power and Positive Self Esteem by Gershen Kaufman and Lev Raphael

What Do You Stand For? A Kid's Guide to Building Character by Barbara A. Lewis

Where Have All the Smart Women Gone? by Alice Ann Rowe

Girls and Young Women Inventors: 20 Stories about Inventors Plus How You Can Be One Yourself and *Girls and Young Women Entrepreneurs: True Stories About Starting and Running a Business* by Frances Karnes and Suzanne Bean

Girls Know Best: Advice For Girls From Girls On Just About Everything, Written by Girls Just Like You by Michelle Roehm

Girls Who Rocked the World from Sacagawea to Sheryl Seoopes by Amelie Welden

Choices: A Teen Woman's Journal for Self-Awareness and Personal Planning by Mindy Bingham, J. Edmondson, and S. Stryker

The Supergirl Dilemma: Girls Grapple with the Mounting Pressure of Expectations – a Girls Inc. survey that provides insights into girls' lives in 2000, on the mounting expectations they face from family, peers, and educators as they struggle to decode confusing messages from the media and reject traditional gender stereotypes at www.girlsinc.org/store/publications.php

Passionate Parenting ... Discovering Your Exceptional Selves

By Kris King

"DISCOVERING THE ways in which you are exceptional, the particular path you are meant to follow, is your business on this earth ..." said Bernie Siegel, MD, a pioneer in supporting cancer patients to change their perception of themselves from being victims of cancer and disease, to being exceptional and courageous patients. I agree with Dr. Siegel. I believe it is our task to accept and explore our own unique talents and gifts... to live our lives becoming more truly our best selves each day *now*...not waiting for a catastrophe to wake us up.

And yet so much of what happens in our lives has nothing to do with these discoveries of your exceptional nature. Much of what we are taught in life is devoted to directing, restraining, and containing ourselves to fit into a certain pattern that is called 'culturally acceptable.' Am I saying that learning to follow the rules isn't important? No...I think some rules are vitally important to our health, welfare and to our community.

What I am saying is that through our acculturation and learning process sometimes the uniqueness, the spunk, the creativity and the dignity of the individual are sacrificed. The intention is good, to create structure, predictability and safety. The results are not always so good...individuals who feel controlled and dependent upon authority figures, bored, and fearful of being judged and not belonging.

I believe we must live and behave in such a way that our children (our own and those we have a responsibility to) learn to appreciate their own magnificence and learn to take action for themselves that **repeatedly reaffirms their accountability, magnificence, and capabilities.** That sounds like a tall order when faced with an irate toddler or teenager! And how do we do this, if we have not learned how to do this for ourselves?

To become an exceptional parent...or to assist others in becoming exceptional people, we must decide that

discovering our own uniqueness is valuable, possible, and worthy of our time and energy... because it will take time and energy! From there on, it is a matter of learning ways that work and using them everyday with ourselves and in our interactions with everyone, especially our children!

The ways that work are simple things, simple actions that show how much you care and what you stand for. Simple things like:

- **taking ownership of your own behavior,** rather than blaming others,
- **receptive listening, rather than judging and rebuttal,**
- **telling the whole truth,** instead of editing or lying,
- **respecting,** rather than disregarding,
- **loving unconditionally,** rather than expecting,
- **creating clear agreements and keeping them,** rather than forgetting,
- **encouraging,** rather than controlling
- **celebrating,** rather than criticizing.

Simple to understand, perhaps not so simple to apply, especially in those moments when you feel the most challenged. However, isn't it amazing we want our kids to practice self-control, when we ourselves cannot? Imagine in those moments of feeling most challenged that you stop, breathe, and take ownership of your own behavior. For example,

"I just noticed that I am speaking loudly and using critical language as I am talking to you. I apologize. I think it is something I do with you when things don't go the way I want them to. I think I am afraid of conflict and don't know how to handle it very well. I feel sad and concerned that I do this with you. What I want is to understand you and for you to understand me. I want to really hear what you are saying. I want to make clear agreements with you

that we both keep to build trust between us. How do you feel about what I just said?" And then, really listening.

This may sound like a mouthful to you and I want you to know with practice you will transform not only the way you communicate, but the level of trust, clarity, love and cooperation between you and your child.

"Those who preserve their integrity remain unshaken by the storms of daily life. They do not stir like leaves on a tree or follow the herd where it runs. In their minds remains the ideal attitude and conduct of living. This is not something given to them by others. It is in their roots ... it is a strength that exists deep within them."
—Unknown Native American

Why wait to be sick or to have a life-changing event come along before you accept and appreciate that you and your daughter are truly exceptional people? Use the actions listed above with yourself and your child for a few days, or a lifetime, and you will be amazed at what you will discover about yourself and your daughter!

With love and gratitude,
Kris King

Note:

The communication technique being demonstrated in the example above can be summarized in the following way:

- Observing what I am doing right now.
- What do I think this is about?
- How am I feeling right now?
- What is it that I really want for myself and for my child?
- Checking for understanding, making sure that my child understood what I said.
- Listening carefully for her feelings and needs.

This technique is powerful because it allows a person to slow down, to carefully attend to everyone's feelings and needs, and to establish empathy with the other person. This sets the stage for successfully resolving conflicts, being accountable for your own behavior, and

creating more trust and connection in your relationships.

Kris King is owner of Wings Seminars/Innovative Learning Group, a Personal Development Center headquartered in Eugene, OR that offers experiential seminars in personal development and communication skills. Kris works with individuals, organizations and business communities in the areas of transformational education, leadership development, teen leadership training, professional and personal coaching, and spiritual renewal. Innovative Learning Group's mission is to inspire and support positive change, creating an abundant, loving and respectful world community. More information can be found at www.wings-seminars.com.

Written for Family Empowerment Network by Kris King, owner of Wings Seminars/Innovative Learning Group. Wings is a Personal Development Center that offers experimental seminars in personal development and communication skills. Please contact Kris King at www.wings-seminars for reprint permission.

Parent as Coach Approach

By Diana Sterling, author of *Parent as Coach*

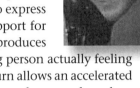

Do you want your children to be authentic, to find their passions and manifest their dreams? Imagine your children knowing that what they experience is a result of a choice they have made. How can we teach our kids to be strong, resilient, self-aware and take responsibility for their own lives? How can we support our children to think through their decisions, to practice their "choice muscle"?

Most of us learn by trying out different ways and discovering for ourselves what is the best fit for us. As parents, the idea of allowing our kids to "figure it out" can be scary, especially for those of us "helicopter parents" who tend to hover and rescue. As your child's abstract brain develops, their need to become independent beings. Parents find their old parenting style is not working. An approach that can be quite effective is to become a "parent coach." A good resource to support you on this is my book, *Parent as Coach: Seven Ways to Coach your Teen in the Game of Life*. It is based on the poem below, written by teens who shared what they learned from the coaching they received from Diana.

The Parent as Coach® coaching philosophy is based on the belief that we first need to understand what human beings are in order to teach and coach them. This includes often misunderstood teens! From this place of understanding, we learn to offer support, ideas, new perspectives, plans for moving forward, and a host of tools and formats to help people create fulfilling and meaningful lives. Above all, we offer love and compassion to all we serve and come in contact with.

Instead of teaching how to manage and control teens, our model helps us as adults appreciate the unique perspective of teens and young adults and to express respect, understanding, and support for who they are right now. This produces uncommon effects of the young person actually feeling respected and heard, which in turn allows an accelerated path for the young person to grow, learn, and produce positive choices and outcomes.

> **Young people require adults who can help them to find their own way in life.**

The Parent as Coach® Approach does not dictate how to grow up; instead, the parent learns how to guide young people to their own positive decisions, solutions, inherent gifts, and the path to a meaningful and purposeful life.

What our young people need is adults who can help them find their own way.

- Teens do not want or need adults who tell them, exactly how, what, and where to do this, and that.
- Teens who feel heard and respected can more readily access their own sense of self and create lives of joy and meaning.
- When teens feel understood they work harder, display more interest and curiosity, and are far more compassionate and easy to get along with.
- When teens feel that they are seen as responsible, they become more responsible.
- When teens feel appreciated, they are more willing to feel and show gratitude.
- When adults open the lines of communication through the Parent as Coach® role, the result can be harmonious and loving relationships that both parents and teens treasure.

As parents it is our responsibility to help our young people to build the confidence to handle the ups and downs of life, the courage to take on new adventures, and the capacity to develop compassion for all living beings. Join the **Parent as COACH®** movement! For more information: www.parentascoach.com

Reprinted with permission from Diana Sterling, CEO of New Generations and author of Parent as Coach: Seven Ways to Coach Your Teen in the Game of Life. Visit www.parentascoach. com for more information.

A Message to Parents
If you Respect me,
I will hear you.
If you Listen to me,
I will feel understood.
If you Understand me,
I will feel appreciated.
If you Appreciate me,
I will know your support.
If you Support me as I try new things,
I will become responsible.
When I am Responsible,
I will grow to be independent.
In my Independence,
I will respect you and love you all of my life.
Thank you, Your Teenager
From Parent as Coach

Women Supporting Women in Their Work

Supporting Each Other in Balancing our Lives Both Inside and Outside our Home

By Madelyn Stasko

"The phrase 'Working Mother' is redundant."
— Jane Sellman

WOMEN TODAY FIND themselves in quite a dilemma as they try to balance their personal, family, and career lives. Women who try to do it all often find themselves feeling depressed, stressed, or completely burnt out. While busily attending to the needs of others at home and at work, women often sorely neglect their own needs for relaxation and self-renewal, following their own passions, and spending time with their women friends. To make matters worse, no matter what decisions a woman makes in terms of balancing her work at home and in the workplace, there are plenty of other women who will criticize her for these choices. Have you ever wondered why we women are so hard on each other when we all have to make difficult decisions in our lives regarding how we spend our time? Our choices are really neither right nor wrong, just different. Wouldn't it be great if we were more supportive of each other as we make our way in the world?

Our complex society places many demands on a woman's time. Not only are we to be "Super-Women," climbing the corporate success ladder and having busy business lives, but we are supposed to be "Super-Moms." Furthermore, we live in a culture that doesn't always appreciate how much work it is to be a mom. We end up feeling guilty if we spend too much time at work, or conversely, too much time at home raising our kids. This puts women in a terrible bind as they struggle to structure their lives. To top it off, women often feel guilty and selfish if they take any time out of their busy lives to nurture themselves. We forget that self-care is not selfish and that we cannot expect to fill another's cup when ours is empty.

It is important for women to look at their life choices and to make sure that they reflect their true values. What are we women unconsciously teaching our daughters when we act like self-sacrificing martyrs within our own homes and workplaces? What do we teach them when we completely ignore our own needs in order to be of service to others? What are we teaching our daughters if we complain about life, as if we are just victims of cruel, outside forces? Finally, what do we teach our daughters when we berate other women for how they choose to spend their time?

It is our belief that whatever life you fashion for yourself, it can be great no matter what it looks like, if you are living your values. The most important thing is to believe in and value the choices you have made on how you spend your time, and to consciously spend your time where it has the most meaning for you. There are some women who will be better at parenting when they are actively engaged in an interesting and exciting career, choosing to spend limited, but quality time with their kids. Other women may find the most fulfillment in being stay-at-home caregivers for their children, if their partners are willing to take on the burden of financial support for the family. Many women try to mix part-time work with full-time mothering. Other families will find ways for both parents to be equally involved in childrearing and financial support. Moreover, the wonderful thing about lives is that they can change: what works for one period of your life may be altered as different needs and circumstances arise within yourself or your family.

Many questions come to mind when women make these kinds of life choices that so affect the lives of their family. Are we personally comfortable with our decisions, no matter what others think of us? Are we behaving in a way that helps our daughters respect other people's choices? Are we raising our daughters in a way that allows them to feel that it is OK for them to live their dreams—whether it is to pursue a career, stay at home or find some way to do both? Finally, are we supporting each other and all of our children in our attempts to balance our work, family and social lives? There is room on this planet for many creative ways to live our lives.

Madelyn Stasko has a daughter and works in banking and financial investments.

Learning to Stand Up for What's Right

By Natalie Rusk

I remember Ms. Tanner, my third-grade teacher, yelling, "Everyone! Stop what you are doing and put your heads down on your desks." Minutes dragged waiting for Ms. Tanner to turn on the lights and say, "You can get back to work now."

Later at the dinner table with my family, I said it wasn't fair. It was always just one group of boys being rowdy. Why did our teacher keep making us put our heads on our desk? "Have you asked her that?" my dad asked.

Didn't he know that kids weren't supposed to question their teacher? Besides, usually Ms. Tanner was nice.

"Do you think you're being treated unfairly?"

"Yes, but…"

My dad shook his head in dismay. "You know, if you don't speak up when you feel you're being treated unfairly, I can't have much sympathy for you. I know I can't respect myself if I don't stand up for what I believe is right." His eyebrows raised, "Let me ask you something. If you talked with her, what's the worst that could happen?"

I imagined the worst. Ms. Tanner would tell me to get out of my chair. Everyone would stare at me. I'd start to cry. She'd point me out the door to the principal's office.

My dad suggested that if approaching Ms. Tanner seemed difficult, instead of talking I might consider writing her a letter. He said when he had to fire a friend —one of the hardest things he'd ever done—he wrote a letter to think out what he wanted to say before meeting and talking it out.

"You could let Ms. Tanner know what you like about her class as well as how you feel about having to spend time with your head on your desk. She might not change her mind, but at least you'd give her a chance to consider your point of view—and you'd avoid building up resentment against her."

After dinner I couldn't stop thinking about it. Talking with her seemed worse than putting my head on the desk every day for the rest of the school year, but now I felt bad just complaining behind her back. I realized I could write out what I might say to Ms. Tanner, and afterwards decide whether to give it to her. I don't recall which words I chose, but I remember printing as neatly as I could on my favorite stationery. I read and reread the letter, then sealed it, brought it to school the next morning, and placed it on her desk.

The next day Ms. Tanner called me to come outside to talk with her while the other students went to recess. My legs felt shaky as I followed her out the door and sat on the stairs in the sun. I could see the light blue pages of my letter in her hand. "I rarely receive letters from students," she said. I looked up at her nervously.

"I appreciate that you wrote and told me what you were thinking. Your handwriting shows some improvement." She smiled at me, and then her voice became serious. "I've thought it over, and what you wrote makes sense. I agree it's not fair to stop the whole class because a few students are being unruly. I will try something else."

The next week, Ms. Tanner asked a few boys to move their chairs next to her desk. She began spending more time helping them while the rest of us worked. We didn't have to put our heads on our desks anymore. I felt relieved and amazed. How could a third-grader's words have such a powerful effect? I hadn't realized I could feel so good about something that had made me so nervous.

This was my first experience with the idea of self-respect. Now that I'm an adult, I try to keep this experience in mind when interacting with young people. I remind myself how important it is not just to listen to girls' thoughts and opinions, but also to coach them about constructive action they can take when they seem to be accepting situations that go against their own sense of what's fair.

Reprinted with permission from Natalie Rusk. Originally published in *Daughters: For Parents of Girls*, Jan/Feb 2004, at www.daughters. com.

Cultivating Hardiness Zones for Adolescent Girls

By Lyn Mikel Brown, EdD

IN THE LAST paragraph of *The Bluest Eye*, Toni Morrison's poignant novel about racism and poverty, the narrator, nine year-old Claudia, reflects on the ineffective magic she and her sister Freida practiced one hot summer's day, believing as they did so fervently, that "if we planted the seeds, and said the right words over them, they would blossom, and everything would be all right" (p. 9). Pecola's baby, conceived in such pain and sorrow, would live; she and Freida would, in effect, "change the course of events and alter a human life." But when the marigolds, those most common and hardy of flowers, symbolic of suffering and despair, do not bloom and Pecola's baby dies, Claudia comes finally and rightly to blame not herself, but the unyielding earth.

> *"I talk about how I did not plant the seeds too deeply, how it was the fault of the earth, the land, our town. I even think now that the land of the entire country was hostile to marigolds that year. This soil is bad for certain kinds of flowers. Certain seeds it will not nurture, certain fruit it will not bear, and when the land kills of its own volition, we acquiesce and say the victim had no right to live."* (p. 160)

I teach *The Bluest Eye* and each year I ask myself and my students, and now you, this question: What if we were to know what Claudia knows in her nine-year-old wisdom: that to alter a human life we need not one caring adult or mentor, not individual resolve, not courage or pull-yourself-up-by-your-boot-straps willpower, but the right soil—the proper pH, the correct nutrients, sunlight and rain, the right hardiness zone?

If you garden, you have a sense of what I mean by a hardiness zone. In your mind you might picture the page from any gardening manual. You know the 1-10 different bands of color running horizontally across the country, warning you to take care what you plant where. Relational hardiness zones tell us that girls need different things to grow well in urban areas than they do in rural or suburban areas, that poor girls need different nutrients than girls who are economically well-off, that white girls in Van Buren or Calais need different soil than white girls

in Waterville or immigrant girls in Portland. Hardiness zones remind us that there is no monolithic girl, not even a monolithic white girl. The idea of hardiness zones requires us to move away from the purely psychological—away from a focus solely on self-esteem or depression or eating disorders, those symptoms of individual stress and distress—and to widen our lens, to consider the social and political landscape in which a girl comes of age.

More specifically, in health psychology, the concept of "hardiness" (Ouellette [Kobasa], 1979, 1982, 1993) describes the stance of an individual girl in relation to a stressful context and points to developmental experiences girls may need to resist the long-term harm of institutionalized sexism, racism and classism. Consisting of three key components, *control, commitment,* and *challenge,* hardiness describes how persons make sense of and respond to stresses in their lives. *Hardiness control* refers to a girl's capacity to make choices in stressful circumstances, her ability to understand her stresses within a larger context, and to have a repertoire of positive coping skills. *Hardiness commitment* describes her individual belief system, sense of purpose, connection to others and recognition that there are resources for her to draw on. *Hardiness challenge* is a relationship to change, in which she feels challenged and mobilized rather than defeated. People who exhibit hardiness challenge "are catalysts in their environment and are well practiced at responding to the unexpected" (Ouellette [Kobasa] 1979, p. 4). Such girls know where to go for support, and they are flexible and persistent.

If we widen our lens in this way to include the cultural and social contexts in which girls live and what they need to thrive, different issues and concerns come into focus. Let me illustrate with an example.

In each of three years of a study of poor and working class urban adolescent girls, Anita speaks with clarity and passion about her hopes for the future and her connections in the present. In eighth, ninth and tenth grade, Anita says she wants to be a lawyer and that "kids, kids, kids," as she explains in eighth grade, are the only thing that might get in her way. In ninth grade she determines that "I ain't going to let nothing get in the way. The only thing that could probably happen is a baby." In the tenth grade, she wants to be a lawyer "because we need some black lawyers up there," and she is taking an elective for students interested in law. A powerful critique of race and class motivates her to "want to achieve in life." She observes, "There's a lot of people that I know that don't want a black kid to be somebody." This same year, her response to the interviewer's question about what might get in her way is less forceful: "If I ever got pregnant." Anita also tells her interviewer that she has been sexually active without using contraceptives.

Perhaps Anita's sense that a baby "could probably happen" to her comes from being the daughter of a woman who had children in her teens. Her mother, she explains in another part of her interview, "is part of me and I'm a part of my mother." Passionately, Anita explains how she and her mother "have trust in each other and we rely on each other" which comes from her mother's tendency to be "very open" with Anita, even open "about sex and boys and stuff." "We are not that different," Anita says, "and we do the same thing because I follow behind her footsteps and sometimes she will follow behind mine." Anita is proud of her connection with her mother and the mutuality within their relationship. A baby does happen to Anita; she follows in her mother's footsteps. She's pregnant by the fall of eleventh grade, when she drops out of school.

We can talk about what happened to Anita in a lot of different ways, most of them point to her or her mother as the source of the problem—we can say she had low self-esteem, that she was depressed, she had poor social skills and so she was easily taken advantage of, that she was the result of bad mothering. In so doing, though, we risk pathologizing and stigmatizing Anita, her mother, or her culture, and we ignore who Anita is and what she has said about her life and relationships. So I don't want to go there. Instead I want to argue that poor girls, including girls who become pregnant like Anita, do not make stupid choices; they make the best of tough situations in which they are faced with few real options for psychological growth and long-term well-being. By exploring the critical importance of relationships within girls' lives, we shift the focus from girls' alleged failures to the relational and environmental contexts that too often cannot fully support them in ways that have been considered to be health promoting. When we do so, we find ourselves asking different questions.

For example, what does it mean for Anita that her capacity to carry out her dreams may depend on a certain disconnection from her mother and the community through which she has come to know her self? And, indeed, perhaps a disconnection from mothering itself. Girls' psychological strength derives from their connections with significant others. Anita's decision to have baby places her in closer connection with her mother as it moves her away from the dreams for a better life that she, and her mother, shared.

Anita's story—a story not unlike that of many poor adolescent girls in Maine—is at the heart of a dilemma facing those of us who want to foster girls' strengths, their hardiness, as they deal with the stresses of adolescence. How can we encourage girls to take positive risks that lead to increased options for economic viability and well-being when taking those risks runs the danger of disconnection from the people they love? If "strength" for adolescent girls implies the capacity to stay mentally and physically whole while being able to achieve, or maintain, middle-class (or better) economic status, then the question of how girls negotiate their relationships with those closest to them, and what girls need from these adults as well as the from their communities and the institutions in their lives, becomes particularly urgent.

This is no simple or straightforward negotiation. Connection to adults and community is essential to girls' mental health and well-being. Those connections are often strained when girls embark on life paths different from the adults they love and who, ironically and poignantly, often themselves encourage these disconnections through their hopes for better lives for them. This lays the groundwork for a psychological mine field: on the one hand, "success" in middle-class terms too often means a betrayal of cultural and familial connections and the terror of isolation while, on the other hand, not achieving such success can mean betraying one's own and one's parents' or community's hopes, economic marginalization and limited notions of identity and social position.

While adolescence is considered to be a time of broadening horizons and efficacy, the sphere upon which girls most often exert power and control is on or with their bodies. Research on girls' experiences of sexuality reveals how fraught girls' psychosexual development really is: sexuality is typically experienced as a physical, psychological or social danger (Thompson, 1995; Tolman, 1992). Rates of sexual abuse increase remarkably for girls between the ages of ten and fourteen (Russell, 1984); research documents the fact that the youngest teen mothers are made pregnant by men who are, on average, ten years their senior (Males, 1993). The realization that their bodies are a site of temptation and conquest provides many girls with a profound sense of anxiety for their own safety and some girls with an illusory sense of power that too often backfires. Girls' real powerlessness in their lives and worlds is implied by the constrained sphere of action—their bodies—upon which they typically act.

Girls' struggles are rooted in systemic problems, such as poverty, racism and sexism that require collective, rather than individual, response. Research suggests that women (and of course men) teachers, counselors, and youth workers need to take a holistic approach to their work with girls. Such an approach should address the individual girl within the social context of her life, her relationships, the systems she encounters and the society in which she lives. To do this, women must possess knowledge of girls' lived experiences of racism, sexism, and classism.

But even this knowledge is insufficient. Every woman's life has been shaped and is continually influenced by these interlocking contexts. Power and privilege (and their absence) can cause divisions among women by distorting their perceptions of themselves and each other and blinding them to the systemic obstacles they each face. Without the opportunity and capacity to examine our own histories of bias, women—with the best of intentions—may mistakenly enact the role of cheerleader: enthusiastically encouraging girls to be confident, courageous and bold, but leading them into hostile territory without preparing them well for the consequences they may face (Ward, 2001).

What connection means for girls is far more complicated than providing her with a mentor. In understanding the struggles and strengths of girls within the communities and contexts in which they live, our notions of health and the units of analysis need to change. Hardiness does just that. It's a concept of health and stress resistance that locates the struggle between the girl and her world, not simply within the individual girl, and that holds the adults in girls' environments accountable for providing girls with experiences and opportunities for them to understand, engage with and potentially transform what limits and harms them—so that they can develop strategies of what Janie Ward calls "resistance for liberation" (Robinson & Ward, 1991; Ward, 2000).

The stress and distress that so many girls experience can be understood as a loss of control in many arenas of their lives, a struggle to create an identity and belief system to which they can wholeheartedly commit, and a sense of isolation within the challenges that face them. Hardiness begins to define areas of knowledge, skills and support that an individual can develop to resist and transform stresses. Through this perspective, the relational and educational contexts—both in schools and other community organizations in which girls find themselves—can be assessed in terms of their capacity to facilitate hardiness or to be "hardiness zones." Girls need experiences in which they exert control over more than their bodies, sexuality or appearance; where they can connect to their own worth, to a positive belief system and to others who will commit to them, and where they can experience support and encouragement to learn and persist in the face of struggles.

What would it mean for the significant adults in girls' lives to provide them with a relational hardiness zone —a context in which girls experience greater control, commitment and challenge? What can we learn about hardiness zones from relationships that girls experience as positive?

Girls' relationships with their mothers are a critical arena for the development of hardiness. Relationships between mothers and daughters present powerful opportunities to develop hardiness zones in those contexts in which self-development and cultural identity often become divided. How can these relationships better support girls? Terri Apter (1990) notes that mothers' culturally-driven expectations of adolescent separation are the lens through which they interpret conflict and questions from their daughters. For the girls, she found, struggles in relationship were about fighting for a new way of relating, not a moving away. Apter found that girls wanted to be engaged in vibrant, searching and challenging relationships— relationships in which they could experience control and commitment—but that mothers, too often, withdrew, teaching their daughters to back down in the face of challenges or conflict (see Debold, et.al., 1993).

Women teachers also hold a possibility of providing relational hardiness zones for girls, but it is a possibility that is complicated by the women's own complex relationships to the systems of power that they represent as teachers. Entrusted with the nurturance and education of girls, women teachers are often "engaged in a kind of socio-cultural balancing" (Hartman-Halbertal, 1996) of themselves, their students and their communities— struggling with the conflicts and contradictions among their roles and identities as women, as mentors and socializers, and as transmitters of patriarchal culture. Listening to a group of white working-class girls here in central Maine, I heard girls refer to this balancing in their descriptions of their women teachers. In spite of their intense anger at their teachers' ambivalences, what the girls seemed to want, what they longed for and seemed unable to attain, was a genuine closeness and the unequivocal support of their teachers. They spoke fondly of those rare occasions when they felt "closer" to a teacher, when "it feels more like she's a person," when a teacher shows "she really cares about us," or when teachers "know how I'm feeling" (Brown, 1998).

Connections between girls and women teachers are complicated and difficult, particularly across class and cultural lines, where women cannot fully read, understand, or identify with the girls in their charge. Such relationships, Lisa Delpit (1995) explains, demand "a very special kind of listening, listening that requires not only open eyes and ears, but also hearts and minds," a willingness to "put our beliefs on hold . . . to cease to exist as ourselves for a moment." It is, she insists, "the only way to learn what it might feel like to be someone else and the only way to start a dialogue" (p. 46-47). Through such a relational stance, girls perceive connection and the commitment of adults in ways that allow girls to hold their hearts and minds together.

Girls' relationships are as complicated as they are important. In schools and in programs, relationships with peers and with adult women become the sites where girls practice and hone their understanding of the social world. Such connections have the potential to provide girls with an environment where they are both heard and free to speak, where they can experience their own voices as substantive, worthy of being taken and responded to seriously. Listening and, through listening, meaningful participation in school and community life (rather than conformity and obedience), is a means by which adults can create hardiness zones for girls.

Tantalizing evidence suggests that the meaningful involvement of young people in school and community programming has a very positive impact on their engagement with school and their health (O'Connor, 1997). Linda Powell's (1994) creation of Family Group within an urban high school provided young people with a place to bring their questions about power and authority as well as their desire for connection with each other and their teachers. One result was an extraordinary improvement in retention rates. In a recent study of 25 school sites nationwide, girls who volunteered in their communities, and who did not have sex education, were less likely to become pregnant, be suspended or fail school courses than girls who took a regular curriculum and had no community experience (Allen, et al., 1997). Speaking of girls' "hunger for an us," and their hope, fears and excitement to "create their own homeplaces" (another way to think of hardiness zones), Michelle Fine and her colleagues (1996) refer to the need for "schools and communities that engage young women . . . in social critique and in activist experiences of social transformation."

In many families, especially those of color, young women form strong relationships with what Patricia Hill Collins (1991) has called "othermothers"—the women who are integral to the strength of caring communities by taking a real and persistent interest in the children of the community. These "other mothers" have relationships with the girls' mothers that serve as bridges across generations and perspectives. They are perceived as "being there" for the girls in ways mothers are not allowed; they are perceived as seeing the girls as "special"; and they are respected and trusted by the mothers. "Othermothers" do not parachute in as mentors but are part of the physical or social community; they are people who nourish a girl's hope through acts of love, courage, and commitment to making the community and the world a better place for girls. In my own research, I hear of the many women in white, working-class girls' daily lives who provide safe spaces for their feelings and thoughts, their questions and social critique—aunts, older sisters, family friends, cousins (Brown, 1998). These women know them, love them, and teach them. It's important that we join these women and honor the power of such relationships in our attempts to create relational hardiness zones.

When young girls seek out relationships with other mothers, they form genuine connections that can make a real difference in their lives. Such relationships, in which girls' questions and women's ambivalences are brought to the surface, provide the scaffolding for public critique and political resistance. So many girls are hungry for such relationships and sites of possibility. These meaningful relationships, echoed in the girls she listened to, cause

Amy Sullivan (1996) to question the traditional role of mentor, a "helping model . . . which often assumes deficiencies in the adolescent," and locates knowledge and power in the adult, and to offer, instead, the role of "muse" and the possibility of "evocative relationships." Such relationships, Sullivan explains, are "distinguished by girls' ability to speak freely; by women's ability to listen to, understand, and validate girls' feelings and experience; and by women's willingness to share their own experience as well."

Girls' relationships with the "muses" in their lives suggest the importance of women who will listen with "open hearts and minds"; who will allow the experiences of girls who are different from them to "edge themselves into our consciousness" (Delpit, 1995, pp. 46-47). Such relationships make room for girls' strong feelings and opinions, out of which come their social critique and a useful examination of the expectations, rules and norms of the culture of power. Without this examination— which depends both on the immediacy and intensity of girls' feelings and an adult's willingness to remain in their presence and to be, in Adrienne Rich's (1979) terms, "a witness in their defense"—girls are less likely to speak out or publicly respond to injustice or hurtful behavior in ways that are effective and constructive. In turn, they are likely to be less hardy.

The caring that girls want and find meaningful from adults is a caring that gives girls the opportunity for self-development through such effective cultural critique. Learning to read the culture critically provides girls with greater hardiness control by giving them a way to understand their context and to see their options; greater hardiness commitment, by providing girls with a sense of shared purpose and connection with others; and greater hardiness challenge by demonstrating the positive benefit and importance of shared struggle.

Girls need safe spaces, home places, in schools, neighborhoods, within kinship networks, as well as within families, "where one can weave whole cloth from the fragments of social critique and sweet dreams" (Pastor et al., 1996, p. 15). The hardiness zones I'm describing are not precious spaces in which girls bond through suffering but spaces where their personal experiences can be understood through systemic analysis and where they can develop skills through being involved in making change within their communities. As Suzanne Ouellette, who first developed the idea of hardiness zones, has said, "If depression is linked to stressful life events, then you need to go in and change the situation in which those events are happening" (Debold, 1995, p. 22). Girls need to be involved in that intervention process, and adults need to take responsibility for creating those spaces and possibilities for change.

Most adolescent girls do not fit media representations and stereotypes (Leadbeater, et. al., 1996). Most girls move through adolescence without succumbing to depression, becoming a teen mother or a suicide statistic. Yet, this is not an occasion for us to pat ourselves on the back. By and large, as girls angrily tell us, we have left them to their own devices to negotiate the divide between their dreams and their commitments to others. In so doing, we force girls, particularly poor girls, to enact betrayal: will they choose their own achievement or their connection with their cultural community and family?

For girls not to face, or internalize, a divide between potential achievement and familial or cultural connection, they need to have adults who provide them with the space and the skills to construct the problem differently, to see different options. They need to have opportunities

to develop a sense of purpose and to experience effective action that takes very seriously what they have experienced within systems of power and unequal resources. Girls cannot act alone to move beyond their

bodies as their only realm of power into a larger arena of possibility. They need adults, and the institutions adults create and are part of, to join them.

In her collection of essays, *In Search of Our Mother's Gardens*, Alice Walker (1983) describes the fruits of her mother's passionate commitment. I'm asking you, now as you listen, to think about yours and to consider our collective work today:

> *My mother adorned with flowers whatever shabby house we were forced to live in. And not just your typical straggly country stand of zinnia's, either, She planted ambitious gardens, with over fifty different varieties of plants that bloom profusely from early March until late November... Whatever she planted grew as if by magic and her fame as a grower of flowers spread over three counties. Because of her creativity with her flowers, even my memories of poverty are seen through a screen of blooms-sunflower, petunias, roses, dahlias, forsythia, sprea, delphiniums, verbena... whatever rocky soil she landed on, she turned into a garden. A garden so brilliant with colors, so original in its design, so magnificent with life and creativity, that to this day people drive by our house in Georgia-perfect strangers and imperfect strangers-and ask to stand or walk among my mothers' art.*
>
> *I notice that it is only when my mother is working in her flowers that she is radiant...she is involved in work her soul must have... Her face, as she prepares the Art that is her gift, is a legacy of respect she leaves to me, for all that illuminates and cherishes life. She has handed down respect for the possibilities-and the will to grasp them.* (p. 241-242)

The soil in Georgia or say, Oregon or Texas or Florida, is good for certain kinds of flowers. Here in Maine we have a short growing season—my manual tells me there are four hardiness zones in Maine alone—our soil is rocky, our land rugged, and as a result we have had to become amazingly creative in sharing gardening secrets and developing hardy plants. We have met challenges and we are here today because we have more work to do. Like our mothers before us, we are the tenders of flowers. Creating relational hardiness zones in our communities and state is about preparing a garden for all variety of girls so they can "bloom profusely." Our work, as Carol Gilligan (1998) says, is about "the perennial flowering of truth" (p. xii). It will take community efforts, on-going conversations and planning, othermothers and muses, but it is our gift, a legacy of respect we leave, it is work our souls must have.

http://www.mainelygirls.org/reports/zones.html

This paper draws from one that Elizabeth Debold and Lyn Mikel Brown wrote together with others. The reference for that paper is: Debold, E., Brown, L., Weseen, S. & Brookins, G.K. (1999): "Cultivating hardiness zones for adolescent girls: A reconceptualization of resilience in relationships with caring adults." In N. Johnson, M. Roberts, & J. Worell (Eds.), Beyond appearance: A new look at adolescent girls. Washington, DC: American Psychological Association.

References:
- Allen, J.P., Philliber, S., Herrling, S. & Kupermink, G.P. (1997). Preventing teen pregnancy and academic failure: Experimental evaluation of a developmentally-based approach. *Child Development, 67,* 729-742.
- Apter, T. (1990). *Altered Loves: Mothers and Daughters During Adolescence.* New York: St. Martin's Press.
- Brown, L.M. (1998). *Raising Their Voices: The Politics of Girls' Anger.* Cambridge, MA: Harvard University Press.
- Collins, P.H. (1991). The meaning of motherhood in Black culture and Black mother-daughter relationships. In P. Bell-Scott et al. (Eds.), *Double stitch: Black Women Write About Mothers and Daughters.* New York: Harper Perennial.
- Debold, E. (1995). *Body Politic: Transforming Adolescent Girls' Health.* A report of the 1994 proceedings of the Healthy Girls / Healthy Women Research Roundtable. New York: Ms. Foundation for Women.
- Debold, E., Wilson, M., & Malave, I. (1993). *Mother Daughter Revolution.* New York: Addison-Wesley.
- Delpit, L. (1995). *Other People's Children: Cultural Conflict in the Classroom.* New York: The New Press.
- Gilligan, C. (1998). Wild voices: Fiction, feminism, and the perennial flowering of truth. In J. Fisher & E. Silber, *Analyzing the Different …Voice.* Lanham: Rowman & Littlefield.
- Hartman-Halbertal, T. (1996). *Mothering in Culture: Ambiguities in Continuity.* Unpublished doctoral dissertation. Harvard University.
- Leadbeater, B.R. & Way, N. (Eds.). (1996). *Urban Girls.* New York: NYU Press.
- Males, M. (1993). Schools, society, and 'teen' pregnancy. *Phi Delta Kappan,* 566- 568.
- Morrison, T. (1970). *The Bluest Eye.* New York: Plume.
- O'Connor, C. (1997). Dispositions toward (collective) struggle and educational resilience in the inner-city: A case analysis of six African American high school students. *American Educational Res. Journal, 34,* 593-629.
- [Ouellette] Kobasa, S. (1979). Stressful life events, personality, and health: An inquiry into hardiness. *Journal of Personality and Social Psychology, 37,* 1-11.
- [Ouellette] Kobasa, S. (1982). The hardy personality: Toward a social psychology of stress and health. In J. Suls & G. Sanders (Eds.), *Social Psychology of Health and Illness.* Hillsdale, NJ: Erlbaum.
- Ouellette, S. (1993). Inquiries into hardiness. In L. Goldberger & S. Breznitz (Eds.), *Handbook of Stress: Theoretical and Clinical Aspects.* (2nd ed., pp. 77-100). New York: The Free Press.
- Ouellette, S. (in press). Personality's role in the protection and enhancement of health: Where the research has been, where it is stuck, how it might move.
- Pastor, J., McCormick, J. & Fine, M. (1996). Makin' homes: An urban girl thing. In B.R. Leadbeater, B.R. & N. Way, (Eds.). *Urban Girls* (pp. 15-34). New York: NYU Press.
- Petersen, A. & Craighead, W. (1986). Emotional and personality development in normal adolescents and young adults. In G.L. Klerman (Ed.), *Suicide and Depression Among Adolescents and Young Adults* (19-52). Washington, DC: American Psychiatric Press.
- Powell, L. (1994). Family group and social defenses. In M. Fine (Ed.), Chartering urban school reform: Reflections on urban public high schools in … the midst of change. New York: Teachers College Press.
- Rich, A. (1979). *On Lies, Secrets, and Silence.* New York: Norton.
- Robinson, T. & Ward, J. (1991). A belief in self far greater than anyone's disbelief: Cultivating healthy resistance among African.American female adolescents. In C. Gilligan, A. Rogers & D. Tolman (Eds.), *Women, Girls & Psychotherapy: Reframing Resistance* (pp. 87-103). Binghampton, NY: Harrington Park Press.
- Russell, D. (1984). *Sexual Exploitation.* Beverly Hills, CA: Sage.
- Thompson, S. (1995). *Going All the Way: Teenage Girls' Tales of Sex, Romance, and Pregnancy.* New York: Hill & Wang.
- Tolman, D.L. (1992). *Voicing the Body: A Psychological Study of Adolescent Girls' Sexual Desire.* Unpublished doctoral dissertation. Harvard Graduate School of Education.
- Walker, A. (1983). *In Search of Our Mother's Gardens.* San Diego: Harcourt Brace Jovanovich.
- Ward, J. (1996). Raising Resisters: The role of truth telling in the psychological development of African-American girls. In B.R..Leadbeater & N. Way (Eds.) *Urban Girls* (pp. 85-99). New York: NYU Press.
- Ward, J. (2000). The skin we're in. New York: The Free Press.
- Ward, J. (2001). Progress Report: The Alliance on Gender, Culture and School Practice. Unpublished report Harvard Graduate School of Education.

Reprinted with permission from Lyn Mikel Brown, co-author of *"Cultivating Hardiness Zones for Adolescent Girls,"* and co-creator of Hardy Girls, Healthy Women, www.hghw.org.

Exploring Self-Esteem

By Kathy Masarie, MD

My golf game was the one thing that kept coming to mind when I first started thinking about self-esteem. One day, I was playing with a woman friend and we were paired up with two strangers. I felt uncomfortable. My muscles tightened up; I could not hit the ball. What was going on with my self-confidence?

SELF-ESTEEM IS A complex issue. It has a different meaning for each one of us. It seems to vary over time and place. What all of us can probably agree on—we all want it for ourselves and we want it for our kids. So, what is it and how do we "get" it?

People with high self-esteem believe they are lovable and capable. This is not conceit, but just a quiet comfort about being who they are. How we feel about ourselves affects every aspect of every interaction with our world. People who feel lovable and capable are willing to risk more. They feel competent handling themselves and they feel they have something to offer others.

All babies have the full potential to like themselves the way they are. All children build pictures of themselves over time by reflections of what those around them think of them and they judge themselves in comparison with others. We all require experiences with success. We all want to feel accepted. If children have love and positive experiences with life, high self-esteem develops. They expect to do well, and do.

Children feel inadequate when they continually fail at tasks they try or if they are told "you are never going to amount to anything." They become convinced they are no good and then refuse to let positive messages in. After getting many negative messages over a long period of time, low self-esteem develops. Many problems have been linked to low self-esteem—alcoholism, drug abuse, crime, teenage pregnancy, school failure, unemployment. It is very clear that there is no simple cure for it. Low self-esteem can improve if children are given a nurturing environment and successful experiences. The earlier this happens, the better.

Yet high self-esteem has the disturbing reputation of being a "cure-all." A person with a learning disability and poor social skills may have low self-esteem, but a complete solution must also address the underlying causes, not just improve self-esteem.

Our ability to nurture our children's self-esteem begins with our own self-esteem. The best chance a child has of securing high self-esteem is to have parents who possess it, model it, and let their modeling instill it in their children. If the parents have a lot of unmet needs, they project them onto their children and expect more than is realistic. Jennifer James explains it best in her audio talk, *Family Self-esteem,* "It's like the child's fable, Old Mother Hubbard, 'If your own cupboard is bare [of self-esteem], it is hard to give anything to others.'" A good place to start building your children's self-esteem is to start with your own. There is a lot written about this. Find what speaks to you. I like Jack Canfield's tapes *How to Build High Self-esteem.*

Research supports that the two most influential experiences you can have to build "full" self-esteem are secure and harmonious love relationships and successful accomplishment of tasks important to you.

To help ensure a good, open relationship with your children, one of the most powerful tools parents have is to listen well. This means, not only to listen patiently to your children's words, but also to have a deep desire to hear and see your children's point of view. Reflecting what they say without judgment lets them know you are hearing what they are saying.

Helping children feel capable is tricky. "Happy-grams, empty praise, smiley-face stickers, 'participant trophies,' and all manner of drivel are lavished upon children under the guise of building their self-esteem," says Nancy Curry, author of *Beyond Self-esteem: Developing a Genuine Sense of Human Value*. She says our culture is already overly obsessed with self-preoccupation and narcissism. How do we strike a balance? One can start by calling attention to what they do well. Ideally, the praise is well deserved, specific, immediate, consistent and focused on the behavior. Seek out environments and activities where your child can feel successful.

Be aware that there are two situations that typically interfere with the growth of children's self-esteem, competition and the adult tendency to step in and "help." Competition pervades our society: in school, in sports and on the job. It serves many valuable functions, but if we only measure ourselves against others, as the "system" does with grades and making the team, we will always lose. There is always someone better.

The tendency to help arises when parents watch their kids struggle with a task and want to show them the "right way," and to save them the frustrations, embarrassment or emotional pain of making mistakes. Unfortunately, it often deprives them of the experience that is truly their own. One 15-year-old said it well, "I wish my parents would do less for me, and more with me."

When we are considering our children's self-esteem, we must realize that they are active participants in their own development. How children view themselves is not just a mirror of how others view them. You have to consider their actual self: their physical abilities, social skills, emotional reactions, and temperament, all of which influence their reactions, behavior, and perceived self.

There are three ideas I want to leave with you.

- We want to strive for a "balanced" sense of self. For most people, self-esteem is like trying to ride a teeter-totter with yourself, trying to balance in the middle. As Curry points out "Good feelings about self can be self-deceptive and narcissistic (excessive pride) and bad feeling can be constructive and energizing (healthy remorse)."

- You don't ever "get" self-esteem. It is an ever-changing, dynamic process that we work on all our lives. For every one of us there is a place where we function better, where we are loved. We all have areas of strength and vulnerability. We may feel very confident managing our kids temper tantrums, but very inadequate on the company softball team.

- To have healthy self-esteem, we need not only a sense of self-worth and meaningful work, but also to be accountable for our actions and to act responsibly toward others. Good citizenship is essential.

How people feel about themselves is important. If we have positive feelings and high self-regard, we have the confidence, energy and optimism to master life's tasks. The more positive experiences you have with yourself, the stronger your self esteem. I'll close by going back to my golf story.

With our encouragement, the two strangers left us after four holes. Immediately, I could hit the ball again. The concept of self-esteem really hit home for me when I discovered I can play golf only with people who love me.

Kathy Masarie is a pediatrician, the founder of Full Esteem Ahead and Family Empowerment Network, and a Parent and Life Coach. She is married to Chip, a medical informatician, and has a daughter and a son (pictured here).

Developing Healthy Self-Esteem in Children

By Marilyn J. Sorensen, PhD, author of *The Handbook for Building Healthy Self-Esteem in Children*

1. Parents must demonstrate love and approval.
2. Encourage more, criticize less.
3. Independence is the long-range goal of parenting.
4. One of the most valuable gifts parents can give a child is their time.
5. Promoting acceptance of diversity encourages acceptance of self.
6. Roadblocks are a natural part of life.
7. Children have a right to find their own path in life.
8. Children are not meant to vicariously fulfill a parent's dreams.
9. Conflict, controversy, and confrontation are all opportunities for growth and change.
10. Ten compliments equal one criticism.
11. Be sure your expectations are appropriate to the age/individual development of your child.
12. Be emotionally available to your child.
13. Show empathy towards your child.
14. Help your child to learn from her mistakes.
15. Always be open to hearing your child's side of a problem.
16. Give your child opportunities to solve her dilemmas.
17. Consider your child's ideas and ways of doing things.
18. Support and encourage your child's ideas and endeavors.
19. Make your home a safe environment.
20. Encourage your child to invite friends to your home.
21. Require that your child participate in family outings.
22. Gradually give your child more freedom.
23. Avoid using your child against your spouse.
24. Don't ever ask your child to take sides between you and your spouse, or ex-spouse.
25. Don't treat your child in ways that you wouldn't treat an adult friend.
26. Avoid blaming your child for your problems.
27. Don't personalize your child's behavior.
28. Don't expect your child to follow in your footsteps.
29. Don't overemphasize appearance and weight.
30. Tell your child often that you love her.
31. Find ways to tell your child that she is important to you and the entire family.
32. Talk to your child with respect.
33. Talk to your child about the meaning of friendship.
34. Allow your child to say what he really thinks and feels.
35. Reminisce with your child about positive memories of time spent together.
36. Don't compare your child with others.
37. Teach your child practical skills.
38. Help your child set reachable goals.
39. Don't expect your child to immediately master a new skill. Be patient.
40. Let your child do for himself or herself.
41. Give your child physical affection.
42. Create opportunities to laugh and play with your child.
43. Model the behavior, attitudes, values and standards that you hope to instill in your child.
44. Apologize to your child when you've acted inappropriately or share with her how you apologized to someone else.
45. Don't put yourself down in front of your child.
46. Model gratitude.
47. Model authenticity.
48. Allow your child to see your mistakes and imperfections.
49. Allow your child to see how you handle your emotions.
50. Show by example that you are trustworthy.

Please check out *The Handbook for Building Healthy Self-Esteem in Children* by Marilyn J. Sorensen, PhD for a thorough exploration of this important topic.

Dr. Sorensen is a clinical psychologist who has developed a healing practice dealing primarily with adults who suffer from low-self esteem. She believes that it is difficult to effectively resolve a child's diminished self-esteem until they are at an age when they can cognitively engage in self-reflection (often at or after adolescence). Families can help immensely, however, by becoming aware of their own patterns of behavior that encourage the development of healthy self-esteem. A parent with low self-esteem often passes on these tendencies to their own children. Improving your own self-awareness and self-esteem will do wonders, inadvertently, for your child. For more on low self-esteem in adults, refer to Dr. Sorensen's book, Breaking the Chain of Low Self-Esteem.

Written for Family Empowerment Network by Marilyn J. Sorensen, PhD, Clinical Psychologist/Author. Founder/Director of The Self-Esteem Institute, Portland, OR. www.getesteem.com. Please mail Dr. Sorensen at mjsorensen@GetEsteem.com for reprint permission.

Taking Risks: Teaching Her To Be Daring

By Tom Flinders, author of *Power and Promise: Helping School Girls Hold on to Their Dreams*

"Of all the virtues, courage is the greatest, because without it, no other virtues are possible."

—George Bernard Shaw

MY BROTHERS AND I used to spend summers with some cousins along a dark-watered river that looped without much notice through the foothills of middle California and into pools that grew warm and mysterious in the sunlight. One of the pools lay at the foot of a rock that rose from the streambed forty feet or so above the water and seemed to glare at us. The pool was deep and the rock pitted, so that you could climb to the top if you wanted to, and (if you wanted to) jump.

We aimed for the still patches in the current. Locking our arms to our sides, we could sink straight through to the sand at the bottom and root ourselves there, stump-like, just above the bedrock. We'd stay down as long as we could, peer into the flowing river above us, watch air bubbles ride to the surface.

This was it, we told ourselves, grinning at each other through the spangled water. We'd stay right there as long as we could, hidden at the clear core of the river.

The Daring Young Men

It would be a mistake to think that all our climbing and jumping was done simply for the thrill of it, though that was certainly part of the payoff. As young boys, we were testing ourselves. We climbed to reach heights, ours as well as the rocks; we jumped to test the depths —within ourselves, as much as those of the river. We were answering a call to find out what we were made of, to see just how wide and far we could reach.

The image glows in my mind against a bright summer sky, an endless satisfaction over the years. But missing from it, I now realize, are my girl cousins. Odd, now that I think of it, because they were with us throughout that summer. We were a close bunch, half boys and half girls, and we were friends as well as cousins, hanging out together, shooting the rapids in old truck-tire inner tubes an uncle salvaged for us, getting into trouble down at the abandoned mine shaft. The girls went everywhere we went, and at the river they swam, horsed around, and laid in the sun. But they didn't go up on the rock. It wasn't out of fear—they could be just as reckless as any of us boys. But in the fifties, even country girls didn't venture beyond a certain, well-fixed feminine propriety. It was boys who tested the limits, not girls, and we had all internalized this core message: males take the risks; females stand aside and offer support. Now, though, their absence from that vivid image seems fundamentally flawed omission, like a landscape without the trees.

By nature, boys are no more (nor less) daring than girls. But they are informed by their culture that proving themselves in acts of physical daring is an essential condition of their manliness. Whether they welcome it or not, boys take risks, push their limits, and in the process learn some important lessons about themselves. It's what boys do.

It's what girls would do, too, given the appropriate cultural mandate, and they too would learn essential lessons. But until just recently we've denied women the risk-taking arena. It has always been the males that we allowed to roam the borders, make the leaps, and plumb the depths. Girls, from early on, are schooled to play it safe and to keep out of harm's way.

If what Shaw said above is true, that everything of value depends upon courage, then in long denying girls the cultural inducements to explore their boundaries and test their limits, we may have denied them qualities essential to a strong sense of self. This denial may help explain the historical underachievement of gifted women and throws some light on why it is, for instance, that despite their pronounced verbal skills, women still publish fewer books than men and have produced fewer literary and artistic classics. Along with talent, art requires solitary time to think and work, and it demands great amounts of risk-taking, whether it's the courage to expose one's innermost feelings, or simply the daring to place one's financial security at stake. Historically, we've denied them all three: time, solitude, and the opportunities to be daring.

This is changing. Women pilot the space shuttle now, run corporations, win Nobel Prizes—but not nearly in proportion to their numbers. The bold, commanding, high-achieving woman is still the exception in corporate boardrooms and congressional delegations. Professional women still have a long way to go before they approach equity with men. The cultural injunctions that virtually prohibited women from being physically daring are even more unyielding. Girls and young women are allowed to be far more physically active now, but the cultural mandates that define daring and physical courage as essentially male enterprises are still locked away in the minds of most of us. If parents want to raise their daughters on a truly equal footing with their male counterparts, then they have to set aside some age-old injunctions and look upon their daughters as being as fully entitled to physical daring and courage as any male.

Kinds of Courage

There is more than one kind of courage, and each is essential to the development of fully self-reliant, creative young adults:

- Physical courage is generally synonymous with "courage" itself, the word having become identified with acts of daring and physical risk.
- Mental courage consists of intellectual and creative risk-taking, placing one's integrity or reputation on the line, and creative problem-solving which may require leaps of faith in one's capacities.
- Emotional courage includes what might be called the courage of the heart, and includes qualities more associated with the feminine, like patience, endurance, fortitude. It also includes a form of courage especially central to girls' healthy emotional development, what Dr. Annie Rogers of the Harvard Project calls the "ordinary courage" to speak what is in one's heart.

Teaching Girls To Be Daring

Risk-taking needn't place a youngster in physical jeopardy. It's mostly a mental quality, though it's expressed through physical challenges. In order to establish it in our girls, we do not have to place them at

risk. Risk-taking, physical or otherwise, means stretching oneself beyond one's apparent capacities. For a toddler, it may mean taking a step while risking a fall, while a ten-year-old might extend her threshold climbing higher into a tree, learning how to swim in the deep end of the pool, or performing in a first piano recital. An adolescent's courage may be tested in a team sport or in a physical activity like diving or skiing, or in taking a lead role in a school drama.

Young Girls

Daring begins in the imagination as a possibility, with images of daring girls and women. And the best way to embed it in your daughter's mind is through story. You can use storytelling skills to embed the images and voices of daring girls and women, traditional and modern:

- Tell (or read) stories of daring women, stories showing that women have every bit as much claim to physical daring as do males. Your young daughter should become as filled with the images of heroic women past and present—from Egypt's Queen Hatshepsut and the Greek philosopher Aspasia in antiquity to women's rights crusader and abolitionist Sojourner Truth, adventurer and aviator Amelia Earhart, Nobel Peace Prize Laureate Aung San Suu Kyi, or astronaut Sally Ride—as boys are of Daniel Boone and Charles Lindbergh.
- Imagine your young daughter as moving within a bubble of security which defines her sense of limits. Ask yourself regularly: How can I help her expand it? How can I broaden her boundaries?
- Spend time outdoors with her. The physical world offers the most visible forms of physical risk-taking. Explore the outdoors with her. Encourage her to climb a tree (providing it's safe), or clamber over a boulder, or jump down from a height. Applaud even her smallest successes. Help her overcome her natural fears of the physical world, while letting her experience the satisfaction of pushing her physical limits.

Preadolescent Girls

As your daughter grows, try to keep nudging her beyond her thresholds of experience. Use the materials and activities that are easily available to you, and stay within her own tastes and natural abilities. But keep extending her capacity to explore new and challenging experiences. And keep mindful of the following:

- Look at your own attitudes. Studies show that parents reward boys for exploring and risk-taking while they reward girls for being obedient and conforming[1]. You need to examine your attitudes towards girls and females in general. Do you think they are more fragile than boys? If so, ask yourself: Is a six-year-old girl any more likely to suffer injury on a bicycle than a six-year-old boy? (The girl is probably more coordinated.) The same can be said for teaching her to swim, to hike, or to jump. Girls are no more fragile than boys, and no less prone to injury. We simply think of them that way.

- Use the same criteria for physical safety with your daughter that you would use for your son. Remember that you want to help her build daring within the context of her physical safety, and the criteria are no different for her than for a boy the same age.
- Help her assess risks and gain confidence in her judgment to stretch herself, but not place herself in harm's way. Much of the confidence in taking appropriate risks comes from experience in making good decisions. Only experience can teach this.

Physical Challenges

I've listed below a few ways to encourage your growing daughter to embrace physical challenges. Have her experiment with some of these, but allow for her own preferences and natural abilities to guide her in trying out new experiences.

- Machines – Get her a bike, or a set of roller blades, or even a scooter, as soon as she has the physical coordination to use them. These require a physical competency that is ideal for developing confidence and daring in a youngster. I recently watched a ten-year-old rollerblading off of a ramp she had built. When she landed, she skated my way with enough swagger and confidence for ten kids. Teach your daughter how to care for her equipment, too. She needs to know that when something breaks or malfunctions, she can learn how to fix it in many instances.
- Water skills – Swimming, diving, and most forms of water play provide ample opportunities for learning to be daring. I got my six-year-old son an inflatable raft that he used to navigate increasingly difficult stretches of water, including a couple of safe but heart-thumping white-water experiences that moved him beyond what he thought was possible at the time.
- The outdoors – Nature offers innumerable opportunities for stretching your daughter's sense of her physical capacities, including her sense of daring,

endurance, and competence as she learns that she can hike a mile (or ten), carry a pack, build a fire, climb a rock, cook a meal, pitch a tent, sleep outdoors.

- Gymnastics or ballet – Many of my students participate in one or the other of these activities, and I think I can spot them by their sense of physical presence. Both provide ample opportunities for a girl's self-confidence and daring to flower.
- Team sports – Soccer, softball, basketball (the sports available to girls in my area) all require her to take risks within an environment of physical skill-building, physical and emotional risk-taking, and connection (teamwork).
- Musical Instruments – Learning to play a musical instrument is an obvious confidence builder, and performing in public is a terrific way to extend her sense of daring.
- Animals – Working closely with live animals, especially large ones, requires a certain amount of daring. Horseback riding includes a wide range of skills and offers many ways to help her extend her willingness to take risks.
- Stories and More Stories – And keep feeding her imagination and sense of possibility. Read books with her about courageous women, and not just those who were physically daring.

Adolescent Girls

When your daughter reaches adolescence, you can continue in much the same vein as above, since physical skills and athletics should continue to form an important part of adolescent girls' lives. It's never too late, if you feel that your daughter has imbibed the notion that girls don't take risks. Now, you might extend her reach to include more adventurous activities like whitewater rafting, rock climbing, skiing, or scuba diving. Have your adolescent daughter meet women who are competent in high-performance, physical activities. Expand her ideas of feminine possibility at an age when the culture's feminine stereotypes threaten to narrow them.

Some Cautions: Do not confuse daring with recklessness. The mountain climbers and whitewater rafters I've met are some of the most cautious people I know. They do not overextend themselves, and do not place themselves in jeopardy. They know that their physical safety depends upon their foresight, preparation and judgment. In fact, appropriate risk-taking teaches one above all the art of assessing risk, and weighing it against one's abilities, equipment, and the nature of the challenge.

And it builds judgment, which becomes increasingly important as girls mature. There is a delicate balance all parents have to strike between protecting their daughters from the real dangers that surround them, and in overprotecting them so that they lack self-reliance. As their daughters near adolescence and become more independent, parents have to rely increasingly on their daughters' judgment—better to build that judgment right from the beginning.

Practicing Mental Courage

For years I have told parents of my GATE students that I often see my role as a teacher of the gifted as teaching their children how to fail. These high-achieving students tend to play it safe in their learning experiences. This wins them good grades, and may even ensure their academic success. But such safe specialization has limits. Real-world achievement in the arts and sciences, the corporate world, in the professions and workplace is based on creativity and innovation which require taking intellectual and creative risks.

Risk-taking is essential to creative achievement in any field. But often because of their academic success, high-achieving students may resist taking mental or creative risks for fear of getting something wrong. So it becomes my job (I reassure my doubting parents) to move these students beyond their insecurities, press them to take some risks in their schoolwork, and hopefully learn the value of trial and error.

"I can't do that!" they'll complain, staring at the complex cosmological model on the blackboard I've asked them to replicate.

"You don't know what you can do," I reply, "until you've tried." Sometimes, after a few hours of trying, a student will walk up with a finished project in hand and a smile on her face, and say, "I didn't know I could do it."

Learning Helplessness

Girls are generally less willing to take intellectual risks than boys. It's not that they are naturally more fearful, but because they have been taught that they need our protection and help. Girls are taught by adults to feel more fragile and less capable of daring than boys. Parents assume that their infant daughters are more fragile than infant males (even though infant girls have a lower infant mortality rate). So to prevent her from experiencing frustration or even a little failure, parents rush in and tie the shoelace or assemble the puzzle even before she asks for help. Studies show that new parents are much more likely to rescue their newborn daughters from a challenge than their sons[2]. Fathers are especially prone to this.

Unfortunately, all this premature coddling sends girls a message that can be disabling: I am helping you because you can't do this yourself. As a result, girls learn a kind of behavioral passivity called "learned helplessness," that arises out of our unconscious belief that females are the weaker sex.

Rescuing

I used to train parent volunteers to work in classrooms, and the most difficult concept I had to teach them was how not to help a child. Their instincts told them to do whatever they could to help a student out of trouble, including finishing the child's work themselves. It is an art to know when to intervene with a child, and when to withhold your active help. It takes some skill to learn where a child's threshold really is, and to gently help her across it, insisting that she do the work herself. Parents face a similar challenge, having to overcome their instinct to protect a daughter from frustration or failure in order to let her find her own strengths.

It is always difficult to stand back while your child experiences frustration, intervening only when you've decided that she is truly out of her depth. It's especially hard when you're emotionally attached. But it is absolutely essential if you are to raise an independent, self-reliant daughter willing to press herself to her limits.

Problem-Solving

Whether intellectual or artistic, problem-solving consists of much trial and error, exploring unknowns and taking leaps. Denying young girls the opportunity to take appropriate risks, physical or otherwise, places them at a disadvantage. Here are some simple strategies you can use to help your daughter learn the skills of problem-solving:

- Identify your own problem-solving strategies to pass along to her. You probably have more strategies than you think.
- Wait until she asks you for help, or seems to be getting too frustrated before you intervene.
- Offer her a strategy rather than a solution when she asks for your help: "Why not look for some corner pieces first? What about putting all the reddish pieces over here? They might go together." These will teach her useful mental strategies that will help her the next time she becomes challenged.
- There are times when you will have to step in with solutions, but keep them minimal. Try to give her only part of a solution so that she may build on it to discover the rest.
- When your daughter has completed a problem, walk her through her thought process: "Notice how you first got the pieces with straight sides, then you found all the yellowish pieces, then . . ." In the flush of her success, she may be happy to hear you dissect her success, while learning some useful strategies.
- Lavish compliments, even for minor achievements. Young people are quick to let you know when they don't want a compliment—until then, your words will give her a strong support that she can learn to solve problems for herself.
- "Here, let me do that for you." Make sure before you say this that you have given her every chance to solve the problem herself. Then instead, say, "Here, let me help you do that yourself."
- Make sure your daughter knows that you are there to support her. The message you want her to receive from you is, "I will give you whatever assistance you need to do this, but you get to do it. And I know that you can."
- Wait until she asks for your help. If she asks how to do something, model it for her, but let her do it herself. If she asks for the answer to a problem, show her where she can find the answer.

Ordinary Courage

"I've lived a lie these past three years. I don't know what to do. I just can't tell her I don't want to be her friend."
—Leslie, a sixth-grade GATE student

- When she attempts a problem that pushes her near her limits, don't rush in and finish it for her. Stand aside and let your body language convey the message that you know she can manage things on her own.

- Help her learn from her failures. "Next time, if you cut along the lines, it should work." Show her how "failing" can give her useful information.
- Testing, Testing . . . You need to find ways to applaud her efforts to test the boundaries of convention. It may result in her getting into trouble or trying your patience. Find a way to balance the need to establish clear limits for her behavior, while making sure you applaud her efforts to probe her boundaries. When you see defiant behavior in your daughter, ask yourself: is there risk-taking here? Is she testing herself as she tests your resolve? And find ways to honor that, even though you may well need to reprimand her.

Emotional Courage

There is a form of courage that is especially crucial to girls' healthy psychological development, especially as they enter adolescence. Dr. Annie Rogers of the Harvard Project writes about what she calls "ordinary courage," the courage of girls to hold onto their real voices in their relationships, even though this may risk relationship itself.[3] Dr. Rogers notes that the earliest meanings of the word "courage" were in fact associated with "heart." (Chaucer, for instance, uses "in hir courages" to mean "in their hearts.") More specifically, Rogers found that the Middle English usage of "courage" included the capacity "to speak one's mind by telling all one's heart." But, by the fifteenth century "courage" had become dissociated from its more feminine qualities and came to mean facing danger without fear, a definition much closer to masculine ideas of physical heroism. Rogers suggests that the historical losses of the word reflect a larger cultural devaluation of feminine forms of courage, like patience or endurance. She argues that there is a correspondence between the historical alteration of the word courage and the losses that girls experience as they come of age in contemporary times.

Watching preadolescent girls struggle to hold onto their voice in the face of cultural silencing, Rogers feels that restoring the word to its broader meanings helps girls' experience become more coherent. It takes courage to speak the truth, especially for young adolescent girls, whose fear of losing relationship is often at the heart of their willingness to trade away their authentic voices. In order to express herself honestly and openly in relationship, a girl must develop this "ordinary" courage to speak honestly, even at the risk of breaking connection with loved ones or friends.

In the "practice of ordinary courage," a girl must learn to:
- Risk relationship when it asks that she be less than her true self;
- Face up to the fear of displeasing others, a difficult challenge for many girls;
- Be willing to have disagreements with friends;
- Tolerate and accept criticism without letting it diminish her sense of self;
- Learn to say no, and to expect her no to be honored.
- Accept the idea that not everyone she meets will like her.

Instructing an adolescent daughter in what Dr. Rogers calls the "practice of ordinary courage" is a formidable task. But if you have been engaging her all along in the parent-daughter relationships encouraging her honesty and modeling your own, respecting her points of view even when you disagreed with them, then you will have helped her immensely towards gaining this "ordinary," but immensely rewarding, courage on her own.

Crossing Anxiety Thresholds

Your daughter also needs to learn that risk-taking will be accompanied by feelings of insecurity and anxiety. Overcoming these anxieties is a large part of becoming bold and daring. One of your jobs as a parent (and mine as a teacher) is to locate her anxiety thresholds and find creative ways to help her over them, increasing her sense of mastery as she grows.

Whenever you observe your daughter facing a challenge, ask yourself: "What is her threshold here. Can I raise it a little?" Usually it means taking her hand and walking her across the threshold, while artfully stepping back and letting go. Make this process a staple of how you support her so that she trusts that you will provide a safety net for her should she overreach. The aim is to nudge her beyond her emotional comfort zone, to where she can experience herself at the full extension of her powers.

There is no reason why learning to be brave, adventurous, and self-reliant should compete with a girl's being connected, nurturing, expressive, and caring. More than anything else, your daughter needs to know from you that she has a rightful place along the conventional boundaries, at the edge of her comfort zone, testing waters, plumbing depths—that she has as much claim as any boy to the high ledge above the pool.

The Daring Young Women

The pool was deeper this time, the rock higher and 100 miles south of the one I jumped off of so many years ago with my cousins. My son and I were on our way back from a camping trip, fighting the summer heat when we found a swimming hole with a waterfall and a series of diving ledges rising up as high as sixty feet. The place was jammed with local kids who must have grown up around there, for nine-and-ten year olds were leaping from the thirty and forty foot ledges. Jumping from the very top were the teenagers, some diving fifty feet and more into the water.

My son took his time getting up to the thirty-foot ledge (I figured I didn't need to do that sort of thing anymore) and finally worked his way off, feeling pretty good as he clambered up out of the pool. We started to leave, then stopped underneath one of the valley oaks when he pointed to the very top of the diving rock. "Look."

Two teenaged girls had stepped out onto the topmost ledge and were smiling down at the water. Then they stepped off and dropped into the pool, holding hands all the way down!

"Awesome," my son said, his head shaking.

"Amazing," I muttered to myself, watching the two puckish faces bob up from where they had splashed down. I found myself both buoyed and delighted at the image of these gutsy kids swinging down together through the summer air—girls testing themselves their way, with courage and connection.

Resources
1. Letty Cottin Pogrebin, "The Stolen Spotlight Syndrome," Ms, Nov/Dec 1993, 60, in Jeanne Elium and Don Elium, Raising A Daughter: Parents and the Awakening of a Healthy Woman, Celestial Arts, Berkeley , CA , 1994, 68.
2. Cited in Marone, page 298.
3. Dr. Annie Rogers, Harvard Educational Review, Vol. 63, No. 3, Fall 1993, 289.

Reprinted with permission from www.TwoRocks.org.

Building Moral Intelligence: 10 Tips for Raising Moral Kids

By Michele Borba, author of *Building Moral Intelligence: The Seven Essential Virtues that Teach Kids to Do the Right Thing*

1. Commit to Raising a Moral Child

How important is it for you to raise a moral child? It's a crucial question to ask, because research finds that parents who feel strongly about their kids turning out morally usually succeed because they committed themselves to that effort. If you really want to raise a moral child, then make a personal commitment to raise one.

2. Be a Strong Moral Example

Parents are their children's first and most powerful moral teachers, so make sure the moral behaviors your kids are picking up from you are ones that you want them to copy. Try to make your life a living example of good moral behavior for your child to see. Each day ask yourself: "If my child had only my behavior to watch, what example would he catch?" The answer is often quite telling.

3. Know Your Beliefs & Share Them

Before you can raise a moral child, you must be clear about what you believe in. Take time to think through your values, then share them regularly with your child, explaining why you feel the way you do. After all, your child will be hearing endless messages that counter your beliefs, so it's essential the she hears about your moral standards. TV shows, movies, newspapers, and literature are filled with moral issues, so use them as opportunities to discuss your beliefs with your child.

4. Use Teachable Moments

The best teaching moments aren't ones that are planned—they happen unexpectedly. Look for moral issues to talk about as they come up. Take advantage of those moments because they help your child develop solid moral beliefs that will help guide his behavior the rest of his life.

5. Use Discipline as a Moral Lesson

Effective discipline ensures that the child not only recognizes why her behavior was wrong but also knows what to do to make it right next time. Using the right kind of questions helps kids expand their ability to take another person's perspective and understand the consequences of their behavior. So help your child reflect: "Was that the right thing to do? What should I do next time?" That way your child learns from his mistakes and grows morally. Remember your ultimate goal is to wean your child from your guidance so he acts right on his own.

6. Expect Moral Behavior

Studies are very clear: kids who act morally have parents who expect them to do so. It sets a standard for your child's conduct and also lets her know in no uncertain terms what you value. Post your moral standards at home, then consistently reinforce them until your child internalizes them so they become his rules, too.

7. Reflect on the Behaviors' Effects

Researchers tell us one of the best moral-building practices is to point out the impact of the child's behavior on the other person. Doing so enhances a child's moral growth: ("See, you made her cry") and highlights the victim's feeling ("Now he feels bad"). The trick is to help the child really imagine what it would be like to be in the victim's place so she will be more sensitive to how her behavior impacts others.

8. Reinforce Moral Behaviors

One of the simplest ways to help kids learn new behaviors is to reinforce them as they happen. So purposely catch your child acting morally and acknowledge her good behavior by describing what she did right and why you appreciate it.

9. Prioritize Morals Daily

Kids don't learn how to be moral from reading about it in textbooks but from doing good deeds. Encourage your child to lend a hand to make a difference in his world, and always help him recognize the positive effect the gesture had on the recipient. The real goal is for kids to become less and less dependent on adult guidance by incorporating moral principles into their daily lives and making them their own.

10. Incorporate the Golden Rule

Teach your child the Golden Rule that has guided many civilizations for centuries, "Treat others as you want to be treated." Remind him to ask himself before acting, "Would I want someone to treat me like that?" It helps him think about his behavior and its consequences on others. Make the Golden Rule become your family's over-arching moral principal.

Dr. Michele Borba is an educational consultant and author who has conducted parent and teacher seminars to over a half million participants. Her latest book is Building Moral Intelligence: The Seven Essential Virtues that Teach Kids to Do the Right Thing *(Jossey Bass Publishers). Information on her publications and seminars can be accessed through her Web site,* www.moralintelligence.com.

DEVELOPING CAPABLE PEOPLE
Guidelines
from the book *Raising Self-Reliant Children in a Self-Indulgent World*
by H. Stephen Glenn and Jane Nelsen

Seven Strategies for Developing Capable People

1 *Recognize* that the rate and intensity with which knowledge, technology, and lifestyle are changing have created conditions in which resiliency and personal resources are critical to effective living and learning.

2 *Encourage* the development of seven resources of highly resilient and capable people:
   a. *Strong perceptions of personal capabilities.* "I am capable of facing problems and challenges and gaining strength and wisdom through experience."
   b. *Strong perceptions of significance.* "My life has meaning and purpose, and I contribute in unique and meaningful ways."
   c. *Strong perceptions of personal influence over life.* "I can influence what I do in life and am accountable for my actions and choices."
   d. *Strong intrapersonal skills.* The ability to manage personal emotions through self-assessment, self-control, and self-discipline.
   e. *Strong interpersonal skills.* The ability to communicate, cooperate, negotiate, share, empathize, listen, and work effectively with people.
   f. *Strong systemic skills.* The ability to respond to the limits and consequences of everyday life with responsibility, adaptability, flexibility, and integrity.
   g. *Strong judgmental skills.* The ability to make decisions based on moral and ethical principles, wisdom, and understanding.

3 *Provide* opportunities in homes and classrooms for children to develop the significant seven. Strategies such as family/class meetings, mentoring, and firmness with dignity and respect can provide opportunities for children to develop all of these resources.

4 *Create and use* rituals, traditions, and service projects as opportunities for growth and empowerment for children.

5 *Increase the use* of dialogue (a meaningful exchange of ideas and perceptions) as the essential process for encouraging closeness, trust, and learning: "What are your thoughts about that?" *Avoid* "Did you? Can you? Will you? Won't you? Is everything okay?" etc. Instead *use* "What? How? When? In what way ___?" etc.

6 *Build closeness* and trust, and convey respect by avoiding the *Five Barriers* and using the *Five Builders* instead:

Barrier #1: *Assuming:* Acting on limiting assumptions about what a person can or can't do, say, think, etc. "I didn't tell you because you always get upset." "You always think ___." "You're too young to try that!" etc.

Builder #1: *Checking:* Giving people a clean slate: "How do you want to deal with this?" "What are your thoughts about ___?" "What will you need to have ready for ___?" etc.

Barrier #2: *Rescuing/Explaining:* Problem solving for a person: "___ is what is happening." "___ is why it is happening." "___ is how to deal with it." "Do it this way." etc.

Builder #2: *Exploring:* Problem solving with a person by letting them try something and then asking: "What did you experience in that situation?" "Why is that significant?" "How might you apply what you have learned in the future?" etc.

Barrier #3: *Directing:* Telling people what to do: "Pick up your shoes." "Put that away." "Don't forget your lunch." "Be sure and ___." etc.

Builder #3: *Inviting:* Asking for participation/assistance: "I would appreciate any help you could give me in straightening up the room." "How do you plan to ___?" "What will you need to do in order to ___?" etc.

Barrier #4: *Expecting: (too much too soon)* Using potential as a standard and discounting people for not being there already: "I was expecting this room to be spotless." "You should know that already." "I appreciate ___ but you forgot ___." etc.

Builder #4: *Celebrating:* Focusing on effort progress and/or what was gained by trying: "I appreciate the effort you have made to clean up this room." "What did you learn from trying to do that?" "What progress do you see yourself making?" etc.

Barrier #5: *Adultism:* Using stereotypes when dealing with people: "Teenagers are like that." "You know better than that! Surely you realize!" "You are too young to appreciate that." "Grow-up!" "Why are you so childish." etc.

Builder #5: *Respect:* Allowing for people's uniqueness and individuality: "What is your perception of ___?" or "Let me check out what you think." "How do you see this issue?" etc.

7 *Improve* your relationships 100% by avoiding the *Five Barriers*. Where can you get that kind of return for doing less? Replace the Barriers with *Builders* and double the positive impact of your contributions!

9 Steps to Raising Money-Smart Kids

By MFS Heritage Planning

There are many ways to teach your children good money sense. You can fall back on stories of how you used to earn, save, and spend money all those years ago. You can fill their heads with lessons on how important it is to be careful and wise with their money. However, the bottom line experience is the best teacher. The key is to have your children learn by doing.

Here are some ways you can encourage your children to save and manage money. In addition to the short-term benefit— having children who realize that money doesn't grow on trees— you will be instilling in them financial responsibility that they can carry with them through adulthood.

> ### Key Points
> Children learn by doing. Give them as many opportunities as possible to
> - save money
> - spend money
> - earn money
>
> Guiding them through real-life transactions is a good way for them to gain an understanding of the value of money and the importance of managing money carefully. Encourage children to earn money outside of their allowances and teach them about prices.

1. Get children interested in money early

When your children are very young (perhaps age three or four), show them how to tell different coins apart. Then give them a piggy bank they can use to store up their change. A piggy bank (or even a wallet or a purse) is a tangible place to keep their money safe.

Using a clear bank is probably best, as this will allow your child to hear, feel, and see the money accumulating. Once the saving has begun, let children spend money on treats, buying things both when there are just a few coins in the bank and when it's completely filled. This way, they will come to realize that a little bit in the bank buys a small treat, but a full bank enables them to purchase something special.

When your children are a little older, try playing games to help them understand the difference between "needs" and "wants." When riding past billboards or watching television, for example, ask them to identify whether each product advertised is a "need" or a "want." Tally their score, and when they've accumulated enough points by guessing 10 or more correct answers, treat them to a "want."

2. Make saving a habit

To get children off on the right foot, make a house rule of saving 10% or more of their income, whether the source of that income is earnings from a neighborhood lemonade stand, their weekly allowance, or a part-time job.

If started early enough in the child's awareness of money, your plan shouldn't run into much resistance. However, if you don't set some sort of guidelines, chances are pretty slim that a child will take the initiative and save on his or her own.

For proof, all you have to do is think back to when you were a child. Can you honestly say you would have saved the money you received from a relative on your eighth birthday without parental guidance? Saving money is a learned skill.

3. Open a savings account in a child's name

Like a piggy bank, a bank savings account can show kids how their money can accumulate. It can also introduce them to the concept of how money can make money on its own through compound interest. Start by giving your child a compound interest table (available for the asking at most banks) to let them anticipate how their money may grow.

Be sure to plan regular visits to the bank. Although these days many people find it easier to save via direct deposit, having your young child see you make regular, faithful trips to the bank can shape his or her own saving behavior.

Being able to participate in something a grownup does makes a youngster feel mature and responsible. In case you have not noticed, children who accompany their parents to the bank invariably want to "fill out" their own deposit slips. Why not do it for real?

4. Encourage goal setting
Have your kids write down their "want" list, along with a deadline for obtaining the items on the list. For example, your child may want in-line skates by the end of the summer or a mountain bike by next year. Visualizing

may give kids the added motivation they need to save.

You might also contribute a matching amount every time they reach a certain dollar amount in savings by themselves. Such a proposition sounds just as appealing to a child as it would to you if your boss told you the company would kick in a dollar for every dollar you saved over $10,000.

Not only will such an arrangement make them work harder to reach their goals, it might also prevent them from thinking they'll be old and gray before they save enough for an item on that wish list.

5. Give regular allowances
Allowances give kids experience with real-life money matters, letting them practice how to save regularly, plan their spending, and be self-reliant. Of course, you should determine the amount of allowance you think fits their age and the scope of their responsibilities.

Some parents feel they do not have to pay allowances because they generously hand out money when their kids need it. But kids who got money from their parents as needed have less incentive to save than the children who receive allowances, even when the total amounts children in each group receive are the same.

While you will, of course, decide for yourself when to start allowances and how much to offer your children, consider the following guidelines:

- *Do not grant too much independence by telling them they can spend their allowances on whatever they wish.* Encourage them to save at least some of their allowance, and advise them to spend the rest wisely.
- *Do not take away allowances as punishment.* Allowances are an educational tool, not a disciplinary one.
- *Carefully consider raise requests.* Discuss with a child why he or she is making such a request. Spare yourself weekly petitions for raises by telling your children they can ask for raises only twice a year, and then stick to your rule.
- *Do not reveal too much about your own finances when justifying reasons not to grant a raise in allowance.* Simply explain that your own budget is limited and that there is no extra money for a higher allowance.
- *Do not be too generous.* Too much money in a child's hands can breed careless spending habits.

6. Help plan a budget
Encourage your children to write down what they buy during the week and how much each item costs. Then write down their weekly incomes. If they do not match up, they will have to prioritize their "needs" and "wants."

To give younger children practice making tough decisions, allow them one special treat—which they pick out themselves—at the grocery store. Having to face 10 or more aisles knowing they can choose something from only one helps children understand that spending means making choices.

Just as you know fixing a leaky roof might mean postponing your Caribbean vacation, your children will realize that opting for an action figure during a store visit means they won't be able to enjoy a candy bar on the way home.

7. Encourage money-earning ventures

To help your children earn money beyond their weekly allowances, suggest that they find creative ways to make money. Encourage them to do special household chores or to seek jobs in the neighborhood such as raking, mowing, pet sitting, or shoveling snow.

Many people in your neighborhood—particularly elderly residents—would love to have a person regularly doing things for them that they no longer can, such as taking out the garbage or raking leaves. This is a perfect opportunity for your child to both earn some money and to do something for someone in need.

Even though by the teen years many children begin earning money on their own by working part-time jobs, continue to encourage that entrepreneurial spirit.

8. Show them the effects of inflation

To show your children how prices have risen over the years, take them to the library to look up ads—for movie tickets, bikes, sneakers in the newspaper archives. (Try finding the year they were born.) Or go on the Internet. The US Bureau of Labor statistics (www.bls.gov) publishes statistics tracking such everyday purchases as bananas and gasoline. It can serve as both a financial awakening and a history lesson for your children.

Once armed with the knowledge that things will almost certainly rise in cost, your children can use their math skills to see how much items they are saving for will cost in the future. For example, a bike that costs $150 today might cost $180 in five years, with 4% inflation.

If they are old enough, let them know there are ways to try to keep ahead of rising prices, such as investing regularly. While investing may not hold any interest for them at this point in their lives, it's important that they know such financial opportunities exist.

9. Most importantly, give them a head start

The money habits your children learn—and witness from mom and dad—will certainly carry over into adulthood. While you may be proud of the 12-year-old who saves enough to buy a $400 bike, you might be even prouder of the 22-year-old who can move into her first apartment without having to ask mom and dad for a loan, or the 32-year-old who can draw on his savings and investments to put a 30% down payment on his first home.

Chances are, after you have imparted all these lessons, when those financial successes come, your son or daughter might even turn to you and say, "Thanks, I owe it all to you."

Other resources in addition to www.mfs.com

- **The National Association of Investors Corporation (NAIC)** find out how your child can join or start an investment club www.better-investing.org
- Karlitz, Gail; Honig, Debbie; and Lewis, Stephen, *Growing Money: A Complete Investing Guide for Kids.* (Price Stern Sloan Publishing, 1999, $6.99)
- Godfrey, Neale S., *Neale S. Godfrey's Ultimate Kids' Money Book.* (Simon & Schuster, 1998, $18)
- Otfinoski, Steven, *The Kid's Guide to Money: Earning It, Saving It, Spending It, Growing It, Sharing It.* (Scholastic Trade, 1996, $5.95)

Reprinted © permission from *MFS Heritage Planning: Helping Yourself, Helping Your Parents, Helping Your Children.* 1-800-MFS-TALK (1-800-637-8255) or check out www.mfs.com.

By the numbers
- **1-to-1.** Matching a child's savings dollar for dollar when they save for a big ticket item like a bike or a new computer game can be a great motivator.
- **2 times a year.** Let your children ask for a raise to their allowance only twice a year. They'll learn that money is a serious topic of conversation.
- **6** is a good age to start paying an allowance. By first grade most children can appreciate that money can buy things.
- **10%** of the money your child receives—as a gift, allowance, etc.—should be earmarked for savings. Learning this concept early helps make savings a life-long habit.

Empowering Our Girls to Gain Financial Independence

By Madelyn Stasko, Women's Financial Specialist

PARENTS WANT TO empower their daughters to leave home with a foundation to gain financial independence. On one hand, we want to gift our girls with the tools and skills they need to create the lives they choose. On the other hand, we want them to learn to use wisely the monies they earn from their endeavors. These two concepts go hand in hand. We want to raise our daughters to both understand their values towards money and to manage their money well. Doing so will empower our children to more fully live and contribute to our society. Parents are already teaching their children a lot about money management in the everyday ways that they earn, spend and allocate their family's financial resources. Taking some time to be thoughtful about how to pass on these values around money will help your entire family to gain fiscal responsibility and financial independence.

Teach Your Child About the Value Side of Money—Explore What Money Means to You.
Do you remember sitting down before you left your parents' house and talking about handling finances, the value of saving and how compounding interest can help them realize financial security? Surveys of groups have shown that very few people have. Traditionally our culture has not openly supported discussing the topic of money. It's been one of those taboo subjects that is not polite to talk about. You probably learned a lot about the emotion of money from your parents modeling what was important to them—you probably spend and use your money today based on some of these observations. We have absorbed these values without a word being spoken. And, our attitudes towards money—whether we're aware of them or not—will be passed down to our children.

A beginning point in teaching your children the real value of money and how to handle your finances is understanding your own beliefs. Here is an insightful exercise to help you understand what money means to you.
- Remember an event/experience from childhood about money.
- Remember your feelings at the time.
- What message did this give you about money?
- What is the impact this belief has on your behavior/decisions today?

Taking some time to ponder these questions is a wonderful way of getting connected with your values. Understanding these values will help you more consciously shape your child's developing philosophy around the value of money. This includes the power of giving back through donations and volunteering. There are some wonderful books to help you explore this dimension of money values further include *Your Money or Your Life—Transforming Your Relationship With Money* and *Achieving Financial Independence*, by Joe Dominguez and Vicki Robin, and *The Energy of Money, A Spiritual Guide to Financial and Personal Fulfillment"* by Maria Nemeth, PhD.

Teach Your Child About the Practical Side of Money—Handling Personal Finances.
In one of the books we recommend, *Yes, You Can Raise Financially Responsible Children*, the author discusses the parent as the CFP—Chief Financial Parent. "You are your children's main resource, guide and teacher in financial education and responsibility."

In her book, *Raising Strong Daughters*, Jeanette Gadeberge emphasizes the importance of teaching girls to be financially responsible. "It does not matter whether your family lives simply, sticks to a modest budget, or has money to burn. Your daughter must learn to be in control of her finances. If she does not learn early, she will not know how to be in charge of her money when she must depend on her ability to support herself."

An experience-based approach to raising financially aware kids allows children to get interested in money at a young age and develop good habits that help them to learn by doing. Children best learn to spend, save and invest by doing so. Giving your kids a budget that covers some of their essential needs lets them learn from their own experience, as long as you do not bail them out when they fail to save for an important purchase. Helping your child gain financial skills gives her a lifelong gift that will ease her life no matter how much money she makes. The skills of saving and investing money are essential for manifesting her dreams.

Online Resources:
- http://www.moonjar.com
- http://www.moneyopolis.com (fun game to play)
- http://kidsmoney.org

Teaching Her 6

Mckenna Miller, 6th Grade, Rosemont Ridge Middle School

Teaching Her

> *"People don't care how much you know—until they know how much you care."*
> —John C. Maxwell

> *"Students don't become what they think they are or what you think they are but they become what they think you think they are."*—Dudley Flood

> *"The bad news is at tender ages, girls are under-encouraged and underexposed to science, math, and technology. The good news is when they're encouraged, they respond with enthusiasm."*
> —Heather Johnston Nicholson, PhD, Girls Incorporated

> *"When asked why her peers stopped calling her a dog and barking at her, she replied, 'I stopped them.' We sighed in relief until we heard, 'I picked out someone worse off than me and started barking at her. They forgot about me and barked at her instead.' "* —Middle-school girl on relational aggression

GOALS

- To discuss ways to positively impact your daughter's learning

- To raise parental awareness of the gender equity issues in the schools

- To recognize the destructive power of verbal, physical and relational aggression, and to learn about ways to reduce this problem

- To recognize the value of the partnership between families and schools in preparing children for the future

Going off to school marks an important milestone in the life of a child. A child moves from the nurturing environment of hearth and home into the larger society of her culture when she starts school. At school, she encounters a diversity of values and experiences that help her to expand her world, and learn about what her culture expects from its young people. Ideally, our educational system works in partnership with parents to support the intellectual, social, psychological and emotional development of our nation's children. Feeling connected to school is an especially important protective factor for our adolescent girls and thus is an area worthy of our attention and energy. Parents who think of school as a collaborator in preparing their children for the future can reinforce their daughter's learning and activities. Parents are in the best position to monitor the psychological and social well-being of their children, and to assist the school and intervene if these needs are not being met. Parents who take an active role in their children's schools can ensure that the educational environment is accepting, caring and supportive, and one that encourages all students to succeed.

Developmental Asset-Building in Schools

Developmental Asset-building within a school is one manner in which communities can maximize success for all their students by encouraging respectful relationships, caring environments, and successful programs and practices. In fact, 5 of the 40 Developmental Assets relate directly to commitment to learning:

- Achievement motivation—Young people try to do their best in school.
- School engagement—Young people are enthusiastic about learning and come to school prepared.
- Homework—Young people in middle and high school spend at least one hour per day completing homework.
- Bonding to School—Young people care about their school.
- Reading for Pleasure—Young people enjoy reading on their own for at least 3 hours per week.

Young people who have these assets will be more successful in school and less likely to engage in risky behaviors. Asset building in schools is a great way for school staff, parents and communities to encourage success for all children.

Within a school community, respectful, high-quality relationships are more strongly correlated with student academic success than are high-powered programs. The article **"Great Places to Learn: How Asset-Building Schools Help Students Succeed"** (p. 6:13) reminds us that children who feel valued and cared about, who have numerous positive role models, and who feel connected to their school are more able to learn and excel. Teachers and parents are both in excellent positions to help build assets within their kids' schools. **"Every Student a Star"** (p. 6:15) outlines how staff in a Texas middle school of 900 kids reached out to "leave no child behind." The principal first put every child's name on a bulletin board and then asked each teacher to place stickers by the names of the 10 kids they felt closest to. What they discovered was that the students who were the most outgoing received the bulk of the stars. More than half of the kids, including those who needed attention the most, received none. The teachers then divided up the kids with no stars and brainstormed about ways they could establish some sort of meaningful connection with them.

Parents are just as capable of creating assets within their kids' schools. Asset building at a school benefits your own child as well as others; it helps create a community where all children feel cared for no matter what their home environments are like. School volunteers often become important mentors for high-risk children whose success depends on finding positive role models outside of their home environments. Parents do not need to have oodles of time or money to become meaningfully involved in their kids' education. Working parents, who face an additional challenge staying connected to their child's school, may be able to broker paid time off in order to volunteer in a classroom. They can also be involved in nighttime or weekend activities.

There are as many ways to be involved in school as there are parents, and taking the initiative to find some small way to contribute to your daughter's school will greatly benefit both your child and your community. Here are some asset-building ideas that can be organized by parents in conjunction with school staff:

- Greet kids as they arrive at school.
- Arrange a school-wide spaghetti dinner to welcome incoming 6th-grade students and their parents.
- Coordinate a community service day with speakers and parent-led volunteer opportunities.
- Attend open houses and join parent organizations.
- Incorporate Art Literacy—a parent-run art history program.
- Create appreciations for teachers.
- Tutor and mentor students.
- Organize evening school-wide festivals or dances.
- Help in classrooms.
- Teach/facilitate an after-school or lunch recess class/club.
- Organize the school's recycling program.
- Start parent-led, grade-level monthly discussion of timely topics.

Small actions can create a huge ripple effect in your community and can increase the number of assets for your child and her school. The power of parents to improve their children's education is really quite unlimited. "At Home in Our Schools" (p. 6:18) is an article that outlines a novel way of creating a sense of community within our schools. A sense of fun and shared community is enhanced by implementing educational activities where the goal is to have everyone participate, where students work collaboratively with families and other students, and where everyone wins and nobody loses. Included in this article are examples of family-focused activities that parents anywhere can initiate in their schools.

Ten months of the year our neighborhood schools are teeming with activity between the hours of 8 and 3, but think of the potential schools have for community-building when class is not in session. Your school can become a community resource where the doors are "always open" to meet the needs of local children, families, and community members. In some regions of our country, school communities have collaborated with cities and counties to create Community Schools, where schools are used when they are traditionally closed. Community Schools can offer school year and summertime activities, homework and reading clubs, tutoring, mentoring, family fun nights, health fairs, and educational activities for the community. Community Schools increase academic success, encourage family involvement, support families, involve community resources and local businesses in schools, and foster local collaboration to benefit schools and optimize their use as a public resource. In some counties, high schools are the sites of health clinics which offer free health and mental health services for local teens.

The way schools are structured can make a big difference in how readily children (or parents) can bond to school. Recall that "Bonding to School" is an asset and protective factor for teens. Community-building becomes increasingly difficult as schools increase in size. Small schools may not be the most financially viable model, but they do create the critical sense of being known and valued. "Thinking Small in a Big School" (p. 6:20) describes a federally-funded initiative to create smaller communities and better bonding within large high schools. A national trend to keep middle school children in their elementary schools, thereby returning to the older K–8 model, echoes the importance of keeping students bonded to school and school values (kindness, respect, hard work, connection to adults) as they move into adolescence. "Fostering Cooperation and Compassion in the Classroom" and "TRIBES: A New Way of Learning and Being Together" (pp. 6:21-6:22) are included to offer a look at educational models designed to create schools that are safe, respectful containers in which children can learn. As schools decrease competition, increase collaboration and improve relationships, students learn skills that will help them succeed in all aspects of their lives. To be bonded to school, our children need to feel that they can be themselves at school and that people care about them.

Recent education trends fueled by an emphasis on test performance, often ignore developmentally appropriate practices and push formal academics for younger and younger children while withholding the arts and recesses. This is counterproductive for our sons and daughters. Education is not about forcefeeding information to our children, but is about involving the whole person in the process of learning. Children (and adults) need breaks and physical activity to feel content and mentally alert and to retain new information. Furthermore, we need to acknowledge the importance of kinesthetic learning which only occurs when children move their bodies. Playgrounds at recess offer rich opportunities for this learning. As parents we have an important role: to be aware of educational trends that are counter-productive and to advocate for healthy, effective practices that educate the whole child. The importance of arts education for our children is poignantly expressed in the article "**The Power of Arts Education**" (p. 6:23).

"**Girls Night Out**" (p. 6:24) describes a wonderful middle school program that helps girls bond to each other and their school by spending an overnight together at school. Sixth grade is an excellent time to start this program. Moms, older teens (mentors), volunteers and girls themselves offer a flurry of activities that helps bond the kids together and set a positive tone for the rest of their middle school years. Many good memories are created for the girls, teens and moms alike. Again, parental advocacy for such programs is instrumental in creating similar opportunities for the children at your kids' schools.

Another way to increase our children's bonding to school and community is to offer them "place-based education" (see *Place-Based Education: Connecting Classrooms & Communities* by David Sobel). In place-based education, students learn **in** the community: for example, through researching its history, researching and reconstructing aspects of a local watershed, or improving habitat for wildlife in an empty lot or at the edges of the schoolyard. Students become actively involved in their community and become resources to the community. David Sobel describes place-based education in this way:

> *Place-based education is the process of using the local community and environment as a starting point to teach concepts in language arts, mathematics, social studies, science, and other subjects across the curriculum. Emphasizing hands-on, real-world learning experiences, this approach to education increases academic achievement, helps students develop stronger ties to the community, enhances students' appreciation for the natural world, and*

creates a heightened commitment to serving as active, contributing citizens.

Getting our children involved with their world rather than simply observing it is more likely to honor the multiple types of intelligence our children possess.

Character Education and School Success

Parent-school partnership is critical in helping children develop positive character traits. The six pillars of character education (www.charactercounts.com) provide us with a shared vocabulary for teaching ethics: trustworthiness, respect, responsibility, fairness, caring and citizenship. Parents of all religious backgrounds agree with these core values. "**Character Counts! From the Inside Out**" (p. 6:25) describes how a character education program was designed at an elementary school with the intent of encouraging ethical behavior and reducing discipline referrals. Can you imagine what kind of impact a similar program could make in the caring environment of your own child's school?

Schools that emphasize Service Learning as part of their curriculum help develop the character of their students while creating a bond between the school and the community. School service learning can happen at many levels:
- Within school service: recycling, school buddies, gardening, teacher assistance
- Whole class projects: sandwiches for the homeless, pulling ivy at the park
- Family service projects: organize recycling, build bird feeders, family garden
- Community projects organized by students
- Volunteering at a local agency (see Session 10)

Service learning connects students to their communities in ways which allow them to see themselves as people who are making a positive difference. These experiences empower and encourage them to develop the skills and motivation to become responsible citizens.

Character education may be helpful in curbing the widespread practice of cheating, an ethical problem that many schools have had to approach as a singular issue, as noted in "**Cheating in High School is Widespread,**

High-Tech and Contagious" (p. 6:26). Many adolescents struggle with impulsive behaviors such as lying, fibbing and cheating, and unfortunately they are facilitated by modern technology such as cell phone texting, Internet access and instant messaging. As parents, however, our role is to stay true to basic values through modeling and using calm respectful communication and consequences when needed.

Helping your child learn how to learn and study effectively is an important parenting role. You are your daughter's consultant, providing the structure she needs to be successful in school. Some of our daughters are "self starters" and need very little supervision with homework at any age. However, most children benefit from family routines for planning the week (at a family meeting) and weeknight family quiet times when all distractions (except music) are turned off and everyone is doing homework, reading or writing. Don't be surprised if at some point you have to track your daughter more carefully, communicate with teachers, and insist that 100% of homework is completed before fun begins. When your daughter has been absent for a period of time or gets behind, she will also need your support in designing a plan to catch up. **"Helping Our Children Learn Study Skills"** and **"Time Management from a Different Point of View"** (pp. 6:28-6:29) offer some good tips for helping children succeed at school.

While it is important for our children to do reasonably well at school, sometimes parents get too focused on grades and lose track of the bigger picture. Being bonded to school and home is actually more important than getting A's, because the bonding is the protective factor that helps keep your teen making safe and reasonable choices during adolescence. This means that if homework completion starts to become a power struggle with your teen, you may need to shift to more of a coaching strategy, which minimizes nagging and recognizes that homework is a contract between your teen and his or her teacher, and involves natural consequences. Teens generally need more support and less pressure from us in navigating the complexity of this developmental period. If school is not going well for them sometimes it is because they are not getting their needs met in that

school; they may need a smaller magnet school or our older teens may be ready to move out of high school and get their credits from your local community college.

Parents are also wise to supervise the number of hours their daughters work in the community as they reach the teen years. A part-time job can be a source of great growth and pride for a girl, as long as the number of hours worked during the school year remains at less than 15 hours per week. Working enables teens to learn lifelong work and money management skills and gives them a role in the community as well as exposure to future career possibilities. You can check out your state's rules about teenage workers at www.familyeducation. com. However, working too many hours (more than 20) during the school year is associated with lower grades and sleep deprivation and interferes with extracurricular activities and social relationships. Contemporary research shows a direct link between the number of hours worked and the likelihood of dropping out of high school (*Student Workers in High School and Beyond* by Stephen Lamb, et. al.). Parents are an essential resource in helping their daughters maintain a healthy balance between their studies and work. Our daughters also need help in learning to handle stress and to "de-stress" in healthy ways. Our teens are often happy when they are busy with school and many activities, but at times they can feel overwhelmed by their lives. Teach and model living a balanced life.

Educational Equity for our Daughters

Encourage your teenage daughter to take upper level math courses and prepare her along the way so she has the option. Give her the support she needs at each level to succeed in math. Three-quarters of high paying jobs require high-level math, and girls who opt out of math will limit themselves unnecessarily. **"Helping Her Avoid Math Anxiety"** (p. 6:30) notes that parent involvement is one of the most important predictors of increased success in math for girls. In elementary school your support may take the practical path of helping her via flash cards to be quick with her math facts. The article offers tips on how parents can incorporate math into their daughters' lives in fun and practical ways that will encourage self-confidence and mastery. Some schools have tried all-girl math classes for adolescent girls. Based on evidence that girls and boys learn better under different conditions, some schools offer a variety of options which include both same-sex and coed classrooms. For an excellent and thorough review of this topic see *"Teaching Boys and Girls Separately"* by Elizabeth Weil, March 2, 2008, *New York Times*.

Girls have made significant academic strides in the past thirty years as a direct result of schools paying attention to improving the educational environment for girls. The Title IX Educational Amendments that were signed into law by the US Congress in 1972 mandated that equal opportunities be given to males and females in all educational programs that receive taxpayer dollars. Over the last 35+ years Title IX has been a strong anti-discrimination measure providing protection against sexual harassment, participation in sports, classes and clubs, as well as in faculty hiring and admission policies. In many ways Title IX has been an astounding success. In fact, girls are now outperforming boys academically in most arenas, and feel more confident and capable within our educational systems than do boys. Girls are also more likely to graduate from high school and college than boys. This can be attributed to a number of factors, which include the nation's efforts to create more equity for girls within schools, the fact that traditional schooling favors the natural learning styles of girls over boys, and the reality that it is more difficult for girls to find gainful employment in a labor force that still favors men.

In spite of recent academic gains, however, it is still important that parents make sure that their own neighborhood school is presenting an education that is equitable for all students: girls and boys. This means being attentive to the overt and subtle messages that students receive that serve to encourage or discourage them from participation, either on the basis of sex, race, or academic ability. Furthermore, it means not pitting the needs and successes of one gender against the other; rather, insist that all children be educated to the best of their ability and with the goal of universal academic success. Be the supportive critic your school needs. Work with educators to identify areas of change and help them make these changes happen. For instance, some schools have never addressed the issues of educational equity, while others

have provided extensive staff training on equity issues related to curriculum, teacher-student interactions, counseling, teaching materials, school activities and environment. Parents concerned about equity issues can ask the principal about how these issues are being addressed in their school. **"Building on the Strength of Girls"** (p. 6:31) discusses this very important equity issue. Although girls have come a long way, there is still a lot that parents, teachers and schools can do to ensure the academic success of all our girls. Title IX has not remedied all areas of educational inequity, in spite of its laudable successes. Sexual harassment is still experienced by a high percentage of girls and women (as well as some boys and men). Our schools need to teach students what sexual harassment is, that it is against the law, and to report rather than ignore it; all of our younger teens are learning to behave respectfully in different situations and we need to give them specific guidance in these areas.

Relational Aggression in Schools

Learning environments need not only to be openly supportive of girls, they need to be safe from harm, harassment and ridicule. Twenty percent of kids sit in class every day in fear of being bullied (Garity, *Bully Proofing Your School, Intervention in School and Clinic*, 32 (4), pp. 235-243, 1997). No one can learn in the face of fear and intimidation; however, physical, verbal, non-verbal and relational bullying occur at alarming rates amongst our youth. The fear of bullying causes many children to miss school in America each day. While most schools do a good job of disallowing physical bullying, other forms of bullying are rampant and can be just as traumatic for children. Verbal bullying includes name-calling, teasing, insults, putdowns, and making threats. Non-verbal bullying carries similar messages but does so with gestures or dirty looks instead of words. Relational bullying involves using gossip, cliques, rumors or other group activities to ostracize, make fun of, humiliate or harass anyone deemed "different" or "not belonging." Relational aggression is unique in that it is used as much in close relationships as it is against one's enemies. Often, the price of belonging to a clique is the requirement to commit relational aggression against others both inside and outside the group. What can parents do about the problems of bullying within their own children's lives and schools?

The first step is to learn about bullying and then raise awareness of this problem in others. To help you with this, we have summarized the key concepts about peer aggression and its solution in the article "**The Problem with Peer Aggression in our Schools Today**" (p. 6:32). There are skills individual parents, teachers, counselors and administrators can learn to help intervene effectively when a bullying incident occurs. Anti-bullying programs can operate with great success, and parents can be instrumental in insisting that they exist. However, the most effective approach to the problem of aggression is to raise the social norm of the school to higher standards for how people treat each other. The only way this can happen is for the entire school community, from the school board to the youth themselves, to implement sustainable interventions and programs to reduce aggression. Many schools with such programs have reduced bullying and relational aggression tremendously and have successfully created a culture of caring within their school community. An excellent article on the type of aggression girls use on each other, "**Interview with Lyn Mikel Brown on Girlfighting**" (p. 6:38), helps us understand that teen girls are angry in part because our culture puts them down and treats them like commodities. We need to teach girls from the beginning not to take their anger out on other girls and give them the media literacy skills they need to see through the negative cultural messages. "**Taking Action to Stop Relational and Verbal Aggression**" (p. 6:40) shares practical ideas that parents and teachers can use daily. Our children must be taught the power of bystanders to avoid allying themselves with bullying and, on the contrary, to speak up for kindness. This takes courage, confidence, empathy, ingenuity, and communication skills—qualities that will benefit our daughters throughout their entire lives.

The journey through school is an important rite of passage for your child. However, the quality of a child's education tends to correlate strongly with the quality of parent involvement in their school community. Parents who partner with schools to improve education truly create benefits for all the children and families within their community. It is the sincere hope of Family Empowerment Network that parents will be inspired to find many small or large ways to get involved in their children's schools. This *Raising our Daughters* discussion group is a perfect place to start networking together and brainstorming ways for each participant to get involved in improving the lives and education of the children in your own school. Research has proven the benefits: your daughter's life and academic success will be greatly enhanced by your efforts to stay involved.

THE 40 DEVELOPMENTAL ASSETS Essential to Every Young Person's Success

The 40 Developmental Assets are research-proven building blocks that support the healthy development of our youth and help them to grow up to be caring and responsible. The following assets relate directly to a child's academic success and experiences at school:

*   Asset #5   **Caring School Environment:** School provides a caring, encouraging environment.
*   Asset #6   **Parent Involvement in Schooling:** Parent(s) are actively involved in helping young person succeed in school.
*   Asset #9   **Service to Others:** Young person serves in the community, one hour or more per week.
*   Asset #10   **Safety:** Young person feels safe at home, school, and in the neighborhood.
*   Asset #12   **School Boundaries:** School provides clear rules and consequences.
*   Asset #21   **Achievement Motivation:** Young person is motivated to do well in school.
*   Asset #22   **School Engagement:** Young person is actively engaged in learning.
*   Asset #23   **Homework:** Young person spends at least one hour on homework each school day.
*   Asset #24   **Bonding to School:** Young person cares about her school.

CIRCLE QUESTION

Share one positive experience your daughter has had in school,
where she has really blossomed and grown.

POSSIBLE DISCUSSION QUESTIONS

1. How do you perceive your school is doing with educating your child and with partnering with parents?
2. How is your child's school doing with building Development Assets? How can you get involved to increase assets at your child's school?
3. In what ways does your child's school show they care about their students? Does your child (and do you) perceive it as a nurturing, caring place?
4. What kinds of community-building activities occur at the school? What would you like to see?
5. What are some specific steps parents can make to enhance communication between home and school?
6. What strategies have helped your child with study skills, time management, and balance of activities?
7. Is character education being taught in the school? How effective is it? How can you help?
8. In what ways can overt and subtle expectations imposed by parents and teachers limit the growth and development of girls (and boys)? Did this happen to you growing up?
9. How does your school manage equity issues in education?
10. What are the key differences between bullying and conflict? Why is it sometimes hard to tell? How would your parenting be influenced by knowing whether it's bullying or a conflict? Share examples.
11. How much peer aggression goes on at your child's school? What is your school doing to address this problem? Discuss the power of empathy and of addressing the "school climate" for systemic change.
12. How can you empower your child to help reduce peer aggression as a bystander? As an aggressor? As a target? What can you do to help reduce peer aggression at your child's school?

PUTTING IT INTO PRACTICE

- Have your child name people at school who show they care about students. Write a personal note of thanks and appreciation to everyone your child names.
- Engage your child in conversations about what she is learning in school.
- Make learning a family affair. Share each other's hobbies and interests.
- Attend all of your child's parent-teacher conferences, open houses, and community nights.
- Help your child explore all the options for education available to her at her school or elsewhere if her current school is not serving her needs. She may not be aware of interesting opportunities.
- Nurture a sense of school ownership in students; include them in decision-making.
- Volunteer in your child's school: classroom, field trips, library, office or on PTA activities.
- If you work full-time, consider taking a half-day off to go on a field trip or offer to help in the classroom.
- Encourage your place of business to give employees time off to volunteer in a school.
- Plan extracurricular activities that bring students, teachers, administrators and staff together for fun and fellowship (i.e., a Bike Safety Fair, Ice Cream Social).
- Encourage your girls to gain skills outside of the "stereotypical female role."

- Discuss with your child the peer aggression she sees in her school and empower her with information on how to make a positive impact.
- Talk with your daughter about the differences between groups of friends and cliques that emphasize sameness, exclusion and meanness. How can you tell when your group starts becoming a clique? Does your group have a Queen Bee (see Rosalind Wiseman's *Queen Bees and Wannabes*)?
- Recognize the difference between friendship and popularity and that friendship is more important.
- Be a good listener and empathize with your child's social pain, but keep it in perspective.
- Monitor yourself and your family and friends very closely to just notice target, bully and bystander behavior.
- Take a step at being the "gossip-stopper."
- Share stories about how you struggled, learned and/or succeeded in supporting a target? A bystander? What worked?
- Discuss situations where you (or your child) either did step up or wished you had stepped up and helped someone being bullied.
- Try not to worry too much!

PUTTING IT TOGETHER—YOUR VERSION

Write down three or four ideas you have been inspired to implement in your own life after reading and discussing this chapter.

1. _____

2. _____

3. _____

4. _____

FURTHER READING

General Education

Challenge Newsletter: Dept of Ed. publication on Creating Safe and Drug Free Schools at www.thechallenge.org

ERIC (Education Resource Information Center) at www.eric.ed.gov

PTA Parent Teacher Resources at www.pta.org

Search Institute: Building Assets in Schools at www.searchinstitutestore.org

Essential Assets for You at www.essentialassetsforyou.com/Education.htm

Great Places to Learn: How Asset-Building Schools Help Students Succeed by Search Institute

You Have to Live It! video by Search Institute, identifies three themes for asset building in schools

Teaching with the Brain in Mind by Eric Jensen

Seven Kinds of Smart: Identifying and Developing Your Multiple Intelligences by Thomas Armstrong

Raising Lifelong Learners: A Parents Guide by Lucy Calkins and Lyle Bellino

Place-Based Education: Connecting Classrooms & Communities by David Sobel

What Do We Say? What Do We Do? Vital Solutions for Children's Educational Success by Dorothy Rich, EdD

At Home In our Schools: A Guide to School-wide Activities that Build Community, Developmental Studies Center

Ways We Want Our Class to Be: Class Meetings that Build Commitment to Kindness and Learning by Developmental Studies Center

Among Friends: Classrooms Where Caring and Learning Prevails by John Dalton and Marilyn Watson

Your Hyperactive Child: A Parent's Guide to Coping with Attention Deficit Disorder by Barbara Ingersoll, PhD

Overcoming Underachieving: A Simple Plan to Boost Your Kids' Grades and End the Homework Hassles by R. Peters

The Pressured Child: Helping Your Child Find Success in School and Life by Michael Thompson, PhD and T. Barker

Is Your Teen Ready for a Job? and *The Five Worst Jobs for Teens* at www.familyeducation.com

Character Education and School Success

What Do You Stand For? A Kid's Guide to Building Character by Barbara Lewis

Character Counts by Josephson Institute Center for Youth Ethics at www.charactercounts.org

Gender-Focused Education

Girls in the Middle: Working to Succeed in School by The AAUW Educational Foundation

Addressing Relational and Verbal Aggression

Schools Where Everyone Belongs by Stan Davis, one of the best, positive resources for primary and middle schools

Queen Bees and WannaBes by Roselind Wiseman, great overview of "girl culture" and aggression

Cliques: 8 Steps to Help Your Child Survive the Social Jungle by Charlene Giannetti and Margaret Sagarese

Odd Girl Speaks Out by Rachel Simmons, a very insightful book for girls <u>and</u> their parents

Bully, Bullied and Bystander: From Preschool to High School—How Parents and Teachers Can Break the Cycle of Violence by Barbara Colorosa

Nobody Left to Hate: Teaching Compassion after Columbine by Elliot Aronson

Best Friends, Worst Enemies: Understanding the Social Lives of Children by Michael Thompson

Mom, They're Teasing Me: Helping Your Child Solve Social Problems by Michael Thompson

The Bully-Free Classroom by Allan L. Beane

Books for Children and Teens

How To Do Homework Without Throwing Up by Trevor Romain

Get Off My Brain: A Survival Guide for Lazy Students by Randall McCutchen

The Teenage Liberation Handbook: How to Quit School and Get a Real Life and Education by Grace Llewellyn

Keeping Ahead in School: A Student's Book about Learning Abilities and Learning Disorders by Mel Levine, MD

My Secret Bully, Just Kidding, I'm Sorry, and *Trouble Talk* by Trudy Ludwig

Bullies are a Pain in the Brain by Trevor Romain

The 6 Most Important Decisions You'll Make by Sean Covey

Great Places to Learn
How Asset-Building Schools Help Students Succeed
by Neal Starkman, PhD, Peter C. Scales, PhD, and Clay Roberts, MS

School must be more than just a place to learn—even a great place to learn. It should be a place to belong.
—Sara Pierce, Senior, Overland HS, Aurora, Colorado

HOW CAN A SCHOOL build developmental assets? The obvious thought might be for the school to concentrate on the five Commitment-to-Learning assets that are part of Search Institute's 40-asset model. Those five assets describe students who care about their school, are actively engaged in learning, are motivated to do well, hunker down over homework each school night, and read for their own enjoyment.

Yet research suggests that practically all the assets play some role in helping to create and sustain a climate for improved student learning. Although schools can't directly affect all 40 assets, they can have a direct impact on more than half, including the assets that research indicates are very important in promoting academic success (see chart).

A look at the key assets related to academic success reveals that most involve *relationships* more than they do *programs*. They are about how students are treated as individuals, how much they feel valued and cared about, the kinds of positive role models they have, and how connected they feel to their school. Researchers have repeatedly found that schooling is as much social—how students relate to each other and to the adults around them—as it is intellectual.

Yet most students do not experience most of these key assets. In fact, only 7 of the 22 developmental assets that schools can directly influence are experienced by half or more of students. For example, only a minority of students surveyed report experiencing school as a caring place, where students genuinely care about each other, and where students get care and encouragement from their teachers.

How can schools go about changing this? *Great Places to Learn: How Asset-Building Schools Help Students Succeed* identifies three strategic areas for action and offers stories from the field. Read on for a sample.

Forming Relationships

No matter who you are, you can potentially form a respectful, asset-building relationship with a young person. In fact, young people can form such relationships

Assets at Work at School	
Assets Schools Can Most Directly Affect	Percentage of Youth Who Report Experiencing Asset*
School Engagement	64%
Achievement Motivation	63%
Positive Peer Influence	60%
Youth Programs	59%
Safety	55%
Bonding to School	51%
Service to Others	**50%**
School Boundaries	46%
Homework	45%
Peaceful Conflict Resolution	44%
Interpersonal Competence	**43%**
Other Adult Relationships	**41%**
High Expectations	41%
Resistance Skills	37%
Parent Involvement in Schooling	29%
Planning and Decision-Making	29%
Adult Role Models	27%
Caring School Climate	25%
Youth as Resources	25%
Reading for Pleasure	24%
Community Values Youth	**20%**
Creative Activities	19%

*Assets in boldface are those that research suggests are most important to academic success. *Sample of 99,462 6th- to 12th-grade youth surveyed in the 1996-1997 school year. Figures from Peter L. Benson, Peter C. Scales, Nancy Leffert, and Eugene C. Roehlkepartain. 1999. A Fragile Foundation: The State of Developmental Assets Among American Youth. Minneapolis: Search Institute.*

that benefit both themselves and others. Consider, for example, the case of the boy who became a mentor.

Hilde Newman, a social worker at Dry Creek Elementary School in Englewood, Colo., tells the story of a boy (we'll call him Max) who had a number of emotional, learning, and motor problems. He was becoming increasingly difficult to teach—or even have in a classroom. But something happened; somebody looked for and found the positive in Max. One of the teachers told Newman that Max did great in her room.

Asked what was different about the situation there, the teacher revealed that the other students in the room were younger than Max, and he seemed to really enjoy working with them and being a leader.

So Max was given the responsibility of teaching several kindergarten students, and he became a mentor. The improvement in Max was dramatic. He began to walk taller, to show more tolerance for behaving in class, and to concentrate on his own work. "He loves helping out," says Newman, smiling. "He told me, 'I've got it worked out. I've got a plan for the kids.'" He was being treated as a resource, not as a problem, and as a result he more than fulfilled people's expectations and blossomed.

Creating an Environment

Lots of little changes are what add up to an asset-rich environment in which students experience comfort and warmth alongside challenges and boundaries. At New Richmond High School in rural New Richmond, *Wise,* an asset-building approach, has brought about wide-ranging innovations, from including students on the hiring committee for new faculty to adding comments about student strengths on each report card.

And for each new student who enrolls, New Richmond extends a warm welcome, sending out a letter of introduction to staff that might go something like this:

Hello! Let me introduce "Marcia," a new student at New Richmond High School. Marcia likes to read and write and indicates that some of her greatest assets include Planning and Decision-Making, Interpersonal Competence, and Cultural Competence.

Sometimes peaceful Conflict Resolution is a challenge for Marcia. When she experiences a conflict with staff, it's helpful for both the staff person and her if another person is there to help work through the conflict. Marcia is also working to improve her assets in the category of Support.

Using Programs and Practices

Asset-building is not itself a program or a practice; it's a philosophy that informs and shapes how we "do" school and a framework that helps schools organize their efforts on many fronts. But many programs and practices can contribute significantly to making a school a great place to learn. Some of these include service learning, peer mentoring and counseling, and youth leadership activities.

Consider Mitchell Elementary School in Denver, Colo., which has created a number of entrepreneurial programs that give learning a real-world flavor. Students

can see the concrete results of their hard work while at the same time building such assets as responsibility, planning and decision-making, and sense of purpose.

The budding young businesspeople run the Mitchell Mart, where they sell flowers and vegetables they've grown in their own garden behind the school; the school store, in which they sell school supplies to other students; and a vinyl-letter business called SPELL, for Students Producing Educational Letters in Learning. Mitchell Elementary School entrepreneurs can also be spotted pulling a red wagon through the school halls. They're headed to make deliveries for the teacher-supplies warehouse, as well as toward a brighter, asset-rich future.

School Resources

Great Places to Learn: How Asset-Building Schools Help Students Succeed, #722, 216 pages, $29.95.
"You Have to Live It." Building Developmental Assets in School Communities, #723, 27 minutes, VHS, $24.95.
Call Search Institute at 877-240-7251 to order.

Every Student a Star
School Staff Reach Out to the Forgotten Half
By Search Institute, from *Assets* Magazine

ALL KIDS ARE OUR KIDS—AREN'T THEY? Recently, Principal Randy Adair at Benold Middle School in Georgetown, Tex., decided to see to what degree the school was truly embracing that philosophy. He began by posting the names of all 900 Benold Students on the walls of the school cafeteria during a staff planning meeting.

"I said that we were going to do an exercise to let the staff know that all really does mean all," says Adair, referring to that title of the book by Search Institute President, Peter Benson. "I gave each teacher ten stickers and asked them to put a star next to the students that they had the closest relationship to."

After completing the task, the teachers and principal stood back and surveyed the cafeteria walls. What they discovered was that a quarter of the students had more than one star next to their names, but more than half didn't have any stars at all! "My immediate reaction was sadness," says sixth-grade language arts teacher Mindy Ellerbee. "We found that the more outgoing students had all of the stickers, and a number of those students who really needed our attention didn't have any."

The staff then brainstormed about those students who didn't have a connection to a staff member, identifying small ways to reach out without necessarily drawing attention to what they were doing. "A lot of these kids don't want a mentor and are suspicious of adults based on their own past relationships," says Adair. He acknowledges it can be a challenge to build bridges to such youth, especially those in high-risk situations who find learning and bonding to the school community difficult.

"I asked the teachers to put a star next to the names of the kids that they would start a relationship with in some way," says Adair. "To start, it could be as simple as saying 'Hi!' to that young person in the hall." Adair calls this strategy "the silent mentor concept."

Ellerbee is taking small steps to connect with her silent mentee, who struggles with low self-esteem. "My goal is not to be any different in his eyes but to raise my awareness of his needs," she says.

Adair says these new relationships will not only improve student self-esteem but will also allow them to excel academically. Ellerbee agrees. "I've found that by talking more about the Assets and raising the level of respect, student put more effort into their work than ever before," she says. "I believe it's because they get the sense that teachers care. The improved performance of Ellerbee's new star in her classroom is proof positive for her.

Reprinted with permission from "Every Student a Star: School Staff Reach Out to the Forgotten Half,"*Assets: The Magazine of Ideas for Healthy Communities and Healthy Youth.* Copyright © Spring 2000, Search Institute ®, Minneapolis, MN; www.search-institute. org. All rights reserved.

Asset-Building Ideas for Teachers

By Search Institute, from *Pass It On! Ready-to-Use Handouts for Asset Builders*

TO TEACH IS TO TOUCH a life forever. Teachers have the potential to be powerful asset builders. In addition to the Commitment-to-Learning assets (21-25), five other assets (3: Other Adult Relationships; 5: Caring School Climate; 8: Youth as Resources; 12: School Boundaries; and 14: Adult Role Models) focus on the important role of a teacher. Below are some suggestions for what teachers can do to build assets. These suggestions are intended to give you some ideas for how to get started. They may need to be modified or adapted depending on the grade you teach; whether you are a classroom teacher, specialist, or resource teacher; and the nature of your school environment.

Asset Building in General

- Post the list of assets in your classroom.
- Devote a bulletin board in your classroom to asset-building messages.
- If your community has an asset-building initiative, get involved.
- Train all volunteers and support staff you work with to the asset framework.
- Plan asset-building learning activities as part of the curriculum (for example, service learning projects, social skills training, or setting aside time to read for pleasure).
- Put an asset-building message on your computer screen saver. One school used the slogan, "Wrap Your Arms around Cherry Creek Kids . . . Build Assets!"

Support

- Greet students by name when you see them.
- Send a letter to parents about the idea of asset building, and then use assets as springboards for discussions in conferences with parents and students.
- Meet with other teachers and brainstorm ways to help students succeed. A school in Wisconsin set up DATES (Developing Assets to Encourage Success) meetings that are designed to help students who are struggling academically.
- Encourage access to at least one caring adult for each student in the building. Homerooms can facilitate this.
- Provide asset-building resources for parents.

Empowerment

- Teach students about the 40 Assets and help them set goals for assets they want to develop (two resources for this are *Me@My Best* and *Take It to the Next Level*, published by Search Institute).
- Provide opportunities for service learning. Help students plan and make decisions about providing service to others.
- Empower students by encouraging them to tell their stories through written and visual autobiographies.

Boundaries and Expectations

- Work with students to set school boundaries or rules. Post a written set of the rules in conspicuous places: hallways, classrooms, the lunchroom, the gymnasium, and other common areas. Create copies of the rules and have an agreement form for students and parents to sign, indicating their willingness to stay within the boundaries.

- Set high and clear expectations for student behavior and learning outcomes.

Constructive Use of Time

- Create visual symbols of assets. For example, cooperative murals can show the importance of working together to strengthen the community. Art students can create self-portraits that reflect their assets.
- Thank other teachers, staff, and students when you catch them building assets.
- Demonstrate sensitivity with respect to student involvement in extracurricular activities. Some teachers make it a practice to always allow at least two nights for students to complete assignments.
- Read biographies or view videos or films about musicians and other artists. Discuss the assets students see in these people's lives.
- Discuss current music, movies, or arts and entertainment and the messages they send. Do they build assets or not?

Commitment to Learning

- Discuss the assets of characters in stories, history lessons, and current events. For example, when studying Romeo and Juliet, talk about how asset deficits can lead to tragedies. Change the tale by building assets for the two main characters.
- Use assets as the focus for assignments.
- Choose a quote of the day with an asset focus and ask students to talk about it.
- Introduce students to web sites that have asset-building themes.
- Read biographies of people who have realized their dreams. Talk about the assets that helped those people succeed.

Positive Values

- Ask students to gather information about their heroes—famous or not. Then have small-group or class discussions about what values these heroes seem to have and how those values guide who they are and what they do.

- As a class, create a list of shared values. See the Positive-Values assets (26-31) as a place to start. Talk about what it takes to uphold these values. Set boundaries and expectations based on these values.

Social Competencies

- Provide a process in the classroom for mutual goal setting and evaluation. Such a process empowers students and actively engages their learning.
- Encourage planning through the use of student agendas and calendars.
- Use resources in your community to help teach Cultural Competence (asset 34). Consider having students organize a diversity-awareness week, a cultural fair, or some other way of learning about each other's backgrounds and cultures.
- Don't let students get away with bullying or fighting. Talk to them about how to solve conflicts peacefully.

Positive Identity

- Use "strength interviews" with students to help them identify their assets and their sources of support.
- Attend concerts, programs, and activities your students are involved in.
- Congratulate successes with a written note, a call home, or verbal praise.
- Create life-planning portfolios that follow a student from the end of one school year to the beginning of the next school year and include goals, dreams, and hopes. They can be an important tool for the student—and for teachers—to keep track of accomplishments and challenges.

The Developmental Assets are positive factors within young people, families, communities, schools, and other settings that research has found to be important in promoting the healthy development of young people.

At Home in Our Schools

A Guide to School-Wide Activities That Build Community
Ideas for Parents, Teachers, and Administrators from the Child Development Project
at the Developmental Studies Center

Creating a Sense of Community

While many of the community-building ideas presented here will be familiar, what may be new is the emphasis on the relationships that form and foster a sense of community—relationships that include everyone, avoid competition, and respect differences but lessen hierarchical divisions between older and younger students, staff members and students, and teachers and parents. As you read the pages that follow, think about your goals for community building and about the school-wide activities your school already sponsors. Then think about ways in which small shifts in focus may better align these activities with your goals.

Consider the following example of how these essential ingredients might be realized in an actual activity, such as your school's annual science fair. How can the "traditional" science fair—in which children compete to create the "best" project in the hope of winning an award—be given a CDP "twist" to create an environment where everyone is included, everyone works cooperatively, and everyone wins?

Traditional vs. Noncompetitive	
"Traditional" Science Fair	Noncompetitive Science Fair
• Individual students create science projects that are displayed in a central area, such as a gym or a library. Students and families view the projects. Prizes are awarded to "outstanding" projects.	• Science experiments and activities are set up around the school in different classrooms. Students and families visit the classrooms and try out the activities. Students and families become more comfortable in school and experience a collaborative learning atmosphere—everyone is a learner.
• Competitive • Goal is to win • Students work individually	• Collaborative • Goal is to participate • Students work with families and other students
• Parents observe • Teachers judge • Some people win, some people lose • Excludes students and families unwilling to compete	• Parents participate • Teachers participate • Everyone wins, no one loses • Includes everyone

Family Projects Fair

A Family Projects Fair begins with families deciding on a cooperative project to do at home—for example, they might document a project that they work on together, such as planting a garden; create a project such as a science experiment or model; or make a display about a family interest, such as baseball or rock collecting. The emphasis should be on the process of working together as a family, rather than on the resulting "product." Families then show their projects at school for the Family Project Fair, during which they can both explain their work to other families in the school community and learn from the other families' projects.

Family Math Night

Family Math is a widely used parent involvement program developed by EQUALS at the Lawrence Hall of Science of the University of California at Berkeley. Together, parents and children attend a series of hands-on workshops where they use math manipulatives such as blocks, pennies, and other easy-to-find objects to understand more about numbers and space and to develop strategies for solving mathematics problems.

Working for a Cause

Each school picks a "helping opportunity that interests its students and staff—such as collecting supplies for disaster victims, raising money for a cause, or working together on a community service project such as a toy drive or walk-a-thon. Students apply their considerable energy and ingenuity to a cause that lets them reach out and contribute to the wider community.

Family Read-Aloud

Family Read-Aloud brings students, families, teachers, and school staff members together in a comfortable environment to enjoy reading. This event helps unite the entire school community around the importance of reading without setting up a competition among students and classes.

Family Science Night

Family Science Night is a high-involvement "messing around" time for children and their parents. Together, families make their way from classroom to classroom exploring a variety of hands-on science activities that students have created in class during the weeks leading up to the event.

These are summary excerpts describing some community-building ideas. Full details on ways of implementing these projects can be found in the book, *At Home in Our Schools: A Guide to School-Wide Activities That Build Community* by Alfie Kohn.

Reprinted with permission from Developmental Studies Center, 2000 Embarcadero, #305; Oakland, CA 94606, 1-800-666-7270, www.dvstu.org. Copyright 1994. All rights reserved.

Thinking Small in a Big School

By Linda West

TRAGIC INCIDENCES OF violence on school campuses prompted Congress to fund the development of small, safe and successful learning environments within large high schools. Three-fourths of high schools have over 1,000 students and half have over 1,500. Researchers and educators believe that large, impersonal schools may lead to increased apathy, isolation and alienation.

The Smaller Learning Communities Initiative is a $45 million federal grant program to develop smaller learning communities so that all students receive more personalized attention in order to make a successful transition to college, careers and productive citizenship. US Dept. of Education research supports that smaller learning environments result in increased student achievement, attendance and connectedness, and a decrease in disciplinary actions, drug and alcohol use.

Across the country, schools are examining ways of reorganizing their use of time, space and student/staff relationships to create safer and more effective learning environments. Southridge High School (SHS) near Portland, Oregon, is one such high school. SHS was designed to house its 1,800 students in 4 smaller, more personalized learning communities of 450 students each. In its second year of the Smaller Learning Communities grant, SHS is seeing the results: student achievement, test scores and academic rigor have increased, absentee and dropout rates have decreased. Says principal, Sarah Boly, "It's about re-inventing the 'American High School.' Smaller learning communities have the greatest potential for personalizing learning and are very supportive of humane treatment of kids. To create a small school, you have to create a democratic school."

So what are the key elements of the SHS initiative? Increase personalization of education and relationships with adults by:

- The neighborhood structure that includes a core group of teachers, parent volunteers, and an advisor, counselor and administrator who provide the student's base for four years.
- More in-depth teacher contact by having 5 classes a day for 70 minutes. (Many schools have 6-8 periods with educators facing upwards of 170 students daily!) Teachers and students alike get to know each other better. In the 9th/10th grade, Language Arts and Social Studies are teamed: teachers have the same students in both classes.

"To create a small school, you have to create a democratic school."

- Assignment of an advisor with whom each student meets 2 to 3 times each week for 4 years to obtain academic support, conduct career and college planning and address important school climate issues. Each advisor has 25 students of all grade levels and a Link Crew Leader, who is a senior trained to serve as a big brother/sister to freshmen.
- Offering of Career Academies: Students focus their studies in one of 6 Career Academies ranging from Science and Technology to Arts and Communication. Students work closely with their Academy Advisor to pursue an individualized course of study that includes a senior project and field experience.
- Completion of a Service Learning requirement: In order to graduate, every student completes at least 60 hours of community service that is tied to their course work, thus making their schooling more authentic and relevant.
- Offering a variety of courses and programs: Based on a trimester schedule, students graduate with 30 credits, as opposed to the standard 24. Students are encouraged to explore their interests, pursue their dreams and prepare for college and career. A strong International Baccalaureate program allows students to earn a full IB diploma or follow their passion in a particular subject area. The Learning Center offers 9th and 10th grade students a daily study period with a peer tutor, resulting in both academic and social success. Students sit in small table groups, not individual desks, emphasizing discussion and interaction, not isolation. Teachers team and make inter-disciplinary connections.
- Valuing student voices: As members of staff committees, students raise questions, address key issues and make proposals on issues ranging from advisory topics to discipline policies.

At SHS, the Small School grant has enabled staff to look at other model programs and collaboratively examine their own teaching. The SHS staff are committed to small school reform that has proven so effective in their work with students.

Linda West is a high school teacher in Beaverton, Oregon.

Reprinted with permission from Full Esteem Ahead, *Wings*, Winter 2002.

Fostering Cooperation and Compassion in the Classroom

By Kathy Keller Jones, MA

IN MANY HIGH SCHOOLS and middle schools around the country, the academic environment encourages students to compete against each other for grades and teacher attention. Students have 6-8 classes like this a day and the competition in the classroom exacerbates competition outside the classroom. Everything becomes a competition: the car you drive, the clothes you wear, the sports you play. This highly competitive atmosphere creates a situation of winners, losers, and those in the middle. The winners and those in the middle will distance themselves from the losers, often teasing and taunting then. We've seen these situations escalate in cases like Columbine and Springfield.

Many schools have tried to counteract the effect of too much competition. In fact, in elementary and preschools, children are encouraged to share, treat others with respect and cooperate, even nurturing students with outdoor classes. All children are included, even those with learning disabilities or physical handicaps. Unfortunately, teaching inclusion and using cooperative learning techniques become less common as children grow older. It is hard to find a high school that has successfully dealt with the negative impact of competition.

The "jigsaw classroom" is a cooperative learning structure and has been used successfully for over 30 years. It was developed by Elliot Aronson, author of *Nobody Left to Hate: Teaching Compassion after Columbine*. The jigsaw classroom is designed to reduce competition and increase cooperation among students. It is successful, because unlike other cooperative learning environments, it requires everyone's cooperation to produce the final product. For example, if in the name of cooperation, we simply put a group of students together to work on a project, the one or two most motivated students will do most of the work and they will resent that they have had to carry the load. The less able and less motivated students will do less, learn less, and end up feeling inadequate. While it seems like this model should have created cooperation, it didn't.

The jigsaw classroom works like this: the class is divided into small groups of 5-6 students. Each group is assigned the task to learn, for example, about World War II. Each member of the group is assigned a different area to become an expert in. For example, one student researches Hitler's rise to power, another is assigned to learn about concentration camps, the others research Britain's role, the Soviet Union's role, Japan's role and the atomic bomb. Each student goes off to research their given area. Then a student researching the atomic bomb may work with students who are also assigned to learn about the atomic bomb but are from different groups. This helps ensure that information is complete and accurate. After all the students have researched their individual areas, the groups reconvene to share their information. Even the students who didn't do their research well, but went to the group meeting on their subject, will have valuable information to share. Each group member has to listen intently to the person reporting or they will not be able to learn the information they may need for the test that follows.

There are many benefits to this style of learning. The jigsaw classroom (www.jigsaw.org) is an efficient way to learn material, but more importantly, it gives every student an important role and requires that everyone listen attentively. Only teamwork can achieve the desired outcomes, and individual and group goals become intertwined. Each student ends up collaborating successfully with a variety of classmates, some of whom s/he might not normally interact with. Ideally a sense of belonging will be created within the classroom. In the same way that competition in the classroom exacerbates competition outside the classroom, cooperation, empathy, and compassion in the classroom will lead to cooperation, empathy, and compassion outside the classroom. Our children of all ages need to be taught in ways and about topics that foster the development of compassion, respect, and cooperation.

Resources:
Check out www.jigsaw.org.
Nobody Left to Hate by Elliot Aronson

TRIBES: A New Way of Learning and Being Together

By Nancy Huppertz

A CLASSROOM IS A microcosm of a community. The members are together on a regular basis, in the same place, and must function together to attain group and individual goals. At the elementary level, the group is usually intact for 5 to 6 hours each day. At the secondary level, groups are together for only 50 or 90 minutes, but they are together every day and, to be most successful, must function harmoniously.

Teachers are trained well in their content areas. They know what to teach and most have acquired skills in how to get the information across to students. What most teachers lack is the skill to turn a room full of individuals into a group that functions well for all its members. What happens in the classroom each day is an important part of a student's educational experience not only cognitively, in terms of the content taught, but emotionally and socially, how it feels to be in the classroom, how s/he is treated by the teacher and other students and whether s/he feels an integral part of what is going on.

TRIBES is a national program that trains teachers how to build community in the classroom. The goal is to make all students feel welcome and viable, to feel as though they are regarded and treated in a positive manner by the teacher and other students, and to have the knowledge, skills and resilience to be successful in a rapidly changing world.

TRIBES is not a curriculum, but a process that uses three phases and a set of community agreements to transform a room full of isolates into a group.

TRIBES begins with INCLUSION. Teachers learn how to take the time to build caring and support within the group by allowing students to get to know each other. A skilled TRIBES teacher knows how to encourage students to participate in inclusive activities without feeling that they have to reveal personal information if they do not wish. Barriers between diverse students begin to crumble as they begin to know and enjoy their similarities and respect their differences.

The next phase of TRIBES is INFLUENCE. Teachers give students a sense of value and offer meaningful participation by modeling and teaching communication skills, some as basic as taking turns speaking, rotating responsibilities in small groups, asking questions, listening, disagreeing without rancor, and problem-solving. TRIBES teachers know not to assume that the students already have these skills. Many adults do not.

Finally, TRIBES recognizes the importance of APPRECIATION. Time is taken to express thanks to other members of the group for working together and students are taught to value the contributions and celebrate the achievements of others.

The community agreements taught early on in TRIBES classrooms include: attentive listening, appreciation, no put-downs, mutual respect, and the right to pass.

Judi Mackey, a middle school principal in the state of Washington, sponsored a TRIBES training for her entire staff. The staff was so enthusiastic about the concepts and process that they began using them in staff meetings as well as in their classrooms. A year later, Principal Mackey reported a decline in absenteeism among students and staff and a reversal in attitudes of substitutes previously reluctant to come to her school—all attributed by Mackey to the implementation of TRIBES.

Schools throughout the US and Canada are using TRIBES to create safe and non-violent schools, engage students in the prevention and management of conflict, make cooperative learning work well, teach students collaborative social skills and provide inclusion and respect for multicultural populations. TRIBES was developed and written by Jeanne Gibbs.

Parents who would like to see a TRIBES training occur in their child's school may contact CenterSource Systems at 1-800-810-1701 to get the name of a TRIBES trainer in their area. The trainer can provide complete information about TRIBES to the principal and may be willing to do a brief overview of TRIBES for a parent group or faculty meeting. Check out the web site at www.tribes.com.

Nancy Huppertz is a gender equity specialist who runs Apogee Training and Consulting, consulting firm specialists in gender equity issues for organizations and schools throughout the United States.

Reprinted with permission of Full Esteem Ahead, *Wings*, Winter, 2002.

The Power of Arts Education: Everything I Need to Know I Learned from My Dance (Art) Teacher

By Georgia Harker

TRYING TO "REACH" our teens, we often listen to their words but miss their meaning. Just like the rest of us, our children communicate in many ways. Encouraging and supporting our adolescents' continuing involvement with the arts is one way to "hear" what they are trying to say and teach life skills.

Linda Smith, my dance teacher, taught me that my dancing is a unique, personal, and important form of expression, but that the underlying experiences are universal. I learned to:

- Not automatically accept my first solution to any problem.
- Keep building my skills to perform my best work.
- Use eye contact.
- Present my work and myself confidently.

Through the arts we learn many things. As a parent and an artist, I'm continually reminded of the power and importance of the arts and arts education in our children's lives. When there are opportunities for self-expression, risk-taking, problem solving, and imagination in a supportive environment, good things happen.

Jan von Bergen, a teacher at the Arts and Communication High School in Beaverton, Oregon, has taught art for 22 years. She believes very passionately that "one of the worst things you could do to teenagers is to take away their expressive outlets. They are vital. It would be like cutting their heads off!" She thinks art education encourages students to dig within, to push themselves, and to improve at something. She believes this is great for building self-esteem.

How does Jan encourage healthy self-esteem in her students? "My approach is always, 'tell me about that,' not, 'what is that?' In spite of teenagers' apparent bravado, they are really very sensitive. You can inadvertently put the kibosh on something that would have been great, by seeming to criticize it. What matters most is not what I see in their work, but what they are trying to create."

Art, music, and theater classes can be havens for students who don't shine in the prescribed ways most schools emphasize. I still harbor a crush on a tall, charming guy I knew in high school. While barely passing most of his other classes, he produced amazing and ambitious creations in Mr. Morrison's art class. Howard Gardner, Harvard education specialist and author, might say my friend displayed "high degrees of visual/spatial and kinesthetic intelligence." Gardner's research into the brain and learning styles led him to identify seven different forms of intelligence, and to call for radical changes in how we teach and raise kids.

In his book, *The Unschooled Mind*, Gardner says that different people learn, think, and respond to the same stimulus differently. We want to acknowledge that and help children build on their strengths. For teens who are more spatially, musically, or kinesthetically oriented, involvement in the arts may be the vital link with school and learning. "To the extent that students feel good about themselves, feel productive, have an opportunity to be critical and creative in the arts," he says, "these can have positive spin-offs in the class and in school."

Anna Montgomery is a family friend whose self-confidence was clearly bolstered by her decision to attend a small, arts-oriented high school. She thought she would feel lost, or be labeled "weird" at a large school, where she finds most of the energy and attention go into fashion and sports. She likes being in a place where self-expression is valued and expected.

Jan von Bergen has great advice for parents: "Allow for different approaches! As much as possible in school and in life, present the important concepts and goals you'd like them to achieve. Then let them decide how to get there. Allow for growth. Help them to take chances, and to stretch out of their comfort zone. Otherwise, they'll never reach new levels of understanding and achievement."

Georgia Harker is a designer and writer who works with her husband Chris, for Cayuse, their software company. She has a daughter and a son.

Reprinted with permission from Full Esteem Ahead, *Wings*, Winter 1999.

Girls Night Out: An Event to Celebrate Girl Power!

By Cindy Easton and Kathy Keller Jones, MA

"I don't like her, she's a prep." "I look way fat in this outfit." "She thinks she's just TOO cute." "My hair is sooo ugly, why can't I look like her." "Check out her bad style, she's a geek." "I'd do anything to go out with that guy!"

HAVE YOU EVER heard these statements or similar ones coming out of the mouth of a middle-school girl? Walk down the hall of any middle school and you'll probably hear a variety of self-deprecating, callous, or "catty" statements like these.

Middle school is a difficult time in a girl's life. Filled with hormonal surges, girls' bodies are changing and taking on a new shape. Friend groups are more defined and labeled: prep, goth, geek, etc. Girls feel pressured to look a certain way, act a certain way, dress a certain way. Their self-esteem is often challenged and frequently declines.

Research suggests that strategies to address the needs of middle-school girls include making them aware at an early age of their worth and power as females and providing opportunities for them to learn about issues such as body image, self-esteem, and relational aggression. Some girls progress confidently through their middle-school years, but many do not and all girls could benefit from a forum that addresses girls' needs.

Girls Night Out, an overnight event at the middle school, is a program that provides middle-school girls with the opportunity to find out more about themselves, increase their self-esteem and celebrate "girl power" in a positive way. It is an event that changes lives. We've seen it happen.

Imagine 100 seventh- and eighth-grade girls from all different walks of life spending the night together listening to inspiring female speakers, sharing about themselves in small groups run by high school mentors, having their hair done and trying out new make-up, running around slamming each other with pillows, belting out bad karaoke tunes on the microphone, making new friends, breaking down barriers, seeing one another from a new perspective, falling asleep in the "wee hours" . . . this is what *Girls Night Out* is all about. Through the use of female speakers, small group activities, themed stations, and games the participants acquire tools and experience bonding that strengthens their self-worth and empowers them as young women.

One seventh grader wrote: "Girls today deal with a lot of ups and downs because of friendships, relationships and school itself. *Girls Night Out* helps girls realize just how special they are and that they can and will become somebody. The event gives girls a chance to make new friends and teaches them how to get along with others . . . the purpose of the event is to have fun, but also to learn."

Another middle school made a sixth-grade girls' overnight the culmination of a friendship class all the sixth graders took in the fall during their Health and Spanish period. The eighth-grade peer helpers organized and conducted the yearly event in which they had participated earlier. The girls set up camp in the auditorium and then got ready for their evening activities by playing mixer games, which facilitated the introduction of another girl. Then it was off to the gym for a "hands-on" self-defense class designed for girls their age (i.e., not scary but very empowering). After that the girls gathered to put on relational aggression skits (the "bad" way and the "good") with their eighth-grade friends. Finally the lights were dimmed for the movie, with hair, nails, beading and other stations going on simultaneously. After a break for preparing for bed, and a pillow fight, the eighth graders went home and the sixth graders enjoyed their nutritious snack while sitting on their sleeping bags in the dark watching the second half of the movie. After the movies, it was quiet time until breakfast.

Girls Night Out is a rewarding way to help our girls bond to each other and to school while learning how great it is to be a girl in today's world.

Cindy Easton developed this program as a middle school teacher at H.B. Lee and is a former marketing, event-planning and development director. Kathy Keller Jones is a school counselor who created a Girls Night Out for sixth graders.

Reprinted with permission from Full Esteem Ahead, *Wings*, Summer 2000.

Character Counts! From the Inside Out

By Liz Swinea, School Principal

"Not one more thing! Our plate is full and overflowing!" teachers are saying. They are bombarded with information, technological advances, and more and more pressure for accountability for student achievement. How can they possibly be expected to teach one more thing? And of all things, why character education? I believe we can't afford to not teach character education, purposefully, systematically, and pervasively. With violence, substance abuse, and delinquency on the rise, there is a sense of urgency to reduce the risk factors that contribute to these problems, while promoting protective processes as preventive measures. Character development—a firm understanding of and commitment to core ethical values is one such protective measure. It is essential to inform and to energize conscientious, proactive decision-making.

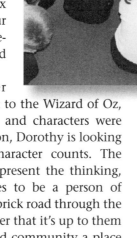

The staff of Lincoln Elementary School identified character education as a means through which we would raise achievement and decrease disciplinary referrals. We specifically chose *Character Counts!*, a nationally recognized, community-based program directed toward developing character in children. Founded by Michael Josephson, the *Character Counts! Coalition* is a project of the Josephson Institute of Ethics. It identifies Six Pillars that "clearly define us at our best"—trustworthiness, respect, responsibility, fairness, caring, and citizenship.

To initiate our Character Counts! program, we compared it to the Wizard of Oz, since we felt that the story line and characters were familiar to most kids. In our version, Dorothy is looking for someplace special, where character counts. The Scarecrow, Tin Man, and Lion represent the thinking, compassion, and courage it takes to be a person of character. They follow the yellow brick road through the Pillars of Character, only to discover that it's up to them to make their school, families, and community a place where character counts. The script was the brainchild of teachers, Cindy Robnett and Kathleen Augsburger.

Each month we study a Pillar of Character, integrating it throughout the curriculum, from reading to math to P.E. Everywhere on campus, kids are "caught" being persons of character and are awarded a coupon, which goes into a weekly lottery for prizes. Daily announcements include brief comments about what character looks like and sounds like—at school, at home, and downtown. We've created a "citizenship" grade on the report card. To earn an A, students must not only follow the rules, they must also provide two hours of community service. We celebrate quarterly success, and students who earn A's three of the four quarters are inducted into the Kids' Character Counts! Club.

Parent involvement is an integral part of our program. Through newsletters from school, and a page in our local newspaper, we keep parents and the community informed of the monthly pillar. We identify vocabulary, and the do's and don'ts specific to the current pillar. This year we'll sponsor several parent seminars to encourage support and to invite input on improving the program.

We've encouraged community involvement by posting kid-made posters in our stores, and requesting patrons to ask our kids about the Pillar of the Month. Kids' Club members march in our community's annual parade in June. As we emphasize community service, we're supporting the community's swimming pool enhancement campaign, setting a goal of $2000 in our own "Pennies for the Pool" project.

The responsibility to teach our youngsters about character rests with all of us—parents, schools, and community members. Yes, it does take a village to raise a child. Thank goodness, we're in it together—for kids' sake!

Elizabeth Swinea ran this program as principal of Lincoln Elementary in Coquille, Oregon. The Character Counts! website is www.charactercounts.org.

Reprinted with permission of Full Esteem Ahead, *Wings*, Winter 1999.

Cheating in High School is Widespread, High-tech and Contagious

By Kathy Masarie, MD

HIGH SCHOOL STUDENTS today find themselves in a competitive environment where grades and test scores determine their eligibility for graduation, upscale scholarships, university admissions and favored academic status. Faced with family and academic pressures to succeed, many students are cheating as a convenient and efficient way to get ahead.

Cheating has become much easier for students now that they have access to computers and the Internet. Numerous websites offer tips on how to cheat and others sell downloadable term papers for $10-$15 apiece. The Internet acts as a multi-billion page encyclopedia, offering endless cut and paste opportunities for students who plagiarize to enhance their own writing.

Classroom cheating has also hit the high-tech age. Students can use small fonts to create crib sheets on business or note cards, which they then use to cheat on tests. Palm pilots can be used to "beam" answers to each other, and calculators can be programmed with algebraic formulas that are supposed to be memorized.

"Students are getting a bottom-line mentality that grades matter, not learning," states Elizabeth Kiss, director of the Kenan Institute for Ethics at Duke University. She notes that cheating starts at ages 11-13, when schools begin to place more emphasis on grades.

Michael Josephson, founder of Josephson Ethics Institute notes that kids do not grow out of cheating. "In fact," he says, "they grow into it. Cheaters are more likely to lie on resumes, expense reports and insurance claims."

The problem of cheating has always been around, but it is getting more common and more acceptable in recent years. A 2002 study by the Josephson Ethics Institute found that 74% of 12,000 high school students nationwide had cheated on a test in the previous year. This represented a 21% increase over a decade before. As well, 38% of the students admitted to stealing from a store within the past 12 months, and over 80% admitted to lying to parents and teachers. Of these students, 43% of them agreed with the statement that "a person has to lie or cheat sometimes in order to succeed." This is a substantial increase from just two years previous, and indicates a growing cynicism amongst our young people.

Josephson notes, *"The evidence is that a willingness to cheat has become the norm and that parents, teachers, coaches and even religious educators have not been able to stem the tide. The scary thing is that so many kids are entering the workforce to become corporate executives, politicians, airplane mechanics and nuclear inspectors with the dispositions and skills of cheaters and thieves."*

A similar 2001 study by Donald McCabe of the Rutgers University Management Education Center found that 75% of 4,500 high school students had engaged in serious cheating, up from 50% in 1993 and 25% in 1963. This study also found that more than half of the students had plagiarized work they found on the Internet, and a similar number did not see anything wrong with cheating. When students were asked why they cheat, most cited academic pressures and the poor examples set by the adult world. McCabe notes, "I think kids today are looking to adults and society for a moral compass, and when they see the behavior occurring there, they don't understand why they should be held to a higher standard."

What can parents and teachers do about this phenomenon of cheating? First of all, it is important to make your values of trust and integrity clear to your students. Children not only need to hear that cheating in any form is a serious offense; they need to watch adults be good role models in their own lives. Kids notice when adults act in untrustworthy or dishonest ways, and frequently copy what they have learned. Honesty, trust and integrity are best taught by example.

Websites, such as www.nocheating.org, offer tips, advice, and free pamphlets to help adults teach values that counteract cheating. Teachers can also educate kids about plagiarism and utilize a number of website services that check term papers with search engines to identify plagiarism. Parents and teachers can help by emphasizing learning over class standing and grades. This may mean taking an active role in redirecting your own academic emphasis and goals for your child, as well as influencing that of your child's teachers and the local school system. Helping your child to get organized is a big help for kids who cheat due to time crunches and/or overextended schedules. This could mean helping your child to schedule time on the calendar to work on bigger projects, limiting extracurricular activities, or brainstorming with your child about ideas and research.

Most of all, it is important for parents to resist the urge to do homework for their child. One study of middle schoolers found that 33% turned in work done by their parents. This sets a terrible example, as it involves kids in cheating with the sanction of their parents and robs them of an opportunity to learn for themselves.

Josephson summarizes: *"The biggest single factor in escalating academic dishonesty is the failure of parents and teachers to diligently teach, enforce, advocate and model personal integrity. It's the adults, not the kids, who have the greatest responsibility to create an ethical culture that nurtures the virtues of honor, honesty and fairness."*

Helping Our Children Learn Study Skills

By Susan Wellman, founder of *The Ophelia Project*

My child wants me to be with her when she studies. I need that time to get things done around the house. How important is it that I study with her?

My son is totally disorganized when he studies. I tell him to clean off his desk; he tells me he likes to work that way. I don't know what to do about it.

Studying each night in our home has become a war zone. Our kids want us to help them, but when we do they just get mad at us. I also have to hassle them to get off the phone or away from the TV. They argue that they study better in front of the TV. It's making me crazy and I'm about to give up entirely. What do you recommend?

DO THESE SOUND like they could have come from your home? You're not alone. All parents struggle with the homework issue. Here are some tips to help parents create a good study environment at home:

1. Choose a good study site where the whole family can be together rather than having children working alone in their rooms.
2. Create a "distraction-free" zone during study times. Turn off the phone so you don't even hear it ring. If your child needs background noise to study, turn the radio on low volume.
3. Make this a time when everyone in the family is studying or reading. Reading together as a family is one of the best ways to encourage the activity.
4. Create an aura in your home where learning is "what we do in our family," just like "we use napkins instead of our sleeves" or "we listen when someone has a concern."
5. Make "learning" not "homework" the task.
6. Correct homework only if your child asks for help and if this is a peaceful activity between you and your child. Reassure your child that the goal is NOT to get everything right. It is to learn the material, eventually, not necessarily all at once.
7. When your child is "stuck" (angry, frustrated, self-deprecating, bored), try these tips:
   - Show a genuine interest in what your child is learning.
   - Ask your child questions that he/she CAN answer—be the learner and allow your child to be the teacher. If you are both clueless about an assignment, suggest questions the child can ask the teacher the next day and be eager to hear the answers when your child returns.
   - When you or your child can't do something, use that moment to role model effective problem-solving skills—ask questions, seek answers, practice and acknowledge that the learning process involves stretching and not always being able to do something right away. If your child can always do the work, he/she is not being challenged.
   - If you see a problem, speak directly with the teacher rather than venting your concerns to your child.
   - Keep the dialogue with the teacher open until you both feel the child is "on the right track." Email works well for many teachers.
8. At dinnertime, make it a ritual for everyone in the family to share one thing new they learned today and one thing they don't understand yet.
9. Create family mantras about school, studying and learning.
   - We are learners and readers.
   - School is an opportunity to learn.
   - Learning is a life-long adventure and it is fun!
   - It's perfectly OK to make mistakes or not learn something right away.
   - Each time you will do a little better.
   - It's not your grades that count.
10. Create a reward at the end of study sessions (not video games), such as:
    - A half-hour family TV program that you all watch together,
    - A bowl of popcorn, dessert or piece of fruit,
    - Play a game or do a hobby,
    - Read to your child from a great book,
    - A phone call to a friend.

Susan Wellman, founder of The Ophelia Project, *has brought relational and verbal aggression prevention into schools all over the country. Previous to this, she taught study skills, then high school and college English. She lives in Erie, PA, is mother to a son and daughter, and has five grandchildren.*

Reprinted with permission of Full Esteem Ahead, *Wings*, Winter 2002.

Time Management from a Different Point of View

By Marydee Sklar, Organizing Coach, Teacher and Tutor

BELIEVE IT OR NOT, you can teach your child time management skills. The trick is to use strategies that match your child's thinking. If you're a parent who is always on time and always plans ahead, your approach using lists and priorities won't work with a child who floats through time. Lecturing them just goes in one ear and out the other. If you're a parent who struggles with being on time and meeting deadlines and you have a child who is also challenged by time issues, there's hope! This article gives you family-tested ideas to help you teach your child the critical life skill of time management.

I've found it useful to divide learners into two groups, based upon behavioral characteristics. By looking at behavior, I have clues about how the learner's brain works. I label these two types of learners as auditory thinkers and visual thinkers.

In my role as a learning coach, I specialize in visual thinkers. This is the group of learners who typically have the most challenges connected to time. Auditory thinkers, on the other hand, seem to have internal clocks and can more easily manage themselves using traditional homework strategies.

If your child exhibits most of the behaviors listed in the box, you can describe your child as a visual thinker. It is critical for visual learners to be taught about time management using methods that match their visual brain. I know this because I am a visual thinker and have visual thinking children. The ideas I use as a learning coach came from problem solving within our family. The list of tools

and ideas below are effective because they keep time in the sight and mind of the visual thinker. I recommend the book, *Mapping Inner Space: Learning and Teaching Visual Mapping (Zephyr Press, 2001)*, by Nancy Margulies for more ideas about visual learning and teaching.

Time Tools and Tips:

- "Face clocks" and wristwatches: Have one in every room, even in the shower! They show how much time remains to finish a task. They help the visual thinker see ahead so they can be on time.
- Beeping digital timers: The continual beeping breaks into the visual thinker's world and brings them back into the present. It works as a reminder to change activities. Visual thinkers have no clue about how long a task really takes, so timing a homework assignment is a good exercise for a child. They'll find that if they stay focused and try to "beat the timer" they'll have time left over for fun!
- Use an assignment book that shows the whole month at one glance. Record assignments on the date they are due. This helps them to look ahead and not forget assignments. Dates for extra-curricular activities, parties and family events should also be written on the calendar.
- Use "to do" lists that are divided into 30-minute increments of time. Block out the time that is taken by activities like sports, dinner and chores. The empty

TRAITS OF A VISUAL THINKER:
- Big picture, creative thinking—not sequential linear thinking
- Spoken and written language lacks continuity of thought
- Usually late; NOW is important
- Last minute or late projects, produces lower quality work
- Trouble planning ahead; lots of procrastination
- Distractible
- Lists and prioritizing don't help scheduling
- Argues with, or ignores verbal reminders to work

TRAITS OF AN AUDITORY THINKER:
- Sequential details
- Organized "linear" language
- Usually on time or early
- Completes projects on time; has time for quality work
- Stays on task
- Works well with lists and reminders

space is where they have time for homework. Once the work is done, the leftover spaces are for fun!

- Plan ahead by planning backwards using the monthly assignment calendar. For bigger assignments and projects, use Post-it-Notes to represent each step.

On each individual task note, write the estimated time required to complete each part of the project from its beginning, through revisions, to the end. Begin by placing the "Done!" note on the calendar space two days before the actual due date. These two days are a cushion for unexpected complications like the printer dying. Then, put all of the remaining Post it-Notes on the calendar by working backward to the beginning task. Your child will have to decide where there is time to work on each piece. After this exercise, your child can concretely see the time needed to complete the project. They know when they have to begin and how they must fit it in with the rest of their life.

Developing good time management skills is a process that has to be learned and practiced in steps, especially for a visual thinker. A child, who can use time well, will feel less stress and be more successful reaching their goals. Be patient with yourself and your child as you teach and model time management skills. Time spent developing these skills is time well spent.

Marydee Sklar is a state-licensed teacher and reading specialist. She coaches individual children and adults who need help with learning, writing and time management. She conducts workshops and gives presentations for groups. You may reach her at marydee.sklar@comcast.net.

Resources

- *Beat Procrastination and Make the Grade* by Linda Sapadin
- *The Procrastinating Child: A Handbook for Adults to Help Children Stop Putting Things Off* by Rita Emmett
- *Perfectionism: What Is Bad about Being so Good* by Free Spirit Press
- *Taming the Tiger* (of Stress) by Free Spirit Press

Reprinted with permission of Full Esteem Ahead, *Wings*, Winter 2002.

Helping Her Avoid Math Anxiety
By Helen Cordes

For 15-year-old Marisa Morales, math doubts began in third grade. "She was having problems with multiplication tables, and she started saying, 'I'm not good at math,'" recalls mom Irene. So when an all-girls after-school math and science group began at Marisa's Texas middle school, Irene immediately signed her daughter up. Last year, Marisa aced Algebra I, and more importantly, "she has so much more self-confidence about math," reports her mom.

WHILE ALL-GIRL PROGRAMS aimed at overcoming math dread are growing, parents can easily boost math confidence at home as well, experts say. "Studies say that parent involvement is the number one predictor of increased success," says Julie Jackson, curriculum coordinator for the Austin, Texas-based Girlstart program. Many of the activities offered by Girlstart, which has benefited more than 12,000 area girls with programs aimed at getting girls enthusiastic about math, science, and technology, can be done at home. Jackson suggests these tactics.

Make everyday math explicit, and let her figure it out. "Shopping is ideal for showing how several math operations help us make decisions," notes Jackson. Sale prices and coupons offer opportunities to use percentages and decimals; budgeting and allowances can be transformed into word problems such as "compute how many weeks of allowance gets you the blue dress compared with the blue jeans at a 30 percent discount." Resist the temptation to jump in and solve it for her, and keep in mind that girls also need to practice figuring out problems in their own way.

Cook with her for another prime math opportunity. "Recipes are wonderful for working with fractions and learning how to change fractions by increasing or decreasing a recipe," says Jackson. Meal planning using grocery store circulars can be fun. Girls can plan a dream meal and figure out the total price for given amounts of food, with discount coupons or two-for-one specials adding still more math practice.

Let your daughter help balance your checkbook and have her review credit card statements to offer exposure both to math and practical living skills. "Girls can also compute salaries and savings scenarios if they babysit or have other jobs, or for planning what jobs they'd like to get," notes Jackson.

Find out what her specific math bugaboo is, and address it. Monitor her homework to see where she's getting things wrong, and confirm with a quick chat with her teacher. Check out resources to sharpen skills in that area, or simply use a real-life example. If fractions are the offender, for example, buy a chocolate bar that breaks into equal pieces and ask her to figure out fractions linked to differing numbers of friends who might share the bar.

Always model a math-positive attitude. "Never say, 'Oh, I'm no good at math either,'" warns Jackson. As math classes get more complicated, many parents may need to brush up themselves. But if so, say something like, "I'm not sure how to answer this problem. But I'm sure we can work it out together if we review the material." If your daughter puts down her own math ability, remind her of times when she's learned something—such as a musical instrument—by practice and patience.

Host an all-girl after-school math funfest or a math-themed party. When girls are in an all-girl group, they feel less self-conscious about making mistakes and have more fun just being themselves, notes Jackson. Try a book such as *The Math Book for Girls* for inspiring math games, or throw a party in which girls create secret-code invitations, chart pizza preferences on a graph, and play probability games.

Resources:
- *The Math Book for Girls* by Valerie Wyatt (Kids Can Press, 2000)
- *She Does Math! Real-Life Problems from Women on the Job* by Maria Parker, ed. (Classroom Resource Materials, 1995)
- *New Moon Money* by the New Moon Books Girls Editorial Board (Crown, 1999; available from www.newmoon.org).
- www.girlscouts.org/moneymatters - The money section of Girl Scouts of the USA's website
- www.girlsinc.org - look under the Smart Girls section for money information

Helen Cordes is on the advisory board of Daughters magazine. Her daughters, 16 and 10, are acing math.

Building on the Strength of Girls

By Nancy Huppertz

This article explores ways to make schools more friendly for girls. Ideally, every child would be looked at individually. Until that time comes, using the "lens of gender" to frame a child's needs in school is one step in the process. There are many boys who will benefit from what is listed for girls and vice versa. Connection, via interests and relationships, is key to success.

AT FIRST GLANCE, it may appear that girls have freedom of choice and they themselves may even argue that they do. So—what are girls missing? The answer to the question today is very different from what it would have been thirty years ago. Equal opportunity laws have given girls equal access to curriculum, to activities and to opportunities to play interscholastic sports. It is illegal to advise girls toward traditionally female courses of study and occupations.

But laws can only do so much. What progress has been made in the school environment, the content of the curriculum and teaching practices? There is a wide variation in implementation of these laws from school to school. Attitudes and behavior of teachers and other school staff toward students can take a long time to change. While we are waiting, girls' participation and aspirations are compromised.

Here is what benefits girls:

Girls need to be taught by teachers who are truly committed to creating a learning environment that does not overtly or subtly convey limits and expectations based on sex. By now most teachers know not to divide classroom responsibilities into "boys' jobs" and "girls' jobs." However, teachers can convey different expectations for students based on sex (or race or other factors) by how they interact with them on a day-to-day basis. Teacher expectations, subtly or overtly conveyed, have powerful impacts on student self-concept. Teachers must learn to interact with students equitably.

Girls need a curriculum that includes them. History should include the contributions and accomplishments of women, and study of social issues and movements as well as political/military issues. Students should be as familiar with Jane Adams as John Adams. History should also include study of legal, social and religious practices that imposed strict limitations on women's participation in every aspect of life. Reading and literature should include stories and books by and about females of all races.

Girls need encouragement toward non-traditional courses of study and occupations. Even though anti-discrimination laws in employment were passed more than thirty years ago, young people still have a sense of "men's jobs" and "women's jobs." There is much that schools can do to raise awareness about the benefits of taking higher-level math, science and technical courses and of the full range of occupational opportunities.

Girls need to hear language used in an equitable, inclusive way. The importance and impact of the use of language is thoroughly established in extensive research. Language conveys and creates the culture. Educators can easily adopt non-biased language by using alternatives to occupation titles that end in "man," not using masculine pronouns as though they are generic—they are not—and not allowing words associated with being female to be used as insults.

Girls need to have their athletic teams encouraged and celebrated as much as the boys' teams and to participate equally. This includes such things as uniforms, practice schedules, facilities, equipment, game times and days, and support by rally, band and pep assemblies. Write-ups in the school newspaper need to be equal for girls and boys. PE classes, with boys and girls together, should emphasize "education"—the skills and rules of sports—rather than "competition." Girls and boys will benefit from learning life-long, noncompetitive activities such as yoga, T'ai Chi and cooperative games.

Girls need to feel safe at school. Schools should have a "No Tolerance" policy for sexual harassment.

Perhaps the most important point is that all the "needs" mentioned above are beneficial to all students, boys as well as girls.

Nancy Huppertz is a gender equity specialist who runs Apogee Training and Consulting, conducting teacher training and consulting in gender equity issues for organizations and schools throughout the United States.

Reprinted with permission from Full Esteem Ahead *Wings*, Winter 2002.

The Problem with Peer Aggression in Our Schools Today

By Kathy Masarie, MD

A deadly combo is a bully who gets what he wants from his target, a bullied child who is afraid to tell, bystanders who either watch, participate in the bullying or look away, and adults who see bullying as teasing, not tormenting, as "boys will be boys," not the predatory aggression that it is . . . . Bullying is not about conflict. It is about contempt for another person. Bullying is a conscious, willful and hostile attempt to harm someone . . . . The cycle of bullying will only be broken when the majority begins to stand up, speak out and step in to stop the cruel acts of the minority.

—Barbara Coloroso, author of *Bully, Bullies and Bystander*

Once thought to be simply an unpleasant rite of passages, bullying can actually result in long-term social, academic, psychological, and physical consequences.

The Challenge, Vol. 11 (3)

In recent years, the ways children hurt each other has received national attention. Nearly all of the school shooters were targets of taunting by their peers. An online rejection by a "boyfriend" led a girl to kill herself; the mother, who posed as that "boyfriend" to avenge her own daughter, may go to prison. We wouldn't send our children to schools where there was no policy on physical aggression, yet we routinely send them to schools where verbal and relational aggression is both rampant and unchecked. To be fair, in former times we didn't have the research to recognize how harmful relational aggression was and we didn't know that verbal taunting could drive someone to extreme acts of violence. Now we do. There is so much we can do, but it takes patience and commitment. And it takes all of us.

While it is easy to dismiss these "stories" as normal rites of passage, research shows that relational aggression is every bit as harmful as physical aggression. Relational aggression is by nature covert, secretive and difficult to

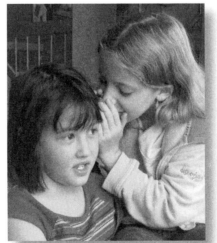

detect. Adults struggle to even be able to identify it, let alone deal with it. Our culture has taken a stand on physical violence in schools and today we rarely see overt fights. However, our children have redirected their aggression to exclusion, gossip, verbal taunting and "sneaky" physical aggression, such as "accidentally" bumping someone.

Forms of Aggression

Aggression takes various forms based on the "weapon" used to hurt another:

- **Physical:** uses physical force such as hitting, tripping, taking a backpack, breaking a pencil.
- **Verbal:** uses words (spoken, written or via email) to tease, taunt, or call names.
- **Relational:** uses the target's social relationships with others to hurt him/her.
    o gossip: spreads rumors about a disliked classmate
    o exclusion: tells others not to play with a certain classmate as a means of retaliation
    o silent treatment: purposefully ignores someone when angry
- **Non-verbal:** uses gestures, dirty looks, eye-rolling, turning one's back to the target

Aggression can also be distinguished as:

- **Direct or overt** (physical and verbal aggression)
- **Indirect or covert** (relational aggression or non-verbal gestures)

There are two additional categories: aggression in self-defense (reactive) versus initiating aggression (pro-active). Even the legal system reflects this concern to understand the "motive."

- **Proactive aggressors** are looking for opportunities to bully and to "raise their social status" by putting others down. For example, forming a group to leave someone out.
- **Reactive aggressors** misinterpret ambiguous social settings. For example, when someone in the cafeteria

spills a drink on a reactive aggressor, s/he immediately assumes it was done on purpose and acts accordingly by turning around and punching the child. It can happen when someone has been bullied repetitively and has become suspicious, thinking "everyone" is out to get him/her.

Bully, Bystander, Target

In any aggressive incident, there are three roles: aggressor, target and bystander. The role of the aggressor is obvious: this is the person leading the bullying. The second character is the "target." "Target" implies just that: a person who was chosen, for whatever reason or no reason, to be on the receiving end of the aggression. Using "victim" here implies a helplessness and weakness. Finally, the bystander(s) on the sidelines have three options: join the bullying and encourage the bullying by egging it on, be neutral and observe it from a distance taking no sides, or sympathize with the target. Those that sympathize are often afraid to help because there is a realistic possibility that they will become the next target.

Target Today; Aggressor Tomorrow

It is important to remember that an aggressor today may have been a target yesterday. In today's world, the best defense (to avoid being a target) is a good offense (by becoming a bully). How many kids do both? Research studies show that if you look solely at relational aggression, about 20-30 % of middle and high school students are *both* aggressors and targets. (This is not true for physical bullies, where targets and aggressors usually stay in one role.) So the kid we see being aggressive toward our child today may have been the recipient of our child's aggression for the past month. It is not always easy to figure out where it started and children have more difficulty identifying themselves as aggressors than as targets. One thing that is clear is that "removing the bully" rarely solves anything as there is always another to take his or her place. Nor does "teaching the target to be more assertive" always help since there is always another target to take his/her place.

Peer aggression happens at all ages, including adulthood. How many days do we hear gossip about someone, avoid talking to someone we are angry with, or leave someone out from an activity we are participating in? Or it may go further: we talk about someone disparagingly at the dinner table or tell our kids not to play with that kid who is "from the wrong side of town," which is prejudice and exclusion.

Examples of Aggression

Felicia was bullied continuously from 3rd through 5th grade at a private elementary school and suffered from migraines and stomach aches as a result. Felicia's mother, a single parent, made repeated efforts to get the school to take action. The school's responses: "Felicia is too thin-skinned". . . Kids will be kids . . . You're mistaken if you think we can stop this." The bullying continued, with no end in sight. Eventually, Felicia's mother had to place her daughter on "suicide watch" when she threatened to kill herself. Felicia, now 11, no longer attends that school and is on the road to recovery from this long-term abusive situation.

The in-group ruled the social life of a third-grade classroom. Four of the twelve girls decide each day who will be allowed to play with them. The rules change daily, but the best way to get in is to criticize another girl. The girls on the "out" haven't figured out how to create their own friendship groups—they just wait to see if maybe today they'll get lucky and be allowed in.

As a quarterback in football, a seventh-grade boy has friends and social standing. Another boy who covets his position starts spreading rumors, behind his back, that he is gay. Friends start avoiding him. He tells no one, asks no one for help. His grades begin to suffer and he loses focus on the team. The coach replaces him with the aggressor.

When Amanda was in 9th grade, her boyfriend broke up with her. At first she was heartbroken, but when he started dating a classmate she became enraged. She sought revenge by spreading ugly sexual rumors about them, which her fellow students were happy to believe. A few months later, she realized what she had done and apologized to the couple and told her classmates it was all a lie. But it didn't work. The rumors had become "true" to her classmates. She couldn't take it back and she was heartsick. With tears in her eyes, she said she would do anything to help other girls not make the same mistake. She became a teen mentor in her school and helped teach younger students about relational aggression.

At an 8th-grade overnight, a few girls posted some rumors on the Internet about several more "popular" girls who they did not like. On Monday, the aggressors were afraid to go to school. Eventually they admitted their wrong-doing and agreed to meet with the targets to talk. They discussed relational aggression and cyberbullying, and the targets were able to speak clearly about how hurt they were. When it was all over, all the girls felt closer to each other.

The Research on Peer Aggression

Most early studies of bullying were on direct verbal (VA) and physical aggression (PA). Relational aggression (RA) has surfaced since the mid 90's, showing that girls bully as much as boys, it is just that girls use a different, more indirect, form of aggression (RA). What is very interest-ing is that some studies reveal the "underlying beliefs" that allow aggression to continue and become more normal. If you believe something is acceptable, you will continue to do it. Even though kids say relational aggression-exclusion is the most hurtful type of aggression, it is the type most commonly used. Research shows when parents are asked, "Would you rather have your child hit, call names or exclude?" they pick "exclude" even though kids say that hurts the most.

- Boys and girls today view relational aggression as the most acceptable aggression, even in preschool.
- RA is the type of aggression most commonly used at all ages by boys and girls together.
- Kids view relational aggression as the most hurtful type of aggres-sion (physical second, verbal third).
- The research confirms that children who use high levels of relational aggression are more likely to approve of it (compared to children who use low levels of relational aggression). This perpetuates the problem.
- If asked about the best way to retaliate when you were "wronged by someone," all ages and both sexes answered "relational aggression."

Short- and Long-Term Effects of Aggression

The consequences of bullying can be serious. Surprisingly, the outcomes look equally bleak whether you are the target or the aggressor. Research shows that low self-esteem is not always present in aggressors. Those who do have low self-esteem, however, tend to get jealous and frustrated easily, need a lot of attention from other people, need to feel accepted, need to be noticed, and need to gain power and control. Other aggressors may feel very good about themselves and their ability to manipulate others and do not take responsibility for what they have done.

Aggressors who use relational aggression may have a lot of friends, but the quality of friendships is poor. They tend to believe they are "close" to their friends and don't want to "share" their friends with others. They score high on exclusivity. They are highly jealous and very manipulative, using relational aggression against friends. For example, they may threaten to tell a friend's secrets, a very powerful threat. They will betray a friend if it serves them well. They are low on warmth and caring. These qualities of jealousy and possessiveness extend into romantic relationships of college students. Most of all, they have difficulty recognizing their hurtful behavior. Relational aggression may work very well in the short term but it has serious long-term effects for the aggressor.

Aggressors and targets are <u>both</u> at risk for:
- Depression
- Drug and alcohol abuse and early use
- Eating disorders, poor body image, self-harm
- Violence: 60% of bullies in grade 6-9 had at least one conviction by age 24[1]
- School failure, suspension, dropping out, absenteeism, avoidance, delinquency, disruptive in class
- Peer rejection, loneliness, isolation
- Low attachment to parents and school
- Low self-worth.

> ### Key Ingredients in Bullying
> - Imbalance of power
> - Repetitiveness
> - Intent to harm

In addition to the risk factors listed above, targets suffer other negative effects. Short-term effects include: humiliation, sadness, distressed affect, confusion, anxiousness, psychosomatic symptoms and poor con-centration. The long-term outcomes for targets also include:
- Insecurity about their place in the social hierarchy, which manifests as social avoidance and anxiety
- Lower levels of leadership
- Fear, which may lead to absenteeism, truancy, or dropping out
- Poor self-concept.

Is It Conflict or Is It Bullying?

One of the most frequent questions we hear is how to tell the difference between aggression and conflict. A key feature of aggression/bullying is that there is an imbalance of power between the target and the bully. In bullying, the bully is always trying to have "power over" the target. The power often comes from other children who join in on the bullying. Another feature is intent to harm. The only one who truly knows "intent" is the bully. Two other key features are distress in the target only and repetition. When two kids are fighting in a situation of equal power, that is conflict, not bullying. Both kids want their way and both kids feel distressed. Conflict resolution skills help with these incidences—hearing each side of the story, helping each to see the other's point of view, brainstorming solutions together. In a conflict, adults may not need to get involved. The intervention in a bully incident is very different: support the target, give clear consequences for the bully, and empower everyone involved with skills to do it differently.

Adults Establish the Social Norms about Bullying

The basic concept of "social norm" is very important because it, more than anything else, is what drives bullying to continue. Social norms are the "expected rules for behavior" and they are driven by beliefs that kids have about the acceptability of a behavior. These beliefs come from the cultural response to behaviors. How would you react to your kid hitting someone versus excluding someone by saying, "You can't come to my birthday party." Even though kids say exclusion is the worst (they would rather be hit or called names), we adults tend to react strongly to hitting but erratically to exclusion. We then have established a "norm" that it is okay to exclude someone. When teachers do not intervene in bully incidents, they create a "social norm" that says it is okay: to bully when you get away with it, put someone down for a laugh, exclude people or spread rumors. Teachers "don't have time to deal with it" but time spent "not dealing with it" is enormous: disciplining bullies, counseling targets, dealing with angry parents—with all of the effort leaving destruction in its wake.

There are social norms within the adult world that perpetuate aggression among adults and between adults and children. Examples include "It's okay to gossip disparagingly about a child who is bullying others and about how 'poorly' that child is being raised by his/her family," and "It's okay to put down a teacher we don't like to our children and other parents."

Intentional versus Accidental Harm

One of the reasons that it is difficult to put a stop to emotional aggression is that it is not black and white. Bullying involves an imbalance of power, but an aggressor may not even realize that he/she is in a one-up position. Because of this, most of us inadvertently find ourselves a bully, a target and a bystander from time to time.

Here we will explore three areas that we all experience everyday: teasing, gossip and exclusion. On one end of the spectrum, these behaviors are normal, everyday interactions. It is healthy to share stories with each other. It is healthy to tease someone you like. It is healthy to exclude people because there is not room to invite everybody, every time. On the other end of the spectrum is the obvious aggression with "intent to harm," repetition and imbalance of power. Aggressors use the excuse that they didn't mean it to hurt and that they were "just kidding," but the aggressor and the target know the difference. Like any other bullying, the bystanders, target, adults and aggressors themselves need to be involved to stop this kind of aggression. In between these two extremes is the "gray zone" where it is sometimes unclear to the "target" whether the damage was done "on purpose with intent to harm" or done innocently and accidentally. The target feels hurt, but only the aggressor knows their real intent. And if the "accidental aggressor" didn't really mean to do it, s/he may not even know someone was hurt. In this case, the responsibility lies with the "target" to let the person know s/he was hurt. This always works better if the "target" and "accidental aggressor" have a good relationship. Someone who is chronically bullied has an even tougher time deciphering this. After repeated bullying, it is a natural defense mechanism to "be on guard for aggression" and it makes it harder to take things light-heartedly.

Social Types and Friendships

Our children are very different in their friendship needs, partially based on temperament, introvert-extrovert, etc. However, no matter which group a child wants to belong to, there are unwritten rules that the "in-kids" learn in order to fit in. There are five invisible rules or social norms described in *Best Friends Worst Enemies* by Michael Thompson: 1) Be Like Your Peers; 2) You Must Belong to a Group; 3) Be In—Or Be Out; 4) Find a Place in the Social Hierarchy; and 5) You Must Play a Role. He reports on research about the eight essential elements a child receives from his/her relationships with other children. Seven of these can be found in the one-on-one friendships your child finds and establishes: affection, intimacy, a reliable alliance, instrumental aid, nurturance, companionship and an enhancement of self-worth. The eighth element is a "sense of inclusion" comes from belonging to a group. This eighth "essential element" is the one with which parents can directly assist their child. Parents can help find or create groups or "safe spaces" where their child can be accepted for being themselves (e.g., religious youth group, close soccer team, Scout troop or an after-school club). Many of these groups can offer your child a wonderful sense of belonging. Pay attention to the fact that there are other groups, of your child's choosing, that may be detrimental to your child's safety and well-being. Sometimes, members of the group will do daring, foolish or mean things they wouldn't have considered doing as individuals. What is encouraging is that social skills needed to make good friendships and be well-liked can be learned, as you can see in *The Unwritten Rules of Friendship—Simple Strategies to Help Your Child Make Friends* by Natalie Madorsky Elman and Eileen Kennedy-Moore.

Popularity

Popularity—that ever-elusive obsession . . . . something nearly all kids want but only a small percentage of kids attain. There are two types of popularity: popular-as-dominance ("bad" popular) and popular-as-decency ("good" popular). Good popularity is what we want for our kids—to be liked for who they are as individuals with qualities such as friendliness, ability to share, kindness, assertiveness, and compassion. According to Michael Thompson, parents who focus more on their child's quality of friendships, as opposed to the quantity and their child's popularity status, foster healthy relationships. Why? It only takes just one good friend to carry you through tough social times. Likeability among one's peers, as opposed to "popularity" with one's peers, is a far more important goal to strive for.

In his book *The Friendship Factor,* author Kenneth Rubin describes popularity as a "reputation bestowed upon an individual by one's social peers." Popular boys are perceived by their peers as those who are the best athletes, wear the coolest clothes, have tough-guy attitudes, have a good sense of humor, and display "advanced" social skills. Popular girls are often described by their peers as attractive, socially competent, fashionable, savvy, financially well off, "sassy," and precocious about boys. The "popularity quest" can wreak havoc on healthy friendships.

Cliques

You can get an idea of the social cliques in your child's school by asking about the school cafeteria, says Margaret Sagarese, co-author of *Cliques, 8 Steps to Help Your Child Survive the Social Jungle.* Most children know who sits where and at which tables they are welcome or not welcome. They could map these out for you, describe the characteristics of each group, and then tell you where they fit in. Asking them, "How does that feel? What group do you want to be in? Why? Which group do you admire most? Which group is mean or a clique?" can give you incredible insight into their lives and help children frame where they fit into the social scene.

Supporting our Children

Some of the most difficult questions we will face as parents are: how to stop your child from bullying other kids, how to protect your child from being bullied, and how to empower your bystander to step in and help. The more we explore these roles, the more muddied the waters become. We all play the bystander at one time or another and most people, adults and children alike, have been on the receiving and giving end of hurting others. Every situation that involves potential bullying is unique, which means each situation deserves special consideration.

"It only takes one friend to buffer the effects of bullying."
Michael Thompson

Support Aggressors: The skills needed to be a bully are the same that are needed to be a leader. When identified, a child who has been bullying can be taught ways to shift his energy into leadership and become an asset to his/her community. Making amends may also be an important part of his or her consequences. You can improve a school by addressing one bully at a time, especially if it is your child, but there is always another to take his/her place. The better goal is to get involved with the PTA and school staff to educate the whole community about bullying and try to establish higher standards of behavior to stop bullying before it starts.

Support Targets: When we ask a group of people why kids get bullied, we get lost in the answers: too fat, too shy, too passive, cries easily, too sensitive, too clueless, too awkward, etc. But we forget the main and really only reason a child is bullied, someone decided to bully them, to solve a problem with aggression rather than non-violently. The focus should be on stopping the bully, not "changing" the target so they won't be picked on anymore. The target should be thanked for reporting the situation. The last thing we want to do is leave targets feeling like it is their fault that they are being bullied.

Support Bystanders: An excellent researcher in the field of bystanders, Wendy Craig, PhD, has shown that bystanders have lots of power when they decide to help. The barriers to helping others in trouble are mostly obvious and the consequences they fear of retaliation by the bully who might then turn on them is very real. Stan Davis wrote a book, *Schools Where Everyone Belongs and Empowering Bystanders in Bullying,* that we recommend you give to your school. He has interviewed hundreds of kids who have been bullied and asked, "What would be the best way somebody watching the bullying could help you?" The overwhelming and surprising answer was "support me afterward." It points to the message Michael Thompson keeps repeating, "It only takes one friend to buffer the effects of bullying."

Teach Empathy: One of the most powerful qualities that will have an impact on decreasing bullying is to foster empathy in our children and in the adults who care about them. Empathy is the "ability to put yourself in another's shoes." Everyone can play a role:
- Adults take the time to intervene when there is an imbalance of power between kids.
- Adults remain neutral and respectful.
- Aggressors learn to get in touch with what they were wanting when they bullied and come up with different strategies.
- Bystanders pay attention to the impact of bullying and intervene (telling the bully to stop, getting help from an adult and/or comforting the target).

- The target focuses on their underlying needs and receives support to become empowered.

Support School-Wide Interventions
- Educate parents, students, and staff with library books, videos, seminars, monthly newsletter articles, and monthly book clubs.
- Support "safe havens" where kids can be themselves: after-school clubs, lunch clubs, and support groups.
- Create Girls'/Boys' Night Out: 8th graders plan it for incoming 6th graders.
- Host "Mix-It-Up" Day, (www.mixitup.org). Everyone sits in a different place in the cafeteria and engages with people they usually wouldn't talk to.
- Support school staff with supervision in risky areas: playground, hallways, and buses.

Resources:

[1] *Bullying at School: What We Know and What We Can Do* by D. Olweus, 1993, Cambridge, MA: Blackwell
Queen Bees and Wannabes by Rosalind Wiseman
Odd Girl Out and *Odd Girl Speaks Out* by Rachel Simmons
Best Friends, Worst Enemies and *Mom, They're Teasing Me* by Michael Thompson
Cliques: 8 Steps to Help Your Child Survive the Social Jungle by C. Giannetti, et.al.
Schools Where Everyone Belongs by Stan Davis at www. StopBullyingNow.org
The Bully, the Bullied and the Bystander by Barbara Colorossa
Raise Your Child's Social IQ by Cathi Cohen
Teaching Your Child the Language of Social Success by Stephen Nowicki, et.al.
The Friendship Factor by Kenneth Rubin

Interview with Lyn Mikel Brown on Girlfighting

From *Daughters: For Parents of Girls* newsletter

When it comes to girl's issues, there aren't many people more expert than Lyn Mikel Brown. This Colby College professor of education and women's, gender, and sexuality studies co-authored with Carol Gilligan the important book Meeting at the Crossroads: Women's Psychology and Girls' Development *(Harvard University Press, 1992). She is also the author of* Raising Their Voices: The Politics of Girls' Anger *(Harvard University Press, 1998), and most recently of* Girlfighting: Betrayal and Rejection among Girls *(New York University Press, 2003).*

Are Girls Fighting More?

There has been a lot of fascination recently about girls fighting. I don't think it's just a coincidence that it comes so soon after girls began getting more serious attention. We've had a decade of women doing girls' programming—Girls Scouts, Mary Pipher, Girls Inc., New Moon, and lots of other people and groups have done amazing work.

Partly as a result of this new attention to girls, girls are much more direct and outspoken now, and that makes people anxious. It's interesting that 10 years ago we were all concerned about girls' loss of voice in early adolescence, and not long after that, the media picked up on girlfighting.

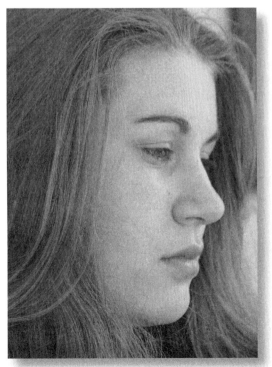

We've got a generation of outspoken girls trying to find their way, but we haven't done a great job of helping them locate the source of their anger and channel it constructively. I want to put the responsibility back on us adults, and have us look much more closely at how the culture and the media treat girls.

Relational Aggression

When girls are angry, the first place that anger goes is toward each other. Especially in middle school, a girl can't be too smart, too fat, too sexual, or too much her own person. The targets of relational violence (social rather than physical cruelty) are often those group members who are challenging the rigid norms of girlhood. Girls police each other, and despite "niceness" shown in front of adults, there is all too often underground bullying going on.

Girls may be attacking each other, but they're not truly angry with one another. Instead, they're angry with things like being objectified in the media, the way boys treat them and overall unfairness to girls in the culture. The problem, then, is not girls; the problem is a culture that puts down girls, treats them like commodities, demoralizes them, and then gets a kick out of watching the divide-and-conquer consequences.

We have to recognize that girlfighting exists and that it's going on all the time. We need to address it before we see it and not just respond when it happens in front of us. We need to start really young with girls, telling them to speak clearly about what they need and to not put down other girls who do so. We need to start early with teaching girls media literacy. And we need to help them notice what makes them angry and get them talking about it.

Adult Intervention: What Kind Helps?

Some adults want to intervene directly in girls' relationships and their fighting. I'm not a big fan of adults micromanaging girls' relationships in this way, by wading right into the fights.

Instead, we need to help girls learn to criticize how the world treats them, and then put them in situations, like nonprofit programs and girls groups, where it's possible to do that. We need to help them talk with each other honestly and build coalitions, and engage in social action projects. If we help girls feel strong, in control, and challenged in their lives, then fights among girls can be addressed within the safety of the groups that they're part of.

When relational aggression happens in a girls' group, that's a safer and more real place to talk about it than when a parent or teacher starts suddenly to address a fight. When you're working with a group of girls and one rolls her eyes at another, you can ask, "When you rolled your eyes at her, what was going on for you?"

Taking on "Nice"

We're always telling girls to be "nice." I have a problem with the way the word nice is full of so many other meanings for girls. Because rather than meaning simply "not cruel," nice also seems to mean quiet, passive, feminine, and less angry and expressive. When we want girls to treat people well, we should avoid using nice and instead use words like kind, civil, and respectful.

However, we need to realize there are risks when a girl doesn't conform to socially acceptable ways of behaving. Many girls conform to protect themselves. If you encourage your daughter to be outspoken, know that there will be consequences for her.

Find social outlets for her outside of school, such as Girl Scouts or a drama program or a sport. It's important, especially for a nonconformist kid, to get out of her school and find other people to connect with who are more like her.

And don't be afraid to encourage discriminating tastes in friendships either. Girls don't need to like and be friends with everyone, they need only be respectful. Encourage girls to choose friends who are affirming, who listen to them and treat them well. Most important, let them know that mistreatment is not a quality of true friendship.

It's true that much of the girlfighting we hear about is media hype. It's part of an old definition of femininity as being about deceit and manipulation. It's certainly not part of us as a gender. I think women and girls are much less likely to fight and undermine each other and more likely to support each other and form coalitions than the media has suggested. Look at what we've done in the women's movement—the anti-rape and domestic violence movements—we've formed coalitions that have really changed our culture.

Junior High: Not All Bad

As adults it's important for us to acknowledge that junior high school is not strictly a relationship wasteland. Girls at 11 can really see what the culture tells women to be, and they can describe the process by which they're encouraged to give up what they know. They struggle openly with it at that point.

Since it is all up for grabs then, what better time to be one of the voices encouraging them to discuss this, and to fight back? We adults should be asking questions about the culture, talking about healthy relationships, body size issues, and all that stuff they're sorting out. To leave them alone with all this seems terribly misguided—it's when they need us most.

Teachers should be a lot more educated about what's going on with girls, and think more critically about gender issues, and how those affect how girls experience school. They also need to be trained to teach media criticism and to help girls distinguish between real girls and media representations of girls.

In the end, the problem with a preoccupation with girlfighting is that girls' solidarity gets lost. I want people to see what's potentially great about girls. I want people to see that fighting isn't what defines them, and it's so small compared with all the other ways they are great.

---

12 Ways to Prevent Girlfighting
Developed by Lyn Mikel Brown, EdD

1. Do Your Own Work
2. Help Girls Understand the School Culture
3. Encourage Discriminating Tastes in Friendships
4. Address Girlfighting When You See It
5. Engage Girls' Anger and Hone a Sense of Fairness and Justice
6. Foster Solidarity among Girls, Women, and Women and Girls
7. Develop Hardiness Zones and Safe Spaces for Girls
8. Question the Traditional Romance Story
9. Develop Media Literacy
10. Encourage Her to Play Sports and Build Physical Strength
11. Practice Voice, Encourage Activism
12. Tell the Truth about Your Lives, Choices, and Actions

Taking Action to Stop Relational and Verbal Aggression

By Kathy Masarie, MD and Sue Wellman

Strategies for Parents

- Never belittle their issues. Be ready to talk with your kids and their friends and get to know their friends' parents too. Listen to them for hours, when they want to talk.
- If you discover your child is involved in relational aggression, take it seriously yet try to maintain neutrality. Don't assume you are getting the whole story. Your child may be a bully sometimes, too. Don't attack the parents of the friends who are "aggressors"—it usually makes things worse.
- Listen empathetically and avoid trying to "solve" the problem. Help them draw out possible solutions that don't include revenge. There is no simple solution.
- Emphasize respect for others as early as possible. De-emphasize popularity. Teach them the difference between popularity and friendship. Talk with your children about the importance of wise choices and doing right in the face of peer pressure. Educate them about relational aggression so they can recognize it, cope better with it and stop it.
- Set limits and intervene when siblings use "bullying" tactics. Teach them to deal with conflict with open discussions. If you don't intervene, they may assume you sanction their strong-arm tactics and verbal abuse.
- Be a good role model. Don't disparage others or make fun of them, especially your kids! Love and respect your children. Learn to say "I'm wrong" and "I'm sorry."
- Exemplify the importance of anger control, respect for self and others, tolerance, empathy and responsibility. "Catch them" enacting these values and show your appreciation.
- Expose children to different kinds and ages of people. Involve them in activities and groups outside of school. Encourage relationships with adults who will appreciate them for who they are.
- Create meaningful activities for your family to share. Don't buy into your kids acting scornful of their family. They want closeness. Give family time top priority.
- Monitor the media in your home. Don't underestimate its power to influence behavior. Many popular TV shows make bullying look chic.
- Get involved in your child's school to reduce verbal and relational aggression.

Strategies for Teachers

- Create a "Catching Acts of Kindness Jar" (or bulletin board). Display it and send home notes to parents.
- Catch teachable moments with purposeful small group interventions in health classes: role-playing difficult classroom situations.
- Be aware of children hurting each other.
- Ask small groups of students about the aggression that is going on in their lives. Create conversations —focus on listening to kids' issues.
- Ask older grades to mentor incoming younger grades—eat lunch together once a week, promoting a kinder climate in the school.
- Foster a sense of belonging with various "clubs" during lunchtime and after-school.
- Adopt a "blueprint" of response for all forms of aggression and intervene immediately.
- Form an advisory group with your colleagues to begin discussing techniques to defuse aggression.
- Create a process for school personnel to respond to verbal and relational aggression.
- Teach lessons on creating a safe school climate.
- Name relational aggression and make sure all the students know how to identify it, how it hurts and that it is not acceptable in your class.
- Contract with students to stop hurting each other.
- Elicit students' help in developing a motto for the positive treatment of everyone.
- Break up cliques by assigning groups.
- Be a positive role model—don't tolerate talk about students or parents in the staff room.
- Form a support group for student victims using mentors to help them role-play situations.

One teacher's approach: "I watch, record all incidents of relational aggression and ACT."

1. Verbally interrupt the behavior with compassionate but firm authority.
2. Achieve separation between the parties.
3. Firmly repeat the "respect/responsibility/group rules." *"I repeat this step for as long as it takes."*
4. Meet with aggressor, parents, and staff to:
   i) Determine the scope of the incident.
   ii) Determine the aggressor's willingness to change.
   iii) Draft a plan of action for the aggressor and all present to sign.
   iv) Monitor the aggressor's behavior with written notations when necessary.

Reprinted with permission from Full Esteem Ahead, *Wings*, Fall 2000.

Making Time for Her 7

Stefani Graap, 8th Grade, Rosemont Ridge Middle School

Making Time for Her

"In the end these things matter most: How well did you love? How fully did you live? How deeply did you learn to let go?" —Jack Kornfield, from *Buddha's Little Instruction Book*

"You will never find time for anything. If you want time, you must make it." —Charles Buxton

"How different our lives are when we really know what is deeply important to us, and, keeping that picture in mind, we manage ourselves each day to be and do what really matters most."
—Stephen Covey, author of *Seven Habits of Highly Effective People*

"If you were starting over today, what would you do differently? Whatever your answer, start doing it now."
—Brian Tracy

"Yet, if we look more closely ... you discover that there is only ever this moment. Life is always now. Be still. Look. Listen. Be present."
—Eckhart Tolle, author of *The New Earth: Awakening to Your Life's Purpose*

GOALS

- To help you explore your priorities in life, and to make time for these priorities

- To help you become aware of the choices you have regarding busyness, clutter and stress

- To support you to align your actions with your values, so that when you manage your time, you engage in those activities that matter most to you

- To explore your satisfaction with the amount of your life energy devoted to work

OVERVIEW

Families today live in a fast-paced, complex world. It is difficult to find time to spend with kids in a world that encourages both parents to work full time away from home and kids to be in several activities weekly. These same families often lack the support of nearby relatives, adequate daycare options, or a supportive community. Contemporary families are also faced with having to somehow protect their children from the larger culture's values and influences that enter our households through electronic and screen technologies, at the expense of our youth's psyches and innocence. The situation can seem hopeless for many parents, who often feel that if they are asked to do one more thing, they will implode. They may give up, feeling like personal and parental failures, without taking into account that they are simply being battered by societal pressures which are not very family friendly.

There is support out there for such dilemmas. It does require taking the time to figure out what works. Each of us has our own unique issues with time, balance, inner peace and work, and each of us will have unique solutions. The important thing is to pay attention to your intuition, your "inner compass" as a clue to what fits for you and your family. We are constantly changing, as are our daughters. Keeping open to new learning and new approaches to what works is helpful.

One answer to family empowerment is to simply take some quiet moments each day to prioritize your time and energy. Focusing your life into what is important and what is not can be liberating and literally life-saving. That is why this parenting guide devotes a whole chapter to "Making Time for Her." To model this concept, we have simplified this chapter. You will note that there are fewer articles to read. Instead, we ask you to take some time to focus on thinking about your own life, looking at how you spend your time, and evaluating what you are getting out of the time you are spending. Do your actions line up with your values? Are you living the life you always dreamed of? Are you able to say "No" to some very good things in life, so that you can say "Yes" to those things that are most important?

The essence of this "time" chapter is illustrated in the following popular story (author unknown, although a version of it is told by Stephen Covey):

A professor stood before his philosophy class and had some items in front of him on a table. When the class began, wordlessly, he picked up a large gallon jar and filled it to the top with fist-sized rocks. He then asked the class, "Is the jar full?" Everyone in the class could see that it was so, and answered, "Yes."

The professor replied, "Really?" He pulled out a bucket of pebbles and poured them into the jar. He shook the jar lightly. The pebbles rolled into all the open spaces between the rocks. Grinning, he then asked the group, "Is the jar full?" By this time, the class was on to him. "Probably not," the students responded. "Good!" he replied. The professor picked up a bucket of sand next and started dumping it into the jar. The sand filled all of the spaces left between the rocks and the pebbles. Once more, he asked the class, "Now, is the jar full?"

"No!" everyone shouted back. Once again, he said, "Good." He then grabbed a pitcher of water and poured in about a quart, until the jar was filled to the brim. Then, he looked at the class and said, "Ladies and gentlemen, the jar is now full. Can anybody tell me the lesson you can learn from this? What is the point of this demonstration?"

One eager beaver raised his hand and said, "The point is, no matter how full your life is, if you try really hard, you can always fit more into your schedule!"

"No," the professor replied, that's not the point. I want you to recognize that this jar represents your life. The big rocks are the important things, those things that, if everything else were lost and only these remained, allowed your life to be full. The pebbles are the smaller things that matter, like your job, your home, your car. The sand and water are everything else…the small stuff. If you put the sand into the jar first," he continued, "there will be no

room for the rocks or pebbles. The same goes for life. If you spend all your time and energy on the small stuff, you will never have room for the things that are most important to you."

"What are the 'big rocks' in your life?" the professor continued. "Pay attention to the things that are critical to your happiness. Play with your children. Take time to get medical checkups. Take your spouse out to dinner. Play another 18. Follow your dreams. Block out time in your schedule for these activities. Amazingly, the other stuff still gets done. Periodically, reflect on how you're doing. Are you putting your big rocks first, or does the small stuff still dominate your life? Set your priorities and when you're planning your month, your week or your day, think back to this story, and take care of your big rocks first."

The first exercise of this chapter, **"Finding Time: An Evaluation of My Values and Activities"** (p. 7:11) relates to this story, and will be used as the basis for your circle question at your next discussion group meeting. How closely do your actions match your priorities in life? Evaluate whether you are getting what you want out of each activity on your list… is each activity worth the amount of time you have invested in it? Are you spending a lot of time doing something that is important but that you are undervaluing? How could your actions and priorities better match up? What kinds of changes could you make to give more time to the activities of greatest value (your big rocks)?

Keep this list of your priorities handy and visible (on the refrigerator, at your desk, etc) and refer to it frequently to help you "choose" the time you want for your daughter and other loved ones. Becoming a conscious consumer of our culture, as well as a judicious creator of your own life, can cure a lot of contemporary woes: stress, a hectic lifestyle, disorganization, unhappiness, loneliness, and lack of intimacy. By putting your time where it is most important, by keeping your "big rocks in the jar," families can put themselves, their children and their most meaningful activities first in their lives. It may be helpful to do the "Finding Time" exercise on a monthly, quarterly or annual basis, so that you can track how well

you are doing on your quest towards leading a life that you long for, with balance and peace.

People who love what they do enjoy life. Parents who live with passion and intention will inspire their children to do the same. And, kids who are excited about life have within themselves one of the most powerful protections around for avoiding high-risk behaviors. The first two articles in this chapter, **"Modeling a Life Worth Living,"** and **"Personal Navigation"** (pp. 7:12-7:14) share ideas about finding passion.

Simplifying your life can often free up time and energy for the "big rocks" that give us the most meaning in life. The article, **"Fifteen Steps to a Simpler Life"** (p. 7:15) is an excellent overview of how to focus on what matters most, how to free ourselves from clutter and how to be more organized. Many of us don't recognize the impact of our "stuff." Not only do we struggle to stay clutter-free, we have to work to afford it, take time to shop for it and have a big enough house to store it, which all takes away energy from our "big rocks."

Today we seem to have too many choices and too little time. Often "time savers" like microwaves, dishwashers, faxes and other electronic devices cause us to pack more into each day. We don't allow them to give us any more leisure time. We tend to pause less and do more. Yet, we do have control over how we use our time. **"Vote with Your Life"** (p. 7:22) talks about how we "vote" every day—with our time, our money and our lives. How do you vote?

Stress is an unavoidable fact of life, and learning to manage stress is a very important life skill for everyone. As parents we need to develop ways of processing some of our stress away from the listening ears of our children. For example, we can process work stress on the way home from work so we can be more present when we are home. Many chores and life obligations can drain us. Housework was a big drain on one Mom. She realized that she was wasting precious mental energy dreading the task. She decided to change her approach. First she evaluated the level of cleanliness that was important to her—clean enough so that she and guests were comfortable. There really wasn't money to hire a cleaning service so she broke down the tasks and the frequency they needed to be done and engaged other family members in the tasks. Her attitude and stress level changed and the house was presentable.

How can we reduce our level of stress and increase our enjoyment? One way is to emphasize connection and relationship. We all get wrapped up in our roles as parents (from homework police to sports fan to chauffeur); we focus on the "doing" and lose track of the importance of "being" together and resetting the rhythm and tone of the family. The pace that matches best with our internal, innate rhythm is the natural speed of children and nature, as Richard Carlson describes in his book, *Slowing Down to the Speed of Life*. Our daughters need de-stressing skills just as much as we do, so consider how you can do this together.

- While you are together at dinner, take turns sharing something that troubled you during the day and something that made you happy—share something "good" and something "bad."
- Sharing appreciations is always a good way to shift the focus from our worries to the things in life which are really important.
- When family members are feeling stressed, it pays to get back to basic self-care—exercise, coziness, connection to nature, laughter, restful sleep, good food—a picnic under a beautiful tree, playing catch outside or at a swimming pool, resting together in a hammock, sitting by a fire reading aloud, singing in the car, watching the sun set or the moon rise or the stars come out, going to a beautiful spot and breathing deeply.
- Our children need to know that exercise and deep breathing—even a good walk—helps cleanse the stress chemicals out of our bodies, as do creative activities such as art, music, and writing. Try doing this together.
- We can share skills we have to reduce stress such as getting perspective ("What is the worst that can happen if…?"), prioritizing, mapping tasks out on the calendar, or resetting our inner talk to be more positive.

- If your teen is very driven and rarely misses school, allowing the privilege of a "personal day" now and then can provide time for focusing on calmness, rest and self-care.
- Our daughters may enjoy some of the excellent books on stress such as *Fighting Invisible Tigers* by Earl Hipp. *How to Stop Worrying and Start Living* is a very useful book for teens and adults who are inclined toward worry. Sean Covey's book *The 6 Most Important Decisions You'll Ever Make* helps teens thoroughly examine the issues in their lives that are most stressful: academics, friends, parents, dating, addictions and self-worth.

Strangely enough, many of us have fallen into a demanding, stressful, parenting style called "helicoptering" that requires us to protect our kids from all pain, be sure they are always happy and do everything we can to mold them into superstars. This means we must involve our children in countless activities so they can get into the "college of our choice" (eloquently described by Nora Ephron in her book *I Feel Bad About My Neck*). These "helicopter parents" are on call 24/7 and are completely exhausted from their self-generated whirlwind of endless activity. Sadly the outcome is the opposite of what they want; instead the kids resent their parents, lack motivation, and are ill-equipped to problem-solve, make decisions, or become self-reliant. **"How to Ground Your Helicopter Parenting"** (p. 7:23) shares tips on what we can do to reduce this unnecessary pressure in our own life and our kids' lives, and at the same time empower our kids to develop healthy competency and decision-making skills.

A powerful way to reduce stress lies in nature. Time in nature helps us to slow down to a healthy speed of life. In fact, Richard Louv, in his book *Last Child in the Woods— Saving our Children from Nature Deficit Disorder* proposes that contact with nature is an essential part of mental, physical and spiritual health. He says,

> *Unlike television, nature does not steal time; it amplifies it…nature offers healing…inspires creativity…Time in nature is not leisure time, it is*

Dear Asset Champion,

Thank you so much for your interest in *Raising Our Sons* and/or *Raising Our Daughters*. These books are a wonderful way to learn more about Developmental Assets and explore ways to build them in your community, one idea at a time.

We wanted to give you some tips to help you get started using your new book(s) effectively.

- Read the introduction, especially the chapter descriptions, so you have a feel for the content.
- Flip through the whole book and read what grabs you or bookmark it for later with a sticky tab.
- Use the book as a reference when you have a specific area of concern. Examples:
  - School Struggles: You might skim over all of Chapter 6: Teaching Him/Her.
  - Conflict or Possible Bullying: Go to the index for bullying, aggression, friendship. If there is serious bullying, you might delve deeper into the topic guided by the many resources.
  - Money Management: Check out the index for money, allowance, financial responsibility.

An incredibly powerful way to build Developmental Assets in your community is to encourage self-led parent discussion groups, using *Raising Our Sons/Daughters* as a guide. It is easy to get a group going by viewing **http://www.family-empower.com/running-a-successful-parenting-group/**. On our website you will find:

- Easy steps on how to get a group started.
- PDF files of flyers you can download to share on the power of parent discussion groups.
- Brief video on how these books were created and how to run successful discussion groups.
- Agenda for an organizing meeting to kick off groups in your community.

Please contact me at info@family-empower.com or (503) 292-4162 if you have any questions.

With admiration for all you do,

Kathy Masarie, MD

www.family-empower.com

Creators of *Raising Our Daughters* and *Raising Our Sons:*
The Ultimate Parenting Guides for Healthy Children and Thriving Families
6663 SW Beaverton-Hillsdale Hwy., PMB 158, Portland, OR 97225
info@family-empower.com   Work 503-292-4162   Cell 503-516-3755

Discover the Power of Networking with Other Parents

As a parent, do you:

Worry that you are not doing enough?

Struggle with embarrassing issues?

Seek ways to reduce power struggles?

Want to do everything you can to be
an effective and competent parent?

Find yourself exhausted and overwhelmed?

Long to be understood?

Networking with Other Parents Is an Untapped Resource That Can Help!

As our families are pulled in different directions, we need a force that can hold us together and allow everyone to thrive. A *Raising Our Daughters/Sons Parent Discussion Group* is such a force. At Family Empowerment Network we believe that when parents talk honestly with one another, they become empowered to parent confidently and effectively.

Form a Parent Discussion Group Using *Raising Our Daughters* or *Raising Our Sons*

is easier than you think!

Gather a group of your friends or parents of your child's friends from school, sports team, youth group, or scout troop.
Set the parameters—ideal class size is 8-12 people who meet for 1 1/2 hours (biweekly/monthly) and whose children are ages 8-16 (although 0-18 also works).
Use the *Raising Our Daughters/Sons* book for discussion group guidelines, questions and action ideas.
Share the leadership tasks.
Everyone is empowered by taking a turn facilitating a meeting.
Spend 1-2 hours prep time reading one of ten chapters from *Raising Our Daughters/Sons*.

The benefits are immeasurable! You will:

- Discover you are not alone and have a safe place to share honestly.
- Be surprised by the wisdom of parents who work together.
- Learn to support each other and each other's children.
- Enjoy an easy, efficient, and cost-effective way to create the life you want.

Testimonial from Professional Author and from Parents

I wish every neighborhood in America would create discussion groups that utilize these marvelous guides. They will help us raise a healthy and happy millennial generation.

Mary Pipher, PhD, author of *Reviving Ophelia* and *Shelter of Each Other*

It is such a relief to know we weren't the only parents struggling with limiting access to media. Our group came up with some great ideas.

Mother of a son and a daughter

I took Raising Our Sons *over two years ago and I still use the communication strategies I learned. I feel like we finally speak the same language.*

Mother of three sons

Family Empowerment Network Family Empowerment Network® was created to support parents and foster healthy families and communities. We believe the most powerful way to reduce risky behavior in our youth and support them to thrive is to enhance communication and connection within our families and to network with other families and teens. This can happen with individuals reading the book or with groups of parents meeting regularly to discuss the material.

Visit www.family-empower.com Today!

Contact Your Local School Coordinator _____ *at* _____

essential investment in our children's health (and also, by the way, in our own).

Some of our best childhood memories are of time spent in nature. Our children need opportunities to play unsupervised in natural settings and our family deepens from time spent together in nature. Pick a place near where you live and visit it frequently to observe nature. Stay up late and watch the stars. Set up a "nature table" at home with treasures collected outside. Go camping. Sit around a campfire. Visit the beach. Sometimes we forget the importance of unstructured play to both children and adults. "It takes a lot of slow to grow" reminds us that our ingenuity, inventiveness, creativity and imagination flourish in down time. Play is critical to healthy child development and teaches many important relationship and problem-solving skills. Summer is a special opportunity for experiencing life with less stress, for bonding with family and nature, and for developing different sides of our selves, as described in the article **"Summertime"** (p. 7:24).

Changing your relationship to money and work are examined in the articles **"Your Money or Your Life: Are You Making a Dying or Making a Life?"** and **"Remaking a Living"** (pp.7:25-7:26). The first explores how work in our society has become so important that we often let our jobs define who we are. Sometimes, by freeing ourselves to think outside the box on the issues of employment, money and security, we can come up with alternatives to doing things the same old way, and create more meaningful life work for ourselves. Family Empowerment Network finds that one of the very best resources for doing this comes from Joe Dominguez and Vicki Robin's book *Your Money or Your Life: Transforming your Relationship with Money and Achieving Financial Independence.* This approach asks readers to contemplate what their life purpose is, and even more importantly, when they intend on enacting it. If not now, then when? Their simple formula shows how ordinary people can simplify their lives, save more money, work less, and increase their happiness and connection with others, while living their dreams. Life is really just a series of choices. By becoming active, conscious participants in these choices, families can jump out of the rat race and into a life of their own choosing.

Many people have found inspiration, peace and purpose in Eckhart Tolle's book, *The New Earth: Awakening to Your Life's Purpose.*

> *Time is seen as an endless succession of moments, some "good," some "bad." Yet, if [you] look more closely, through your own immediate experience, you find there are not many moments at all. You discover that there is only ever this moment. Life is always now… A vital question to ask yourself frequently is: "What is my relationship with the present moment?"*

Our article on **"Mindfulness"** (p. 7:28) elaborates on this concept. By paying attention to what is going on in your and your daughter's life right now, experiencing it fully and accepting it, one can find a sense of calmness even when there are emotional storms around us. Mindful meditation can happen anywhere and anytime.

Focusing on breathing is a powerful way we can all learn to be present. When our child interrupts us and we react with anger and sharp words, we inadvertently teach our child to do the same. Thich Nhat Hanh, internationally renowned Zen master, peace activist and Nobel Prize nominee suggests we can stop this pattern of "passing negativity down the generations" by saying:

> *Breathing in, I see myself as a five-year-old*
> *Breathing out, I smile with compassion at my child*

He shares this advice with children:

> *Breathing in, I am calm. Breathing out, I smile. Next time you are angry or jealous of your brother or sister, or when you are unhappy with a friend, stop and do this exercise.*

Parents who really want to teach their children how to live fully, how to deal with stress effectively, and how to find balance between family, work, and fun in their lives, must model these behaviors themselves. These parents notice where their time, money, and attention flow, and keep these aligned with their own values.

_____

CIRCLE QUESTION

From the first article of this chapter, **"Finding Time: An Evaluation of My Values and Activities,"** describe how closely your actions and time match your values. Share what "big rocks" you commit to include in your life that are not there now?

POSSIBLE DISCUSSION QUESTIONS

1. Do you think you have enough time to spend with the children in your life? If not, what gets in your way? What are some "small steps" you could take to change this?

2. How do you "vote" with your time, money and life? If you knew you had six months to live, would you live differently? How could you give more time towards putting your "big rocks into the jar of life"?

3. How is your daughter stressed? What does she typically do to relieve stress? How does her stress affect you?

4. Do you often find yourself asking your child to hurry up? What is her usual response? Is there enough transition time between activities and free time to another allow her to assimilate life lessons and experiences?

5. How are you stressed? What do you typically do to de-stress? How does your stress affect your daughter and your other family relationships? What are some ways that your family schedule could be less stressful?

6. Do you find yourself drained by "un-dones?" If yes, make a list and focus on doing, deleting, delegating.

7. How can you tell when involved, supportive parenting turns into over-involved, "helicopter" parenting that is actually detrimental to your child?

8. Is healthy eating and exercise a priority in your family? If yes, do you model it by exercising regularly yourself?

9. Do you schedule downtime for yourself? Does your daughter have downtime?

10. How can we support our daughter to safeguard her time? Minimal part-time job? Only one sport per season? Cell phone rules? Strive for two nights at home per week? Other suggestions?

11. Would you be willing to take less pay for more time off? If you lost your job tomorrow, how would you feel? Frantic? Relieved? How might you make your work more meaningful?

12. How would you rate your life if your family was happy but your job had lower social prestige? You lived in a smaller house? You drove an old car? You had fewer clothes or gadgets for the house?

13. How might you be able to make your own workplace more family friendly?

PUTTING IT INTO PRACTICE

- Take some time each day to remember your dreams, hopes, wishes and values you had when you started your family. Update your ideas and focus your energy on the most important ones.

- Share your hopes, dreams and ideals with your daughter, and work on ways to make them happen.

- Place your list of priorities in a visible place, and revisit the "Finding Time" activity regularly.

- Have your daughter and other family members do the "Finding Time" activity, and discuss together how well each of you are doing at matching your values with your time commitments.

- Find others who are on a path of living balanced lives, and ask about their first or subsequent steps.

- Carefully evaluate what you say "yes" to.
- Give yourself permission to do less and find extraneous commitments to jettison.
- Limit your nights away from home.
- Decrease the amount of screen time in your home.
- Practice mindfulness. Learn to enjoy activities in the moment; fully immerse yourself in an activity without watching the time.
- Model the behaviors you want to see in your daughter.
- Rather than tell your daughter to hurry up, tell yourself to slow down or start earlier for more transition time.
- Use family meetings to plan downtime fun for everyone.
- Find others in your community interested in the voluntary simplicity movement, and share ideas.
- Read *Your Money or Your Life* or take the Voluntary Simplicity Discussion Course from www.nwei.org.

PUTTING IT TOGETHER—YOUR VERSION

Write down three or four ideas you have been inspired to implement in your own life after reading and discussing this chapter.

1. _____

2. _____

3. _____

4. _____

FURTHER READING

Voluntary Simplicity

The Simple Living Guide: A Sourcebook for Less Stressful, More Joyful Living by Janet Luhrs at www.simpleliving.com
Simplify Your Life: 100 Ways to Slow Down and Enjoy the Things That Really Matter by Elaine St. James
Voluntary Simplicity Discussion Course, Northwest Earth Institute (NWEI) at www.nwei.org, 503-227-2807
Healthy Children, Healthy Planet Discussion Course at www.nwei.org
The Organized Parent: 365 Simple Solutions to Managing Your Home, Your Time, and Your Family's Life by Christina Baglivi Tinglof

Finding Peace Within

The New Earth: Awakening to Your Life's Purpose by Eckhart Tolle
Shelter for the Spirit by Victoria Moran
Inner Simplicity by Elaine St. James
Building Unity by Paul Werder
Slowing Down to the Speed of Life: How to Create a More Peaceful, Simpler Life from the Inside Out by Richard Carlson
Seven Habits of Highly Effective People by Stephen Covey

Addressing Clutter and Stress

Clear Your Clutter with Feng Shui: Free Yourself from Physical, Mental, Emotional, Spiritual Clutter Forever by Karen Kingston

Simplify Your Time: Stop Running and Start Living/ Simplify Your Space: Create Order and Reduce Stress by Marcia Ramsland

Less Stress, More Success: A New Approach to Guiding Your Teen Through College Admissions and Beyond by Ken Ginsburg, MD and Marilee Jones, Dean of Admissions of MIT

Balancing Life and Work

Your Money or Your Life: Transforming Your Relationship with Money and Achieving Financial Independence by Vicki Robin and Joe Dominguez

Getting a Life by Jacqueline Blix and David Heitmiller

The Millionaire Next Door: The Surprising Secrets of America's Wealthy by Thomas Stanley, PhD and William Danko, PhD

Resources for Youth

Fighting Invisible Tigers: A Stress Management Guide For Teens by Earl Hipp

Perfectionism—What's Bad About Being Too Good? by Miriam Adderholdt-Elliott and Jan Goldberg

Create a Personal Stress Management Guide at www.aap.org/stress/teen1-a.cfm

WEBSITES

Northwest Earth Institute at www.nwei.org

Simple Living Newsletter at www.simpleliving.com

Simple Living Network at www.simpleliving.net

The New Roadmap Foundation at www.newroadmap.org (from authors of *Your Money or Your Life*)

Wings Seminars: promote transformational shifts in consciousness at www.wings-seminars.com

Finding Time: An Evaluation of My Values and Activities:

Part 1:

Write here a list of all your daily activities during an average week, along with the approximate times spent on each activity.

When you are done, tally up the time spent on each activity, and divide by 7 to give an estimate of the time spent on each activity daily. List the top ten activities, in order of most time spent on them, in the list at the lower right-hand side of this page.

Part 2:

Write down a list of your top priorities in life:

From your list of priorities, mark the ten most essential ones, and list these in order of importance in the lower left-hand side of this page.

Top Ten Priorities (by importance):

1. _____
2. _____
3. _____
4. _____
5. _____
6. _____
7. _____
8. _____
9. _____
10. _____

Top Ten Activities (by time spent):

1. _____
2. _____
3. _____
4. _____
5. _____
6. _____
7. _____
8. _____
9. _____
10. _____

Modeling a Life Worth Living

By Shann Weston

"FINDING MY PASSION" has never been a one-time event. I used to live and die for horses. Then it was John Lennon. I loved my years of homesteading, raising food and running sled dogs in Alaska. I was an ardent environmentalist. I became an expert on being pregnant and having babies when it was my time. These days, I am passionate about resuming running, writing, and my kids. In coming years I'll expect new passions. Recently I have wondered where the capacity for creating passion comes from. What inspires me to find and pursue these interests? What guides me through the dark times and rekindles my basic passion for life?

Many self-help and inspirational books do their best to illuminate the meaning of life. If I could gain such wisdom by osmosis, I would surely have it by now. But there's nothing like raising kids to show me the gap between what I "know" and how I live. When I addressed that gap deeply, I got a succinct, if not simple, message back: To teach life's lessons, I must learn to live them. It comes down to this: If I want my children to understand what it means to be creative, joyful, physically fit, engaged in their own spiritual journey, pursuing meaningful work, involved with community, connected to the earth, celebrating family

and friendships, I must model being an adult doing these things. When things don't go well—when illness or setbacks or depression come visiting, I must model facing the truth and creating a strategy to change, accept, or heal it.

Of all the challenges involved with raising and teaching kids, for me, the greatest task of all is to live my own life as fully as I can, and model to my children what I am doing. I have to learn to freely share my own stories, struggles and lessons, to remember that actions do speak louder than words. If my husband and I are silent with our own life's wisdom and history, what do our children have to go on? We spark our own motivation daily by recognizing how quickly the media could fill that void. The essence of this question is: When our children are out on their own, what will they have to refer back to? What I remember is how my parents lived day to day, how they responded to the twists and turns of life, not what they said about how life should be accomplished.

Modeling a life worth living asks me to take risks—"to show, not tell." The children witness my efforts, sometimes clumsy, to write poetry again, make a new friendship, go for a challenging job, try yoga or meditation, sing in public, formulate my own authentic spiritual truths, and give kids a hug even when they seem to asking for the opposite. My ongoing inspiration is my memories of teachers who loved kids, loved their subject, loved learning, AND SHOWED IT. Their words are long since gone. What I remember is their passion, and if today I pick up Shakespeare or history or science, it will be with the memory of their shining eyes and modeled enthusiasm.

Sometimes taking action means giving myself opportunities to enter into the stillness of life, to be quiet and conscious. I look at my cat or dog as they doze or stare off into space and think they have great lessons to teach us busy humans. Our family balances between jobs, sports, music lessons, friends, entertainment, homework, chores and community activities. We are ready for action all the time, perhaps addicted to it. A few too many quiet moments produce cries of "I'm bored." It's not just our lives, but the whole society and the times we live in. That's why it feels so difficult when we stand up against the force of the flow, and create a ritual, a moment in time, a quieting space to just be, to feel grateful and to celebrate what we've accomplished. Each week, we plan a few sit-down dinners, candles and all, despite everyone's hectic schedules. The phone is turned off. We say a blessing before the meal and share our day. Some days it works better than others, but it has become "tradition," and so we continue to re-create it every week.

I recognized recently that teenage angst is contagious to close family members. In a recent episode with it in our family, I returned to a favorite book, *Man's Search for Meaning*, by Victor Frankl, a survivor of a Nazi concentration camp. Frankl tells us clearly to stop asking about the meaning of life, rather to think of ourselves as being questioned by Life, daily and hourly. Life is asking how we will respond to each loss, each obstacle, each success. Everything else can be taken away but that fundamental freedom to choose our attitude and action to everything Life presents to us.

In the camps, Frankl lived a life where death, pain, and hunger were constant companions. He decided that if his life were to have meaning during its productive and comfortable times, it must also have meaning in times of suffering. That's an uncommon thought these days. It implies that Life's lessons are not easily mastered—and suffering can be a great teacher if we grant permission for its presence. Thinking that we can avoid suffering—for ourselves or our children—is, in itself, responsible for a lot of emotional pain. Life asks us how we will respond to the bad times. We are faced with many choices, including ignoring the pain, tranquilizing it, and facing up to its source. Sometimes finding the way in the midst of personal suffering gives great meaning to life.

Frank noted that those who had a sense of purpose developed faith in the future which served them better than physical strength. In the middle of our shared teenage/family angst, I read these chapters with sudden comprehension. The purpose of our existence changes day by day. The purpose of my existence now is to model my truths, commit fully to my life and to be the best parent I can be. I answer the meaning of my own life by surrendering to the spiritual act of loving my kids and the kids whose lives I touch. That love allows me to see their shining potential, and help them believe in it. That is what will help them survive the

lures of drugs and other distractions. I hope to teach my children by example to find and articulate their truths, to recognize their talents as gifts, to treat mind, body and soul with respect and gratitude, to enjoy their relationships with friends, family and nature, to search out what gives them joy and solace, and to go to the center of their beings for wisdom and strength.

Shann Weston is a writer and founder of Positive Legacies, *an organization devoted to leaving the world a better place than we found it. With a Masters of Science in Natural Resources from the University of Alaska, she has a life-long passion for whales and marine life. She lives in the San Juan Islands and has two daughters.*

Author's Note on Finding Passion

Dear Friends,
"To do good things in the world, first you must know who you are and what gives meaning in your life."
Paula P. Brownlee

We often don't take time to reflect on what is really important to us, to explore who we are and what we stand for. Are we doing something we really love and getting lost in it? Finding passion can give our lives fulfillment. For me, getting outdoors for a bit every day makes me feel whole, even when it is raining.

Children and parents can help each other find passion. Our children, who are naturally spontaneous, can keep us in the moment. I had a blast making a gargoyle out of clay with my son's art literacy class. On the other hand, as parents we can provide our children with opportunities to find their own passions. We can even explore with them. Sometimes your child may pick up on your passion, like my friend who shares her love of playing the guitar with her daughters. However, children may not share the same passions as their parents. Your child may even explore passions shared with an adult mentor. We can encourage them to discover what "sparks the light within them" and then kindle that spark in whatever way we can.

Kathy Masarie is a pediatrician, founder of Family Empowerment Network and a Parent and Life Coach. She has a daughter and a son.

Reprinted with permission from Full Esteem Ahead, *Wings*, Winter 1999

Personal Navigation

By Molly Krupa

As a teenager, finding a passion saved my life. I had been full of passions as a child: horses, soccer, gymnastics, and piano. As I entered junior high school, though, these interests were extinguished in the face of societal pressures. Through television and my peers, I "learned" that popular young women were not supposed to be active, loud, or covered in mud. The length of my fingernails and the color of my lipstick became more important than the topics I learned in my advanced classes or the score of my basketball game. My happiness also lost importance. Instead, what was "cool" dominated my existence. My guide to this coolness was soap operas, fashion magazines, and my popularity with the opposite sex. I was miserable.

When I was eighteen (and extremely difficult to get along with), my parents generously supported a dream that I had held since my childhood. I began flying. The physical separation from society's expectations gave me a much needed respite. While up in the air, I did not

have to look at pencil thin women with hair styles that I could never achieve. I did not have to behave like that actress, or look like that model. I only had to be a good pilot. Beyond that, I could begin to be me again.

Flying literally gave me the distance to see society more clearly. However, I do not believe all teens need to take up a passion as dramatic as aviation. A young person's mind only needs to be truly engaged, in a space free of commercial advertising, powerful stereotypes, and pressure from peers. For me, once my world became flying, I could see the discrepancies between my world and the world which had previously set all the rules. My new world had power, and that power began to flow towards me.

Not surprisingly, the most glaring disparity between my former and new worlds lay in the expectations of women. Before, when a joke about the fragility or incompetence of females was passed, I would giggle or act demure. For this complicit response, I was rewarded by the person who made the jest. I also internalized the comments. However, when these jokes were directed towards my ability as a pilot, I no longer thought them funny. Not only that, I knew these "jokes" (and I began to wonder, are these really jokes, or disguised attacks?) were absolutely wrong. I was an excellent pilot.

I began to see a connection between sexist remarks and societal expectations of women. When my long fingernails got caught in the cockpit controls, I cut them, and then thought, "How convenient that their desire for long fingernails matches their expectations of an incapable female pilot." I wondered how many of these connections existed, and became increasingly aware of such societal traps. Aviation gave me the power to see, and also an identity that I cared about enough to want to protect.

A passion gives a young person a purpose in life, a purpose not obscured by media and peer influence.

Moreover, when a teenager finds a passion, she finds a conduit through which her childlike fascination with life itself is rediscovered.

Aviation, which judged me by my flying skills only, liberated me from other standards. As I cast off these other, often harmful, standards, I was able to be myself. Not only did I start living again, but I gained the skills and knowledge needed to protect myself in the face of future adversities. **I believed in myself.**

At the time of this article, Molly Krupa was working as a carpenter in Southeast Portland.

Reprinted with permission from Full Esteem Ahead, *Wings*, Winter 1999

Fifteen Steps to a Simpler Life

By Victoria Moran, author of "Simplifying," excerpted from *Shelter for the Spirit*

I LOVE TO GO TO Susan's house. There's space between the furniture. You can see the wood floors. At Christmas she can put up a tree without rearranging her living room. There are empty places on the bookshelves for more books. There is room in her house for gifts and guests and possibilities. That's because Susan knows how to simplify.

Maybe she was born with the capacity to cull the inconsequential from the basic. Perhaps her mother had it, too, and her grandmother, and they passed it down like a recipe or a figure of speech. But those of us who didn't grow up with a knack for simplifying can learn how to do it later in life. We have to learn how, if we want a home and a life that nurture our spirit.

Cluttered rooms and complicated schedules interfere with our ability to treasure the moment. Ironically our houses and apartments—where some of our best moments can be—seem to attract clutter and complication like a magnet. Mail, both the welcome and the unsolicited, is delivered; purchases are unloaded; items accumulate. After several years spent in one place, it can feel as if moving would take more effort than climbing Mount Everest.

And think of the hours in the day. Are they packed so tightly they make your basement and garage look orderly by comparison? That's true for most of us. We fill hours, children of the Great Depression fill pantries: to the brim —just in case. The things the majority of people find the least time for are exercise, healthy meals, meditation, time with their spouses and children, and pursuing their dreams. Some couples even have to book appointments for making love. It's not an extra sitcom there isn't time for; it's the indispensables that are dispensed with.

You may be familiar with the sense of uneasiness, even desperation that can accompany a growing awareness of how much "stuff" is pressing down on you. There are various stopgap responses to it: a garage sale to deal with object overload, a weekend away as a break from incessant responsibilities. With the proceeds from the sale we shop again, and when we get back from our trip there's more to do than ever.

The only sure way out of the miasma of excess is to embrace simplicity, although our cultural ambivalence toward the concept can get in the way. Sometimes we like simplicity. We say, "These are great directions—really simple," and "Her dress was simple and elegant." Other times we're not so sure. "Simple living" can conjure up visions of voluntary poverty, subsistence farming, and '60s dropouts. To clear away some of the confusion, let's examine simplicity, first by looking at what it is not.

Simplicity is not poverty and lack. If you've experienced those, you know that juggling bills and chasing checks don't simplify anybody's life.

Simplicity is not self-denial. It is an indulgence, providing you with a wealth of time and space.

Simplicity is not going back to the land. Unless that's your chosen way to live and you know what you're in for, you'll end up with more complications than you ever dreamed of in Cleveland.

Simplicity is not boring. Contrary to popular belief, the alternative to incessant activity and acquisition is not vast emptiness. Instead it means experiencing life more fully than ever.

Simplicity is not giving up what you need. It is having everything you need with the bonus of being able to find it.

Now, what simplicity is:

Simplicity is discerning the essential from the unessential. Even with a commitment to living simply, you'll have lots of possessions and pas-times that aren't essential to your survival or your spiritual well-being. You just won't mistake these extras for necessities.

Simplicity is having room for the unexpected. In a simplified life an unforeseen challenge—or a sudden blessing—can be incorporated without a lot of shifting and upset.

Simplicity is savoring life. It is having a truly memorable lunch with a friend because you didn't try to cram in breakfast with another one that morning as well as tea with a third in the afternoon. It's being charmed by the ceramic bowl on your kitchen table every time you see it, rather than having so many ceramic bowls that you no longer notice any of them.

Most of all, simplicity is freedom. It's freedom to choose what you want in your life because you're not letting in everything that shows up. It's freedom to do what you want because you're not already committed to more obligations than you can handle and the maintenance of more objects than you'll ever use.

There are probably hundreds of ways to decrease the complexity of anyone's domestic domain. To keep things truly simple, though, I'll stick with five time-tested ways to simplify your space and 10 others to do the same for your time.

Five Surefire Ways to Simplify Your Space

1. Chop Up Your Credit Cards

I'm not opposed to shopping. I like it, in fact. And I like it more since I chopped up nearly all my credit cards. I did. Right down the middle and again through that corner that said "expiration date." Since then, I have sought to live by the principle of, by and large, only spending money I have. A hundred years ago, that was common sense. Today it seems wildly radical.

Since I stopped shopping with money I didn't have, my life has simplified on every level.

Operating on a pay-up-front basis, I rarely make impulse purchases and therefore don't acquire a lot of intensive-care items: bric-a-brac that demands polishing, clothes that demand dry cleaning. I am released from the culturally entrenched notion that everything I admire I should buy, and everything cheap that I remotely admire I must buy. Now I buy what I need and I buy what I love. And my house is looking more like Susan's.

Remember how good it felt when you were a kid and bought a toy or a present for Mom with your very own money? That's how it feels to pay cash, because you are shopping with your very own money. And you'll have more of it because there will be fewer bills to dog you.

However you wish to conduct your personal financial dealings, making even a minimal effort to charge less and pay cash more can guarantee you the following:

- You will end up with less junk you wish you'd never bought, and your environment will be less cluttered.
- You will look better in your clothes and feel better in your house because everything that goes on your body or in your rooms you will absolutely adore.
- With fewer bills, you'll have additional discretionary income and the satisfaction of being more fully in charge of your financial life. Your expenses will be easier to keep track of, and because cash is so tangible, money itself will become more meaningful.
- When you buy something you truly want— especially something you've "saved up for"—you'll

feel like a million bucks. And you'll greatly improve your chances for having a million bucks since you won't be shelling out a fortune in interest every month.

2. Insist on Quality

I have a crocheted vest that I bought when I was 18 and worked at a specialty store over the holidays. The vest seemed expensive at the time, but it was skillfully crafted of good yarn. In the many years that have passed since I was 18, I've sent innumerable garments to rummage sales, charity, and the rag bag. I still wear that vest, though, and it is still beautiful. Quality is never outdated.

When you're thinking of adding something new to your wardrobe or to your environment, let quality be the keynote. Quality does not necessarily mean cost, and it certainly doesn't mean the current status value of that particular item. It means only allowing into your cherished space those things that either serve a useful purpose or bring you genuine pleasure.

The highest-quality objects in my home are those made by my daughter. Her artwork, needlework, clay creations, and poems are more valuable to me than a wall full of Rembrandts. Next in quality are the heirlooms—and I don't have many—that connect me with other important people in my life or my heritage. For example, I have a quilt my great-grandmother made. It is folded on top of our piano—fitting because the quilter raised two daughters selling Steinways after she was widowed in 1910.

Also high on the quality scale for me are memorabilia of my own life and travels, books signed by their authors, gifts from people I like being reminded of, and items that by their shape, texture or color make me glad they're in my everyday world. Only you know what denotes quality to you. In general, an object made by hand touches the soul in a way something mass processed cannot. Items whose quality is determined by their practicality can come from almost anywhere, but those whose value derives from more subtle attributes are seldom found in big, barnlike discount stores. They're occasionally made of plastic, but not very often.

Look around the room where you're sitting. What things there meet the dual criteria for quality, in that they are both practical and aesthetically pleasing? Which ones have a definite purpose and are regularly used for that purpose? Which ones simply make you happy because they're in your field of vision? What else is in the room? The "what else" is what stands between you and the simplicity of space your spirit craves. Clothes you don't wear, books you don't read, little statues that don't do anything and you've never liked anyway make indirect demands that rob energy. You see them, but they don't reward your eyes. You have to shove them aside when you look for what you're really going to use. If you have too many of them, maintaining a sense of order will be impossible.

Test the contents of each room in your house or apartment with these two questions: "Is it serving a purpose?" and "Does it make me happy?" Remember, you only need a "yes" answer to one of them for the object at hand to be earning its keep. This querying can be the makings of a massive mental garage sale of "what else." Take those same questions with you when you shop. Envision your intended purchase in the place you've set aside for it. Will it be functional or genuinely promote happiness? If so, it's worthy taking on. If not, you're sabotaging your simplicity.

3. Do a Seasonal Closet Cleaning and Excess Purge

Paying cash and insisting on quality diminish the likelihood of accumulating simplicity-diminishing junk, but it creeps up on all of us. Moreover, what is useful to us changes as our lives change. An overview of your home is in order every season. Do the two-question test on each room and storage place and eliminate excess accordingly.

Closet cleaning can be like sending your soul to a spa. As you discard the worn-out, the worthless, and the size 5 jeans that haven't fit in decades, you discard ways of thinking that no long fit either. You don't have to belabor the point: "I am now cleaning out my closet and my mind." Just clean your closet. Your mind will respond.

Once you've done the major eradication that starts the process, subsequent seasonal purges will be quick and easy. Remember: You're not giving up what adds to your life. Simplifying does not mean paring down to cold and stark. As long as what's on display or in storage

serves you in any way, it can be a welcome part of your simplified lifestyle.

When you exercise discernment about everything, accepted or purchased, that stays in your house, you will find yourself in the presence of something rare and wonderful: unsaturated space. This emptiness opens the door to all those things that will enrich your life in new ways. What you want and need now is far more likely to make its way to you when you make a place for it. By eliminating the unnecessary, you create the void. Nature does her best to fill it. You decide with what and how much.

4. End the Paper Chase

The mail is here. My simplicity is at stake. There are the weekly grocery ads that come unsolicited, the pizza delivery flyers, the catalogs from every mail-order company on earth as penance for having once ordered a set of sheets and pillowcases.

I carry the entire bundle to my desk. I put the envelopes in the recycling basket; the bills go in a file until bill-paying day. I take magazines to the breakfast room since I read them in the morning with my cereal and fruit. I read the letters last when I can spend time with them. If I'm in a hurry, I put them in a special basket and read them later. If someone has taken the time to write to me, I want to give that letter more attention than I give the light bill. Everything else I either tend to immediately file or toss for recycling.

One way to get less junk mail is to answer each piece with a postcard that says, "If I have ordered from you or contributed to your organization in the past, I appreciate that association. However, I wish to have my name immediately and permanently removed from your mailing list." (I had postcards printed with this message.) It also helps to put a note with every subscription, order, or contribution asking that your name not be passed on to other companies or organizations. And you can write to the Mail Preference Service, Direct Marketing Association, P.O. Box 9008, Farmingdale, NY 11735-9008, asking that your name not be sold to lists. But you'll need to write every five years. Direct mailers are better than bloodhounds for finding and refinding potential customers.

We know our copious consumption of paper is environmentally reckless, but it has a personal price as well. All that paper goes into our homes and detracts from the beauty we should see there. Having to sort, read, and dispose of it takes away from the time we have to spend there. So deal with as little paper as necessary and set up a workable filing system for the rest.

A filing cabinet is a most useful piece of furniture. When I got mine, Frankie Grady, a self-confessed filing ace, helped me set up a very workable system. Here are her suggestions:

- Determine how you do paperwork: in one place, wherever it's sunny at the moment, whatever. Use the equipment that suits your style: a stationary cabinet, a file on wheels, or mini-files you can carry.
- Use a container equipped for hanging files. Inside each main compartment, use labeled file folders for each subcategory. The hanging files can cover broad, general headings like "house" or "finances," but avoid anything as all-inclusive as "miscellaneous." Example: Hanging file—Car. File folders within that hanging file—Repair and maintenance, Insurance, Titles and Registration.
- Clear out a file or two every season, just like your rooms and your closets. Be willing to part with unnecessary written and printed matter. The backs of used pages make fine scratch paper, fax-sending paper, kids' drawing paper.
- Put your important documents in a safe deposit box, and keep an updated list of what that box contains in your filing cabinet or computer.
- If you have a computer, file as much as you can electronically. Every once in a while clean out your hard drive, too. Excess is draining, even when it's byte-sized.

5. Organize—But Only After You've Simplified

Simplification and organization are often confused, but they're not the same. You could conceivably organize every bit of extraneous accumulation that's in your house right now. You could hang it on pegboards, stack it neatly on shelves and in cabinets, put it in drawers with those nifty little dividers, stick it on bulletin boards with matching pushpins, and place it by category in those see-through, stacking plastic boxes. In *Clutter's Last Stand*, Dan Aslett's classic on unfettered living, he calls such organizing aids "junk bunkers." If we didn't have so much junk, we wouldn't need all those places to keep it.

But be forewarned: If you organize before you simplify, things will be disorganized again in no time.

> Cultivating spirituality for simple living involves locating and exploring those places in our soul that ring like jubilant wind chimes to the breezes and whispers of the divine.

This is not because you're a hopeless slob without a prayer for redemption. It is because excess cannot be organized. If it could, it wouldn't be excess.

Ask 10 friends if they think they're organized or not. Unless everybody you know is a CPA, eight out of the 10 will probably say they're dreadfully disorganized. It's a myth. We just think we're disorganized because we live in a time and place overflowing with junk.

If you practice the first four Surefire Ways to Simplify Your Space, you will find your environment becoming organized with minimal effort. When you remove from a desk drawer the broken rubber bands, dried-up pens, loose change, and year-old receipts, what remains looks pretty good. So what if there's a paper clip in with the postage stamps? That drawer is, for all intents and purposes, organized.

You can organize further if you enjoy doing it, but it isn't necessary. Too much concern over tidiness and organization can defeat your purpose of making your home friendly to human beings, starting with yourself. We all have an internal clutter/order tolerance level. Some people need houses that look like Marine barracks when the sergeant is due in for inspection. Others aren't comfortable unless there are half-read books on the tables, and open sewing basket by the big chair, and last night's Scrabble board left out.

Find your tolerance point and compromise with the tolerance points of the people you live with and the conditions of your life. If you put the well-being of living things ahead of arranging objects, you will be somewhat less organized but quite a bit happier.

The Time of Your Life

The other day I watched an attractive, professional-looking mother approaching a department store entrance at a trot, her little girl galloping behind her at two arms' length. The child was five, maybe six, one of those ages that only lasts a minute and never comes back. "Hurry up," the mother said several times. Her daughter tried to comply, while respecting the childhood conventions of studying cloud formations, running the fingers of her free hand along the turquoise railing, and of course not stepping on any cracks.

I was angry with her mother and I don't even know her. Well, in one sense I don't know her, but in another I know her intimately. She's just me in a different phase of life. I said "Hurry up" to my daughter a thousand times and she obeyed implicitly. She hurried so well that she's a teenager now, and it took her no time at all. Hurrying ourselves and those close to us is a harsher activity than we realize. We tend to be short tempered when we are short on time. When we have the time to be patient, we usually are. When we have the time to listen, we usually do. When we have the time to help, we're glad to pitch in. Without the time, we feel pressured and annoyed.

As we add more activities to our to-do list, we become like a debtor adding creditors to the roll in an attempt to pacify those he already has. There is no bankruptcy court for people whose time account is chronically overdrawn, but you can recognize them. They're always racing. They can't sit back and enjoy themselves. They're terrified of "wasting time." They suffer from stress-related illnesses. Their relationships are strained. Their schedules are so full that even they don't know what's happening tomorrow. Misplacing a planner seems like losing a limb.

Too many physical objects to work around and care for can diminish our serenity, but too many obligations, too many activities and too many hours at the office will wipe it out completely. We've heard Ben Franklin's phrase "Time is money." In our era, time is better than money. *The American's Use of Time Project* done at the University of Maryland showed that 48 percent of Americans earning less than $20,000 a year would give up a day's pay every week for a day of free time. Seventy percent of those earning more than $30,000 a year would do the same thing. We crave more time and we're willing to pay for it. Of course, the richest person alive can't buy more than 24 hours a day. That used to be enough. Now, in spite of increased life expectancy and a bonanza of labor-saving apparatuses, the pace of life is more often than not a mad rush.

An occasional jam-packed day is exhilarating. A part of me likes the stimulation I can get from over-scheduling and arriving where I'm going, out of breath, just in time. It feels like sliding into home plate with the crowd cheering. But of course, nobody is cheering, and when I collapse at home after an overly rushed day, I bring the agitation with me. Everything is here to soothe my soul—a delightful daughter, congenial pets, art and music handpicked to suit myself—but I'm too tired to notice. A couple of things had to take place to make me want to simplify my time. The first was that I saw my incessant busyness interfering with my closest relationships. The second was that serenity started to feel better than stimulation. It was like switching from strong coffee to herbal tea. At first it's wretched, but after a while it feels better to be naturally composed than artificially energized.

Ten Surefire Ways to Simplify Your Time

1. Say "No"

Just as you're saying "no" to gadgets you won't use and clothes you don't wear,  you can say "no" to activities that aren't genuinely meaningful to you. Developing the habit of politely but consistently saying "no" when you want will give you more time at home and more peace when you're there.

When something is important to other people, they assume it should be equally so to you. The art museum docents think you should be one. The neighborhood crime watch people think you should drive patrol two hours a week. Everybody in the Save-the-Rainforest group thinks you should carry a sign this Saturday. Maybe you should. And maybe not. Our lives are multifaceted. We are workers, students, householders, losers, parents, and friends. All these identities can be part of the tapestry of our destiny. Our task is to balance the many roles we play and refrain from volunteering to understudy everybody else's. It can be tough to say "no," especially to causes we recognize as worthy. The goal is to realize that, since we can't help with everything, our time and stamina need to go into what truly speaks to your hearts.

2. Tithe Your Time

Tithing money—donating one tenth of all income to the church, to people in need or some other deserving cause —is a way of orderly giving. It not only enriches society, but those who do it believe that the practice blesses them with greater prosperity. (John D. Rockefeller's famous "Ledger A," on which he wrote his income and expenditures from boyhood, included a regular tithe.)

Time can be tithed also. You don't have to get specific—10 percent of waking hours—but you should be conscious of giving some time every week or month to something outside yourself. If lack of time is a problem, giving it away may not seem like a viable solution. But when you plan to spend a portion of the hours you've allotted in service of others, you will better organize those that are left. Be sure you tithe your time to something that genuinely moves you, and say "no" without guilt to anything that doesn't. This way it will be easy to remember that you're giving a gift, not serving a sentence.

3. Put Things With Feelings First

Balancing your checkbook is probably not as important as listening to your child. Having a romp with the dog should usually take precedence over waxing the kitchen floor. That's because bank accounts and linoleum can wait until a more convenient moment. Things with feelings can't. Because the hours in the day are finite and many of them are already taken up with sleep, meals, working, bathing, and the like, it's crucial that our discretionary time be spent where it means the most. Put things with feeling first—including yourself.

4. Allow More Time

Whatever it is you have to do, allow a little more time than you think it will take. That way, if it takes longer than you thought it would, you're covered. If it doesn't, you have some spare time, some breathing minutes. Leave for your appointment before you really need to. You can drive slower. If you get there early, you're not wasting time. Bring a book and read it. Bring your journal and write in it. Bring your spirit and meditate.

If you're expecting guests, plan for their arrival in advance of the appointed hour. That way you can rest before they're ringing your doorbell, and truly enjoy their visit once they finally get there.

5. Prioritize With the ABC Method

Priorities change from day to day, which is why the ABC method of meeting them works so well. When you make your list of what you want to accomplish each day, label every item with a letter: A – priority, it must be done today; B – important, it needs to be done soon; C – necessary, it should be done sometime.

If you only get through your A list, you've done everything you have to. The following day, a B or two is likely to rise to the A category. Eventually even the C's will be promoted—or they'll fade into insignificance.

6. Stay Well

Nothing is more time-consuming than being sick. Days and weeks can be devoted to an illness, and more are eroded by having to use them to make up for lost time. If you are a hurrier, one way to get less sick is to stop

hurrying. Colds and the like tend to pounce on hurriers mid-rush. It's as if the body and mind conspire to force a rest on those who refuse to take one otherwise.

We can't always prevent coming down with something, but if we're aware of our state of health and take care of it on a consistent basis, we can substantially hedge our bets. How are you taking care of yourself right now? How is your nutrition? How much rest do you get? Are you frequently outside to get fresh air and a little sunlight? Do you meditate daily or have another routine for stress reduction? Have you sought out health care providers you trust and with whom you can communicate freely? The time you spend preserving your health is like time invested in a savings account; you'll get it back plus interest.

7. Let the Machine Get It

Pavlov's dogs salivated at the sound of a bell, and we respond just as habitually: We answer the phone. We run in from the garden to answer the phone. We leap from the shower and track a rivulet as we dash in a towel to answer the phone. In the midst of a wonderful dinner or the part in the bedtime story where the bears just walk in on Goldilocks, we say, "Just a minute," and answer the phone.

Let the machine get it. Pick up the calls that are important, and be grateful to the callers who didn't leave messages. They just gave you something precious: time.

8. Turn Off the TV

Television can be educational, motivational, and uplifting. Families can watch quality programs together and discuss their meaning. TV can help us understand the world around us and people who are different from ourselves. Is that how you use TV? Me neither.

Regardless of what we choose from the televised menu, one thing is clear: Watching television takes time. The average American will spend one year of life just watching the commercials. If you want more time to enjoy your home, get to know your family, unleash your creativity, or ponder spiritual truths, turn off the TV. You may just want to turn it off from time to time and use that 30 or 60 minutes for something else. Or you may want to turn it off, unplug it, and give it away. Whatever choice you make, you and your television—and your VCR and your computer, for that matter—have a relationship of which you are in charge. How much time to you choose to spend with electronic companionship? Spend that much and no more. This is your life, not a pilot for an upcoming series.

9. Put Off Procrastination

My mother has lots of "do it now" phrases: "Never put off until tomorrow what you can do today." "A stitch in time saves nine." "The early bird catches the worm." The early bird also doesn't have to come up with an excuse or pay a late fee.

If you look around your life and find a great many things undone, perhaps you're trying to do too great a number of things. Procrastination can be a problem for anyone, but it usually strikes life by necessity. If you're attempting to do more than there is time to do, something has to be put off. And then something else. Before long you're lamenting that you can't finish any of it.

If this is your situation, go back over the previous Surefire Ways to Simplify Your Time. Choose the one that you think would make the most difference in the time you have, and do it for a week. That alone should give you the time you need to take care of your most pressing procrastinated issue.

Procrastination itself is a time robber. It takes time to worry about a task, plan additional ways to put it off, talk about how awful it is, and feel guilty over not having done it. If you want more time and something needs doing, do it. Then you'll have time left over.

10. Schedule In Fun

Even when time is a problem, most of us get our work done. We keep our houses reasonably clean. We care for our children. We take the car in for an oil change. We write to our parents and the friends who moved to Seattle, at least every once in a while. We do what we have to do. What we want to do, however, may never get done.

Right now put down this magazine and get out a pencil and a piece of paper. Write down everything you want to do before you die. It doesn't have to be reasonable. Just write it. Locate my best friend from sixth grade. Write it. Learn to speak Icelandic. (Why not? Lawrence of Arabia did.) Write it. When you catalogue your heart's desires, it sets in motion a chain of events that is indeed uncanny. It's as if your subconscious reads the list and sets about to make it happen.

My daughter made such a list, a poster actually, when she was seven. It had things on it like, "Go to China," "Go to Paris," "Be in a movie." These seemed fantastic at the time—it was when we were living in a cabin in the Ozarks and sharing one closet. Amazingly, a surprising number of the events she entered have come to pass for her, including China, Paris, and the movie—even though it was a nonspeaking part in a low-budget horror flick.

We were conditioned early in life to see work as more valuable than play, but play is the work of children. In school we had courses that were "solids" —math, grammar, Latin, history—and "non-solids" —art, music, poetry, sports. But what makes life worth living today, the fact that you can conjugate a verb, or that you can still recite Sara Teasdale and serve a pretty decent tennis ball?

Program your mind with this: Recreation is required. It is not optional. Look at the word: recreation. The time you give to it recreates your soul. There's no waste in that.

Bringing Simplicity Home

Eliminating the chaos from our drawers and from our days invites our spiritual self to make its presence known. In his book *Adventures in Simple Living*, Rich Heffern writes: "Cultivating spirituality for simple living involves locating and exploring those places in our soul that ring like great jubilant wind chimes to the breezes and whispers of the divine. Simplicity… frees us from clutter so that we can wake up to and hear the great chiming within us."

Because "the great chiming" is inside us, it's available to us any time and any place. Chances are, though, we'll hear it at home. At home we're in our own time and our own space—time and space we've cleared out to be amenable to chiming and such.

When the physical amenities of our homes are the necessary and the beautiful, just walking through a room can inspire us. When our calendars have substantial white space, like a well-funded advertisement, we have more time to spend in this place where we can most thoroughly be ourselves. A simplified life seems easier. And remarkable joy comes from simple things—like having work to do that matters, and having people to love who matter a lot.

Permission granted by Gideon Weil, Senior Editor, HarperOne Publishers, a division of Harper Collins. From *Shelter for the Spirit: Create Your Own Haven in a Hectic World* by Victoria Moran, Harper Perennial 1998. Moran is a certified life coach, motivational speaker, and the author of other books including *Fit from Within, Fat, Broke & Lonely No More,* and the best-selling *Creating a Charmed Life.* To learn more about her work or subscribe to her free ezine, "The Charmed Monday Minute," visit www.victoriamoran.com.

Vote With Your Life

By Janet Luhrs, author of *The Simple Living Guide, a Sourcebook for Less Stressful, More Joyful Living*

DID YOU KNOW THAT the choices you make every day are about who you are as a person? Each choice we make is like a vote. Most of us think of voting as only the action of going into a voting booth and choosing whether we want a Democrat or Republican, school levy or not, or a new city council member.

We vote every minute of every day. We vote with our time. We vote with our money. We vote with our life. How's that? Here is an example from my own life. Each time one of those new mega-discount stores opens up, I groan and moan as I pass by, complaining that our sense of community is going out the window, that life is becoming increasingly isolated and sterile, and how I miss the little Mom and Pop stores where the proprietors actually know your name and care about your day. For years, I grumbled about this, yet when I wanted to get good deals, I'd drive on over to the warehouse store, load up my cart, and cram my shelves at home with all of my good deals. I had this vague sense that it didn't feel right, but I did it anyway, rationalizing that it saved me so much money.

I stopped one day and thought about this dual life I was leading. Complaining, but still shopping. I realized I needed to start voting with my choices. I needed to decide which was more important—saving money or encouraging a sense of community and smaller stores. Was I willing to pay more for toilet paper and a jar of jam in order to keep my local store in business? Was I willing to save a little money in exchange for the incredible hassle of driving to one of those mega-stores, fighting for a parking place, wading through a vast and overwhelming maze of stuff, and standing in line for an eternity with a sea of humanity that could care less about my day?

I voted for intimacy and community. I'm not renewing my discount warehouse card. This doesn't mean I'll never again set foot in a warehouse store, because my life isn't about rigid absolutes. It does mean that I no longer will carry a card, and I will instead find another provider for the items I once bought at the warehouse store.

How can you live more in alignment with your values?

1. **Vote with your time.** If you say your family is the most important part of your life, then why are you at your office until 7:00 P.M. every night? If you say

it's because you have a boss to please or you need to earn more money, then admit it and realize that you have just voted for money or your boss over your family. In my book, *The Simple Living Guide,* I wrote about a friend who owns a public relations business. He decided early on that his family was most important, and as a result, he turns down work if it means staying at his office past 5:00 P.M. or on weekends. If you say your kids are the most important to you, how often during the day do you tell them that you love them? How much time do you spend with them? If your marriage is most important, how much effort are you putting into keeping it thriving?

2. **Vote with your money.** If you love having cute little boutiques and bookstores in your neighborhood, why are you driving miles to the nearest shopping center filled with mega-stores? Decide whether money or neighborhood is more important and spend your money accordingly. Voting with your money is also about how much you spend and on what. If you are envious of people who retire early or work part-time, then why are you making car payments, TV payments, big house payments and so on? Why is your wardrobe so elaborate? You get the picture. If you want more free time, spend less money so you don't have to work as many hours.

3. **Vote with your life.** Are you leading the kind of life you've always dreamed of? If not, why not? How are you spending your money and your time that is not in alignment with who you are? Does what you do for a living fit with your values? Are you in it just for the money? If so, then money wins your vote. There is nothing wrong with money getting your vote as long as it feels like a good fit inside.

Keep this voting idea in mind as you go through your day. Take note of where your votes feel right and where they don't. And remember too, we're not perfect, and life is fluid. What may seem right this year may not fit next year. What fits for one person may not fit for another. Our job is simply to stay conscious and aware.

How to Ground Your "Helicopter" Parenting
By Kathy Masarie, MD

"Helicopter parent" is eloquently described by Wikipedia:
....a parent who pays extremely close attention to his or her child's experiences and problems. These parents rush to prevent any harm or failure from befalling their children and won't let them learn from their own mistakes, sometimes even contrary to the children's wishes. They are so named because, like helicopters, they hover closely overhead, rarely out of reach, whether their children need them or not. An extension of the term, "Black Hawk parents," has been coined for those who cross the line from a mere excess of zeal to unethical behavior, such as writing their children's college admission essays.

Helicoptering starts out with bringing forgotten homework and lunch to school and goes on to berating the teacher for an "unfair" grade or overly helping on school projects. It evolves to calling your kid at college to be sure s/he got up for class or flying to Harvard to protest your child's biology grade or demanding the college provide more desirable plumbing for your child studying abroad in China. Colleges and now even companies are actually hiring extra staff to ward off helicopter parents.

One outcome is that parents are stressed and worried to the max. A study by the Society for Research in Child Development determined that helicopter parents reported "more sadness, crying and negative beliefs about themselves, and less joy, contentment and life satisfaction," whether the children were succeeding or failing. Helicoptering's message to the child is that "you are too ineffective to succeed on your own"; however, we all need to learn how to cope with adversity to be effective in life. How can a 22-year-old who can't address setbacks, disappointments, goals and progress at the university level, adjust to a complex job situation and an independent adult life?

Caring for our children's welfare and helping them out along the way is a fundamental part of a parent's role. But we baby boomers have made this nurturing an extreme sport. Some reasons for this parenting phenomenon are:

- Technological advances that allow 24/7 connection. This makes it easy to cross the line from involved to over-involved. The cell phone has become "the world's longest umbilical cord."
- Parent's concern for their children's safety, after school shootings, 9/11 and campus assaults.
- Rejecting the less engaged, "latch-key" parenting style today's parents were raised with.

So what are some antidotes?

1. **Consider what is the best support to enable your child to succeed toward independence,** to learn to make his or her own decisions and become self-sufficient. That answer will vary from child to child.
2. **Connect and communicate with your child.** When your kid complains about an unfair math grade, get curious about what your child sees as the problem behind it rather than storm the school. It may be s/he just wants to vent or that your child doesn't realize the value of completing an unpleasant task in realizing a long-term goal (of getting into the college he/she wants).
3. **Model healthy listening and conflict skills.** If a parent "bullies" a teacher or administrator into doing what they want, the message the kids learn is: "Might makes right." The teacher's perspective on the issue can be very insightful.
4. **Be involved in your child's education.** The Harvard Family Research Project found that teens whose parents play an active role do better in school and are more likely to enroll in college. Communicate regularly with the teacher, volunteer on projects the teacher or school needs in ways that don't stress you out.
5. **Offer support rather than rescue.** Communicate that you are not going to step in every time a child needs help. We can ask our kids, "What are you going to do to solve this problem?"
6. **Allow every opportunity for your child to practice making his/her own decisions.** Think of yourself as a life coach who provides structure, and gives suggestions. However, your child needs to "step up to the plate." Start small when they are young and gradually give them more responsibility as they grow.
7. **For every intervention ask yourself, "Is this action going to lead my child toward independence, competence and confidence or take away from it?"** In this way we give our children what they need: roots to grow and wings to fly.

> **You're a Helicopter Parent if you:**
> - Equate "love" with "success"
> - Feel ashamed when your child fails
> - Fight your child's battles for him/her, such as protesting an unfair grade
> - Take over your child's school projects
> - Start sentences about your child with "we," as in "We are applying for scholarships."
> - Are preoccupied with the details of a child's activities, practices, schedules and performances
> - Lurk on Facebook or MySpace to see if your child is hanging out with any bad seeds
>
> By Erin Wade 8/15/05
> Dallas Morning News

Resources:
Mom Needs an "A": Hovering, hyper-involved parents the topic of landmark study by Kay Randall at www.utexas.edu/features/2007/helicopter/

Summertime

By Peg Edera

EVERY YEAR PREPARING for summer brings us a new set of dilemmas: our work schedules are conflicting; our daughter's interests have changed; her friends are out of town every week that we are in town; we signed up for her favorite camp too late to get in, etc. Every fall, as I glance back at our summer, I see a myriad of missed opportunities, bad ideas, good ideas poorly executed (and really fun stuff.) As I look back today on my daughter's 10th summer I have decided that my goals for this year need to be clearer and simpler.

There is so much cool stuff to do and so much pressure on us all to do more that it is easy for us to forget about those long summer afternoons of our own childhoods.

I could just drift around, play with other kids, help Mom make jam, get bored and complain. What happens when we forget that those are real options—real activities that have great opportunities for learning? As a kid, I played more games of cards over tuna sandwiches than I can count. What happens when our time is so packed we don't have those simple memories of tuna and cards?

My idea is to find a balance. Last summer one practical thing we did was to schedule our daughter with a camp every other week, some of them being half-day camps. This proved to be a great balance for us all. My husband and I were lucky enough to be able to manipulate our schedules so that one of us was home during the non-camp weeks. It gave our daughter a lot of structure and experience as well as a lot of "down" time. (She also got very involved by helping to choose and schedule her camps, and clearly felt like her summer was HER summer.)

A friend of mine grew up going to three camps a summer. She could pick a one-week camp for each of the 3 A's: athletics, art and academics. Another friend of mine has made sure that her kids are involved in at least one volunteer activity each summer, helping her kids to remember that the world is filled with ways we can help and that simple acts really make a difference.

For us, summertime involves family members coming into town for a few weeks. This is a balancing act requiring great finesse in our household. We try to be available for spontaneous plans as well as organized family get-togethers. The result has frequently been frayed tempers and late nights catching up on the day-to-day obligations of life. Last year I learned how to say "No" and our lives changed. I planned only one dinner party and two special outings. These seemed less hospitable and I worried about hurt feelings, but I emerged from those weeks with several lovely memories and enough energy to weed the garden. Simplify, clarify and balance. This may be my new summer mantra.

In recent years a topic of increasing importance to me has been our spiritual lives. Going to a place of worship is, of course, a good option, but what if you are out of town most weekends? As I've grappled with this I've come up with a few small things we've included in our busy days. One is to notice the things we really love and the things that bring us a sense of wonder, and to make sure they are in balance. One small ritual we have at dinner is to say something we are thankful for in our day. Just noting what is special for each other brings a small awareness of the spirit to our table.

Another thing I have trouble balancing is trips. Our trip planning is frequently so hectic that there is a missed opportunity in it—engaging my daughter in the plan. What do we need; how do we get it; who will take care of the dog; what is our route to the destination; what does she most want to do when she's there? So often our lives are scheduled so tightly that we depart weary and worried that we have forgotten something. What would happen if we completely reframed our idea of a trip to include the preparation as part of the family fun? It sounds like a minor revolution in scheduling for us but the possibility is enticing...thrilling, even.

As I write this I am aware that our list of summer dreams has begun its morning glory-like growth.

We'll be sure to make some of these dreams into reality . . . and we'll still fit in the tuna sandwiches and the card games.

Peg Edera is a businesswoman, now a spiritual coach, facilitating labyrinth walks and workshops, writing poetry and working as a substitute teacher. She lives in Portland and has a daughter.

Reprinted with permission from Full Esteem Ahead, *Wings*, Spring, 2003.

Your Money or Your Life:
Are You Making a Dying or Making a Life?
By Joe Dominguez & Vicki Robin, authors of *Your Money or Your Life*

ONCE UPON A TIME "earning a living" was the means to an end—the means was earning, the end was living. For most employed people, work for pay now dominates their waking hours. Living is what can be fit into the remaining time. Is this really "making a living," or is it more like "making a dying"?

What is the place of work in our lives? Benjamin Franklin said that if everyone labored three hours daily, there would be no need for anyone to work more than that. Dr. Frithjof Bergmann, author of *On Being Free,* agrees: "For most of human history, people only worked for two or three hours per day."

But thanks to the Industrial Revolution, by the late 19th century, work had expanded to fill 60 hours per week. Workers began to fight for a shorter work week. Champions for the workers claimed that fewer hours on the job would decrease fatigue and increase productivity. Indeed, they said, fewer hours was the natural expression of the maturing Industrial Revolution; it would free the workers to exercise their higher faculties, and democracy would enjoy the benefit of an educated and engaged citizenry.

But along came the Depression and the work week, having fallen to 35 hours, started climbing again. Why? During the Depression, people equated free time with unemployment. In an effort to boost the economy and reduce unemployment, the New Deal established the 40-hour work week. Workers were educated to consider employment, not free time, to be their right as citizens.

During the last half century, this has created a push for full employment. There have been more people with more "disposable income," which meant increased profits, which meant business expansion, which meant more jobs, which meant more people (consumers) with yet more disposable income. Consumption has kept the wheels turning.

The fabric of family, culture and community that gave meaning to life outside the workplace has begun to unravel, and paid work has become an end in itself. At work, we now seek answers to the perennial questions of: "Who am I?"; "Why am I here?"; and "What's it all for?"

We want jobs to provide the exhilaration of romance. It's as if we believe there is a Job Charming out

there—like the Prince Charming in fairy tales —that will fill our needs and inspire us to greatness. We've come to expect that we can somehow have it all through our job: status, meaning, adventure, luxury, respect, power, tough challenges and fantastic rewards! Like the princess who keeps kissing toads looking for a handsome prince, we go from job to job looking for personal fulfillment.

Perhaps worst of all, we look to our jobs to provide us with a sense of identity. Remember the question we were asked in childhood, "What do you want to be when you grow up?" The very question reveals the problem. It asks what you want to "be," yet you are supposed to answer it with a "do." Is it any wonder so many of us suffer mid-life crises as we face the fact that our "doing" doesn't even come close to expressing our "being"?

Our focus on money has robbed us of the pride we can feel in who we are as people and the many ways we contribute to the well-being of others. Our task now is to retrieve our birthright of knowing ourselves as human beings rather than human earnings. As we simplify our lives, "earning a living" can take its place again as a means to the end of a whole and fulfilling life.

Editor's Note: Your Money of Your Life *has been an incredibly impactful book in prioritizing our energy toward connection, family, balance and community over paid work.*

Reprinted with permission of Health Directions, LLC. To subscribe to *Simple Living* by Janet Luhrs, visit www.simpleliving.com or call 1-888-577-6164.

Remaking a Living
By Brad Edmondson

YOUTH AND FREE TIME are both wasted on the young. Fifteen years ago, I lived on a remote desert ranch and would think nothing of climbing a hilltop to spend the afternoon watching cloud banks roll across the mountain ranges. I didn't have any "family" nearby, but I was rarely alone. I didn't have a "job" either, although there were always plenty of important things to do. I had a luxurious amount of free time and I didn't realize it.

I learned that in the desert you can see wind, hear lightning, and smell water. As I was out walking one day, a violent storm came over the pass and bore down on the ranch. Taking shelter between two boulders, I heard the blue arcs of cloud-bound lightning; smelled ozone and the essence of sage in the newly moist air; and saw small whirlwinds being pushed before the storm with sand and tumbleweeds rising within them to heights of 30 feet.

Although I didn't earn any money or make any good career moves that day, I remember it vividly. Now in the middle of a typically frantic workweek, you can stump me just by asking what I had for dinner last night.

Most people with full-time jobs must fight for every hour of free time. But even if you spend your days in a building where the windows can't be opened, the wind still blows as it always did, and the rain still falls. These simple things can offer great joy and meaning to those with time available to notice, just as men fresh out of prison have been known to cry at the taste of beer. First, however, you have to draw the line at work. You have to break loose from a life of breakfast business meetings and three-day dashes to the seashore that were supposed to be relaxing vacations.

There are several ways for people of even modest means to evade being trapped in an unrewarding career and to live more meaningful, leisurely lives. All of them involve making decisions about what is essential and what can be discarded. If the current trend heralded by Time magazine and other dedicated followers of baby-boom behavior holds true, we are likely to see a heartening upheaval in the next decade: millions of people following Thoreau's advice to "simplify, simplify." Instead of quietly battling desperation, they will quietly whittle away at their complex lives until only the heartwood is left.

There's some evidence that this trend may be more than this year's fashionable fad. According to a recent survey by the Gallup organization, most baby boomers say that they won't increase the time they spend at work in the next five years. In fact, almost half of boomer women and 37 percent of men expect to cut back on their work hours.

The problem with this retreat from work is that in most cases it hasn't been accompanied by a retreat from consumer desires. Relearning the values of frugality and thrift may not be difficult for the generation who began life during the

Depression, but it won't be nearly as easy for younger generations. Regardless of the values espoused during the '60s and '70s, baby boomers and younger adults are more oriented to the cash economy and consumer values than any other generation in American history. We still believe that we are entitled to a better life than our parents had, although we remain confused about what "a better life" really means.

Decreasing your income without decreasing your consumption is impossible for everyone except the federal government. Getting off the typical American treadmill of earning and spending will mean living by a new set of values. You won't even need to take up residence on the shore of Walden Pond or shuck everything for an organic hazelnut collective in the wilds of Oregon. Indeed, it may be possible for harried people to live much as they do now and be much happier. It all boils down to where you draw the lines.

Here are a few suggestions:

Ask your boss for a break instead of a raise. The nation's population growth rate is slowing down and so is growth in the nation's labor force. This means that highly skilled, trusted workers will become harder and harder to find as the 1990s roll on. Employers will be forced to make concessions to hold onto these kinds of workers. And unions will be in a better position to bargain for shorter and more flexible work hours. Management will give more serious consideration to a wider range of job benefits, from paid childcare leave and sabbaticals to flex-time and telecommuting.

Work part of the time at home. This delightful way to step back from your career can also be relatively painless, if your boss goes for it. If you're used to a high-pressure office environment, this option can seem almost like not working at all. You get up when you feel like it and wear what you want. When it's time to take a break, you can knead bread or watch the bird feeder instead of wandering aimlessly through beige corridors or gulping coffee.

Taking work home can actually increase the quality of your work. I find that going home to work is like escaping to a sanctuary. At the end of the day, when your housemates return, the house is clean, the work is done, supper's ready, and you're the hero.

Substitute community for cash. Most young and middle-aged Americans were raised in the suburbs and lived within the small confines of a nuclear family. When family labor couldn't provide something, the family paid cash for the extra product or service. Now, the combined efforts of economic stagnation and a pervasive desire to simplify could force a large and positive shift in values. It could teach highly individualistic people that collective behavior is often a cheaper, more satisfying way to solve a problem than cold cash.

Relying on your friends, and being there when they ask the same from you, is one of the most effective ways to reduce your dependence on paid products and services. This could mean forming a childcare cooperative instead of paying through the nose at a good day-care center, throwing potluck dinners instead of patronizing trendy restaurants, or putting up vegetables from a community garden instead of buying fresh produce flown in from South America.

Reprinted with permission of Brad Edmondson, who currently lives in Ithaca, NY. The article was originally published in *Utne Reader,* July/August 1991.

A master in the art of living
draws no shape distinction
between her work and play,
her labor and her leisure,
her mind and her body,
her education and her recreation.
She hardly knows which is which.
She simply pursues her vision
of excellence through whatever
she is doing and leaves
others to determine
whether she is working or playing.
To herself, she always seems
to be doing both.

Unknown

Mindfulness

By Glenda Montgomery

Though we live unconsciously, "on automatic pilot," every one of us can learn to be awake. It just takes practice.

—Jack Kornfield, from *Buddha's Little Instruction Book*

I ARRIVED ONE DAY at my daughter's school and as I threw the car into "park," I lurched into awareness, as if suddenly awaking from deep sleep. I was there, at the school, yet how did I get there? I had no memory of the drive. I couldn't remember a single sight from the route nor whether the lights had been green or red. I had arrived safely, and so I believe that I had driven safely, but my body had been on autopilot while my mind leaped and jumped from solving anticipated problems with the class I was going to teach the next day to rehashing a conversation I'd had with my husband in the morning to launching into planning my shopping list for next week's groceries. I'd been in "monkey mind" and it had been so compelling that I had literally no awareness of my life during the moments that I had been living it.

My cavorting thoughts had caused a minor roller-coaster of anxious emotion and completely robbed me of 20 minutes of my life. The fact is that the only moment we have control of is the moment we are living right now. Jon Kabbat-Zinn of the Stress Reduction Clinic at the University of Massachusetts and author of *Coming To Our Senses,* says that much of our stress and discontent is from being caught up in analyzing and reliving our past and worrying about our futures rather than being present and fully living our "now." He extols the value of "mindfulness meditation" which includes being in silence while focusing on breath or on physical senses while letting go of thought. Mindfulness meditation focuses on deeply experiencing the present moment in its stillness and emptiness.

Kabat-Zinn has led many research studies on the benefits of mindfulness meditation. He has found that it significantly lowers anxiety and negative emotions, reduces blood pressure and increases levels of antibodies, leaving people not only less stressed but healthier and happier. Well-known authors Wayne Dyer and Deepak Chopra, describe an experiment in the set of tapes called *Creating the World the Way You Really Want It To Be,* in which serotonin levels were measured in the brains of each of many meditators before a large group meditation session began. Serotonin is a neurotransmitter which induces feelings of calm. The higher the levels of serotonin in your brain, the greater sense of calm you experience. After the meditation session, the levels were measured again. Virtually every one of the meditators experienced a rise in their serotonin levels with a corresponding rise in their sense of peace. What is further fascinating is that people in the general vicinity of this large group meditation session ALSO experienced a rise in their serotonin levels. This supports what we already know intuitively: when we are with calm people, we too begin to feel calm.[1] Think of the positive influence your meditation practice could have not just to you but to the people around you!

Mindfulness meditation can take place anywhere. It is simple, yet its results can be profound. Some people merely focus on the in and out of their breath, saying, "In" and "Out." Others run through their senses: What am I seeing right now? What sensations am I feeling right now . . . in my toes, in my legs, in my belly, in my chest, in my shoulders, in my neck, in my face? What do I smell right now? What sounds can I hear right now? When we notice our thoughts push back, we gently let them go. We can simply say, "thoughts" and imagine them being blown by a light breeze as we resume our breath and our attention to the present moment.

You don't need a meditation cushion or quiet room or any equipment to practice; you don't even need to be sitting down. You can experience the beneficial results of mindfulness meditation just by giving your FULL attention to what you are doing at any given moment. You could wash the dishes as a practice of mindfulness, or practice while eating a meal or while taking a walk. It is a time to give your monkey mind a rest and to fully engage in the "Now." I have begun to practice mindfulness meditation as I drive. I turn the radio off, and try to be present. I focus on colors and sights and sounds. I check in with the sensations of my body and relax the tension I've accumulated by rushing through my day. I listen to my breath in and out, and any thoughts that want to crash in on my peace, I circle in an imaginary balloon, which I let float away. I find that I am calmer, more connected and I always know exactly how I got to where I am going.

Resources:
[1] *There is a Spiritual Solution to Every Problem* by Wayne Dyer, pg 99
The New Earth by Eckhart Tolle
Coming To Our Senses by Jon Kabbat-Zinn

Written for Family Empowerment Network by Glenda Montgomery, Certified Positive Disipline Instructor in Portland, Oregon at www.positiveparentingpdx.com. For reprint requests, contact www.family-empower.com.

Keeping Her Safe 8

Shelby Lindstedt, 8th Grader, Private School

Keeping Her Safe

"Setting an example is not the main means of influencing another, it is the only means." —Albert Einstein

"We all know that love leads to sex for girls, and sex leads to love for men."
—Conversation of two adolescent girls

"Children have never been very good at listening to their elders, but they have never failed to imitate them."
—James Baldwin

"That's how you grow up: experiences. The only way to get experiences is to take risks. When you're growing up you've got to find out. Well, I've heard all this stuff about sex and drugs and driving and you have to try out a little bit of everything and from that you build your own plan, your own lifestyle, and become the person you are when you become developed."
—17 yr-old answering, "What's appealing about taking risks?"
from *The Culture of Adolescent Risk-Taking*

"Where citizens are activated, where local coalitions are at work, where parents are making an issue of underage and heavy drinking, where there is pressure on local police—that is where we see changes that limit [adolescent binge drinking]."
—Alexander Wagenaar, from *Dying to Drink*

GOALS

- To help parents understand that a goal of adolescence is for teens to form their own identity and this often involves experimenting with boundaries and risk-taking behavior

- To encourage parents to know that they can be the first line of defense between their daughter and common health and safety risks

- To give parents tools to communicate better with their girls about high-risk behavior and to intervene earlier

- To help parents recognize signs that their daughter might be in trouble

- To help parents establish support structures which encourage healthy decision-making

3

OVERVIEW

Protecting our children from risky behaviors is one of the most important and distressing jobs of parenthood and one that can leave parents feeling afraid and powerless. The bad news is that sexual promiscuity, depression, suicide, violence, drugs and alcohol are serious problems confronting our nation's youth, regardless of how sheltered their environment. All of our kids will be exposed to or affected by these problems well before high school graduation. Most of our teens will experiment in some ways before they graduate from high school. The good news is that there is still a lot that parents can do to instill skills in their children that are essential for successfully surviving the adolescent years. These skills include the ability to:

- Learn from one's own life experiences,
- Look at issues from multiple perspectives,
- Develop effective decision-making skills.

Our daughters have tremendous ability to make good choices if they have practiced and have learned to live with the consequences of these choices. Parents can also be a great help to their teens by guiding them into "positive" risk-taking activities and by creating family and community support that provides a feeling of belonging and significance.

To some of you, this chapter on keeping your daughter safe may feel overwhelming; however, we believe that knowing what can happen in the world of today's youth can be used to empower you as a parent. Accurate information, combined with proactive support can move you from a feeling of powerlessness to a feeling of empowerment. You can make a difference in your daughter's ability to safely navigate the rough waters of adolescence. This chapter will give you both information about the dangers and difficulties inherent in the world of adolescence and specific, proven ways you can have a positive impact on the choices your daughter makes at this time in her life.

One critical task of adolescence is to move from making decisions based on resistance to outside authorities (parents, teachers, society, peers) to making reasoned choices that are based on values and needs. There is no more important time to use respectful, positive discipline parenting skills than when it comes to risk-taking behaviors. Parents will want to share information with their teenagers about sex, relationships, violence, drug use and chemical dependency and to empower their teens to deal effectively with these issues. What our kids do with that information will be their choice. We can improve the chance of healthy choices if we avoid creating a family atmosphere that invites rebellion, where risky behaviors become a power struggle in which everyone loses. Sometimes our kids might even agree with what we are demanding—for example, "You will not drink"—and yet their intense desire for choice and autonomy will lead to resistance. Since our teen's world is far beyond any parent's ability to control, parents will be better off focusing on positive interactions that will help their teens develop strong self-discipline and self-knowledge skills.

Creating a strong sense of love and connection to family and community has long been proven to greatly diminish problem behaviors in teenagers. One study of 12,000 youths, summarized in our first article **"Connecting Teens and Parents: The Vital Link"** (p. 8:18), found that good connection and communication with parents was the most highly protective factor against risky behaviors. This, of course, brings us back to the Developmental Assets. A child who has at least 30 of the 40 assets is much less likely to experience problem alcohol use, drug abuse, early sexual activity or violence, as shown graphically in **"The Power of Assets to Protect"** (p. 8:19). Another proactive tool that works is to network with other adults to create a "web" of support for each other and for your children. A *Raising Our Daughters* discussion group is a great place to start networking and connecting with other adults who care.

Risk-Taking and Adolescence

Discussing teens' safety issues can be very scary, especially for parents of younger children. All of us find it hard to believe OUR children will ever engage in risky behaviors. However, risk-taking is developmentally NORMAL during adolescence. Since all parents want to know what they can do now to support their children in making healthy choices later, we invite you to consider the two threads of thought in this chapter's articles. One thread addresses what parents can do now for prevention and the other thread helps identify and deal with problem behaviors once they develop. Those parents who want to know the details of risky behavior can read all the articles. Others, especially those with younger children, may find this overwhelming and will want to use them later as reference materials. We encourage all of you to participate in the group discussion of risk-taking behaviors, regardless of the amount of reading you have done before the meeting. Our goal is to get parents thinking about long-term parenting strategies that will lessen the chances that their teenagers will make risky choices that will have lifelong negative consequences. Being knowledgeable on these topics (as opposed to overreacting or jumping to conclusions) puts parents in the best possible position when their teens want to talk honestly about their lives or those of their friends.

Risk-taking in youth is normal, but the kinds of risks taken vary widely. For some teens, it might entail climbing a mountain or trying out for a school play, while for others, it entails smoking, drinking, or sexual activity. One thing to recognize is that many "risky behaviors" in youth can be considered "normal" adult behaviors. In their quest to become adults, some teenagers will take these "normal" behaviors too far, as in binge drinking, promiscuity, sniffing glue or using "club drugs" such as ecstacy at a rave (all night concert). Many would say that there is **no** behavior that teens do that is not modeled for them somewhere in the adult world. This creates a conundrum for parents: how are we to forbid our youth those activities that our teens see as the hallmarks of adulthood to which they aspire? Perhaps the strongest antidote to this double bind is keeping a strong line of communication, love and acceptance (with age-appropriate limits) flowing between ourselves and our teens, even if we don't always approve of their behaviors. If parents don't go out of their way to share unconditional love with their teens, it is likely that our kids will look for love and acceptance elsewhere, most likely with their peers. Parents who want to have as much influence on their teenagers as their peer culture will need to show their

teens, through actions and words, that they are loved and respected, even if they choose differently than their parents would like.

We now know from brain imaging studies that our teens' brains are a work in progress. With puberty (11 to 14 years of age), the emotional part of the brain (the amygdala) gets charged up to seek rewards and stimulation. The pre-frontal cortex of the frontal lobes, which helps us with reasoning, problem-solving, considering long-term consequences, and inhibiting impulsivity, is not fully mature until 18 to 25 years of age (earlier in females than males). Most young adults continue to have cortex maturation until their late 20's. You can see that the teen brain is like a "fast car with no brakes." This means that we adults have even more proof that our teens need us. Our respectful dialog, negotiation and limit-setting, and gradual expansion of boundaries help them to learn how to put on the brakes and be more discerning. As parents we can facilitate and encourage healthy risk-taking for our teens, such as sports which push their personal limits, sharing one's poetry, handling sexual situations responsibly and safely, and speaking one's mind. These points are highlighted in the article: **"Teens and Risks"** (p. 8:20).

This chapter discusses common safety issues for today's adolescents, including body image, healthy relationships and sexuality, violence, depression, suicide, substance abuse, and motor vehicle safety. Our hope is that you can educate yourself on these issues in time to introduce preventive parenting actions—or at least to intervene with your child as early as possible—before problem behaviors turn into persistent, negative habits. We owe it to our kids to understand the myriad dangers they will face in everyday life so that we can prepare them to face these head-on and with strength of character.

If at any point you are feeling nervous or overwhelmed by what you are reading and wish you could just skip this part of parenting, join the club; you are welcome to skip over any topic for now or to go straight to the articles that share information in a gentler style with solutions on every page. Then you can come back to this Overview or to the Circle Question from a place of empowerment rather than fear.

Body Image

With hundreds of images of abnormally thin, scantily-clad women flashing past us every day in magazines, movies, billboards and TV sitcoms, it is difficult for our daughters to feel good about themselves. More than 98% of women and girls will compare poorly with the feminine "ideal," as the average model at 5'8" weighs only 110 pounds. Additionally, girls learn early that they are often valued more for their looks than for their brains or abilities in our fast-paced culture. As a result, our daughter may take unnatural measures to look the way she thinks she should, which may involve some rather bizarre looking getups. It is helpful to recall that few of your own peers dress now like they did as adolescents and that fashion is a relatively benign form of rebellion and individuation. Within limits, it's usually best to let kids have control over this arena.

Diets and eating disorders are rampant amongst our girls. As parents, we need to be knowledgeable about the stages of eating disorders and provide a counterpoint to the negative media messages, while teaching a healthy joyful relationship to food and its preparation for our daughter and her friends. If your daughter is showing signs of anorexia or bulemia you will need to get professional help and make sure she is not spending time on Internet sites (Pro-Ana sites) which promote eating disorders. The following articles highlight these issues: **"Her First Diet"** and **"Body Image and Eating Disorders"** (pp. 8:22-8:23). As a parent, one of the best gifts you can give your daughter is to value her opinions and actions and to model for her in all your relationships that it is truly what is on the inside that counts. Your daughter's looks and weight are really her own issues: criticism or compliments on these issues by parents are best avoided. It is healthier to compliment the functionality of your daughter's body, and to encourage her to use it in active pursuits. Mothers can help their daughters by modeling healthy relationships with their own bodies. Dieting rarely works—97% of all diets fail—it is better to eat moderately several times a day with a wise balance between good quality foods and junk foods and practice healthy exercise habits. Help your daughter understand how empty calories like soda pop (and alcohol) either put on excess weight or

substitute for calories that her body needs from healthy foods (diet pop has its own drawbacks). Teach her about the importance of breakfast for an alert morning and to one's metabolism. Be sure to listen to yourself; be careful not to put yourself or others down due to looks or weight. Families who eat dinner together create an atmosphere of healthy eating and connection that has been proven to be protective against risk-taking behaviors during adolescence. Furthermore, girls who learn healthy eating habits at home are less likely to develop serious eating disorders when they go off to college and no one is watching over them.

Sexual Activity/Healthy Relationships

Dealing with our kids' sexuality is probably one of the most difficult jobs for parents. After all, we want our teens to have sex … not today, but someday. This is different than many of the other behaviors in this chapter, which we would like our kids to avoid altogether. It is an extremely tricky task to help our daughters develop a healthy sexual identity and a sense of healthy sexual behavior, while at the same time postponing sexual intercourse until they are "old enough" to be mature and responsible about it. This job is easier if parents acknowledge that their teenagers are sexual beings: our kids will have sex someday whether we want them to or not, and our job as parents is to prepare them as best we can for that day. This includes giving them information on the advantages of postponing that day.

One thing is clear. Our children will get the best information from us, rather than their peers. They want accurate information, even if it makes both of you uncomfortable. Accurate sexual information has been shown in multitudes of studies to be an effective tool of prevention. In the US, sex education and easy access to condoms and contraceptives have repeatedly been shown to actually delay the onset of sexual activity by an average of one to two years. European youth, exposed to bare-breasted women on the beach, good sex education in their schools and easy access to contraceptives, delay sexual intercourse about 1½ years beyond their American counterparts.

There is NO EVIDENCE that education about sexuality makes a teen more likely to have sex. Our Puritan roots have allowed this rumor to flourish and deprived our nation's children of reliable, life-saving information about responsible and safe sexual behaviors. There is nothing wrong with a family value of "waiting until marriage" as long as the parents also recognize this is not a fail-proof plan. Many youth, saturated in abstinence education, are simply not prepared to use condoms and contraceptives when the "moment" suddenly arrives. This story tells it all:

> When European boys are asked if they carry condoms, they say, "Of course I do. I love and respect my girlfriend and want to be prepared if something should happen." When American boys are asked that question, they say, "Of course I don't. I love and respect my girlfriend too much to expect that it will happen."

But it does happen. Remember that European youth delay sexual intercourse 1½ years beyond their American counterparts and have much lower rates of sexually transmitted diseases and pregnancy. Teenagers are sexual beings. Parents cannot prevent the onset of sexuality in their teens, but they can promote safe and responsible sexual behaviors (something that's modeled poorly for our teens by adults and the media, unfortunately). Talking about sexuality does help, and teens need to know that there are a whole range of sexual behaviors they can engage in safely other than intercourse. It is very important to ensure that our teenagers have open access to medical care for their contraceptive and sexual health needs. Your teen daughter will also want to know where to take her friends if they need birth control or the "morning after" pill. Some families may decide to keep a supply of condoms available in their homes and allow teenagers open access to them. It may be difficult for parents to accept that their children will make their own decisions about when to become sexually active. This can be easier to live with, however, if parents know they have done a good job of educating their kids about the responsibilities that must accompany this decision and about the value of "waiting."

Our culture's puritanical denial of teenagers' sexuality has had an unfortunate outcome: it has led to an epidemic of adolescent ignorance, "pregnancy by accident" and sexually transmitted diseases. Some kids think that if they have oral sex, they are not really "sexually active" and hence are not at risk for sexually transmitted diseases. They are. Other kids don't realize that it is possible to get pregnant on your very first encounter or while engaging in sexual activities other than vaginal intercourse. This lack of awareness of responsible and safe sex practices has led to a relatively new trend among some teens of "buddy sex," where friends trade sexual favors with no strings attached. Parents can provide information and a counterpoint to this casual attitude toward sexuality, as well as listening to the stresses of modern teen life. The articles, **"Can You Talk [With Her] About Her Body?," "Sexual Myths,"** and **"Communication Tips for Parents"** (pp. 8:24-8:28) offer ways to start talking with your daughter about her body and sexuality. A good place to start is to share information with your daughter about normal pubertal development. The easiest time to talk about sexuality is when situations arise that naturally lead to discussions, i.e., teachable moments. Starting these talks early in life and continuing them through puberty will desensitize the topic of sexuality in your household and will make it easier for your daughter to ask you for information or advice. Most teens want their parents to be honest and to share their knowledge and feelings about sexuality with them, but they are unlikely to start these conversations themselves. Parents who can manage to overcome their own difficulties talking about sexuality with their children, and who do so in a matter-of-fact way, can greatly benefit their children's health and sexuality. Teens need support and acceptance dealing with the struggles of growing up in a sexualized culture, as noted in **"Talking Back: Ten Things Teens Want their Parents to Know About Teen Pregnancy"** (p. 8:31). Also, teens who have developed a level of comfort talking about sexual issues within their own homes are much more likely to be able to talk to their potential sexual partners about these issues and much less likely to engage in casual and unsafe sex.

Healthy Relationships

Parents play a significant role in helping their daughters learn to create responsible, healthy and safe relationships with others. Our girls need to learn to speak up for themselves when it comes to sexual activity. They need to know that there are one hundred sweet steps between someone liking you and having sex (in spite of what they see in the movies). They have years to walk along that path and, in the meantime, they can speak up about what they like and don't like. Our daughters need to be able to identify sexual harassment: someone is trying (often repeatedly) to get power over you by saying or doing something sexual that feels uncomfortable. Teach your daughter the "Three No Rule": if someone asks her to go out three times and she says, "No," the other person needs to drop it or it becomes harassment. They need to learn to speak up clearly if they are being harassed since ignoring sexual harassment only makes it grow. A respectful person will stop when they hear that you don't like what they are doing, so if the harassment doesn't stop, a girl needs to get help. As bystanders, girls can also help stop sexual harassment by speaking up when they see it happening to others. Girls need to know that sexual harassment is now against the law and have some information about how people have handled different situations. Look for the teachable moments.

As parents, it is also our responsibility to intervene in a teenage relationship if we suspect abusive behavior, even if our daughter resents it. Some girls who believe it is their duty to have sex or that aggression is an acceptable means for men to satisfy their sexual needs are simply modeling behavior they see at home or in the media. It is important to talk with our daughters about healthy relationships and the respectful treatment of women. More importantly, it is essential for parents to model healthy relationships in their own lives and to raise their daughters with love and respect, without the threat of violence, ridicule or shame. As mothers, we have to demand respect from all the men in our lives, especially our children's father, if we want to see our girls expect respect from the men in their lives. Sharing with your daughter the information in the articles **"Recipe for a Healthy Relationship," "Dater's Bill of Rights,"** and **"Abuse in Teen Dating Relationships"**

(pp. 8:32-8:34) will help both of you to evaluate your significant relationships for signs of healthy respect. Healthy relationships exhibit the following qualities: self-esteem of both members, mutual respect, trust, open communication, nonviolence, personal responsibility, mutual interests/friends, shared decision-making, non-controlling behavior, non-abuse of drugs, and responsiveness to the other person saying "No."

Violence

Girls now live in a country where around 40% of homes have guns (US Department of Justice at www.ncjrs.gov/pdfiles/165476.pdf), where popular culture glorifies violence and where the suicide and homicide rates in youth are quite high. All of our children need to know the rules around firearms regardless of whether there are any in your family. If they see a firearm that is not in a locked case, or their friend wants them to look at a gun, they need to leave the area immediately and tell you. Let them know that each year some kids die because of curiosity about firearms or because someone thought the gun "wasn't loaded."

Prevention of violence is a prime concern for today's parents. In a study by the Family and Work Institute entitled "Youth and Violence: Students Speak Out for a More Civil Society," 1000 youth were asked how to stop violence in America (a complete report can be found at www.coloradotrust.org). These kids suggested stopping emotional abuse (such as gossip and put-downs), embracing diversity (so kids value differences rather than "sameness"), and getting support from important people in a youth's life. Modeling healthy relationships in your daughter's life, establishing deep connections with her, and teaching anger control and peaceful conflict resolution are important ways to diminish the toll of violence in her life.

Community efforts at violence prevention can be very effective. Schools often have an anti-violence program that parents can actively support. The National Center for Injury Prevention and Control's book, *Best Practices of Youth Violence Prevention, A Sourcebook for Community Action* at www.cdc.gov/ncipc/dvp/bestpractices.htm, contains many ideas for community-wide prevention strategies. One activity that PTA's and community groups concerned about youth violence can support is the initiation of media literacy education for kids, since violence is often glorified or romanticized in the news and entertainment media.

Personal safety is especially important for our daughters since they can be the targets of aggression. We want our daughters to feel empowered (not scared) and embrace practical guidelines that keep them safe. Our teen daughters can move safely around most of our communities during the day and can remain safe in the evenings as long as they travel in groups. Self-defense classes are wonderful ways to empower our daughters; check to make sure that the content is age-appropriate. You may want to take a mother-daughter class. Teen girls need to know that alcohol can put them or their friends at risk for acquaintance rape. Explain that even a little alcohol can cause the lowering of inhibitions (that normally guide what is okay for us) as well as our ability to speak up for ourselves effectively. This, combined with the fact that alcohol can cause aggressive behavior in some boys and men, puts a girl who isn't sober at great risk. As girls and guys become old enough to attend parties in the community, they need to make a commitment to look out for each other and make sure they are all safe, i.e., always go with a trusted buddy or group. Let your daughters know that having sex due to the influence of alcohol could be a very unsafe (pregnancy and STDs), abusive, and demoralizing way to experience sex. Therefore, they have to be savvy in high school and college to avoid circumstances and situations where this could happen (e.g., parties with much older teens, parties with drinking contests, or fraternity parties). Finally, girls need to know that rape is never the girl's fault and it is important to report the rape and get medical and social support. These topics are often too scary for younger girls, but as your daughter gains more freedom to make her own choices about where and how she is going to socialize, she needs to be realistic.

Depression and Suicide

Suicide is the 3rd leading cause of death for children ages 15-24. Sixty percent of these deaths were from firearms. For every completed suicide, there are 48 attempts. Girls attempt suicide more frequently but are less successful since boys use more lethal means. When children are highly depressed or suicidal, all guns should be removed from the home and prescription drugs and knives should be secured. Over the past 25 years, there has been a five-fold increase in the youth suicide rate, and most of these youth were clinically depressed. The key to reducing suicide is to better recognize the symptoms of depression in our youth. Depression can manifest in a variety of behaviors in our children and can include feeling sad, failing at school, engaging in violent outbursts and using drugs. Girls who are depressed are particularly inclined toward self-harm, such as cutting marks on their wrists or other parts of their body, so keep your eyes open. Girls report that "cutting" helps reduce their stress; this shows just how habit-forming this behavior can become and how much help girls need in handling their feelings in healthy ways. Girls who are cutting need to be connected with mental health professionals.

"**Depression in Girls**" (p. 8:35) will help you differentiate between normal teenage moodiness and clinical depression, as well as when to get help from a mental health professional. It should be noted that lesbian and gay youth have a higher risk of depression and suicide than other kids. Helping our teens to get constructively involved in community activities and community service, giving our kids opportunities to connect with nature, and working on a warm, open parent-teen relationship are all protective factors for our daughters. Adolescence is a stressful time and too much lonely brooding in one's room (nowadays often accompanied by online and other screen activities) is not healthy for teens. We need to teach our teens how to reduce stress in healthy ways.

Substance Abuse

Although many of our adolescents are doing well and making choices that protect themselves from harm, a significant proportion of teens put their health at risk in a variety of ways. Alcohol use among teens and young adults is of particular concern, especially since binge drinking (5 or more drinks on the same occasion) has become the norm for many of our youth, girls and boys alike. We now know from brain imaging studies that large amounts of alcohol (like other drugs) can cause long-term damage to the developing brain. And research shows that young teen brains (15 and younger) are particularly susceptible to alcohol addiction. Even moderate use by teens impairs learning and memory to a much greater extent than it would for an adult user. What is a parent to do? After all, some of us tried drugs ourselves as adolescents and most of us drink some alcohol as adults, and now we don't know how to deal with our own children who are using drugs and alcohol! Take heart, you are not alone! Our kids live in a pleasure-seeking and drug-using culture, and their choice to "use" is influenced by many factors outside the family and cannot be blamed upon parents. However, parents who want to deal constructively with their child's relationship to drugs and alcohol can help their kids in the following ways:

- Talk openly about drug dependency in the family.
- Model a healthy legal relationship to alcohol and drugs.
- Inform yourselves about common drugs and the continuum of use from abstinence to chemical dependency (see www.theantidrug.com).
- Share your own values with your children.
- Set clear rules and expectations and age-approp-riate consequences.
- Teach assertiveness, delay of gratification and long-term planning/goal setting skills.
- Foster emotional honesty with your kids.

Be prepared for those difficult questions your children will ask you about your own behavior. It is okay to avoid detailed answers, but it is important not to lie since you are trying to teach honesty. (You can plead the "5th Amendment"; however, that may be interpreted as a "Yes.") **"The Power of Parents"** (p. 8:37) reminds us of the important influence parents can have in raising children who are wise about alcohol.

There *are* known risk factors for problem substance abuse. One of the biggest risk factors is starting use in the early teen years. The Surgeon General's "Call to Action: To Prevent and Reduce Underage Drinking (2007)" reports that around 40% of adults who started drinking before age 15 say they have the signs of alcohol dependence. That rate is 4 times higher than adults who didn't drink until they

were 21. Other serious risk factors include: a family history of substance abuse, the modeling of excessive alcohol use at home by parents or older siblings, busy parents who don't take the time to supervise or connect with their daughters, affluence (resulting in too much money and free time), and access to alcohol. During our children's adolescence, we need to lock up, or better yet, remove alcohol from our home as well as prescription drugs such as pain-killers. The distorted view that prescription drugs are safer than street drugs has contributed to a rash of serious drug abuse, over-dose, and death using drugs from medicine cabinets.

It is important to realize that many teens will experiment with alcohol and/or marijuana, and some will go toward chemical dependency. The more that our child hangs out with a "cool" crowd, the earlier experimentation may happen. Since we know that early use is a risk factor, it often pays for parents to assertively intervene when drug or alcohol use becomes apparent in our younger teens. One family discovered that their 8th-grade twins were beginning to smoke marijuana. They explained why that was against their family standards and how it might affect their ability to succeed at school, and that they would be taking the twins to have monthly urine analysis tests until they were 15. If they had a positive test (marijuana can be detected up to one month after use), they could not get their driver's permit when they turned 15. This assertive, clear approach was very successful with their children and the experimentation stopped. The parents also voluntarily shared this information in an 8th-grade parent meeting, which was very useful for other parents.

Nicotine, in all forms is another illegal drug of choice for our teens. If we can persuade our teens not to use nicotine until age 18 when it is legal, it is very unlikely they will be interested. Fortunately, cigarette use has been decreasing in the last few years, but nicotine comes in many forms. Since nicotine is very addictive, it is easy for our teens to become addicted if they begin smoking or chewing. What begins as an attempt to feel cool or part of the crowd easily turns into a form of self-medicating for anxiety or stress or a way to control eating. If our children become addicted they may need medical assistance to stop, as well as help handling stress and anxiety in healthier ways.

As our teens grow older than 15 or 16, our "control" over them gradually lessens and we will be more effective if we focus on what we can influence, such as the quality of our home/community environment and our relationship, so they can still receive our guidance and coaching. For older teens who are experimenting (and most teens will at some point), one effective long-term parenting goal is to help your teen honestly assess her level of drug use, so that she can avoid progressing to more serious levels of use. Above all, it is important to keep communicating with her and knowing what she is doing rather than setting down inflexible rules that will push drug use underground and out of the sphere of our influence. Parents can give their teens a safe place to learn from their mistakes and be careful not to buffer their kids from the negative consequences of their drug-using behaviors. They can continue to show their kids unconditional love and acceptance and have faith in their kids. This can be very hard for parents who were raised with rigid rules and who feel a lot of external pressure from others to exert the short-term parenting strategy of control. However, honesty is a much more effective, respectful and safe long-term approach. Kids who are exploring alcohol use in high school have the benefit of their parent's watchful eye and intervention. With this influence, the teens can learn about setting limits, using discretion and why this is important. This skill will help them for the rest of their lives, especially when they go off to college where binge drinking is rampant. Using drugs or alcohol can be an especially dangerous problem for college kids who have never discussed these issues with an adult and who do not have adequate knowledge or self-discipline to monitor their own use of chemical agents. This difficult parenting subject is covered in **"Teenagers and Drugs"** (p. 8:38).

Another area that needs to be addressed is our society's lackadaisical attitude about underage drinking. With alcohol dependency affecting at least 10% of our adults, this should come as no surprise. However, communities of people can come together to prevent underage drinking, and all of our teenagers greatly benefit. One Mom we know routinely called every party her teen was invited to and just asked, "Hey, I was wondering if you needed any help with the party at your house next week? Can I help chaperone? Can I bake anything?" This was her way of making sure the parents knew there was a party at the house and that they would be there. Her teen, now in college, survived this ordeal and is happy Mom helped with difficult situations. Some high schools provide guidelines for parents on how to increase the likelihood that their child will stay alcohol- and drug-free, such as **"Safe Teen Parties in Your Home Guidelines"** which describes how to hold a "substance-free" party. High schools can also offer drug-free activities or parties for special events often associated with drinking, such as graduation. Parents working together can exert tremendous preventive pressure toward keeping youth activities drug- and alcohol-free.

Many of our healthy teens surround themselves with peers they can trust and look out for each other as they navigate through their adolescent world. These teens have often made advance agreements before they arrive at a party. They know that teens are vulnerable to acquaintance rape, fighting, and alcohol poisoning, and they are careful to look out for their friends to make sure that everyone is safe. They may have decided not to drink. They will have a designated driver if they need one. They will leave as a group if a get-together becomes uncomfortable.

If you find your daughter is experimenting with alcohol or marijuana, there are several steps, in addition to staying connected with her, that you can take to support minimum consumption:

1. Reduce access by removing all alcohol from your home and talking to her friend's parents about doing the same. Kids can often gain access easily to "locked" cabinets.
2. Do not leave your home unsupervised overnight.
3. Do not enable underage drinking. Be crystal clear with your daughter that you will not allow an underage youth to drink in your home. Serving alcohol to an underage youth is an incredible risk to the youth's and to your own emotional health. It may also harm your financial health since it is against the law. You can be sued even if nothing significantly negative happens to the youth you are serving alcohol to. (Some families choose to serve small amounts of alcohol to their teens as part of special family occasions or rituals to help them form healthy associations with alcohol. This differs significantly from including teens in adult social drinking.)

4. Let her know there will be consequences to drinking. If she gets in trouble with the authorities or drinks and drives, she will lose access to a car.
5. Connect with the parents of your daughter's friends to create a safety net for them. Consider meeting monthly over dinner.

One of our long-term goals for our teens is to increase the chances they are safe and grow up free from addiction. Some of our teens, however, will abuse alcohol and/or drugs to the point of addiction. Teens who are abusing and addicted to drugs/alcohol will rarely have the insights and coping skills of normal teenagers. As their parent, you are going to need outside help from community resources if you suspect your child has problem substance-abuse behaviors. If you are concerned about your daughter's drug or alcohol use, ask her to honestly answer to herself the questions on addiction on the last page of the article **"Teenagers and Drugs"** (p. 8:42).

Automobile Injuries and Graduated Licensing

The leading cause of death for children in the US, ages 1 to 24, is motor vehicle crashes.[2] Teenagers are known to take risks with cars. They like speed, feel invincible and are aggressive drivers. They are also inexperienced, immature, over-confident, and are less able to perceive hazards. 10,000 American sixteen-year-olds die every decade from driving under the influence of immaturity and inexperience. These accidents are characterized by the following:

- When a teenage passenger dies, 1 out of 4 times, the driver is a teenager.
- The vast majority of crashes with teens have no alcohol or bad weather involved.
- Speed, immaturity, inexperience, peer pressure from other passengers and night driving are the biggest contributors to teenage car crashes.
- 16-year-olds have the most crashes, and 16- to 19-year-olds have more crashes than the elderly.
- Fatigue is a major contributor to car crashes.
- When teenagers die in car crashes, they are usually not wearing seatbelts.

The highest risk for young drivers is driving at night with other teens in the car. This sets the stage for peer pressure leading to immature and dangerous behaviors. A car is a 3000-pound weapon, and it is important for your teen to understand that driving is a privilege that will be revoked for irresponsible behavior. Also, to counteract the modeling of unsafe driving habits that are common on prime-time television, it is important for parents to model consistent use of seat belts and to exhibit law-abiding and respectful road behaviors.

Since we are unlikely to raise the driving age to 18, as in European countries, "graduated" licensing is the next best approach. Research has shown that graduated licensing successfully reduces adolescent death and injury. Within two years of implementing these laws, deaths of new drivers went down an impressive 33% in Oregon, as noted in **"Facts about Risky Driving and Graduated Licensing"** (p. 8:45).

Teenagers can also be protected against fatal mistakes by having them sign the "no questions asked" **"Contract for Life"** (p. 8:46) sponsored by SADD (Students Against Destructive Decisions). Parents realistically can't stop their children from using drugs or alcohol, but they can make sure that they don't put themselves or others in danger by driving or riding in a car under the influence. This is a healthy investment in your daughter's survival.

Conclusion

There are certain adolescent developmental tasks which parents cannot derail. These include:
- Individuating and outgrowing childhood dependence on parents,
- Forming an identity in sexual, intellectual and moral realms of self-concept,
- Developing a separate identity that includes personal lifestyle preferences, and vocational/career goals,
- Exploring risk-taking behaviors as a means of self-exploration and confidence-building.

We can help our daughters to navigate safely through these developmental tasks by staying closely connected with them and talking with them about high-risk behaviors and today's tough issues. This may mean getting help for our girls who are aggressive, depressed, rageful or suicidal. Parents can also work to build connections and assets for their daughters within their own communities. Finally, there is one powerful tool for successful parenting. This is an often untapped resource and an idea that Family Empowerment Network advocates for wherever we go: NETWORK WITH OTHER PARENTS. You can bet that your daughter is very networked with her friends, especially if she is trying to get away with something. Talk to other parents. Confirm the plans you hear from your daughter. Check out the curfews and driving records of your daughter's friends by asking their parents. When a problem does come up, you will then have the support of invested parents to help you through it. This is especially nice to do before girls get their driver's license, which gives them incredible freedom and a strong desire to explore boundaries.

Clearly, keeping kids physically, emotionally and socially healthy is a job of great magnitude for parents in the twenty-first century. But there is hope. Skills that will help you through this difficult job include awareness, education, diligence, setting clear boundaries big enough for lots of choices, good listening, and continuous communication with your daughter. You will be surprised how quickly adolescence passes once you are finally through it. Then, you will know the joy of appreciating the adult your daughter's adolescence shaped, honed and produced.

---

[1] Mueller TE, Gavin LE, Kulkarni A. *The association between sex education and youth's engagement in sexual intercourse, age at first intercourse, and birth control use at first sex.* J. Adol. Health. 2008 Jan; 42 (1): pages 89-96.

[2] National SAFE KIDS Campaign dedicated to prevent unintentional childhood injury. www.usa.safekids.org

---

THE 40 DEVELOPMENTAL ASSETS Essential to Every Young Person's Success

There are many Developmental Assets that help a teen to be safe in her environment and resist negative influences. Notice how much the categories of Boundaries, Social Competencies and Positive Identity stand out here.

SUPPORT/ EMPOWERMENT

- **Asset #3 Other Adult Relationships:** Young people have at least 3 adults in their lives who support them.
- **Asset #4 Caring Neighborhood:** Young people have the care and support of people who live nearby.
- **Asset #7 Community Values Youth:** Young people know they are valued by the adults in their community.

BOUNDARIES

- **Asset #10 Safety:** Young person feels safe at home, school and in the neighborhood.
- **Asset #11 Family Boundaries:** Family has clear rules and monitors the young person's whereabouts.
- **Asset #12 School Boundaries:** School provides clear rules and consequences.
- **Asset #13 Neighborhood Boundaries:** Neighbors share the responsibility for monitoring youth's behavior.
- **Asset #14 Adult Role Models:** Parents and other adults set good examples for young people.

CONSTRUCTIVE USE OF TIME

- **Asset #17 Creative Activities:** Young people are involved in music, theater or other arts 3 hrs/week.
- **Asset #18 Youth Programs:** Young people are involved in sports, clubs or organizations 3 hrs/week.

POSITIVE VALUES

- **Asset #31 Restraint:** Youth believes it is important not to be sexually active or to use alcohol or drugs.

SOCIAL COMPETENCIES

- **Asset #33 Interpersonal Competence:** Young person has empathy, sensitivity, and friendship skills.
- **Asset #34 Cultural Competence:** Young people know and respect people of different racial and cultural backgrounds.
- **Asset #35 Resistance Skills:** Young person can resist negative peer pressure and dangerous situations.
- **Asset #36 Peaceful Conflict Resolution:** Young person seeks to resolve conflict nonviolently.

POSITIVE IDENTITY

- **Asset #37 Personal Power:** Young people believe that they have control over "things that happen to me."
- **Asset #38 Self-Esteem:** Young people feel good about who they are.
- **Asset #39 Sense of Purpose:** Young people believe their life has a purpose.
- **Asset #40 Positive View of Personal Future:** Young people are hopeful and confident about their future.

CIRCLE QUESTION

Which safety issue is of greatest concern to you? Share the ways or situations
in which you talk to your daughter about these sensitive topics.

DISCUSSION QUESTIONS

1. Share what you did as a youth that was "risk-taking." How does that impact your parenting?

2. What changes in children's behavior might be a clue that they have become involved in something unhealthy or that something is disturbing them? How do you separate "moody" from the signs of serious problems such as eating disorders, depression, and drug or alcohol abuse?

3. What behaviors do you engage in that you want your child to avoid, such as anger outbursts, impulsivity, smoking, excessive drinking, or dieting? In what ways can you modify what you do in order to provide more positive modeling for your child?

4. How have you connected with neighbors? Share how you might form an agreement with them about letting you know if they see suspicious or problem behaviors with your child.

5. How have you facilitated relationships with teachers and other adults in your daughter's life so that they could more easily let you know if there were any problems?

6. When we see our child's friend engage in risky behavior, is our first reaction to "keep her away"? What are ways we could intervene that might be more successful?

7. What do you think about "nothing good happens between midnight and 5 am"? Do you employ curfews? If yes, what time on weeknights? Weekends?

Body Image

8. What are some things we as parents can do to decrease our society's obsession with how we look?

9. What changes can you make in your eating habits and feelings about your own body to help your daughter grow up free from eating disorders?

10. How might you help your child feel comfortable about her appearance, even if it doesn't conform to popular standards?

Sexuality

11. What surprised you the most about the information on sexuality and youth?

12. Have you talked to your daughter about the pros of abstinence, the benefits of delaying her first sexual experience, as well as where to go to get contraceptives if she needs them? If yes, share how you had this conversation, and if no, what are the barriers to having this conversation? Strategize overcoming these.

Violence

13. Does your daughter struggle with impulsivity and anger? Do you? What helps with this?

14. What does your daughter need to know to prevent acquaintance rape and sexual harassment?

15. What steps would you take if you think your daughter is being harassed?

16. Talk about violence concerns in your neighborhood, community or school. What could you do to help decrease some of these problems?

17. Discuss a planned reaction with your daughter if a friend pulled out a gun to "show-off."

18. How can you distinguish moodiness from depression?

Drugs

19. "Just Say No" and similar campaigns alone are not effective in keeping kids from trying sex, alcohol, cigarettes and drugs. What does work?

20. Imagine your daughter had a party while you were out of town. Role-play with each other how you would talk with her about this, keeping your anger at bay and maintaining respect and openness.

21. What would you do if you suspected your child was taking drugs or drinking alcohol? Talk about the different reactions you might have to experimental use, social use, regular use or addiction.

PUTTING IT INTO PRACTICE

- TALK to your kids about tough issues. Start early before anyone else gives them incorrect information or explanations that lack the values you want to instill.
- Create an open environment for communication in which your children can ask any questions and share honestly—on any subject—and freely and without fear of consequence/embarrassment/ridicule.
- Use teachable moments that arise in everyday life as occasions for discussion.
- Try to be honest when you answer her questions; it will strengthen her ability to trust.
- Be patient. Let her know that she is worthy of your time.
- Communicate your values—frequently, not just once.
- Really listen → Effectiveness as a parent is more from what you hear than what you say.
- Spend time with your child.
- Network with other adults—other parents, your neighbors, relatives and friends—so she feels like there is a "conspiracy to help her turn out OK."
- Establish clear boundaries but be open and flexible so everything doesn't become a hiding game.
- If you are afraid of your daughter, seek help immediately.
- Avoid commenting on anyone's appearance/weight in front of your child, including her own.
- Practice healthy habits as a family.
- Review the "Dater's Bill of Rights" with your child, help make sure she knows what a safe, respectful relationship is all about.
- Find out what sex education your children are receiving in school. Use it as a discussion starter.
- If you have a depressed teen, get professional help, alert the school, and secure meds and weapons in your home. Check out www.helpguide.org/mental/depression_teen.htm to help you assess depression.
- Role-play refusal skills or assertiveness skills with your child that she can use when being pressured to engage in unhealthy behavior.
- Take a self-defense class with your daughter to reinforce these assertiveness skills.
- Children "do what you do." Model good behavior regarding substance abuse (cigarettes, alcohol, or drugs) and violence (temper outburst, verbal or physical abuse). Don't drink, drive, or model "road rage."
- Remove risk factors from your home: TV and computer in the child's bedroom, guns, prescription drugs, and alcohol.
- Sign the drinking and driving "Contract for Life" with your teenager.

PUTTING IT TOGETHER—YOUR VERSION

Write down three or four ideas you have been inspired to implement in your own life after reading and discussing this chapter.

1. _____

2. _____

3. _____

4. _____

FURTHER READING

Books for Youth

Fighting Invisible Tigers: A Stress Management Guide for Teens by Earl Hipp

What's Bad about Being So Good: Perfectionism by Jan Goldberg and Caroline Price

What Are My Rights?: 95 Questions and Answers about Teens and the Law by Thomas Jacobs

Depression Is the Pits, But I'm Getting Better: A Guide for Adolescents by E. Jane Garland, MD

Help Me, I'm Sad by David Fassler, MD and Lynne Dumas

When Nothing Matters Anymore: A Survival Guide For Teens by Bev Cobain, RNC

Highs! Over 150 Ways to Feel Really, Really Good...Without Alcohol or other Drugs by Alex Packer

Understanding the Human Volcano: What Teens Can Do About Violence by Earl Hipp

The Care and Keeping of You: The Body Book for Girls by American Girl

The Right Moves: A Girl's Guide to Getting Fit and Feeling Good by Tina Schwager and Michelle Schuerger

Risky Behavior

Positive Discipline for Teenagers by Jane Nelsen, EdD, and Lynn Lott, MA, MFT, see chapters: "Are Your Own Unresolved Teen Issues Getting in Your Way?" and "What To Do When Your Teen's Behavior Scares You"

The Romance of Risk: Why Teenagers Do the Things They Do by Lynn Ponton, MD

Talking With Kids about Tough Issues: A National Campaign to Support Parents at www.talkingwithkids.org

Can We Talk? Family Activity Book and video series, great training package for families by the National Education Association Health Information Network at www.neahin.org/canwetalk/index.html

Body Image and Eating Disorders

Body Language: New Moon Talks About Growing Up by New Moon Publishers

Nourishing Your Daughter: Help Your Child Develop a Healthy Relationship with Food and her Body by Carol Beck

Food Fight: A Guide to Eating Disorders for Preteens and Their Parents by Janet Bode

The Secret Language of Eating Disorders by Peggy Claude-Pierre, Founder of the Montreux Clinic

The Beauty Myth: How Images of Beauty Are Used Against Women by Naomi Wolf and William Morrow

Eating Disorder Awareness Prevention at www.edap.org/facts.html or www.nationaleatingdisorders.org.

Sexuality

Promiscuity: The Secret Struggle for Womanhood by Naomi Wolf

The Sex Lives of Teenagers: Revealing the Secret World of Adolescent Boys and Girls by Lynn E Ponton, MD

All About Sex: a Family Resource on Sex and Sexuality by Planned Parenthood

The National Campaign to Prevent Teen and Unplanned Pregnancy at www.teenpregnancy.org

Violence

Dating Violence: Young Women in Danger by Barrie Ley

But I Love Him: Protecting Your Daughter from Controlling, Abusive Dating Relationships by Jill Murray

Sexual Harassment and Teens: A Program for Positive Change by Susan Strauss and Pamela Espeland

Safe at Last: A Handbook for Recovery from Abuse by David Schopick and Suzanne Burr

Sexual Harassment: High School Girls Speak Out by June Larkin

Secrets in Public: Sexual Harassment in Our Schools by Nan Stein, Nancy Marshall and Linda Tropp, NOW Legal Defense and Education Fund and the Wellesley College Center for Research on Women

Ten Talks Parent Must Have with Their Children about Youth Violence by Dominic Capell, talks for 4th–8th graders

Helping Teens Stop Violence: A Practical Guide for Counselors, Educators and Parents by Allen Creighton and Paul Kivel

Best Practices of Youth Violence Prevention: A Sourcebook for Community Action by National Center for Injury
Prevention/Control at www.cdc.gov/ncipc/dvp/bestpractices.htm

Depression

Growing Up Sad: Childhood Depression and Its Treatment by Leon Cytryn, MD and Donald McKnew, MD

Lonely, Sad and Angry: How to Help Your Unhappy Child by Barbara Ingersoll, PhD and Sam Goldstein, PhD

Conquering the Beast Within: How I Fought Depression And Won…And How You Can, Too by Cait Irwin

Youth Suicide Prevention Pamphlets by Kirk Wolfe, MD at www.oregon.gov/DHS/ph/ipe/ysp/spubs.shtml

Youth Suicide Prevention Program at www.yspp.org

Suicide Prevention at www.yellowribbon.org/Msg-to-Teens.htm

Depression Awareness at www.psychologyinfo.com/depression/teens.htm

American Assoc. of Pediatrics at www.aap.org/advocacy/childhealthmonth/prevteensuicide.htm

American Assoc. of Suicidology at www.suicidology.org/displaycommon.cfm?an=1&subarticlenbr=25

The Nemours Foundation at www.kidshealth.org

National Mental Institute of Mental Health at www.nimh.nih.gov

American Psychological Association at www.apa.org

Center for Mental Health Services at www.mentalhealth.org

Drugs

"What to Do When Your Teens Behavior Scares You" chapter from *Positive Discipline for Teenagers* by Jane Nelsen

Dying to Drink: Confronting Binge Drinking on College Campuses by Henry Wechsler, PhD and Bernice Wuethrich

Broken Bottles, Broken Dreams: Understanding and Helping the Children of Alcoholics by Charles Deutsch

Parents. The Anti Drug at www.theantidrug.com

Partnership for a Drug Free America at www.drugfree.org, www.drugfreeamerica.org/talk_listen.htlm

Join Together at www.jointogether.org/news/headlines/inthenews/2008/games-contribute-to-youths.html

Al-Anon and Alateen at www.al-anon.alateen.org

Automobile Injury

Not My Kid Campaign by Trauma Nurses Talk Tough at www.legacyhealth.org/body.cfm?id=1018
www.teensafedriver.com or www.aigteengps.com

Teen driving at www.teensafedriver.com or www.aigteensgps.com

MEDIA EDUCATIONAL FOUNDATION: excellent videos for adults or youth at www.mediaed.org

Overall:	*Reviving Ophelia,* interview with Mary Pipher on risky behaviors
Body Image:	*Recovering Bodies,* on eating disorders
	Slim Hopes: America's Obsession with Thinness
Sexuality:	*Girls: Moving Beyond Myth,* on the sexual dilemmas young girls face
	Teen Sexuality in a Culture of Confusion
	Hip-Hop: Beyond Beats and Rhymes, a riveting look at manhood, sexism, homophobia
Violence:	*Tough Guise: Violence, Media and the Crisis in Masculinity*
	Date Rape Backlash: Media and the Denial of Rape
	Dreamworlds 2: Desire, Sex and Power in the Music Video
Drug Use:	*Selling Addictions and Deadly Persuasion,* the advertising of alcohol and tobacco
	Pack of Lies, lies by tobacco industry to keep America addicted
	Spin the Bottle, about binge drinking, student deaths
	Game Over, about video and computer game addiction

Connecting Teens and Parents: The Vital Link

By Marta Mellinger

WE ALL KNOW ADOLESCENCE can be a time of great risk. As parents, we want to do all we can to help our children to move safely through the teen years and into adulthood. But what can we do? What protects teens? What empowers them to choose wisely and avoid risky behaviors?

A national scientific study was undertaken by the Adolescent Health Program at the University of Minnesota and the University of North Carolina.[1] Thirteen names are listed as co-authors, indicating the breadth of the collaboration. This research explored specific risks in adolescents' lives while seeking to identify factors within the home and school that help children avoid risky behavior. The findings of the study are profound.

Over 12,000 adolescents in grades 7 through 12 were drawn from an initial national school survey of over 19,000 around the country. Eight behaviors were considered: emotional distress, suicidal thoughts and behaviors, violence, use of cigarettes, alcohol, and/or marijuana, age of sexual debut, and pregnancy history.

The results of this comprehensive study showed that the single most important factor in helping children move safely through the teenage years is how close they feel to Mom and/or Dad.

The term "close" is defined as children perceiving they are loved, wanted and cared for by the way their

parents treat them. Secondly, children are supported most at school by feeling that teachers treat them fairly and that they are "connected" at school, and feel a part of the school and its activities. The study says the most important influence is that feeling of connectedness.

This study reinforces for professionals—counselors, teachers, educational administrators, and health professionals—what parents know intuitively. It asks all professionals to focus more attention on the relationships being built, and to help build them. And, it reinforces for parents that the absolute core of parenting adolescents is that we must take the emotional risk to stay connected.

Ever since I became a parent, I've been told that the "work" of the teenager is to establish his or her independence. I'm of a generation that embraced the motto "Do Your Own Thing," and there's an attitude about parenting teenagers that goes along with that. I've heard it said that as my kids become middle-schoolers, it's going to be "hell." People say the girls will push me away, and that by the time they reach high school, I won't see them much, if at all. We'll have fights; I won't know them or their friends. The picture is of a path leading away from me, their father, and family life.

As my own ten-year-old daughter approaches adolescence, will I let her "do her own thing"? Will I accept that this "moving away" is part of these "hell years" and allow her to emotionally distance herself from me and the family—as TV tells her to, as the movies tell her to, as much of our society tells us she should? Or do I take the risk to commit to sustaining our connection—even when she doesn't seem to want it?

Right about now, I have a choice to make. As she moves on to 11, 12 and 13, will I continue to reach out? Will I ask for her sharing by sharing myself? Will I sustain our "hokey" family rituals, enthusiastically plan family vacations she wants to skip? "Yes," I now say with more assurance. That's my job as her parent—to sustain the fragile flame of connection, even when the winds of our world are trying to blow it out.

Now, at least, I have science affirming what I've always intuitively known—in the larger scheme of things, it's our love that counts.

---

[1] "Protecting Adolescents from Harm", JAMA, Journal of American Medical Association, 278 (10):823-32, 9/10/97

Marta Mellinger, founder of The Canoe Group, a shared practice of four passionate professionals who help organizations develop new ways to succeed in rapidly changing times. With her husband of 23 years, she has two young adult daughters and is proud that they still call and come home regularly.

Reprinted with permission of Full Esteem Ahead *Wings,* Fall 1997

The Power of Assets

By Search Institute, from *The Asset Approach: Giving Kids What They Need to Succeed*

On one level, the 40 Developmental Assets represent common wisdom about the kinds of positive experiences and characteristics that young people need and deserve. But their value extends further. Surveys of almost 150,000 students in grades 6–12 (ages approximately 11–18 years) reveal that assets are powerful influences on adolescent behavior. Regardless of gender, ethnic heritage, economic situation or geographic location, these assets both promote positive behaviors and attitudes and help protect young people from many different problem behaviors.

0–10 assets   **11–20** assets   **21–30** assets   **31–40** assets

Promoting Positive Attitudes and Behaviors

Our research shows that the more assets students report having, the more likely they are to also report the following patterns of thriving behavior.

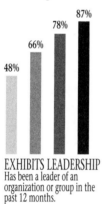

EXHIBITS LEADERSHIP
Has been a leader of an organization or group in the past 12 months.
48% 66% 78% 87%

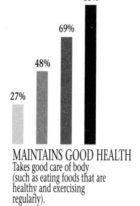

MAINTAINS GOOD HEALTH
Takes good care of body (such as eating foods that are healthy and exercising regularly).
27% 48% 69% 88%

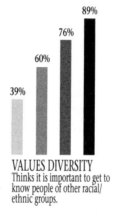

VALUES DIVERSITY
Thinks it is important to get to know people of other racial/ethnic groups.
39% 60% 76% 89%

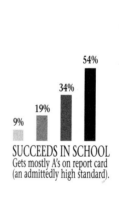

SUCCEEDS IN SCHOOL
Gets mostly A's on report card (an admittedly high standard).
9% 19% 34% 54%

Protecting Youth from High-Risk Behaviors

Assets not only promote positive behaviors, they also protect young people: The more assets a young person reports having, the less likely he or she is to make harmful or unhealthy choices. *(Note that these definitions are set rather high, suggesting ongoing problems, not experimentation.)*

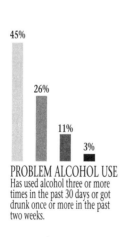

PROBLEM ALCOHOL USE
Has used alcohol three or more times in the past 30 days or got drunk once or more in the past two weeks.
45% 26% 11% 3%

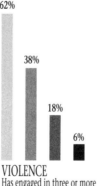

VIOLENCE
Has engaged in three or more acts of fighting, hitting, injuring a person, carrying a weapon, or threatening physical harm in the past 12 months.
62% 38% 18% 6%

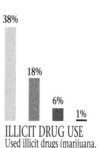

ILLICIT DRUG USE
Used illicit drugs (marijuana, cocaine, LSD, PCP or angel dust, heroin, or amphetamines) three or more times in the past 12 months.
38% 18% 6% 1%

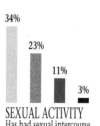

SEXUAL ACTIVITY
Has had sexual intercourse three or more times in lifetime.
34% 23% 11% 3%

Teens and Risks

By Kathy Keller Jones, MA

ADOLESCENCE IS A TIME OF risk-taking. Young people experiment with life, take on new challenges, and try out how things fit together in order to define and shape both their identities and their knowledge of the world. In other words, adolescents are learning how to think and how to act. Risk-taking is actually one of the ways that teens develop their cognitive abilities. The scary part for parents, however, is that the part of the brain which drives teens to seek out exciting new experiences develops much earlier than the part of the brain which regulates risk-taking behavior. The emotional center of teens is activated by their new hormones around age 12, while the frontal cortex, which enables us to reflect about consequences, delay gratification, and plan ahead, matures between 18 and 25 years of age. The connection between the emotional and cognitive parts of the brain, however, may not fully mature until around age 30. Knowledge about youthful brains helps us to realize how important adult influence is during those teen years.

Lynn Ponton, a practicing clinical psychiatrist and psychoanalyst, has written an interesting book, *The Romance of Risk*, which can help us to understand rather than fear adolescent risk-taking.

> *Teens need risks in order to grow; they need parental support in order to take those risks. If the risk-taking becomes dangerous, then, of course, parents must act. But when we assume that all adolescent risk-taking is bad, we fail to recognize both the very real dangers some risks pose and the tremendous benefits that others can yield.*[1]

Understanding the importance of risk to teen development helps parents to support teens in this area of their development, including encouraging healthy risk-taking of interest to their child, e.g., arranging for rock climbing lessons for a teen who wants to learn to climb. Risk-taking can promote more complex thinking, increase confidence, and help develop a young person's ability to do healthy risk-taking in the future. Even unhealthy, unsanctioned risk-taking sometimes has positive outcomes for teens. Teens who are caught breaking the rules or doing something foolish, for example, learn from the consequences of their actions that it is risky to do impulsive things and it pays to think ahead. This is particularly true, however, if parents are empathetic and also allow teens to experience the consequences of their actions. Recognizing teens' needs for adventure can help us to interact with them without blaming and fueling rebellion. Teens want to separate but they also want to be recognized by adults for the unique people they are and will become. Healthy adolescents are both connected and independent.

One of the real risks in today's times is that teens can become disconnected from their families and their friends can become more important to them than their family. Healthy teens are usually close to their friends and their family. Dr. Ron Taffel is a psychotherapist who has worked with teens and parents for over 30 years. He became curious about why children were doing worse things at earlier and earlier ages. He informally studied 250 teens, 1000 parents, teachers and counselors. What he discovered was that in many cases, the world of teens and commercial pop culture had overpowered the parents. Peers and media become a "second family"[2] to today's teens—a family which provides comfort and an attitude of live and let live. This second family, however, lacks the rules and standards that the first family used to have. Taffel also talks about how parents participate in this process by being unwilling to set and follow through on rules, i.e., they "abdicate their authority."[3] When peer culture supports children in a way that parents do not, our kids are vulnerable both to the consumerism fed to them by large corporations and to unhealthy high-risk behaviors.

Cynthia Lightfoot, in her book *The Culture of Adolescent Risk-taking,* describes adolescent risk-taking as a "transformative experience."[4] She found that youth associated risk-taking with feeling independent and mature. The youth she surveyed saw risk-taking as a challenging or novel experience with the possibility of unknown or unintended consequences. Teens mentioned the pleasure and excitement of changing the status quo, including the chance to learn about themselves and their abilities. Sometimes risk-taking also had social positives such as creating shared memories. Ten percent of the teens Lightfoot interviewed thought risks were appealing because they are an act of defiance or rebellion. The excitement of what is forbidden is a big draw to teens. A 17-year old had a party while her parents were gone but she was very careful to "leave no trace" and not allow anything "bad" to happen. Afterwards she felt proud of her ability to do this well and was glad she took the risk of being caught. Teens often take risks that help them to feel more like an adult.

How can we promote independence, growth, and risk-taking in our teens while also protecting them? Younger teens need several years of clear rules and consequences with gradually increasing freedom. Remember, their frontal cortex needs your help. Older adolescents need to be setting boundaries more collaboratively with their parents and they need room for independence while still living with the family. This also means strengthening the "first family" so the "second family" stays in its place. Teens need to feel the presence

of at least one (preferably more) supportive guiding adult who is willing to listen, dialog and negotiate, while remembering to not take everything personally. Families need to have comfort time together. Parents will need to bend their own perspectives somewhat to understand and participate in the teen's world. Parents must learn to deal constructively with teenage lying, which is how teens protect their freedom. Parents can share risk assessment skills they have used in their own life. Finally, parents can encourage and support teens in finding positive ways to take risks based on their teen's interests and needs.

Some Examples of Positive Challenges and Risks:
- Sports, pushing your personal limits,
- Interpersonal risks, assertively speaking your mind,
- Pushing academic limits, trying a difficult subject,
- Auditioning for performances,
- Challenging cultural biases,
- Confronting hardships, developing resources,
- Experimenting with creativity,
- Involvement in community action projects,
- Learning new skills,
- Handling sexual situations responsibly and safely,
- Getting a job.

References:
[1] Ponton, *Teens and Risk,* p. 12
[2] Taffel, *The Second Family*
[3] Taffel, *The Second Family,* p.26
[4] Lightfoot, *The Culture of Adolescent Risk-Taking*

Her First Diet

By Carol Beck, author of *Nourishing Your Daughter: Help Your Child Develop a Healthy Relationship with Food and Her Body*

AT SOME POINT DURING adolescence, nearly all our daughters try to lose weight. Maybe it happens when a girl is 10 and a growth spurt thickens her waist, or when she is 12 and wants to wear smaller jeans. For many girls, first diets are events they move through and beyond. But for others, that first diet is an initiation into a lifelong struggle with food and body size. Here's how you can help.

Understanding Why

If your daughter is restricting her food intake, ask her to tell you about her diet. She is likely to focus on calories, fat grams and the size of her body. Adolescent girls are acutely aware of their hips, thighs, stomachs, breasts and upper arms—all places women naturally store fat. Listen to your daughter carefully without interrupting. Resist the urge to correct her false perceptions. Then help her explore the reasons for her diet by asking, "If your diet worked and you became the size you want to be, what would happen? How would your life be different?" This is your opportunity to learn who your daughter wishes to be and what's missing from her life.

> Her diet may be a way of asking "Am I good enough? Can I be who I really am?"

Girls often believe that if they look "right," they'll be accepted and loved. They diet as a way of asking, "Am I good enough? Can I be who I really am, or must I mold myself to fit what others urge me to be?" Let your daughter know your love for her doesn't fluctuate with the numbers on a scale.

Diet Myths

Because there's so much information available about weight loss, most girls assume they know all they need to know about dieting. In fact, they seldom do. No one-size-fits-all diet from a magazine or weigh-loss center is likely to suit your daughter's adolescent body. If she is truly overweight, have her talk with her pediatrician, a therapist or a nutrition counselor about healthy eating habits. In the meantime, address these two myths popular among girls:

The magic formula. Many of my adolescent clients believe they know the magic dieting formula—eat fewer calories and exercise more. But that's not the whole story. Explain to your daughter that metabolism happens only in her muscle cells, so she needs to nourish her muscles with enough protein and carbohydrates at each meal to make her metabolic rate burn at its peak. If she's exercising more but going hungry, her body will not burn fat efficiently. Over time, this pattern actually lowers her metabolic rate, making it more difficult for her to lose weight. At mealtime, you might ask her, "What protein and carbs will you feed those hungry muscles?"

Excluding Pleasure

Many girls try to diet by avoiding all fatty foods and desserts. In truth, cutting out all pleasurable foods always backfires. The girl who deprives herself of fat and of the satisfaction it gives her body, eventually feels deprived. She develops cravings, gives in and binges. Then she feels guilty, deprives herself again and gives in once more. This is how some girls establish a cycle of dieting and failing that lasts well into adulthood. Encourage your daughter to eat reasonable amounts of the foods she loves, even those high in fat.

Messages from Home

You may want to use your daughter's first diet as an opportunity to look at your own relationship with food. What messages do you send her about dieting and weight? Do you feel comfortable serving as her role model? If you struggle with your weight, don't hesitate to see a professional. Then you'll be better able to guide your daughter.

For helpful information, suggest your daughter read *The Care and Keeping of You: The Body Book for Girls* (Pleasant Company, 1998) or *The Right Moves: A Girl's Guide to Getting Fit and Feeling Good* (Free Spirit, 1998). Even more important, encourage her to notice her body's messages. When is she hungry, and when is she full? Which foods help her feel energetic and which ones make her sleepy or tired? Each time you remind her to tune in to her body's messages, you help her get to know her body better and, ultimately, love it more.

Body Image and Eating Disorders

By Kathy Keller Jones, MA

ANOREXIA AND BULIMIA are serious issues: they affect over one million American women a year, 5-15% of whom eventually die as a result. Up to one-half of the others never fully regain their health after the ravages of starvation weaken their bodies. Anorexia and bulimia are eating disorders that overwhelmingly affect highly achieving adolescent girls and young women. Anorexia involves starving oneself even to the point of multi-organ failure: the results may include (but aren't limited to) infertility, heart failure, immune system dysfunction, sleep disturbances, gastrointestinal atrophy and death. Bulimia is characterized by a pattern of overeating, then purging via self-induced vomiting or laxatives. Both eating disorders are characterized by a girl's preoccupation with thinness, and are exacerbated by the images of unrealistically thin women in the popular media. As well, anorexics and bulimics are commonly people-pleasers who expect nothing less than perfection from themselves, and who are extremely sensitive to rejection and outside expectations. Psychological issues of control, separation and independence also play a role in these eating disorders. Control over food intake becomes a central theme in these girls' lives that separates them from feeling or dealing with other difficult issues facing them.

> Young girls, emulating the images they see in the media, may starve themselves in order to look thin, sexy and sophisticated.

Prevention of anorexia and bulimia best starts long before girls start thinking of themselves as fat, which now commonly occurs at around ages 9 or 10, regardless of body build. Some prevention strategies include:

- Starting early, teach your daughter about healthy eating habits and demonstrate them in your home.
- Avoid using the giving or withholding of food as a reward or punishment. Encourage a positive approach towards food as sustenance, not as a substitute for love, support or comfort.
- Make peace with your own body and set a good example with your own diet and exercise patterns.
- Love your daughter unconditionally. Let her weight and eating habits be her own business; teasing and criticizing your daughter about her body does not help her to feel loved, honored or appreciated.
- Encourage fathers to have warm, close, respectful relationships with their daughters, especially as they enter puberty.
- Girls learn early that society values women's bodies, not their minds, and when you criticize or make fun of other women's appearance, you feed into this. Make positive comments and critiques about other women in front of your daughters. Accepting women who don't meet your physical ideals and acknowledging the women in your life for their many-faceted talents other than beauty can make a huge impression on your own daughters.
- Recognize and be sensitive to the fact that developing—or under-developing—breasts are an issue of constant concern for all young women, including your daughter.
- Our girls get heavy exposure to models, whose bodies are 24% underweight. Give her plenty of access to accurate information about real women's bodies and take the opportunity to discuss her issues around body image and eating disorders.
- Explain to your daughter the difference between image and substance, and encourage her to pursue the latter, even though it takes more effort.

When girls and young women feel valued and admired for who they are and what they do, it may help them to stop obsessing about how they look. The best place for this to happen is in the home.

Resources:
- *Things Will Be Different for My Daughter* by Mindy Bingham, Sandy Stryker, and Susan Allstetter Neufeldt, PhD
- *Reviving Ophelia: Saving the Selves of our Adolescent Girls* by Mary Pipher

Can You Talk About Her Body?

By Lynda Madison, PhD and Amy Lynch from *Daughters: For Parents of Girls* newsletter

(A mom and her 10-year-old daughter work together in the kitchen)
Mother: "I've been thinking we should talk about growing up. I mean, you're starting to change."
Daughter: (rolls her eyes) "Uh, right."
Mother: "Are there any questions you'd like to ask?"
Daughter: "I don't think so." (moving toward the door) "Actually, I know all this already."

Maybe you know how this mom feels. You need to talk with your daughter about physical changes, but somehow the conversation never goes the way you plan. Meanwhile, her body hurtles through an extraordinary transformation, its most profound since infancy.

No Longer a Little Girl
Around age 7 or 8, a girl's adrenal glands begin to release androgens, and puberty begins. Soon, the bones in her legs and arms grow long. Her hips widen, her breasts bud, the hair on her legs grows course, her waist becomes fuller, and her weight climbs. Two years before boys begin to change, girls go through a growth spurt and sprout underarm and pubic hair. They gain heightened energy and athletic prowess. Their sweat glands become more active, and they develop body odor. Their skin becomes oilier and more prone to pimples. Meanwhile, a girl's emotions shift into high gear, too. Her feelings and reactions become more intense, and she has new sexual feelings

> All these changes are hard to talk about. They're complicated, personal, potentially embarrassing, and fraught with emotion.

—not adult sexual desire, but intense crushes and a heightened awareness of people who are attractive to her. Finally, usually around age 12, girls get their periods, marking what is medically defined as the end of puberty. Reaching puberty usually takes about four years, but five or six years is normal, and so is only two.

All these changes are hard to talk about. They're complicated, personal, potentially embarrassing, and fraught with emotion.

Ambivalent Reactions
Girls have many different reactions to the profound changes of puberty. Your daughter may be aghast to discover hair growing under her arms when she is 10, but comfortable with her period when it begins two or three years later. It's absolutely normal for her to feel betrayed by her body during this time, but it's also normal for her to be exhilarated about her newly curvaceous self. Many girls go back and forth between wanting to grow up and wanting to stay kids.

That was true of 12-year-old Leslie, a girl I saw in my practice. She had learned about menstruation in a human development class, but her mother had never talked with her about it. When her first period came, Leslie longed to share her feelings with her mother, but didn't know where to begin. She feared that her mother didn't care, or that there was something shameful about the way her body had changed.

All these changes are hard to talk about. They're complicated, personal, potentially embarrassing, and fraught with emotion. A whole range of reactions, from joy to loss to confusion, is perfectly normal for daughters and parents alike. But if we don't talk to the girls we love, they become as confused and hurt as Leslie was. It's our job to reassure our daughters that they are exactly who they are supposed to be right now—no longer little girls but not yet young women. Someone new in the making.

Finding Words
These ideas may make conversation easier:

Gentle guidance. Whether you're her mom or her dad, your daughter needs your guidance as her body changes. Left to the messages she gets from the media,

Listening In

"I have to admit I keep changing the subject when my dad talks to me about puberty."—Adria, age 11

"My mom came out with something about me changing, right out of the blue. I thought she would never mention anything like that. I didn't think she had the nerve. Since we weren't in public, it was okay."—Annaluz, age 13

"It's annoying. My parents expect me to be open about it, but sometimes I'm shy." —Elizabeth, age 11

"My mom tells me little stuff now and then. That's okay. I wouldn't want her talking to me more than that. This is private." —Paula, age 12

she may assume that puberty marks adulthood or it signals readiness for sexual activity. It's up to us to say, "This is a really amazing in-between stage that prepares you to become an adult later on. But not quite yet. Right now you're still a girl."

First steps. When your daughter is about 8, buy her some books about puberty. Look for friendly, reassuring texts like *The Care and Keeping of You* (Pleasant Company, 1998), *The Period Book* by Karen and Jennifer Gravelle (Walker, 1996), or *Body Language: New Moon Talks About Growing Up* (New Moon Publishing, 1999). Simply having these books around encourages questions and conversation, and talking about changes before they happen is always less embarrassing. If you skipped this step when your daughter was 8, do it now. It's never too late to show her that you care. Once her puberty is underway, suggest a shopping trip to a drug store buy things she'll need as she changes. To reduce embarrassment, buy fun items like nail polish and shower gel along with deodorant, tampons, and a razor. At home, set aside a special drawer or shelf in the bathroom where she can store her things.

Lots of little talks. Supporting your daughter through puberty means having lots of little talks and check-ins with her, rather than one big talk. Try matter-of-fact, specific openers such as, "I have read that some girls get their periods at 9 or 10. Has anybody in your class started yet?" or "If you're going to play basketball this year, let's buy you a sports bra so you'll be comfortable." Not all your comments will result in heart-to-heart talks. Still, they remind your daughter that you're there to answer her questions.

A sympathetic ear. Growing breasts may ache or twinge. Periods sometimes arrive with cramps or mood swings. Be sure your daughter knows that some discomfort is normal; otherwise she may fear something is wrong. Offer a sympathetic ear along with a heating pad, back-rub, or pain reliever.

A Note to Dads

Your daughter needs to hear from you during puberty. While it's never appropriate for you to comment specifically about her body shape, it's important that you say things like, "You're going to be a beautiful young woman" and "I'm so proud of how you're growing up." Of course, if you're raising your daughter alone, or she doesn't see her mother often, she'll need even more support from you. These ideas may help:

Admit it's awkward. Tell your daughter that talking about this isn't easy for you either. Remember that simply listening sympathetically when your daughter talks about feelings or uncertainties is a comfort to her. Try, "This is new for both of us." Buy books about puberty for her, and read them before you give them to her.

Call in reserves. Tell your daughter that you want her to have a woman to talk with, too. If her mother isn't available, ask your daughter to decide on someone she trusts, such as the mother of a friend, an aunt, or a grandmother. With your daughter's consent, enlist this woman's help. Ask her to shop with your daughter for things she'll need, and make sure it's okay for your daughter to talk to this woman any time.

If you are matter-of-fact about your everyday support, then your daughter will be, too. She'll always remember that you were there for her when she needed you.

Take Two

If talking is difficult, these words may help:

Mother: "I know you're well informed, but I need to have this conversation with you for my own peace of mind."

Mother: "You know, I think we avoid having these talks because they are embarrassing. Let's agree to have short talks. That will help."

Mother: "It's embarrassing to talk about growing up, but I remember how many questions I had at your age. You can write them down if you want to, or e-mail them to me, or leave a note on my pillow."

Resources:
- *The Care and Keeping of You: The Body Book for Girls* (Pleasant Company, 1998). Head-to-toe guide to everything from bad breath to bras.
- *The Period Book* by Karen and Jennifer Gravelle (Walker, 1996). All a girl needs to know about her menstrual period.
- *Body Language: New Moon Talks about Growing Up* (New Moon Publishing, 1999). Girls and adult writers on bras, eating disorders, body image, etc.
- *Our Daughter's Health: Practical and Invaluable Advice for Raising Confident Girls Ages 6-16* by Sharon L. Roan (Hyperion, 2001). Great parental guide to girl health.
- *Keep Talking: A Mother-Daughter Guide to the Preteen Years* by Lynda Madison (Andres McMeel, 1999). Interactive exercises to help you talk with your daughter about puberty, peer pressure, and more.

Sexual Myths
By Susan Chappell

DOES YOUR DAUGHTER think she can't get pregnant if her period isn't regular yet? Or that she can't get a sexually transmitted disease (STD) or HIV by having oral sex? And here's another myth that girls fall prey to—that we, their parents, are too old to understand anything about sex today.

In our information-saturated culture, it's easy for us to assume that adolescents are well-informed and that the era of sexual myth is long past. In fact, Nathalie Bartle, author of *Venus in Blue Jeans: Why Mothers & Daughter Need to Talk about Sex* (Houghton Mifflin, 1998), has found that girls usually know less than we assume. "As soon as you do a little probing," says Bartle, "you find that girls' knowledge is like a puzzle sold at a yard sale for a quarter. The box looks full, but when it's time to put the pieces together, you discover glaring holes."

What's Missing?

Many of those gaps and misconceptions are about the emotional impact of sexual activity. The "sex-is-no-big-deal" myth is powerful among teenagers, girls and boy alike. What can we do to combat it? "Always talk about sexuality in the context of relationships," Bartle advises. "Otherwise, girls think that understanding the vocabulary of mechanics of sex is the same as understanding sex."

We parents often fear that giving a girl information means we're giving her permission to be sexually active. In fact, just the opposite proves true. Studies show that the more we talk with our daughters about sex in a context of care and concern, the more likely they are to delay sexual activity. If there's one lesson girls learn when we discuss sex with them honestly, it's the lesson we want them to remember most—wait.

The Most Common Misconceptions

Our daughters are the real experts on what myths are most popular right now, and that's whom Dr. Lynn Ponton relied on in her research for *The Sex Lives of Teenagers: Revealing the Secret World of Adolescent Boys and Girls* (Dutton, 2000). "In talking with girls, I found that the most prevalent myths they believe are about orgasm, desire, masturbation and oral sex," says Ponton. "The very topics we talk about least openly in our culture."

Ponton has found that the single most common myth among girls these days is that they can't get HIV or STDs from oral sex. "Girls often think oral sex is completely safe," says Ponton. "They need to know that whenever body fluids are involved, they can get STDs. Recently, minority girls have had higher rates of HIV than other girls, so they may be particularly at risk for believing this myth."

Girls have high expectations for their first sexual experiences, and as a result, myths abound about orgasm. In her research, Ponton found that girls often think there's something wrong with them if they don't reach orgasm in their teens. Or they expect to have an orgasm that's like a male orgasm. "Girls whose parents give them honest, reliable information about desire and arousal don't have to worry so much about whether they're normal," says Ponton. "They're better prepared to decide 'yes' or 'no' responsibly because they know more about the sequence of things and what's likely to come next."

> Sexual behaviors and risks have changed since you and I were teens, but the hearts of girls have not. They still want love and sex to go together.

Myths about Relationships

Because most girls value relationships highly, they are especially vulnerable to myths about love and desire. All of these ideas are false. Here are a few myths we need to talk about with our daughters as they become teens:

- If a girl has sex with a guy, he'll begin to love her,
- Having oral sex is no big deal, and you have to do it if you want to have a boyfriend,
- Girls fall into two categories—those who have sex with everybody (sluts) and good girls,
- Good girls don't fantasize about sex, but bad girls do all the time,
- Feeling attraction for a person of the same sex automatically makes you gay or lesbian.

Myths about Intercourse and Pregnancy

Just as when we were young, girls still believe lots of myths about intercourse and pregnancy. Here are a few examples:

- People meet, fall in love and have sex immediately, don't they?
- A girl can't get pregnant unless she has an orgasm.

A girl can't get pregnant the first time she has intercourse, if she's having her period, or if she has intercourse standing up. A girl can't get pregnant if the boy she has intercourse with has already ejaculated earlier in the day. If a boy pulls out before he ejaculates, this prevents pregnancy. As soon as a girl takes a birth control pill, she is protected from pregnancy. Douching is a method of birth control.

- Condoms are too small for a lot of guys. Condoms are not a good method of preventing pregnancy and STDs because they break a lot.
- Once a boy is aroused, he has to have sex or he'll suffer physical pain/damage.

Be sure your daughter knows that not one of these ideas is true.

Myths about Teens

When it comes to myths, we parents believe our share of them, too. For example, it's a myth that your daughter doesn't want to hear from you on sexual topics. A recent study by the National Campaign to Prevent Teen Pregnancy revealed that girls between the ages of 12 and 14 list their parents as their biggest influence regarding sexual decisions. Friends and media come in second and third. Your daughter may be embarrassed or appear resentful when you offer her information about sex, but she needs and wants your guidance.

As you attempt to talk with your daughter, don't give in to another myth prevalent among adults—that all teens are irresponsible and sex-crazed. Recent studies have found that most girls believe sex should take place only between people who care deeply about each other. Even girls who have become sexually active with one partner wait an average of 18 months before having intercourse with a new partner. Granted, sexual risks and behaviors have changed since you and I were teens, but the hearts of girls have not. They still want love and sex to go together.

Talking the Talk

Regardless of your daughter's age, she will encounter sexual myths. Begin talking with her now at a level that's appropriate for her.

A good place to start when she is young is with her own body. Let your daughter know it's healthy to explore her body, and be careful not to overreact if she asks about subjects such as masturbation.

Acknowledge her first period as a special event that may prompt questions. Many girls learn the basics of menstruation, but they may have trouble understanding their monthly cycles, including when they ovulate. Encourage your daughter to keep a monthly calendar on which she tracks her menstrual cycle, her moods and how she feels during each phase.

No matter what your daughter's age, admit to her that sexuality is not a simple subject. Let her know it's normal to have lots of questions. If, for any reason, you simply cannot talk to your daughter about sex, find someone who can. A therapist, an aunt, a school counselor, a physician or another caring adult may be able to help.

> No matter what your daughter's age, admit to her that sexuality is not a simple subject. If, for any reason, you simply cannot talk to your daughter about sex, find someone who can.

Conversations about sex aren't easy for any of us. Yet each time you acknowledge your daughter's sexuality and supply her with facts with loving support, you debunk the myths she'll hear—including the one that says you're too old to understand anything about sex today.

Debunking the Myths

We recommend these resources as conversation starters:

- *The Period Book: Everything You Don't Want to Ask (but Need to Know)* by Karen and Jennifer Gravelle (Walker, 1006). A delightful book full of down-to-earth answers.
- *Growing Up: It's a Girl Thing: Straight Talk About First Bras, First Periods and Your Changing Body* by Mavis Jukes (Knopf, 1998). For your 10-to-12-year-old, a warm yet frank book about puberty.
- *It's a Girl Thing: How to Stay Healthy, Safe and in Charge* by Mavis Jukes (Knopf, 1996). This book is for older girls and includes basics about sexual activity and birth control.
- *Ophelia Speaks: Adolescent Girls Write About Their Search for Self* by Sara Shandler (Harper Perennial, 1999). Stories for older teens written by girls about desire, sexual encounters and relationships.
- National Campaign to Prevent Teen Pregnancy. Ideas to share when you talk with your daughter at www.teenpregnancy.org.

Communication Tips for Parents (Regarding Sexuality)

SIECUS Publication for Parents

Here are some tips to get parents started:

- **Parents are the primary sexuality educators of their children.** Children want to talk about sexuality with their parents and to hear their values. It is not just a parent's right, it is their responsibility. Your children need to hear your point of view. Children often want to hear about your growing up. They want to hear stories about your youth and how you dealt with issues. This can often help them with their own struggles.

- **Be an "askable parent." Reward questions.** It is never a good idea to tell your children to wait until they are older before you will answer their questions. When children ask questions, you have a chance to help them learn. Reward a question with, "I'm glad you came to me with that question." Say this before you respond to what was asked. It will teach them to come to you when they have other questions. If you don't know an answer, tell your child you will look it up and tell them later. Be sure you follow through. You might want to go to the library and look up the answer together.

- **Find "teachable moments."** Difficult situations are often "teachable moments." They offer a chance for you to teach your children what you know or believe about sexuality. You can even make use of a TV show that you believe sends the wrong message. Turn it around and say, "I think that program sends the wrong message. I want to tell you what I believe and why."

- **You don't need to wait until they ask a question.** Many children never ask questions. When our children are young, we don't wait until they ask to teach them they should look both ways before

crossing a busy street or touching a hot stove. Some things are essential for them to know. It is the job of adults—and especially of parents—to teach our children how to get along in the world. Learning about sexuality is the same. You need to decide what is important for children to know, and then tell them before a crisis arrives. Think through your own values about sexuality: What messages do you want to give your children about love, nudity, gender roles, intimacy, privacy, etc?

- **It is okay to feel uncomfortable.** Relax. Very few adults have had a formal course in sexuality, and it is hard for many adults to talk about sexual matters. You can let your children know you are uncomfortable, but you will talk to them anyway because you love them and want to help. It is also okay for parents to set limits. You do not have to give specific answers to questions about your own sexual behavior.

- **Talk about the joys of sexuality.** This might include telling them that sexuality is natural and healthy, that loving relationships are the best part of life, and that intimacy is a wonderful part of adult life.

- **Listen, listen, listen.** When children ask questions, thank them for asking, and ask them why they want to know or what they already know. That may help you prepare your answer.

- **Facts are not enough.** In addition to sharing facts and thoughts, do share your feelings, values and beliefs. Then tell your child why you feel that way. Pre-teens and teens often seem to reject their parents' values—especially when they feel their parents want to impose their point of view with "because I say so!" Most of us have very good reasons behind our beliefs. Telling our children the why behind our values teaches them to think. Children also need help in seeing the difference between thoughts, feelings and actions. Parents can help their children understand that while it is normal to have all kinds of sexual thoughts and feelings, they are in charge of their own behavior, and they do not have to act upon their thoughts and feelings.
- **Know what is taught about sexuality in your schools, churches, temples, and youth groups.** Urge these groups to include sexuality education in their programs. While young people often joke, tease and talk about sexuality among themselves, it is more helpful when trained adults lead those talks.
- **When you talk with your children about sexuality, you are telling them that you care about their happiness and well-being.** You are also sharing your values. This is one of the real joys of parenthood.

- **Be aware of the "question behind the question."** The unspoken question, "Am I normal?" is often hiding behind many questions about sexual development, sexual thoughts and sexual feelings. On the surface, these questions may sound like, "What is the oldest (or youngest) that a girl got her period?" or "Can a flat-chested girl nurse a baby?" Behind each of these questions (and hundreds more) is the unspoken question, "Am I normal?" Reassure your children as often as possible.

Talking With Infants And Toddlers (0-2 Years)

Of course, infants and toddlers do not need to know the facts about sexuality. But children this age are beginning to learn about their sexuality, and you are their main teachers. Naming all the parts of their body teaches them that their entire body is natural and healthy. ("This is your arm, this is your elbow, this is your vulva/penis, this is your knee," etc.) Reacting calmly when they touch their genitals teaches them that sexual feelings are normal and healthy. Holding them, hugging them, talking with them and responding to their needs all lay the groundwork for trust and open discussions as they grow older.

Talking With Preschool Children (3-4 Years)

Children at this age are learning about their bodies. They learn about their world through play. They begin to ask questions about where babies come from and they can understand simple answers. They do not understand abstract ideas or adult sexual behaviors. They can learn simple things such as bathing, washing their hands, brushing their teeth, eating good foods and napping. They can begin to accept the need for privacy. The best thing a parent can do at this age is to create a home where children will feel free to ask questions about their bodies, health and sexuality. Children then will learn that sexuality is one of the things that can be talked about in their home.

Talking With Young Children (5-8 Years)

Children at this age are able to understand more complex issues about health, disease and sexuality. They are interested in birth, families and death. They have probably heard about sex and AIDS from TV, their friends or adults. They may have questions or fears about sex and HIV/AIDS. Children at this age can understand basic answers to their questions based on concrete examples from their lives. For example, if your child cuts his/her finger and blood appears, this is a good time to explain how germs (things that make you sick) can get into the blood system from cuts in the body. They can understand simple answers to questions about their bodies and reproduction.

Talking With Preteens (9-12 Years)

Children at this age are going through all the changes of puberty. They are concerned about their bodies, their looks, and what is "normal." For some young teens, this time marks the start of dating, early sexual experiences and trying drugs.

Because of the strong social pressures which begin at this age, it is important that you talk about sexuality, regardless of what you know about your children's sexual or drug experiences. As a concerned parent, you must make sure your children know about prevention NOW. During the changes of puberty, preteens are very curious about sex and need to be given the basic, accurate information. They need to know what is meant by sexual intercourse, homosexuality and oral, anal and vaginal sex. Preteens need to be told that sex can have consequences, including pregnancy and diseases, including HIV infection. They should be told why sexual intercourse is an adult behavior and why it is a good idea for young people to wait to have sex. They need to know how HIV is transmitted, how it is not transmitted and how to prevent transmission, including talking a bit about condoms. This may seem like a difficult task, but it will give you a chance to teach your children the values that you hope they will adopt in their lives. It is also the time to let your children know that they can come to you with any of their questions about sexuality.

Talking With Teens (13-19 Years)

Parents should share their family's values about sexual behaviors. Teenagers and preteens should be told that the best way to prevent becoming infected with STDs, HIV or becoming pregnant is by not having any type of sexual intercourse.

Many parents want to tell their children to wait to have intercourse at least until they are no longer

teenagers. However, most children today are not waiting—the majority of Americans have intercourse by their twentieth birthday.

Therefore, most parents also want to make sure that their children can protect themselves. We can explain to our children that if they are going to be involved in sex, they must protect themselves against teenage pregnancy and sexually transmitted diseases, including HIV.

Parents can talk about the full range of sexual behaviors that people find pleasurable. Many of these activities are "safer sex"—they cannot transmit HIV or cause pregnancy. This means talking to your teens and preteens about kissing, hand holding, caressing, masturbation and other sexual behaviors that do not involve penetration.

Social pressure to try sex and drugs can be very strong for teens. Therefore, at this age, regardless of their personal experience with sex or drugs, all young people must know:

- Not having sexual intercourse (abstinence) is the best method for preventing sexually transmitted diseases and pregnancy.

- For teenagers who are going to have sexual intercourse, they must use condoms for each and every act of intercourse, including oral sex, anal sex and vaginal sex. Only latex (rubber) condoms should be used. Condoms are very effective at preventing pregnancy and diseases. In fact, using a condom is 10,000 times safer than not using one.

- Teenagers should avoid all drugs including alcohol. Drugs and alcohol impair good decision-making and may suppress the immune system. Sharing needles of any kind puts people at risk of HIV— that includes injection drug-use, skin-popping, injecting steroids, ear and body piercing and tattooing.

Reprinted with permission from *Communication Tips For Parents.* © *SIECUS. Now What Do I Do?* (New York: Sexuality Information Council of the United States, 1996). www.siecus.org/pubs/pubs0004.html.

Talking Back:
Ten Things Teens Want Their Parents to Know about Teen Pregnancy
Survey by the National Campaign to Prevent Teen Pregnancy

TEENS HEAR ADVICE all the time but they don't often get asked for their advice. The National Campaign to Prevent Teen Pregnancy asked teens from all over the country:

If you could give your parents and other important adults advice on how to help you and your friends prevent teen pregnancy, what would it be?

1. Show us why teen pregnancy is such a bad idea. For instance, let us hear directly from teen mothers and fathers about how hard it has been for them. Even though most of us don't want to get pregnant, sometimes we need real-life examples to help motivate us.

2. Talk to us honestly about love, sex, and relationships. Just because we're young doesn't mean that we can't fall in love or be deeply interested in sex. These feelings are very real and powerful to us. Help

> Teens are precariously balanced between the sexual values they hear at home and those they are faced with daily in our sexualized culture.

us to handle the feelings in a safe way—without getting hurt or hurting others.

3. Telling us not to have sex is not enough. Explain why you feel that way, and ask us what we think.

Tell us how you felt as a teen. Listen to us and take our opinions seriously. **And no lectures, please.**

4. Whether we're having sex or not, we need to be prepared. We need to know how to avoid pregnancy and sexually-transmitted diseases.

5. If we ask you about sex or birth control, don't assume we are already having sex. We may just be curious, or we may just want to talk with someone we trust. And don't think giving us information about sex and birth control will encourage us to have sex.

6. Pay attention to us before we get into trouble. Programs for teen moms and teen fathers are great, but we all need encouragement, attention, and support. Reward us for doing the right thing—even when it seems like no big thing. Don't shower us with attention only when there is a baby involved.

7. Sometimes, all it takes not to have sex is not to have the opportunity. If you can't be home with us after school, make sure we have something to do that we really like, where there are other kids and some adults who are comfortable with kids our age. Often we have sex because there's not much else to do. Don't leave us alone so much.

8. We really care what you think, even if we don't always act like it. When we don't end up doing exactly what you tell us to, don't think that you've failed to reach us.

9. Show us what good, responsible relationships look like. We're as influenced by what you do as by what you say. If you demonstrate sharing, communication, and responsibility in your own relationships, we will be more likely to follow your example.

10. We hate "The Talk" as much as you do. Instead, start talking with us about sex and responsibility when we're young, and keep the conversation going as we grow older.

A Recipe for Healthy Relationships

By The Raphael House, from *Take Care: A Guide to Safe Relationships*

Do you know what you're looking for in your relationships? Do you know what a healthy relationship looks like? Is it just about being physically attracted to another person or liking each other a lot? Those are certainly important things to think about, but is that all there is? Not according to the young people we talked to. According to them, the recipe for a healthy relationship would contain the following ingredients:

- **Self-Esteem**
  People who believe in themselves and their own worth are more able to believe in the worth of their intimate partner.
- **Mutual Respect**
  People in healthy relationships respect each other's opinions, feelings, goals and decisions even if they don't always agree with each other.
- **Trust**
  People in healthy relationships are honest and open with each other at all times. Trust builds over time and is based on consistent' honest behavior.
- **Open Communication**
  People in healthy relationships are not afraid to express their needs, concerns and feelings. They listen attentively while their partners do the same.
- **Nonviolence**
  People in healthy relationships do not hit, threaten, or otherwise scare each other. They do not use words to hurt each other.
- **Personal Responsibility**
  People in healthy relationships take responsibility for their own actions and feelings. They do not blame each other if they lose their temper or make a bad decision.
- **Mutual Friends & Interests**
  People in healthy relationships continue their own interests and friendships outside of their romantic relationships.
- **Shared Decision-Making**
  People in healthy relationships use communication and negotiation to make decisions about their activities. One person does not dominate the decision-making.

- **Non-Abuse of Drugs**
  People in healthy relationships do not pressure each other to use alcohol and other drugs. They do not "get high" to make the relationship better.
- **Hearing "No!"**
  People in healthy relationships don't pressure or force the other person to have sex or do things they are not comfortable doing.
- **Non-Controlling Behavior**
  People in healthy relationships are not jealous or possessive of each other.

"After several abusive relationships, I've finally learned what I want from a partner. Love, respect and honesty are the most important things to me. In past relationships, I've lost a part of myself. I found myself giving up my own interests, hobbies and even friendships to please the other person."

—Cassie, age 19

"I think that respect for each other as people is key. Stay respectful and understanding even if you're mad at each other. Don't be sexist—that's old school."

—Marcus, age 17

Reprinted with permission of the Raphael House. *Take Care: A Guide to Safe Relationships* is a Raphael House prevention project in Portland, Oregon. Contact: (503) 222-6507. www.raphael-house.com

Dater's Bill of Rights

By National Crime Prevention Council

◆ I have the right to refuse a date without feeling guilty.

◆ I can ask for a date without feeling rejected or inadequate if the answer is no.

◆ I do not have to act macho.

◆ I may choose not to act seductively.

◆ If I don't want physical closeness, I have the right to say so.

◆ I have the right to start a relationship slowly, to say, "I want to know you better before I become involved."

◆ I have the right to be myself without changing to suit others.

◆ I have the right to change a relationship when my feelings change. I can say, "We used to be close, but I want something else now."

◆ If I am told a relationship is changing, I have the right not to blame or change myself to keep it going.

◆ I have the right to an equal relationship with my partner.

◆ I have the right not to dominate or to be dominated.

◆ I have the right to act one way with one person and a different way with someone else.

◆ I have the right to change my goals whenever I want to.

Reprinted with permission by National Crime Prevention Council, 1000 Connecticut Avenue NW, 13th floor, Washington, DC 20036. www.ncpc.org

Abuse in Teen Dating Relationships

By Jeannie La France

"When I first met him I thought he was great, but slowly things began to change. He would go with me everywhere and cause a big fight if I talked to other guys. Once he threw a glass at me at a party and it broke on the wall behind my head. Everyone just laughed. Once he threw me up against a locker at school and I slapped at him to try to get away. The security said it was just 'a slapping match between kids.' I thought no one cared. It took me two years to get out, and he still drives by my house every week; he still scares me."

—Anonymous Teen

TEEN DATING VIOLENCE is when one person in a romantic relationship uses emotional or physical or sexual abuse to gain power and keep control over the other person. Teen dating violence happens more than we think. Nearly one-third of all teenagers will have been in an abusive relationship by the time they reach their twenties. It's important to be able to tell if you or your friend's relationship is abusive so you can start taking steps to help yourself or your friend be safe. Below are some questions to help you.

Am I In an Abusive Relationship?

- Are you ever afraid of the person you are dating?
- Do they say no one else would ever go out with you?
- Do they embarrass you in public? Do they call you names or put you down?
- Does the person you're dating tell you where you can go, what to wear or who you can hang out with?
- Do you feel pushed or pressured into sexual activities? Do you feel like you will "get in trouble" if you say "no"?
- Is the person you are seeing really nice sometimes and really mean other times? (Almost like they have two different personalities?)
- Does this person ever threaten to kill themselves or hurt anyone else if you leave them?
- Does this person ever shove, grab, hit, pinch, hold you down or kick you?
- Does this person ever say it is your fault if they hurt you or yell at you?
- Does this person make frequent promises to change? Do they say you are "making it too big a deal?"

If you have answered "yes" to any of these questions, then you or your friend is in an abusive relationship. What can you do? Here are some suggestions ...

If Your Friend Is In an Abusive Relationship:

- Be patient. Leaving relationships takes a long time.
- Don't spread gossip; it could put them in danger.
- Tell them the abuse is not their fault and they don't deserve it, no matter what.
- Be non-judgmental. Be a good listener.
- Don't ignore it or pretend it isn't happening.
- Support your friends in making their own choices, don't boss them around.
- Make safety plans with them about going between classes or to and from school.
- See if you can tell a supportive adult.
- Call crisis lines like National Domestic Violence Hotline at **1-800-799-SAFE.**

If You Are In an Abusive Relationship:

- You could tell people what is happening. If the first people you tell are not helpful, find other people. Try thinking of supportive adults to tell.
- You could call a crisis line. They are confidential, all ages and you can be male or female.
- You could join a support group for young women who have been abused.
- You could take a self-defense course.
- You could look into legal action. The school may have helpful policies or you could get a court restraining order to keep the abuser away from you.
- You could go to a shelter.
- Believe in yourself. Abuse is not your fault no matter what anyone says. You deserve a life without abuse.

Dating violence happens in all kinds of relationships. When it is between a boyfriend and girlfriend, 95% of the time it is the boyfriend abusing the girlfriend. Dating abuse can also happen in same-sex relationships. Abuse can happen in any relationship no matter what race the people are, how much money they have or where they live. The important thing is that no matter who the people are, dating violence hurts.

Reprinted courtesy of Jeannie La France and the Bradley-Angle House, www.bradleyangle.org. 503-232-7805 PO Box 14694, Portland, OR 97293. The National Domestic Violence Hotline is 1-800-SAFE.

Depression in Girls

By Kathy Keller Jones, MA

15-year-old Whitney Meers started wishing she were dead. Her family had just moved to Florida, and she went from being a popular, straight-A student to being the lone "dork" sitting at the back of the class. "I cried about everything," she says. It got to the point where Whitney could barely stand to be awake. "I'd come home from school around 4:30 and sleep. I avoided everybody."

One day, on the way home from the mall with her parents, Whitney pushed open the car door and tried to jump out. Her mother grabbed her just in time and took her straight to the hospital. That's when Whitney finally got help for her depression. Ironically, she was one of the lucky ones. Most of us who suffer from depression do so in silence. We don't understand that we are not to blame for the feelings of worthlessness and isolation, and that, in fact, these feelings are caused by a disease.[1]

ADOLESCENCE IS A TIME of angst for most teens because their minds and bodies and lives are in the process of a massive makeover. They may feel very insecure, confused and hate life at times. The teen girl's brain is actively reorganizing and pruning neuronal circuits, which influences her thoughts, feelings and actions. In her book *The Female Brain*, Louann Brizendine, MD, a neuropsychiatrist, describes the teen brain changes in great detail:

Once estrogen and progesterone levels climb at puberty, her responsivity to both stress and pain start to rise, all marked by new reactions in the brain to the stress hormone cortisol. She is easily stressed, high strung, and she starts looking for ways to chill out (p.35).[2]

How can we distinguish between normal moodiness and emotionality in our teen girls and clinical depression? One in eight teens suffer from depression according to *A Parent's Guide to Recognizing and Treating Depression in Your Child*.[3] Before the hormones of puberty start to change our daughters' childhood personalities, boys and girls are equally likely to experience depression. However, by 15 years of age, girls are twice as likely to be depressed, and genetics can play a role.[2] Boys, however, tend to be more covert about depression so they may be under-diagnosed.

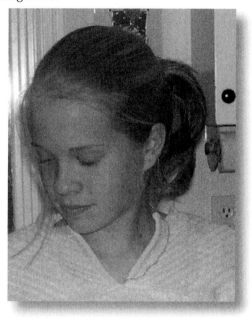

We all feel sad or depressed at times, but clinical depression is more than just feeling "down" or "blue." Here are some ways you can identify clinical depression:

- The feelings go on for an extended period of time.
- The feelings continue to get worse.
- Things that have worked in the past to reduce these feelings aren't working.
- The feelings interfere with day-to-day functioning.[3]

Adolescents may experience a drop in grades, withdrawal from friends and difficulty with relationships, feelings of hopelessness, poor self-esteem, increased substance abuse, changes in eating and sleeping patterns, self-destructive behaviors such as cutting, and suicidal and other dark thoughts. Depression is not just a feeling, but a state of being fueled by a biochemical imbalance. Neuroscientists hypothesize that women's "sensitivity to fear, stress, genes, estrogen, progesterone, and innate brain biology (p. 132)"[1] all play important roles in female depression. "Many gene variations and brain circuits that are affected by estrogen and serotonin are thought to increase women's risk of depression (p. 132)."[1]

What can you do if you recognize signs of depression? If your daughter is seriously depressed such as the teen described at the beginning of this article, it is critical to get professional help promptly and keep your daughter safe. Listen attentively to your child's concerns and avoid trying to talk her out of her feelings. Remember that the most important step toward overcoming depression is facing it and asking for help. This means finding a medical professional and a therapist who both you and your daughter feel is supportive. Our daughters are very intuitive and their healing will be facilitated by professionals who '"speak" to them.

If your teen does not seem clinically depressed but is in a funk, you can support her in some of the following ways:

• Focus on overall health. Help her get organized around her nutrition. Sometimes a high quality woman's formula/multi-vitamin with iron and omega-3 fish oils can help our girls feel healthier and more stable emotionally. Explain the importance of breakfast to alertness and keeping our metabolism functioning optimally. Talk about what a healthy diet is and how it helps us to feel better emotionally and physically.

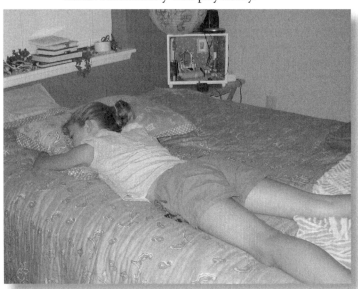

• Explain the relationship between exercise and stress reduction and help her organize physical activities that make sense for her. Remind her that fun activities such as swinging on swings and having water fights are also excellent ways to fight moodiness.

• Work on the quality of relationship you have with your daughter. Having a parent who listens, who cares and tries to understand, and who has faith in you can go a long way.

• Although all teens like some alone time in their room, too much room time and online time can be depressing. If possible, keep computers and TV out in family space rather than in your child's room. Help your daughter join organized activities and youth groups that get her out in the neighborhood and the community.

• Help her find ways to help others in the area of her interests. Encourage hobbies such as photography that give her a new perspective.

• Let your daughter know that smokers are twice as likely to develop depressive symptoms as those who never took a puff.[1] Explain that alcohol is a depressant.

• Encourage your daughter to use music and dance to express herself and to take up a cool instrument.

• Pets, yours or the neighbors, can be a wonderful way to feel calmer and loved.

Your daughter may also need help in supporting a friend who is depressed. Explain what depression is and encourage her to listen to her friend and help him or her find help. Check in with your daughter to see how things are going. Teach your daughter that when we are concerned about a person's safety we need to take immediate action and get help. Encourage her to use resources at school and in the community. Depression affects people throughout their life span so adolescence is a time when teens can learn to identify symptoms in themselves and others and develop a plan of action to create a healthy life.

For more information on depression, see the websites and books at the end of Chapter 8 Overview.

Resources:
1   Brody, L. "Hearts of Darkness," *Jump* magazine
2   Brizendine, L. *The Female Brain*, "The Teen Girl Brain"
3   *A Parent's Guide to Recognizing and Treating Depression in Your Child, Washington State*, www.yspp.org

The Power of Parents:
Teens Say Parents a Leading Influence in Helping Them Stay Alcohol-Free

By Emily Moser, MPA, MA

"Peer pressure is overrated; parents are huge." —Oregon teenager who said parental influence was a major reason she chose to be alcohol-free.

THIS TEEN IS FAR FROM ALONE. A survey a few years ago by the respected Roper organization found that 76 percent of youth ages 8 to 17 said parents were a leading influence in their decision about whether to drink.

It can be easy for parents to dismiss the enormous power they have to educate and equip their kids to steer clear of alcohol. Our culture is awash in alcohol advertising that promotes the false notion that everyone drinks, with no consequences, and it can make parents feel undermined when it comes to helping their children make the healthy choice to not drink. But research underscores that parental influence is the key to keeping kids alcohol free. Among the most important steps parents and other caregivers can take are to educate themselves about the harms of underage drinking, to share those facts with their children, to express their values on the importance of not drinking until age 21, to establish rules and clear consequences for their behavior, and to take opportunities to strengthen the connection with their kids.

It's critical that parents start talking with their kids when they are young about the harms of underage drinking because alcohol is the No. 1 drug problem among youth. About one in three eighth-graders and half of 11th-graders consumed alcohol in the past month, according to the Oregon Healthy Teens Survey. And too many teens who drink aren't just having a cocktail at the end of the day; they are drinking a lot in one sitting.

The risks associated with youth drinking are serious. Alcohol is a major cause of death among young people. The part of the brain that controls planning, delayed gratification and judgment develops last. Pouring alcohol on top of that affects a youngster's ability to make sound decisions, like whether to ride in a car with a driver who has been drinking. Beyond the sobering safety consequences, underage drinking has serious health risks. Scientific research has found that regular drinking can harm a child's brain. Studies show that tremendous brain development occurs during the adolescent and teens years, and that the brain is not fully developed until our mid-20s. For parents, helping kids make the healthy choice to stay alcohol-free falls into the same category as making sure they wear a helmet when they ride their bicycle or a seat belt when they get in a car. It is very important to emphasize that underage drinking is not an inevitable rite of passage for underage youth.

What strategies can parents apply today to protect their kids from alcohol and other drug use? A strong family bond is proven to be one of the most important factors. Here are a few suggestions to help build closeness and trust—even through everyday activities:

- Spend time doing fun things as a family, like cooking and eating dinner together, playing board games, watching a movie, shooting baskets or going to community events.
- Take advantage of everyday moments to tell your children that you love them and to share your values and expectations.
- Your child may have opinions, fears and concerns about substance use. In addition to sharing with your son or daughter the facts about alcohol and other drug use, ask them open-ended questions and listen to their perspectives.
- Help your child develop the skills to refuse offers of alcohol from their peers and others. Together, practice responses they are comfortable saying.
- Take a look at the example you're setting with your kids. What message are you sending about things such as your own alcohol use? If you do not drink, explain to your child why. If you enjoy an occasional drink, talk with your child about moderation and why the legal drinking age is 21 (studies show the law has saved lives on the road and prevented injuries, and it has kept countless adolescents and teens from drinking at early ages). And let your son or daughter see you say "no" to a drink from time to time, too.
- Remember that parenting doesn't have to be done in isolation. You'll find other parents share many of the same concerns and challenges about raising kids. Together, you can establish standards of behavior, explore ways to build your parenting skills through classes and seminars, and become an even better parent.

Written for Family Empowerment network by Emily Moser, MPA, MA, Director of Parenting Program at Oregon Partnership. Reprinted with permission from Emily Moser at emoser@orpartnership.org. 503-224-5211, or www.orpartnership.org.

Teenagers and Drugs

By Kathy Masarie, MD

Serenity Prayer: "God grant me the serenity to accept the things I cannot change, the courage to change the things I can, and the wisdom to know the difference."

THE SERENITY PRAYER says it all when it comes to intervening in teen drug use. (We consider alcohol a "drug" in this article.) When a parent is clear about what they do and don't have control over, they can be extremely effective in reducing teen substance abuse. What a community of caring adults do have control over is a support structure that encourages healthy choices. What we don't have control over is the moment when our teen is faced with the choice of taking drugs or alcohol. That moment lays 100% in his or her hands. Our teens know this. What we as parents can do to focus our energy on what we do have control over: empowering our teens to make healthy decisions and fostering an environment that makes it difficult for them to drink. At the same time, we can work to help create a cultural norm that glamorizes a healthy life-style rather than a life-style of drinking and drugs.

Connection with Your Teen Is Key

Connectivity with parents is a vital element in reducing alcohol and drug use. Parents who have good communication with their teens can share all of the information listed below. Their teens hear it and trust the information because they know their parents are honest, open and have their well being in mind. Teens with a trusting connection with their parents know their parents are not trying to control them or take away their autonomy and are sharing this information to help them stay alive, stay healthy and stay safe. Even though our teens might not always make the choice we hope for, we have done our job as competent parents to support a good decision. If our teens choose to use drugs or alcohol, we want to know so we can help them. Teens with a good relationship with their

parents will tell their parents when they are struggling with a serious problem; they trust their parents will actually help them and not over-react with anger and consequences. One of the best sources of information on long-term parenting strategies comes from Jane Nelsen's book, *Positive Discipline for Teenagers.*[1]

Be Aware of Family Patterns That Invite Chemical Dependency

Genetics and family patterns are very influential in whether a teen will become addicted. Parents who hide the embarrassing stories about alcoholism in the extended family are setting their kids up. Our kids need to know these stories and they need to hear them early.

Alcoholism is a disease that develops when alcohol reacts with a person's particular body chemistry. Depending on a person's physical make-up, it may take a lot of drinking to trigger alcoholism or it may take just a little. Each person is born with a certain level of risk for developing this disease. Teenagers can become alcoholics in 6-18 months while it usually takes older people several years, partially because a young person's liver metabolizes alcohol more rapidly than an adult's does.[2] A teen who feels "like she has come home" when she drinks can be an addict even if it's her first time. Teens may build up a tolerance to the drug, requiring more and more alcohol to achieve the same affect. A teen who "holds his liquor" can be genetically predisposed to alcoholism.

Creating a home environment that is free of chemical dependency is an important first step to protecting our teens from drugs. One in four US children, sometime before the age of 18, lives with a family member who abuses alcohol.[3] Children model what they learn at home; parents who look at their own relationship with drugs and alcohol can evaluate whether they are modeling unhealthy behaviors. Households with problem drug or alcohol users teach kids to use chemical agents to numb their feelings, emotions and fears. Wanting a healthy lifestyle for your teen can be a great motivator for healing dysfunctional family patterns.

Talk to Kids Early to Influence "Alcohol Expectancy"

Our brains store information in memory so we are prepared for similar situations (otherwise every moment would be an overwhelming new experience). This stored automatic information is called "expectancies." Researchers are now finding that expectancies play an important role in alcohol use. Children acquire their alcohol expectancies very early—even as young as 3 or 4 years old. Young children often have negative expectancies that alcohol makes one sick or mean. Over time they are exposed to the community norms that make drinking seem "cool": ads everywhere marketing alcohol to teens, movies where there are rarely negative consequences to drinking, MTV spring break promotion of binge drinking, and so on. By 5th-6th grade, children's expectancies may shift to the positive effects of alcohol to be socially successful, happy, sexy, etc. Individuals who have strong positive alcohol expectancies drink more and are at risk for abuse.[4]

Inform Yourself about Your Community Norms

Even though parents are fearful of drug and alcohol abuse, there is a tendency to think "not my kid" when in comes to alcohol and drugs. Just to give you a general idea, nationally norms from 2005[5] are:

Age	% of Teens who Have Used Alcohol	
	Males	Females
12	10%	9%
14	32%	33%
16	60%	62%
18	73%	76%

Nearly 50% of college-aged men and nearly 40% of college-aged women binge drink (5+ drinks in a row) monthly.[6] Find information about the rates of alcohol use among teens in your community, the severity of use, the rates of deaths and complications from drugs and alcohol, how they get the alcohol, and strategies the high schools, police and community are doing to curtail the problem.

Why Do Kids Do Drugs and Alcohol?

Ask yourself why you drink and teen's reasons are similar: it is fun, it feels good, it makes one feel more comfortable socially (part of the group, less shy or boring, happier). Teens are hormonally charged for risk, and they see alcohol as exciting, cool and sexy. They like the escape from boredom and their life of school and chores. They want to be like the "cool" guy who sold them the drugs or their music and movie idols who glorify drugs. Some girls take speed to lose weight. Boys may associate alcohol with sex. Kids who are over-controlled or over-protected may use drugs to rebel against their parents (even when they don't really want to). Using drugs and alcohol fits into the norm of the culture they live in. Again, like some of the adults in the culture, kids are looking for "quick fixes" to feel good, especially if they are feeling lonely or depressed and want to numb out painful problems or feelings.

One thing very different about teens is that they drink to get drunk. Although they may use less frequently than adults, when they do drink they consume on average 5 drinks on a single occasion. This is binge drinking and can have serious consequences.[7] There is now a "coming of age" ritual to drink 21 shots on your 21st birthday, which of course can be lethal.

Sex, Lies and Alcohol, a Media Education Foundation video[6] discusses several other causes of drinking that come from cultural norms. For men, there is a bravado pressure to "hold your liquor." Boys will consciously work to raise their alcohol tolerance to avoid being called "girl" or "wuss." They also have drinking competitions to see who can drink the most. Girls are socialized on one hand to be good (get good grades, be a virgin, be nice), yet on the other hand, the media airs messages that being "bad" is attractive, sexy and "cool." Alcohol is the perfect solution: be "good" by day and "bad" by night. It is a way to experiment with sex and still be "innocent" by saying, "It was not my fault. The alcohol made me do it."

Share Information with Your Teen

Parents who can share what they know about the many facets of drug abuse and dependency, and who do so in a non-threatening manner can help provide their kids with the information they need to make good decisions for themselves. We now know that

- Kids who start drinking under 15 are 4 times more likely to become addicted. Every day the first drink is delayed is a plus. Age of first use is also associated with a variety of other problems, including early and unwanted pregnancy, depression and suicide. [8]

- Alcohol-dependent teens have impaired memory, altered perception of spatial relationships, and verbal skill deficiency even when not actually drinking.[9]
- Alcohol poisoning can look similar to being drunk. Knowing the difference can save their friends' lives. Signs are confusion, stupor, coma, not responding to pinching of the skin, vomiting or urinating while sleeping, breathing slowly 8 times/minute or breathing irregularly with 10 seconds between breaths, and low body temperature where the skin is cool, clammy and looks pale or somewhat blue. Do not put a friend to bed in this state. Stay with them, protect them from vomiting, and call 911.
- Acquaintance rape is now such a common occurrence that colleges encourage their new students to have buddies who watch out for each other at a party. Teach this system to your teen, even if they aren't planning on drinking. Some girls get so drunk (or are drugged) that they are not even sure what happened when they wake up the next morning.

Understand That Drug Use Exists Along a Continuum from Benign to Crippling

The drug use continuum stretches from abstinence, experimental use, social use, regular use, and problem use to chemical dependency. It is important for anyone who wishes to monitor the results of their own drug use to understand where they lie within the continuum of use. Although most parents would like their kids to choose abstinence, it is unlikely that most kids will choose this path (again look at the rates of use in your community and high schools). Parents can have conversations with their kids about the progressive nature of chemical dependency and about the responsibility of each person to monitor their own drug-using behaviors. Teens can learn that it's OK to get help before they hit bottom. They can choose to learn from their mistakes, change to a different level of drug use, or get into treatment for problem drug behaviors. This is more likely to happen if parents are willing to keep a door open for honest, non-punitive discussions, even if they don't agree with the choices their children have made.

Beautiful Boy: A Father's Journey Through his Son's Addiction gives insight into teen drug abuse. David Sheff recounts how he first found his son using pot at 13 and thought things were OK until he discovered he had lost his son to meth at 18. He shares the long, agonizing struggle to get him back. His 25 year-old son, clean for 2 years, shares his version of the experience in *Tweak*,

including the sordid details of turning to prostitution for drugs and serious infections from dirty needles.

Share Your Values

It is important to be honest about your own values when it comes to drugs. However, sharing values is not the same as imposing them on your children, and "imposing" your values on your kids is impossible anyway. Most importantly, it is critical to model the responsible behaviors you want your child to have with regard to drugs, and to think about long-term strategies that will protect your child. Having a plan to pick up a child who is intoxicated without fear of punishment or reprisals, for example, can save lives. Teaching kids to be responsible with their behaviors must take precedence over controlling their behaviors. Denial creates an environment where kids can be ignorant of the dangers of alcohol and drug use and can be fatal.

Give Teens a Safe Place to Learn from Their Mistakes

The only true way to protect kids from chemical dependency is to allow them a safe place to work out on their own how they feel about using drugs. Kids will either be open about their drug use or they will hide it; much will depend on the relationship they have with their parents. Supporters of connected parenting believe that parents are much more likely to be able to influence their teenagers if they have a respectful, honest, and open relationship with their teen. This includes not over-reacting to a mistake about drug use, respecting the dignity of their teen and having faith in the ability of their teen to learn from their experiences and use what they have learned to help them to make healthy choices.

Foster Emotional Honesty

Emotional honesty helps parents to achieve connection with their teen without trying to control or abandon them. This skill must be learned and practiced. Putting an arm around a teen, admitting your own fears, and asking them to help you understand what is going on for them is not the same as condoning negative behaviors. But it does let the teen know that you love them and are curious about them, and that you respect their ability to process how their behaviors are affecting their own lives. Listening to your teen's point of view does not mean that you agree with them. It DOES mean that you show them that you are interested in understanding their world.

Use Long-Term Parenting Strategies

Parents who are clear about their long-term parenting goals can more easily enact strategies that may be difficult for parents in the short term. Empowerment is a long-term parenting strategy that helps kids develop self-discipline and responsibility. Supporting kids in their strengths and refusing to support them in their weaknesses is the key to empowering teens, especially when it comes to chemical abuse. Another long-term parenting strategy is to decide what YOU will do, discuss this with your child in a kind, firm and non-punitive way, and be especially careful to carry through on your own commitments. This teaches children to be accountable, trustworthy and in charge of their own behaviors, since you are not trying to control theirs.

When it comes to substance abuse, we can parent a bit differently for younger (under 16) versus older (16 and up) teens. Because drugs can be so devastating on a young teen brain, we can use more clear boundaries to delay use every day we can. When our teens are older and autonomy is even more important, clarity, connection and good "coaching" questions to help them think through situations will be more effective tools. Kids appreciate and value your full honesty. Honesty about "Our family rules and values are for health and not doing drugs or alcohol. We also know we can't stop you if you decide to drink or do drugs. That will be your decision. What we can share with you is that every day you wait is better for your brain."

Long-term parenting strategies are not easy, and come only with study, contemplation and practice. The reward is a child who possesses the internal skills to make good choices for themselves when faced by the myriad of bad choices available to them in a free, democratic society.

Don't Rescue or Buffer Children from the Consequences of Their Behaviors

Learning to have faith in teenagers to make their own decisions also means you have to learn not to rescue or buffer them from the negative results of their own choices. Letting children start this learning process early in their lives will mean that they have lots of experience with good decision-making skills before they have easy access to drugs and alcohol. This also means not abandoning them if they do get into trouble. Being a supportive presence while they figure out how to extricate themselves from the mess they have made teaches kids self-discipline and responsibility. Loving kids in spite of their mistakes and not taking their behaviors personally will help kids to navigate the world successfully.

Allow for Differences

It is highly unlikely that your kids will feel just like you do when it comes to drugs and alcohol, primarily because you have had a lifetime of experiences upon which to base your opinions. Your kids also will need life experiences upon which to base their own opinions. Respecting differences will go a long way towards keeping communication open and honest between you.

Show Love and Unconditional Acceptance

The message of love and unconditional acceptance in spite of behaviors or differences can go a long way towards minimizing the effects of drugs and alcohol in the lives of children. Appreciating your child's uniqueness and place in the family can take many forms, but does take some conscious thought.

Some Specific Ideas Helpful to Reduce Substance Abuse and Dangerous Behavior:

- Have your child sign a Contract for Life before they get a driver's license—see last article of this chapter.
- Never let other people's underage kids drink in your home (even at 20). Not only are you potentially encouraging alcohol dependency and damage, you might lose all financial security from a civil lawsuit if something happens to that kid.
- Remove alcohol from your home: Since up to 70% of alcohol comes from kids' homes, remove it from yours (and encourage other families to do the same).
- Let your kid know if there are any incidents with drugs or alcohol there will be a delay of their driver's permit/license.

Create a network of support with other parents, since given our kids' brain development, some might not be able to make sound decisions, even when good information is shared with them. The frontal lobe that gives people the ability to have good judgment and make long-term plans is poorly developed in teens until they are 18-25 years of age. Consider connecting with people with "mature frontal lobes," parents, especially parents of your child's friends. Meet monthly with parents of your child's friends to discuss timely topics. Then if there is "an incident," you have already established trusted relationships. Start this as early as you can, even when kids are in 5th grade.

Host talks through the local high school PTA to share information with other parents. A great panel to present to both parents and kids 6th grade and up is: trauma nurse or doctor[10], lawyer, policeman and representative from your state Liquor Control Commission. One mom found that having her 15-year-old son and his friends attend this panel discussion helped her enforce the "We will not have kids underage drinking in our home" even into the college years. Her son understood the threat of a lawsuit better than the threat to a friend's health.

Community Support to Address Substance Abuse

If "nothing else to do" is a cause of teen drinking, help your community to create safe spaces and teen-friendly activities, like teen-run coffee shops with weekend entertainment by high school performers.

The message teens receive when alcohol advertising is pervasive throughout the community landscape is that drinking is central to a desirable life. Not only is it acceptable, it is expected. The linking of community events to alcohol through sponsorship also sends teens the message that alcohol is integral to fun and community. You can work with others in your town or city to reduce the impact of the alcohol industry on local teens by educating the community and lobbying local government officials to restrict location, content and pervasiveness of outdoor advertising as well as minimizing or eliminating alcohol industry sponsorship of events.

Know When to Get Help

Getting help is a wise investment in a family's health. Few sport teams can thrive without a coach, and there are times when any family may need coaching to learn new skills, see new perspectives and learn from its mistakes. When drug or alcohol use enters into routine, problem or addictive use, families will benefit from help that is available in many forms in the community. Accepting help does not mean failure; it means that a family is dedicated to optimum health for everyone.

Look for the Signs of Addiction, and Get Help

The attitude of an adolescent who is chemically dependent is very different from that of normal teenagers, who have periods of moodiness and unhappiness interspersed with equally long periods of time when they are engaging and happy.

Chemically dependent persons also have difficulty expressing feelings, look for external rather than internal positive strokes, and are willing to continue doing what doesn't work over and over and over. A pattern of thinking and acting in these ways leads to a desire to numb feelings, and drugs and alcohol are often the treatment of choice for such teens. Seeking professional help for chemically dependent teens can be life-saving. Although it would be nice to believe that parents could send kids off for a miracle "cure," it is more likely that the whole family will benefit from family counseling. Chemical dependence develops within a web of relationships at home and in the community; helping your child may entail learning some new ways of relating with each other at home. It is also helpful to have support from a professional with expertise in teen substance abuse and to enlist her advice so that you can create a home environment that will facilitate your child's return to sobriety.

If you are concerned about your teen's drug or alcohol use, you can tell your daughter that you are worried and you want her to give herself honest answers about the following questions that indicate a chemical dependency. It is important to remember that a very common symptom of alcoholism is denial, sometimes lasting decades.

- Do you find yourself lying about your use to friends, family and yourself?
- Are others concerned about your use?
- Do you plan your days around your "next high," at the expense of other things you want to do (schoolwork, friends, and/or sports)?
- Do you use in the morning?
- Can you "handle your liquor" better than your friends?
- Have you had a "run in" with the police?
- Have you continued to use in spite of past problems like fights, lost items, arguments?
- Are you getting drunk/high on a regular basis and experiencing hangovers or "blackouts"—forgetting what you did while using?
- For you, are drugs necessary to have fun?

- Are you feeling run-down and depressed?
- Is alcohol interfering with your life in any way?

If you answered "Yes" to 3 or more of these questions, it is time to get an evaluation from an addiction specialist. Often the whole family gets involved in the solution.

Have Faith

It is important for parents to remember that they themselves are successful survivors of adolescence. Indeed, most teenagers grow up and do not remain as adults who they are as teenagers. Growing up in an empowering and loving environment can make the adolescent journey less harrowing. Parents who have faith in their teens can increase the chances that their teen will avoid a pattern of drug abuse, because they are communicating to their teen faith in their ability to make choices, to learn from their own experiences and to function successfully in this world of many temptations. Trust does not mean sticking your head in the sand. Parents who are able to "let go," not only keep open communication and continue to check in with their teens, but also trust that their teen can handle challenging situations and learn from the mistakes he or she makes. These parents trust that their teen is constantly evolving, growing up into a wonderful person.

Resources:
[1] *Positive Discipline for Teenagers: Resolving Conflict with your Teenage Son or Daughter* (1st Ed), and *Positive Discipline for Teenagers: Empowering your Teen and Yourself Through Kind and Firm Parenting*, 2000 by Jane Nelsen & Lynn Lott.
[2] *Reality Matters: Under the Influence*, Discovery Education, 2005
[3] Grant, BF, *Estimates of US Children exposed to alcohol abuse/ dependency in families*. Am J Public Health 90 (1): 112-115.
[4] Dunn ME, Goldman MS, 1998. *Age and drinking related differences in the memory organization of alcohol expectancies in 3rd, 6th, 9th, 12th graders*. Consult Clin Psychol 66 (3): 579-85.
[5] Substance Abuse and Mental Health Services Administration, *2005 National Survey on Drug and Health*
[6] *Sex, Lies and Alcohol* from Media Education Foundation video. See www.mediaed.org for discussion guides.
[7] *The Surgeon General's Call to Action: To Prevent and Reduce Underage Drinking: What It Means to You*. www.surgeon general.gov/topics/underagedrinking/FamilyGuide.pdf
[8] Grant, BF, Dawson DA, 1997, *Age of onset of alcohol use and its association with DSM-IV alcohol abuse and dependence:* Results from the National Longitudinal Alcohol Epidemiologic Survey. J Subst Abuse 9: 103-110.
[9] Brown, SA, Tapert SF, Granholm E, Delis, DC, 2000, *Neurocognitive functioning of adolescence: Effect of protracted alcohol use*. Alcohol Clin Exp Res 24 (2): 164-171.
[10] *Not My Kid* Presentation by Legacy's Trauma Nurses Who Talk Tough, www.legacyhealth.org/tntt.

FOR PARENTS TO LOOK AT THEIR OWN USE

Alcoholics Anonymous

Alcoholics Anonymous, Families Anonymous, Al-anon and Alateen are all fantastic support structures for anyone who is struggling with alcohol themselves or alcoholics in their lives.

www.aa.org   www.alanon.org.
www.familiesanonymous.org
www.al-alon.alateen.org/questions.html

Twenty Questions to Evaluate if You're an Alcoholic

www.step12.com/alcoholic-20-questions.html

Take this 20-question test to help you decide whether or not you are an alcoholic.

1. Do you lose time from work due to drinking?
2. Is drinking making your home life unhappy?
3. Do you drink because you are shy with other people?
4. Is your drinking affecting your reputation?
5. Have you ever felt remorse after drinking?
6. Have you ever got into financial difficulties as a result of drinking?
7. Do you turn to lower companions and an inferior environment when drinking?
8. Does your drinking make you careless of your family's welfare?
9. Has your ambition decreased since drinking?
10. Do you crave a drink at a definite time?
11. Do you want a drink the next morning?
12. Does drinking cause you to have difficulty in sleeping?
13. Has your efficiency decreased since drinking?
14. Is drinking jeopardizing your job or business?
15. Do you drink to escape from worries or trouble?
16. Do you drink alone?
17. Have you ever had a complete loss of memory as a result of drinking?
18. Has your physician ever treated you for drinking?
19. Do you drink to build up your self-confidence?
20. Have you ever been to a hospital or institution because of drinking?

What's your score?
- If you have answered YES to any one of the questions, there is a definite warning that you may be an alcoholic.
- If you have answered YES to any two, the chances are that you are an alcoholic.
- If you answered YES to three or more, you are definitely an alcoholic.

Dear Parenting Guide Participant,
You can make an impact in your community! Here is a letter you can encourage to be inserted into your high school's "Back to School" package. It is an effective way to share information and network your high school community to reduce teen drug and alcohol use.

Safe Teen Parties in Your Home: *"It takes a village to raise a child."*

Dear Parents: This note is a vehicle to network our community to work together to reduce the impact of drug and alcohol use in our teens. This sheet addresses common pitfalls. By coming together, we can create a community where substance access and places to have unsupervised parties are reduced. After signing this form, an asterisk will be placed by your teen's name in the student directory to distinguish you as a family who will do your best to keep your home safe from teenage drug/ alcohol use.

Thank you,   HS principal _____ and PTA president or HS Safety Committee: _____

- Model respectful use of alcohol and prescription drugs in your home.
- Ideally, remove the alcohol and prescription drugs from your house (up to 70% of alcohol teens use comes from their own home).
- Don't leave teens home alone without adult supervision, especially over the weekend. A party of 80 can happen in 1-2 hours with cell phones.
- If you do go away for the weekend, be sure to ask all of your direct neighbors to keep an eye on the house. Also ask an adult friend your teen likes or a neighbor, if they would support your teen in a dangerous or difficult situation.
- Be aware of where your child is when he/she goes out. Call parents where parties are held.
- Know your teen's friends and his/her parents. Make a point of keeping in touch with these parents. Communicating and connecting with each other is ESSENTIAL. Our kids will benefit if we network as effectively as they do.
- Hold your child accountable for his/her behavior. Many parents remove car privileges when their child abuses alcohol or drugs.
- Do not serve alcohol to other teens in your home. It is not "safer." Teens brains are more susceptible to damage and addiction than adults at all ages up to 21 years-old (especially if <15). Also, if something happens to that teen, you are libel and can lose your assets in a civil lawsuit.

Tips for parents whose teen is planning a party
- Make a guest list and stick to it (uninvited guest are not allowed to attend the party).
- Restrict entry and exit areas to deter guests from bringing in contraband or drinking out in their parked car or from a bottle hidden in the yard.
- Establish one area for coats and bags and monitor it.
- Set a beginning and end time to the party.
- Make it clear to your teen and all the guests that alcohol and other drugs are not allowed. Put away your alcohol, valuables, weapons, and breakables.
- Define an area for the party; do not allow party-goers in other areas (bedrooms, garages, etc.).
- Have sufficient chaperones to monitor the areas and the partygoers. Frequently monitor the party area as well as areas that are off-limits to guests.
- Establish a signal that your child may use if he/she needs help. For example, when your child says, "Sorry I forgot to take out the garbage" on the phone, it can be code for, "Come pick me up right now." Another example is: pulling at his/her ear when asking to spend the night is code for you to say, "No."
- Be prepared to call a guest's parents if he/she appears to be "under the influence" or brings alcohol or drugs to the party.

--*Cut here*--

PLEASE SIGN HERE AND YOUR FAMILY HOME WILL BE DESIGNATED AS A "SAFE HOME"
I have read the Safe Home guidelines and will do my best to prevent teenage drug and alcohol use in my home.
Please put an asterisk by my family's name in the student directory so others will be aware of our commitment.

Name _____ Date _____

Facts about Risky Driving and Graduated Licensing

- The best, most well-intentioned teenager can makes poor decisions and exhibit inappropriate behavior, especially when under the influence of alcohol and other drugs.

- 10,000 sixteen-year-olds die every decade because of driving under the influence of immaturity & inexperience.
- One American teenager dies every three hours in an alcohol- or drug-related crash.
- Approximately 450,000 teens/year are arrested for driving under the influence of intoxicants.
- 67% of fatal teenage crashes had another teen driving.
- Teens can be sued and a 20-year judgment filed.
- Every weeknight from 1 pm-1 am, 1 of 13 drivers are drunk.
- On weekends from 1 am-6 am, 1 of 7 drivers are drunk.
- Remember the highest risk for young drivers is at night or with other teens in their car. This is when peer pressure can lead to immature, dangerous behavior.

Graduated Licensing: Insurance Institute for Highway Safety Recommends:

- 200 hours or 6000 miles to be logged by the teen before they are granted privilege as principle driver.
- Graduated licensing: Systematic & progressive, it limits opportunities for immature behavior. Peer pressure can lead ANY teenager to ignore rules set by adults. The highest risks for young drivers are: driving at night or with other teens in the car. This is when peer pressure is most likely to lead to immature and dangerous behavior. Oregon has a good model for graduated licensing which parents can use with their own family.
- Teach teen passengers to remain awake to help the driver stay alert. Fatigue is a major contributor to car crashes.

Graduated Licensing in Oregon: A Good Example for Everyone

To get this started in your state, contact your state's Department of Motor Vehicles or government officials.

The Law	Beyond the Law
LAW: Six months of driving with a permit.	Parents may want to extend this time frame.
LAW: At least 50 hours of adult-supervised (older than 21) training plus a safety course, or an additional 50 hours of adult-supervised training. Keep a driver's log to document this.	Parents riding with a young driver after 50-100 hours who find they still need to caution the young driver about speed, signals, tailgating, traffic conditions, weather conditions, etc., may want to increase the hours of supervised driving.
LAW: In the first six months, a teen can carry no one younger than 20-years-old, except immediate family.	It might be safer without siblings as they may be the hardest to control of ALL. Reminder: Licensing a teen to make life more convenient for parents is not advisable.
LAW: In the second six months, a teen can carry no more than three passengers younger than 20, except family.	When adding passengers, parents can expand beyond the law to allow ONLY ONE passenger for three months and add additional passengers SLOWLY.
LAW: Curfew between Midnight and 5:00 am unless it is work-related, to or from a school event, or with a licensed driver 25 or older.	47% of crashes involving teenage drivers occur between 9:00 pm and 6:00 am.

Reprinted with permission from the *"NOT MY KID"* Campaign Parent Handbook. Materials and Program made possible through funds from ODOT, TSD and NSTSA Section 410 Grant, and "Trauma Nurses Talk Tough: Family Education." www.legacyhealth.org/tntt

Contract for Life

A Foundation for Trust and Caring

This Contract is designed to facilitate communication between young people and their parents about potentially destructive decisions related to alcohol, drugs, peer pressure, and behavior. The issues facing young people today are often too difficult for them to address alone. SADD believes that effective parent-child communication is critically important in helping young adults to make healthy decisions.

Young Person

I recognize that there are many potentially destructive decisions I face every day and commit to you that I will do everything in my power to avoid making decisions that will jeopardize my health, my safety and overall well-being, or your trust in me. I understand the dangers associated with the use of alcohol and drugs and the destructive behaviors often associated with impairment.

By signing below, I pledge my best effort to remain free from alcohol and drugs; I agree that I will never drive under the influence; I agree that I will never ride with an impaired driver; and I agree that I will always wear a seat belt in a moving car.

Finally, I agree to call you if I am ever in a situation that threatens my safety and to communicate with you regularly about issues of importance to both of us.

_____

Young Person

Parent (or Caring Adult)

I am committed to you and to your health and safety. By signing below, I pledge to do everything in my power to understand and communicate with you about the many difficult and potentially destructive decisions you face.

Further, I agree to provide for you safe, sober transportation home if you are ever in a situation that threatens your safety and to defer discussions about that situation until a time when we can both have a discussion in a calm and caring manner.*

I also pledge to you that I will not drive under the influence of alcohol or drugs, I will always seek safe, sober transportation home, and I will always wear a seat belt.

_____

Parent/Caring Adult

Editors Note: We have permission to use the contract as it is written above. Consider altering it to offer your teen an "unconditional" ride home. Perhaps even make an arrangement with a cab company or a caring neighbor to drive him or her home. If safety is your top priority, do not put up any barriers that would decrease the chance of your teens taking you up on your offer to get home safely.

Reprinted with permission of SADD, Inc. SADD–Students Against Destructive Decisions is "students helping students make positive decisions about challenges in their everyday life" with many great resources at www.sadd.org.

Lindsay Nelson, 8th Grade, Rosemont Ridge Middle School

Supporting Her

> *"I love you not only for what you are, but for what I am when I am with you. I love you not only for what you have made of yourself, but for what you are making of me. I love you for the part of me that you bring out."*
> —Elizabeth Barrett Browning

> *"To the world you may be one person, but to one person you may be the world."*
> —Heather Cortez

> *"Physical fitness is not only one of the most important keys to a healthy body; it is the basis of dynamic and creative intellectual challenge."* —John F. Kennedy

> *"In our present cultural environment, sports may well be the best antidote for the body preoccupations that squelch the creativity of so many American girls. Even as toddlers, we need to encourage the idea that what your body can do is far more important that what it looks like."*
> —Joan Jacobs Brumberg, author of *The Body Project*

GOALS

- To understand the value of "safe havens" where your daughter can be her authentic self and be accepted

- To appreciate the value of including other adults in your daughter's life and the benefits of rites of passage celebrations

- To see sports activities and exercise as a way to achieve physical fitness, mental and emotional well-being, and to encourage all girls to do some form of exercise

- To encourage trainings where coaches and parents can learn about developmentally appropriate expectations, making sports fun, and the importance of encouraging all athletes equally

- To encourage team sports where team work, discipline, and a sense of fair play are more important than winning

OVERVIEW

Connected, engaged, and committed communities and families are more likely to raise kids who are resilient and successful at transitioning from adolescence to adulthood. Strengthening the connections and commitments between children and adults within a community supports the healthy development of all our children and is the cornerstone of the Search Institute's Developmental Asset program. One way that parents can build assets in their daughter's life is to make sure that she becomes involved in supportive community activities that involve cooperation, build on her strengths, and expose her to a diversity of people of all ages, races, abilities and genders. By encouraging honest and healthy relationships with others, parents can help their daughters build positive visions of themselves, their capabilities, and their futures as valued members of a caring community.

This chapter focuses on supporting our daughters within their community by involving them in support groups, mentoring relationships, coming of age rituals, fitness and sports. These activities have in common an opportunity for your daughter to develop genuine, caring and honest relationships with herself, as well as with others in her community. A girl can feel both acceptance and a strong sense of belonging when she becomes an essential part of a special relationship, a community ritual, a team effort, or a group that meets regularly to share some kind of mutual hobby or interest. This strengthens her ability to know and trust herself and to be honest, genuine and comfortable in her relationships with others. This really pays off during adolescence, when a child's ability to make good choices depends upon having a strong sense of self, a positive view of her place in the world, and a safety net of valued, involved mentors and family friends who can help her set a course of moderation through stormy adolescent waters.

Empowerment Groups

Support groups for girls take many forms and can be created by anyone with a sincere desire to engage girls in enjoyable and enriching activities. Such support groups provide a safe haven for girls to bond, interact and have fun together, while encouraging positive values and healthy relationships. Group activities geared specifically for girls can be found within child advocacy organizations such as the Girl Scouts of America, Camp Fire, and the YWCA. Younger girls especially seem to like the activities and camps offered by these organizations. However, since children often lose interest as they mature, it may be up to you to find or create an appropriate support group for your daughter. Any group that meets regularly over time will become an important source of support, acceptance and enrichment for her.

Over the last fifteen years we have seen the blossoming of girls' empowerment groups designed specifically to give girls a chance to have a voice and to listen to others' voices. These groups create a setting where girls can be their authentic selves and examine their feelings and the realities of growing up in today's world. They are led by school counselors, teachers, parents, young and older adult women and parents, all dedicated to supporting girls to be resilient and thrive.

The first set of articles in this chapter are included to give parents some good examples and guidelines on the kinds of girls' support groups that they can initiate. "Empowerment Groups for Girls" (p. 9:15) shares current research that shows how valuable girls' groups can be in increasing self-efficacy and decreasing self-harm, as well as increasing attachment to school and decreasing alcohol use. "Get Girls Talking Through a Girls' Circle" (p. 9:16) gives a first-hand example of a mother who took the training and led a girls' circle that included her daughter. Girls Circle (www.girlscircle.org) is a tremendous resource for anyone—teen or adult—who would like to create community for girls. They offer several books and ideas for starting girls' groups. Rosalind Wiseman, author of *Queen Bees and Wannabees,* has designed a curriculum for a girls' group called "Owning Up" (www.rosalindwiseman.com). Girls Inc. (www.girlsinc.org) also offers several ideas on their website and trainings for leaders.

Mother-daughter groups are a particularly important medium for bonding with our daughters. SuEllen Hamkins and Renee Schultz, in their book *The Mother-Daughter Project* (www.themother-daughterproject.com), explain how mothers and daughters banding together can help our girls remain strong, confident, and whole through adolescence. They began a monthly mother's group and then a monthly mother-daughter group when their daughters were 7. The book details the activities they did with their daughters from age 7 to age 17. The article **"The Mother-Daughter Project: Start Your Own Mother-Daughter Group"** (p. 9:17) will help you to create more support for both you and your daughter. Mother-daughter book clubs are also a fun and satisfying way to bond with your daughter and provide her (and yourself) with a greater community (see *Mother-Daughter Book Club* or *100 Books for Girls to Grow On* by Shireen Dodson). Another example of a great mother-daughter group geared for 5th or 6th graders is the Choices Program (advocacypress@girlsinc. org). One activity in this program has girls looking for jobs in the paper, renting or buying houses within their incomes, making budgets and thinking about how they will support themselves and their families in the future. Mothers share with the group their own adolescent experiences and concerns, creating a bond between members that often lasts well into the high school years.

Parents or adults who are willing to commit to an activity with a group of girls over time can have an enormously positive impact on the lives of these girls by simply caring about them and sharing in life's lessons. In addition, such groups offer adults a way to get to know their daughters and neighborhood youth better. For example, discussions that occur at a parent-child activity can be a great tool for parents to better understand how their daughter and her friends view the world. Hiking, biking or sports clubs that meet after school or on the weekends can be very popular with girls and are a fun way to share physical activity with youth. Churches and synagogues often have youth groups and activities already in place and they often welcome kids from their community regardless of religious denomination. You can get a feel for the flavor of any established program by talking to the leaders and the families already involved in the program. **"Safe**

Havens: Support Groups for Youth" (p. 9:18) reviews many ways that you can help girls get involved with groups in the community where they feel accepted for who they are.

School remains another arena where girls benefit from additional support, especially if they are in an environment where bullying or relational aggression is a problem. Lunchtime activities, clubs, intramural sports and after-school activities sponsored by the school or by interested parents can be an exceptional way to give kids a place to feel at home and to bond to school and to other teens. Since bonding to school is a critical protective factor for teens, it is wise for parents to encourage their children to take advantage of extracurricular activities at school. Finding or creating supportive activities within your community in which your daughter can participate may take some creativity and time, but the rewards of giving your daughter a sense of belonging far outweigh the effort.

Mentoring

The Search Institute has shown that young people do better if they have 3 or more non-parent adults in their lives from whom they receive support, care, guidance and advocacy. Other organizations have demonstrated similar findings. The Big Brothers/ Big Sisters of America found that young people with mentors are about one-half as likely to use illegal drugs or skip school and about one-quarter as likely to use alcohol. Unfortunately, few of our youth benefit from adult mentoring. A 1997 Multnomah County, Oregon survey of 10,000 youth found that only one-quarter of kids surveyed could identify an adult they looked up to as a role model, and 6 in 10 had no adults other than parents involved in their lives. These results correlate closely with the Search Institute's national findings in their Developmental Asset research.

A mentor can be any caring adult who makes an active, positive contribution to the life of a child who is not his or her own. A mentor can be anyone who has experienced life and who cares enough to pass their own lessons along to a young person in a supportive way. A mentor is a friend, a guide, a coach. He or she may be a grandma, an uncle, a neighbor, a co-worker, a sport coach, a family friend, or someone down the street who shares an interest with your child. Sometimes mentoring relationships develop naturally; however, parents may need to actively seek out an appropriate adult and set up a formal mentoring relationship for their daughter. This may feel awkward at first, but the rewards are manifold.

Stan Crow trains people all over the US on mentoring and rites of passage programs and helps run the Rites of Passage Journeys program in Washington. He eloquently defines a mentor as one who is a "journey master, one who takes a measure of responsibility for this other person." The article **"How Girls Benefit from Having Mentors in their Lives"** (p. 9:20) explains how to mentor teen girls through thirteen serious yet common life crises. **"Teenagers Can Be Mentors, Too"** (p. 9:25) reminds us that teenagers can feel the same sense of competence, generosity, and meaning that we feel when they mentor younger children. Mentoring also helps teens escape from social and academic pressures and remember how to play. Finding a way to become personally involved with youth and parents within your community as a mentor will enrich your own life and your teen's life, as well as the lives of others in your community.

Coming of Age Rituals

Parents may wonder why coming of age rituals are presented here as a way to support your daughter's development. **"Cherishing Teens Reconnects Communities: The Power of Coming of Age Ceremonies"** (p. 9:26) reviews the historical and modern day importance of these rituals. Most indigenous societies from around the globe mark the passage of their members from the world of childhood into the benefits, freedoms, restrictions and responsibilities of adulthood with some sort of community ritual. Traditionally, a coming of age ceremony has been an important milestone for youth. In the process, young people understand that they are an important member of a larger community and experience within themselves a newfound capacity for increased decision-making, responsibility, and accountability for their own actions.

Our American melting pot has resulted in the loss of any common ritual that marks the beginning of a girl's journey towards womanhood and that establishes her as an important member of our society. Girls, however, yearn for proof of their adulthood. As a result, young women have largely replaced community coming of age rituals with ones of their own creation: rituals that tend to be harmful and/or dangerous. Activities such as smoking, using drugs, getting drunk, being sexually promiscuous, getting pregnant, driving and other high-risk activities tend to be used as proof of adulthood by youth in our culture. Unfortunately, these behaviors are often carried out without community sanction and without any thought as to the impact of these actions upon self or others. Wouldn't it be better to acknowledge the milestone of emerging womanhood in our daughters by creating a ritual that surrounds our girls with caring women and family members and helps our daughters to see themselves as capable, compassionate and responsible?

One of the few examples of a coming of age ritual that has survived through the ages in America is the Jewish practice of Bat Mitzvah. This ceremony initiates girls into their faith as full-fledged members at age 13, requiring a period of study, reflection and instruction prior to the ceremony. Parents of other faiths may have to create their own coming of age rituals to mark one of their daughter's special birthdays or milestones. Two families describe their unique ways of welcoming their daughters into young adulthood in the articles **"Coming of Age Book: Gifts from Wise Women to Honor a New Phase of Life"** and **"Coming of Age Quilt"** (pp. 9:28-29). Wisdom Quilt (www.wisdomquilts.com) is a resource for families who would like to use quilting as a way to teach the values of peace, creativity and community, as well as create new family rituals.

There are many ways in which we can help teens celebrate this transition. Other examples include a special gathering of mentors who pledge to support a girl in her passage to adulthood, a mother/daughter wilderness adventure, a year-long study and support group, a church-sponsored program, or a specially designed experience offered by an organization which specializes in rites of passage for youth. "**Lessons of Nature**" (p. 9:30) will give you ideas of how to use the natural world for inspiration and analogy in a ritual of your own creation.

Finding a coming of age ritual that fits within your own family circumstances and is reflective of your daughter's personality and preferences is a work of creativity and love. Your daughter may not understand or fully appreciate the significance of a coming of age celebration in the moment, but in the long run, it will become a valuable memory, an invitation into the wonders and responsibilities of womanhood, and a reminder, not only of the loving community that surrounds her, but of the strength and goodness of her own special place in the world.

Fitness

A healthy girl is a physically active girl. We support our daughter by cultivating her interest in living an active life. Families, communities, and schools all play a role in teaching our daughters that their bodies were made to move. Families are in the best position to cultivate their daughter's athletic interest by being active together (e.g., tossing a ball, swimming, biking, playing tennis, roller blading), spending lots of time outdoors, giving her equipment of her own, taking her to women's sporting events, limiting screen time, and promoting an active life for fun and fitness rather than competition and slimness. Remember that the experiences our daughters have in the first 12 years of their lives become part of their self-identification: "I enjoy doing … I am good at …" Girls who exercise and play sports see their body functionally, rather than as an ornament. That means better mental health, better physiological health, better social interaction, and more camaraderie for our girls.

The article "**Family Fitness**" (p. 9:31) reminds us that there are many avenues to experience the growth, health, and transformation that can come from physical activities. Modeling commitment to a healthy lifestyle is crucial for our daughters. Families can guide (or don't guide) their children in the many ways to be physically active: active lifestyle, outside play, fitness programs,

individual sports and team sports, to name a few. This section will discuss the importance of fitness to a girl's self-esteem and health, recent research findings, life lessons that sports convey to our daughters, using sports as a vehicle for good communication, and getting the most out of organized sports, including tips for coaches.

Many children thrive in individual sports and these sports often have much more lasting value over a lifetime. Parents can find out what kinds of non-competitive sports and activities are available in their community. Club sports, intramural leagues, recreational leagues, the YWCA, and parent- or student-led activity groups are a few alternatives to more organized sports. "**Sports Clubs Can Lead to Lifelong Enjoyment**" (p. 9:32) reminds us that we can create our own sports clubs that are truly family-friendly and fun. Some elementary schools are using *Girls on the Run* (www.girlsontherun. org) to teach girls about self-respect and healthy living through running.

Participation in sports is a vehicle for healthy child development. Although a lot of the research has been done on organized sports, the results are relevant for all physically active people. At their best, sports promote responsible social behaviors, greater academic success, confidence in one's physical abilities, an appreciation of personal health and fitness, and strong social bonds with individuals and institutions. The discipline and work ethic that sports require can be of benefit throughout one's life. Sports provide a venue for helping young people work toward an ethical understanding of fair play, sportsmanship, integrity and compassion. "**How Girls Win Self-Esteem**" (p. 9:33) describes how playing sports can help create stronger, more confident and powerful girls who have the skills to think strategically, take risks, and work cooperatively toward a common goal.

The Women's Sports Foundation (www.womensports foundation.org), in cooperation with Harris Interactive, recently completed a comprehensive nationwide survey, which provides us an inside view of girls' (and boys') participation in physical activities. "**Go Out and Play**" (p. 9:36) reports many of these findings. The report confirms that youth sports are a satisfying resource for families, and that they are linked to improved physical and emotional health, academic achievement and quality of life. They find that there is still a gender gap for physical activity and sports participation between boys and girls, but primarily in urban areas. For example, the National Federation of State High School Associations (2003) reported that nearly 1 of 2 boys participate in high school sports and only 1 out of 3 girls. (Before Title IX, however, girls' participation in sports was 1 in 27!) Research shows, however, that girls do take part in a wider *array* of sports and exercise than boys. The report also clearly states that interest in sports and exercise is about opportunity and encouragement rather than gender.

Every girl deserves the opportunity to be healthy and physically fit, but the solutions to the gender gap are often complex. The following are some things that interfere with girls' involvement in an active lifestyle, according to the Women's Sports Foundation:

- Working parents often insist that their daughters stay inside after school.
- Screen time of all sorts precludes physical activity.
- Recess and physical education are disappearing from many schools.
- Parents worry about the safety of their daughters staying after school for exercise.
- Many of our youth sports programs are male-oriented.
- When available space for exercise and athletic programs is limited, boys' programs win out.
- Girls may not have role models for being fit.

There is a dramatically clear relationship between female health and physical activity. The Women's Sports Foundation has summarized the medical research as follows:

- Exercise during a woman's reproductive lifetime lowers the risk of breast cancer.
- Female athletes are significantly less likely to smoke.
- Female athletes are less likely to use most illicit drugs.
- Female athletes are less likely to be sexually active

or get pregnant.
- Women and girls who participate in regular exercise suffer lower rates of depression.
- Female athletes have a lower probability of considering or planning a suicide attempt.

Active girls are also less likely to have problems as adults with obesity, high blood pressure, elevated cholesterol levels and sedentary lifestyle. Not only does physical activity develop muscle tone, strength, and aerobic capacity, it also provides girls with heightened natural defenses against the ravages of stress and sleep disorders.

Girls in high school sports have higher educational aspirations in the senior year, better school attendance, higher math, science, and honor class enrollment and spend more time on homework. High school athletes are often required to sign contracts saying they will not use drugs or alcohol during the season, which supports them in making healthier choices. Furthermore, the relationship between physical activity and positive physical and mental health is firmly established. Getting girls involved in fitness, therefore, warrants the serious attention of parents, educators, sports leaders, and public health officials, as a way to head off the daunting risks adolescent girls face.

Youth sports can be a wonderful vehicle to improve your communication with your daughter. **"Tell Me More: Connecting through Sport Talk"** (p. 9:38) is one of the best articles we have seen on giving parents specific ways to communicate with their children that will work with any topic of discussion. Sports and fitness activities are best used as a tool for learning life-long lessons, as one gifted coach tells us in the article **"Learning Life Lessons through Sports"** (p. 9:40). This dad coach shares that team-building, working effectively with others, and encouraging one another are all lessons that can be learned through team experience. In fact, sports offer our youth rich experience through which to mature socially, morally and emotionally.

Organized sports have largely displaced the neighborhood "pick up games" of the past, where young children spent hours playing games, making up and enforcing their own rules and generally spending time together learning about each other and fair play. Skills of leadership, collaboration, cooperation, communication and organization grew out of this informal, peer-organized sport play. Many of today's kids, who are so used to being organized by adults, don't even consider organizing physical play on their own. However, some children will take this on. Be grateful if your child is one who does, and encourage any steps towards this peer-generated play, as the skills that are developed and practiced will be beneficial through life.

Honor the Athlete/Honor the Game

As mentioned, there are many benefits to organized sports but because recruitment of children for teams happens very early, we as parents must be aware of the issue of developmental appropriateness. Elementary school-aged children are developing a cognitive understanding of complex concepts such as the difference between ability, task difficulty and effort, offensive and defensive strategies, teamwork, and the fact that losing does not mean failure. Children whose parents and coaches focus on skill development during the childhood years attain the positive social, emotional and physical outcomes that we all want to see from their sports experience. Therefore, early childhood involvement in sports should emphasize instruction more than competition and should be based in fostering a love of physical fitness and of "the game" while ensuring that enjoyment remains a primary goal.

Be clear about what you want your girl to learn and gain from sporting activities, and make judicious choices about the organized sport programs that you will allow your kids to be involved with. It pays to look carefully at your daughter's sports programs to be sure they are teaching the values that are important to you. Parents can enhance the quality of sports programs by actively insisting that these positive qualities be incorporated into the structure of their daughter's team sport programs. Parents or programs which are over zealous and overstress the need to win can be especially harmful to youth. No child benefits from feeling that their parents' approval is tied to success in sports. On the contrary, our children benefit from playing the

game for its own sake. Parents who have a talented child are particularly susceptible to getting caught up in the possibility of getting scholarships for their child. The rationale for prolonged training seasons and high intensity training is often to produce optimal performance outcomes. However, the data on burnout and attrition support the contention that for almost all young athletes, such periods of intensive training have no justifiable physiological, psychological or educational benefits.

Attrition is a major problem with organized sporting programs. It is well underway by age 10 and peaks at ages 14-15, such that 50% of all sports participants will drop out by the time they reach early adolescence. The number one reason kids drop out is because "it is no longer fun." The organizational structure of school sports is another cause of this drop off, as school-based team membership and sports offerings can only offer participation to 50% of the kids involved in sports on the non-school level. Should your athlete fail to make the high school team, or if she is not interested in competing at that level, you can research and find out what kinds of non-competitive sports are available in your community.

Tips for a Positive Coaching Experience

Another index of the quality of a child's experience in youth sports is determined by the competence of the coach. Unfortunately, many youth sport coaches do not have the essential skills that are prerequisites for coaching young athletes. Coaching youth requires not only knowledge of specific skill development for the sport in question, but also an awareness of how to effectively work with children at different developmental levels in order to inspire and motivate them while keeping the "big picture" of fun, movement and improvement towards mastery in mind. Most coaches are volunteers with little formal training. This, coupled with a coach turnover rate estimated at 50% per year, leads to many problems with coaches and coaching every year. **"Positive Coaching Alliance"** (p. 9:41) describes an organization that was developed to help coaches and parents "create a positive culture around youth sports." Workshops are carried out by this organization in many cities around the nation to help adults create programs where kids will experience practices and games as fun, and where kids can tap into a joy of playing that will last a lifetime. **"My Life as a Bobcat"** (p. 9:43) describes one coach's growth as a coach as his players grew. **"Asset Building Ideas for Coaches"** (p. 9:44) is an excellent handout to share with your child's coaches and coaching association.

Parents have a powerful role in encouraging their daughters to remain physically active throughout their lives and facilitating participation in sporting activities that will enhance their daughter's overall health and success. Through modeling a lifelong commitment to exercise and physical wellbeing, parents do much of the work to ensure that their daughter will follow suit. Cultivating the spirit of play, age-appropriate skill building, and healthy attitudes toward winning allow our girls to utilize sports as a positive avenue of growth, learning and wellbeing. Whether your daughter is involved in an organized, competitive sports program or not, a critical message for her to receive early in life is that moving her body vigorously and often will allow her to thrive. Being fit will inspire a joyful life in which she will be able to fully offer her gifts to the world.

THE 40 DEVELOPMENTAL ASSETS Essential to Every Young Person's Success

The 40 Developmental Assets are research-proven building blocks that support the healthy development of our youth and help them to grow up to be caring and responsible. The topics in Chapter 9, Supporting Her—support groups, coming of age rituals, mentoring, and fitness—relate directly to more than half of the assets, both internal and external. What you can do is focus on supporting her with external assets that can lead to the blossoming of the internal assets.

- Asset #1 **Family support:** Family life provides high levels of love and support.
- Asset #3 **Other adult relationships:** Young person receives support from three or more nonparent adults.
- Asset #5 **Caring school climate:** School provides a caring, encouraging environment.
- Asset #7 **Community values youth:** Young person perceives that adults in the community value youth.
- Asset #10 **Safety:** Young person feels safe at home, school, and in the neighborhood.
- Asset #14 **Adult role models:** Parent(s) and other adults model positive, responsible behavior.
- Asset #15 **Positive peer influence:** Young person's best friends model responsible behavior.
- Asset #18 **Youth programs:** Young person spends three or more hours per week in sports, clubs, or organizations at school and/or in the community.
- Asset #28 **Integrity:** Young person acts on convictions and stands up for her or his beliefs.
- Asset #29 **Honesty:** Young person "tells the truth even when it is not easy."
- Asset #30 **Responsibility:** Young person accepts and takes personal responsibility.
- Asset #33 **Interpersonal competence:** Young person has empathy, sensitivity, and friendship skills.
- Asset #35 **Resistance skills:** Young person can resist negative peer pressure and dangerous situations.
- Asset #36 **Peaceful conflict resolution:** Young person seeks to resolve conflict nonviolently.
- Asset #37 **Personal power:** Young person feels he or she has control over "things that happen to me."
- Asset #38 **Self-esteem:** Young person reports having a high self-esteem.
- Asset #39 **Sense of purpose:** Young person reports that "my life has a purpose."

CIRCLE QUESTION

Is there a group your daughter belongs to where she can she can be her authentic self? Are there other groups you know about that might be valuable for her?

POSSIBLE DISCUSSION QUESTIONS

1. Would you consider starting a Girls' Circle or a parent-daughter group?
2. Who are the adults your daughter can talk to about important issues and questions? How can you create a sense of extended family that brings many other adults into your children's lives?
3. Share activities in your community that you think are powerful for supporting our youth.
4. Describe important adults in your life when you were growing up and their influence on you.
5. Does your daughter have Developmental Asset *#3 Other Adults Relationships: Young person receives support from three or more nonparent adults* (53% of 150,000 surveyed) or *#4 Caring Neighborhood: Young person experiences caring neighbors* (37% of 150,000 surveyed)?
6. How can your daughter benefit from having other adults in her life? Does this idea bring up hesitations or resistance for you?
7. Did you have a coming of age experience? How might a coming of age event benefit your daughter? How do think you might organize a ceremony or event for your daughter?
8. How do you model fitness for your daughter?
9. What can you do to maximize family activities for bonding and fitness? Share what you do now. Does your family spend more time watching sports (including watching your child) or actively participating in sports?
10. What physical activities is your daughter involved in?
11. Are her activities teaching her teamwork, sportsmanship, integrity, compassion, and sense of fair play, as well as skill development?
12. Discuss examples of adult conduct you have seen before, during, and after a youth sporting event.
13. Are you consistently modeling the moral and ethical behavior you want your daughter to exhibit? Do you help your daughter see the positive values of both winning and losing?
14. Are there coaching clinics available in your area? Does your league use these services? What will you do to promote healthy coach-parent-youth athlete relationships on the next team your daughter is on?
15. Do you make a point to attend field trips, academic events, and school social gatherings as well as your child's athletic events? How does your support for athletic and academic success differ?

PUTTING IT INTO PRACTICE

- Show girls—your own and others you know—you care about them:
  - Give them your time.
  - Look at and greet every girl you see.
  - Talk with girls about their interests.
  - Invite a young people to an activity you think they might enjoy.
  - Welcome neighborhood kids and your daughter's friends into your home.
- Encourage Empowerment Groups at your daughter's school through the school counselor and PTA funds.
- Start a girls' group with your daughter and some of her friends.

- Go to The Mother-Daughter Project website and consider starting a mother-daughter group.
- Involve other adults and families into your daughter's life by planning events with neighborhood or family friends: games, picnics, camping trips, bike rides, and hikes.
- Take part in youth-serving programs through schools, community organizations and churches.
- Invite caring adults and mentors into your daughter's life. Trust them.
- Imagine and create a coming of age event or ceremony for your daughter and enact it.
- Model healthy exercise habits and eat a balanced diet. Have healthy, easy snack foods available.
- Enjoy alternative exercise activities with your daughter—dance, yoga, rock-climbing, kayaking, martial arts. Make daily physical activity a family priority and exercise or play a sport with your daughter often.
- Help your daughter start a low-key sport club in your neighborhood.
- Encourage your daughter to go out for a sport and take your daughter to women's athletic games.
- Find out what kinds of coaching clinics are available in your area and find ways to have your daughter's coaches attend. If they are not available, check out www.positivecoachingalliance.org for ideas.
- Encourage a pre-season meeting of parents and coaches to discuss expectations that the coach has of the parents and the players and what the players and parents expect of the coaches (e.g., playing time, parent behavior during games, rules, sportsmanship, etc.).
- Deal with problems with your daughter's team or coach experience EARLY.
- Talk to other parents or coaches who are yelling inappropriately to the referees or players.
- Attend your daughter's academic, music and art interests with the same vigor you attend her sporting events.
- Evaluate your values concerning pro sports and help keep them in proper perspective for your daughter.
- If you have limited time, show her she is important by interacting directly with her off the field, rather than watching from the sidelines. Remember it is OK to not attend every game, especially if you need time alone or need to exercise yourself.

PUTTING IT TOGETHER—YOUR VERSION

Write down three or four ideas you have been inspired to implement in your own life after reading and discussing this chapter.

1. _____

2. _____

3. _____

4. _____

FURTHER READING

Empowerment Groups

The Girls' Circle Facilitator Activity Guide, Complete Set, Facilitator's Manual, many other resources at
www.girlscircle.com

The Mother-Daughter Project: How Mothers and Daughters Can Band Together, Beat the Odds and Thrive Though Adolescence by SuEllen Hamkins, MD And Renee Schultz, MA

Mother-Daughter Wisdom; Understanding the Crucial Link Between Mothers, Daughters and Health by Christiane Northrup, MD

The Mother-Daughter Book Club and 100 Books for Girls to Grow On by Shireen Dodson

Great Books for Girls: More Than 600 Books for Girls 2-14 by Kathleen Odean

Choices: A Teen Woman's Journal for Self-Awareness and Personal Planning by Mindy Bingham, Judy Edmondson, and Sandy Stryker

Women Helping Girls with Choices: A Handbook for Community Service Organizations by Mindy Bingham and Sandy Stryker

Mentoring

Connect 5: Finding the Caring Adults You May Not Realize Your Teen Needs by Kathleen Kimball-Baker

Daughters of the Moon, Sisters of the Sun, Young Women and Mentors on the Transition to Womanhood by K. Wind Hughes and Linda Wolf

Big Brothers/Big Sisters of America: Little Moments, Big Magic. Contact (215) 567-7000 or www.bbbsa.org.

Mentor promotes, advocates and is a resource for mentors and mentoring initiatives worldwide at www.mentoring.org

Rites of Passage

Crossroads: The Quest for Contemporary Rites of Passage by Louise Carus Mahdi, Nancy Christopher, Michael Meade

Nature and the Human Soul: Cultivating Wholeness and Community in a Fragmented World by Bill Plotkin

Betwixt and Between: Patterns of Masculine and Feminine Initiations by Louise Carus Mahdi, Steven Foster, Meredith Little

Rites of Passage Journeys at www.ritesofpassagejourneys.org

Prairie Star Coming of Age Program. Contact Beth Brownfield at bethbrown@aol.com

Coming of Age: Deepening Ties within Your Congregation at uucoa@mac.com

Fitness and Sports

Dr. Rob's Guide to Raising Fit Kids: A Family-Centered Approach to Achieving Optimal Health by Robert Gotlin, DO

Your Active Child: How to Boost Physical, Emotional, and Cognitive Development Through Age-Appropriate Activity by Rae Pica

Sports Her Way: Motivating Girls to Start and Stay with Sports by Susan Wilson

Good Sports: Winning, Losing, and Everything in Between by American Girl Library

The Double Goal Coach: Positive Coaching Tools for Honoring the Game and Developing Winners in Sports and Life by Jim Thompson of the *Positive Coaching Alliance* at www.positivecoach.org

Whose Game Is It, Anyway?: A Guide to Helping Your Child Get the Most from Sports, Organized by Age and Stage by Richard Ginsburg, Stephen Durant, and Amy Baltzell

Raising Our Athletic Daughters: How Sports Can Build Self-Esteem and Save Girls' Lives by Jean Zimmerman and Gil Reavill

In These Girls, Hope is a Muscle by Madeleine Blais

See Jane Win: The Rimm Report on How 1,000 Girls Became Successful Women by Dr. Sylvia Rimm

Winning Ways: A Photo History of American Women in Sports by Sue Macy

Books and Movies for Youth
Rites of Passage

Into the Forest by Jean Hegland

Finding New Harmony, Then and Now, Women's Rites of Passage by Elizabeth Belden and Judith Beckman

Borderlands by Peter Carter

Fitness

New Moon Sports: Stories, Poems, Interviews, Advice on Why We Love Sports and Choosing the Right Sport for You
Into Thin Air by Jon Krakauer (mountain climbing)
It's Not About the Bike by Lance Armstrong (bike racing)

Movies

"A League of Their Own"	"Chariots of Fire"
"Bend It Like Beckham"	"Bad News Bears"
"Cutting Edge"	"Breaking Away"
"Gracie"	"Field of Dreams"
"Finding Forester"	"Million Dollar Baby"
"Remember the Titans"	"Annie O"
"Rudy"	"Blue Crush"

Empowerment Groups for Girls

By Kathy Keller Jones, MA

ONE OF THE MOST valuable things we can do for our teen girls is to give them a chance to have a voice and an ear to listen to other girls' true voices. In the words of Beth Hossfeld, founder of *Girls Circle,* we can help our girls to "trade in their security of silence or facade of indifference and experience the sense of belonging, strength, and possibility that comes with using their voices." Adults can encourage and support girls' communities in many ways (as described on the *Girls Inc.* website at www.girlsinc.org):

- Affirm girls' right to speak up and speak out.
- Learn from girls about their issues and perspectives.
- Affirm girls' thoughts and feelings and encourage them to channel their enthusiasm, anger, joy, or frustration into positive action.
- Help girls to envision the possibilities, and then work toward big goals, such as justice, equity, and environmental preservation.
- Encourage respect. Help girls create diverse communities that recognize girls' similarities and celebrate their differences.

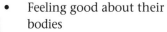

Excellent curricula for starting an empowerment circle for girls are available from *Girls Inc., Choices* and *Girls Circle.* Empowerment groups combat depression, eating disorders, self-destructive behaviors and delinquency, while building self-esteem. As Beth Hossfeld says, "they encourage girls to speak out and build relationships rather than to alienate themselves in silence" or to act out. Through the curricula of these groups, girls are encouraged to be themselves and cross clique lines to build positive relationships. As Mary Pipher writes in *Reviving Ophelia,* teens "need to feel they are part of something larger . . . that they are emotionally connected to a whole."

Girls Circle provides particularly effective curricula and the success of their empowerment circles has been verified by research. The programs are organized around the following common themes: friendship, being a girl, body image, diversity, connections between mind, body, and spirit, expressing individuality, relationships with peers, identity, and paths to the future. The Girls Circle National Research Project (see the Ceres report by J. Roa,

A. Irvine, and K. Cervantez) conducted pre- and post-participation surveys that reflect the outcomes of the 8-to-12 week sessions. A great variety of girls participated in the 2007 study—about half the girls were white, 71% were high school age, 81% were heterosexual, some girls were teen mothers, half of the girls had been suspended from school, and some had been arrested. The results follow:

After participating in a Girls Circle, the teens reported an increase in six valuable skills:

- Finding things they have in common with other girls
- Trying to see beyond other girls' tarnished reputations to their true selves
- Telling adults what they need
- Feeling good about their bodies
- Picking friends that treat them the way they want to be treated, and
- Being able to tell people what they mean to them.

Participants also reported an improvement in four long-term outcomes:

- A decrease in self-harming behavior
- A decrease in alcohol use
- An increase in attachment to school
- An increase in self-efficacy.

These wonderful skills and outcomes are ones we would like to see in all of our teen girls as they grow into young adults. Girls' empowerment groups can clearly play an important role in supporting our young women in becoming healthy adults. Use some of these excellent resources to start a group in your community. Take a look at *Girls Circle's* new curriculum for mothers and daughters called "Daughter Circle: The Heart of the Matter."

For Empowerment Group Curricula to start your own group contact:

Girls Circle	www.girlscircle.com
Girls Inc.	www.girlsinc.org
Choices	www.advocacypress.com/choice
Owning Up	www.rosalindwiseman.com

Get Girls Talking Through a Girls' Circle

By Niki Smith

AS MY DAUGHTER WAS approaching 10, I read Mary Pipher's *Reviving Ophelia*, which left me feeling disheartened and a little panicked. Although my daughter was still doing great, I worried that she would soon start hating me, and I wondered if there was anything I could do to prevent that. I figured that if others were reading *Ophelia* too, then someone out there must be doing something to help parents positively influence our girls' transition into womanhood.

What I found was Girls Circle, a nonprofit organization that trains adult facilitators to get girls talking with each other. A friend and I signed up right away for an intensive, two-day training at the YWCA in San Francisco. One of our trainers, a founder of Girls Circle, began the workshop by exploring her own motivation. "When I discovered the satisfaction of sitting with a group of women and talking about my life, I thought, 'Why should girls have to wait until they're adults to experience this kind of communication?'"

The training emphasized how to ask girls questions that elicit conversations. It wasn't as easy as it sounds. How do you ask girls to talk about their strengths when so much of what they see in this culture portrays young women as nothing more than window dressing?

Within weeks of the training, Maria and I sent flyers home with girls from my daughter's school about starting our own Girls Circle. Seven girls responded, and we went for it. Unknowingly, we had scheduled the first meeting on a field trip day, leaving only three girls who could attend. Already nervous, my insecurities grew as I learned that the two girls other than my daughter hated each other because of a teasing incident at school.

We opened the circle with each girl lighting a candle and saying one word about how she was feeling. We defined the rules of the circle, decorated journals, and discussed the day's topic, "Being a Girl," in which we asked the girls to discuss the pros and cons of girlhood.

The highlight of that discussion occurred when Anna said, "A bad thing about being a girl is when a girl who doesn't like you gets her friends to be mean to you." Almost simultaneously, Bella, the girl who had teased her, sadly nodded her head and said, "I know and I'm sorry."

In that moment Bella truly understood the pain that her teasing had caused Anna. She told Anna how uncomfortable she'd felt about participating in the teasing and that she'd felt pressured to do so. It was amazing to witness these girls connecting. As facilitators we really hadn't done anything except provide the space and the opportunity; the girls had all the answers right there. The exchange did not transform Anna and Bella into best friends, but it did help them understand each other better.

In the seven weeks that followed, girls spoke up about the pain of their parents' divorces, voiced concerns about their physical development, and revealed fears ranging from kidnapping to sewer rats. Some girls got more out of the sessions than others did, but in general, the more they shared the more they benefited.

Facilitating a girls' circle was enormously challenging. Discussions could quickly deteriorate into giggling fits or my daughter would complain that I was too strict, causing me to wonder whether it was worth the strain on our relationship. But, in the end, Girls Circle was one of the most rewarding things I've done. It's the most effective means I've seen of promoting communication among girls. At an age when cliques are common and conversations beyond gossip are not, Girls Circle allows girls to hear their voices, share their lives, and discover their wisdom.

Niki Smith is a Bay Area writer. For more information on Girls Circle check out www.girlscircle.com.

The Mother-Daughter Project: Starting Your Own Mother-Daughter Group

By Kathy Keller Jones, MA

WHAT A DELIGHT IT was to discover SuEllen Hamkins, MD and Renee Schultz, MA's book, *The Mother-Daughter Project: How Mothers and Daughters Can Band Together, Beat the Odds, and Thrive Through Adolescence.* As a school counselor, I already knew how much our girls long for time with their mothers as they enter into adolescence. The same girls who are seemingly pushing their mothers away in their search of their identity will admit that what would make the most difference to them would be bits of undivided attention and attentive listening from their mom. At times it is heartbreaking to witness how upset our teen girls can be when they feel unsupported. As girls face the complexities of adolescence in our times, they need to feel their most knowledgeable ally, their mother, at their backs. SuEllen Hamkins and Renee Schultz are committed to the principle that mothers and daughters can sustain close relationships through adolescence and that this will not interfere with, but enhance our daughters' growth toward independence. They also feel that mothers and daughters need the support of other mothers and daughters to thrive. *The Mother-Daughter Project* is a step-by-step guide to creating a support group, which can help you and your daughter to thrive, and head off the disconnection that our culture often encourages. *The Mother-Daughter Project* book and website, www.themother-daughterproject.com, are filled with practical information for creating more community for both of you.

SuEllen Hamkins and Renee Schutz started their group over a decade ago when their daughters were seven. At that age the girls had no resistance to the idea of a mother-daughter group and were eager to play games with their mothers and their friends' mothers. This group stayed together over 10 years, through the girls' high school years. You can see a wonderful clip of this story done for the Today Show on www.youtube.com. The mothers met monthly without the girls for about a half year before the mother-daughter group began. In this way they got to know each other well and map out ideas for future meetings. The trust that develops from compassionately hearing and guarding the tender and difficult stories women tell will determine the strength of the group. The website gives specific ideas on how to organize your group of 3 to 6 women and how to structure each meeting. Creating this women's support group is excellent modeling for our daughters. The mothers continue to meet once a month and eventually begin the once-a-month mother-daughter activities.

The mother-daughter groups are designed to be playful while fortifying our girls' self-esteem. *The Mother-Daughter Project* is filled with activities that fit developmentally with our daughters as they grow. For example, the chapter on nine-year-olds prepares them for changes ahead by welcoming cycles. How would our lives have felt differently if we had learned to recognize and welcome natural cycles? The chapter connects girls with moon cycles and goddesses and eventually to the moon dance of their own bodies, culminating in a special ritual. The book outlines activities for 7- to 17-year-olds that explore key issues, such as girls' friendships and puberty, when they are younger, and more challenging subjects, such as body image, drugs, sexuality and violence against women, as they mature. The adults marveled at the strength and confidence their girls showed in adolescence and found that the group really did protect their daughters from the perils of teen culture.

Of course, your daughter may not be seven, and you may wonder whether it is possible to start a group when she is older. Although it is easier to start a group when your daughter is ten or younger, that doesn't mean that you can't start a group with older girls. A teen will be secretly thrilled when you let her know that now that she is maturing you want to find new ways of connecting with her and keeping a good relationship. You may be able to involve her in forming the group, although she may need to be encouraged to include girls who are not her closest friends. On the other hand, your teen daughter will be happier if the other girls are girls she respects and feels she could grow to trust. Mother-daughter groups encourage connection and provide mentoring for our daughters from other women, while giving our girls a voice and critical information. This puts our daughters in the best possible position for navigating adolescence with health, direction, and love.

Check out: www.the motherdaughterproject.com.

Creating "Safe Havens" for Youth

By Kathy Masarie, MD

ALL OF US LONG TO be part of a group where we feel accepted for who we are. This group can be hard to find in school unless you are a jock or popular. As ironic as it seems, being a good student may not be enough in a culture that models "nerd bashing" as a sport in movies. Providing interest groups outside of sports and academia can foster comfortable settings for kids to be themselves, especially for teens who are shy, loners or outcasts. When funding for schools dwindles as it has in some states, we see fewer and fewer of these interest groups, such as art, band and foreign language, being provided by schools.

As parents, we are in a powerful position to create these "safe havens" for our children, whether in our homes or at school during lunch, after school or in the evening. One of the most important things a parent can do for their youth is to start to understand the world their child is living in. Being part of a support group of adult and youth interacting with each other is an excellent way to accomplish this. All interactions—youth-to-youth, youth-to-adult and adult-to-adult—are valuable. As an adult facilitator, it is important to work toward empowering the youth to take charge of and choose activities for the meetings.

We can't expect the kids to be immediately open. Initially, the youth may not share that much with the group. As they get more comfortable they open up. One mother-daughter hiking club found that it took about a year of just being together before the girls started opening up to the other adults in the group (it might take boys longer). Eventually there were very strong bonds that developed between the adults and the youth.

General Structure

One or two adults and group of youth. This can work with a parent facilitator who understands youth. Sometimes a teen will open up to a non-related facilitator in ways they feel too inhibited to do when someone's parent is there. Young adults, religious educators and school counselors are especially effective at facilitating discussions among teens about their life struggles and issues. If teachers are involved in after-school or lunch clubs, they should be reimbursed generously.

One parent/one child (mother-daughter, mother-son, father-daughter, father-son) groups. This is an excellent way for parents and youth to understand each other better, especially the intergenerational interactions between unrelated pairs. This sets up a natural buffer for your children even outside the group, as the other youth and adults who get to know and love your child will be looking for him/her when there is trouble or need.

Gathering with families regularly. When our kids are little we naturally socialize with other families with children of similar ages. When we keep meeting for holidays, regular potlucks or outings, our children grow up together and feel at home with the other children and adults.

Age to Start

It is ideal to start a group while your child is in grade school or the first part of sixth grade. It is difficult to start a group when your child becomes "cool" and you become an embarrassment, as often happens during the middle school and early high school years. However, if you started a group earlier they will often ride right through these tough years. They don't want to quit something they are enjoying. It is never too late; my daughter was happy to start a mother-daughter book club in 10th grade when someone else's mom suggested it.

Meeting Times

Regular: weekly, monthly or yearly

Irregular: "when you have time" but if you don't have some structure/leadership you may never get around to meeting.

After-school clubs: This is a great place for schools to offer programs they wish were part of the curriculum (language, art, music, theater, book club).

Lunch clubs: For those kids who don't fit into the social scene, lunch can be an excruciatingly long time to be exposed to loneliness or harassment.

General Activities

Any common interest the youth and adults share can bring a group together. It could be an outdoor adventure, craft activity or even meeting at a restaurant together.

The list below is by no means a complete list but is designed to expose you to some different styles and formats that have worked. Don't let yourself be limited by these choices.

- *"Name Your Group"*—playful activities such as pizza parties, swimming, baseball game, art projects. Let the kids' interest drive the activities. One group we know meets every other month for mom-daughter activities of the girls choosing. Every other month the moms meet alone for a discussion on parenting.
- *Youth Groups*—in religious settings can provide the safest havens for kids who don't fit-in in traditional settings, especially since the theme is centered on acceptance of our differences and loving one another.
- *Coming of Age programs*—in religious settings can be a fantastic experience. They can challenge teens to think for themselves and to start to take more responsibility, while formally recognizing the important transition from childhood to adolescence. Otherwise our teens are more likely to do their own rituals of smoking, drinking, drugs or sexual promiscuity to "prove" that they are older.

Empowerment Groups

Empowerment groups are run by non-related adults to discuss issues which concern youth: for example, self-esteem, gossip, exclusion, friendships, risky teen behavior, media, over-focus on athleticism and other burning issues. These groups are particularly effective at helping children deal with interpersonal interactions and relationships.

- *The Girls Circle*—www.girlscircle.com
- *Girl's Empowerment Circles*—Girls Inc. at www.girlsincnw.org
- *BAM! Boys Advocacy and Mentoring*—at www.BAMgroups.com
- *Boys Councils*—at www.boyscouncil.com

Fitness and Sports Groups

It is very important for youth to learn to move their body while they are young and to get in the habit of exercise before they are 10 years old. For girls, the added bonus is that they see their body functionally rather than as an ornament. For boys, the added bonus is "action talk"; they will open up more easily while moving their body. For both, it can be a place where cooperation is more important than competition. Examples:

- *"Sports Clubs"* —around any activity. An alternative to long baseball practices and games is to have a baseball club that meets once a week. Think of any sport you can and there could be sport club around it.
- *Girl's Sport Clubs*—a weekly after-school club that meets to play and do alternative sports such as yoga, self-defense, kick boxing, and hip-hop dance
- *Action Club*—meet weekly to go for a hike, bike riding, roller-blading or different adventures.

Adult and Child Groups

- *Mother-Daughter Project*—empowerment group for moms and daughters (www.motherdaughterproject.com)
- *Book Club*—read and discuss a book monthly
- *Movie Club*—watch and then discuss movies
- *Campfire, 4-H and Scouts*—programs from kindergarten to high school. They have great curriculum, leadership training and support.
- *Science Club*—after-school science club run by moms, such as MAD Scientist or AWSEM: Advocates for Women in Science, Engineering and Math at www.saturdayacademy.org
- *Choices or Challenges*—for middle-schoolers and their parents

Family Gatherings

- Monthly potlucks or block dinners; holidays
- Yearly outdoor adventures: camping, backpacking, rafting, fishing, to name a few
- Family camps offered by local camps or churches

Lunch Clubs: "Safe havens" during lunch breaks

- *Library Fun*—nearly all schools have their libraries open during lunch, but not all quiet kids like to read. Some libraries set up a puzzles area with a 1000-piece puzzle to work on over time.
- *Game room*—this is a room full of board games and a couple foosball tables for active kids who don't want to go on the playground.
- *Support groups*—this is a great time for counselors (or outside facilitators) to work with kids who are in conflict: a group of girls who seem to attack each other, a group of kids who need to learn social skills or a group of boys who don't communicate well.

How Girls Benefit from Having Mentors in Their Lives

By Jody Bellant Scheer, MD

"The problems of adolescence deal with deep and moving human experiences. They center on a fateful time in the life course when poorly informed decisions can have lifelong consequences. The tortuous passage from childhood to adulthood requires our highest attention, our understanding, and a new level of thoughtful commitment." —David Hamburg, President, Carnegie Corporation of NY[1]

Why Girls Need More Than Parents Can Give

Many mothers think that their relationships with their daughters are wonderful. They may think, "I'm not worried about her. We have a great relationship. My daughter tells me everything."[1] Counselors often hear this from mothers. Pegine Echevarria, a social worker and counselor who has written the book *For Our Daughters: How Mentoring Helps Young Women and Girls Master the Art of Growing Up*, states that she has heard words like these from many parents. But, she adds, "the truth is, your relationship with your daughter may be great, but that doesn't mean that she will share everything of importance with you, and it certainly doesn't mean she's getting all the advice and guidance she needs as she approaches womanhood."[2]

The reason why girls don't confide in their parents at this age is partly due to the nature of normal child development. The developmental task of adolescence is to separate from family and to explore the larger world. In order to prepare for adulthood, adolescents need to individuate, explore their own separate personalities, and learn to exert control over their own identities, sexuality and destiny. During this period of development, independence from parents and family is sought, hormones are raging, and peers and the media exert a very strong influence over behavior. Due to this normal developmental pattern, our girls often do not consult their own parents about the very behaviors and issues that are most likely to cause them harm or to permanently impair their future abilities to succeed.

Paradoxically, adolescence is also a time when young people are seeking strong adult role models.

Unfortunately for teens and preteens in our society, adolescence is now often a time when many of our children are getting less adult interaction than they want or need. Recent studies show that many teenagers spend two or more hours alone after school each day, without any adult contact at all.[1] A 1997 Multnomah Co, OR survey by The Commission on Children, Families and Community asked 10,000 young people about their lives, values, wants, and support. The findings revealed that "most youth feel unwanted and unneeded by our community and don't have positive role models in their lives."[3] If positive adult role models are missing from our girls' lives, then this is certainly something that parents can do something about! We can make sure to provide our girls with a community of adult friends and mentors who can offer support and guidance during their often tumultuous and sometimes dangerous journey through adolescence.

Why would you want to provide outside adult female support for your daughter? Isn't it enough that your connection with your daughter is full of moments of intimacy, caring and mutual respect? Ms. Echevarria, whose book outlines a successful series of ideas and strategies to make a positive difference in the lives of girls through mentoring, thinks not. She states, "the sobering fact remains that you can't guide your daughter through this [adolescent] period on love alone. You need help."[2] She emphasizes the need to "bring someone else into the life of your daughter, someone who you trust implicitly, and who will know things about your daughter that you won't know."[2]

What Girls Gain from a Mentoring Relationship

Girls are navigating a series of serious emotional, physical, emotional and developmental challenges between the ages of 9 and 18. They are breaking away from the family, as well as coming to the immense realization that every time they enter a room, they are making a sexual statement simply on the basis of the development of their body. Echevarria reminds us that after puberty, a girl's body is perpetually on display and has a powerful effect on others. "Girls are often unprepared for these [physical] changes—but the necessity that they develop identities separate from their role within the family keeps them from reaching out to parents as they might have done a few years earlier."[2] In addition, the social environment within which every girl grows up nowadays is distinctively complex and can be scary, with "tough choices that carry difficult implications. Yet [your daughter] must—and she will—learn to make those choices outside of [the parental] sphere of influence."[2] This is why developing a close emotional relationship with a caring, trusted, non-parental older woman is such an essential part of the maturation process of girls. Such caring mentors can discuss questions and issues that concern girls of this age and can provide girls with guidance and support from a neutral party. Mentors are much less likely than parents to get emotionally charged or reactive over important issues and, as such, are often much easier for girls to confide in.

Girls benefit in other ways from a mentoring relationship. Research overwhelmingly shows that mentoring is an effective tool for enhancing the positive overall development of all youth, provided that the mentor can provide sustained support, guidance and concrete help when the child goes through a difficult time, enters a new situation, or takes on new tasks.[4] Research also suggests that mentoring relationships are most successful when they persist for at least 18 months, less time than that can leave a vulnerable child feeling abandoned by yet another adult. In a 2002 study using scientific evaluations of mentoring programs, Child Trends, Inc. found that youth were likely to enjoy multiple benefits from well-designed mentoring, which include the following:

1. **Academic advantages.** Mentored youth had fewer absences from school, better attitudes toward school, a better chance of going on to higher education after high school, and a trend toward higher grades.[4]
2. **Health and safety gains.** Mentored youth were 46-70% less likely to initiate drug use and 27%-50% less likely to initiate alcohol use during a study period of 18 months. Mentored youth were 33% less likely to hit others, half as likely to

commit a major criminal offense and showed an overall decrease in the development of "problem behaviors."[4]
3. **Social and emotional gains.** Youth who participated in a mentoring program had more positive attitudes toward the future and the elderly, and exhibited more helping behaviors than youth in control groups. Many of the youth in mentoring programs also reported improved parental and peer relationships and an increase in their overall sense of self-worth.[4]

Although research and common sense supports mentoring relationships as extremely beneficial for our girls, it also seems true, as author Echevarria points out, "that today's far-flung, media-saturated, divorce-damaged family structures have left more and more girls and young women adrift without such role models."[2] So, it is left to parents to find a way to point our daughters towards a trustworthy role model—an aunt, a cousin, a neighbor, a grandmother, a Girl Scout leader, a teacher, a coach, or some other caring adult woman—and help facilitate an ongoing connection between them.

Your Daughter Won't Tell You Everything!

There seem to be a number of life crises which most of our adolescent daughters will face either directly or indirectly where having an established mentor relationship is an especially important asset. Based on her many years as a counselor and a mentor herself, author Echevarria believes girls will be much more likely to discuss a series of 13 life crises with a mentor rather than with their parents.[2] This is not because girls are trying to be dishonest or duplicitous. Girls don't talk about these particular crises with their parents because they fear disappointing them, they are afraid to challenge parental belief systems, and/or they don't want to admit to their parents that they have critical issues or problems looming in their lives. Girls often want information on various behaviors or issues in order to make educated choices for themselves, but fear parents will lecture them, limit their ability to make choices for themselves or punish them for their questions. Also, adolescent girls are experiencing a developmental phase that leads them to believe that they must solve their intimate problems by themselves, outside of the family nest.

Therefore, Echevarria states, "no matter how good your communication is with your daughter, no matter how well things seem to be going on the surface, there are things she will not and cannot tell you—things she needs desperately to tell someone. And that someone has to be an adult woman—a mentor—typically someone who makes a subtle first move to reach out to the girl. Establishing oneself as a mentor is an art that must be practiced, but it's not that difficult to learn. Once the connection is made, the difference a mentor can make in the life of a young girl can mean the difference between life and death."[2]

13 Life Crises your Daughter is More Likely to Talk with a Mentor About:

The following life crises represent occasions in your daughter's life where having a mentor is especially important.

Crisis #1: I had sex last night. A 1999 study of high school girls shows that about 50% have had sex, have had four or more sexual partners, and more than 33% have had sex within the past 3 months.[5] The truth is that our daughters are being raised in a society where the media is saturated with sex and sexuality. Casual and irresponsible sex are represented everywhere as the norm. You may have reared your daughter with a firm grounding in strong morals and values, but the reality is that most of our teenagers succumb to peer pressure and societal influences and become sexually active at a young age. In fact, close to 1 in 10 high school girls had their first sexual experience before the age of 13.[5]

Although parents may not be happy with this sexual reality, it can be life-saving for our daughters to receive appropriate education and support should they decide (as they do in great numbers) to have sex. While it is essential that parents talk with their daughters about sexuality, the reality is that girls will often share more about this area of their lives with a mentor. A mentor can help guide your daughter toward making responsible decisions about her sexuality, as well as help her make sense of some of the "sales talk" she is likely to encounter from boys. As well, a mentor can help your daughter understand how the media exploits youthful sexuality for economic gain, and promotes safe sex practices as archaic or unnecessary.

Crisis #2: I had unprotected sex. Do you think I have a sexually transmitted disease? Of the 36% of high school girls who were sexually active within the past 3 months, only half of them used condoms, even though 91% noted that they had studied about AIDS and HIV in school.[5] Teenagers are notoriously prone to thinking that bad outcomes happen only to other people, and for engaging in risky behaviors that put them at risk for unprotected or unplanned sexual encounters. Studies show that nearly 40% of sexually active girls admitted to using drugs or alcohol before sex, which may help to explain why nearly 1 in 10 high school girls have been forced to have unwanted sex[9] and why the HIV/AIDS epidemic is gaining such a stronghold among young women. For young people aged 13-19, 61% of new HIV infections occur in females, with the largest percentage of these infections being transmitted via heterosexual unprotected sex. African American and Hispanic girls are most at risk, accounting for 75% of these new infections.[6] In addition, 25% of sexually active teens will acquire an STD (sexually transmitted disease) other than HIV each year.[7] A trusted mentor can be instrumental in reinforcing the gravity of the decision to become sexually active, and can supply important information about birth control, personal safety, and safe sexual practices—something you can't do if your teenager decides, as is common, to "take you out of the loop."

Crisis #3: I'm pregnant. Each year, 10% of young women aged 15-19 and 20% who have had intercourse become pregnant. Most of these pregnancies are unplanned.[7] Girls will most often talk first with someone other than their parents about their pregnancy, because they are afraid of what their parents will say or do. A mentor can be a neutral party who can help young girls problem-solve and make good choices about their pregnancy. A mentor can be a vicarious parental ally who can help guide your daughter to get adequate medical help, counseling, family support and reassurance. Currently, about 56% of teen pregnancies end up with live births.[7] To optimize a healthy outcome, a teenager needs support from the start of her pregnancy, a time when she may be afraid or unwilling to get support directly from her parents.

Crisis #4: I've been smoking for awhile—everybody at school does. The gender gap between girls and boys using tobacco has disappeared in recent years, with girls starting to smoke at high rates in spite of massive public health efforts to educate youth about the dangers of tobacco. In 1999, 70% of high school girls had smoked at least once in their life, with nearly 33% of these having smoked before the age of 13.[5] By 2001, 61% of high school seniors reported ever smoking, with 30% of these having smoked within the past 30 days.[6] A mentor can be a trusted, impartial influence for a girl to talk to about the risks and realities of smoking, including such issues as how smoking ages skin, alters appearance and body odor, costs a lot, and hurts unborn children. Since the natural history of a smoker is someone who starts smoking as a young teenager and spends most of his or her adult life trying (unsuccessfully) to quit, nipping the smoking habit in its earliest stages is in the best interests of your teenage daughter. A teen's mentor can be a strong ally when it comes to helping your daughter quit smoking.

Crisis #5: I got drunk last night. Alcohol use among teenagers is rampant. 80% of all high-school girls had had a drink sometime in their lives, while 50% had drank within the past 30 days.[5] More disturbing, 33% of high school girls had ridden in a car in the past 30 days with a driver under the influence of alcohol, and 9% had driven themselves after drinking.[5] A mentor can serve as an important sounding board for your daughter regarding issues of alcohol and drugs, as well as personal safety. Mentors can also guide your daughter or her friends to counseling and treatment resources, if needed.

Crisis #6: I want to kill myself. In the past 25 years, the rate of suicide among young people ages 15 to 24 has tripled.[10] Suicide is now the third leading cause of death among young people aged 15 to 24, and the fourth leading cause of death among persons aged 10 to 14.[11] In 1999, 1 in 4 high school girls had seriously considered suicide within the previous 12 months, and 11% had made a suicide attempt. Having a trusted

mentor to turn to in such situations can be life-saving. **Crisis #7: I throw up after each meal.** Eating disorders are a pronounced risk for our adolescent girls in our thin-obsessed society. Of girls in 5th to 12th grades, 1 in 6 had binged and purged (4% on a regular basis), 3 in 5 had dieted and 1 in 3 thought they were overweight.[9] Adult female friends can be literally life-saving in reinforcing healthy self-esteem and eating habits in our daughters. As well, they can help guide our daughters to the understanding, often by personal example, that successful women come in all shapes and sizes.

Crisis #8: My mom doesn't care about me; she's not interested (or she won't give me any privacy). "13% of girls surveyed reported having no one to turn to when stressed, overwhelmed, or depressed, or for information about health. Nearly half did not name their mother as the person to whom they would turn for emotional support."[2] Such feelings of neglect or disinterest can be related to conflicts with parents over issues of privacy and autonomy. Girls who enter into such power struggles with their parents will often escalate their irresponsible and rebellious behaviors, which in turn leave parents trying ever more desperately to control their teenager's behavior. This often escalates into a vicious cycle that leaves both parties feeling betrayed and hopeless. A calm, mature, accepting adult friend can help your daughter to put her life into a more healthy balance. Girls desperately need to feel valued and loved in spite of their behaviors; frankly, during times of crisis, this may be easier to accomplish for an adult somewhat removed from the intimate family sphere.

Crisis #9: I hate myself. Adolescent girls show a high degree of depressive symptoms, mood swings and low self-confidence in recent surveys. These factors also tend to increase as girls grow older, in stark contrast to the trends noted in young men.[1,5,9] Surveys show rates of depressive symptoms in young girls to be between 25% and 36%, with about 10% showing severe symptoms.[1,2,9] Parents of girls with self-hatred or depressive symptoms are often unaware of their daughters' suffering, and many girls relate that they have no one to turn for support during times of depression or stress.[9] It is important for our daughters to have a trusted adult mentor to talk to when they are feeling down, and who can break through a teenager's habitual "everything's fine" (when it's not) attitude.

Crisis #10: I want the pill (or I need to talk to a doctor). The leading reason that girls do not get health care is that they don't want to tell their parents about their situation, in fact 40% of girls noted this concern.[9] When our daughters need health care, they will benefit from having a mentor to help them access it. Mentors can be an important source of information as well, helping our daughters to make self-care decisions that are responsible and sometimes life-saving.

Crisis #11: He hit me. 26% of high school girls reported some form of physical, sexual or date-related abuse in their lives; 29% of these girls had told no one of their abuse.[9] These reports mirror the experience of counselors, who find that many girls do not tell their parents about being involved in an abusive relationship, and often blame themselves for it. Mentors can offer your daughter some hope of extricating herself from such relationships by offering empathy, guidance and insight about dealing with men who show a need to abuse or control others. Mentors can also bolster a girl's sense of self worth and dignity, such that she gains courage to break off relationships that damage her stability, either physically or emotionally. This is another instance where a mentor can have a life-changing or even life-saving impact on your daughter for years to come.

Crises #12: An older male friend (or relative) keeps coming on to me. The majority of sexual abuse occurs at home, as a result of a family member or friend, and occurs more than once. "Girls are often sworn to secrecy or physically threatened in an effort to maintain silence. They may have serious reactions of shame, guilt and self-hatred following these episodes."[2] Mentors are often easier to talk to regarding these issues, and are often perceived by girls as less threatening or judgmental than family members. Mentors will almost certainly bring the problem to your attention immediately, and initiate the process of getting much needed help for your daughter.

Crisis #13: This guy made me do something I didn't want to do. Nearly 1 in 10 high school girls reported having had forced sex against their will.[9] Girls who start having sex at the youngest ages are most at risk.[7,9,12] Among Oregon teenagers in 1999, 62% of girls who started having sex before age 13 reported having been

forced to have unwanted intercourse.[12] A mentor who has an ongoing investment in the life of your daughter can be an important ally in helping her to avoid negative or abusive relationships. For a girl who is already involved in such an entanglement, having an ongoing relationship with a trusted mentor who truly values her can help her recover from the abuse and extricate herself from relationships with men who cause her psychological, sexual or physical trauma.

References:

1. *Great Transitions: Preparing Adolescents for a New Century,* a report of the Carnegie Corporation of New York, 437 Madison Ave, New York, NY 10022, 4/26/02.
2. *For All Our Daughters: How Mentoring Helps Young Women and Girls Master the Art of Growing Up* by Pegine Echevarria, MSW, Chandler House Press, c. May, 1998.
3. "1997 Youth Asset Survey," The Commission on Children, Families and Community (Multnomah County, OR). 421 SW 6th Avenue, Suite 1075, Portland, OR 97204.
4. "Mentoring: A Promising Strategy for Youth Development," by S.M Jekielek MA, K.A. Moore PhD, E.C.Hair, PhD, and H.J. Scarupa, MS. Feb. 2002. *Child Trends Research Brief,* Child Trends Inc., 4301 Connecticut Ave, Suite 100, Washington, DC 20008.
5. "Youth Risk Behavior Survey, 1999 results," published 2001, part of the CDC Youth Risk Behavior Surveillance System (YRBSS), an annual national survey including 9th to 12th graders. Center for Disease Control, 1600 Clifton Road, Atlanta, GA 30333.
6. "Young People at Risk: HIV/AIDS among America's Youth," 3/11/2002. Center for Disease Control & Prevention, National Center for HIV, STD, and TB Prevention, Division of HIV/AIDS Prevention. 1600 Clifton Road, Atlanta, GA 30333.
7. "Teen Sex and Pregnancy," Revised 9/1999, *Facts in Brief.* c. 2000, The Alan Guttmacher Institute, 120 Wall Street, 21st Floor, New York, NY 10008.
8. "High School and Youth Trends: 2001 Monitoring the Future Study (MTF)," 12/19/01, The National Institute on Drug Abuse, National Institute of Health, US Dept of Health and Human Services, 6001 Executive Blvd, Room 5213, Bethesda, MD 20892-9561.
9. "Report on The Commonwealth Fund Survey of the Health of Adolescent Girls," 11/97. Study done 1996-1997 with girls in 5th to 12th grades. The Commonwealth Fund, One East 75th Street, New York, NY 10021
10. "Teen Suicide," by Richard O'Connor, PhD, c. 2000 by Focus Adolescent Services, an internet clearinghouse of information, resources and support at *www.focusas.com.*
11. "Some Things You Should Know About Preventing Teen Suicide," by the American Academy of Pediatrics, c. 1998 by American Psychiatric Association, 1400 K Street NW, Washington, DC 20005.
12. "Sexual Activity Decreasing Among Oregon Teens Age 15-17: Survey Results, 1999." March 2001. *Oregon Health Trends,* Series No. 58, published by the Center for Health Statistics, Oregon Dept. of Human Services, Health Division, 800 NW Oregon St., Suite 225, Portland, OR 97214

Teenagers Can Be Mentors, Too!

By Susan Hopkins

As BOTH TEACHER AND parent, I am heartened by the expanding chorus of voices promoting parent involvement. I hear a renewed sense of mission in the messages that caring adults are delivering: TALK to your daughter about her self-image, VOLUNTEER in her classroom, MAKE TIME for a family meal, and so forth.

The media are joining in, with activities and strategies to help families prepare their teenagers for a successful transition into adulthood. Wisely, teachers and others who care about adolescents are sharing the stage with parents. Parents are realizing that kids are watching the adults in their lives, tuning in to examples of wisdom and self-esteem. Indeed, a theme in these discussion guides has been modeling a life worth celebrating; modeling our own efforts as adults—toward good health, good sportsmanship, and self-respect.

As strongly as I endorse this approach, it appears to flow in only one direction, adults as leaders; youth as followers. No matter how inspiring the leadership, however, teenagers can more easily embrace healthy adulthood after they themselves have had an opportunity to lead, and serving as a positive role model for a child is a priceless opportunity to do so. Leadership is another step on the path toward adulthood that I feel is too valuable to ignore.

My children spend their days in multi-grade classrooms. We who support mixed-age classrooms recognize that children best explore what they know when called upon to teach it. Children can proudly claim their own knowledge and expertise as they patiently pass it along to someone else. Teaching in small, everyday interactions helps them to feel both competent and generous toward those who are coming up from behind.

For most teenagers, the adults closest to them— teachers and parents and coaches—appear to have the right answers and to see through any mistakes. No matter how patient and respectful their approach may be, adults are more experienced and appear to be more knowledgeable. With such "together" adults all around, a teenager may be reluctant to risk the failure of trying new ideas, new hobbies, or new ways of connecting. But when a teenager mentors, tutors, or coaches, s/he becomes the expert in the eyes of the young followers.

This can result in the confidence boost to take intellectual risks and explore ideas.

Paradoxically, mentoring children serves another important purpose for teenagers. As with anyone, a teen occasionally needs a break from striving toward self-control and competence. Destructive ways of "taking a break" are all too obvious today, as adolescents abruptly turn away and establish their own contrasting identities. Mentoring children allows teens a healthier choice for escaping from social and academic pressure. They can re-visit childhood. I watch as my friends' teenagers eagerly play with my small children. For these teenagers, "helping me with the kids" is a dignified opportunity to have a really good time in the fort-building, secret-sharing world of childhood, which was their own refuge not so long ago. The challenge for teenagers is to gain inspiration by emulating worthy adults, while honoring their own desire to hang on to childhood. Being with children gives a teenager a respectable excuse to relax and linger awhile, to make the most of, well, playtime. Now that's a skill worthy of passing along to adults!

For an adolescent, serving as a mentor to a younger child can contribute to self-esteem, add to a sense of belonging in the community, and help bridge the passage from childhood to adulthood. When we encourage our teens to mentor others, we send a powerful message: "We believe you are someone to look up to, just as we hope you look up to us."

Susan Hopkins is a teacher, writer, and mother to a girl and a boy. She hopes to combine teaching with her former career as a city planner to develop programs to guide youth in creating livable communities.

Reprinted with permission from Full Esteem Ahead, *Wings*, Spring 1999.

Cherishing Teens Reconnects Communities:
The Power of Coming of Age Celebrations
By Glenda Montgomery

THROUGHOUT THE WORLD, ritual and community-based celebration have marked the transition between the life of a child and the life of a young adult. Guided by elders and others who have been taught and tested before them, youth have learned necessary adult skills, been challenged, taken risks and have been acknowledged and embraced by their societies. The time and attention given towards these endeavors benefited not only the youths but their communities as a whole. Unfortunately, our modern western culture is a great exception in the diverse history of humankind because of our lack of established Rites of Passage. By failing to jump in and actively engage with our youth in this vital time of their lives, our culture alienates and confuses them. As a society, we tend to fear teenagers and their worlds. We end up collectively shunning youth at a time when they are driven developmentally toward pushing at the edges of their known world, taking risks and demanding new roles. Instead, we could be training them and skillfully guiding their energy within the embrace of the larger community, as they do where Rites of Passage are an integral part of community life. Not only do our youth miss out, our whole communities suffer from this void.

Today, in land-based, season-focused cultures (most of the world!), vibrant rituals and rites are practiced to mark Coming of Age. There is common structure in virtually all of these; they tend to have three phases:

- The first marks the leaving behind of childhood and of the day-to-day life of a child. It often is literally a "leaving behind." Hair is sometimes cut and the youth may leave his or her childhood home to spend time with other youth and elders.

- The next phase is one of "grounding down to be fashioned anew." It is a time of intense acquisition of skill-based knowledge and of ordeal, when youths learn what they are made of and are tested emotionally, physically and spiritually.

- The final phase is reintroduction back into the community. This is a time of celebration and reunification, when the society acknowledges that the youth is no longer a child and now carries different rights and responsibilities.

The recognition ceremony often provides a sense of renewal for the entire community. In fact, Rites of Passage are an integral part of community life. Not only do our youth miss out, our whole community suffers.

In our society we idolize the individual and individualism. As a result, the skills of collaboration, mediation, compromise, group problem-solving, listening and personal contribution are not given the status as those of being a leader, a rebel, or a star. We do not actively support or recognize the skills that are so crucial for the continued surviving and thriving of any community. In fact, we don't know what skills we *should* help children to pursue nor how to teach them. Youth end up being confused by our culture's mixed messages and our inaction.

Furthermore, today when there is great competition in the labor market, young people are required often to depend on their parents for a much longer period of time than what was traditionally the case. Because of attending higher education and/or requiring financial support, sometimes youth do not leave behind their childhood home, childhood domestic responsibilities, patterns and expectations until their mid-twenties.

While transition from childhood to adulthood is no longer clear, our culture makes it clear that transition from adult to elder results in marginalization. Elders who in other places are honored for their life experience and entrusted with the guidance of the youth, in our culture are relegated to insignificant or indulgent roles in children's lives.

In this world of unsure transition, contradictory messages of what is important, fear and shunning from the greater community and a developmental drive to individuation and risk-taking, teens are taking initiation into their own hands. High risk behavior, hazing, gang activity, drinking and drugs, tattoos, and even random acts of violence and denigration against the larger community can be parts of these self-imposed initiations. This separation from childhood and community is not guided and overseen by elders towards positive goals as it is in cultures where the rites of passage are integral to growing up and it often does not culminate in the ritualized and celebratory reintegration with the society at large, which is so important. Instead, this separation isolates and breeds mistrust.

The book, *Crossroads: The Quest for Contemporary Rites of Passage*, states:

> *One reason for the great demand of psychiatric services for adolescents today may be the absence of socially sanctioned rites of passage. Throughout human history these rites have served humanity well. The desire for some rites and rituals at puberty as well as at the end of the teen years is natural, even today. Young people seem to want the real thing . . . There is truly a hunger for initiation . . . Together with the culture, the community and the individual elders offering nurturing guidance and support, whole villages are needed to help raise our children, to help them survive.*

Not only do socially sanctioned programs of rites of initiation help *youth* survive and thrive, they are equally important for the survival of a thriving, healthy community.

What do we do then, given the absence of most universally accepted rites of passage in this culture, its ambivalence to youth, the largeness of the task and its importance? There are three ways you might provide your child with a profound Coming of Age experience. You might want to send your adolescent to one of the many excellent Rites of Passage camps; you might want to start or become involved in a local community or church-based program, or you may want to create a Coming of Age celebration just for your own child at your home.

There are many companies that specialize in taking youth into the natural world and guiding them in groups through Coming of Age rites of passage. Many incorporate all of the three stages: leaving behind, learning/testing and reuniting. Research some on the web and see what might be right for your teen:

- www.theritejourney.com
- www.ritesofpassagejourneys.org
- www.outwardbound.org

All of these are excellent choices to research and utilize.

If you have a school community, religious community or neighborhood that is interested in a program to do at the community level "in house" to guide a group of teens or preteens through a period of initiation and coming of age, there are a few excellent choices that you can explore. Usually the program arrives as a book or manual with "how to" instructions to help you with your community effort. Two excellent resources are:

Prairie Star Coming of Age Program: by Beth Brownfield
Order a copy at Bethbrown@aol.com
Coming of Age: Deepening Ties within Your Congregation
Order a copy at uucoa@mac.com

Finally, you can create your own homespun Coming of Age celebration to honor your son or daughter. Bring together "elders" to teach skills and act as guides in these transition years; honor the path your son or daughter has walked as a child so far and celebrate the adult they are evolving into. With a gathering of family and friends, celebrate your adolescent and reaffirm the importance of their unique qualities, skills and knowledge. Reassure them that they have the support of the group and of individuals within the group as they are tested and challenged on the journey to adulthood.

It is time for us to build anew the rites and rituals of passage that mark the transition from child to emerging womanhood and manhood. Youth hunger for them; our communities suffer from lack of them. It is time for us to remind our youth that they are valued and are part of a place where they are both needed and cherished.

Written for Family Empowerment Network by Glenda Montgomery, parent coach and Certified positive Discipline Instructor in Portland, OR and mother of a girl and a boy, www.positiveparentingpdx.com. For reprint requests, contact www.family-empower.com.

Coming of Age Book:
Gifts from Wise Women Honor a New Phase of Life
By Georgia C. Harker

I REMEMBER YEARNING to reach the magical age of thirteen. I don't recall my birthday, but that summer my grandmother introduced me to Europe and I now see that trip as the beginning of my journey into adulthood. She and I still laugh about scenes from a London disco and memories of our trip thirty years ago.

When my daughter, Ayla, approached thirteen last year, I decided to mark the occasion. Mary Pipher's warnings of a hostile culture inspired me, along with anthropological and spiritual lessons from scholars like Joseph Campbell. Traditional societies publicly acknowledge the coming of age of their youth. "Growing up" in many non-Western communities still begins with ritual, celebration, and often a test of strength or courage. I think that our media-barraged youth need these, too. They need a clear message that, instead of solo agents, they are connected to a broad web of caring people.

I wanted to remind Ayla of her extensive, loving community and to acknowledge her new status. I also thought she'd like an enduring gift, so I settled on a book and a group celebration.

A month and a half before assembling it, I sent letters to about 30 women requesting pages for Ayla's book. These women included her closest relatives and family friends plus a few favorite teachers. I explained the secret gift being produced, and why we wanted to mark this impending occasion. I asked for their contributions—a favorite poem or Ann Lander's column perhaps, or wisdom born of 20/20 hindsight—and that each woman share something with Ayla on her 13th birthday that she wished a "wise woman" had shared with her way back when.

Along with the letter, I included three sheets of acid-free paper, trimmed to 8x10" to fit scrapbook pages, a large manila envelope addressed to me at work (to guard the surprise), plus a return deadline and surprise party date. Three or four weeks before the party, I sent invitations to local friends.

Each returning envelope was like a visit and a hug from some of our favorite people in the world. Stories, artwork, poetry, and love filled the pages. Photos showed Ayla's great-grandmother as a flapper, and her great-aunt playing the trumpet, just as Ayla does. Advice ran the gamut, covering pretty much everything she'll ever need to know! My mother wrote "Find someone who thinks you walk on water and stick with them." Many voices advised "Respect yourself and cherish friendships with women." Together the pages create a tapestry of family history, of an extensive support system that's always there for her, and of many paths leading to fulfillment and adventure.

Assembling the book took longer than expected, but thanks to friends who let me monopolize their dining room for a few days, it all came together. Allow two weeks for this. Page one holds a photo of a lanky, pre-thirteen-year-old Ayla grinning from behind little sunglasses in Baja, Mexico. The invitations to participate in the book and the celebration come next, followed by a powerful bundle of words and images.

Ayla's celebration took place on a sun-dappled day beneath a friend's leafy grape arbor. Encircling the wary honoree, seated on blankets, ten women plus her best friend, Justine, explained their connection and greeted her. Our ritual incorporated music, fire, a quest to locate the book, and a little pain burning a scrap of her still-beloved blankie. Finally, Ayla was invited to become part of the circle.

Afterwards, we all felt changed. We wondered aloud how different the world might be if every child were initiated in some intentional and loving way. What if we each knew that our own circle was out there and we could just open our book to be reminded of that again and again?

Georgia Harker is a designer with husband Chris, and has two children, Ayla and Graham.

Reprinted with permission from Full Esteem Ahead, *Wings*, Spring 1999.

Coming of Age Quilt

By Kathy Masarie, MD

THERE ARE MANY WAYS to celebrate "coming of age." In our society, we acknowledge age 16 with the right to drive a car, and age 18 brings voting privileges and "adulthood" status. Another important birthday is 13, the emergence of adolescence; however, only the Jewish religion seems to recognize it.

This is a crucial time in the life of a youth. Thirteen-year-olds want proof that we agree they are no longer children. They thrive better with more than their nuclear family to celebrate their growth. They mature best in a supportive community. A Coming of Age quilt can be the centerpiece of a ritual that acknowledges this milestone. For my daughter Kaitlin's 13th birthday, her adult female friends and relatives contributed quilt squares, which were sewn together into a quilt.

All the participants presented the quilt to her at a celebration. Each woman described what her quilt square meant and made a promise of how she would help Kaitlin through adolescence. This was a way of building a community of adults who care about Kaitlin and what happens to her as she grows through her teen years.

The idea of this quilt came from Mary Pipher's book, *The Shelter of Each Other.* On page 254, Pipher tells the following story:

"A friend of mine who is a single parent planned a coming-of-age ceremony for her daughter's thirteenth birthday. In the spring, she sent all her women friends who had known her daughter quilt pieces and asked them to stitch or draw a picture on the piece. The picture was to depict an experience the woman had had with the daughter. In the summer, all of these women met the mother and daughter for a weekend of camping, hiking, and feasting. Saturday night around the fire, there was a ceremony. Each woman showed and explained her picture."

"Then they gave the girl a gift—a promise of one way she would help the daughter grow up. One woman said she would teach the daughter to garden; another

offered to help her write papers and college applications, another could teach her French and another could help her learn to sail. The girl sat in the middle of the circle beside the fire. She listened to the stories and the offers. The women gave her hugs and congratulations. The next morning in the sunlight, they sewed the quilt together."

After Kaitlin heard this story, she told me she would like a quilt like this. I love it best that it was her idea! She made a list of the women she would like to have make her quilt squares. Four months before the party, two 6 1/2 inch muslin squares (one extra in case of mistakes) were sent out to 28 women, including her grade-school teachers. They could use anything to decorate the square. Tie-dye, permanent markers, beaded words, photo collages and traditional quilting were just a few of the techniques used. To complete the quilt, we cut some squares out of Kaitlin's baby blanket and sheets. The corner squares were photos from her childhood, which were transferred onto the fabric at a local copy shop. Many were able to attend the coming of age ceremony.

After the presentation of the quilt, each person told what her quilt square represented and made a promise to help Kaitlin in the future. Those who could not be present wrote notes that were read out loud. Her sewing teacher promised to help with a sewing crisis; her piano teacher promised to take her to recitals; a friend promised to help her understand the value of female friendships; her aunt promised to share creativity and her grandmas promised unconditional love. As we told these stories, each woman made one tie on the quilt. Most of us were teary-eyed the whole time. At the end of the ceremony, everyone shared cake and laughter. Now, Kaitlin has a community of women interested in her growing up, each with ties to her through their commitments, in addition to their friendship.

Reprinted with permission from Full Esteem Ahead, *Wings*, Winter 1998.

Lessons from Nature
By Marta Mellinger

RITES OF PASSAGE OFTEN draw on lessons from the natural world. It is in nature that we may be still enough to know our true selves. Teens will learn merely by spending time surrounded by nature and paying close attention, but adults can use the outdoors to guide and deepen a teen's experience. Asking thought-provoking questions and using the natural world as an analogy for "life" are two ways that an adult can enrich a teen's learning from an experience of nature. Here are some "rules" and questions compiled from an exercise where a Coming of Age group, after much discussion and preparation, separates from one another for a solo experience in the woods, where they took a journal and spent a number of hours in silent contemplation.

The Six Rules of a Milestone Solo Experience in the Woods

1. NUMBER ONE RULE FOR LIFE: PAY ATTENTION TO WHERE YOU ARE.
2. Don't be afraid to ask for help. Blow your whistle loud if you get lost, injured or have a real emergency. If you hear someone else blow their whistle, head back home and check in before rushing off into the woods to the rescue.
3. If you lose your way, return to the last milestone. If you lose your milestone, stop immediately, see where you are and use your whistle.
4. You need to see your last milestone to stay on path.
5. You can "come home" any time.

6. Life's about learning to learn, and learning what is needed to trust yourself and your choices.

If you think about these rules as "rules for life" what do they tell you that you need to remember? How do you think about each one as it applies to your life right now? How might you think about each one as it might apply to your life at age 21?

Milestone Questions

Moving through the land is the same as moving through life. If done well, it requires looking for answers, finding solutions, asking and being willing to receive gifts, noticing details (which way is the sun, that rock is in my right hand), envisioning your future and discovering your purpose. You may have lots and lots to think about without these questions. That's great. But here are some things you might want to consider now while sitting in the woods—or later on.

- Write a note to yourself at age 21. What do you want to be sure to remember about this time in your life? What do you want to remember to ask yourself about your life when you reach 21?
- Make a list of all the living beings you have seen on your milestone walk. Close your eyes for a while and imagine an animal coming to you and offering words of counsel and encouragement. What animals do you imagine? What did your animal guide say?
  - What are you searching for in life and how will you know when you have found it?
  - How will you recognize the need to slow down, use your senses to tune in and find your path, the paths that have heart (meaning) for your life?

  - Will you be able to accept that you will make mistakes along this journey; can you become comfortable not knowing the answers? In what ways do you want to be treated differently when you return home? Are there any specific privileges you would choose to ask for that you believe would help you grow in your independence? In what ways would these privileges help you grow.

Marta Mellinger founded Canoe Group to help organizations succeed in rapidly changing times. She has two young adult daughters.

Family Fitness

By Kathy Keller Jones, MA

It is impossible to read the news nowadays without being reminded about the abysmal state of our children's fitness. We have an epidemic of overweight citizens and the number of obese and overweight children has more than doubled since 1970. Obese children are beginning to have the same problems adults' experience, such as diabetes and heart disease. We are inadvertently creating a culture that is unhealthy for many of our youth. We know many of the elements that have contributed to this, so how do we create healthy communities for our children where making healthy choices comes more naturally?

The family teaches and models physical health in so many ways. It is natural that we teach our children to brush their teeth, bathe, and sleep well, and it is equally important that we teach them to be active every day and to eat well. That all sounds straightforward, but it turns out it is not. Powerful forces, such as the many screens  in our homes, our own fears of letting kids go outside, our busy lives, commercialism, the plethora of junk food, and the fact that we drive everywhere, are interfering with what was natural for previous generations. Kids went out every day and played actively, they ate homemade dinners with their families, had much less screen time, more imaginative play and more freedom to roam the neighborhood. In today's world it takes a conscious and concerted effort to maintain a healthy lifestyle for our families.

We can make a commitment to duplicate some of the positive conditions of a healthier past and to teach our children the joys of movement and the outdoors, as well as the satisfaction of doing activities together. Parents will need to encourage healthy eating habits and active play, while at the same time limiting the unhealthy influences. That means, in part, having systems and limits that work for all sorts of electronic devices, making sure that computers and TVs are in "public" home spaces, eating dinner together whenever possible, and making time for free play, family play and active family fun. In this way family food preparation and fitness become family priorities.

As we know, fitness can take many forms, all of which involve movement and reasonably healthy food intake. Our younger children are fit, for example, when they play actively everyday, walk to school with their family and go swimming once a week. Free play improves motor skills, provides an outlet for energy, and encourages kids to use their imagination. Elementary-aged children also need free play, and they grow in confidence when they develop skills and try out new activities. Kids need a balance between being in their bodies in their own authentic way, responding to their own inner rhythm, and learning new physical skills through enjoyable physical activity. Teens can be involved in individual or group sports, or commit to working out several times a week. One girl ran with her father in the early morning hours from middle-school on, and even though they ran in silence she felt very bonded to her father through their common fitness goal.

The family acts powerfully when they change their behavior in the direction of fitness. For example, they decide to walk or ride bikes to school rather than drive. They plan healthy meals, cook together, and stock the house with healthy snacks. They have a common understanding about why they spend less time on screens and more time having fun together: biking, playing catch, hiking, playing active games such as tag, exploring local parks, playing touch football, swimming at family swim, roller-blading, shooting baskets, you name it. The family can save money toward buying equipment that encourages active play, visit secondhand stores and stock the garage with balls and other fun equipment. Some families organize fun neighborhood games such as softball, volleyball, or badminton. When our family commits to outdoor activities like fishing, camping, and cabin trips, we are committing to a healthy active lifestyle. Fitness is a priority and a lifelong commitment and families have a golden opportunity to start their children on the right track.

Sports Clubs Can Lead to Lifelong Enjoyment

By Kathy Masarie, MD

Do you want to get away from the hassles of car-pooling, weekend games, dinner-hour practices, and over-zealous competition, and still have your child enjoy a sport? A sports club may be the answer. This is what I call a group of kids and an adult mentor who get together once or twice a week to enjoy their sport. It attempts to mimic what we grew up with: backyard sports where kids just gathered Saturdays on the grade school field for a pickup game. Today most of us live far apart and we are uncomfortable letting our kids just go off for hours at a time. Sports clubs can help kids build skills in a sport while providing low-key, low-cost fun. A sport that we love can provide us with lifelong thrills and benefits.

My sports club experience involved my son Jon when he was in the third grade. We had finished T-ball where everyone got to play equally. On the other hand, we had heard horror stories about baseball leagues —cut-throat competition, frequent practices, three-hour games, over-involved parents and intense coaches who focused only on winning. We decided regular baseball would take too big a bite out of family time with only questionable benefits. So, we organized all the kids who weren't participating in baseball to meet at our local grade school field right after school at 3:00 PM. Since most coaches didn't finish work until after 4:00 PM, the fields were free until then.

About 10 players met every Friday afternoon for eight weeks. We had matching baseball caps and snacks and drinks at practice. We did drills and played "work-up" (a scrimmage game). Occasionally, kids from a regular team joined us for an actual game. Everyone's skills improved, and we were all home by 4:30 PM for real family time.

Here's another example. Ann Garrett, a Physical Education teacher at a local elementary school, started a running club. Passionate about kids being active, she disliked the intensity she saw in organized sports. She wanted kids to have fun and get fit at the same time. She thinks kids naturally want to move their bodies and find something they enjoy. Her goal was for club members to be fit enough to compete in a local 5K run. About two months before the race she sent a flyer home with the fourth and fifth graders. The response was about 35 kids who then worked out for an hour twice a week as a group, and a third time on their own. They did warm-ups and relay games and then ran through the neighborhood, rewarded with Popsicle's at the end of practice. Parents sometimes joined them. All kept logs of their mileage. The day of the race everyone wore matching hats, used the buddy system, and had parent supervisors.

If a sports club is not for you, there are other choices. Some children are more suited to a non-traditional sport. My favorite story concerns a mom who took up rock climbing for fun. Her son, Bryan, joined her and now is a successful, national competitor. And best of all, they spend time together. If you focus on family fitness, everyone benefits. Too many families exercise separately. Personally, I'd rather do sports with my kids than sit on the sidelines watching. Remember—"the family that plays together, stays together." Getting your child into a sport he or she enjoys can lead to competence and enhance mental and physical health. Success in a sport builds confidence and carries over into the rest of our lives.

Reprinted with permission from Full Esteem Ahead, *Wings,* Spring 1998.

Aerobics • Archery • Backpacking • Badminton • Ballet • Baseball • Basketball • Bike racing • BMX bike riding • Bowling • Boxing • Canoeing • Capoeira • Cricket • Croquet • Cross-country skiing • Curling • Dancing • Diving • Downhill ski • Dragon boat racing • Fencing • Fishing • Folk-dancing • Footbag • Frisbee • Frisbee Golf • Gymnastics • Hackey sack • Hiking • Horse riding • Ice hockey • Ice-skating • Jogging • Karate • Kayaking • Lacrosse • Martial Arts • Mountain biking • Mountain climbing • Orienteering • Parachuting • Poekoelon • Pull-pull-pedal (ski, canoe, bike) • Racquetball • Recumbent bikes • Rock-climbing • Rodeo • Roller-blade hockey • Roller-blading • Rowing • Rugby • Rythmics • Sailing • Scuba diving • Skateboarding • Sculling • Snowboarding • Snow shoe • Snow shoeing • Softball • Special Olympics • Squash • Surfing • Swimming • Soccer • Synchronized swimming • Table tennis • Tae Kwan Do • Tai chi • Taiko (drumming) • Tennis • Track and Field • Triathlons (swim, bike, run) • Ultimate Frisbee

How Girls Win Self-Esteem
By Mary C. Hickey

Organized sports build confidence, teach risk-taking and encourage teamwork. Here's why girls need equal time on the playing field.

WHEN CYNTHIA KUHN was in junior high school back in the 1960s, the epitome of achievement for her was winning a coveted slot on the cheerleading squad. For her two daughters, however, being a cheerleader doesn't hold the same appeal. They'd rather be on the team, playing basketball.

Maggie, 14, is a point guard on her school's varsity team. Katie, 12, plays in their town's recreational league. Kuhn says she's thrilled that her daughters have chosen to play sports rather than follow in her footsteps as a cheerleader. "You get a lot more out of life being right in the center of the action than you do by watching from the sidelines," she says.

For as long as there have been Little League baseball and peewee football teams, youngsters have benefited enormously from participating in organized sports. In past generations, those benefits were bestowed primarily upon males. But thanks to changes in attitudes—and changes in laws—young girls today have more opportunity to reap the same rewards. The number of girls playing sports has skyrocketed. In 1971, about 4 percent of female high-school students participated in interscholastic sports, according to a report by the Women's Sports Foundation, a nonprofit educational organization in East Meadow, New York. In 1991, that number jumped to over 30 percent.

And that bodes well for the future. "Greater female sports participation is going to make stronger, more powerful women with a clearer sense of their capabilities," predicts Ellen Wahl, program director for Girls Inc., a New York City-based organization that helps girls overcome the effects of discrimination. Wahl and others believe that sports participation will help make girls happier and healthier adults—and maybe more successful in the workplace as well.

Evidence is mounting that the skills acquired on the playing field will help to level the field for girls in the professional world. A 1993 survey of 1,566 white-collar women by the Women's Sports Foundation revealed that a significant number credited past participation in organized sports with the development of traits essential to workplace success. "They learn teamwork, cooperation, risk-taking. I think they're developing a lot of skills that are going to give them an edge in the work world of tomorrow," says Marjorie Snyder, Ph.D., associate executive director of the foundation.

The Lasting Benefits

Anyone who's ever swung a tennis racquet or lobbed a volleyball knows that girls will reap immediate rewards from playing sports. Athletic involvement contributes to an individual's physical and mental well-being. Mothers of female athletes say they've seen their daughters acquire confidence and self-esteem by scoring a goal in a soccer game or batting a baseball far into right field. They observe a direct relationship between a child's sports involvement and her sense of responsibility and levels of determination and self-discipline.

"My daughter is extremely conscientious about getting to her practices and her games on time because she knows her teammates are counting on her, and she doesn't want to let them down," says Edie Journey, who lives and works in Libby, Montana. Shasta, now 13, plays tennis, basketball and fast-pitch softball.

Because these lessons are learned at such an impressionable age, they are likely to remain with a girl long after she hangs up her softball jersey. "When young girls play sports, they develop habits and attitudes that will say with them for a lifetime," says Ellen Wahl.

The physical benefits alone are significant. Research has found that children who play sports are likely to be more physically active as adults. The physical competence they develop affects their state of mind as well, sports psychologists say. For instance, if a girl sees she can be aggressive on the tennis court, she may be more comfortable acting aggressively in other areas of her life. If she learns that with effort and perseverance, she can run a mile longer than she originally thought, she may be more prone to undertake challenges at school or work.

"You learn to think strategically, take risks, work cooperatively toward a common goal," says Peggy Kellers, EdD, head softball coach and consultant for Sports Psychology at the University of Virginia. "These are things that you incorporate into other areas of your life."

New Model for Success

Some experts even suggest that sports participation may help women break through the barriers that have hindered advancement to the highest levels of business. Jane Tear, a consultant who advises corporations on gender issues, says that many women have been held back in the past because they subscribe to a "model of achievement" that does not conform to corporate culture.

Tear's theory goes like this: Girls, because they were more comfortable in academic settings in their formative years, tend to subscribe to the "academic model of achievement." Boys, who were more likely to be comfortable in physical activities, internalize a "sports model of achievement." Tear contends that the sports model reflects the realities of corporate life.

For starters, she notes that organized sports emphasize team effort. One player may be good, but without the best efforts of his teammates, he may lose the game. The same is true in business. A person may have a good idea for a product but it will never be a success in the market without support from the entire company. Girls who never play sports may not learn this lesson. In school, girls' achievements are typically based on individual effort. If a girl does well, she gets an A, no matter how her classmates do. Girls also learn that if they work hard enough, they can get all A's. "In the educational model girls learn that you get what you deserve," Tear says. "Everyone can get an A. There is no shortage of A's."

Children who play sports, however, quickly learn that no matter how hard they work and how well they play, they may lose the game. "There are serendipitous factors," Tear says. For instance, maybe the wind was blowing in the other team's direction, and that made it easier for them to score goals. "Men, because of the model they've internalized, can brush off disappointment and move on to the next thing," Tear says.

The academic success model has another important difference from the sports model. In school, risk-taking is a private endeavor. A girl's term paper, for instance, is generally only seen by the teacher. And the earlier drafts—the "practices," so to speak—are not seen by anyone at all. In sports, all practices are in full view of teammates and coaches. Consequently kids who play sports become more comfortable taking risks, a trait essential to professional and career advancement.

More at Ease on the Job

There is another asset for girls who play sports: As women, they'll be more comfortable in traditional, male-dominated workplaces. "So much behavior in the corporate world is modeled on the sports world," says Judi Brownking, who left an executive position with American Express to return to teaching and coaching track at Michigan State University.

She switched careers so she could teach girls the lessons that were so important to her success in the corporate world. "You learn to be competitive. You learn time-management skills. You develop the ability to set goals. You learn how to win and lose, and to do both gracefully," Brownking says.

"I think my daughters will be better equipped to deal with the working world than women of my generation were," says Cynthia Kuhn.

Fair Play for Girls

The number of school-age girls involved in athletics has been climbing steadily since the late 1970s, thanks in large part to a law that bans sexual discrimination in schools receiving any federal funds.

That law, Title IX of the federal Education Act, requires that schools provide equal opportunities for male and female athletic programs. "As soon as programs for girls became available, there were plenty of girls who wanted to participate," says Peggy Kellers, EdD, former executive director of the National Association for Girls and Women in Sports, and now a sports psychology consultant.

Girl's participation in organized sports still lags far behind that of boys, however, with about one third of high-school girls playing interscholastic sports compared to half of boys, according to the National Federation of State High School Associations (2003).

Many school districts are trying to narrow that gender gap. The Montgomery County School District in Maryland, for instance, appointed a task force to study the issue, and is implementing a number of recommendations on how to expand opportunities for girls. Kellers says, "I think people understand that girls, just like boys, benefit from sports, and they want to make sure there's equal opportunity to realize those benefits."

For more information on the law, or ideas on how to expand sports for girls in your community, contact the National Association for Girls and Women in Sport, www.aahperd. org/nagws.

Reprinted with permission from author Mary Hickey. First appeared in *Working Mother* magazine, January 1994.

Go Out and Play: Youth Sports in America

Executive Summary by Don Sabo, PhD, Phil Veliz, MA and Women's Sports Foundation

THIS STUDY MEASURES THE nationwide participation rates of girls and boys in exercise and organized team sports. The central focus is on how the intersections among families, schools and communities are related to children's involvement and interest in athletics and physical activity. Some of the personal and social benefits associated with children's athletic participation are also identified and discussed. The athletic interests and involvements of girls and boys are examined from childhood through late adolescence, including entry into sport as well as drop-out patterns.

American families display a wide array of cultural, economic, racial and ethnic characteristics. Despite this diversity, all families have two things in common. First, they nurture children from infancy through young adulthood. Second, parents do not raise their children in isolation. Family life unfolds within an institutional web that includes schools, churches, community organizations, after-school programs, government, economic forces and—central to this study—sports. It is within this wider social matrix that children's athletic ability and interest in physical activity take shape and either blossom or dwindle.

The findings and conclusions in this report are based on two nationwide surveys. The Women's Sports Foundation commissioned Harris Interactive to complete a school-based survey of youth drawn from a random selection of approximately 100,000 public, private and parochial schools in the United States. The nationwide sample consists of 2,185 third- through 12th-grade girls and boys. In addition, phone interviews were conducted with a national cross-section of 863 randomly selected parents of children in grades 3 through 12. Parents were asked how they think and feel about their children's interest and involvement in sports and physical activity. African-American and Hispanic parents were over-sampled in order to deepen understanding of the needs and experiences of underserved girls, boys and their families.

This report confirms that sports are a resource for US children as well as their families. Children's athletic participation was associated with higher levels of family satisfaction. Sports and physical activity were also linked with improved physical and emotional health, academic achievement and quality of life for children.

A complex picture of gender differences in athletic opportunities and physical activity emerges from this study. There is a nationwide gender gap in physical activity and sports involvement between girls and boys. The size of the gender gap, however, does not stretch uniformly across the country and all age brackets. In many communities, girls show similar levels of athletic participation and interest as boys. In other communities, however, access to sport and physical activity for girls appears to be thwarted by economic disadvantages and inadequate school resources. Young urban girls, especially, have a narrower window of opportunity for becoming involved with sports than their male counterparts and girls from suburban and rural communities. One in four 9th- to 12th-grade girls has never participated in organized or team sports in urban schools, compared to about one in six urban boys. In short, progress on the gender front in U.S. sports has been made, but it remains uneven, and it is often poor and mainly urban girls who are being left behind.

Some of the major findings documented by this study are summarized below within four main themes.

Participation In Sports And Physical Activity: The Gender Gap

1. **A Gender Gap Exists in Sports and Physical Activity—But It Is Uneven.** Girls generally are not as involved with sports and physical activity as boys. However, the gender gap is wide in some areas and narrow in others. Whereas similar rates of sports participation between girls and boys exist in suburban communities, urban and rural girls are less involved than their male peers. Variations in the gender gap in athletic participation often appear to be driven by economic disparities, race and ethnicity, and family characteristics. These variations strongly suggest that girls' and boys' participation in sports and exercise is primarily shaped by access and opportunity.

2. **Interest in Sports and Exercise Among Girls and Boys Is About Opportunity and Encouragement, Not Biology.** Girls' and boys' interest in sports and exercise varies by grade level, school location and income level. In some communities boys and girls show similar levels of interest in sports, while in other communities, boys' interest levels are higher than those of girls. Parents very often feel that their daughters and sons have similar interest in sports, especially when their children are younger (3rd through 8th grades). In short, interest in sports can often vary more within genders than it does across genders. And finally, boys tend to overestimate their interest in sports, while girls lean toward underestimating their athletic interests. For example, 42% of 3rd- to 8th-grade boys who are non-athletes said that "sports are a big part of who they are," compared to 16% of non-athletic girls. Female athletes, moreover, are often involved with several clubs and organizations outside sport, whereas male athletes focus more singly on sports.

3. **The Gender Gap in Physical Education.** Urban girls are the "have-nots" of physical education in the United States, with 84% report having no PE classes at all in the 11th and 12th grades. Rural girls in the same grades are not far behind with 68% reporting no PE classes. Across the country, young low-income children—both girls and boys—are underserved with regard to school-based physical education. Generally, more boys attend PE classes than girls, especially in urban and rural schools.

4. **Girls Now Take Part in a Wider Array of Sports and Exercise Activities than Boys.** Girls explore a wider array of sports and exercise activities than boys do, including traditional, recreational and newly emerging sports such as cheerleading, dance, double Dutch and volleyball. Boys focus more on traditional sports and exercise activities, which, most often, take the form of organized school and community sports.

5. **Girls Have a Narrower Window of Opportunity in Sports.** Girls enter sports at a later age than boys (7.4 years old, compared to 6.8 years old). The widest gap between the age girls and boys enter sport appears in urban communities (7.8 and 6.9 years old, respectively). Girls also drop out sooner and in greater numbers than boys. Girls' late start may set them up for failure in sports during the middle-school years (6th through 8th grades).

Sports and Family Life

1. **Sports Are an Asset for U.S. Families, and Families Are a Resource for Young Athletes.** Children's involvement with sports is associated with higher levels of family satisfaction. Youth sports can help build communication and trust between parents and children. Sports help parents and children spend more time together. These positive connections are particularly evident in dual-parent families, but they also resonate in single-parent families.

2. **Many Parents Say Their Daughters Are Being Shortchanged.** While a majority of parents say they want similar levels of athletic opportunity for their daughters and sons, many believe that their schools and communities are failing to deliver the goods. Many parents are aware that girls are getting fewer opportunities in sports and physical activity than boys are. More African-American and Hispanic parents feel schools and communities are failing their daughters.

3. **More Dads Need to "Step Up to the Plate" to Mentor Young Female Athletes.** Non-family members are the top two people girls mentioned as their mentors in exercise and sports—coaches and physical education teachers. For boys, in contrast, dads and coaches top the list of main mentors. 46% of boys and 28% of girls credit their father for teaching them "the most" about sports and exercise. While mothers and fathers provide similar levels of encouragement and support for both their daughters and sons, many girls may be

shortchanged by dads who channel more energy into mentoring sons than daughters.

Children's Well-Being and Development

1. **Sports Help Create Healthy, Well-Adjusted Children.** Sports are a health and educational asset for U.S. girls and boys. Organized sports are associated with children's general health and body esteem, healthy weight, popularity, quality of life and educational achievement. Female athletes often derive greater benefits from athletic participation than their male peers.
2. **Participating in Organized or Team Sports Helps Enhance Girls' Quality of Life.** Girls who do not currently participate in a team sport are less content with their lives than girls involved with sports. Sports involvement enhances the quality of life for girls.
3. **The Benefits of Athletic Participation Unfold Long Before High School.** Many of the social, educational and health benefits linked to sports participation begin during the elementary school years. The positive contributions of athletic involvement to youth development are especially visible among 6th- to 8th-grade girls and boys.

Diverse and Unrecognized Populations

1. **Sports are Racially and Ethnically Diverse, but Inequities Are Very Real.** Youth sports are racially and ethnically diverse. 15% of all girls and 16% of all boys who participate in sports are African-American. 17% of female athletes and 15% of male athletes are Hispanic, while Asian girls and boys comprise 8% and 12%, respectively, of children who play sports. And yet, proportionally fewer girls of color are involved with sports than white girls. Girls of color are also much more likely than their male counterparts to be non-athletes. The same discrepancies across racial and ethnic groups do not exist among boys. Girls of color are doubly hit by both gender and race discrimination in sport.
2. **Children with Disabilities.** About 9 out of every 100 U.S. families have a child who has a disability that can interfere with sports and exercise. Most sports and physical activity programs are currently designed to meet the interests and needs of children without disabilities. Some sport leaders and educators assume that children with some kind of disability are not capable of being physically active or just not interested in sports. The findings in this study, however, show that children with special needs are interested in

sports and exercise, and many of their parents want to see more programs offered in schools and communities. A gender gap in sports and exercise activity does exist among children with disabilities, and it is the boys who are less physically active than the girls. Finally, the exercise frequency of both girls and boys with disabilities declines more sharply than their counterparts without disabilities from the elementary through middle school and high school years.

3. **Boys in Immigrant Families Are More Likely than Girls to Play Sports.** This is the first study to gather some basic facts about athletic participation among children in immigrant families. 23% of children have at least one parent born outside the United States. Compared to boys, girls in immigrant families report lower rates of athletic participation. Many immigrant parents also hold more traditional attitudes toward girls' and boys' interest in sports.

Policy Recommendations

This research report is designed to foster public discussion and policy debate over the state of girls' sports and physical activity in the United States. In order to fulfill its strategic research initiative, the Women's Sports Foundation seeks to unite and educate local and national nonprofit organizations, government agencies, schools and sport organizations that serve the interest of girls' health and empowerment through physical activity. A National Policy Advisory Board was created to review the findings of this study and to identify key policy recommendations. The members are recognized leaders from academic research, education, health and sport.

The findings in this study form an evidence-based foundation to help policymakers assess the current state of U.S. girls' and boys' physical activity and sports. The Center for Research on Physical Activity, Sport & Health has worked with the Women's Sports Foundation to develop nine clusters of policy recommendations to advance the health and well-being of both girls and boys through sports and physical activity. See the final section of the complete report.

Tell Me More and Other Great Tips on Connecting with Your Kid

By Positive Coach Alliance at www.positivecoach.com

Empowering Conversations with Your Child

When we think about what makes people friends with each other, a number of things come to mind. For example, our friends like us and enjoy spending time with us, as we enjoy them. And what is it we mostly do when we are together with our friends? Mostly we talk and listen to each other.

Conversations are the glue between people, the essential element in a strong relationship. Relationships wither without communication, and the very best form of communication is the conversation. Many parents fall into the trap of thinking that it is their job to talk and their child's to listen. Actually that's only half-right. It is also our job to listen and the child's job to talk. It's a wonderful thing when a parent and child can really talk to and hear each other.

It is important that parents intentionally seek out conversations about sports with their athletes. Here are some suggestions for how to engage your child in a conversation about sports.

1. Establish Your Goal—A Conversation Among Equals: A conversation is something between equals. Kings didn't have conversations with their subjects. They told them what to do. Prepare yourself for a conversation with your child by reminding yourself that sports is her thing, not yours. Remember that you want to support her, to let her know that you are on her side. Your goal is not to give advice on how to become a better athlete. It should be to engage your child in a conversation among equals, one of whom (you!) is on the side of the other (her!).

2. Adopt a Tell-Me-More Attitude: Brenda Ueland penned one of the most important essays on relationships ever written, "Tell Me More": "When we are listened to, it creates us, makes us unfold and expand. Ideas actually begin to grow within us and come to life." Adopt the attitude that you want your child to tell-you-more ("I really want to hear what you have to say."), and then listen to what he has to say—even if you don't agree with it or like it—and you will begin to tap into what Ueland calls the "little creative fountain" in your child.

If you are very tired, strained … this little fountain is muddied over and covered with a lot of debris … it is when people really listen to us, with quiet fascinated attention, that the little foun-tain begins to work again, to accelerate in the most surprising way.

Think of your conversation with your child as an Olympic event with judges. A conversation that rates a 9 or a 10 is one in which the child does more talking and the parent more listening. Set your goal before you start, and go for it.

3. Listen! In many instances you may know exactly what your child can do to improve. However, this is a conversation, remember? Your goal is to get your child to talk about her sports experience, so ask rather than tell. Save your tellings for another time.

4. Use Open-Ended Questions: Some questions lend themselves to one-word responses. "How was school today?" "Fine." Your goal is to get your child to talk at length, so ask questions that will tend to elicit longer, more thoughtful responses.
- "What was the most enjoyable part of today's practice/game?"
- "What worked well?"
- "What didn't turn out so well?"
- "What did you learn that can help you in the future?"
- "Any thoughts on what you'd like to work on before the next game?"

5. Also ask about life-lesson and character issues: "Any thoughts on what you've learned in practice this week that might help you with other parts of your life?" Even if you saw the entire game, the goal is to get your child to talk about the game the way she saw it, not for you to tell her what she could have done better.

6. Show You Are Listening: Make it obvious to your child that you are paying attention through use of nonverbal actions such as making eye contact as he talks, nodding your head and making "listening noises" ("uh-huh," "hmmm," "interesting," etc.).
Listening is one of the greatest gifts you can give your child! Ueland again:

> Who are the people, for example, to whom you go for advice? Not to the hard, practical ones who can tell you exactly what to do, but to the listeners; that is, the kindest, least censorious, least bossy people that you know. It is because by pouring out your problem to them, you then know what to do about it yourself.

7. Let Your Child Set the Terms: William Pollack, MD, author of *Real Boys: Rescuing Our Sons from the Myths of Boyhood*, notes that children have different "emotional schedules" that determine when they are ready to talk about an experience. Forcing a conversation right after a competition (when there may be a lot of emotion) is often less successful than waiting until the child gives an indication that he is ready to talk. Boys may take longer than girls to talk about an experience, so look for prompts that a child is ready. And conversations don't have to be lengthy to be effective. If your child wants a brief discussion, defer to his wishes. If he feels like every discussion about sports is going to be long, he'll likely begin to avoid them. And don't be afraid of silence. Stick with it and your child will open up to you.

8. Connect through activity: Sometimes the best way to spark a conversation is through an activity that your child enjoys. Playing a board game or putting a puzzle together can allow space for a child to volunteer thoughts and feelings about the game and how he performed. This is especially important for boys, who often resist a direct adult-style of conversation.

9. Enjoy: The most important reason why you should listen to your child with a tell-me-more attitude: Because then she will want to talk to you, and as she (and you) get older, you will find there is no greater gift than a child who enjoys conversations with you.

Guidelines for Honoring the Game

The key to preventing adult misbehavior in youth sports is a youth sports culture in which all involved "Honor the Game." Honoring the Game gets to the ROOTS of the matter and involves respect for the Rules, Opponents, Officials, Teammates and one's Self. You don't bend the rules to win. You understand that a worthy opponent is a gift that forces you to play to your highest potential. You show respect for officials even when you disagree. You refuse to do anything that embarrasses your team. You live up to your own standards even if others don't. Here are ways that parents can create a positive youth sports culture so that children will have fun and learn positive character traits to last a lifetime.

- **Before the Game:**
  1. Make a commitment to Honor the Game in action and language no matter what others may do.
  2. Tell your child before each game that you're proud of him or her regardless of how well he or she plays.
- **During the Game:**
  1. Fill your children's "Emotional Tank" through praise and positive recognition so they can play their very best.
  2. Don't give instructions to your child during the game. Let the coach correct player mistakes.
  3. Cheer good plays by both teams (this is advanced behavior!)
  4. Mention good calls by the official to other parents.
  5. If an official makes a "bad" call against your team? Honor the Game—BE SILENT!
  6. If another parent on your team yells at an official? Gently remind him or her to Honor the Game.
  7. Don't do anything in the heat of the moment that you will regret after the game. Ask yourself, "Will this embarrass my child or the team?"
  8. Remember to have fun! Enjoy the game.
- **After the Game:**
  1. Thank the officials for doing a difficult job for little or no pay.
  2. Thank the coaches for their commitment and effort.
  3. Don't give advice. Instead ask your child what he or she thought about the game and then LISTEN. Listening fills Emotional Tanks.
  4. Tell your child again that you are proud of him or her, whether the team won or lost.

Reprinted with permission from Positive Coaching Alliance. Check out more great resources on healthy coaching at: www.positivecoachingalliance.org.

Learning Life Lessons through Sports

By Kathy Masarie, MD and Coach John Child

Positive Self-Critique

John Child's coaching style started with his management role at work. When he started a review with "you are doing 'this' wrong," people would shut down and get defensive. So he started asking, "Tell me what you're proud of," and then asked, "What's sub-par?" He found people to be surprisingly honest. It was easy for John to just "coach" them along to figure out solutions for improvement.

When John started coaching his child's team, the same thing happened. Kids shut down when told what they were doing wrong, not unlike the adults. Over time he developed a routine. Early in the season, after the first game, he starts the practice with what he thinks the team did well, then poorly as a team. Then he asks the kids to share something they were proud of and something they want to work on. He picks the kids with naturally out-going personalities first. Without fail, they pick something accurate in their self-critique. There are always 3-4 shy, non-athletic kids who find this process very painful, but John helps them through it. Every 2-3 games he repeats this, and gradually the shy ones have their hands up in the air as fast as the others. In addition, they start to critique themselves as a team and to see what the other team didn't do as a team. This leads them to think for themselves on the field.

> Team sports are a great place to learn life lessons.

Team Building: Start Early

Team sports are a great place to learn life lessons.
1. We belong. In addition to their team name, the team develops a song and a banner. Each game the kid who tried especially hard takes the banner home (John starts this at age 9. Every kid gets picked by the end of the season).
2. Empowerment—everyone counts: If you show up to practice you get equal playing time.
3. Everyone does something well and even the "best" have their weak points. We want the kids to be proud of themselves and to be proud to be on the team. We want them to learn to critique themselves.
4. Life is not fair. There will always be bad referees, people make mistakes. It is no big deal. (John deliberately makes bad calls in practice so they get used to it. "Bad calls" occur many times in life, too.)

5. Winning is just a by-product; success is something more. John likes to start with his soccer teams early at the kindergarten coed level and stay with them until they enter classics or high school. His "average" caliber kids have a lot of fun and also win most of their games.

Parents

"The best way to deal with problems is to avoid them," says John. "At the first team meeting, our parents sign pledges: 'At games I will yell for the team—I will not yell at a particular kid—I will not give specific directives—I will be on time.' However, I tell them kids are responsible for getting ready and getting their parents there on time."

"Most important way to deal with parents is to not single anyone out." If some kids have been late, the entire group hears, "Some of you have been getting to practice late. That's not fair to everyone else." If there is a serious issue, he recommends talking to the parent in private. No confrontation on the field. If the parent is psyched out by a bad call, let them "know you noticed it too and that you will deal with it. It's not helping anybody to be screaming."

> **ATTENTION ADULTS:**
> 50% of kids drop out of youth sports by age 13.
> Number one reason: "It's not fun anymore."
> **LIFE LESSON HAVE FUN!**

Two new tips:

1. "Let parents know what skills you are having the kids concentrate on—passing or trapping the ball. This helps the parents focus on those goals, rather than just on scoring."
2. "Don't coddle your girls." From the girls' moms he's hearing, "Do they have to practice for 1.5 hrs? Do they really need to practice two times a week?" He coached boy's teams for years and never once did a mom worry that their boys were working too hard.

John Child is the father of a son and a daughter.

Reprinted with permission from Full Esteem Ahead, *Wings,* Spring 2002

Positive Coaching Alliance:
Transforming Youth Sports so Sports Can Transform Youth
By Harmony Barrett

It's another afternoon of watching your son and his baseball team play their cross-town rivals. The coaches have been preparing the boys all week to crush the other team—the enemy. You chat with the other parents, but as a group, you are careful to keep your distance from the other teams' parents. No making friends with the enemy! One dad sitting near to you yells orders at his son, criticizing his every move. You hear the Head Coach tell the players to run over anyone who gets in their way.

Suddenly, your son hits a ball into right field, the right fielder picks it up and throws it to first base, just as your son's foot hits the bag—the referee calls him "Out!" The coaches jump up from the bench and charge towards the official, parents start yelling out insults, and the players join in on the barrage of objections. In the middle of the commotion, your son turns around and looks directly at you for guidance. Your next move will send him a myriad of messages, from how to handle conflict and what respect means, to the values you hold for him and the importance of healthy competition.

As we find ourselves in an increasingly problematic youth sports culture, a movement is emerging to curtail the growing aggression among youth, parents, coaches, and officials at youth sporting events, as well as belittling and negative coaching techniques.

The Positive Coaching Alliance (PCA), a national organization out of Stanford University, reports that in any given year, more than 4 million coaches work with more than 40 million young athletes in the US. Ideally, this experience "provides opportunities for children to learn important lessons about determination, commitment, hard work, teamwork, and empathy while acquiring increased self-confidence and positive character traits" (www.positivecoach.org). Sounds great, doesn't it? Isn't this exactly the experience we want for our kids? The question remains, how did we get so far away from this ideal vision of youth sports?

That is exactly the question the PCA is trying to answer; but, more importantly, they are trying to create a culture where kids love to play the game while maintaining a healthy sense of competition.

"Positive coaching is very difficult because of the arena we are in," said Rob Baarts, a former professional soccer player who now coaches for a Soccer Club in Portland, Oregon. Baarts noted that, while professional sports have positive effects on youth sports, the influence from the inflated importance put on professional teams and players has trickled down to younger players. Sometimes parents and coaches have inflated expectations of kids.

Furthermore, the PCA provides an arena for parents, coaches, and leadership members to feel empowered to make changes in their local areas. Primarily, they achieve this by promoting the Positive Coaching Mental Model, defined by three main themes:

1) Redefining what it means to be a winner: "The problem in sports right now is the 'win at all costs' mentality. What we're trying to do is change that to the Positive Coaching Mental Model. A Positive Coach is a 'Double-Goal Coach' who wants to win and also helps players develop character, so they can be successful in life. Winning is important, but the second goal, helping players learn 'life lessons,' is more important," explained Baarts.

He suggests that coaches work to develop character by making it clear to their players that effort and learning are more important than not making mistakes. This reduces anxiety and raises confidence.

Some coaches have developed a mistake ritual with their players to let the person who made the blunder know that it is okay to forget about it. One such ritual is called "the flush," where everyone on the court or field mimics flushing a toilet when someone makes a mistake, as if they are flushing it away … to "let it go."

2) Honoring the Game: Honoring the Game is getting to the ROOTS of the matter and involves respect for the Rules, Opponents, Officials, Teammates and one's Self. Don't bend the rules to win. Understand that a worthy opponent is a gift that forces you to play to your highest potential. Show respect for officials even when you disagree. Refuse to do anything that embarrasses your team. Live up to your own standards even if others don't.

It is important that coaches model behavior that they expect of their players, such as respecting the officials. If the coach doesn't agree with the official, but does not speak up, it is their responsibility to explain why they didn't argue the call and to validate the kids' frustrations. This will promote healthy responses in the future by the kids and help them to focus on the game while moving past the officials' calls.

3) Filling the Emotional Tank: A Positive Coach is a positive motivator who refuses to motivate through fear, intimidation, or shame. Baarts compared this technique to filling the tank of a car: filling kids up with positive feedback keeps them going and keeps their energy up, which makes them more coachable and more apt to listen. On the contrary, negative criticism drains them so they run "out of gas."

A positive way to build team unity is to hold a "Winners Circle," where each player says one thing they were proud of in the game and one thing they think they need to work on. Or, each player says something positive that they saw someone else do.

Youth Tell What Coaches Need to Know
YMCA coach Nick Firchau has heard kids say::

When coaches yell at us, it makes me feel bad. We're trying to do something good. I think couches should encourage us.
　　　　　　　　—Jessica, 11, 5th grade, plays softball

Coaches make you practice and that's good. If they're really bossy, or if they're pushing too hard, then it is not fun. But if they push you hard but not too hard, then it makes you do something. And usually you are not doing it. Parents shouldn't be competitive at my age. It depends on what they yell, but I think if they are booing the other team then it's not good.
　　　　　　　　　　—Jon, 10, 4th grade, plays soccer,
　　　　　　　　　　baseball, basketball

When coaches yell, you get discouraged. They should make you want to do the sport instead of not wanting to do it. Coaches shouldn't order you around like they're your mother or father.
—Selena, 9, 4th grade, ice skating

Coaches shouldn't yell at us, because we already know what we're trying to do. When coaches yell at me, it makes me feel like an idiot. —Michael 8, 2nd grade, plays baseball

Positive Coach Alliance offers workshops to educate coaches, parents, and youth sports leaders (including Board of Directors, the registrar, officials' representatives, field administrators, and head referees) about positive coaching and positive interactions between these entities. These workshops are delivered through partnerships with cities, schools and local and national youth sports organizations. Check out www.positivecoach.org to find out how to start a positive sports environment for the kids in your community.

Harmony Barrett was the Program Manager for Full Esteem Ahead and now lives in Boulder, CO.

Reprinted with permission from Full Esteem Ahead, *Wings,* Spring 2002.

Healthy Coach-Parent Partnership
1. Recognize the commitment the coach has made.
2. Make early, positive contact with the coach.
3. Fill the coach's emotional tank with positive feedback.
4. Don't put the player in the middle by talking with the coach directly when you don't like something.
5. Don't give instructions during a game or practice
6. Fill your child's emotional tank.
7. Fill the emotional tank of the entire team.
8. Encourage other parents to "Honor the Game."

My Life as a Bobcat

By Fred Edera

I WAS THE ONLY PARENT to show up at the 1st grade team meeting, so I became the coach. With the help of two other parents, we had a season and the kids had a good time. We made up some exercises to play in practice. We named the team the Bobcats and the kids had a great time chasing the ball in a pack. I am glad we didn't know the game that well, because we would have overwhelmed them with strategy and driven them away. Our secret to success was to let the children have a good time and be sensitive to when we were impeding enjoyment—and to bring really good snacks. If you asked one of our 1st graders about the game, he or she would probably have said, "It was great. We had Rice Krispie Snacks." They always thought they won the game, regardless of the score. I had fun, so I signed up for next year.

> "The children don't think they are learning skills. They think they are having fun playing games."

In second grade, the Bobcats went from co-ed to a girls' team. I went to my first coaching clinic that summer, a six-hour, specific clinic sponsored by the Portland Youth Soccer Association (www.oregonyouthsoccer.org). My new assistant coaches and I look forward to them every year.

In our first clinic, we learned many short, enjoyable games that teach soccer skills. Several variations of tag teach the players to run with a soccer ball while looking up, which is a crucial skill. Other games include running, and children will run forever while playing, even though they don't like to run laps. All the games were designed to have each girl kicking a soccer ball as often as possible. The Bobcats loved it. They ran, kicked and got in shape. I am particularly drawn to the least adept players—since I was one. Our practice games kept them moving, kicking and learning, and they improved. Everybody learns: what a discovery!

The clinics taught us what to expect developmentally. For example, second graders play "My Ball" and don't pass, and you can't make them. What a relief. We were doing a good job, after all. We had produced engaged players who wanted the ball, wherever it was. They were learning to play this game, on their own, natural schedule. Some of the 3rd graders learned to pass and to play defense with a plan in mind, but many of the Bobcats were not ready for these skills.

This year's Bobcats are 4th graders, and they are putting the entire game together: passing, predicting where they should be, working together to create plays, and communicating with each other on the field. They learned how through our practice games and their own maturity. Let me make this perfectly clear. I can't show them how; I do not have a sophisticated "game plan" each Saturday. They are making the connections between what we practice and how to use it in a game. They try things and experiment. They are starting to see the whole field, and where everyone needs to be. We couldn't have forced this knowledge into the 2nd graders with Vulcan mind melds. I'm glad we didn't try.

We have all grown closer over the years. I am an important person in the players' lives. Our families have grown closer, too. Everyone expects a phone call early in August. Our practices begin in the last, hot days of summer. Soccer is a season in our lives. I get more excited each year as the girls learn together. I love watching some of the girls become exceptional players, but my single biggest thrill is finding that some of the slower, less confident girls have learned that they are pretty good athletes. They may never make varsity, but they will remember that they can do well in sports. I'm pretty sure that I will run into the players later, during their teenage years, and I look forward to hearing what they accomplished.

Fred Edera is married to Peg Edera, a spiritual coach, and father to Mia. When he's not coaching soccer, he's a math tutor.

Reprinted with permission from Full Esteem Ahead, *Wings*, Spring 2002.

Family Empowerment Network Recommended Handout for Coaches and Parents

A healthy experience on a sport team can be an incredible way to build assets in a child's life. Potential Developmental Assets include: #3 *Other adult relationships*; #7 *Community values youth*; #8 *Youth as resources*; #14 *Adult role models*; #16 *High expectations*; #18 *Youth programs*; #26 *Caring*; #30 *Responsibility*; #31 *Restraint*; #32 *Planning and decision-making*; #33 *Interpersonal competence*; #36 *Peaceful conflict resolution* and #38 *Self-esteem*. Coaches can be powerful, important mentors in your child's life. Have Fun!

For information on 40 Developmental Assets, check: www.search-institute.org
For information on discussion guides to support parents, check: www.family-empower.com

Asset Building Ideas for Coaches:

Coaches teach young people not only the rules and strategy of games but important lessons about life as well. You can help young people develop confidence and self-esteem, help them learn to resolve conflicts peacefully, teach them ways to take care of their health and well-being, and help them develop skills for communicating with others. Here are a few ways coaches can be asset builders:

- **Learn the names of all the players on your team** and call them by name. Make a point to talk at least once with each player each time your practice or play.
- **Create and maintain a positive atmosphere.** Two top reasons young people participate in sports are to have fun and to spend time with their friends. Winning is not one of their top reasons.
- **Focus on helping players get better, not be the best.** It will reduce players' fear of failure and give them permission to try new things and stretch their skills (asset #16: High expectations).
- **Know that highly competitive sports can often cause a great deal of stress for young people.** The intense pressure that goes along with trying to be the best can sometimes lead to unhealthy outcomes such as substance abuse and/or disorders. Be careful not to push young people too hard and learn about the warning signs of possible problems.
- **Care about your athletes' lives outside of the sport** and show them that they are valuable people as well as team members.
- **Adapt your teaching style and language to the players' age level.** Young children do not always know sports terms. Use words and concepts they understand. On the other hand, older youth may be more successful when they understand the big picture of what they are trying to accomplish as well as the specific skills or strategies needed.
- **Set goals both for individuals and for the team.** Include young people in setting these goals.
- **Catch kids doing things right.** Be quick to praise a player's efforts. The best feedback in immediate and positive.
- **Use the sandwich method of correcting a player's mistake.** First praise, then constructively criticize, then praise again.
- **Always preserve players' dignity.** Sarcasm does not work well with young people. They may not always remember what you say, but they always remember how you said it.
- **Insist that all team members treat one another with respect.** Then model, monitor, and encourage respect. Have a zero-tolerance policy for teasing that hurts someone's feelings.
- **Be specific about a code of conduct and expectations** for athletes, parents, spectators, and team personnel.
- **Encourage athletes to do well in school** and to be motivated to achieve.
- **Respect other activities and priorities in athletes' lives.** Avoid conflicts with their other commitments and respect their need for time with their families.
- **Find ways each child can participate,** even if he or she is not particularly skilled in the sport.
- **Listen to and encourage your athletes' dreams,** concerns, and desires—sports-related or otherwise.
- **Develop leadership skills in young athletes** by giving them opportunities to lead practice drills and develop a team code of conduct.
- **Take time at the end of practice to have the group offer positive comments about each player's performance that day.** Make sure no one is left out.
- **Split up cliques on the team by mixing up groups for drills and scrimmages.**
- **Plan a community service project for the team.** It teaches players to give something back to the community.
- **If you have an end-of-season gathering, take time to say a few positive things about each player.** Avoid Most Valuable Player awards and other "rankings." Focus on the relationships, the improvements of the team, and the unique contributions of each player.

Creating Community 10

Andrea Millen, 14 yrs. Private School

Creating Community:
Building a Culture that Cares about Kids

"It is in the shelter of each other that the people live."
—Irish Proverb

"Do not pray for an easy life, pray to be a strong person."
—Anonymous

"Thousands of candles can be lighted from a single candle and the candle of life will not be shortened. Happiness never decreases by being shared."
—Buddha

"Whatever you can do or imagine, begin it; boldness has beauty, magic and power in it."
—Goethe

"You can create the life you dream about—the family life you long for. Just decide you want a 'connected, thriving family', vision it, and then commit to it. The rest will follow."
—Kathy Masarie

GOALS

- To solidify a vision for yourself, your daughter, and your family and to plan the steps you will take to create a nurturing, supportive, and connected family and community.

- To use the Developmental Assets to build on what is strong and positive in your family and community.

- To integrate regular volunteering into your family activities, as well as actively contributing to a strong, inclusive community.

- To establish a personal plan for staying connected to other parents and their daughters.

OVERVIEW

In our first chapter, we asked parents to make a list of positive visions and wishes for your family and your daughter. This is a good time to look at that vision again, as your discussion group reads this last chapter and you start to think of next steps to nurture your daughter's mental, social, and emotional development. Over the past nine sessions, you have discussed and shared some difficult issues that families and girls may face in today's world. Remembering a positive vision for your daughter will help empower you to network within your own family, with other parents, and with your community to create a positive and supportive environment for your daughter and for all children. It is our hope that you will bring these visions to fruition.

Family Empowerment Network believes that parents are the best resource for helping their children thrive in the transition from childhood to adulthood. Parents can foster an environment at home and within their community that supports their children's emerging competence, caring and responsibility. We sincerely hope that you will take the information you have learned from *Raising Our Daughters Parenting Guide* and apply it constructively within your lives. A group of committed individuals like yourselves, choosing to take the time and effort to make a difference, can truly turn positive visions for our youth into realities.

Families Making a Difference

Changing your daughter's world for the better starts at home. Families are the most important source of encouragement, caring, support, and unconditional love for our children. Connection to family is one of your daughter's greatest protective factors. Families are more important than ever now that we are living in a time when our outside culture is often discouraging and even harmful to the healthy development of our children. Dr. Stephen Covey, in his book *The Seven Habits of Highly Effective Families*, encourages parents to clearly understand the power they have to create the kind of nurturing family life that will inspire and protect their children. He states:

One of the best parts of being a family is that you can encourage one another. You can put courage into one another. You can believe in one another. You can affirm one another. You can assure one another that you are never going to give up, that you see the potential, and that you are acting in faith based on that potential rather than on any particular behavior or circumstance. You can be bold and strengthen one another's hearts and minds. You can weave a strong and secure safety net of encouraging circumstances in the home so that family members can cultivate those kinds of internal resiliencies and strengths that will enable them to deal with the discouraging, anti-family circumstances outside.

Mary Pipher, in her book, *The Shelter of Each Other: Rebuilding our Families*, echoes these same sentiments. She reminds us that much of what ails families today is related to our toxic culture. When our kids have problems with sexuality, addictions, or school failure, for example, it is simply not helpful to shift the blame to parents or teens. Our popular culture significantly endangers the healthy development of our children.

Pipher suggests that modern American families think of themselves as immigrants within their own culture. Immigrants, like families in modern America, must find ways to straddle two different cultures, the family culture and the outside one, each with its own set of values and behaviors.

We are all immigrants today living in a culture whose stories are not our stories and whose values are not our values. Families are stronger when they acknowledge this and unite to resist the messages and influences that would harm them.

To survive, the immigrant family must use discretion to pick the best values and behaviors, while rejecting negative or harmful outside forces. Faced with these difficulties, families who unite together will flourish, while those who attack each other from within will flounder. Likewise, families can embrace the wonders and joys of modern living, while limiting the impact of and exposure to harmful technologies, influences and behaviors. In this way, families can successfully learn to work together, to enrich their relationships and to create healthy communities in spite of the difficulties encountered in the outside world.

More than any single factor that parents can control, studies have repeatedly shown that "feeling cared about and connected" during one's youth is the key to a safer adolescence and a happy adult life. In Chapter 8: "Keeping Her Safe" (p. 8:18), we shared the National Longitudinal Study of Adolescent Health, a survey of over 90,000 youth, which found that there were two factors (out of more than one hundred) that most protected children from negative outcomes during adolescence. The first protective factor was a feeling of connectedness at home, defined as closeness to parent(s), perceived caring by parent(s), and feeling understood, loved, wanted and paid attention to by family members. The second protective factor was a feeling of connectedness at school, defined as being treated fairly by teachers, feeling close to and having good relationships with students and teachers. Again, we can see the supreme importance of relationships to the healthy development of our children. In a fascinating sociological study of eight teens living in a well-off suburb, Patricia Hersch, author of *A Tribe Apart*, helps us to understand from the inside out how much teens need parents, teachers and other adults to be involved in their lives and how overwhelming their lives can be without enough adult presence. The good news is that creating connected relationships costs very little. It does, however, require giving our children a significant investment of our time and energy, learning ways of relating to our children that are loving, empowering and supportive, and setting limits on screen time. In **"Slow Down: You're Movin' Too Fast … For Real Connection"** (p. 10:14), Marta Mellinger shares some sage advice for families from Simon and Garfunkel:

Slow down, you move too fast. Gotta make the morning last. Just kickin' down the cobblestones— lookin' for fun, and feelin' groovy.

Taking the Time to Build Assets
Taking the time to build deeper connections in our families and communities is what this last chapter of

Raising Our Daughters is about. This is called community building: creating the world of connection that we want for all our children. If our intention is to build a healthy, supportive family and community for our children, regardless of where we live, how are we to do this? One answer brings us full circle back to the Developmental Assets. Increasing the assets in your daughter's life is a research-proven way to enrich her relationships, to protect her from risky behaviors and to help her feel more connected with her family and community. Asset building can be summarized in three words all of us can remember: CONNECT WITH KIDS. Kids grow and develop best when surrounded by caring, nurturing adults who are actively involved in their lives. The authors of the book *What Young Children Need to Succeed* state that making Developmental Asset building a part of your everyday life is easy:

All you need is the belief that children are important and that people need to be there to support them, guide them, and cheer them on. Building Assets in children helps you bring out the best in them—and in you. You can begin to build children's assets in 3 simple steps: believe that children deserve your attention and care, make a commitment, and act… Asset-building can be as simple or complex as you'd like. It can use a little of your time or a lot of it. It all depends on what you want to do. Many people prefer to start small. If this is true for you, follow the ABC's of Asset-building and do easy, quick things to build Assets in children. If you want to have a greater impact, use the XYZ's of Asset–building as a guide to building Assets in deeper, long-term ways. Building Assets can take only a few minutes of your time—or years of your life, depending on what you choose to do. You can choose to build Assets in 3 major ways: as an individual, as part of an organization, or as part of a community. It doesn't matter which way (or ways) you choose. All that matters is that you start.

There is a saying that a vision without action is just a dream. Likewise, building connection and healthy relationships in your family and community requires positive intention coupled with action. Peter Benson,

ABC's of Asset Building	XYZ's of Asset Building
• Quick	• Slower
• Offer immediate results	• Lead to long-term results
• Don't take long	• Take more time
• Need little preparation	• Require preparation
• Simple	• More complex
• Spontaneous	• Intentional
• Easy commitment	• Greater commitment
• Requires little energy	• Requires more energy

From the book *What Young Children Need to Succeed*, by Jolene Roehlkepartain and Nancy Leffert.

the founder of the Search Institute, explains the core asset-building principles in **"Adding Up Assets"** (p. 10:15):

* The 40 Developmental Assets provide a common language.
* Assets are contagious.
* Assets protect and enhance.
* Assets are fragile.
* Community capacity is enormous and unlimited.
* Unleashing capacity requires a critical mass.
* Youth can be asset builders.
* Asset building is a movement.

"Listen up, Adult Advocates: How Can Adults Be More Supportive of Young People?" (p. 10:16) reminds us that if we want to build assets for youth we need to remember to be present, reach out, be consistent, listen, be clear, be willing to share power, be engaged and be sincere. This chapter will help you to picture clearly what you want for your children and design a plan for increasing assets in your daughter's life.

Building Assets One-on-One

Asset building can be simple, as easy as a smile, and can take myriad forms. It takes only one person at any one time to make changes that benefit one's own child or a whole community. It could be as simple, yet challenging, as being home every day to welcome our teens when they arrive home. Sometimes we build assets through unique family rituals that provide a lifelong sense of bonding to family and/or nature, such as an annual camping trip. In other situations, the attempts of one individual can change the life of a young person. **"Making a Difference**

One by One" and **"Asset-Building Stories About the Power of Individual Action"** (pp. 10:17-10:18) will give you ideas about how you can create community for your daughter and how one simple step can lead to a rich future. **"Brewing Up Assets: A Friendly Adult Stirs in Some Support"** (p. 10:19) is a great reminder to all of us that in our everyday lives we either leave time to connect or we don't.

Building Assets with Neighbors and Friends

Families, parents, and daughters thrive when they feel part of a greater community of neighbors and friends. These overlapping communities involve people of all ages who feel cared for and secure and support each other. We don't always get to choose the makeup of our neighborhood, but an asset-building perspective helps us to take initiative in creating community within our neighborhood (as shared in **"Asset-Building Ideas for Neighbors and Neighborhood Groups"** (p. 10:20)). Some neighborhoods have a focal point such as a park, a pool, a community garden, a basketball net, or a sledding hill, which can be used to enhance everyone's connection to the neighborhood. One of the authors was fortunate enough to grow up in a community where an elderly couple opened their pool to the neighborhood in the mornings. Neighbors set up a complete swim instruction program for all ages, and neighborhood teens helped out; the summer culminated in an evening water show complete with homemade costumes. Although this example required a pool with very generous owners, most neighborhood bonding activities—from badminton tournaments to 4th of July bike parades to weekly pizza nights—do not. **"May Day Basket Celebration"** (p. 10:21) shares a delightful neighborhood-based activity that enhances community while building assets for all of the neighborhood's children. In addition to being lots of fun, the annual May Day photo collage of the neighborhood children enables every neighbor to recognize every child. This makes it easier, especially for elderly neighbors, to engage with the children.

In addition to creating community in our neighborhoods, asset-building parents can organize with other adults to create family magic. Some family magic is created with our own extended families of cousins, aunts and uncles and grandparents. Daughters who can spend time with loving grandparents, aunts and uncles are lucky indeed. However, for those of us who are not close to family, or may only see them once or twice a year, creating a sense of family with friends becomes increasingly important. Some families with younger children band together to form babysitting co-ops where families take care of each other's children, moms meet monthly for "Mom's Night Out" and the families get together for holidays and even weekend getaways. Even though the families don't live in the same neighborhood, the children grow up feeling like they are part of a community of people who know them well, welcome them into their homes, and care deeply for them. "Asset-Building Stories about the Power of Neighbors and Friends," "Get-Away Weekend," and "Family Magic" (pp.10:22-10:24) will give you many ideas for bonding with other families. Finally "Why Aren't There More Dads' Groups?" (p. 10:25) addresses the isolation dads can feel because men do not bond via groups as readily as women. As we know, parents who feel supported—moms or dads—are better able to parent wisely.

Building Assets Through Schools

As we wrote in detail in Chapter 6, schools are an important milieu for asset building, from teachers reaching out to students and families, to parents volunteering and being involved in learning. Further-more, feeling bonded to school is one of the top protective factors for teens. Stephen Covey's book, *The Leader in Me,* shows how schools can develop internal assets in our kids by directly teaching leadership, communication, and initiative skills, as well as getting business and civic leaders involved in the process. School is also such an excellent opportunity for parents to meet other parents and children. Walking and riding bikes to school, carpooling, volunteering, attending school events, and staying after school while children play on the playground and parents talk are all great ways to connect. When our schools are "community" schools where the doors are always open to meet

community needs, the possibilities for building assets grow exponentially. "Asset-Building Stories about School Connection" (p. 10:26) will give you ideas for building community at your schools. "SUN—Schools Uniting Neighborhoods" (p. 10:27) is an excellent example of how to create a community-responsive school. SUN schools open their doors to the whole neighborhood for afternoon, evening, and weekend classes and events, essentially becoming a neighborhood community center.

Asset Building Through Volunteering

Volunteering or service learning is one of the most powerful of asset builders, since you can build several assets at once. "Virtues of Volunteering" (p. 10:28) shares the many ways volunteering can support your daughter. She will:

- Feel useful and valued by the community,
- Learn that she has something to offer and can make a difference,
- Build skills and develop a sense of personal competence,
- Enhance her self-esteem,
- Create a supportive network of relationships with other adults and with healthy peers.

Research shows that people who volunteer are happier. Kids in service to others learn there are interesting people out in the world if they make the effort to get to know them. Volunteering enhances girls' engagement with the community and feelings of social responsibility towards others. Adults who volunteer with kids are often amazed by how much kids know and how skillful they can be. Some projects can also provide a parent and child with one-on-one time, working together with a common purpose. Volunteering as a family adds significantly to a feeling of family cohesion.

In our culture, boys (and men) particularly need to be encouraged to volunteer, as described in "Let's Get Girls and Boys Equally Involved in Volunteering" (p. 10:30). "Volunteering—The Youth Perspective" (p. 10: 31) gives us insight into how satisfying volunteering can be from a teen's point of view. The article describes four teen service projects: painting a house, helping students learn English, raising money to help others, and volunteering to help adults with their computers. How do we help our kids and ourselves to get involved? **"Connect with Kids by Helping Them to Help Others"** (p. 10:33) takes us step-by-step through the process of coming up with community service ideas. Finally, **"Hands On Portland: Volunteering Made Easy"** (p. 10:34) describes a model organization that connects volunteers with needs in Portland, Oregon. This website connects volunteers with opportunities at scores of organizations in the metro area, making it incredibly easy for busy people to volunteer. Your community can duplicate this wonderful non-profit idea, which is win-win for everyone. These articles show that volunteering is not limited by gender, age, occupation or working full-time. Taking an interest in children and improving our communities can happen at all levels of our society.

Building Assets in the Greater Community

Asset building can also affect the community at large for parents who have the motivation to work on this level. For example, the entire community can learn about the 40 Developmental Assets if the local newspaper dedicates a weekly column to spreading the word about asset-building ideas. Local businesses can also get connected with schools and develop assets in a variety of ways, from encouraging employees to volunteer at schools to developing a school-to-work program where students participate in business activities. **"Asset Building Stories about Businesses and the Greater Community"** (p. 10:35) shares several asset-building projects instigated by parents that affect whole communities. Parents in some states have created **"Stand for Children"** (p. 10:37) groups, a grassroots advocacy movement that lobbies to improve children's lives from educational needs to health needs and rights. They have demonstrated that banding together can transform political policies.

How would our communities look if many of our local businesses became family-friendly workplaces and encouraged their employees to volunteer with children in the community as tutors, mentors and classroom resources? **"Businesses—Join Up and Volunteer Today"** (p. 10:38) shows how one community's businesses give back to the community. **"Take Your Kids to Work Day"** (p. 10:39) is another excellent way to forge a connection

between families and business. As in all school-to-work programs, kids learn about careers, and adults learn from and become bonded to kids and teens.

In many other industrialized nations, the importance of parenting is acknowledged and supported by both government and industry. In modern America it receives much less support than it deserves. Sylvia Hewlett and Cornel West, professors at Harvard, created a task force that networked parents around the country to create a blueprint for parents' rights, as described in their book *The War on Parents: What We Can Do for America's Beleaguered Moms and Dads*. The Bill of Rights is a vision for how our country could improve the assets of parents and families. This approach and Internet advocacy groups such as MomsRising.org attempt to change the structure of our society in order to support and nurture families.

A Parent's Bill Of Rights

Mothers and Fathers are Entitled to:

1. Time for their children
   - Paid parenting leave
   - Family-friendly workplaces
   - A safety net
2. Economic security
   - A living wage
   - Job opportunities
   - Tax relief
   - Help with housing
3. A pro-family electoral system
   - Incentives to vote
   - Votes for children
4. A pro-family legal structure
   - Stronger marriage
   - Support for fathers
   - Adoption assistance
5. A supportive external environment
   - Violence-free neighborhoods
   - Quality schooling
   - Extended school day and year
   - Child care
   - Family health coverage
   - Drug-free communities
6. Honor and dignity
   - An index of parent well-being
   - National Parents' day
   - Parent privileges

What would it look like if we had a culture that actually honored these family rights at all levels of our society, from schools to businesses to government? What if we all knew and operated from the idea that the health and well-being of our children reflects the health and well-being of all of us, like "canaries in the mines"? What if we greeted each other every day with the question the Masai greet each other with, "How are the children?"

Your Action Plan

Congratulations! You have completed reading and discussing the many chapters of *Raising our Daughters* and it is time to take action. Read **"Family Empowerment Network: Final Session of Raising our Daughters"** (p. 10:40) and think about how you would like to continue nurturing your new awareness and connections. To help prepare yourself to take action and actively increase the assets in your daughter's life, take out (or recreate) your list of positive visions and wishes for your daughter from Chapter 1, your list of 40 Developmental Assets that is posted on your refrigerator, and your nine lists of "Putting It Together" ideas from each of the previous chapters. Using these ideas, fill out the form **"Next Steps: A Tool for Creating a Vision and Taking Action"** (p. 10:41). Now you have a list of ideas that will keep you on track towards actively building the world you want for your daughter. This form can be used again and again, whenever you have specific or general goals that you want to achieve within your family or your community. It helps to keep your vision and intention clearly in mind, and to recognize honestly where you are along the way. Delineating these two things clearly will make it easy to plan your action steps to accomplish your vision.

To enhance the success of your goals and action steps, here are some coaching tips from life coach, Kathy Masarie:
- Write your goals in the present tense as if they already happened.
- Focus on what you have control over.
- List concrete actions that are doable and can be measured in some way. That way, you will be able to know when you have accomplished each task.
- Put a timeline on each action step and post the form where you will see it often.
- Keep in touch with your discussion group and support each other. Share how and what you are doing and consider working together to build assets.

Creating a Culture That Cares

In the end, creating a new culture of acceptance and connectedness for our daughters begins with one person at a time. However, there are cultures in the world that place a priority on connecting with and celebrating their youth, which is illustrated in this vivid example from author Barbara Kingsolver (from *High Tide in Tucson: Essays from Now or Never*):

As I walked out the street entrance to my newly rented apartment, a guy in maroon high-tops and a skateboard haircut approached, making kissing noises and saying, 'Hi, gorgeous!' Three weeks earlier, I would have assessed the degree of malice and made ready to run or tell him to bug off, depending. But now, instead, I smiled, and so did my four-year old daughter, because after dozens of similar encounters I understood he didn't mean me, but her.

This is not the United States.

For most of the year my daughter was four we lived in Spain, in the warm southern province of the Canary Islands.

I struggled with dinner at midnight and the subjunctive tense, but my only genuine culture shock reverberated from this earthquake of a fact: people here like kids. They don't just say so, they do. Widows in black stop on the street to have little chats with my daughter. Routinely, taxi drivers leaned out the window and shouted 'Hola, guapa!' My daughter, who must have felt my conditioned flinch, would look up at me wide-eyed and explain patiently, 'I like it that people think I'm pretty.' With a mother's keen myopia I would tell you, absolutely, my daughter is beautiful enough to stop traffic. But in the city of Santa Cruz, I have to confess, so was every other person under the height of one meter. Not just those who conceded to be seen and not heard. Whenever Camille grew cranky in a restaurant (and really, what do you expect at midnight?), the waiters flirted and brought her little presents, and nearby diners looked on with that sweet, wistful gleam of eye that I'd thought diners reserved for the dessert tray. What I discovered in Spain was a culture that held children to be its meringues and éclairs.

Isn't this the culture we all crave for all of our children? We can make a difference. Nothing has ever changed in this world without the thoughtful, committed work of a creative group of individuals. Family Empowerment Network's mission is to create families and communities where children are truly valued, supported and cared for, as described in **"Our Dream for our Daughters:**

Authenticity, Self Love, and Self Acceptance" (p. 10:42). How would our lives change if we loved our children and ourselves unconditionally? We hope that you will take stock of your own family and community, and then take action toward making this vision a reality in your own life.

"Never doubt that a small group of thoughtful, committed citizens can change the world. Indeed, it's the only thing that ever has."

—Margaret Mead

THE 40 DEVELOPMENTAL ASSETS Essential to Every Young Person's Success

The Search Institute's "40 Assets" inventory and survey was introduced in Session 1. The following are the assets that can be built through community building and creating "safe havens" of support for youth.

- **Asset #3**   **Other Adult Relationships:** Young people have at least three other adults in their lives giving them support in addition to parents.
- **Asset #4**   **Caring Neighborhood:** Young people have the care and support of people who live nearby.
- **Asset #7**   **Community Values Youth:** Young people know they are valued by the adults in their community.
- **Asset #8**   **Youth as Resources:** Young people serve useful roles in their school, family and community.
- **Asset #9**   **Service to Others:** Young people volunteer one hour or more per week to help others.
- **Asset #13**   **Neighborhood Boundaries:** Neighbors share with parents the responsibility for monitoring young people's behavior.
- **Asset #14**   **Adult Role Models:** Parents and other adults set good examples for young people.
- **Asset #15**   **Positive Peer Pressure:** Youth's best friends model responsible behavior.
- **Asset #17**   **Creative Activities:** Young people are involved in music, theater or other arts three hours per week.
- **Asset #18**   **Youth Programs:** Young people are involved in sports, clubs or organizations at least three hours per week.
- **Asset #19**   **Religious Community:** Young people are involved in spiritual growth.
- **Asset #26**   **Caring:** Young people feel that it is important to help others make the world a better place.
- **Asset #27**   **Equality and Justice:** Young people believe in fairness and equity and are committed to social justice.
- **Asset #34**   **Cultural Competence:** Young people know and respect people of different racial and cultural backgrounds.
- **Asset #37**   **Personal Power:** Young people believe that they have control over the direction of their life.
- **Asset #38**   **Self-esteem:** Young people feel good about who they are.
- **Asset #39**   **Sense of Purpose:** Young people believe their life has a purpose.

CIRCLE ACTIVITY

This last week, you will have a group activity instead of a circle question.

- Take your individual Next Steps Action Plans and share with each other.
- Copy the outline of the "Next Steps: Making a Vision and Taking Action" on a large piece of paper.
- Brainstorm as a group and decide on one project that you would like to accomplish together, and place this in the Vision Box. This could be a group celebration with your daughters, a group picnic, a school or community project, or any other service activity that you could work on together to increase the feeling of connectedness within your community.
- Fill in the current reality box describing where you are now.
- Brainstorm the action steps needed to make your vision happen.
- Brainstorm how you will continue meeting.

This process is a great way to honor yourselves and each other for successfully completing your *Raising Our Daughters Parenting Guide.*

DISCUSSION QUESTIONS
1. How has this *Raising Our Daughters* discussion group impacted your life and your parenting?
2. If you have had a positive experience with *Raising Our Daughters,* how might you create other ROD groups within your child's school or community?
3. Where can you find support in your own life for your challenging job as a parent?
4. What kinds of community support exists for children and families in your community that you could be a part of?
5. How do you build assets in your neighborhood or greater community?
6. How can you build volunteering into your own life and that of your child?

PUTTING IT INTO PRACTICE
- Go through all your "Putting It Together—Your Version" lists from the previous 10 chapters. Mark three of your favorites, put them on your calendar and do them.
- Show girls—your own and those you come into contact with—that you care about them:
    - Give them your time.
    - Look at and greet every girl you see.
    - Talk with girls about their interests.
    - Invite a young person to an activity you think they might enjoy.
    - Welcome neighborhood kids into your home.
- Make a point of getting to know the people in your neighborhood. Host a community event—like a neighborhood potluck, the porch cookie campaign, or making May Day Baskets.
- Get involved in your neighborhood organization, a Mom's or Dad's support group, or organizations within your kid's school.
- Plan an event with extended family and friends like a bike trip, softball game, summer BBQ, or a camping trip.

- Educate your community on Developmental Assets: put out flyers in the library or schools and start an asset-building column in your local newspaper or school newsletter.
- Fill out the asset checklist—both you and your child—(p. 1-33) and compare the differences and similarities.
- Encourage your daughter to build relationships through service projects, volunteering, or mentoring. Choose a family volunteering project and do it.
- Take part in youth-serving programs through schools, community organizations and congregations.
- Invite caring adults into your daughter's life.

PUTTING IT TOGETHER—YOUR VERSION

Collect your top ten favorite ideas from all the previous overviews.

1. _____

2. _____

3. _____

4. _____

5. _____

6. _____

7. _____

8. _____

9. _____

10. _____

FURTHER READING

What Teen's Need to Succeed by Peter Benson, PhD

All Kids Are Our Kids: What Communities Must Do to Raise Caring and Responsible Children and Adolescents by Peter Benson, PhD, President of the Search Institute.

A Tribe Apart by Patricia Hersch

The Leader in Me: How Schools and Parents Around the World Are Inspiring Greatness, One Child at a Time by S. Covey

The War on Parents: What We Can Do for American's Beleaguered Moms and Dads by Sylvia Ann Hewlett

DVDs

At the Table: Youth Voices in Decision Making from Community Partnerships with Youth, 6319
Constitution Dr., Fort Wayne, IN 46804 (219-436-4402). 15-minute video features youth leaders and
adults who have successfully incorporated meaningful youth involvement into their organizations.

Boos for Teens

The Kid's Volunteering Book by Arlene Erlbach
Kids with Courage: True Stories about Young People Making a Difference by Barbara Lewis
The Kid's Guide to Service Projects by Barbara Lewis
160 Ways to Help the World: Community Service Projects for Young People by Linda Duper
*The Kid's Guide to Social Action: How to Solve the Social Problems You Choose and Turn Creative Thinking into
Positive Action* by Barbara Lewis
What Do You Stand For? A Kid's Guide to Building Character by Barbara Lewis

Other Resources

Working mother's rights at www.momsrising.org

The Best of Everything Social Action Resource: A collection of successful social action and social justice projects
for children and teens. Contains lists of resources, such as books, DVDs, and programs, poems, stories,
and quotations. Detailed information on a "Random Act of Kindness" program, and quilt–making with
children. Contact Beth Brownfield at (360-738-8899) or bethbrownf@aol.com.

Search Institute (Developmental Asset Building): 1-800-888-7828 at www.search-institute.org

Big Brothers/Big Sisters of America at www.bbbsa.org

Youth Volunteer Corps and the Youth Involvement Network: Provides resources for youth volunteers to
find and conduct community service projects in their area. 1-888-828-9822 at www.yvca.org

Activism 2000 Project: Youth-led initiatives at www.youthactivism.com

Smart: Volunteer coaches help early school-aged children become confident readers at
www.getsmartoregon.org.

Hands on Portland: Connects volunteers with community needs at www.handsonportland.org

Friends of Trees: Brings people together to plant city trees and restore urban natural areas at
www.friendsoftrees.org

Friends of the Children: Professional mentors serve high-risk children at www.friendsofthechildren.org

Americorps Community Service Program at www.americorps.org

Green Corps at wwwgreencorps.org

Service and Conservation Corps at www.corpsnetwork.org

LeapNow: Alternative international service-oriented college program at www.leapnow.org

Slow Down: You're Movin' Too Fast For Real Connection

By Marta Mellinger

Slow down, you move too fast.
You gotta make the morning last.
Just kickin' down the cobblestones
Lookin' for fun, and feelin' groovy ...
                    —Simon and Garfunkel song

Slow down

We bemoan our fast-paced, information age world. Listening, really listening, requires that we truly slow down. To listen, first we must be in one place long enough for our teen to sit down beside us. Driving carpool is not such a bad thing. Doing dishes side-by-side isn't either. But do sit down together as often as possible. Slow down long enough to sit down.

You move too fast

If you quiet your mind, you can open your heart. Inside each of us is a personal voice. Some of us have judging voices, or idea-generating voices. Some are always thinking about what to do next. Many of us are busy thinking about what we want to do or say next, instead of concentrating on what our teen is saying to us right now. Concentrate on each word and each pause and each nuance, instead of thinking about what to say next. Watch body language.

You gotta make the morning last

"Make the morning last" is a way to remember to be "in the moment" with our teens. That's where they live. THEIR reality is that they will be a teenager forever; what happened yesterday is monumental. And that WE cannot POSSIBLY understand. Forget trying to "understand." Let them know that you just want to listen. Then, just listen. Listen as if their life depends on your understanding of their life and their perceptions. (And . . . forget trying to tell them your own.)

Just kickin' down the cobblestones

The absolutely best time to listen may be when teens are hanging out. Talking to parents can feel risky because teens both want and don't want to care about what we think. When they are with their friends, or watching TV, or on vacation, we can listen. Talking together becomes less of a big deal, when we're all just hanging out together. Choose the easy times to "practice your listening skills."

Lookin' for fun

Knowing, really knowing, your teen is fun. Trying to change your teen is NOT fun. (And that is another article: If a teen is in trouble, or really needs "saving," this article is not for you.) Look for fun in listening, the fun of knowing who they are turning out to be.

And feelin' groovy

Feel—and notice—your feelings while you're listening to your teen. But ALWAYS remember you don't have to tell THEM how you feel. If they say, "My best friend got a tattoo," you may notice that you feel anxious. Anxiety can lead even the most listening parent to say something like, "Tattoos might affect Nick's future career options." But if instead we notice anxiety, we may zip our judging parental lips and listen long enough to hear what our teen thinks about tattoos. This may actually be MORE interesting than their response to our anxiety. Feel your feelings, own your emotions, and (most of the time) choose to listen instead.

Marta Mellinger is the founder of The Canoe Group—a shared practice of four passionate professionals who help organizations develop new ways to succeed in rapidly changing times. With her husband, she parents their two college-aged daughters and is proud that they still call and come home.

Reprinted with permission of Full Esteem Ahead, *Wings,* Spring 2001.

Adding Up Assets

By Peter Benson, author of *Sparks: How Parents Can Help Ignite the Hidden Strengths of Teenagers*

Both for the novice and the old hand, Search Institute® president Peter Benson offered these core asset-building principles in his keynote address at a Healthy Communities – Healthy Youth Conference in Denver.

- **The 40 Developmental Assets provide a common language.** Language is consciousness and consciousness has so much to do with dictating action. The Assets create a language of possibility that breaks change into small molecules and suggests we all have capacity. With the asset language, we can begin to reframe the human imagination about responsibility, capacity, and change.

- **Assets are additive.** More is better. Remember, this is a culture always looking for the quick fix, the panacea, the one thing we can do that will make everything worthwhile and healthy for our kids. There isn't one thing. It's about weaving a fabric.

- **Assets protect and enhance.** There are over 25 years of scientific research that continue to demonstrate again and again how the Developmental Assets help "inoculate" young people from some of the dangers of the world and help to enhance many forms of thriving—like school success, like showing up as a leader, like the affirmation of diversity.

- **Assets are fragile.** In every community that has done the assessment of Developmental Assets—and that's many, many communities now—one of the things that we discover is a rupture in the developmental infrastructure. Most American young people are now living in towns and cities with huge capacity, but where that capacity is dormant.

- **Community capacity is enormous and unlimited.** The question is: Can we awaken community power? Recently, at the Jimmy Carter Presidential Library in Atlanta, I saw a quote from Carter that said, "The only position in America more important than president is citizen." The President cannot build community for you. CEOs aren't going to build your community. Your superintendent and legislators aren't going to build your community. I think what Carter is telling us is that it's about neighbor and parent and bus driver and parishioner. It is about peer influence. It is about the people of community knitting the fabric of community.

- **Unleashing capacity requires a critical mass of human beings.** This is hard work. This requires communication and engagement with adults of all walks, with kids of all walks, so that they get it deeply, so it becomes a heart work. This is about taking advantage of the moment and the opportunities before us to connect, to engage, to know, to look deeply inside, to pay attention.

- **Youth are asset builders.** Young people, think about your power with your peers. You know how important peer influence is. You have such important credibility and integrity with the kids you hang around with. Imagine your power to build assets in your peers. Imagine your own power for building your own assets. Don't wait for adults to build them. In many communities, what I see is that teenagers don't want to have a whole lot to do with smaller kids. Get over it. Use your power.

- **Asset building is a movement.** By placing ourselves in the context of a movement, rather than simply implementing programs, we can learn from the history of sustainable movements. One of the things we know is that sustainable movements trigger acts of symbolic power. Rosa Parks comes to mind. The Boston Tea Party comes to mind. What in your communities are the symbolic acts that touch the imagination and the heart?

Listen Up, Adult Advocates
Ideas that Work, Opinions that Matter, Research that Illuminates
Written and compiled by Kalisha Davis

How CAN PARENTS and other adults improve how they support young people? We attended Assets for Colorado Youth's State Youth Summit in August to get the inside scoop. Youth sharing their honest opinions, ideas, and solutions included Katrina Harris, 14, of Denver; Mary Hottenroth, 15, of Steamboat Springs; Katrina Robertson, 18, of Denver; Lucia Sanchez, 17, of Greeley; and Kendra Youngren, 16, of Greeley.

How can adults be more supportive of young people?

Be present

There are a lot of youth I know who are in bad situations. They have adults in their households who aren't positive role models. They need to heal. They need adults to support them who are willing to spend the time. You have to be willing to walk with them.

Reach out

Adults need to make more time for youth because, more likely than not, youth are not going to be the ones to come forward. Adults have to seek them out.

Be consistent

If you start mentoring once a week, it's usually better to keep that. If you say, "I'm more busy than I was before, so I think I'll take away some of my time," that kid is going to feel rejected.

Listen

When kids have problems, they have to be able to talk to their parents without consequence. If parents say, "I'm never going to let you do this again," kids won't feel comfortable talking. You have to work through it together.

What can adults do in meetings to make youth involvement more meaningful?

Be clear

You need to speak English. We don't want every single detail. Give us a general outline. Let us know what's going on.

Be willing to share power

I don't see why we have to classify each other as youth or adult. Why can't we just call each other coworkers? We're working together, aren't we?

Be engaged

A lot of times adults meet and it's boring. The adults don't even seem to be into what they're doing, but when youth come in with new ideas, all of a sudden things just start rolling again.

Be sincere

Adults ask what we want and they're not sincere. You have to want to do it. We can see through the fakeness.

Making a Difference One by One

By Peter Benson, PhD, author of *All Kids Are Our Kids*

MOBILIZING INDIVIDUALS FOR action may seem inefficient and time-consuming. It is harder to show progress on a grand scale. But, one by one, individuals can have a tremendous impact. In every community that begins this work, we hear the stories of one person who has made a difference. It took one person to turn around Deon Richardson of St. Louis Park, the first community to embrace asset building as a framework for community action.

Ninth grade wasn't a good year for Richardson. Every day he would skip class. He would write graffiti on the walls and the school lockers. He got into fights. By the end of the school year, he had only earned half of an academic credit.

One of his teachers, Tom Bardal —a health and driver's education teacher—noticed. He often sought out Richardson and would talk with him. He noticed that when Richardson skipped class, he often headed to the gym to shoot baskets with his peers who were also skipping class.

"I could see how basketball was very important to him," Bardal says. "He had potential not only as an athlete but as a student as well." Bardal also happened to be the varsity basketball coach, and he often encouraged Richardson to try out for the team. But Richardson kept turning him down.

"I never had time for it," Richardson says. "I never wanted to play [on a team]."

Bardal didn't give up, however. "He would talk to me during my freshman year, and I would just push that all to the side," Richardson says. "But then my sophomore year came around . . . and he said I could be one of the best if I would really try."

Despite Richardson's skepticism, he decided to try out for the team. He made it. "I never had anybody tell me I was good," Richardson says. "He was the first coach who told me I could be somebody. He was the first one. And that's why I think I will thank him right now for being there. Otherwise, I would have still been on that wrong path."

Not only did Bardal take an interest in Richardson's playing ability, but also in his schoolwork. He checked on Richardson every day to see if he was attending class. He talked to Richardson's other teachers. When he found out that Richardson was skipping study hall, he brought Richardson into his room to help him with his homework. "I saw a kid with potential and that's what teachers are all about," Bardal says. "We can talk about curriculum and teach it day in and day out, but sometimes that's not as important as turning a kid's life around."

Still, Bardal credits Richardson for making most of the changes. By his junior year, Richardson had caught up on all his academic credits by going to summer school and attending after-school classes. Today his favorite subjects are English, math, and chemistry, and he's getting A's and B's. He's now comparing colleges. "I want to go into business," Richardson says. "I want my own business. I think it would be cool to have your own business. And basketball is something I can fall back on."

Where does Richardson think he would be now if he hadn't changed? He figures he would be in jail. Or he would have seriously hurt someone by now.

"When he was a ninth grader, I thought, this kid isn't going to make it," says John Headlee, assistant principal of St. Louis Park High School. "Now he is one of the leaders on the basketball team. All the kids respect him. He's a success story."

The respect is far-reaching. When the junior class voted to choose two to three peers to be on the Natural Helpers Committee (a program that provides peer support for students), Richardson was chosen.

"Kids now say, 'Hey, if Deon can do it, anybody can do it,'" Richardson says. "There's good stuff in everybody. And I tell them, instead of going out looking for trouble, go home and read a book. And they look up to me. They admire me for that."

Reprinted with permission from John Wiley and Sons, Inc. From *All Kids are Our Kids: What Communities Must Do to Raise Respectful and Caring Children & Adolescents* by Peter Benson (1997).

Asset-Building Stories about the Power of Individual Action

Parent Networking Diffuses a Tough Situation (from Mike Roach, owner of Paloma Clothing)

Through participation in a *Raising Our Daughters* parent group, I learned how to handle a situation like an invitation to a coed sleepover, something that happens in high schools these days. I now understand why saying, "NO WAY!" to my daughter doesn't work or foster our relationship. (And, of course, "Yes" isn't an option either!) I learned instead to connect with the parents of the other girls invited so my daughter wasn't the only one excluded and arrange for an alternate activity that was less likely to lead to risky behavior —like an all-girl sleepover at our house on the same night complete with pizza and videos. It's so affirming as a parent to have the tools to diffuse these potentially dangerous situations without alienating my daughter. And this is only one of the tools I learned!

Dusty's Garden

Dustin Hill, a 12-year old middle-schooler, wanted to build a garden to grow fresh vegetables for Sisters of the Road Café, a nonprofit public lunch café that serves low cost, basic comfort foods in exchange for cash, food stamps or labor at the restaurant. Dustin learned about community service when he was little; his family would gather apples and mittens at Christmas time for the homeless. He applied for a mini-grant for the lumber for raised beds, soil and seeds. He persuaded eight other students and some neighbors to help him. When a cancerous tumor on Dusty's leg was diagnosed and successfully removed, the other youth tended the garden. He pitched in on crutches.

Raising our Daughter's Parent Group Blossoms and Grows (from Diana Zapata)

I was inspired to form a parenting group when my ten-year-old daughter had several teary nights in a row. I could tell how frustrated she was with the budding relational aggression happening around her and I didn't really feel equipped with the tools to help her through. I was determined begin the Raising Our Daughter's (ROD) curriculum with other interested parents. This group was a great way to start the process, and we began to bond as a community of concerned parents. Both Moms and Dads attended the first year. We were not afraid to open up. This created a recipe for trust that we still have today. Our group has evolved over the years, but we are still thriving.

- First we had Moms and Dads with the ROD curriculum. It was a little advanced for fourth-grade parenting—but this got us going!
- The second year we evolved into an all Mom's group, discussing our own challenges as Moms, wives, daughters and professionals.
- The third year we formed a mother/daughter support group with our sixth-graders and studied the Choices curriculum, that teaches girls about making good choices during the middle and high school years and how their choices, good and bad, will affect them. This was an excellent activity for us.
- The fourth year, we had our seventh-grade girls decide which direction we would take. They decided to have book discussions every other month and activities such as cooking classes or printmaking the other months. It was a great community gathering each time. The biggest disappointment was when not everyone could make it (which always happens).

I think it works for us because we trust that our conversations/meetings are confidential. I always feel supported, knowing that my daughter's situation is not so unusual and we are not the only ones going through this stage of the game! We also try to support each other's children, as a "go to" person, besides the parent. Not many have really done this yet—but the choice is there. So what started out as a simple *Raising Our Daughters* group four years ago has turned into a great group of supportive families who love to get together on a regular basis. I have enjoyed this community so much and hope it continues well into the high school years—so we'll see!"

Brewing Up Assets: A Friendly Adult Stirs in Some Support

By Kay Hong, Asset Magazine, Search Institute

THE OTHER DAY, I decided to treat myself to a really good cup of coffee on the way home from a hard day's work. Feeling tense, I walked into my favorite coffeehouse with my briefcase on my shoulder. "Hello, Jeremy," I said and watched as the face of the boy at the counter lit up. "Hey, where've you been?!" he asked. I pleaded a busy work schedule then we chatted a little about what books we'd been reading. I had to go, but he made my day by calling out, "You should come in more often!"

One my way out, I saw Carly rise out of her chair with a gangly teenage grace and move toward me with an intense expression. We hugged and I whispered in her ear, "Is something going on?" She said yes, and began to tell me about a new boyfriend who wanted her to have sex with him, and what did I think? We spoke about safety and respect, about being good to yourself, and being careful. We laughed a little and hugged again, then I picked up my coffee and headed home with an unexpected feeling of warmth and satisfaction. A few short weeks ago, such scenarios were simply not a part of my daily life.

How did the change happen? When I first started working at Search Institute, I felt a need to balance out big-picture thinking about community change with my own closer look at the realities of young people's lives. I have no children of my own, but as I learned more about the developmental assets, I became fascinated with the broader possibilities of informal asset building and I wanted to extend my reach. I decided to concentrate in an intentional way on asset #3, other adult relationships, and to take to heart the admonitions we often put in our publications—to say hello to the community's young people, to call them by name, to form relationships with them—and see if such gestures really work.

I started with a small experiment. At the grocery store one day, when a teenage clerk with numerous earrings and an unusual hairstyle rang up my purchases in a moody silence, I gave myself a little internal push and complimented him on his hair, asking him what he did to make it look that way. He looked up at me in surprise, smiled a little, and revealed his combination gel-and-finger-combing technique while we finished the transaction. He thanked me, and as I walked away, I heard him greet the next customer in line. Encouraged, I made a simple remark about the weather to the girl who was wheeling out my groceries—a comment that led to a friendly discussion of the future outdoor jobs she might consider.

Given those successes, I've continued with my experiments, and now enjoy several warm, fun-filled relationships with teens at the coffeehouse I frequent. What has meant the most to me, and what I hadn't expected, has been the great gift of their trust. Their confidences bring opportunities for everyday asset building in their wake, and I feel a deep responsibility for responding as wisely and lovingly as I can.

We joke together over cappuccino and Rice Krispy bars and talk about boyfriends and girlfriends. Jeremy asks what it's like to be a writer and editor, and Carly asks how to know when you're really in love, and Tom asks me how to break up responsibly with a girl he's been dating. Jon tells me his dad yelled at him for not disabling his mom's car the night before, so she drove drunk and was arrested, and I assure him it's not his fault. I tell them all that their lives are just beginning, and that they'll keep making mistakes and learning new things and changing and growing all through their time on this earth. And I tell them that talking with them and listening to them helps me keep learning things too.

Kay Hong has been an editor at the Search Institute for three years.

Asset-Building Ideas for Neighbors and Neighborhood Groups

From *Pass It On! Ready-to-Use Handouts for Asset Builders*

A NEIGHBORHOOD IS MORE than a place where people sleep or grab a bite to eat. A neighborhood can and should be an important community in which people of all ages feel cared for and secure. This kind of neighborhood isn't the norm in most communities, but with a focus on asset building it could be. Two of the 40 Developmental Assets, #4: caring neighborhood; and #13: neighborhood boundaries, focus specifically on the important role neighbors have in building assets. Here are ideas on how neighbors can build these and other assets:

Individuals

- **Learn the names of kids who live around you.** Find out what interests them.
- **Treat neighbors of all ages with respect and courtesy;** expect them to treat you with respect and courtesy too.
- **If you live in an apartment or condominium,** spend time in gathering places, such as front steps, courtyards, meeting rooms, pools, laundry rooms, and lobbies. Greet and talk with others there. If you have a front yard, hang out there.
- **Take personal responsibility for building Asset #13: neighborhood boundaries.** When you see someone in the neighborhood doing something you think is inappropriate, talk with her or him about why it bothers you.
- **Find other neighbors who want to make a long-term commitment to Asset-building.** Begin developing strategies for working together to build assets in your neighborhood.
- **Take time to play or just be with the young people on your block and or in your building.** Encourage them to talk and then listen to what they have to say.
- **Invite neighbors (especially those with children and teenagers) to your home.** Get to know each other and find out what you have in common.
- **Once in a while, leave a message** (with chalk on sidewalks or by hanging notes on doors) saying how much you appreciate a certain neighbor. Do this for neighbors of all ages.
- **If you have children, talk to other parents about the boundaries and expectations they have for their children.** Discuss how you can support one another in areas where you agree.
- **Figure out what you can provide for young people in your neighborhood.** Can you set up a basketball hoop? Can you offer some space for a neighborhood garden? Can you give one hour of your time on weekends to play softball with young people who live near you?
- **If you have concerns about your neighborhood, talk with other neighbors about your feelings.** If others share your concerns, gather a group to work on addressing them. Even if you don't solve all of the problems, you'll strengthen your neighborhood in the process.
- **Attend a game, play, or event** that a neighborhood child or teenager is involved in. Congratulate the young person after the event.
- **Be aware of graduations and other major events** in the lives of children.
- **Once you know your neighbors, find out more about their extended family and friends.** Some elderly people have grandchildren who visit. Or parents may have custody of their children on certain days of the week. Get to know these young people who periodically visit.
- **Pay attention whenever you see a young person.** Take time to smile and say hello. If you have a few moments, ask a few questions and express your interest in her or him. Do this while you're walking, waiting for a bus, or waiting in line somewhere.

Groups

- **Start a neighborhood group. Focus on safety,** neighborhood improvement, or just having fun.
- **Organize a neighborhood book swap.** Ask neighbors to donate books they've already read and have everyone come to find new books.
- **Meet with neighborhood parents and other concerned adults to find out how neighbors can help children and teenagers with homework.** Consider finding adult "study buddies" for kids.
- **Start a neighborhood check-in program.** Form small clusters and check in with each other on a regular basis. If someone needs help or support, gather a group to pitch in and help out.
- **If you have problems with crime or safety in your neighborhood, regularly talk with your local police department** to find out what is being done to address the issues. Ask them what you and other neighbors can do to make a difference.

May Day Basket Celebration
By Lori Delman and Carolyn Quatier

Do you want the kids in your neighborhood to help build closer community? Do you want your neighbors to know your kids and build stronger relationships? Do you want your kids to feel they are doing something really worthwhile and valuable, to connect with parents and other adults—young and old in your neighborhood—and to have fun doing it?

If yes, then we've got a great neighborhood project for you... delivering flower baskets on the first of May. Celebrating May Day in this way brings neighbors out of their homes, after being cooped up all winter and is a wonderful "springtime ritual." Here are two May Day Celebration stories.

Lori's Story

For the past five years, I have invited over the "street kids"—what my six-year-old daughter calls the children on our suburban block. Our project each May 1st is to make flower baskets for each of the block's households. "It's fun at the May Day Party because we get to work on a project together," says thirteen-year-old Lucy.

In addition to the beautiful little baskets that all the kids help make, we created a photo collage of all the neighbor children and included a copy with each basket. This collage turned out to be a hit not only with the children—who love to be on "display"—but also with households that don't have children but want to feel more connected and to know who the kids are. This gives their parents the benefit of an extra set of "eyes and ears" watching over them. Even more important, it makes it easier to talk with a kid whose name you know. The best is the empowerment felt by some of the preteen girls on the block who now want to be in charge of the photo collage layout.

In small ways this tradition has helped build community and to know the value of being a connected neighbor. The first year of this project, a neighbor called to thank us for bringing back the warm, cohesive atmosphere she felt the block had when she was raising her children 30 years ago. Older generations are nostalgic about the days when all neighborhood children attended the same school, making block friendships much easier. Our neighborhood is reflective of the current period of diverse school choices—we have five grade schools, three middle schools, and two high schools represented. Our kids love this chance to connect with the kids from all the schools.

Carolyn's Story

Eight years ago, Kathy Masarie and I introduced our neighborhood to this May Day tradition. We have streamlined the process by getting several parents involved: bringing snacks, buying flowers, building the cones, making May Day tags, collecting photos, making the photo collage, updating our neighborhood phone and email directory. With our larger suburban lots, we are spread out and tend to spend time isolated in our backyards. Almost every May Day, we also become a "Welcome to the Neighborhood" party for new families. Sue Gregoire said, "We were new to the neighborhood, so it was nice for our children to see so many other kids their age. It was a creative activity and a great way to connect with every person in the neighborhood." Emily captures the essence of the appeal, "It was fun because I got to leave the flowers on the doorstep, ring the doorbell, and run away. I also met my new neighbors and now we carpool together."

May Day baskets are simple, fun, and resonate with every generation's hearts. Consider opening up your children's experience to this wonderful, connecting ritual.

Lori Delman is a part-time pharmacist, enjoys her book club and garden and is mother to twin girls. Carolyn Quatier loves gardening and teaching sewing to children and is mother to three girls and a boy.

Reprinted with permission from Full Esteem Ahead, *Wings,* Winter 2001.

Asset-Building Stories about the Power of Neighbors and Friends

Building Community—One Porch at Time (from *Assets Magazine, The Neighborhood Porch Cookie Campaign, Findlay, OH)* "I had fond memories of sitting on the porch sharing with family and friends while growing up," says Brahm, a Hancock County (Ohio) extension agent. After hearing a talk about the importance of assets in building youth and family resiliency, she decided to do more than just share her own porch cookies and lemonade.

Brahm brought her Porch Cookie Campaign idea to several community leaders from the United Way, youth and religious groups, the police department, and the media. Together they developed a plan that included plenty of print and broadcast promotion. People who send in pictures or favorite stories of their porch parties are eligible for prizes. Now in its second year, the campaign runs from May through Labor Day.

The possibilities for porch parties are endless. Here are a few examples: a homeless shelter invited previous residents for a porch party, a retirement center had a porch party with a daycare center, a city councilman invited residents of his ward to two parties through newspaper ads, children had porch parties with their dolls, the block watch program adopted the campaign as a project, United Way invited staff from neighboring offices for cookies and lemonade.

Why has the campaign been successful? Says one mother of two boys: "It was fun, didn't cost much, and took little time. You didn't even have to clean your house!"

Camaraderie and Networking at Work (from Adrienne Greene) We started a *Raising Our Daughters* discussion group at work with about 8 members nearly 5 years ago. Since then, 4 of us continue to meet over lunch and seek out each other when we have parenting issues that need another perspective. Raising teens is challenging work, and it has been extremely rewarding to have a confidential support network of co-workers to rely on. I know it's provided me with a sense of confidence and friendship.

A Safe Network of Friends for My Daughter (from Nellie Nix) *Our Raising our Daughter's* group means knowing that there are nearly a dozen moms—and dads, too—that I trust. I trust their opinions, though they're varied and sometimes different from mine. And since my daughter is close friends with many of their girls, it's so nice to know that I can trust that she'll be safe when she's with them.

Men's Bike Group Unites Families (from Glenda Montgomery) When my husband found out that some men in the neighborhood were getting together to ride bikes on Sunday mornings, he pulled out his 20-year-old bike from a forgotten corner of the garage. It got dusted off and cleaned up and carried him along to join the group, providing an opportunity for my husband to connect with other men and, in turn, to connect all the men's families to one another. He's now been riding for nine years. During these years, the bike group has become the core of our neighborhood experience. The kids feel like cousins, and the couples enjoy hanging out. We've gone camping and have an annual Christmas progressive dinner. When the weather is not rainy and cold, the men ride as often as they can. The high point of their year is the "Reach the Beach," an organized ride in May when the men ride 100 miles from our neighborhood in Portland to Pacific City on the Coast. The families pack up food, clothes, and supplies and caravan down to the beach in time to cheer on their Dads and husbands as they cross the finish line. The rest of the weekend is about free flow fun. The kids are a happy gang, representing a span of almost a decade, from 9 to 18 years old. For them, this weekend is like their Christmas. It is full of laughter and freedom, friendship and tradition and layer upon layer of fun memories. They truly can't remember their lives before we began making this annual pilgrimage and they look forward to it passionately every year.

Iron Mountain Day Camp (from Kathy Keller Jones) After 3 neighborhood girlfriends had their first week at overnight summer camp at ages 11 and 12, they decided that they could earn money and have fun by organizing the neighborhood children in a week-long half-day camp. After all, they already knew all the songs, crafts, and skits they would need. Thus began the Iron Mountain Day Camp in our large yard. In addition to developing many skills in the teens, the day camp brought together all of the younger children in the neighborhood and their families into one happy group and developed a tremendous sense of cohesion in our neighborhood.

A Getaway Weekend for Parents and Kids or
How to Let your Hair Down Instead of Pulling it Out!
By Jane Blackman

As a SINGLE MOM for 15 years, I've had plenty of one-on-one time with my daughter, Holly. We've done lots of day trips and weekend excursions together. One special trip that we took last fall added a new dimension to our time together that proved very rewarding—a Seaside weekend getaway with three other moms and their daughters. For the girls, it was a chance to be with their buddies doing something different and fun. For us moms, it provided an opportunity to share mutual concerns, issues and questions about raising our daughters. For both, it was a time of discovery about who we were and how others perceived us. We packed enough food and games for a month in the Outback and had a ball. The weather was sunny and mild enough to allow for lots of walks and even a two-hour surrey ride for the girls. Our rental house was a bit musty and the beds we shared had seen better days, but no one minded. This is how it worked. None of the moms knew each other except in passing. The common denominator was our sophomore daughters, who had known each other since middle school. One mom found a house to rent in Seaside just a few blocks from the beach and issued the invitation. She picked a weekend when the kids had Friday off so we were able to get an early start that morning. Each mom/daughter team brought whatever snacks they wanted plus the food to prepare one of the main meals for the weekend. We divided meal chores ahead of time so we'd know who was fixing what. There were no rules about time for bed or getting up and that worked just great. The girls had a separate bunkroom off the porch that allowed for privacy and "girl talk." We moms enjoyed tea and conversation in the breakfast nook before the girls appeared for the day and the hubbub began. We planned indoor activities for nighttime, including a scavenger hunt with prizes. The last evening together ended with a circle share. Each person gave a one-word description of everyone else in the circle. I don't know which I enjoyed hearing more, what the girls had to say or what the moms had to say. It was a very moving experience. Weekend getaways are an ideal way to spend time with your children. And the presence of other parents and kids adds texture and insight that is invaluable. In Holly's words, "I think it's important for kids to spend time with their friends' parents. You get a whole new perspective from them and it helps develop a great support system." All of us voted to make the getaway an annual event. My only regret is that we didn't start it years ago. I can't wait for our next adventure!

Some suggestions for organizing your own getaway:

• Keep it simple. Plan easy menus, bring one change of clothes. Limit everyone to one set of towels. Consider bringing a sleeping bag instead of doing linens.

• Look for bargains. Our lodging cost only $25 a night per person. Take advantage of off-season rates and shop the Internet for values (www.cabins.com is one example).

• Be flexible. One of the moms couldn't come so we ended up with an extra girl. We "adopted" her for the weekend and she had a great time. One mom snored and one needed a firmer mattress so we designed extra sleeping quarters in the living room the second night.

Jane Blackman is mother of a young adult daughter. She is the founder of A Festive Heart (www.festiveheart.com), teaches wellness workshops and has a private energy healing practice in Portland, OR.

Reprinted with permission from Full Esteem Ahead, *Wings*, Spring 2003.

Creating Family Magic

By Jody Bellant Scheer, MD

I AM HOPELESSLY nostalgic for the long weeks of summer when my kids were young. My kids, our neighbors and I spent hours swimming off our houseboat decks, building rafts and forts, reading books, working on projects, and exploring our nearby waterways in a variety of small watercraft. While the kids in my neighborhood lived in a rich and inviting natural environment that encouraged activity and creativity, one of their greatest assets was the way they became part of a community of adults and children who interacted often and cared about one another. Our houseboat community consists of 29 homes and 60 to 70 people, including about a dozen kids, who for years ran in a pack together. Some of the advantages of this arrangement were that our children experienced a variety of family styles and rules; they interacted with kids of a mixture of ages; they developed on-going relationships with adults other than their own parents; and they benefited from the collective creativity of a group of adults who worked together to enrich their lives during the long summer months.

For parents who don't live in such a ready-made community, finding other families who wish to share in some group activities can be a great way to build community and offer similar advantages to your own children. Networking with neighbors, churches, schools, community centers, as well as your children's friends, can help parents find other families willing to embark on some group adventures. The possibilities for shared activities are endless and need not take a lot of time, money or effort to create. When I asked my own children about their favorite childhood memories, they did not mention the more exotic and expensive trips we made together. Instead, they remembered contests amongst the neighborhood kids to see who could run the farthest down the hot, black moorage walkways before

having to jump into the water to cool off, floating in big herds of inner tubes down the length of our moorage, and playing in the mud, clay and sun on the shores of our slough. They remembered with relish the spontaneous picnics where we invited anyone home on the moorage, young to old, to join us for a collective meal on our deck or at a nearby beach. In today's society, it may seem odd to ask an older housewife or elderly neighbor to join in some family fun, but for us, it worked to the advantage of all parties involved.

Other group projects can be more intensive. My kids, husband, neighbors and I planned activities that included neighborhood camping trips, group hikes, museum visits, road trips, community gardens and varied explorations of the kids' interests. Our neighborhood built a tree house and playground when our children were little and a basketball court when they grew older.

Several summers, moorage families hosted Asian exchange students and enjoyed sharing the Pacific Northwest with them and each other. One spring, a neighbor invested in a variety of wood supplies and their boys created a multitude of forts, vehicles and projects over the course of the whole summer with their buddies. Weeks of entertainment were provided for my nieces and their friends, who organized a family theater production about pioneers, complete with vintage clothes and props they made themselves. Weekly projects, such as a book club, sewing circle or game night, can regularly bring kids and parents together to share over the course of a summer. Any project where adults and kids can work together, where kids can exercise creativity and independence, and where the outcome is less important than having fun in the process is worth the effort to create and will greatly enrich all of your lives. Creating such family magic will give you years of memories to cherish, and it will entice your children to come home for more once they've left the nest!

Jody Bellant Scheer, a pediatrician, lives on a houseboat and has three young adult children.

Reprinted with permission of Full Esteem Ahead, *Wings*, Spring 2003.

Why Aren't There More Dads' Groups?

By Joe Kelly, author of *Dads and Daughters*

A LOT OF DADS have to be doing something else before we feel ready to start talking to each other about our kids. A jog, a card game, a yard project, a round of golf, or any number of other "guy" activities can serve as safe places for us to jump in, or at least stick our toes in to test the water. For others of us, a more formal, organized setting dedicated specifically to talking about raising daughters works best.

Whenever I mention men's groups, there's at least one guy in the audience who rolls his eyes or makes a wisecrack. Men's groups have a bad reputation with many men; they're considered weird, bizarre, creepy, or just plain ridiculous. There are probably men's groups that are all of these things, but that doesn't mean that every men's group is. It doesn't mean that we can't start up groups with our own rules; and it's also no excuse for staying silent about our fathering.

A big part of the problem is that there simply aren't enough men's or fathering groups out there. The smaller number of groups, the smaller the variety, and thus the fewer chances for a dad to find a group in which he'll feel comfortable. Somebody must be responsible for this shortage, and that somebody is me and you. It looks like we've been too afraid to take the risks and do the work to get what we need from one another.

I think we haven't formed or sustained groups because we're afraid. It takes courage to admit we don't know everything and to ask other fathers for help. It takes leadership to keep the conversation going even when other fathers say they are too busy to participate.

I'm part of a loosely organized book group made up of a half dozen men who I don't know all that well.

There's a business consultant, a city planner, a naturalist/teacher, a psychiatrist, and a man who manages his wife's chiropractic office.

> I have to set aside my expectations when I talk fathering with another dad.

We've discussed novels, a collection of environmental essays, a memoir about sailing to Greenland, and even a volume of poetry. These are all pretty safe topics and while no one has revealed any deep, dark secrets, we really enjoy each other's company. Recently I tried to push the envelope a bit by picking Will Glennon's *The Collected Wisdom of Fathering* (Conari Press, 2002), my favorite fathering book.

I thought the conversation got off to a slow start. It seemed as if there was more off-the-topic small talk than usual, and a couple of the guys didn't seem as enthusiastic about the book as I am. We only talked about our kids a little, and only after prodding each other with plenty of questions.

When the group broke up for the evening, I was disappointed, for I'd hoped we might be ready to use our father experience to jump into a deeper level of conversation. I didn't feel as if that hope had been fulfilled.

The next day, however, I got a phone call and two e-mails from the guys thanking me for the topic and saying it was the best meeting we'd had yet. They were excited and stimulated by a conversation that I had considered halting and uncertain. They've mentioned several times since how much they enjoyed the discussion. And I learned something important here.

I have to set aside my expectations when sitting down to talk with another dad. What I think is irrelevant might be central for him; a conversation I find stumbling and disjointed might be the first time he's ever spoken to another father about being a dad—and those words might amount to great eloquence for him. It turns out that our book group's halting discussion of fathering had laid a foundation for more interesting and personal talk down the road. It's slow going, but it's progress.

Asset-Building Stories about School Connection

"Ramp Up" as Our Kids Enter Adolescence (from Mike Roach, Paloma Clothing, Portland) I have always known that the most valuable gift I could give my daughter was time. I invested a lot in those early years and was starting to think about slowing down. Adolescence is just on the edge of the radar screen in 4th grade when I took the *Raising Our Daughters* class and realized I needed to "ramp up," not slow down. One activity I learned about that I wanted for all the kids as they entered middle school, was a Girls/Boys Night Out—spending the night together at the school, having lots of fun, but also talking about importance of healthy friendships and treating others with respect. So when Isabel was in 5th grade I started volunteering at the middle school and made that happen for all the 6th graders the next year. Just learning the importance of "knowing a name," helped me memorize the names of the 60 other kids in her 5th grade I didn't already know. When I saw them in middle school, a big smile would beam across their face as I "high-fived" them by name. I think they think, "I must be important if someone else's dad went out of his way to learn my name." I was also inspired to create a coming of age book for Isabel when she turned 13 and distribute a letter on asset-building ideas to her coaches. I also helped foster a $500 grant for *Raising Our Sons'* and *Raising Our Daughters'* groups for anyone who wanted to take them in our middle school to broaden the base of parents who understand that being involved in helping other people's children also helps your own child.

Dads and Doughnuts

When one middle school received a $500 mini-grant, they decided to use it in a way that would bring dads and other male role models together with kids. The 5th and 6th grade students each sent their special male figure a personal invitation to come to their school one morning on the way to work. The mini-grant funded doughnuts, muffins, juice and coffee. The students explained their educational program and provided their guests with information on how to enhance children's ability to survive and thrive by getting more involved and building assets in children's lives.

Dragon's Breath Café

In addition to raising reading levels, Janet Muller, a third-grade teacher, wanted to instill in her students an enthusiasm and love of reading. With funds from a small grant, she transformed her classroom into a small, cozy café with hot chocolate, warm, fresh cookies, black and white checkered tablecloths, and little tagboard dragons. Students and their parents came together one evening a month to share thoughts and lessons learned from their book-of-the-month. Questions encouraged critical thinking.

Bike Club

Tom Bright, a middle school teacher, wanted to teach practical skills as well as science in his classroom. He received a $500 mini-grant and used it to fund bike repair and pay for bike maintenance equipment. His repair shop opens up twice a week during lunch. As the weather improves, he hopes to involve parents and other community members and to assist with organizing bike rides after school and on weekends.

Walking to School Builds Community (from Glenda Montgomery)

While visiting Toronto I helped walk my friend's kids to school. I was curious because in suburban America we tend to drive our kids to school. I was delighted by the scene that unfolded before me. My friend's kids were bundled in their snow gear. As we spilled out onto the front porch the same scene was being enacted on all of the other front porches. Parents followed brightly-hued little bundles down the front steps and onto the street. On both sidewalks people made their way in happy clusters towards Queen's Street, the main thoroughfare. There, we met up with a steady stream of more parents holding hands with yet more kids. People called out to one another, smiled and waved happily as each side street stream of school-bound groups joined and headed east together. Across from the urban elementary school, a crossing guard greeted both children and parents alike and we crossed Queens to join the cheerful throng of dads, moms, nannies and children building snow men, making snow forts and milling about on the school grounds. It was like the scene of some idyllic winter movie from the past. When a bell rang, I thought that the moment would be over, kids would disappear and we'd turn around and head home. But instead, the kids ran to hug their kneeling parents in a chaotic jumble of snowsuits and mittens and scarves, then moved up to the building and stood in their classroom lines. My friend and I joined the rest of the adults, who hung out behind the lines of children and chatted. When a second bell sounded, the kids turned around and waved goodbye to their parents who smiled and waved back. The ritual of another day's beginning was finished. What a joyful way to begin the day! Why can't we, in the US, take the time to enact this lovely community-building ritual instead of the one we overwhelmingly choose: a stressed rushing to school, isolated in our own greenhouse, gas-emitting vehicles, to drop our kids at the curb?

SUN—Schools Uniting Neighborhoods

By Julie Salmon

YOUR SCHOOL IS TEEMING with activity between the hours of eight and three. But when the bell rings and the kids go home, not much else happens—the occasional after-school activity, maybe a parent/teacher conference or two, sports on the weekends, or a few yearly fundraising events for families. Otherwise, you're driving elsewhere to seek services and activities for your family—unless your child goes to a SUN school.

SUN, or Schools Uniting Neighborhoods, is a collaboration of city, county, state and schools in Portland, Oregon. Its purpose? To open the school building every day late on school days, over weekends, and during the summer to respond to the needs of children, their parents and the community. SUN schools are busy schools. Their doors are almost always open, and people in their community use their facilities to fill a myriad of needs.

SUN Schools have five basic goals:

- To provide enrichment activities for families that tie into student success, healthy development and good behavior
- To increase family involvement in the schools
- To increase community and business involvement in the schools
- To improve the collaboration among school districts and community-based groups and businesses
- To use schools as a public resource.

Diane Meisenhelter, coordinator of the SUN school at Buckman Elementary in southeast Portland, explains that Buckman became a SUN school in 1999 after first extensively surveying the community to assess its needs. Parent volunteers, operating under the assumption that people don't always respond to just one way of communicating, took a multiple approach in surveying. They put out questionnaires in school newspapers. They asked parents, staff and students to respond to surveys. They went out into the neighborhood and talked to people on the street, in shopping areas, and door-to-door. They sat with kids at lunch tables and got their "laundry lists" of ideas. They met with student advisory groups and the PTA. They did in-depth family assessments with a cross-section of families. All in all, Meisenhelter says they spoke to more than 1,000 people to figure out what kinds of activities might work best for their community. Next they applied to Multnomah County and the City of Portland to become an official SUN school.

There are currently 13 SUN sites in the Portland area. All SUN schools receive grant money from Multnomah County to administrate the program. After qualifying as a SUN school, Buckman volunteers went to work meeting their primary purpose: filling vacant classrooms with people. After only one year, Buckman "extracurricular" activities include:

- 30 after-school classes serving over 200 kids
- An expanded summer school program.
- "Themed" learning days for kids who need an extra boost during teacher planning days
- After-school homework and reading clubs
- Family fun nights at least once a month
- Health fairs for families
- Healthy heart club to promote exercise and fitness for families
- Working with the local Food Bank, offering classes that teach cooking and nutritional information for families who could use this extra boost
- Translations for ESL families
- Support groups for new families
- Families and Schools Together, or FAST, classes which promote family empowerment and community-building.

> **WHAT IF....?**
> *There was a way to help all kids succeed?
> *There was a way to involve all families in their child's education?
> *There was a way that the whole community would feel connected to your school?
> *There was a way that schools were open from 7 a.m. to 9 p.m.? On weekends? In the summer?

Student and parent evaluations revealed that children got very excited about what their classes were doing and this seemed to bolster confidence and self-esteem. The teachers agree. "We saw a few students blossom and gain confidence in areas they had shied away from."

Why not use your local school building as a centerpiece of your neighborhood, using it to enhance the lives of the community during the hours that it usually has locked doors? If you'd like to open up your local school's doors to your community, check out the SUN web site at www.sunschools.org.

Julie Salmon is the mother of three children and is a freelance writer/editor and lifelong volunteer.

Virtues of Volunteering

By Julie Salmon

THE SUMMER LOOMS before us, not exactly those lazy, hazy days of our own youth, because it's our children we're talking about. In an effort to avoid taxiing to the mall or movies and patrolling TV, we flip through camp catalogues and class schedules, looking for just the right activity to fill their time. But the price tags are so high, the rewards hazy, the choices confusing. What to do? Consider volunteer service!

"Youth gain basic skills, a sense of community, and a sense of power through volunteering," says Sabrina Burke, coordinator of Youth Involvement Network, a Camp Fire-sponsored program designed to help youth, ages 11 to 17, become more involved in their community. Volunteering "gives natural, tangible benefits back to your son or daughter" and it doesn't cost a cent.

Volunteering can also help instill in your child certain personal assets necessary for growing up healthy, caring and competent. A decade of research conducted by the Search Institute and undertaken by the Multnomah Commission on Children and Families has identified at least forty assets that kids need to succeed. Their research shows that on the average, youth have only nineteen of the forty, leaving them vulnerable to many negative influences. Getting involved in their community as a volunteer, however, provides several important assets. Some are:

- Learning that the community values them
- Developing relationships with adults
- Developing a sense of purpose
- Allowing them to be valuable resources
- Service to others, at least one hour per week

- Bringing adult role models into their lives
- Positive peer influence—having friends who set good examples
- Developing a sense of caring, empathy, and sensitivity

The Commission and the research behind the Take the Time program have found that the more assets a person has, the less likely she or he will get involved in dangerous or self-destructive activities. Volunteer service is a rich resource for counteracting some of those negative influences.

It has never been easier to find the right service job for your child. Camp Fire's Youth Volunteer Corp works to connect young people with community organizations that can use their help. It provides training and technical assistance to both the youth and the organizations. It has even created a website to help kids plug into just the right service opportunity. Finding the right spot for the right kid is an important part of YVC and its technical arm, Youth Involvement Network.

"A huge part of the Youth Volunteer Corp," says Vanessa Diamond, the AmeriCorp Team Leader at the YVC, "is to make people realize that service isn't just service. It has to be meaningful. It has to be rewarding. I think that's what sells the youth on it. They actually do make a difference."

Kids can sign up for two-week stints throughout the summer. They can work with the elderly, repair houses, plant trees, learn to landscape, work with disabled kids —you name it. The opportunities are boundless, and each one can give your child tangible benefits. There are also several other opportunities throughout the year.

Volunteering is not only about giving, which is reward in itself, it is also about learning. Every project teaches skills, from empathy, compassion, and knowledge of how other people struggle, to life skills, such as painting, construction, and knowing what it really costs to raise a family. These are topics that schools don't usually include in their curriculum.

Volunteering gives kids an important role in our community. It allows them to realize some of their potential right now, rather than existing simply as people in waiting. "In my opinion, people under eighteen are one of the last really disenfranchised groups of folks," says Burke. "They are treated like 'future beings'.

Volunteering gives them a role in the here and now. They can be empowered by the feeling "I can effect change," and by a sense of belonging.

OK, the benefits are clear, but how do you motivate your child to get involved? Burke feels that younger kids, ages 11 or 12, don't usually require a lot of motivation. Older teens are harder to motivate. Burke encourages talking to them about how a volunteer experience can help a teen get a better job than flipping burgers. For example, she's seen many young people gain experience for landscaping jobs by working in community gardens or volunteering with the park department. Real work experience and letters of recommendation are invaluable when applying for work.

Volunteering with a friend, or being invited to volunteer by a friend, can also be motivating. "If they go with someone else and they have fun, they'll do it again," says Burke. It might be necessary to get two friends together and strong-arm them into trying it the first time. After the first few days, though, they'll want to come back.

Even better is being invited by a friend who already volunteers. Diamond believes it places young people in the "I am important to society" category. The volunteer is telling her friend "Hey, it's really fun, but we need your help." In addition, volunteering with a friend helps to build initial confidence. To show up somewhere to volunteer and not know anyone can be really scary.

Burke has one more piece of advice for parents. She encourages parents to emphasize the positive aspects of the volunteer work. For example, if your child went to the Multiple Sclerosis Society and stuffed envelopes, instead of saying "Oh, that's boring," say, "That's how organizations spread the word about their cause."

Once your child is volunteering, success is almost assured. Volunteering may be especially beneficial to those kids who don't particularly shine in other aspects of their lives; for example, academics or sports. "Anybody can be a successful volunteer," says Diamond. "All they need to do is have compassion and the motivation to do it. There is no failure in volunteering if you stick with what you're going to do, and you do it with a good heart."

Julia Salmon is a freelance writer/editor and lifelong volunteer. She spends most of her time and effort, however, raising her three children.

Reprinted with permission from Full Esteem Ahead, *Wings*, Spring 1999.

Research Shows Connection between Volunteering and Emotional Well-Being
By Kathy Masarie, MD

Happy people invest more hours in volunteer service[1] and volunteer at higher levels for charity and community service groups, including religious, political, educational and health-related organizations[2] than do unhappy people. So, does this show that it takes a happy person to volunteer or does it mean that when you volunteer, you become happy? According to research, people may in fact feel a rush of happiness when they help others.[3,4] Reward centers in the brain are activated when people help a charity—even when they do it through paying taxes.[5] There is evidence, though, that as distance comes between a donor and the person receiving help, the benefits are not as great. For instance, giving money may distance the donor from the recipient, whereas volunteering time has social, identity and connection implications that are highly beneficial to creating happiness. [6,7,8]

Much in our lives adds to our feelings of subjective happiness; close friends, pets, a satisfying love life, physical health and laughter, to name a few; however, one avenue to happiness is often overlooked, and that is the blossoming of happiness as a result of giving of yourself to others … through volunteering. [9]

[1] Thoits, Peggy A. and Lyndi N. Hewitt (2001), "Volunteer Work and Well-Being," *Journal of Health and Social Behavior,* 42 (June), 115-131.
[2] Krueger, Hicks and McGue (2001), "Altruism and Antisocial Behavior: Independent Tendencies, Unique Personality Correlates, Distinct Etiologies," *Psychological Science, 12* (Sept), 397-402.
[3] Gilbert, Daniel (2006), *Stumbling on Happiness,* New York, NY: Vintage Press.
[4] Williams, Tonya P. and Angela Y. Lee (2007), "Me and Benjamin: Transaction versus Relationship Wealth in Subjective Well-being," Under review at *Journal of Personality and Social Psychology.*
[5] Harbaugh, William T., Ulrich Mayr, and Daniel R. Burghart (2007), "Neural Responses to Taxation and Voluntary Giving Reveal Motives for Charitable Donations," *Science,* 316 (June), 1622.
[6] Reed, Americus II, Karl Aquino and Eric Levy (2007a), "Moral Identity and Judgments of Charitable Behaviors," *Journal of Marketing,* in press.
[7] Vohs, Kathleen D., Nicole L. Mead and Miranda R. Goode (2006), "The Psychological Consequences of Money," *Science, 314,* 1154-1156.
[8] Vohs, Kathleen D., Nicole L. Mead and Miranda R. Goode (2007), "Money Changes Personal and Interpersonal Behavior: The Self-Sufficiency Hypothesis," University of Minnesota Working Paper.
[9] Liu, Wendy and Aaker, Jennifer, "The Happiness of Giving: The Time-Ask Effect," J. of Consumer Research. Oct 2008

Let's Get Boys and Girls Equally Involved in Volunteering

By Nancy Huppertz

MANY PEOPLE HAVE the perception that volunteerism is something that only women do. That belief recalls a time when women did not comprise nearly half of the paid work force and when larger numbers of women than today were not employed outside the home.

The notion of volunteerism being a female responsibility began at an early age. While boys were mowing lawns, shoveling snow and delivering papers, most often for pay, girls were volunteering in hospitals as candy stripers. Later, it was, for the most part, women who attended PTA meetings and provided other adult volunteer services. The perception persists, even though female and male roles have undergone dramatic change.

> Just as all occupations are now open and available to females and males, it is important that all volunteer opportunities be similarly open to all.

Today, with nearly equal numbers of women and men in the workforce, it would seem to follow that equal numbers of women and men should be available and willing to do volunteer work in the community. And just as all occupations are now open and available to females and males, so should all volunteer opportunities be similarly open to all.

Youth volunteerism serves a number of purposes. Perhaps the most important is instilling a sense of altruism, of giving something back to the community, of helping others just because it is the right thing to do. Second, it is an opportunity to learn a variety of life skills that might not be offered in school. The National Service-Learning Cooperative has issued a document called "Essential Elements of Service-Learning." It sees service learning, an organized form of volunteerism, as among the methods that "tries to create thoughtful and meaningful contexts in which students can be motivated to not only acquire new knowledge, but to retain and creatively transfer what they have learned throughout their lifetime as successful citizens and workers." The range of skills is wide, from care-providing at a nursing home or day care center, to carpentry on a Habitat for Humanity project. Altruism and meaningful contexts are valuable for character development and intellectual growth for all young people ... male and female.

Finally, volunteerism provides an opportunity to learn at an early age how to interact and work with a variety of people. "Communication with diverse individuals" is one of the Essential Elements in the National Service Learning document, as is "participation by diverse groups." Given a choice, most people will choose to associate with others similar to themselves ... such as by sex, race or some other characteristic. The opportunity to meet and work with others who are different will serve students well when they go on to function in a diverse society.

Parents and those in charge of volunteer or service learning programs must be vigilant about not limiting young people's opportunities according to their own preconceived, gender-based notions about appropriate kinds of activities. They must also be alert to attempts by the volunteer sites to stereotype work according to sex or to exclude students by race. The days of "Send me three strong boys ..." are over, happily replaced by, "Send me three people who can do ..." Within the guidelines of safe, honest, and non-exploitative work, students should have the freedom to choose what they want to do.

Recently, a team of high school students, including both males and females, was sent to the home of an elderly man to help him with home maintenance and repair. All of the students expected to be working outside, but when they arrived he gave the boys jobs outside and asked the girls to do the inside housework. All the students would have benefited from doing both kinds of work.

The many benefits of service learning and volunteerism should be open and available to all.

Nancy Huppertz is a gender equity specialist who runs Apogee Training and Consulting, a firm that does consulting in gender equity issues for organizations and schools throughout the United States.

Reprinted with permission from Full Esteem Ahead, *Wings*, Spring 1999.

Volunteering—The Youth Perspective

Gal Pals Go Painting

By Molly Krupa, a college graduate

JUSTINE, 13, and Kaitlin, 15, volunteered last summer through the Youth Volunteer Corps. Their two-week project involved painting a house. The location of the project was significant for Kaitlin and Justine. It was the first time they had really paid attention to a neighborhood different from their own. In fact, when I asked what they had learned from the experience, the people and the neighborhood seemed to have had more of an impact on them than any of the work skills they had learned. Both girls enjoyed the exposure to the people they met; in particular, the stories one neighbor shared with them while they painted. The opportunity to experience life in a different setting, coupled with the reward of helping others, is what made the Youth Volunteer Corps most worthwhile for these girls.

Justine and Kaitlin had some advice for others who have thought about becoming involved:

- If possible, sign up with a friend. Meeting others is often easier if you are already with at least one familiar person.
- Examine the projects well, and pick one that really interests you.
- Be prepared to do hard work!

Justine, Kaitlin, and I also talked about requiring volunteering for high school graduation. To my surprise, both favored mandatory volunteering. Though kids might at first be disgruntled about yet another requirement, "Once they experience volunteerism, they'll like it!"

Molly Krupa is applying to medical school.

Sharing a Love of Words

By Clara Settle, a high school senior

"SINCE I COULDN'T speak English, I felt like I didn't know anything." That's what 13-year-old William said when I asked him what it was like to come to the United States a year-and-a-half ago, after spending most of his life in Guatemala. In exchange for helping William learn English, he gave me something valuable in return—a new perspective.

What began as a community service project has turned into one of my favorite parts of the week. Every Tuesday I go over to my former middle school and help tutor ESL (English as a Second Language) students. In that classroom, the common language is not English or Spanish. Instead, the most important and universal sign is a smile, or a laugh, and the students I work with have plenty to go around. What I do is fairly simple, but is no doubt very important to the kids I help. I give them an hour of my time and share with them my love for my language, something that is easy for me to give. I might help them work on spelling, go over reading questions, or finish up homework. However, I think one of the best things I can do is talk to them.

When I am talking to William, he seems shy, and almost afraid. I try to smile a lot, and maybe that helps. I can understand that confidence is a little hard to come by when you aren't sure how to express yourself in a new language. For William, neither of his parents speaks English, and his friends speak "English a little bit ... but more Spanish." He says that the only person that he can speak English with is his sister and even she isn't fluent. "My sister is 16. She is in high school." He says with pride. I smile and say that I'm in high school, too. His eyes light up. While our conversations might not have much to do with the book they're reading, or the spelling test they're studying for, I know that he has to challenge himself to talk to me and to understand me.

Another boy I look forward to seeing is Max, who, like William, came from Guatemala. He is open and talks to me, even though he might not say it exactly how he wants. He just talks, and I listen. He is not entirely fluent in English, but I've noticed that what he says often comes through crystal clear. His attitude itself would be inspirational, but what impressed me even more was to learn about what he had gone through. He left his family in Guatemala four years ago to come to the US, a country where he did not speak the local language at all. Then, he was transferred to school after school, never staying in any place for very long. I try to imagine what this must be like. In the end, I can't begin to possibly understand how it is that, after all of it, Max is sitting in front of me laughing and smiling.

The Big Help

An Interview with
Mia (11) and Maggie (13)
By Lisa Sloan

WHAT IS THE Big Help?
It's a way we make money that we can give away to help others.

How do you make the money?
We do jobs for money: things like babysitting, yard work, house cleaning, car washing and pet care. We will also type for you or draw a portrait—basically anything people will pay us money for. We did a lemonade stand, too, and sold things we didn't need anymore at a garage sale.

What made you think to start it?
We read a section in American Girl Magazine about girls who were helping people and we wanted to do that. They also talk a lot at school about charity work. We thought it would be pretty cool.

How did you decide what to do?
Well, we fought a lot in the beginning. Then we just made a list of things we were good at and made prices for each thing. We put up signs and handed out our flyers to our neighbors and we got lots of work.

Has it been successful?
Oh, yes! The first year we made $38. (Another friend helped that year too) and we donated it to the People's Bank. It was really cool to get a letter from them saying they used the money to buy mattress for someone. The second year we made $102 and the third year we made $200. Both of those times we gave the money to the Neighborhood House. They gave us a tour and thanked us for what we did.

What has been the best part of the Big Help?
We really like doing the jobs we offer, especially babysitting! It also feels really good to be helping someone else.

Will you to it again?
Definitely! We will do this or something like it forever!

Reprinted with permission from Full Esteem Ahead, *Wings*, "Volunteering the Youth Perspective," Spring 1999. "The Big Help, Spring 2003.

Teens Triumph over Techno-Tribulations

From *Assets* Magazine

YOUR COMPUTER'S NOT working. You live in a small community, and help could be days coming. Who are you going to call? If you live in the Dassel-Cokato area of Minnesota, you can contact a techno-savvy high school student who will fix your problems at no charge, thanks to the Computer Service Club (CSC).

The CSC grew out of an effort to meaningfully engage youth who were idle after school. "A Search Institute survey and local data indicated that nearly half of our youth did not participate in any extra-curricular activities anywhere," says Gary Herman, coordinator of Dassel-Cokato Area Character Counts Initiative. The club answered an important need for many of the nonparticipants—and the community.

Flo Osness had difficulty using e-mail and called the Computer Service Club. "I had just gotten my computer," says the senior citizen. "Everything was new to me." CSC sent out Ryan, age 17, to guide her through the new computer woes. "Oh, he gets a good report from me," says Osness. CSC not only provides a real service to the community, it helps students develop a wide range of assets.

Reprinted with permission from "Teens Triumph over Techno-Tribulations," *Assets: The Magazine of Ideas for Healthy Communities and Healthy Youth.* Copyright © Autumn 1998, Search Institute ®, Minneapolis, MN; www.search-institute.org. All rights reserved.

Connect with Kids by Helping Them to Help Others

By Harmony Barrett and Jennifer McCoy

IN A TIME WHEN MANY children are receiving brand new TVs and expensive clothing in place of parental involvement in their lives, other parents are developing productive and fun ways to connect with their kids. One such parent, Jennifer McCoy, felt that many of the activities in kids' lives, such as sports and school, fostered competition and a "me" attitude rather than compassion for others. So she developed an avenue to show, rather than tell, them what values she holds important.

In 1999, with the help of her children, Katie and Riley, she started *Kids That Care,* a group of 2nd to 6th graders who gather donations to help nurture children moving into foster care. So far 500 backpacks filled with toiletries, toys, and comfort items have accompanied foster children to their new homes, providing them with things of their own during this difficult transition. The group deals directly with the local county Department of Human Services.

In addition to getting supplies donated, the students have raised money through activities such as baby-sitting at a local church for a parents' night out and selling fresh flowers in vases they painted.

Jennifer said she could have found an established group in the community with the values she was looking for, but "I don't like just dropping my kids off," she said. "I guess … I felt I needed to be part of the community, too." Together, by creating an activity to share, she and her daughter have been brought closer together during the middle school years, when parents and their children often drift apart.

They hope other parents might try to form community service groups of their own, maintaining that the commitment can involve just a few hours a month if well organized. The children don't have to meet often. They also are considering changing it to an after-school enrichment class to involve more children.

This idea is just one of many for community service projects that parents and kids could start or be involved in together. Jennifer has generated the following tips for parents who are interested in starting a community service project of their own:

1. Come up with an idea: Inspiration can come from a book, newspaper article, something mentioned by a family member or friend, or a need identified by a social service group.
2. Research: Contact a local social service agency or organization to find out more about the community needs, programs already in place, and what help would be welcomed.
3. Remain flexible: An agency or organization might refer you to another, more suitable one or make suggestions on how to modify the project.
4. Spread the word: Tap existing networks such as classmates, sports teams and neighbors to find children and parents interested in joining the effort.
5. Get help: Approach local businesses and schools for help with supplies or meeting places. Recruit other parents to assist in the work and supervision.

Kids That Care represents a positive movement in our culture—parents and kids rising as equals to social challenges and finding new ways to share important experiences and values together. As always, actions speak louder than words. *Kids That Care* has demonstrated that the gift of involvement and giving extends far beyond any toy. You (and kids you know) can do it, too.

Harmony Barrett lives in Boulder, Colorado. She is always interested in finding new ways to stay involved in kids' lives and help inspire them. In addition to Kids That Care, Jennifer McCoy volunteers in many arenas, her childrens' schools and community. She is the mother of two.

Reprinted with permission from Full Esteem Ahead, *Wings,* Winter 2002.

Hands on Portland: Volunteering Made Easy

To build community and enrich lives by providing a gateway to service and empowering volunteers

By Kathy Masarie, MD

HANDS ON PORTLAND IS a treasure in Portland, Oregon. It is a one-stop-shop for done-in-a-day volunteer projects and it can be mimicked in any community. Through this website you can explore what really grabs you as a volunteer—from working in gardens, tearing up ivy, painting, serving meals, shopping, washing cats … who knows until you've tried it. A family can sign up for

an activity once and move on to a new one. Eventually the hope is that you will get "hooked" and stick with a certain activity. Take Michael who washed cats for the Humane Society one Saturday afternoon when he was in middle school. When his service-learning requirement came up in high school a few years later, he knew where to go. He went beyond just filling up his hours. He liked the work and knew he was committed to the cause.

Hands on Portland breaks down a lot of the barriers that make volunteering difficult—it does the research

for us by finding and listing meaningful work; it breaks down the commitment to "doable" proportions and makes the process of signing up online really easy. All you have to do is go on their website, www. handsonportland.org, each month and pick the opportunities that await you. Here is a sampling of opportunities:

- Care for cats as they await adoption
- Repair bikes for low-income youth at the Community Cycling Center
- Play soccer with Ugandan refugees
- Get involved with the Transportation Alliance Bike Safety Program
- Serve a meal at a homeless shelter.
- Shop or deliver groceries for house-bound folks for Store to Door (a personal favorite)
- Do yard work for elderly with Project Linkage
- Play and do crafts with children at low-income apartment for Human Solutions
- Make cards for juvenile residents of Good Neighbor Center
- Organize school supplies or clothes at the PTA Clothing Center
- Paint Friends of the Children headquarters
- Beautify our world with Friends of Tryon Creek, Portland Community Garden, and Metro-Oxbow Park.

It was Fran Loosen, a committed volunteer in Portland, who decided that her city needed a central "clearing house" to connect willing volunteers with projects that required volunteer help. The result of her work has been extraordinary. The ease with which a person or family can volunteer for meaningful work has inspired the community to volunteer even more. What Fran did for her community by creating Hands on Portland can be replicated anywhere.

Contact www.handsonportland.org to see how you might get started in your community.

Asset-Building Stories from Our Greater Community and Businesses

Pulling People Together to Build Assets in Our Community (from Ann Lider, Co-Founder of LO-ABC Coalition) I was in one of the first *Raising Our Daughters* classes. I was really struck by how powerful the assets are and how many people come back to the assets as the "glue" to support kids in a healthy way. I met with my neighbor, Jann Lane, to brainstorm about asset building in Lake Oswego, OR, and we came up with the LO-ABC coalition. Jann helped bring together the mayor, our schools, and local businesses, including the town newspaper. This became way bigger than I ever thought it would be but we grew step-by-step. Our passion helped keep things going when we got overwhelmed or discouraged by funding struggles.

County-Sponsored Mini-Grants

"Take the Time" was a successful program of the Multnomah County Commission. For several years mini-grants of up to $500 were given to creative projects that helped build the 40 Developmental Assets in the lives of young people. Individual proposals for how the money could be spent were reviewed by volunteer adults and youth from the Portland, OR community. It is astounding how far a small amount of money can go, when combined with passion, determination and support of others. People were very creative, coming up with ideas that connected youth and adults, empowering kids with learning skills that they could use now and as adults and working to strengthen communities and schools. Any community can bring groups together into a coalition that funds and finds grants that can be given out to people who are willing to organize projects for the well-being of our youth. The results of many small projects can be powerful and influential.

Community Centers Build Community (from Glenda Montgomery)

Things have changed in Albuquerque, New Mexico. I'm glad they have. As a young professional couple, my husband and I had a blast starting out our married lives in Albuquerque; there was plenty for us to do to keep active and happy. But, when we had our kids, we noticed what Albuquerque didn't have many of at the time: community centers. There was one run-down YMCA near us, and we couldn't find any sign of a vital community center. As a young mom at home, I felt isolated and alone. I took my kids to the park every day, and because we could afford it, I took them to a private athletic club to learn how to swim. That was it. When I moved to Portland, Oregon, I couldn't believe the difference: a thriving community-center system linked my kids and me into feeling a sense of community and offered classes such as art, clay, woodworking, dance, cooking and swimming; and all of these were just a selection of classes offered to kids from 2 to 4 years old! It seems in Portland that every neighborhood has its own heart and this tends to be its Parks and Recreation Center. As a new mom in Portland, my days were easily filled with indoor park, "Tots and Moms" classes, yoga, aerobics, and a variety of other recreation center activities that allowed me to meet other at-home moms while my kids met friends who shared common passions. Daddy-

daughter dances, teen nights and basketball and volleyball drop-in leagues brought whole families together and connected them to other families. Through our move, we realized how crucial a community center system is to the building and nurturing of community feeling and to the quality of the lives of kids and families.

Company Sponsors School Programs and Provides Adult Volunteers. Tony Arnerich of AM&A, an investment firm, gets his employees involved with young people. The firm divides its employees up between three schools. There, 35 employees volunteer on company time to the tune of 1-2 hours per week. Activities range from reading tutors to a girls' club focusing on leadership skills, math and science clubs, and a study hall program. AM&A also hired a full-time coordinator to keep the programs running smoothly.

What motivates this business? The desire to show kids that they are important and so is their education. And Americh adds, "There is a huge but subtle business advantage in what we are doing. When you hire people who are willing to give back to the community, you get great people."

Church Youth Groups Provide Opportunities for Kids to Be Welcomed and Appreciated 15-year-old Sam seemed pretty introverted. He wasn't doing very well in school and hadn't committed to any kind of activity outside of class. Frankly, his mother was worried about him. He stayed home, watched movies and played guitar. He had no interest in sports. He had a couple of friends he hung out with, but he wasn't a part of anything … he didn't have a group. That changed when his best friend Karl took him to his church youth group. Sam wasn't sure to begin with, but with Karl as a buddy who was already a part of the community, Sam didn't have to work hard to become integrated. Where Karl was welcomed, Sam was too. Eventually, Sam found his niche. The kids in youth group were friendly and open. The leaders were excellent, providing Sam with a strong male role model that he didn't have in his single-mom household. They organized fun activities and outings that Sam began to take part in regularly, even if Karl was

unable to attend. He was going out and experiencing things that he would not have experienced otherwise. He began to feel comfortable and accepted and began to join in when the youth group went to services in the church. Sam and Karl played guitar for the congregation and were acknowledged and appreciated for their talent and their willingness to share that talent. Sam became known and welcomed by the larger group. When the

youth group became counselors for the children's summer camp, Sam realized that he was good working with kids and they showed their appreciation by looking up to him and using him as a role model. Now Sam's mother reports that her son is much more self-confident. He has come out of his shell and is aware of his talents and strengths and has a place to use them where they are acknowledged and are meaningful. He knows he can be himself and be appreciated for who he is by both adults and kids, for his wacky sense of humor and for his talents, and even just for his presence. What a gift! Church youth group allowed Sam to create a world for himself where he could be himself and where he enjoyed being. It took a vital high school youth group with strong adult leadership, a welcoming community, and the invitation of a friend.

What About Boys? National Resources for Boys AND Girls. The Ophelia Project was created to take up the cause of girls in our society. When it provided excellent resources to enhance the safety, health, self-esteem, competence and well-being of girls, people began to ask, "What about boys?" Relational aggression, bullying, health and well-being issues all exist for boys as well, but weren't being given the same attention. That was when the Boys Initiative was born. Instead of reinventing the wheel, The Boys Initiative was spawned from the Ophelia Project and brought together the same resources, though gender-specific to boys and their specific gender needs. They also tapped into resources for boys in the community that already existed. Speaker's bureaus, teacher-leader trainings and workshops for kids were set up, following the organizational pattern already in use by the successful Ophelia project and using many of the same workshop ideas and trainings. Just like the Ophelia project, Boys Initiative offers programs at schools, community centers and libraries. It is committed to violence prevention, leadership development and peer support. Like the Ophelia Project, it functions as a resource to help create a world where kids can safely grow up to become competent, capable, compassionate members of society. The Boys Initiative stresses that "With the addition of a gender-specific perspective and accurate information about social and emotional development, youth and teen programs can be much more applicable, effective, and long-lasting." Both the Ophelia Project and The Boys Initiative are incredible resources. Check out: www.theopheliaproject.org and www.boysinitiative.org.

Stand for Children:
Grassroots Group Influences Government Decision-Making
By Glenda Montgomery

JONAH EDELMAN, THE Executive Director of Stand for Children, believes passionately in the power of grassroots movements to enact real change in our society. He also believes passionately in our responsibility to America's children: "To me, children are the most oppressed group in our society and our ill-treatment of them is a litmus test of where and who we are." Edelman explains that many caring Americans support advocacy groups that provide our politicians with information about our failure to support the health and well-being of children; yet he says, "I think that (having) good information is a necessary condition, but it is not a sufficient condition for change. The average politician knows that kids don't have health insurance and that schools don't have enough funding, and they choose not to address it because there's limited funding and competing priorities that are supported by more influential interests."[1] We parents need to become the influential interest that makes politicians pay attention. We can do that, he says, by banding together to build a powerful and persuasive force, able to push forward transformation at the very top ... on a political level.

Jonah Edelman's two passions converged as he helped to organize "Stand for Children Day" in Washington DC on June 1, 1996. More than 300,000 people showed up to make it the largest rally for the well-being of children in American history. [2] In 1998, he co-founded "Stand for Children" in Oregon, a grassroots organization of parents and other adults interested in the health, education and well-being of children, who work together to gain the political clout necessary to affect electoral and legislative change. Stand for Children focuses on supporting political candidates who demonstrate their commitment to the welfare of children. It builds effective local and statewide networks of advocates to convince elected officials and voters to invest in programs and public education to help children to become successful, productive citizens who thrive. Local chapters and teams of volunteers research key concerns, decide together on a focus issue, set specific goals for change and work in coalition with other organizations to produce significant results. Stand for Children has now grown to 2000 members and seven chapters.

Stand for Children has had great success in Oregon:
✓ **Helped elect a 60% pro-schools supermajority to the Oregon House of Representatives in 2008** by playing a key role in the successful campaigns of Brent Barton and Greg Matthews, who replaced incumbents with weak records on children's and education issues.

✓ **Helped secure $242 million to make urgent health and safety repairs to 48 Salem-Keizer schools, and build a middle school and three elementary schools** to relieve overcrowding by playing a key role in passing the largest bond measure for schools in the state's history.

✓ **Played a key role in renewing the Portland Children's Investment Fund,** which supports more than 60 cost-effective, proven programs delivering before- and after-school mentorship, early childhood education, child abuse prevention and intervention, and support for foster children (programs serve 16,000 Portland kids each year).

✓ **Prevented the loss of 160 teachers in Eugene** by helping renew the 4-J School District Local Option Levy, generating about $15 million per year—10% of the District's funding.

✓ **Enabled most school districts to begin to reduce class sizes and restore essential programs** by helping secure a K-12 appropriation of $6.245 billion for 2007-2009—the first reinvestment in more than a decade.

✓ **Increased teacher quality and retention** by designing and winning legislative approval for the Oregon New Educator Mentor Program, providing mentors for nearly 1,000 new K-12 teachers.

✓ **Confronted the epidemic of childhood obesity** by helping craft and pass statewide legislation requiring the removal of unhealthy snacks and drinks from school vending machines, student stores, and a là carte lines, thereby improving Oregon's national school nutrition rating from an F to an A-.[3]

Since 1998, other successful Stand for Children organizations have come together in Tennessee, Massachusetts, and Washington State. If you are interested in becoming involved in Stand for Children in any of these states or if you are interested in beginning a Stand for Children in your state, visit www.standforchildren.org.

---

[1] www.aecf.org/MajorInitiatives/RelatedInitiative/ProgramProfiles
[2] www.huntalternatives.org
[3] www.standforchildren.org

Businesses—Join Up and Volunteer Today

By Kathy Masarie, MD

AT A TIME WHEN it is so clear that involvement in the schools and in the community is critical to healthy youth, many companies are reaching out to help. They are setting up company-wide projects, making it convenient for everyone to get involved. Some are even giving employees paid time off to volunteer. Only 20% of US families consistently attend school programs and 40% never do. A study conducted by the Mattel Foundation discovered that lack of time was noted as a particular problem for many employees, particularly low-income parents. Employees said they need the support of their employers to provide them the flexibility to visit schools during working hours. Here are a few of the stories of employer support we have heard about.

> Lack of time is a major barrier keeping parents, especially low-income parents, from attending school programs.

There is a program that is reaching out to get adults involved in the schools. It is called "8 for Kids" sponsored by The Greater Hand-in-Hand Coalition and Children First for Oregon. It encourages businesses to provide employees with 8 hours of paid leave (or more) per year to be specifically used for school visits. This could include parent-teacher conferences, volunteering in the schools or mentoring a student. LSI Logic allows employees up to 40 paid hours to participate in children's school activities. The City of Portland is encouraging their employees to get involved as "a caring adult in the life of a child" through the school volunteer programs.

> Employer flexibility is essential for allowing parents the opportunity to visit their children's schools during working hours.

Small companies can be successful with employee volunteer programs too. S and J Heating and Air Conditioning gives their 12 employees eight hours of paid volunteer time per year, allowing these fathers to get involved in their child's education. Sheri Renhard, the former owner, said it was a win-win situation. Since they adopted the "8 for Kids" contract (available from Children First for Oregon), they have seen less sick leave, a higher retention rate and have actually come out ahead financially.

Morgan Anderson at Intel's Human Resources Department says they encourage volunteering by giving matching grants—for every hour their employee volunteers, the place where they are volunteering receives $5, which at 15,000 hours added up to $74,000 donated last year. Intel even provides their own volunteer opportunities, such as Smart Reading, Boys and Girls Club, and Adopt-A-Family at Christmas.

Hanna Anderson gives back to the community in many ways. The company supports its workers by providing excellent benefits, including paying for almost half of employees' childcare costs and allowing for a flexible work week so that parents can go to children's doctor appointments, attend teacher conferences, run errands, or even volunteer. This company organizes volunteer opportunities and allows up to 16 paid hours annually for volunteer time. In addition, Hanna Anderson donates $100 to the classroom of each employee's child. The children are encouraged to decide how the money should be used in the classroom. This teaches them that their parent's employer cares about their education and future, as well as giving them a taste of altruism themselves.

Portland General Electric has supported its employee's efforts to enrich their communities for many years. Most of PGE's employees this year have already committed at least 16 hours of volunteer service through PGE-sponsored volunteer activities or by volunteering in their own neighborhoods or schools. Power Generation is the volunteer program of the employee's children. PGE puts money, people, and power into the communities where its employees live and work. Their success can even be seen with their retiree's commitment to community. They become very active volunteers after leaving their paid work. "It's just in us," a PGE retiree reports.

How about asking your employer to join in and begin creating a family-friendly workplace? If you own a business, use the stories above as examples to follow. How can we expect our kids to give back to the community and care for one another if we adults don't model it?

Reprinted with permission from Full Esteem Ahead, *Wings,* Spring 1999.

Take Your Kids to Work Day: Building Community in Business

By Sue Strater

Having been involved with the "Take Our Daughters to Work" Day at a previous employer, I was interested in starting it with my new company. This national program helps pre- and early-adolescent girls stay strong and confident by having them explore what contributions they can bring to the workplace. Being the mother of two boys, I wanted to expand the program to give girls and boys (ages 6 to 15) exposure to working adults, career choices, and our work environment. So, in 1998 at our company, Medicalogic, we started Kids Day, held on the national day for "Take Our Daughters to Work" (the fourth Thursday in April). Our first year, we had 45 children—belonging to 150 employees—participate. Three years later, we had 70 kids turn out, many for the third year in a row. My son, Zack, an 8-year-old, liked the idea of meeting new friends and seeing old friends each year at this event.

Planning

I set up a core team with volunteers from different departments—representatives from Software Development, Customer Support, Marketing, and Human Resources. A diverse team representing different careers met weekly at lunch for 5-6 weeks prior to the event. Our objectives were:

- Have the kids learn about our company and how we develop products.
- Have the kids learn about different careers.
- Have the employees learn from the kids.
- Make it fun for everyone.

The first meeting, we brainstormed potential activities in four categories—product-related, community-based, career-oriented, and fun. The other meetings covered areas like identifying trinkets for the kids, e.g. T-shirts, ordering food, registering kids so we knew the number and ages, identifying and getting materials, and finding rooms for the day. We divided the children into groups of about 12 for many events, and mixed boys and girls of all ages together—older kids helping the younger ones. Jenny, a 13-year old, said she "learned how to work well with younger kids" from being at Kids Day.

The Day

The day started with a few minutes together to cover rules and expectations, followed by a 15-minute talk by one of the executives. One year, the CEO gave a slide show about his personal and career choices while growing up. Another talk by our Product Development V.P. showed how the company started and grew. The kids were together for pizza lunch with parents and at the end for fun time—games, face painting, and more food. Each year, the kids created an art project that became part of Medicalogic's work environment. The first year, they created a mural on a lunchroom wall—putting paint on their hands or feet and leaving their mark. Another year, kids drew pictures of themselves in a career in which they were interested. We framed these to hang in conference rooms for employees to enjoy. To learn about our company, its products and customers, the kids role-played doctor, nurse or patient and created a medical chart on a computer. Another year, they simulated a surgical operation. To help the kids learn about different careers, employees played 20 questions with the kids who, in turn, tried to figure out what the employees did. One year, the Audubon Society came and the kids built birdhouses to take home. We placed some of the birdhouses on the wetlands next to our offices.

Lessons Learned

Make the activities hands-on and fun, get money budgeted for it, and include a member from Human Resources in your planning so they integrate the day's result into the company's culture. Take initiative and organize your own Kids Day! It's a tremendous learning experience for kids and employees. The kids might also learn one more thing: their parent's company cares about them.

Sue Strater works in Quality Assurance for a software organization and is the mother of two boys.

Reprinted with permission from Full Esteem Ahead, *Wings*, Winter 2001.

Final Session of Raising Our Daughters

By Family Empowerment Network

CONGRATULATIONS! You have completed Family Empowerment Network's *Raising Our Daughters Parenting Guide*. We hope you have found strength in reading and collaborating with others, and it is our sincerest hope that you will remain connected as the next few critical years pass. It could be a quick chat in the halls, keeping an eye out for each other's kids or a more regular monthly or quarterly gathering. Talk with each other about how this might happen.

If you enjoyed the book, please encourage others to participate, purchase books of their own, and start a discussion group. This will foster the building of a community of people committed to our children. Consider becoming a mentor to help new groups to form in your community. It can be as simple as setting up a meeting to share your experience with others interested.

WHERE TO GO FROM HERE . . .

Individual Readers
If you have read this book on your own and liked it, we recommend that you start a group now. After reading the book, you now realize what a great difference it could make for you to create a support group for yourself. Get a group of friends or the parents of your daughter's friends together and discuss one chapter at each meeting. This will help make what you read come alive with possibility and will add richness and depth to your experience.

Discussion Group Readers
Many people find the continued connection and support from other parents invaluable, as their children move through adolescence. Many groups that end up staying together have a project or shared vision. This direction may have come up in the discussions as you went along, or may come up now as you pool all your ideas and see where you want to go. Here are just a few of many ideas:

Continued Regular Gatherings
Support Group
- You have shared for many sessions now—don't stop. Meet monthly over topics, books, videos, events, lunch or community activity. Some groups have even repeated this curriculum.
- Attend local lectures or conferences together.

Parenting Book Club
- Continue to learn by reading one parenting book a month and discussing it. Pick from our TOP TEN (p. 1: 10)

Parent-Child Book Club
- This is an awesome way for a group of kids and parents to bond, no matter what age you start

Mother-Daughter Group or Father-Daughter Group
- Start a mother-daughter or father-daughter group for fun, play, volunteering and learning together.

Parent-Child Gathering
- Bring both Mom and Dad and kids together. Let the kids plan the agenda.
- Consider a self-defense class together—everyone deserves that extra safety information.
- Volunteer together! Choose a project and jump in!

Parent Education and Networking
Seminars - bring a parent seminar to your school, community group or business
Build Community by Fostering more* Raising Our Sons *or* Raising Our Daughters *Discussion Groups
- If you have a son, consider starting a *Raising Our Sons* Discussion Group.
- Be a Parenting Group Organizer: set up a meeting via school newsletter/emails for parents interested in ways to support their sons and daughters proactively. Share experiences from your parenting group.
- Share your experience with the school counselor, or other staff member who might be interested in a group.

Project-Based Activities
- Get youth involved in leadership: start school-based volunteer activities or a Student Advisory Board.
- Start a *Parent Resource Committee* on your PTA to offer more resources and get more parents involved in the school.
- Bring *Girls' Night Out* or *Boys' Night Out* to your middle school—kids help plan it with teen mentors, who help run it.
- Bring *Turnoff* Week to your school with a parent-education program sent home.

Even if you don't start another formal activity, just keep talking to one another. Wave to your neighbors; say hello to kids as you pass them; go to PTA meetings; get involved in your community. You've taken a giant first step—just keep going!

Next Steps: A Tool for Creating a Vision and Taking Action

Step #1 Think of an inspirational vision or goal for you, your daughter and/or your family.
Don't limit yourself by thinking about how it will happen. Tap into what you really long for. Write it out in the present tense (as if you already had it). Is it something you have 100% control over? For example, rather than "I have a healthy relationship with my daughter" which reqires cooperation on her part, say "I prioritze connection and good communication with my daughter," which you have control over.

Step #2 Describe your present reality, where you are now. Include what interferes with achieving your goals. How do you support yourself now and how do you get support from others?

Step #3 List the action steps you will take to achieve your goal with a timeline attached. Include how to support yourself and what support would be helpful from others in achieving your goals.

	ACTION STEP	DUE DATE
1		
2		
3		
4		
5		
6		
7		
8		
9		
10		

CELEBRATION: Plan how you will celebrate when you have achieved your goal(s).

My Dream for All of Us: Authenticity, Self-Love and Self-Acceptance

By Kathy Masarie, MD, founder of Family Empowerment Network™

YOU SEE THIS PHOTO of my daughter when she was about 18 months. I remember this day. You can see the aliveness and sureness in her stride. She is confident, open, and most importantly, loving and accepting herself unconditionally. She was clear about herself then, where she fit in the world. She knew she was loved and that she mattered. When was the last time you loved yourselves unconditionally? When you felt "worthy" and "enough?" When was the last time your daughter loved herself unconditionally or your son loved himself unconditionally?

This is the dream I have for all of us—not only for our daughters and sons—but for parents, professionals, and all caring adults.

It is not about being perfect. Who is perfect anyway? If we were, it would be boring. What makes each and every one of us completely fascinating and lovable are our quirky differences, for better AND for worse.

When each of us can accept and love ourselves unconditionally, we can take on the world. When we are aware and accept what pulls us down, we can change it. When we share honestly what gets in our way, it empowers others to do the same. Together, with all of us open and authentic, we can direct our energy outward and contribute in a way the world has never seen.

Your daughters and sons are already part of a fantastic generation who have the loyalty of their traditionalist grandparents, the optimism of the boomer generation, tempered with the caution of the Gen X generation. With this rock-solid base, these realists can do the work needed to shift our direction from destruction and greed toward a life-sustaining society. What can you do to foster this?

You are now at a pivotal point. You have completed the *Raising Our Daughters* or *Raising Our Sons Parenting Guide*. We so hope your journey has been fruitful. What will you do with these new-found connections with other parents? In what ways will you commit to stretching yourself as a parent and caring adult? Knowing the importance of connection, how will you find more ways to connect with your own daughters and sons and with the other children in your neighborhood? How will you sustain the energy and keep this momentum going? Use the love, support, and empowerment you feel now to focus on what makes a real difference for your family. Have faith that when you start extending yourself, others will too, and watch the magic as the connected neighborhood you helped create starts to overlap with other connected communities. Together we will all contribute, one small step at a time, to building a culture that cares for our children and our children's children, and we will build a world in which every one of us will be accepted, supported and able to thrive.

> *If not now, when?*
> *If not us, who?*
> —Attributed to J.F.K.

Wishing you the best on your life-long journey as a parent. Have fun and enjoy the ride.

Love,
Kathy

RAISING OUR DAUGHTERS
ACKNOWLEDGMENTS

Session 1 : What's Happening to My Daughter?

ROD 1:7   Excerpt from Pipher, Mary. *Reviving Ophelia: Saving the Selves of Our Adolescent Girls*. New York: Putnam Publishing Company, 1994. Page 20. Used with permission of Putnam Publishing Company.

ROD 1:7   Excerpt from Brown, Lyn Mikel, Ed.D. "Cultivating Hardiness Zones for Adolescent Girls." Keynote: Girls' Health Summit, June 1, 2001. Page 3. Reprinted with permission from Lyn Mikel Brown, co-author of "Cultivating Hardiness Zones in Adolescent Girls" and co-author of *Hardy Girls Healthy Women*. This paper can be printed in full from www.hghw.org/docs/HardinessZones.pdf.

Session 2: What Influences Her

ROD 2:7   Excerpt reprinted with the permission of William Pollack, who is the author of *Real Boys: Rescuing Our Sons from the Myths of Boyhood, Real Boys' Voices,* and *Real Boys' Workbook: The Definitive Guide to Understanding and Interacting with Boys of All Ages.*

ROD 2:9   Excerpt from TV Timer - Bob: The Latest in Electronics and TV Time Management at www.familysafemedia.com/tv_timer_hopscotch_bob.html.

Session 4: Celebrating Her Emerging Womanhood

ROD 4:7.   Excerpt from Brizendine, Louann, M.D. *The Female Brain*. New York: Broadway Books, 2006. Page 8.

Session 5: Empowering Her

ROD 5:4   Excerpt from Pipher, Mary. *Reviving Ophelia: Saving the Selves of Our Adolescent Girls*. New York: Putnam Publishing Company, 1994. Page 23-24. Used with permission of Putnam Publishing Company.

ROD 5:4   Excerpt from Girls Inc. Girls Bill of Rights[SM]. Reprinted with permission of Girls Incorporated®. Accessed June, 2009 at www.girlsinc.org/about/girls-bill-of-rights.

ROD 5:6   Excerpt from "Developing a Hardy Personality." *From Things Will Be Different For My Daughter: A Practical Guide to Building Her Self-Esteem and Self-Reliance* by Mindy Bingham and Sandy Striker, with Susan Neufeld, copyright © 1995 by Mindy Bingham, Sandy Stryker and Alison Brown, Cerier Book Development, Inc. Used by permission of Penguin, a division of Penguin Group (USA) Inc.

ROD 5:9   Excerpt from "Five Ways to Cut Spending" from *Start Smart: Money Management for Teens How to Save, Spend and Protect Your Cash*, FDIC Consumer News, Summer 2006 at www.fdic.gov/Consumers/Consumer/news/cnsum06/sum_06_bw.pdf.

Session 6: Teaching Her

ROD 6:6   Excerpt from Sobel, David. *Place-Based Education: Connecting Classrooms and Communities.* Orion Society, 2004. Page 7.

ROD 6:32   Excerpt from brief quotes on pp. xvi, 5, 13, 20 from *The Bully, The Bullied, and the Bystander* by Barbara Coloroso. Copyright © 2003 by Barbara Coloroso. Reprinted by permission of HarperCollins Publishers.

Session 7: Making Time for Her

ROD 7:7   Excerpt from Tolle, Eckhart. *The New Earth: Awakening to Your Life's Purpose.* New York: Plume, 2006. Page 204.

ROD 7:23   Excerpt from "Helicopter Parent." <u>Wikipedia, The Free Encyclopedia,</u> Wikimedia Foundation <u>http://en.wikipedia.org/wiki/Helicopter_parent.</u>

ROD 7:23   Excerpt from Wade, Erin. 'You're a Helicopter Parent if you' from "8 Ways to Avoid Helicopter Parenting," The Dallas Morning News, August 15, 2005. Reprinted with permission of The Dallas Morning News.

Session 8: Keeping Her Safe

ROD 8:20   Excerpt from Ponton, Lynn. *The Romance of Risk.* New York: Harper Collins Publishers, 1997. Page 12.

ROD 8:35   Excerpt from Brizendine, Lynn. "The Girl Brain" from *The Female Brain*, New York, Broadway Books, 2006. Page 35.

Session 9: Supporting Her

ROD 9:28   Excerpt from Mahdi, Louise Carus. *Crossroads: The Quest for Contemporary Rites of Passage.* Open Court Publishing Company, 1996. Page xvii.

Session 10: Creating Community

ROD 10:4   Excerpt from Covey, Stephen. *The 7 Habits of Highly Effective Families.* New York: St Martin Press, Franklin Covey Company, 1997. Page 358. Reprinted with permission of Franklin Covey Company.

ROD 10:4   Excerpt from Pipher, Mary. *Shelter of Each Other.* New York: GP Putnam Sons, 1996. Page 81

ROD 10:5   Excerpt from *What Young Children Need to Succeed* by Jolene Roehikepartian and Nancy Leffert, copyright © 2000 (pp 287-288). Used with permission of Free Spirit Publishing, Inc., Minneapolis, MN; 800-735-7323; <u>www.freespirit.com.</u> All rights reserved.

ROD 10:9   Excerpt from pp. 99-100 (303 words) from *High Tide in Tucson: Essays from Now or Never* by Barbara Kingsolver. Copyright © 1995 by Barbara Kingsolver. Reprinted by permission of HarperCollins Publishers.

Permissions

All material in this list is copyright protected. Please contact authors directly for reprint requests.
For permission of material not listed here, please contact www.family-empower.com.

Session 1: What's Happening to My Daughter?

The 40 Developmental Assets® framework, articles, handouts, data and statistics included in this publication have been reprinted with permission from Search Institute, 615 First Avenue NE, Suite 125, Minneapolis, MN 55413; 1-800-888-7828, www.search-institute.org. All rights reserved. The following are trademarks of Search Institute: Search Institute®, Developmental Assets®, MVParents℠, and Healthy Communities • Healthy Youth®.

The list of **40 Developmental Assets®** is reprinted with permission. Copyright © 1997, 2006 Search Institute®. All rights reserved. No other use is permitted without prior permission from Search Institute, 615 First Avenue NE, Minneapolis, MN 55413; www.search-institute.org.

"Fast Facts About Developmental Assets for Youth" Reprinted with permission from *Pass It On! Ready to Use Handouts for Asset Builders* Handout [#3]. Copyright © 1999, 2006 Search Institute®, Minneapolis, MN; www.search-institute.org. All rights reserved.

"The Power of Assets" Reprinted with permission from *The Asset Approach: 40 Elements of Healthy Development.* Copyright ©2002, 2006 Search Institute®, 615 First Avenue, NE, Minneapolis, MN 55413; www.search-institute.org. All rights reserved.

"How You Can Build Assets" Reprinted with permission from *The Asset Approach: Giving Kids What They Need to Succeed.* Copyright © 1997 Search Institute®, 615 First Avenue NE, Minneapolis, MN 55413; www.search-institute.org. All rights reserved.

"Asset Building Difference" Reprinted with permission from *Pass It On! Ready to Use Handouts for Asset Builders* Handout [#6]. Copyright © 1999, 2006 Search Institute®, Minneapolis, MN; www.search-institute.org. All rights reserved.

"Are Americans Afraid of Youth" Reprinted with permission from Kathleen Kimball-Baker, "Are Americans Afraid of Youth," *Assets: The Magazine of Ideas for Healthy Communities and Healthy Youth.* Copyright © Summer 1999 Search Institute®, Minneapolis, MN; www.search-institute.org. All rights reserved.

"The Girls Report" *What We Know and Need to Know About Growing Up Female--Overview and Executive Summary.* Reprinted with permission from Lynn Phillips and the National Council for Research on Women, 11 Hanover Square, 24th floor, New York, NY 10005. All rights reserved.

"Hardy Girls" by Tom Flinders. Chapter Three from *Power and Promise: Helping School Girls Hold on to their Dreams.* Reprinted with permission from website www.tworocks.org.

"The Asset Checklist" Reprinted with permission from *The Asset Approach: Giving Kids What They Need to Succeed.* Copyright © 1997 Search Institute®, 615 First Avenue NE, Minneapolis, MN 55413; www.search-institute.org. All rights reserved.

Session 2: What Influences Her

"Some Media Facts to Get Us Started" Reprinted with permission of Carol Ann McKay and Dr. Riva Sharples. Carol Anne McKay has worked as a nurse and an attorney and is currently teaching law in upstate New York. Dr. Riva Sharples is an Associate Professor with the Contemporary Media and Journalism Department, University of South Dakota.

"Our Children and Consumerism" Reprinted with permission of Carol Ann McKay and Dr. Riva Sharples (see above). Originally published in *The Ophelia Project Newsletter*, Aug 2003, www.opheliaproject.org.

"Fear Sells: Is No News Good News?" Reprinted with permission of Carol Ann McKay (see above).
"Sick and Ailing: Teen Girl's Magazine Health Coverage" by Lynette Lamb. Reprinted with permission, from *New Moon Network: For Adults Who Care About Girls*; Jan/Feb 2001. Copyright New Moon Publishing, Duluth, MN, www.newmoon.org.

"Internet Literacy: Safe Surfing in the Online World" Reprinted with the permission of Media Think: committed to strengthening critical thinking skills for understanding media, and empowering people to shape media that better serves the needs of individuals and communities (formerly Northwest Media Literacy Center) at www.MediaThink.org.

"CyberbullyingNOT: Stopping Online Social Aggression" Reprinted with permission of Nancy Willard, author of *Cyberkids and Cyber Savvy Teens* at www.cyberbulling.org.

"TV-Free Families: Why—and How—They Unplug" by Nelle Nix. Reprinted with permission from Nelle Nix *Metro Parent: Serving the Families of the Portland Metropolitan Area*, April, 2004, © *Metro Parent* at www.metro-parent.com. All rights reserved.

"12 Tips to Tame the Tube" Reprinted with permission of National Institute on Media and the Family: Building Healthy Families through the Wise Use of the Media. For reports on media research, latest recommendations, and more media tips see www.mediawise.org or contact 612-672-5437.

"Media Literacy in Action" Reprinted with the permission of Media Think (see above).

Session 3: Parenting Her

"Positive Discipline Guidelines" Reprinted with permission from Jane Nelsen, EdD, MFT, author of "Positive Discipline Guidelines," www.positivediscipline.com. For information on Jane Nelsen's seminars, please contact jane@positivediscipline.com.

"Taking Charge: Basic Concepts of JoAnne Nording's Caring Discipline" Written for Family Empowerment Network by JoAnne Nordling, author of *Taking Charge: Caring Discipline That Works, at Home and at School* and director of Parent Support Center at www.parentsupportcenter.org. For reprint information, please contact JoAnne Nordling at 503-796-9665 or info@parentsupportcenter.org.

"Parent's Job: Set Aside and Let the Kids Become Heroes" Reprinted with permission of Lionel Fisher. Originally from the Oregonian 9/25/04. Lionel Fisher is the author of several personal growth self-help books, including *Celebrating Time Alone: Stories of Splendid Solitude* (Beyond Words Publishing, 2001).

"Mother Monster from the Black Lagoon" Written for Family Empowerment Network by Glenda Montgomery, parent coach and Certified Positive Discipline Instructor in Portland, Oregon at www.positiveparentingpdx.com. For reprint information, please contact Glenda Montgomery at www.positiveparentingpdx.com.

"Peaceful Parenting: How to Turn Parent-Child Conflict into Cooperation" from *Greater Good Magazine* Volume 4, Issue 3, Winter, 07-08. Reprinted with permission of Sura Hart and Victoria Kindle Hodson, MA. Sura and Victoria are co-authors of three books: *The Compassionate Classroom: Relationship Based Teaching and Learning; Respectful Parents, Respectful Kids: 7 Keys to Turn Family Conflict into Cooperation;* and *The No-Fault Classroom: Tools to Resolve Conflict and Foster Relationship Intelligence* (2008). They also offer consultation and workshops based off their website at www.k-hcommunication.com.

"Tips on Running a Successful Family Meeting" Written for Family Empowerment Network by JoAnne Nordling (see above). For reprint information, please contact JoAnne Nordling at 503-796-9665 or info@parentsupportcenter.org.

Session 4: Celebrating Her Emerging Womanhood

"Moontime Celebrations" by Janet Rudolph from *New Moon Network,* Jan/Feb 2001. Reprinted with permission from *New Moon Network: For Adults Who Care About Girls*. Copyright New Moon Publishing, Duluth, MN, www.newmoon.org.

"Girls and Desire" by Christine Schoefer of *New Moon Network,* Jan/Feb 2001. Reprinted with permission of *New Moon Network: For Adults Who Care About Girls.* Copyright New Moon Publishing, Duluth, MN, www.newmoon.org.

"If She Thinks She is a Lesbian" by Lynne E. Ponton, MD. © New Moon Girl Media, all rights reserved. Reprinted from www.daughters.com with permission of New Moon Girl Media www.newmoon.com and Joe Kelly www.TheDadMan.com. Originally published in Daughters, July 2001.

"Relationships with Family, Friends, Self, and Others" by Barbara A. Lewis. Excerpted from *What Do You Stand For? A Kid's Guide to Building Character* by Barbara A. Lewis, copyright © 2005. Used with permission of Free Spirit Publishing Inc., Minneapolis, MN; 1-800-735-7323, www.freespirit.com. All rights reserved.

"When Our Kids Fight with Friends" Written for Family Empowerment Network by Glenda Montgomery, parent coach and Certified Positive Discipline Instructor in Portland, Oregon at www.positiveparentingpdx.com. For reprint information, please contact Glenda Montgomery at www.positiveparentingpdx.com.

"Fun Things To Do When You're Alone" by Barbara A. Lewis (see above).

"Compassionate Connection: Attachment Parenting and Nonviolent Communication" and "The Steps of NVC" by Inbal Kashtan. Reprinted with permission of the author. Excerpted from her book, *Parenting From Your Heart: Sharing the Gifts of Compassion, Connection and Choice,* and also published in Mothering, Jan/Feb 2002. For copies of Inbal Kashtan's booklet, go to www.cnvc.org. For her CD, *Connected Parenting: Nonviolent Communication in Family Life,* and for workshop information, go to www.baynvc.org. All rights reserved.

"Parenting for Peace" by Inbal Kashtan. Reprinted with permission of the author. Excerpted from her book, *Parenting From Your Heart: Sharing the Gifts of Compassion, Connection and Choice* and also published in Paths of Learning (Spring 2003) and California HomeSchooler (Oct 2002). All rights reserved.

"Transforming Children's Anger" by Inbal Kashtan. Reprinted with permission of the author. From PuddleDancer Press Quick Connect, October 2006. All rights reserved.

Session 5: Empowering Her

"Passionate Parenting" Written for Family Empowerment Network by Kris King, owner of Wings Seminars/Innovative Learning Group. Wings is a Personal Development Centre that offers experiential seminars in personal development and communication skills. Please contact Kris King at www.wings-seminars for reprint permission.

"Parent as Coach" Written for Family Empowerment Network by Diana Sterling, CEO of New Generations and author of *The Parent as Coach Approach: The Seven Ways to Coach your Teen in the Game of Life.* Visit www.parentascoach.com for more information. Please contact New Generations International at support@parentascoach.com for reprint permission.

"Learning to Stand Up for What's Right" by Natalie Rusk, from *Daughters: For Parents of Girls,* Jan/Feb 2004, www.daughters.com. Reprinted with permission from Natalie Rusk.

"Cultivating Hardiness Zones for Adolescent Girls" Reprinted with permission of Lyn Mikel Brown, co-author of *Cultivating Hardiness Zones for Adolescent Girls* and co-creator of Hardy Girls, Healthy Women: all girls and women experience equality, independence, and safety in their everyday lives. Visit www.hghw.org.

"Developing Healthy Self-Esteem in Children" Written for Family Empowerment Network by Marilyn J. Sorensen PhD, Clinical Psychologist/Author. Founder/Director of The Self-Esteem Institute, Portland OR, www.getesteem.com. Please email Dr. Sorensen at mjsorensen@GetEsteem.com, for reprint permission.

"Taking Risks: Teaching Her to Be Daring" by Tom Flinders, author of *Power and Promise: Helping School Girls Hold on to their Dreams.* Reprinted with permission at www.tworocks.org.

"Building Moral Intelligence: 10 Tips for Raising Moral Kids" Reprinted with permission of Michele Borba EdD, author of *Building Moral Intelligence: The Seven Essential Virtues that Teach Kids to Do the Right Thing* at www.micheleborba.com.

"**Developing Capable People**" Reprinted with permission of Stephen Glenn and Jane Nelsen, authors of *Raising Self-Reliant Children in a Self-Indulgent World* at www.empoweringpeople.com. Jane Nelsen is also the author of *Positive Discipline* and *Positive Discipline for Teenagers*; www.positivediscipline.com. For information on Jane Nelsen's seminars, please contact jane@positivediscipline.com.

"**Nine Steps to Raising Money Smart Kids**" Reprinted with permission of MFS Fund Distributors, Inc. Helping Yourself, Helping Your Parents, Helping Your Children. Check www.mfs.com for more financial information. All rights reserved.

Session 6: Teaching Her

"**Great Places to Learn: How Asset-Building Schools Help Students Succeed**" Reprinted with permission from Neal Starkman PhD, Peter C. Scales PhD, and Clay Roberts MS, "Great Places to Learn," *Assets: The Magazine for Ideas for Healthy Communities and Healthy Youth.* Copyright © Autumn 1999 by Search Institute®, Minneapolis, MN; www.search-institute.org. All rights reserved.

"**Every Student a Star: School Staff Reach Out To The Forgotten Half**" Reprinted with permission from "Every Student a Star: : School Staff Reach Out To The Forgotten Half," *Assets: The Magazine for Ideas for Healthy Communities and Healthy Youth,* Copyright © Spring 2000 Search Institute®, Minneapolis, MN; www.search-institute.org. All rights reserved.

"**Asset Building Ideas for Teachers**" Reprinted with permission from *Pass It On! Ready to Use Handouts for Asset Builders* Handout [#28]. Copyright © 1999, 2006 Search Institute®, Minneapolis, MN; www.search-institute.org. All rights reserved.

"**At Home in Our Schools: A Guide to School-Wide Activities That Build Community**" Reprinted with permission of Developmental Studies Center, 2000 Embarcadero, #305; Oakland, CA 94606, 1-800-666-7270, www.devstu.org. Copyright 1994. All rights reserved.

"**Helping Her Avoid Math Anxiety**" by Helen Cordes. © New Moon Girl Media, all rights reserved. Reprinted from www.daughters.com with permission of New Moon Girl Media www.newmoon.com and Joe Kelly www.TheDadMan.com. Originally published in *Daughters*, May/June 2003.

"**Girl Fighting**" by Lyn Mikel Brown. © New Moon Girl Media, all rights reserved. Reprinted from www.daughters.com with permission of New Moon Girl Media www.newmoon.com and Joe Kelly www.TheDadMan.com. Originally published in *Daughters*, July/Aug 2004.

Session 7: Making Time for Her

"**Fifteen Steps to a Simpler Life**" Permission granted by Gideon Weil, senior editor, HarperOne Publishers, a division of HarperCollins and Victoria Moran. From *Shelter for the Spirit: Create Your Own Haven in a Hectic World* by Victoria Moran, Harper Perennial (1998). Moran is a certified life coach, motivational speaker, and the author of other books including *Fit from Within, Fat, Broke & Lonely No More*, and the best-selling *Creating a Charmed Life*. To learn more about her work or subscribe to her free ezine, "The Charmed Monday Minute," visit www.victoriamoran.com.

"**Vote With Your Life**" by Janet Luhrs from *Simple Living*. Reprinted with permission of Healthy Directions, LLC. To subscribe to *Simple Living* by Janet Luhrs visit www.simpleliving.com or call 1-888-577-6164.

"**Your Money or Your Life: Are You Making A Dying or Making a Life**" by Joe Dominguez and Vicki Robin, authors of *Your Money or Your Life*. Reprinted with permission of Healthy Directions, LLC. To subscribe to *Simple Living* by Janet Luhrs visit www.simpleliving.com or call 1-888-577-6164.

"**Remaking a Living**" Reprinted with permission of Brad Edmondson, who currently lives in Ithaca, NY. The article was originally published in *Utne Reader*, July/August 1991.

Session 8: Keeping Her Safe

"**The Power of Assets**" Reprinted with permission from *The Asset Approach: 40 Elements of Healthy Development,* Copyright ©2002, 2006 Search Institute®, 615 First Avenue, NE, Minneapolis, MN 55413; www.search-institute.org. All rights reserved.

"**Her First Diet**" by Carol Beck author of *Nourishing Your Daughter: Help Your Child Develop a Healthy Relationship with Food and Her Body.* © New Moon Girl Media, all rights reserved. Reprinted from www.daughters.com with permission of New Moon Girl Media www.newmoon.com and Joe Kelly www.TheDadMan.com. Originally published in *Daughters,* April, 2001.

"**Can You Talk About Her Body?**" By Lynda Madison, PhD and Amy Lynch. © New Moon Girl Media, all rights reserved. Reprinted from www.daughters.com with permission of New Moon Girl Media www.newmoon.com and Joe Kelly www.TheDadMan.com. Originally published in *Daughters,* Dec, 2001.

"**Sexual Myths**" by Susan Chappell. © New Moon Girl Media, all rights reserved. Reprinted from www.daughters. com with permission of New Moon Girl Media www.newmoon.com and Joe Kelly www.TheDadMan.com. Originally published in *Daughters,* Jan, 2001.

"**Communication Tips for Parents**" Reprinted with permission of © SIECUS. From *What Do I Do?* (New York: Sexuality Information Council of the United States, 1996). www.siecus.org/pubs/pubs0004.html.

"**Talking Back: Ten Things Teens Want Parents To Know About Teen Pregnancy**" Reprinted with permission of National Campaign to Prevent Teen Pregnancy, © 2001. Contact www.teenpregnancy.org/tip.

"**A Recipe for Healthy Relationships**" Reprinted with permission of the Raphael House from *Take Care:: A Guide to Safe Relationships. Take Care* is a Raphael House prevention project in Portland, Oregon. Contact: (503) 222-6507 or www.raphaelhouse.com.

"**Dater's Bill of Rights**" National Crime Prevention Council © 1997. Reprinted with permission from National Crime Prevention Council, 1000 Connecticut Avenue, NW, 13th floor, Washington, DC 20036. For more information check out www.ncpc.org.

"**Abuse in Teen Dating Relationships**" by Jeannie LaFrance. Reprinted courtesy of Jeannie LaFrance and Bradley-Angle House, PO Box 14694, Portland, Oregon, 97293. www.bradlegangle.org, 503-232-7805. The National Domestic Violence Hotline is 1-800-799-SAFE.

"**Power of Parents – Teen Drinking**" Written for *Family Empowerment Network* by Emily Moser, MPA, MA, Director of Parenting Programs at Oregon Partnership. For reprint permission contact Emily Moser at emoser@orpartnership.org, 503 244-5211, or www.orpartnership.org.

"**Did You Know: Facts about Risky Driving**" and "**Graduated Licensing in Oregon**" by Cathy Bowles, Trauma Nurses Talk Tough Not My Kid. Reprinted with permission from the *"NOT MY KID" Campaign Parent Handbook.* Materials and Program made possible through funds from ODOT, TSD and NSTSA. Section 410 Grant and "Trauma Nurses Talk Tough: Family Education" at www.legacyhealth.org/tntt.

"**Contract for Life**" Reprinted with permission from SADD, Inc. SADD– Students Against Destructive Decisions is "students helping students make positive decisions about challenges in their everyday life" with many great resources at www.sadd.org.

Session 9: Supporting Her

"**Get Girls Talking Through Girl's Circles**" by Niki Smith, © New Moon Girl Media, all rights reserved. Reprinted from www.daughters.com with permission of New Moon Girl Media www.newmoon.com and Joe Kelly www.TheDadMan.com. Originally published in *Daughters,* Jan/Feb 2004.

"**How Girls Win Self-Esteem**" Reprinted with permission from author Mary Hickey, originally published in *Working Mother,* January 1994.

"Go Out and Play: Youth Sports in America" by Don Sabo PhD and Phil Veliz MA, October, 2008. Reprinted with permission from Women's Sports Foundation founded by Billie Jean King located at Eisenhower Park 1899 Hempstead Turnpike, Suite 400, East Meadow, New York 11554. For more information contact (800) 227-3988 or info@ womenssportsfoundation.org. This report may be downloaded in its entirety from www.WomensSportsFoundation.org. All rights reserved.

"Tell Me More and Other Great Tips on Connecting with Your Kids" Reprinted courtesy of Positive Coaching Alliance. Check out more great resources on healthy coaching at www.positivecoach.org.

"Asset Building Ideas for Coaches" Reprinted with permission from *Pass It On! Ready to Use Handouts for Asset Builders* Handout [#37]. Copyright © 1999, 2006 Search Institute®, Minneapolis, MN; www.search-institute.org. All rights reserved.

Session 10: Creating Community

"Adding Up Assets" Reprinted with permission from Peter Benson, "Asseteria: Adding Up Assets," *Assets: The Magazine of Ideas for Healthy Communities and Healthy Youth.* Copyright © Autumn 1999. Search Institute ®, Minneapolis, MN; www.search-institute.org. All rights reserved.

"Listen Up Adult Advocates" Reprinted with permission from Kalisha Davis, "Asseteria: Listen Up Adult Advocates," *Assets: The Magazine of Ideas for Healthy Communities and Healthy Youth.* Copyright ©, Summer 2000. Search Institute ®, Minneapolis, MN; www.search-institute.org. All rights reserved.

"Making A Difference One by One" by Peter L. Benson from *All Kids Are Our Kids.* Reprinted with permission of John Wiley and Sons Inc.

"Brewing Up Assets" Reprinted with permission from Kay Hong, "Brewing Up Assets: A Friendly Adult Stirs in Some Support," *Assets: The Magazine of Ideas for Healthy Communities and Healthy Youth.* Copyright © Spring 2000 Search Institute ®, Minneapolis, MN; www.search-institute.org. All rights reserved.

"Asset Building Ideas for Neighborhood Groups" Reprinted with permission from *Pass It On! Ready to Use Handouts for Asset Builders* Handout [#27]. Copyright © 1999, 2006 Search Institute®, Minneapolis, MN; www.search-institute.org. All rights reserved.

"Building Community—One Porch at a Time" Reprinted with permission from "Building Community—One Porch at a Time," *Assets: The Magazine of Ideas for Healthy Communities and Healthy Youth.* Copyright © Autumn, 1998 Search Institute℠, Minneapolis, MN; www.search-institute.org. All rights reserved.

"Why Aren't There More Dad's Groups?" by Joe Kelly. © New Moon Girl Media, all rights reserved. Reprinted from www.daughters.com with permission of New Moon Girl Media www.newmoon.com and Joe Kelly www.TheDadMan. com.

"Teens Triumph over Techno-Tribulations" Reprinted with permission from "Asseteria: Teens Triumph over Techno-Tribulations," *Assets: The Magazine of Ideas for Healthy Communities and Healthy Youth.* Copyright © Autumn, 1998 by Search Institute®, Minneapolis, MN; www.search-institute.org. All rights reserved.

Index

About the Authors

KATHY MASARIE, MD is generous in heart and in spirit. Her caring commitment to the well-being of families touches all facets of her life. As a pediatrician, she spent extra time to get to know each family. As the founder of Full Esteem Ahead, a non-profit to support families, she worked with thousands of caring adults to help kids stay healthy and thrive. As a parent and life coach, she proactively improves family dynamics for connection and success. Through all of this, her focus has always been on prevention and early action. She wants to share with caring adults everywhere what she has learned from her life's work with children and families. These two books, *Raising our Sons* and *Raising our Daughters Parenting Guides,* are the realization of that dream. She lives in Oregon with her husband, and considers her son and daughter to be her greatest teachers and inspiration in life. They are now two strong, authentic young adults. Her other passions in life include biking, a commitment to life-long learning and connection with family and friends.

JODY BELLANT SCHEER, MD is a pediatrician whose dream is creating healthy relationships and peaceful co-existence within all families, institutions and communities of the world. She has worked for over 27 years with sick newborns, premature infants and their families in Portland, OR. She is co-founder of Medical and Educational Relief International Association (MERIA), Inc, a nonprofit working to provide essential medical and educational services worldwide. As well, she regularly volunteers as a physician in developing countries, serves as a volunteer and Board member of numerous non-profit organizations, is a foster parent, and teaches compassionate communication skills to medical, parent and community groups. She loves spending time in nature through hiking, kayaking, and traveling to diverse corners of the world. She lives with her husband on a houseboat in Oregon, where they enjoy frequent visits from their three adult children and large extended family.

KATHY KELLER JONES, MA is a developmental psychologist and licensed school counselor. For nearly 25 years she has supported elementary and middle schools by teaching social-emotional skills to students, conducting group and individual therapy, consulting with staff and parents, and creating school-community connections. She currently teaches parenting classes and consults with parents on the many challenges of doing their job well. In addition to working with children and families, Kathy has worked as a writer and a research psychologist. She is interested in the individual's search for meaning and the importance of one's connection to nature. She has an MA from Ohio State University, and post-graduate training in her areas of special interest—Jungian/archetypal psychology and play therapy. She and her husband live in Oregon and share the joys of nature with their adult children and their partners, two dogs, a cat and two chickens.